EXPLORING ART

A Global, Thematic Approach

FOURTH EDITION

Margaret Lazzari
Gayle Garner Roski School of Fine Arts, University of Southern California

Dona Schlesier
Emerita, Divine Word College

 WADSWORTH
CENGAGE Learning™

Australia • Brazil • Japan • Korea • Mexico • Singapore • Spain • United Kingdom • United States

WADSWORTH
CENGAGE Learning

**Exploring Art: A Global, Thematic Approach,
Fourth Edition**
Margaret Lazzari, Dona Schlesier

Publisher: Clark Baxter

Senior Development Editor: Sharon Adams
 Poore

Assistant Editor: Ashley Bargende

Editorial Assistant: Elizabeth Newell

Media Editor: Kimberly Apfelbaum

Executive Marketing Manager: Diane
 Wenckebach

Marketing Coordinator: Loreen Pelletier

Senior Marketing Communications Manager:
 Heather Baxley

Senior Content Project Manager: Lianne Ames

Senior Art Director: Cate Barr

Print Buyer: Julio Esperas

Rights Acquisition Specialist, Image: Mandy
 Grosko

Production Service: Lachina Publisher Services

Text Designer: Frances Baca

Cover Designer: Cabbage Design Company

Cover Image: *Kente Rhapsody* by El Anatsui
 Ghana 2001, © Peter Horree/Alamy

Compositor: Lachina Publisher Services

For product information and technology assistance, contact us at
Cengage Learning Customer & Sales Support, 1-800-354-9706

For permission to use material from this text or product,
submit all requests online at www.**cengage.com/permissions**.
Further permissions questions can be emailed to
permissionrequest@cengage.com.

Library of Congress Control Number: 2010941936

ISBN-13: 978-1-111-34378-1
ISBN-10: 1-111-34378-0

Wadsworth
20 Channel Center Street
Boston, MA 02210
USA

Cengage Learning is a leading provider of customized learning solutions with
office locations around the globe, including Singapore, the United Kingdom,
Australia, Mexico, Brazil, and Japan. Locate your local office at:
international.cengage.com/region

Cengage Learning products are represented in Canada by Nelson Education, Ltd.

For your course and learning solutions, visit **www.cengage.com**

Purchase any of our products at your local college store or at our preferred
online store **www.cengagebrain.com**

Instructors: Please visit **login.cengage.com** and log in to access instructor-
specific resources.

Printed in the United States of America
2 3 4 5 6 7 15 14 13 12 11

BRIEF CONTENTS

CONTENTS

Part II

WHY DO WE MAKE ART? 125

PREFACE

Fifteen years ago, we took a risk in writing the first edition of *Exploring Art: A Global, Thematic Approach.* All other competing art texts covered almost only Western art, and in chronological order. There had never been a book that covered art from around the world, and presented it thematically. Would our approach be meaningful to our readers?

Today, a global approach to art seems critically important, equivalent to a global perspective in relation to culture, communication, politics, economics, and so on. With this fourth edition, more and more people are turning these pages and taking a world art tour. We are grateful to you for letting us be your guides to a wide range of art that embodies human dreams, visions, desires, fears, and speculations.

Our book examines essential art ideas and makes them concrete using examples from around the world. Western and non-Western art is represented from ancient through contemporary times. There is a high percentage of artwork by women. In our thematic approach, we discuss art in context with human survival, religion, politics, social protest, family structure, sexuality, technology, and entertainment. Rather than dry chronologies, our chapters present topics of deep interest to students, all made visible in art. In addition to the thematic content, there are introductory chapters that help define art, present the basic elements of art and architecture, examine the full range of media, and lay out the fundamental concepts in art criticism.

We have exciting new features for this edition, which enrich the thematic and global approach that has been the foundation of all four editions of *Exploring Art.*

NEW CONTENT

Part I, which contains the Foundation Chapters 1–5, has been extensively revised. Specifically, there is expanded coverage of Media in Chapter 3, with 25 percent more images than in the third Edition. This increases students' understanding of the qualities inherent in various art materials. Indeed, all five Foundation chapters have new images and many diagrams have been improved. Chapter 4 has been revised especially in sections on writings about art. Chapter 5 is a condensed version of information formerly covered in two separate chapters. This provides better flow for the entire Part I, and allows the instructor more time to cover the Theme Chapters in Part II.

The fourth edition's theme chapters (Chapters 6–15) have been extensively revised as well. Each chapter has an enticing and engaging new beginning, starting with a "Preview" that summarizes what will be covered in the following pages. Next is a cluster of features that improve the students' historical and geographic understanding of the art in this book. The "History Focus" briefly covers world history within a designated time period, and artwork from the chapter is tied to the events discussed in the History Focus. A detail map and a two-page "World Art Map" containing all of the chapter art examples locate the works in geographical context. The final component of these historical and geographic features is a two-page "Timeline," which places each artwork from the chapter in chronological order and in context with major world events and cultural achievements of the time. This new format will pique the students' curiosity, and provide them with greater background for each artwork.

In addition to the new beginning to each theme chapter, there are other important revisions to Chapters 6–15. In our coverage of artwork, we have used a new comparative approach with an emphasis on focus figures that open each topic discussion, followed with several related art examples for contrast. Focus figures are usually Western based, followed by an array of examples of world art that deal with a similar theme. In Chapter 12, we have added a discussion of the mind interconnected with the body, for a new overall focus of "Mind and Body." Finally, the fourth edition is now 15 rather than 16 chapters, which will allow for more time in the semester for instructors and more flexibility in their class plans. Instructors can add or subtract material to suit their own areas of expertise.

The entire approach of this book is to offer alternative learning formats that can be combined into existing teaching formats. The themes and topics are of great interest to even the newest students of art, so it is easier for instructors to engage them and to show that studying art is relevant in their lives today.

NEW ILLUSTRATIONS

The images in the fourth edition have strong representation of non-Western, Western, and contemporary art, as well as art by women. Included are stunning images of African artwork, such as the *Beadwork* by Masai women and a *Double Mask* from Cameroon. From the Islamic world are examples of remarkable Persian miniatures, three mosque examples, a Moslem prayer rug, and more. Contemporary art is experiencing phenomenal growth in China now, and we include works by notable artists such as Cai Guo-Qiang and Huang Yong Ping. New works from South America include the Incan *Silver Representation of a Maize Plant* and the contemporary *Carnival at Olinda*. From Asia is a new image of a Hindu relief carving and an ancient Vietnamese *Drum*.

The fourth edition also features artwork by artists not seen in previous editions. This includes Pipilotti Rist, Arata Isozaki, Damien Hirst, El Anatsui, Judith Baca, Kiki Smith, Tony Oursler, Robert Gober, Yoshitomo Nara, Wangechi Mutu, Olafur Eliasson, Gerhard Richter, Roberto Matta-Echaurren, Juan O'Gorman, Ann Page, Joseph Beuys, and Rirkrit Tiravanija.

Along with historical artists, contemporary artists continue to be well represented in this book, with works by:

Kutlug Ataman	Maya Lin	Martin Puryear
Dale Chihuly	Takashi Murakami	Faith Ringgold
Christo/Jeanne-Claude	Bruce Nauman	Jaune Quick-to-See Smith
Richard Serra	Shirin Neshat	Frank Stella
Andy Goldsworthy	Louise Nevelson	Andy Warhol
David Hockney	Frank Gehry	Barbara Kruger
Catherine Opie	Leon Golub	Cindy Sherman
Lucien Freud	Bill Viola	Yoko Ono
Kara Walker	Yinka Shonibare	Chris Ofili
Jenny Holzer	William Kentridge	Mariko Mori
Tim Hawkinson	Claes Oldenburg	

GLOBAL COVERAGE AND THEMATIC APPROACH

The key ideas in *Exploring Art: A Global, Thematic Approach* are (1) understanding and appreciating the world's art and (2) examining art in the context of human needs within world cultures. Students are enriched and challenged when studying art in the context of themes and ideas, and they see that these themes appear in every culture, across the ages. The themes (*Survival and Beyond, Religion, The State,* and *Self and Society*) show art to be a meaningful endeavor that deals with basic human concerns. By studying integrated global art traditions, the students can see the similarities that connect cultures as well as their differences.

HISTORICAL MATERIAL

With this fourth edition, students can learn about artwork chronologically and geographically as well as thematically. The theme chapters (6–15) open with three integrated historical and geographical features that contains chronological summaries of world history and important developments in religion, culture, and technology. World art maps, detail maps, timelines, and cross-references make further historical or geographic connections. Students are made aware of the larger social, political, and cultural context that serves as a background to the art they are studying.

We hope you enjoy the wealth of world art that is presented in this book.

ANCILLARY PACKAGE FOR INSTRUCTORS:

Online Digital Image Library

This presentation tool makes it easy to assemble, edit, and present customized lectures for your course using Microsoft PowerPoint. The online library provides high-resolution images (maps, diagrams and the fine art images from the text) for lecture presentations, either in an easy-to-use PowerPoint presentation format, or in individual file formats compatible with other image-viewing software. A new zoom feature allows you to magnify selected portions of an image for more detailed display in class. You can easily customize your classroom presentation by adding your own images to those from the text.

Instructor Website

Here you can find an Instructor's Manual with a unique integrated transition guide for teaching art appreciation with a global thematic approach. This site also contains the Test Bank with multiple-choice, matching, short-answer, and essay questions in ExamView® computerized format, as well as text-specific Microsoft PowerPoint slides created for use with JoinIn® on Turning Point® software for classroom personal response systems. ("clickers").

FOR INSTRUCTORS AND STUDENTS

CourseMate

Cengage Learning's Art CourseMate includes interactive learning, study tools, and exam preparation tools that support the printed textbook. Use Engagement Tracker to monitor student engagement in the course and watch student comprehension as your class works with the printed textbook and the textbook-specific website. An interactive eBook allows students to take notes, highlight, search and interact with text-specific embedded media (such as quizzes, flashcards, and videos). Resources include interactive foundations modules that demonstrate the most essential visual elements, principles of design, style, form, and content; image flashcards of fine art featured in the text, maps, and illustrations; video footage of art classes, such as drawing, painting, lithography, wheel working, sculpture, plaster casting, architecture, glassblowing; interactive timelines that allow students to look at themes chronologically; Video Study Tools narrating the iconography and themes of key works of art and comparisons; podcasts comparing works of art through dialogue; glossary term flashcards, critical thinking essay questions, internet exercises, chapter quizzes, and more.

Slide Guide

The SlideGuide provides a place to take notes alongside representations of the art images shown in class. It features reproductions of the images from the book, with full captions, page numbers, and space for note-taking.

ACKNOWLEDGMENTS

We wish to thank once again the entire team at Wadsworth Cengage whose efforts and creativity help shape *Exploring Art*. They encouraged us to make some big leaps in our handling of historical material in this fourth edition. Our acquisitions editor, Clark Baxter, is always supportive and always helping us to think innovatively about the book. We continue to be incredibly lucky to work with the ever-efficient, ever-thoughtful Sharon Adams Poore, our development editor. She has seen us through three editions now, and we hope the partnership continues! Thank you Kimberly Apfelbaum, media editor, and Ashley Bargende, assistant editor, for your work on the many student and instructor resources and Elizabeth Newell, editorial assistant, for helping us all. We also express our gratitude to Diane Wenckebach, marketing manager.

Of course, a book is nothing without its production staff, and we have been very fortunate to work with some outstanding people. We are grateful to Lianne Ames, project manager, Cate Barr, Art Director, Megan Lessard at PreMediaGlobal, and Annie Beck at Lachina Publishing Services for pulling all the details together. We would also like to thank Anna Meliksetian, California State University, Northridge, for creation of the Testbank and Tutorial

Quizzes, Karen Schifman, California State University, Northridge, for her work on the Instructor's Manual (with integrated transition guide) and Web site assets, as well as Cheryl Dullabaun, California State University, Northridge, for her work on the PowerPoint slides and JoinIn.

Our sincere thanks to the reviewers for their input; Sarah E. Bremser, Kapiolani Community College/University of Hawaii; Nicole Cardassilaris, Ball State University; Christian Conrad, Texas Tech University; Susanne W. Howard, Columbus State University; Pamela A. Lee, Washington State University; Lynn Peters, Moraine Valley Community College; Ruth Pettigrew, Colorado State University; Aditi Samarth, Richland College; Terrell Taylor, Meridian Community College; Paul Valadez, The University of Texas Pan American; Heather Weber, Waubonsee Community College.

We are grateful to our respective teaching institutions for their continued support. Dona thanks Divine Word College and its president, Fr. Michael Hutchins S.V.D, as well as the college's administration. She has been highly honored as Professor Emerita by the College upon her retirement in 2008. For Margaret, her gratitude goes to the faculty and staff of the Roski School of Fine Arts of the University of Southern California. Each of us has taught bright, caring students who come from all kinds of backgrounds, some from distant lands. They continually motivate us to make each edition of this global, thematic art appreciation book better than the one before.

Thank you to our families and friends who have provided interesting perspectives, good advice, and moral support throughout. They are too many to name. Margaret thanks her sister, Fran McDaniel, who is a great sounding board for ideas. Both of us especially thank Dona's husband, Douglas Schlesier, and also Margaret's husband and daughter, Michael Dean and Julia Lazzari-Dean. Julia has grown up in the years that have passed since we started the first edition, and Dona has seen her two young grandsons through the beginnings of their lives and has watched them growing up very fast. The wonder of these new lives continues to inspire us. And we thank each other, once again, for our mutual support and collaboration. Our admiration for each other has only grown deeper.

May there be peace and tolerance in our world.

May the appreciation of world art help to get us there.

Margaret Lazzari
Dona Schlesier

I

INTRODUCTION TO ART

Art has a richness and an intelligence that illuminate our lives. The more we know about art, the more our existence is enhanced by it. The chapters in Part 1 lay a foundation for understanding art.

Art is not what you see, but what you make others see.

—Edgar Degas

I never paint dreams or nightmares. I paint my own reality.

—Frida Kahlo

Art is the Queen of all sciences communicating knowledge to all the generations of the world.

—Leonardo da Vinci

I found I could say things with color and shapes that I couldn't say any other way—things I had no words for.

—Georgia O'Keeffe

I am for an art that is political-erotical-mystical, that does something other than sit on its ass in a museum.

—Claes Oldenburg

Every child is an artist. The problem is how to remain an artist once he grows up.

—Pablo Picasso

From around the age of six, I had the habit of sketching from life. I became an artist, and from fifty on began producing works that won some reputation, but nothing I did before the age of seventy was worthy of attention.

—Katsushika Hokusai

A work of art reflects its origins but at the same time it should be able to reach out to people.

—El Anatsui

When the subject is strong, simplicity is the only way to treat it.

—Jacob Lawrence

Art should reveal the unknown, to those who lack the experience of seeing it.

—Jaune Quick-To-See Smith

. . . it's easy for us to depict things of this physical world, of the way we live now, but it's very difficult to depict things that are not seen but have a profound effect on us.

—Cao Guo Qiang

Art is everywhere, except it has to pass through a creative mind.

—Louise Nevelson

For me nature is not landscape, but the dynamism of visual forces. . . . These forces can only be tackled by treating color and form as ultimate identities, freeing them from all descriptive or functional roles.

—Bridget Riley

Whether I'm painting or not, I have this overweening interest in humanity. Even if I'm not working, I'm still analyzing people

—Alice Neel

1.1 *Porch of the Caryatids*, Erechtheum, Acropolis, Athens, Greece, ca. 421–405 BCE.

1

A HUMAN PHENOMENON

Art is strictly a human phenomenon. Only human beings make art to better understand life or to communicate emotions or ideas to others.

PREVIEW

This chapter explores the often-asked question, "What is art?" No single definition of art absolutely applies for all times and places. Generally, however, art is a primarily visual medium that expresses ideas about our human experience and the world around us. Art engages our attention in a way that our everyday environment cannot.

It continues by exploring the potentials and parameters of art making, which allows us to originate something or to cause some object to come into being. In some cultures, art making is tied to artistic expression and innovation, whereas in others, following precedents is essential.

Lastly, cultural aesthetic systems and art categories are discussed. Various cultures have developed their own categories and aesthetic norms that identify in detail what art is for them. In the United States today, groupings are made around fine art, popular culture, craft, or style. Other categories are possible, such as place of origin or thematic content.

TOWARD A DEFINITION OF ART

No definitions are universal, timeless, and absolute. All definitions are framed within a culture's systems of knowledge, and these systems shift and evolve. Therefore, to answer the question "What is art?" we would have to ask: What is art *for whom* and *when*? It was not the same for the Mayans in Mexico in the 1400s as it was in the ancient Greek city of Athens, exemplified by the *Porch of the Caryatids* (Fig. 1.1). For the United States at the beginning of the twenty-first century, a good definition of art would be this: *Art is a primarily visual medium that is used to express ideas about our human experience and the world around us.* This definition holds true for many other cultures and periods, but not for all.

A few decades ago, a definition of art circulated in the United States, saying in effect that art is whatever the artist says is art. There is some truth in this, as artists often have taken the lead in defining new art forms long before society accepted them. However, when we view the long history of art, we see the greater truth to this definition: Art is whatever a society or a culture says is art. What does this mean? Basically, the definition of art is not universal and fixed in all its details, as we saw earlier. It fluctuates, because cultures are alive and changing.

To get a better idea of what art is for a specific culture, we will center our inquiry on four major areas: function, visual form, content, and aesthetics.

Function

Art functions. At the time a work of art is made, it is intended to do a job within a culture, as in the following examples:

- Art assists us in rituals that promote our spiritual or physical well-being.
- Art reflects customs related to food, shelter, and human reproduction.
- Art communicates thoughts, ideas, and emotions.
- Art gives us pictures of deities, or helps us conceive of what divinity might be.
- Art serves and/or commemorates the dead.
- Art glorifies the power of the state and its rulers.
- Art celebrates war and conquest, and sometimes peace.
- Art is a means for protesting political and social injustice.
- Art promotes cohesion within a social group.
- Art records the likenesses of individuals and their environment.
- Art educates us about ourselves and the world around us.
- Art entertains.

Of course, music, dance, or literature does similar things, as do other fields of human endeavor. But one way to measure whether a work of art is "good" is to determine its intended function, and then see how well it succeeds.

Art also can function as cultural records that can tell us about existing and past cultures: how they were structured, what they valued, what was considered ideal, what roles men and women had, and so on.

Let us start with two sculptures with similar functions in their original cultures, which was to symbolize and strengthen the power of a ruler. Figure 1.2 is from Nigeria, *Veranda Post: Female Caryatid and Equestrian Figure,* carved before 1938 by Olowe of Ise. This carved column supported a courtyard roof in a local king's palace among the Yoruba, a people in West Central Africa. To visually reinforce the king's power, he sits on a small horse holding a pistol and spear, at the top of a vertical stack supported by a smaller figure (caryatid) below. Equestrian sculptures like this among the Yoruba are symbols of regional authority, for a ruler who can conquer with power and strength.

Figure 1.3 is another sculpture intended to assert authority. In the *Equestrian Statue of Marcus Aurelius,* from the Roman Empire around 175 CE, the emperor sits atop a striding horse, and perhaps a now-lost enemy cowered beneath the raised hoof. Among the Romans, this type of sculpture was the ultimate symbol of imperial dignity and power. The godlike Marcus Aurelius is oversized compared to the horse, and his lack of armor and outstretched hand may refer to the fact that he was a philosopher as well as emperor.

Both of these sculptures are now in museums, where their function is no longer to assert the authority of those rulers. Rather, today, the function of these sculptures is to educate the general public about other cultures, to provide visual pleasure, and to entertain. Scholars also study these works, gleaning considerable information about the historical moments from which they come.

From Chapter 6 onward, we will study the functions of hundreds of artworks in greater depth.

Visual Form

Art has visual form, which allows the work to be seen or touched, and its ideas to be communicated. The subtleties of visual form are what make nuances of meaning possible. Visual form includes:

- Formal elements, such as line, shape, color, texture, mass, volume, space, and so on
- Overall composition (which is the arrangement of those formal elements), its size, its internal balance, and so on
- Materials from which the artwork is made

1.2 OLOWE OF ISE. *Veranda Post: Female Caryatid and Equestrian Figure*, Yoruba, before 1938. Wood, pigment, 71″ high. Metropolitan Museum of Art, New York.

In Nigeria in Africa, this sculpture was meant to reinforce the power of the local king.

1.3 *Equestrian Statue of Marcus Aurelius*, Rome, c. 175 CE. Bronze, approx. 11′ 6″ high. Musei Capitolini, Rome.

This sculpture was also meant to reinforce the ruler's power, but in this case, in Ancient Rome.

Visual form is carefully considered and manipulated in an artwork, both to help it better fulfill its function and to enhance its visual appeal. Looking at the formal elements and composition of the *Veranda Post*, it is evident that horizontal elements are minimized, while verticality emphasizes the authority of the king on top. Olowe of Ise, the most famous Yoruban master sculptor of his time, was known for his inventive visual forms, which he enhanced with deeply carved surface details. The inventive forms and rich details make this artwork even more appropriate to represent a powerful leader.

Materials are significant as well. The *Equestrian Statue of Marcus Aurelius* is hollow-cast bronze, a costly material sculpted using a difficult process. Because of the strength of bronze, this statue can be more than eleven feet high, have amazing surface detail, and be supported on three horse legs. Bronze allowed the statue to survive for nearly

1.4 SANDRO BOTTICELLI. *The Birth of Venus,* Italy, c. 1482. Tempera on canvas, approx. 5′ 8″ × 9′ 1″. Galleria degli Uffizi, Florence.

The content of a work of art includes its imagery and its cultural references. Some content is obvious, but other is hidden.

2,000 years, much of it outdoors. The very material of bronze is essential in this truly royal portrait.

Every work of art has visual form, which we will study throughout the book. In addition, visual form is discussed in depth in Chapter 2, The Language of Art and Architecture. Art materials are studied in Chapter 3, Media.

Content

Art has content, which is the mass of ideas associated with each artwork and communicated through the following:

- The art's imagery
- Its symbolic meaning
- Its surroundings where it is used or displayed
- The customs, beliefs, and values of the culture that uses it
- Writings that help explain the work

Content can both be immediately apparent and require considerable study. Just by looking at Sandro Botticelli's *Birth of Venus* (Fig. 1.4), from 1482, and Pablo Picasso's 1907 painting, *Les Demoiselles d'Avignon* (Fig. 1.5), you see immediately that both are paintings with multiple figures in the composition, and female nudity is at least part of the subject matter. *Venus* is painted in a more realistic, traditional style. The blocky, simplified *Demoiselles* appears to

be more modern and less interested in popular ideas of beauty. Both artworks seem balanced side to side, with a figure in the middle.

However, much content is not readily apparent and requires deeper study. *The Birth of Venus* celebrates an ancient Greek myth and glorifies the beauty of the human body, in this case, female. When it was painted in 1482, it reflected the ideals of the early Italian **Renaissance**, but its depiction of a pagan deity was at odds with the Catholic Church at that time.

Les Demoiselles d'Avignon originally was to be a brothel scene of prostitutes with their male customers. Picasso made radical changes in progress, ending with an image of intertwined figures and space that began an art movement known as **Cubism**. Three faces were influenced by African masks, like the *Ceremonial Mask known as a Mboom or Bwoom,* from Kuba, Booshong culture of Central Zaire, from the nineteenth to twentieth centuries (Fig. 1.6). The painting reflects its cultural moment, because African artworks like the *Mask* were being brought to Europe through colonial trade, and they dramatically influenced

1.5 Pablo Picasso. *Les Demoiselles d'Avignon*, Spain/France, 1907. Oil on canvas, 8′ × 7′ 8″. The Museum of Modern Art, New York.

Artwork reflects the cultural moment when it was made, in this case, the modern era at the beginning of the 20th century.

Western art. Also indicative of its time was Picasso's blending of figure and space, which echoes the theories of scientists like Albert Einstein on the fundamental nature of matter, energy, and space.

Likewise, the *Ceremonial Mask known as a Mboom or Bwoom* has its own obvious and hidden content. Clearly, it is a decorated helmet mask, made of wood, beads, shells, and pieces of cloth. Less apparent is the fact that it was originally used in African **masquerades**, traditional celebrations that blended dance, art, song, and ritual. Masquerades are reenactments of creation events, spirit works, and ancestor stories that are important to the African people who stage them. This mask represented the people over whom a king asserted his authority (see Fig. 1.11).

For more on how meaning is embodied in art, read Chapter 4, Deriving Meaning.

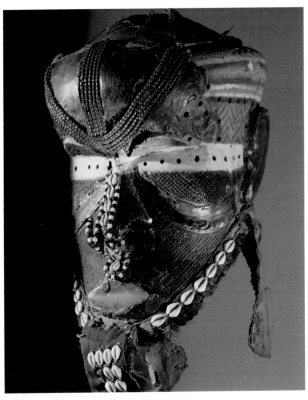

1.6 *Ceremonial Mask known as a Mboom or Bwoom*, Kuba, Central Zaire, 19th–20th centuries. Wood, beads, shells, cloth. Head-sized. Museum of Central Africa, Tervuren.

Influences can cross cultures. The works of modern artists such as Pablo Picasso were influenced by African masks.

Aesthetics

Art is an aesthetic experience. Aesthetics is the branch of philosophy that deals with art, its sources, its forms, and its effects on individuals and cultures. Writings on aesthetics date back to the ancient Greeks. Thinkers from India, Japan, China, and Western cultures have written for centuries about aesthetic issues. In several African, Oceanic, and Native American cultures, art practice demonstrated a clear aesthetic long before there was written material about it. You are thinking aesthetically when you read a book like this one. Aesthetics goes beyond individual tastes or preferences. Aesthetics is a critical reflection on art within a culture and reflects the preferences of a large segment of the culture's population.

In the eighteenth and nineteenth centuries in the West, aesthetics focused on the idea of beauty, and the standard for beauty was ancient Greek sculpture, such as the *Porch of the Caryatids* on the Erechtheum (Fig. 1.1). This approach led to the notion that aesthetics was essentially about beauty and that beauty could be universally defined for all times and places. That universalist position is discredited now, because there is no worldwide agreement about what constitutes beauty and because philosophers today consider many qualities other than beauty as significant attributes of art.

CREATING ART

Perception, Response, and Expression

The visual *perception* that is required for making or looking at art is focused and concentrated. Most of our everyday visual experience is disorganized and not memorable. With art, however, the artist carefully places colors and shapes, not simply to copy our everyday environment, much of which we ignore. Rather, art is designed to be arresting, to engage our attention, to make us look and to be aware of our act of looking, and potentially to be enriched as a result. That gift of engaged vision, in contrast to our everyday inattentiveness, is one of the greatest benefits of art.

All artwork reflects the artists' *response* to the world, specifically, their point of view, values, and individual experiences. Many artists also make work that responds to the art of others. Think of the thousands of flower pictures you have seen in your life, including paintings or photographs, on calendars, wallpaper, wrapping paper, linoleum, fabric, and so on. Every one of those representations of flowers was based on the artist's or designer's experience.

Even though art is a response to the world, only some art is made "from life," with the artists' subjects in front of them. Other works come from memory or

reflection. Figure 1.7 is a delicate scroll painting entitled *Lotus Flowers and Ducks*, from thirteenth-century China. Generally, traditional Chinese paintings were not made directly from life, because the Chinese believed memory and repeated experience allowed the artist to capture the broad essence of flowers rather than the specific details of one particular bloom.

Clearly, art reflects humankind's perceptions of and responses to all aspects of spiritual life and earthly life, from birth to death and the hereafter, and of everything in between. Yet each artist or each culture might express these life experiences differently. Figures 1.8 and 1.9 are two different *expressions* of spiritual traditions. The *Zen Stone Garden* (Fig. 1.8), from 1185–1333, is located at the

1.7 *Lotus Flowers and Ducks*, China, 13th century. Hanging scroll. Paint on silk, 50.4″ × 30.7″. Museum fuer Ostasiatische Kunst, Staatliche Museen zu Berlin, Berlin.

All artworks reflect the artists' responses to their life experiences and to the world around them.

Buddhist Daitokuji Temple and monastery complex in Kyoto, Japan. The *Zen Stone Garden* is a still, dry landscape meant to aid quiet meditation, which Buddhists believe is essential for spiritual growth. The white rocks can stand for the cosmic void, the emptiness of the mind, the flow of water, a journey, and so on, while the large, dark rocks represent material substances and worldly events. Figure 1.9 is a *Gopura* (or gateway) to the *Sri Meenakshi Amman Temple* at Madurai, India, a destination for thousands of pilgrims who attend the Hindu festivals there. This 150-foot-tall tower is covered with deities and attendants, so richly decorated and brightly painted that the surface almost seems to pulsate. This architecture embodies the Hindus' celebration of the divine force that animates the abundant life forms on earth.

Both the *Zen Stone Garden* and the *Gopura* seek to instill a sense of spiritual awareness, but how different each is. Yet each represents its creators' responses to the spiritual and natural worlds, as they experienced it.

1.9, left *Gopura, Sri Meenakshi Amman Temple*, 17th century. Madurai, Tamil Nadu, India.

This artwork is also meant to provide a spiritual experience, but in this case within the culture of India and Hinduism.

Artistic Creativity

Creativity allows us to originate something or to cause some object to come into being. What that means exactly can vary from culture to culture. In the United States today, creativity is often thought to have two essential ingredients. The first is innovation, or the making of something that is new. The second is self-expression, which refers to individual artists' own styles and personal concepts of the world, all of which are embedded in their unique works of art.

However, innovation and artistic self-expression are not always necessary ingredients in creating artwork. For some great art, the artists followed formulas or copied other works, because their culture valued the re-creation of old forms more than innovation. Also, some artists today devote their work to critiquing existing culture, rather than creating something new.

Jaune Quick-to-See Smith's *Genesis* (Fig. 1.10) contains aspects of innovation and self-expression, at the same time as she is re-creating old forms. On the expressive side, Smith has applied thick, gestural strokes of oil paint on top of a collaged layer of newspaper articles, photocopied images, and pieces of fabric. On the side of preserving old forms, in this case referring to Native American creation myths, she has incorporated native symbols, sculptures, and lines from stories, along with glorifying the buffalo, an animal with mythical standing. She has blended traditional native imagery and mythology

into late-twentieth-century art styles. To Smith, all her works are inhabited landscapes, full of life, an essential native idea.

CONNECTION In the lower-right corner of *Genesis*, Jaune Quick-to-See Smith has drawn an image of a 700-year-old Native American ceramic vessel called *Mother and Nursing Child* (see Fig. 7.32), showing the importance of re-creating and preserving old forms.

As evident in the discussion of *Genesis*, creativity can be a complex mix of old and new. Although psychologists have not fully identified the creative process in art making, some contemporary artists believe it begins with a formative stage, as an artist responds to a problem, a vivid experience, or a commission. This may be followed by periods of intense research or experimentation. The making of the artwork comes next, which may be quick or may take years. Picasso worked for two months in 1907 on *Les Demoiselles d'Avignon*.

1.10 JAUNE QUICK-TO-SEE SMITH. *Genesis*, 1993. Oil, collage, mixed media on canvas, 5' × 8' 4". Museum of Art, Atlanta.

Art is often innovative and unique, while at the same time borrowing from existing styles and symbols.

The making of *Gopura* from Madurai undoubtedly took much longer, even with the combined efforts of many craftsmen. In the case of **performance art**, often no art object is made, but the artist initiates some actions, which are the art.

Once the work has been completed, or even while it is in process, artists critically assess their work. Other critiques come from peers, curators, writers, academics, and the audience. All of this feedback provides a certain degree of affirmation.

Who is creative? Artists and designers are, but so are scientists, writers, researchers, and so on. Although we think of creativity as residing in the individual, it has a social dimension as well. Support from others allows a person's creativity to bloom. Creativity comes easily to children, but it must be nourished in adolescence, when negative social pressure and self-criticism can cause us to stifle what is part of our natural human heritage.

CATEGORIES OF VISUAL ARTS

Some peoples, both past and present, have no word that corresponds to ours for art. For example, masquerades

1.11 Mwashamboy (kneeling) and Bwoom (standing) maskers in a royal ceremony among the Kuba. Late 20th century. Democratic Republic of Congo.

Categories of art may not be the same in all cultures. For example, the art form of the masquerade is important in Africa, but not in North America.

in sub-Saharan Africa blur the boundaries between areas that Western cultures might consider very distinct, such as art, ritual, and social cohesion. In Figure 1.11, masqueraders are performing in the court of the Kuba king. Their masks and roles re-create archetypes that deal with the beginnings of the Kuba people, the rights of the king, and basic social values for young men. The standing performer to the right is wearing a mask similar to the *Mboom or Bwoom Mask* in Figure 1.6. Another example of different categories for art comes from the Japanese, who did not necessarily think of paintings as fine art until the late nineteenth century, when the concept of art history was exported from the West along with the idea of painting as fine art. The Japanese also value flower arranging and traditional puppetry as higher art forms than do Western cultures.

CONNECTION For more on Japanese Bunraku puppetry, see Fig. 15.20.

In the United States today, we are inundated with images and visual objects. They surround us in galleries and museums and are everywhere in mass media and in stores. Some of these images are considered art, but others are called popular culture. Crafts sometimes are distinguished from art. The following section includes some of the groupings made in the United States today for visual objects.

Fine Art

Fine art is a Western category of refined objects considered to be among the supreme cultural achievements of the human race. Fine art is believed to transcend average human works and may be produced by only the best artists with unique sensibilities. To be appreciated, fine art requires sensitivity on the part of its audience. One definition of fine art is simply that it is what is displayed in art museums.

> **CONNECTION** For more on the development of museums in general, and art museums in particular, see Chapter 5, Making Art, Using Art, and Preserving Art

The category of fine art has always been evolving. It is different now from what it was before 1800 or so:

> "highbrow" and "lowbrow" . . . were both popular. Shakespeare appealed to lower class audiences; and the same can be said of most stage literature, of music (including grand opera), and of the visual arts. Norms now taken for granted did not exist; audiences were not demurely appreciative but highly demonstrative. . . . Relatively little was sacred. (Wallach 1998: 14)

Since 1800, we can see that what was considered art in the United States has changed radically. Fine art included painting, sculpture, and architecture in the early and mid-nineteenth century in Western industrialized nations. It was heavily influenced by Greek, Roman, and Italian Renaissance art, mostly sculpture, like the *Porch of the Caryatids*, which is our chapter opener. That Greek/Roman-inspired model of fine art was so pervasive that when Théodore Géricault painted *The Raft of the Medusa* (Fig. 1.12), critics were horrified, because it was too realistic, too likelife, not transcendent of the moment, and not enough like "art." The painting, which shows starving survivors of a shipwreck just as they are being rescued, created huge sensations wherever it was displayed, and it caused political turmoil, because it dramatized a shipwreck that was caused in part by its incompetent captain, who was a political appointee. Looking at the painting today, it may be hard to imagine that some critics thought it was not art.

Another major shift in the category of fine art occurred at the beginning of the twentieth century. Contemporary painting became very important, and artists like Paul Cezanne broke conventions in the ways that space and form are depicted. *Landscape at Aix, Mount Sainte-Victoire*

1.12 THÉODORE GÉRICAULT. *The Raft of the Medusa,* 1819. Oil on canvas, 16′ 1″ × 24′ 1″. Louvre, Paris.

Many writers did not consider this painting to be a work of art when it was first made, because it did not conform to the concept of fine art at that time.

(Fig. 1.13), from 1905, is a fractured, disjointed representation of a scene. By the mid-twentieth-century, **avant-garde** art had broken away from representation at all. The critic Clement Greenberg defined avant-garde art as "art for art's sake" and "pure poetry." He stated: "The avant-garde poet or artist tries in effect to imitate God by creating something valid solely on its own terms, in the way that nature itself is valid. . . . [A] work of art or literature cannot be reduced in whole or in part to anything not itself" (Greenberg 1939: 5–6).

In recent years, fine art as a category has expanded to include film, photography, prints, and, most recently, installation, performance, video, and computer art. In addition, definitions of fine art are in flux when Western people look at art from other cultures. In 1880, works like the *Mboom or Bwoom Mask* would not have been displayed in art museums in the United States or Europe, but they are now.

Popular Culture

Popular culture in Western nations consists of magazines, comics, television shows, advertising, folk art, tattoos, customized cars, graffiti, video games, posters, websites, calendars, greeting cards, dolls, souvenirs, toys, movies

1.13 PAUL CEZANNE. *Landscape at Aix, Mount Sainte-Victoire*, 1905. Oil on canvas, 23 ^{1}/$_2$″ × 28 ^{1}/$_4$″. Pushkin Museum of Fine Arts, Moscow.

Frequently, the most recent works of art challenge viewers and their ideas of art. When Cezanne made this painting, he broke with the traditional ways of depicting space and form.

(as opposed to film or cinema), and snapshots and commercial photography (as opposed to fine photography). Popular art is often perceived as being more accessible, inexpensive, entertaining, commercial, political, naive, or colorful than fine art.

Fine arts and popular culture can be seen as part of a continuum that contains much of the visual imagery that Western culture produces. Popular culture images and objects may share many attributes of high art. The work is often highly creative, innovative, and expressive. It shares the same attributes of function, visual form, and content. It reflects the values and structures of our social systems, political hierarchies, and religious beliefs. Popular culture is studied in many academic areas, including visual culture, art history, philosophy, and anthropology. Some objects from popular culture eventually "become" art, for example, popular prints like *Las bravisimas calaveras guatemaltecas de Mora y de Morales*, by José Guadalupe

Posada (Fig. 1.14). Now carefully preserved in a university library, this print was originally inexpensive and widely distributed like an editorial cartoon, with large, running skeletons (*calaveras*) that represent two assassins who brought death and chaos to Guatemala.

Some artists want to occupy the space between high art and popular culture. For example, *Tan Tan Bo*, from 2001 (Fig. 1.15), is by the contemporary Japanese artist Takashi Murakami, who produces paintings, designer handbags, and installations of large-scale inflatable art, like enormous Mylar helium balloons. His work is a blend of U.S. and Japanese fine art, popular culture, and **anime** (contemporary Japanese animation), and always reflects a self-conscious consumerism. Murakami also sells multiple-edition prints of works on paper and canvas through galleries and on artnet.com.

A subcategory of popular culture, called **kitsch**, is by comparison shallow or pretentious, or overly calculated to be popular. Objects or images are kitsch if they display an emotional appeal that is generalized, superficial, and sentimental. Unlike the best of fine art or popular culture, kitsch does not provide an original experience, a uniquely felt emotion, or a thoughtful, introspective moment. *The Smithsonian Institution's 150th Anniversary Float* in the Rose Parade (Fig. 1.16), with its collection of images from astronauts to the first airplane to pandas to butterflies to baseball, is meant to appeal to all and offend none. The museum buildings appear diminutive and cute, and not like a site of serious research.

Like all other categories of visual art, the idea of kitsch is evolving and changing. Critics such as Susan Sontag have reclaimed some kitsch as "camp," which means that objects

1.14 JOSÉ GUADALUPE POSADA. *Las bravisimas calaveras guatemaltecas de Mora y de Morales,* 1907. Pictorial broadside verse, full sheet, printed recto and verso, lavender paper; zinc etching. University of New Mexico.

The boundary between fine art and popular culture are often blurred. This poster, which was inexpensive and widely distributed at the time it was made, is now collected in libraries and museums.

1.15, top TAKASHI MURAKAMI. *Tan Tan Bo*, 2001. Acrylic on canvas mounted on board, 11' 9" × 18' 1" (3 panels). Tomio Koyama Gallery, Tokyo.

In this painting, the imagery resembles Japanese animation and is another example of the blurring between fine art and popular culture.

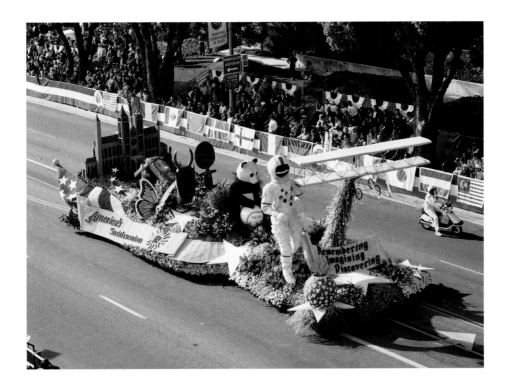

1.16, bottom *The Smithsonian Institution's 150th Anniversary Float* in the 1996 Rose Parade in Pasadena, California.

Artwork that is sentimental or calculated to please may be considered as kitsch.

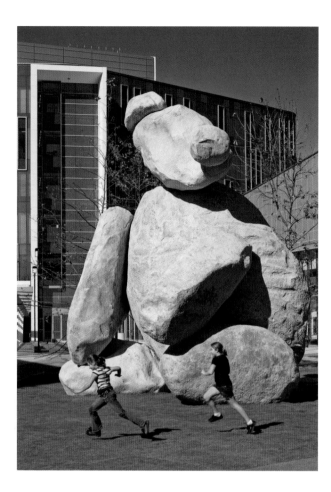

1.17 TIM HAWKINSON. *Bear*, 2005. 23′ 6″ high, 370,000 lbs. Stuart Collection, University of California, San Diego.

This work is a cross between a toy and monumental art.

1.18 *Gheordez Prayer Rug*, Turkey, 18th century. White mihrab (prayer niche) with two Turkish floral columns. Wool, height 65 ³/₄″, width 48 ³/₄″. Museum fuer Angewandte Kunst, Vienna, Austria.

This rug is an example of an object that could be classified as fine art or as craft.

and images of such extreme artifice (and often banality) have a perverse sophisticated and aesthetic appeal, and that they revealed "another kind of truth about the human situation" (Sontag 1966: 287). Other artists incorporate and transform sentimental or cute items in their work. The artist Tim Hawkinson, who is known for his inventive, humorous, or fantastic art, created the nearly 200-ton stone *Bear* (Fig. 1.17), a cross between a teddy bear and *Stonehenge*. There is an interesting association between the surfaces of a soft, fuzzy childhood companion and the rounded, weathered surfaces of ancient stones.

CONNECTION Stonehenge contains circles of ancient, enormous boulders, presumably set up for agricultural rituals, and is located in southern England. See Figure 8.26.

Craft

Craft refers to specific media, including ceramics, glass, jewelry, weaving, and woodworking. Craft usually involves making objects rather than images, although craft may involve surface decoration. Often, craft objects have a utilitarian purpose or perhaps evolved from a utilitarian origin. In addition, however, they display aesthetic and/or conceptual dimensions that go beyond mundane use. Like the distinction between fine art and popular culture, the art/craft distinction is culturally specific and in flux.

The *Gheordez Prayer Rug* (Fig. 1.18), from eighteenth-century Turkey, is a good example of an object that might be categorized as craft or art. Like other woven objects, it is craft, but its aesthetic qualities and ritualistic uses carry it beyond utilitarian function. The intricate pattern echoes tile work in mosques, and the white niche in the center is

1.19 MARY CASSATT. *Mother and Child*, 1897. Pastel on paper, 21″ × 17 3/4″. Musée d'Orsay, Paris, France.

This artwork is representational in style. It mimics the appearance of things in the natural world

like a **mihrab**, an architectural feature in a mosque that marks the direction of Mecca.

Stylistic Categories

Style is the manner of artistic expression characteristic either of an individual artist, of a historic period, or of an entire civilization. So a rose might be a rose, but the styles of representation of it are not the same. Before looking at artists' or cultures' styles, it is helpful to have a basic vocabulary describing stylistic attributes.

Style Vocabulary

Art that is **naturalistic** generally contains recognizable imagery that is depicted very much as seen in nature. Mary Cassatt's *Mother and Child* (Fig. 1.19), from 1897, is rendered in a naturalistic style. From repeated and long observation, Cassatt was able to capture the intense attachment a mother may feel toward her child. This work

is also **representational**, as it contains entities from the world in recognizable form.

In **idealized** art, natural imagery is modified in a way that strives for perfection within the bounds of the values and aesthetics of a particular culture. The *Veranda Post* (Fig. 1.2) and the *Equestrian Statue of Marcus Aurelius* (Fig. 1.3) are both rendered in idealized styles, yet they are quite different because each culture had its own definition of ideal. In African figurative sculpture, it is common to see oversized heads in idealized imagery (the figure is often divided into thirds: one-third is the head, and the other two-thirds are body and legs). Marcus Aurelius's large size and dignified gestures are ingredients for an idealized image.

Expressive or **expressionist** styles of art communicate heightened emotions and often a sense of urgency or spontaneity. Expressive styles frequently appear bold and immediate, rather than carefully considered or refined. They often feature distorted or abstracted imagery and may appear asymmetrical or off balance. Textured surfaces and thick paint application signal an expressive style.

1.20 WASSILY KANDINSKY. *Jüngster Tag (Last Judgment)*, 1912. Underglass painting with ink and color, 13 1/4" × 17 1/2". Musée National d'Art Moderne, Centre Georges Pompidou, Paris.

This painting is expressionistic in style, with its bold colors and the immediacy with which it was painted.

Wassily Kandinsky's *Jüngster Tag* (Fig. 1.20), from 1912, is an example of expressionist painting, as seen in the bold colors, strong contrasts from black to white, vigorous lines, and exploding, fragmented forms.

The term **classical** has several related meanings in reference to style. It can refer to art that is orderly, balanced, clear, and well proportioned vertically and horizontally, like *The Birth of Venus* (Fig. 1.4) seen earlier in this chapter. In this sense, classical is the opposite of expressive. Classical also describes a point in the evolution of styles: classical works represent the full development of a certain style, in contrast to its early formative stage or its late transformation into another style. When written with a capital C, Classical refers specifically to the art made in ancient Greece in the fifth century BCE. Figure 1.1, *Porch of the Caryatids*, is an example of Classical Greek art.

Surreal refers to art with a bizarre or fantastic arrangement of images or materials, as if tapping into the workings of the unconscious mind. Meret Oppenheim's *Object* (Fig. 1.21) is a fur-lined cup, which mixes and thus undermines the pleasures of two senses in a dreamlike way. The fur is sensual to touch, but miserable to taste, even though the cup should be delivering taste treats to the tongue. The title in French means *Luncheon in Fur*, which could refer to luxury or even sexuality, and yet humor is also a prominent part of the piece.

Nonobjective (nonrepresentational) art contains imagery that is completely generated by the artist. Frank Stella's *Abra III* (Fig. 1.22), 1968, focuses on the interrelation between colors and shapes, and nothing else beyond what a person sees while looking at the painting.

The term "abstract art" is often used to mean the same thing as "nonobjective," but there is an important distinction. **Abstracted** imagery may or may not be recognizable, but it has been derived from reality by distorting, enlarging, and/or dissecting objects or figures from nature. Pablo Picasso's *Les Demoiselles d'Avignon* (Fig. 1.5) is an example from earlier in this chapter of abstracted imagery,

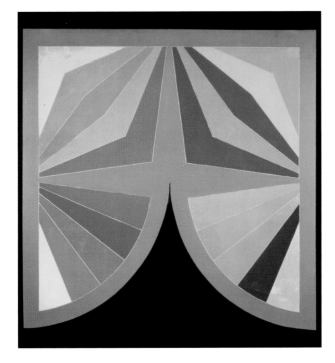

1.21, *above* Meret Oppenheim. *Object (Le Dejeuner en fourrure)*, 1936. Fur-covered cup, saucer, and spoon. Cup, 4 ³/₈″ diameter; saucer, 9 ³/₈″ diameter; spoon, 8″ long; overall height, 2 ⁷/₈″. The Museum of Modern Art, New York.

The surreal style in art often features bizarre or fantastic combinations of elements.

1.22, *left* Frank Stella. *Abra III*, 1968. Acrylic on canvas, 10′ × 10′. Collection of the artist. New York.

Nonobjective art contains invented imagery that does not imitate the appearance of things in the natural world.

distinct and coherent as a group. Stylistic differences make the art of ancient Egypt readily distinguishable from the art of, say, seventeenth-century France. Cultural styles reflect and express the cultures from which they come. Along with language, religion, and social customs, the styles of art and architecture form a culture's identity.

A few definitions are helpful here. **Culture** can mean the totality of ideas, customs, skills, and arts that belong to a people or group. This cultural totality is communicated or passed along to succeeding generations. A **culture** may also be a particular people or group, with their own ideas, customs, and arts. A **civilization** is a highly structured society, with a written language or a very developed system of communication, organized government, and advances in the arts and sciences. A country and a people with a high degree of social and cultural development can also be called a civilization.

So, when referring to ancient Egypt, we may call it a civilization, as it was a structured society with government, written language, and the arts and sciences. We may also refer to Egyptian culture—that is, its collective ideas, customs, and

but it is still representational in the sense that the imagery is recognizable and taken from the world around us. Kandinsky's *Jüngster Tag* (Fig. 1.20) is more abstract than *Demoiselles*.

Cultural Styles

A **cultural style** consists of recurring and distinctive features that we see in many works of art emanating from a particular place and era. Stylistic traits help us identify works from ancient Egypt, for example, and see them as beliefs, and the articles of art that it produced. Most important here is our ability to distinguish the Egyptian style of art, as one representation of its cultural identity.

Cultural styles are recognizable across a broad spectrum of art objects created by a people. These art objects share content and many formal qualities. For example, during the seventeenth-century reign of King Louis XIV of France, the court style, which was ornate and lavish, could be seen in everything from architecture to painting, furniture design, and clothing (see Fig. 5.4). Even hairstyles were affected. Men and women wore enormous, elaborate powdered wigs as they attended court events in fabulously decorated halls. Some hairstyles apparently even had jeweled model ships "floating" among the curls and waves. You can see broad cultural styles around you today. What qualities do you see shared by contemporary art, popular music, and the latest ads for clothing?

On the other hand, different cultural styles become apparent when studying a particular art form that appears across the globe. For examples, Islamic mosques are built around the world to provide a place for Muslims to congregate and pray together. Local solutions are different from each other, as we can see with the *Grand Mosque* at Djenne, in Mali, Africa (Fig. 1.23) and the *Badshahi Mosque* in Lahore, Pakistan (Fig. 1.24). Both are imposing, dramatic buildings with towers, yet each design is influenced by its cultural preferences and by locally available building materials.

Cultural styles are not static but evolve as a result of many circumstances, such as changes in religion, historical events such as war, and contact with other cultures through trade or colonization. Before the twentieth century, European art since the 1400s emphasized the human form in a naturalistic, idealized, or Classical Greek–inspired manner, like *The Birth of Venus* (Fig. 1.4). We already saw that the art of Europe changed profoundly because of African influences, which is especially apparent in works like Picasso's *Les Demoiselles d'Avignon* (Fig. 1.5).

Artists' Styles

Style can also refer to the distinguishing characteristics of one artist's work. Individual artists can develop unique, personal styles, like the artist Vincent van Gogh, who is famous for his expressive paintings rendered in thick paint with broad areas of strong colors. Using a palette knife, he

1.23 *Grand Mosque.* 1906–1907. Djenne, Mali.

All mosques have certain necessary features, but here they are translated into architectural styles favored by North Africans and using materials readily available to them.

1.24 *Badshahi Mosque*, main entrance. 1672–1674. Lahore, Pakistan.

This is a mosque translated into a Pakistani architectural style.

1.25, *right* VINCENT VAN GOGH. *Portrait of Mme. Ginoux (L'Arlesienne)*, 1889. Oil on canvas. 23 1/2″ × 19 1/2″. Galleria Nazionale d'Arte Moderna, Rome.

Vincent Van Gogh is well known for his unique painting style, yet even his work reflects cultural and artistic influences.

applied his paint quickly, and he frequently defined forms with bold lines around and through them. His unique style, readily distinguished from other European painters, can be seen clearly in his *Portrait of Mme. Ginoux (L'Arlesienne)* (Fig. 1.25) from 1889.

Nevertheless, van Gogh's unique style shares attributes with other artists of his time, including Impressionists such as Claude Monet (see Fig. 14.14) and Post-Impressionists such as Georges Seurat (see Fig. 13.29), Paul Cezanne (Fig. 1.13), or Paul Gauguin (Fig. 1.26). All of these artists applied paint in a direct, bold manner. They often chose subject matter from everyday life. They usually painted in oil and used bright-colored, thick paint (called impasto), rather than thin washes of subdued color.

Paul Gauguin and Vincent van Gogh were closely associated for a while, sharing lodgings and painting together, as evident in Gauguin's *Woman in a Coffeehouse, Madame Ginoux in the Cafe de la Gare in Arles* (Fig. 1.26). Each painting has shared and unique qualities. Note the similarity in Madame Ginoux's pose, but the differences in her attitude, in the overall scene, and in the color choices.

Some artists seek to develop their own styles and some do not. In twentieth-century U.S. and European art, innovation and unique personal style often were marks of artistic value. This has changed somewhat in the last few decades, as more U.S. and European artists have created work in collaborations or even incorporated copies of other images, so that a unique, individual style no longer necessarily denotes quality.

In some cultures, copying a venerable artwork is valued more than producing a new, unique object. For example, ancient Egyptian artists had a distinct style of rendering figures that was so well established and effective for their culture that very little change occurred in it over thousands of years. It was more important for the Egyptian artists to follow canons of representation than to invent new imagery or new ways to depict it. We see similar attitudes in some Chinese landscape paintings and in medieval Europe, where new religious manuscripts were carefully copied from old manuscripts. In the nineteenth and twentieth centuries, Native American artists from the Pacific Northwest also copied old forms that had meaning for their people, while investing new spirit and vigor in them. And Jaune Quick-to-See Smith's *Genesis* (Fig. 1.10) has Native American myths and old art forms featured in a contemporary painting.

CONNECTION Today, Native American sculptors of the Pacific Northwest continue to make works that share traits of traditional carvings like Arthur Shaughnessy's *Interior House Post* (Fig. 13.15).

Other Categories

There are other ways to categorize art. Disciplines such as drawing, photography, or sculpture may be grouped as separate categories. Some cultures have art forms that do not translate directly into Western categories, such as Japan's ancient puppet theater (Fig. 15.20) or the masquerade in Africa (Fig. 1.11). We will see all of these forms again in subsequent chapters.

Chronological categories follow a cultural style as it develops through the years, like "a history of Renaissance Art," or "a survey of art from the Middle Ages." A geographic approach studies the art from a particular area, usually also in chronological order, for example, "the art of Africa" or "the art of the American West."

Yet another approach is thematic, in which a group of fundamental ideas forms the basis for discussing art from many different cultures. This book is organized in that way, with Chapters 6 through 15 looking at art associated with human survival, political systems, religion, and our bodies, culture, and relationship to nature and technology.

Other divisions are possible. All observers of art could create their own categories for grouping artworks, and these areas can vary according to preference. You are part of a living, growing culture, and the final word has not been written about it.

1.26 PAUL GAUGUIN. *Woman in a coffeehouse, Madame Ginoux in the Cafe de la Gare in Arles,* 1888. Oil on canvas, 28 ³/₄″ × 36 ¹/₄″. Pushkin Museum of Fine Arts, Moscow.

Note the similarities and differences between Gauguin's and Vincent van Gogh's paintings of Madame Ginoux.

2.1 INTERIOR OF DOME. Mosque, Cordoba, Spain. Umayyad caliphate (Moorish). 961–966 CE.

2

THE LANGUAGE OF ART AND ARCHITECTURE

We communicate ideas through languages: oral and written language, numbers, music, and, of course, art. For the language of art and architecture, the grammar consists of (1) the formal elements and (2) the principles by which those elements are composed or structured. The basic vocabulary of art consists of these elements and principles.

PREVIEW

In this chapter we will learn about the language of art and architecture by defining their visual elements and the principles of their arrangement in composition. The elements of art are line, light and value, color, texture and pattern, shape and volume, space, time and motion, and chance, improvisation, and spontaneity. The principles of composition are balance, rhythm, proportion and scale, emphasis, unity, and variety. We will see that some artworks are strictly visual, whereas others engage our senses other than just vision.

In architecture, it is necessary to also consider structural systems, which are necessary to keep buildings standing. Common structural systems in traditional buildings include load-bearing walls; post-and-lintel architecture; wood frame construction; and arches, vaulting, and domes. These can range from simple structures to highly complex, ornate constructions, as in the Interior of the Dome, of the Mosque at Cordoba (Fig. 2.1). Recent innovations in materials or structural systems include steel frame buildings, reinforced concrete structures, truss and geodesic construction, and, finally, suspension and tensile construction.

FORMAL ELEMENTS

Words are basic elements of oral and written languages. Likewise, the basic units of visual arts are the **formal elements**: line, light and value, color, texture and pattern, shape and volume, space, and time and motion. Some works also contain the elements of chance, improvisation, and spontaneity, as well as engage senses other than sight.

Line

Mathematically, a **line** is a moving point, having length and no width. In art, a line usually has both length and width, but length is the more important dimension.

Lines made with some material are **actual lines**. They physically exist and can be broad, thin, straight, jagged, and so on. **Implied lines** in an artwork do not physically exist, yet they seem quite real to viewers. For example, the dotted line has several individual, unconnected parts that can be grouped into a single "line." The top of Figure 2.2 shows both actual and implied lines.

Lines have **direction**: horizontal, vertical, diagonal, curved, or meandering. A line's direction can describe spatial relationships in the world. Something is above something else; a path leads from left to right; an object starts at one location, and then moves to another. Horizontal lines may imply sleep, quiet, or inactivity, like the recumbent human body. Vertical lines may imply aspiration and yearning, as if defying gravity. Diagonal lines suggest movement, because they occur in the posture of running animals and blowing trees, whereas curving lines may suggest flowing movement. These are guidelines, not rules, because the overall context affects the understanding of specific lines. In *Shoki the Demon Queller*, c. 1849–1853, by Utagawa Kunisada (Fig. 2.3), the man's upper body leans to the left, implying movement, as does the diagonal line of his sword. His robe's sweeping curves and jagged diagonal lines imply a furious energy.

Line quality conveys emotional attributes. *Shoki the Demon Queller* contains lines of many different qualities, such as the thick strokes at the bottom hem of Shoki's robe, the fine wispy lines of his beard, or the crisp lines of the sword blade. Line quality can express a range of emotions, such as precision, fragility, roughness, anger, refinement, whimsy, vigor, and so on. Contrast the thick, angular lines of *Shoki* with the thin, playful lines of Paul Klee's *They're Biting* (Fig. 2.4). Also, the arrangement of lines can seem organized or disorderly. In *They're Biting*, from 1920, the lines seem arranged whimsically or randomly. Other groups of lines could be in different arrangements, for example, rigidly parallel alignments that suggest order or structure.

One single line is essentially two-dimensional in nature, but certain kinds of lines can indicate the volume of three-dimensional objects, as seen in the foot drawings at the bottom of Figure 2.2. **Gesture** lines are rapid, sketchy marks that mimic the movement of the human eyes when examining a subject. Gesture lines are the basic elements of gesture drawings, which are like maps that show the location, size, and orientation of one part of what you are drawing in relation to other parts, but without details. The foot gesture drawing in Figure 2.2 indicates the changing directions of the lower leg, the arch of the foot, and the toes. It also shows the thickness around the ankle and the way the toes flatten against the ground. Gesture lines are often preliminary marks that are covered over as the drawing progresses. However, gesture lines have a quick, energetic quality that some artists like to maintain through to the finished drawing.

Figure 2.2 contains examples of all the following kinds of lines that depict three-dimensional objects. An **outline** follows the outer edges of the silhouette of a three-dimensional form with uniform line thickness. Outlines flatten a three-dimensional form into a two-dimensional **shape**, which is discussed more on page 36. **Contour lines** mark the outer edges of a three-dimensional object, but with varying line thickness and with some internal detail. Objects are clearly identifiable in contour line drawings. **Cross-contours** are repeated lines that go around an object and express its three-dimensionality. Cross-contour lines are usually preliminary, exploratory marks, but some appear in a final drawing, like the belt around *Shoki*'s waist. Lines can also produce **tones** or **values** (different areas of gray), as in parallel lines of **hatching**. Parallel lines in superimposed layers is **crosshatching**, which can be seen both in the foot drawing in Figure 2.2 and in Albrecht Durer's *Artist drawing a model in foreshortening through a frame using a grid system* (Fig. 2.5). Crosshatching with few layers can appear as a light gray, while multiple layers appear as darker grays.

Linear elements can exist in space. Any thin string, rope, wire, chain, stick, or rod used in a sculpture can function like a line. The length of the *Royal Linguist's Staff* from Ghana in the 1900s (Fig. 2.6) gives it an obvious linear quality. Advisors/translators who attend local rulers carry these staffs as signs of their position; the sculpture on top refers to local proverbs. In architecture, columns are linear elements. Exposed beams or thick steel cables also are linear, as seen later in this chapter in Gunter Behnisch's and Otto Frei's Olympic Stadium, Munich (see Fig. 2.44).

ACTUAL LINES: irregular
regular

IMPLIED LINES: dotted
broken
pointing action

DIRECTION: vertical
horizontal
diagonal

LINE QUALITY:

flowing   meandering   calligraphic   jagged

LINES THAT DEPICT THREE-DIMENSIONAL OBJECTS:

gesture   outline   contour   cross-contour   hatching   cross-hatching

2.4 PAUL KLEE. *They're Biting*, 1920. Drawing and oil on paper, 12¼″ × 9¼″.

This contains meandering, playful lines.

2.3 UTAGAWA KUNISADA. *Shoki the Demon Queller*, c.1849–1853. Woodblock print, 14″ × 9¹/₂″. Burrell Collection, Glasgow.

Most lines in this print are bold and calligraphic, except for in the hair and beard, where fine lines depict texture.

2.5 ALBRECHT DURER. *Artist drawing a model in foreshortening through a frame using a grid system* from "Unterweysung der Messung" (Treatise on Perspective). Woodcut.

Many thin, parallel lines create the illusion of a gray tone. Groups of parallel lines layered on top of each other create darker gray tones.

Light and Value

Light is the basis for vision and thus necessary for art. **Light** is electromagnetic energy that, in certain wavelengths, stimulates the eyes and brain. The sun, moon, stars, lightning, and fire are natural light sources, whereas incandescent, fluorescent, neon, and laser lights are artificial. In art and architecture, light might be an actual element, as in Figure 2.7, showing Bruce Nauman's neon sculpture, *Human/Need/Desire*, 1983, here totally illuminated, but which actually alternates between "desire" and "need" to suggest the fluctuating motivations for human behavior. In buildings, the control of light is an essential design element, whether with skylights, windows, or artificial lights.

Most art does not emit or manipulate light itself, but reflects **ambient light**, which is the light all around us in our world. In two-dimensional art, artists use **value**

2.6, *left* *Royal Linguist's Staff.* Akan Culture, 1900s. Asante Kingdom, Ghana. Wood, gold leaf, 65 $^1/_2''$ high.

A long, thin, three-dimensional object can act like a line in space.

2.7, *bottom* BRUCE NAUMAN. *Human/Need/Desire*, 1983. Neon tubing, transformer and wire, 7' $10^3/_8'' \times 70^1/_2'' \times 25^1/_4''$. The Museum of Modern Art, New York.

This is an example of an artwork that is light-emitting.

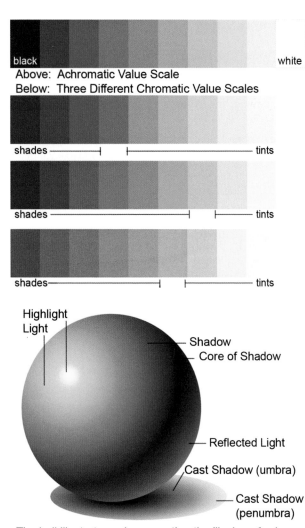

black   white

Above: Achromatic Value Scale
Below: Three Different Chromatic Value Scales

shades ———————┤ ├——————— tints

shades ———————————————┤ ├——— tints

shades———————————————┤ ├——— tints

Highlight
Light

Shadow
Core of Shadow

Reflected Light

Cast Shadow (umbra)

Cast Shadow
(penumbra)

The ball illustrates values creating the illusion of volume.

to represent the various levels of light that reflects off of objects. **Value** is one step on a gradation from light and dark. **Tone** is another word for value. In an **achromatic value scale** (Fig. 2.8), the value extremes are white and black, with the continuum of gray tones in between. Value can also be associated with color: red can still be red, but it can be lighter or darker, or different values of the color, as in the **chromatic** value scales in Figure 2.8.

Artists can carefully manipulate gradations in values to create the appearance of natural light on objects. This is called **shading** or **modeling**, and it can be seen in the drawing of the ball in Figure 2.8. Renaissance Italians used the term **chiaroscuro** to describe these light-dark gradations that can depict objects in space. For example, in Rosso Fiorentino's *Recumbent Female Nude Figure Asleep*, 1530–1540 (Fig. 2.9), the value range of reddish-brown chalk, from dark to light, is clear.

A range of values can express emotion, too. Stark, high-contrast drawings may carry a strong emotional charge, like *Shoki the Demon Queller* (Fig. 2.3), whereas the more subdued tones in Fiorentino's drawing may lull the viewer.

2.8, *left* Value Diagram.

2.9, *bottom* Rosso Fiorentino. *Recumbent Female Nude Figure Asleep*, 1530–1540. 5″ × 9 1/2″. British Museum, London.

In this drawing, shading mimics light washing across the human form.

2.10 Louise Nevelson. *Mirror Image I*, 1969. Painted wood, 117 $^3/_4''$ × 210 $^1/_2''$ × 21''. Collection of the Museum of Fine Arts, Houston, Texas.

This is a completely black sculpture, but we see a range of dark gray values, caused by light hitting and reflecting off the raised areas.

Sculpture and architecture may have value difference simply because of the many angles at which light hits and reflects off their three-dimensional surfaces, as with Louise Nevelson's *Mirror Image I*, 1969 (Fig. 2.10), with carved wooden forms inside of stacked boxes. Everything is painted black, but the light bouncing off of various surfaces appears as gray or as black. Other sculptures may have tonal variation caused by both their three-dimensionality and variations in their painted surface.

Color

Color is a wonderful phenomenon that people are lucky to enjoy. Color is visible in **refracted** light, when a prism breaks a light beam into a **spectrum** of color, or in a rainbow after a storm. Color is also visible in **reflected** light,

when objects around us absorb some of the spectrum and bounce back the rest. Those rays that are reflected to our eyes are the color of the object.

The properties of color are hue, value, and intensity. **Hue** is the pure state of color in the spectrum and is that color's name, such as red, blue, yellow, green, violet, and orange. **Value** in color is lightness and darkness within a hue, as we already saw in Figure 2.8. When black is added to a hue, a **shade** of that color is created, whereas the addition of white results in a **tint** of that color. **Intensity** in color is the brightness and dullness of a hue. Synonyms for intensity are **chroma** and **saturation**. A high-intensity color is brilliant, vivid, and saturated, whereas a low-intensity color is faded or dull. We see high-intensity colors in the spectrum. Black and white have value but not intensity among their properties. **Neutral** colors are very low-intensity colors such as cream, tan, or beige. In Thomas Gainsborough's

2.11 Thomas Gainsborough. *Mr. and Mrs. Andrews*, 1750. Oil on canvas, $27\,^{1}/_{2}'' \times 47''$. National Gallery, London.

Areas of saturated color include Mrs. Andrew's dress and the foreground greens and yellows. Neutral colors were used on Mr. Andrew's attire and the tree trunk.

Mr. and Mrs. Andrews (Fig. 2.11), the most saturated color is the blue satin dress, modified with tints and shades. In Mr. Andrews' neutral-color jacket, the variations are mostly value changes. Foreground greens are warm and intense compared to the cool, blue-gray greens in the distance. **Local colors** are the colors we normally find in the objects around us. In this painting, the blue dress, yellow hay, and gray-and-white clouds are all in local colors.

Artists mix colors through one of two systems: additive and subtractive (Fig. 2.12). The **additive color system** applies to light-emitting media. In additive color systems, absence of all light produces darkness (or black), and all light added together results in the brightest, whitest light at the center of Figure 2.12A. In our diagram, we see what happens as red, green, and blue lights are mixed. Theater lighting, performance art, light displays, and computer and video monitors use the additive color system.

In the **subtractive color system**, artists mix pigments to control the light that is reflected from them. **Pigments** are powdered substances ground into oil, acrylic polymer, or other binders to create paints. In the subtractive color system, white is a pigment that reflects almost the entire spectrum of light. Black absorbs almost all light, reflecting back very little. Our diagram shows the mixing of red, yellow, and blue. Mixing more and more pigments gives darker results, as the mixture increasingly absorbs the available light, as we see in the center of Figure 2.12B.

Primary colors combine to produce the largest number of new colors. Various art media have their distinct primary colors. For example, for light-emitting media, the primary colors are red, blue, and green, as we see on our additive color system diagram. **Secondary colors** result from mixing two primary colors. Again, in light-emitting media, the secondary colors are yellow, cyan, and magenta. For paints and pigments, the primary colors are red, yellow, and blue, while the secondary colors are orange, green, and violet. Mixing one primary color with one of its neighboring secondary colors produces **tertiary colors**. Blue-green is a tertiary color in paint. **Analogous colors** are those that are similar in appearance, especially those in which we can see related hues, such as yellow, yellow-orange, and orange. Analogous colors are next to each other on the color wheel. **Complementary colors** are opposites of each other and, when mixed, give a dull result. In paint, red and green are complementary colors. The color wheel again shows us this relationship. We can see the various colors on the **color wheel** in Figure 2.12C, which applies only to color mixing with paints and pigments.

Many color images we encounter in our lives are commercially printed, including the color images in this book. Commercial printers use semitransparent inks, with these primary colors: yellow, magenta (a bright pink), and cyan (a bright blue-green), plus black added for darkness and contrast. The secondary colors are blue, red, and green. You can easily see these primaries, and their resulting mixtures, if you use a strong magnifying glass while looking at a newspaper's color photograph. You encounter these same inks and the same CMYK (cyan, magenta, yellow, black; K = black) primaries in your home computer printer.

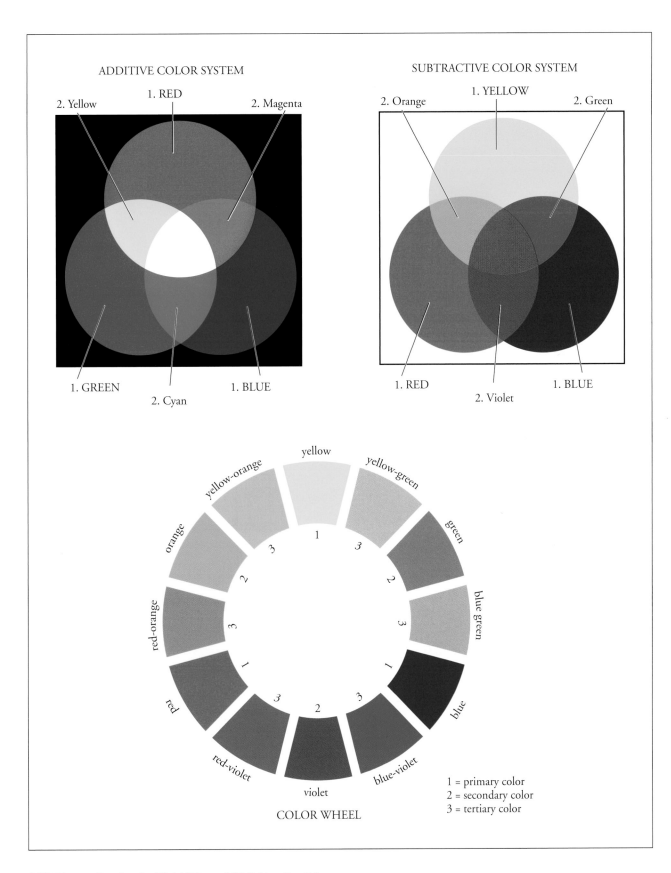

2.12 Diagram Showing the (A) Additive and (B) Subtractive Color Systems, and (C) the Color Wheel for Mixing Pigments.

	Paint	Light-Emitting Media (e.g., Computer Monitor)	Commercial Printing or Computer Printer
Color System	subtractive	additive	subtractive
Effects of Environmental Light Levels	more room light, the brighter the colors	less room light, the brighter the colors	more room light, the brighter the colors
Primary Colors	blue, red, yellow	red, green, blue	cyan, magenta, yellow, black (CMYK)
Secondary Colors	violet (blue + red)	yellow (red + green)	red (magenta + yellow)
	green (yellow + blue)	cyan (green + blue)	blue (cyan + magenta)
	orange (red + yellow)	magenta (red + blue)	green (yellow + cyan)
Complementaries	blue – orange	red – cyan	cyan – red
	red – green	green – magenta	magenta – green
	yellow – violet	blue – yellow	yellow – blue
Mixture of All Primaries	gray or dull neutral	white	black

2.13 Chart Showing Color Properties in Various Media.

Color printouts are made basically from mixtures of these colors. (However, your home printer may feature a wider range of ink beyond the basic CYMK in order to give more saturated results.) The chart in Figure 2.13 sums up the primary and secondary colors in various media, plus other color attributes.

Color perception is **relative**, meaning that we see colors differently depending on their surroundings. Light-emitting media are much more dramatic in dim light, like watching television in the dark. In a very bright room, the television image is barely visible. Conversely, reflective media need a lot of light to be seen well. A spotlight on a painting makes its colors vivid, whereas a dim room makes them difficult to see. Because natural light is constantly changing, our visual perception is also, so there is no single, fixed, permanent state that the painting "looks like."

We also experience **relativity of color perception** when we look at certain combinations of colors. In Figure 2.14, the colors in the center of the top row of squares appear to be different even though they are exactly the same, while the dull pink squares in the lower row appear to be the same but are different. Eye fatigue also affects our color perception. Stare at the white dot in the center of the "flag" printed in Figure 2.14 for one minute. You will notice as the minute wears on that you have trouble seeing the colors, which at first were so clear and bright. After the minute has passed, look at a white wall to see an afterimage of the flag, with colors shifted to red, white, and blue. Because of eye fatigue, your eyes see the complements, or opposites, of the printed colors.

Colors associated with the sun and fire, such as yellows, reds, and oranges, are considered **warm**. Colors associated with plant life, sky, and water, such as greens, blues, and violets, are **cool**. Warm and cool colors can affect an audience both physically and emotionally. Certain colors in the surroundings can actually influence your alertness, sense of well-being, and sense of inner peace.

Colors can be symbolic and, thus, associated with ideas or events. The colors of a country's flag are tied to concepts of national identity and patriotism. Certain colors might mean a holiday or a celebration, such as red and green for Christmastime in Western cultures, or red for a wedding in Asian cultures. One color may be associated with different, and even contradictory, ideas. For example, you might think of blue in relation to the ethereal, to purity, or to depression. Yellow might mean cowardice, or it might mean youth, spring, and rebirth. Associations change from culture to culture (so the red for weddings in Asia becomes white in Western cultures).

Texture and Pattern

Texture is a surface characteristic that is tactile or visual. **Tactile texture** consists of physical surface variations that can be perceived by the sense of touch. Sculptures often have distinctive tactile textures, as in the *Lion Capital* from Sarnath, India (Fig. 2.15), c. 250 BCE. The gleaming smooth sandstone on the lion's legs contrasts with the rough texture of the lion's mane. Sometimes a medium has an inherent texture. For example, mosaic is a method of creating a picture out of small, colored glass or stone pieces, which are affixed to a surface, as seen in

The three small center squares above seem to be different shades of orange, but they are all the same.

The two small pink squares above seem to be the same . . .   . . . but they are different.

Stare at the white dot at the center of the flag for 30 seconds, then look at a white wall. It will appear to be red, white, and blue. Color perception shifts due to eye fatigue.

2.14 Relativity of Color Perception.

Figure 2.16, *Detail of Deesis Mosaic in Hagia Sophia*. Each mosaic piece reflects ambient light in a slightly different direction. **Visual texture** is illusionary. In *Mr. and Mrs. Andrews* (Fig. 2.11), Gainsborough manipulated the paint to create the illusions of lustrous satin, bristly hay, and fluffy clouds, even though the painting surface is flat.

Texture can be simulated, abstracted, or invented. **Simulated** textures mimic reality, as in *Mr. and Mrs. Andrews*. Texture can be **abstracted** as well, meaning that it is based on some existing texture but has been simplified and regularized. The mane on the *Lion Capital* is an abstracted texture. **Invented** textures are apparently products of human imagination.

Building materials often have unique textures. Just think of marble, stone, wood, concrete, cloth, glass, stucco, plaster, metal, brick, or glazed tile, each with a different visual appeal, each with its own texture.

Texture and pattern are related: if a pattern is reduced drastically in size, it is often perceived as a texture, and if a texture is greatly increased in size, it is likely to be perceived as a pattern. The lion's mane on the *Lion Capital* can be read as either texture or pattern. **Pattern** is a configuration with a repeated visual form (or forms). **Natural patterns** occur all around us, in leaves and flowers, in cloud and crystal formations, in wave patterns, and so on. In natural patterns, the repeated elements may resemble each other but not be exactly alike. The intervals between elements also may vary. The tree branches and furrows in

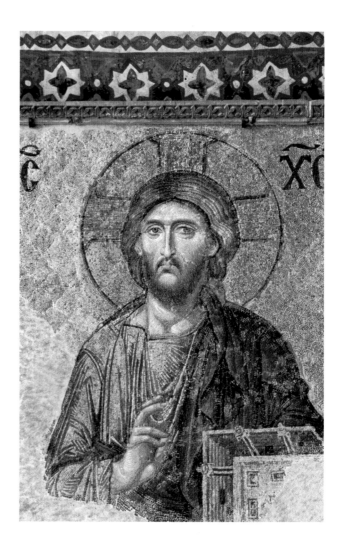

2.15 *Lion Capital* of column erected by Ashoka at Sarnath, India, c. 250 BCE. Polished sandstone, approx. 7′ high. Archeological Museum, Sarnath.

The careful carving of the sandstone results in smooth surfaces and areas of distinct texture.

2.16 *Detail of Deesis Mosaic in Hagia Sophia.* Believed to be 1185–1204. Mosaic tile.

Some media, like mosaic, have a texture that is inherent in the materials themselves.

the field in *Mr. and Mrs. Andrews* (Fig. 2.11) simulate natural patterns. **Geometric patterns** have regular elements spaced at regular intervals. They are common in math, interior design, and art. The Chilkat *Blanket* (Fig. 2.17) is covered with bold patterns abstracted from human and animal forms. The eyes overall were intended as a form of protection and power.

Pattern in art is often an organizing element, as with the *Blanket*, and the extensive use of pattern makes a striking visual impression. Some patterns are totally invented, some are geometric, some contain highly abstracted forms (like the *Blanket*), and some are inherent in the materials, like wood grain. Pattern also functions as **decoration** on objects such as wrapping paper, wallpaper, or fabric design. Pattern's function in these instances is to give visual pleasure.

Pattern serves various functions in architecture. It creates visual interest, whether it is a repeated structural

element or surface decoration. In the *Great Mosque of Cordoba* (Fig. 2.18), pattern appears both in the multiple arches and in the beige and terracotta banding, which is ornamentation that is not structurally necessary. Figure 2.1 is another view of the mosque interior, with more structural and surface pattern. These patterns may function to direct your eye to certain features of a building, like entrances. Pattern can also have symbolic value. In Islamic religious architecture, the amazing, rich patterns express the idea that all the wonder of creation originates in Allah.

Pattern is also an important tool for thinking visually. Pattern helps organize ideas and concepts into visual **diagrams** that make relationships clear. Pattern is the basis of flowcharts, street maps, mechanical diagrams, and floor plans. We see patterns in the creative work of many artists, engineers, and scientists. Pattern is inherent in almost all structural systems in architecture, which is evident in the diagrams later in this chapter (pages 47–50).

2.17 *Blanket.* Tlingit people, Chilkat style. Mountain goat wool and cedar bark, 31″ × 71″, excluding fringe. The Newark Museum, Newark, New Jersey.

The black and yellow patterns are abstracted from human or animal features and have a geometric quality.

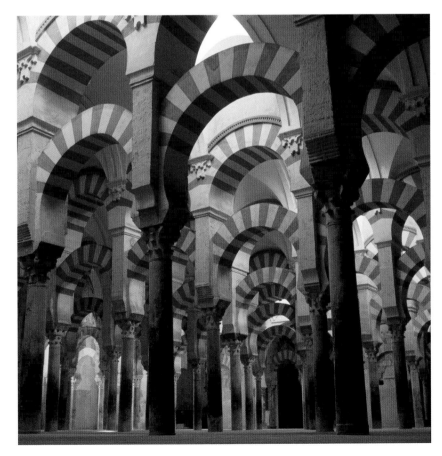

2.18 *Great Mosque of Cordoba*, interior, 786. Cordoba, Spain.

The arches are a vast network of pattern, and the color banding adds to the intensity of the pattern.

2.19 Martin Puryear. *That Profile*, 1997–1999. Stainless steel, bronze, 540″ × 360″ × 136″. Getty Museum, Los Angeles.

This sculpture encompasses a large volume but has little mass.

Shape and Volume

Shape is a two-dimensional visual entity. **Regular shapes** are **geometric**. We have names for many regular shapes, such as *circle*, *square*, *triangle*, *hexagon*, and *teardrop*. **Irregular shapes** are unique and have no simple, defining names. Instead, they are the color patches of a cat's fur, star clusters in space, or the outline of a human body. Irregular shapes are often **organic** or **biomorphic**, in that they resemble living beings. Shapes can be defined by outlines, or by an area of color surrounded by another area. *They're Biting* (Fig. 2.4) contains many abstracted, biomorphic, outlined shapes.

 Volume is three-dimensionality, in contrast to two-dimensional shape. Like shape, volumes can be regular or irregular, geometric or biomorphic. Shape and volume may simulate reality, may be abstracted from reality, or may be invented. Martin Puryear's *That Profile* (Fig. 2.19) is a regular volume, but its name suggests that it is abstracted from a biomorphic form. Volumes may have more or less physical bulk, or **mass**. An open or wire-frame structure, like *That Profile*, can have a large volume but little mass. The solid stone *Lion Capital* (Fig. 2.15) has both volume and mass.

 Shape and volume are key elements in architecture. Look at the buildings around you. What are their predominant shapes? What volumes do they enclose? How much mass do the structures have? What spaces surround them?

Space

In this section, we look at three kinds of space in relation to art: (1) the space in two-dimensional artwork; (2) the space of sculpture and architecture, which is both the area it occupies and the voids it contains; and (3) the space of performance art, installation, and intermedia work.

 First, space in two-dimensional art: two-dimensional art has **planar space**, the height and width of the picture surface. In *They're Biting* (Fig. 2.4), the fish, boat, and fishermen are distributed across the height and width of the picture plane. Yet, artists can create the illusion of deep space on the flat surface of two-dimensional art. Overlapping imagery and placement on the page are two simple ways. Again, in *They're Biting*, the fish at the bottom of the picture seem closer than the boat and buoy near the top. And the boat and buoy themselves are pushed forward because they overlap the horizon, which then is moved back.

 More complex illusions of space are created through **perspective**, a group of methods for creating the illusion of depth on a flat picture plane. **Atmospheric perspective** (or **aerial perspective**) refers to the light, bleached-out, fuzzy handling of distant forms to make them seem far away. We have already seen two works that illustrate atmospheric perspective: (1) Durer's *Artist drawing a model* (Fig. 2.5), where foreground shapes are bold and heavily shaded, versus the light, linear handling of the distant landscape; and (2) *Mr. and Mrs. Andrews* (Fig. 2.11), where the distant landscape is less colorful and less detailed.

Another kind of perspective is **linear perspective**, which operates on the theory that parallel lines appear to converge as they recede. They seem to meet on an imaginary line called the **horizon line**, or at eye level. The horizon line corresponds to the viewer's eye level in a picture, determining what the viewer perceives as "above" or "below."

The three types of linear perspective—one-, two-, and three-point—are shown in the diagram in Figure 2.20. In **one-point perspective** (2.20A), the frontal plane of a volume is closest to the viewer, and all other planes appear to

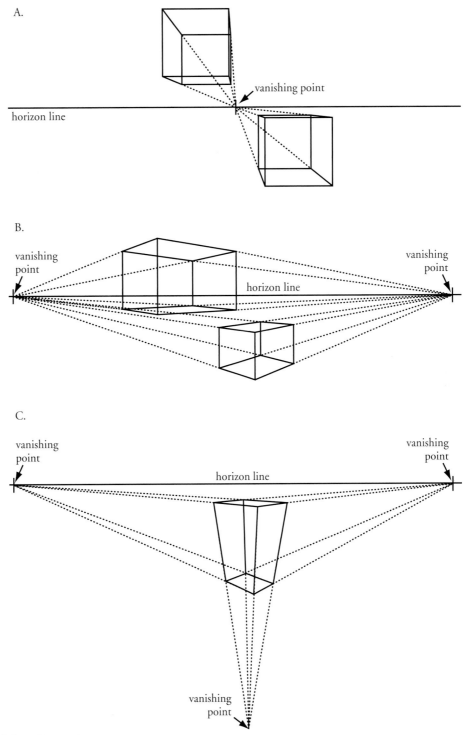

2.20 Diagram of Linear Perspective.

2.21 Ronald W. Davis. *Cube and Four Panels*. 1975. Acrylic on canvas, support: 110 $^1/_2''$ × 130 $^3/_4''$. Albright-Knox Art Gallery, Buffalo, New York.

Two-point perspective creates the illusion of an enormous, cavern-like interior space.

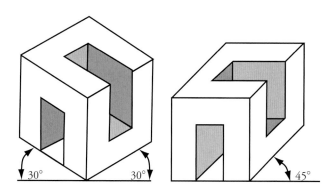

2.22, *left* A. An example of an ISOMETRIC projection. B. An example of an OBLIQUE projection.

recede to a single vanishing point. In **two-point perspective** (2.20B), a single edge (or line) of a volume is closest to the viewer, and all planes appear to recede to one of two vanishing points. In **three-point perspective** (2.20C), only a single point of a volume is closest to the viewer, and all planes seem to recede to one of three vanishing points. Figure 2.5, *Artist drawing a model*, is a precise exercise in one-point perspective. Ronald W. Davis' *Cube and Four Panels* (Fig.2.21) is an example of three-point perspective. In this case, the eye level of the viewer is above the cube and sides recede in three directions.

Two other systems to show space in a picture are isometric perspective and oblique perspective. **Isometric perspective**, which is especially used in architectural drafting, renders planes on a diagonal that does not recede in space (Fig. 2.22A). The side planes are drawn at a thirty-degree angle to the left and right. In **oblique perspective**, a three-dimensional object is rendered with the front and back parallel (Fig. 2.22B). The side planes are drawn at a forty-five-degree angle from the front plane. Figure 2.23 is *Festivities*, a detail of a Japanese screen depicting popular festivities from the Muromachi period. Oblique perspective is used to depict the architecture and people behind the fence, under the cloud.

Artists may use **multipoint perspective** in an image, so that various sections conform to different perspective systems. They also may use amplified or distorted perspective to give their image dramatic emphasis. In *The Morning Anxiety*, 1912 (Fig. 2.24), by Giorgio de Chirico, the perspective gives the painting the fractured space of a dream or a memory. The white building stretches out to the horizon line, while the dark building at right looms tall and recedes to a different vanishing point. The silhouette of a train occupies an even different, frontal space. The strange lighting and shadows contribute to the sense of ill-ease.

Now, let us turn to space in sculpture and architecture, which consists of the footprint occupied by the structure and also the voids and solids within each piece and immediately surrounding it. Look again at Martin Puryear's *That Profile* (Fig. 2.19), which is so memorable because of the large empty space that the framework contains and the sky and landscape seen through it. The voids and solids in Louise Nevelson's *Mirror Image I* (Fig. 2.10) create a rhythmic dance of dark shapes and even darker voids.

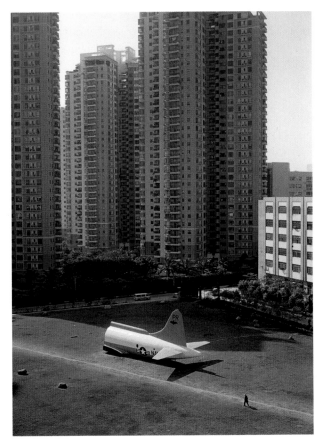

2.23, *above left* *Festivities*, detail of a screen depicting the popular festivities that took place at Shijo-gawa, Kyoto. Late Muromachi period, 16th century. Seikado Library, Tokyo.

The artist has used oblique perspective to give a sense of space going back from the lower right to the upper left.

2.24, *above right* GIORGIO DE CHIRICO. *The Morning Anxiety.* 1912. Oil on canvas. 32″ × 25″ MaRT (Museo di arte moderna e contemporanea di Trento e, Rovereto, Italy).

In this example of multipoint perspective, the dark structure seems to be overly tall while the white building stretches back to the horizon, resulting in an unreal or illogical depiction of space.

2.25, *left* HUANG YONG PING. *Bat Project I (Shenzhen)*, 2001. Replica of an American spy plane from middle of body to tail. China. Barbara Gladstone Gallery.

The location of an artwork affects what it means.

Finally, space in installation or performance art can be particularly significant, because part of the meaning comes from the environment. Huang Yong Ping's installation, *Bat Project I (Shenzhen)*, 2001 (Fig. 2.25), is a replica of a U.S. spy plane that collided with a Chinese plane in April 2001 and had to land in China, which caused an international furor. Huang's reconstruction of the back half of the plane was to be exhibited as part of a major international exhibition amid skyscrapers in the city of

2.26 MARCEL DUCHAMP. *Nude Descending a Staircase (No. 2)*, 1912. Oil on canvas, 57 $^{7}/_{8}''$ × 35 $^{1}/_{8}''$.

Motion is implied by the repeating shapes in a downward direction.

Shenzhen. Before the installation was finished, the replica was removed without the artist's permission, because officials feared that it might damage international relations between the United States, China, and France (a sponsor of the exhibition). It was later installed (again without the artist's knowledge) as a permanent feature in an amusement park. Thus, the impact of the same piece of art, which was too sensational for a major exhibition, was neutralized by the amusement park location.

Time and Motion

A lot of art is static; it does not move. Yet time and motion can still be important elements. **Time** is the period that viewers study and absorb the message and formal qualities of an artwork. Motion can be implied, as in Marcel Duchamp's *Nude Descending a Staircase (No. 2)*, from 1912 (Fig. 2.26). Factors that contribute to its illusion of motion are (1) the rhythmic repetition of abstracted forms in a walking pattern, and (2) the descending arrangement of elements from the upper left down to the lower right.

However, motion is integral to film/video, interactive digital art, kinetic sculpture, and performance. In these works, time and motion are related, as motion cannot exist without time, and motion marks the passage of time. Chinese artist Cai Guo-Qiang's *Black Rainbow: Explosion Project for Valencia, Spain*, 2005 (Fig. 2.27), is one of a series that occurs in cities such as Edinburgh and Beijing. These black rainbows were intended as omens of international unease, and although violence and explosive materials are frightening, they can also attract with their power and beauty. In a matter of mere minutes, the loud explosions are set off, and black smoke appears in the sky, spreads into a rainbow-like arc, and then dissipates.

With architecture and large sculpture, we cannot grasp all their features in an instant, from a single point of view. These works unfold in time as we move through them or around them. For example, a traveler first sees the twenty-nine Ajanta Caves as doorways and porches carved into a curving hillside in west central India. This modest outside view does not prepare the viewer for the amazing *Ceiling of Cave 26* in a darkened, columned hall with a shrine to Buddha, all cut out of the living rock (Fig. 2.28). Yet even more unfolds in time and with the viewer's motion. To one side in Cave 26 is *Parinirvana* (Fig. 2.29), or a sculpture of the death of Buddha, behind a row of columns.

2.27 CAI GUO-QIANG. Black Rainbow: Explosion Project for Valencia, Spain, 2005.

Some artwork moves and changes in time and is not in fixed form. In this case, the change was rapid.

2.28 View of the *Ceiling of Cave 26*, one of the many caves at Ajanta dating back to 700 CE. Maharashtra, India.

See Figure 2.29 for another view of the cave interior. Art can be spatially complicated, which requires viewers to walk around to see it all.

2.29 A second view of Cave 26 at Ajanta. *Parinirvana* between the columns. Cave 26 (chaitya hall). Late 5th century. Ajanta Caves, Maharashtra, India.

Looking up gives one view of the cave; looking to the side is a completely different experience.

Chance/Improvisation/Spontaneity

Many artists purposely allow for chance, improvisation, or spontaneity, to add something unexpected in their work or to make it unique each time it is seen. Some aspects of chance are created by uncontrollable factors, such as atmospheric conditions at the moment that Cai Guo-Qiang's *Black Rainbows* exploded into the sky. Some artists embrace chance and weave it into the very form of the work.

CONNECTION Allan Kaprow's *Household* (Fig. 15.23) was a Happening performed by several men and women, who worked from a simple premise but were free to improvise as the performance unfolded.

Engaging All the Senses

Although we tend to think of art in visual terms, many artworks appeal to other senses as well. Cai Guo-Qiang's explosions are one obvious example. The *Ajanta Caves* stimulate sound, smell, temperature, and visual sensations. Film, video, interactive digital art, and performance have sound components to accompany the visual.

African masquerades are art forms that incorporate art objects, singing, dancing, and community celebrations and rituals. The performances of the *Masqueraders of Burkina Faso* (Fig. 2.30) bring spirits among the people, promote community well-being, and ensure good crops and other necessities. Masks are not considered static sculptures but are integral parts of the larger masquerade art form. The masks and raffia costumes also disguise the performers' identities.

PRINCIPLES OF COMPOSITION

The arrangement of the formal elements in a work of art is called its **composition**. The principles of composition are balance, rhythm, proportion and scale, emphasis, unity, and variety.

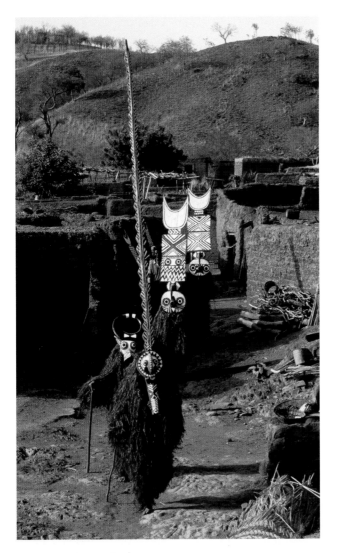

Balance

Balance in an artwork results from placing the elements so that their visual weights seem evenly distributed. *Weight* generally means the amount of attention an element commands from the viewer. For example, large shapes demand more attention than small; complex forms have greater visual weight than simple ones; and vivid colors are visually weightier than faded colors. In **symmetrical balance**, visual weight is distributed evenly throughout the composition. If an imaginary line is drawn vertically down the center of the work, one side would mirror the other, as in the Chilkat *Blanket* (Fig. 2.17). **Asymmetrical balance** is achieved by the careful distribution of uneven elements. In *The Morning Anxiety* (Fig. 2.24), the bright and dark areas are approximately balanced around a central vertical axis. **Radial balance** results when all the elements in the composition visually radiate outward from a central point. Radial balance is often an organizing principle in spiritually based art, featured in mandalas, church windows, temple plans, and mosque domes (Fig. 2.1). The magnificent *Angkor Wat* temple in Cambodia is laid out in a modified radial plan (Fig. 2.31).

2.30, left *Bwa Masqueraders.* Burkina Faso.

Art forms such as performances, masquerades, and film engage more senses than just vision.

2.31, below *Angkor Wat,* Central Temple Complex, Cambodia, c. 1113–1150 CE.

Symmetry and radial balance add to the grandeur of this enormous temple complex.

Rhythm

In a composition, **rhythm** is the repetition of carefully placed elements separated by intervals. These recurrent visual "beats" move the viewer's eye through the composition in jerky, smooth, fast, or slow ways. Rhythm is related to pattern, but it affects the entire composition.

Regular rhythm is smooth and even, where some visual element is systematically repeated with a standard interval in between. Closely related is **alternating rhythm**, where different elements are repeatedly placed side by side, which produces a regular and anticipated sequence. In architecture, rhythm is often alternating solids and voids. **Eccentric rhythm** is irregular, but not so much so that the visual beats do not connect. In the bas-relief of the *Churning of the Ocean of Milk*, from Angkor Wat (Fig. 2.32), we see examples of regular rhythm (the heads), alternating rhythm (the legs), and eccentric rhythm (the dancing spirits overhead). The relief shows an eternal, cosmic struggle in which demons and gods churn the ocean for precious things that have been lost. The visual repetition is a fitting expression for this rhythmic physical struggle.

Proportion and Scale

Proportion refers to the size of one part in relation to another within a work of art, or the size of one part in relation to the whole. The small dancers at the top of *Churning of the Ocean of Milk* are proportionally much smaller than the larger figures below. For another example of proportion, return to the *Bwa Masqueraders* to see how large the masks are in relation to the dancers' bodies and, even within the masks, the size relationship between the face area and the elaborate forms above them.

Scale is the size of something in relation to what we assume to be normal. Figure 2.33 shows a real scale shift upward, with cars driving through *The Binocular Entrance to the Chiat Building* (sculpture by Claes Oldenburg and Coosje van Bruggen; architect, Frank O. Gehry).

Proportion and scale are expressive devices. The *Binocular Entrance* is meant to be dramatic, memorable, and humorous. The tall sculptural forms on the masks of the *Bwa Masqueraders* suggest their otherworldly power. **Hieratic scaling** is a device that points to the highest-ranking person in the scene, as in *Parinirvana* (Fig. 2.29), where the reclining Buddha is enormous compared to all other figures around him. Scale in architecture is its

2.32 *Churning of the Ocean of Milk*. Bas-relief. Angkor Wat, Cambodia.

Rhythm is an organizing principle of composition that places repeating elements in regular, alternating, or eccentric arrangements.

2.33 Claes Oldenburg, Coosje van Bruggen, and Frank O. Gehry. *The Binocular Entrance to the Chiat Building,* 1985–1991. Venice, California.

The binoculars are on a larger scale than everything else around them.

overall size in relation to the human body, which also has expressive potential. Large-scale buildings dwarf and overwhelm people, whereas small buildings often seem comfortable to the individual.

In real life, most people see art in reproductions. Sometimes there are internal clues regarding scale, such as the cars in *The Binocular Entrance* (Figure 2.33), but often scale can be very uncertain, with no way of knowing how large an artwork actually is. Reading the caption gives you some information, but you have to exert your imagination to really see the piece. This chapter contains several reproductions of three-dimensional works. Can you remember which was the largest: *Human/Need/Desire* (Fig. 2.7); *Mirror Image I* (Fig. 2.10); *The Lion Capitol* (Fig. 2.15); or the Chilkat *Blanket* (Fig. 2.17)?

Emphasis

Emphasis is the result of one or more focal points in an artwork. When there are several focal points, lesser ones

are called **accents**. In Figure 2.26, *Nude Descending a Staircase*, the lightest tones are the most emphasized. Emphasis in architecture means that one part of a building becomes a focal point. Architects often use ornamentation for emphasis. The *Binocular Entrance* is obviously the focal point on that building.

Unity and Variety

Unity is the quality of overall cohesion within an artwork. **Variety** is the element of difference within an artwork. They would seem on the surface to be mutually exclusive qualities, but, in fact, they coexist in all artworks, evoking in viewers a fascination that makes them keep coming back and keep looking. In *Nude Descending a Staircase*, unity is achieved with the brown palette, and also with the shapes, which are simplified geometric versions of the human body. Variety is introduced with the varying angles of the shapes and the changes in lighting.

In architecture, unity is the quality that makes the disparate architectural parts coalesce, whereas variety adds opposing elements to buildings. It is interesting to see how architects use nature to create variety in their designs. House plants add variety to the interior, while planter beds and gardens relieve the austerity of the exterior. Within neighborhoods, rows of houses are juxtaposed with green-belts and parks.

CONNECTION An extreme example of variety is the density of Manhattan relieved by the expansiveness of New York City's *Central Park*, designed by landscape architects Frederick Law Olmsted and Calvert Vaux (Fig. 15.8).

STRUCTURAL SYSTEMS IN ARCHITECTURE

So far in this chapter, we have studied formal elements and principles of composition that apply to both art and architecture. Now we turn to structural systems, which apply to architecture only. Structural systems enable buildings to stand up and enclose space, using materials like brick,

2.34 El Castillo, ninth–tenth centuries, elevated view. Chichén Itzá, Mexico.

This structure is nearly solid stone. The small temple on top is an example of load-bearing construction, with its walls uninterrupted except for a few small doors.

stone, wood, steel, and concrete. Structural systems and materials strongly influence the design and visual appearance of buildings.

Traditional Building Methods

Load-Bearing Construction

Early architecture was made of shaped earth, bones, wood, or stacked stone. Builders used whatever materials were locally available. The igloo made of ice blocks is one example. Ancient houses in China were dug right out of the earth. In many places, people stacked material to create solid walls that were usually thicker at the bottom to provide stability. Early roofs were often lightweight, impermanent material like reeds or thatch, as in the sun-dried brick structures in the ancient Near East. This kind of architecture is called "load bearing" because all areas of the walls support the structure above them, and the walls have few openings.

An extreme example of a load-bearing structure is *El Castillo*, a Mayan pyramid and temple at Chichén Itzá, in Mexico (Fig. 2.34). The pyramid base is almost solid, with

BASIC POST-AND-LINTEL MODULE
Arrows indicate the downward distribution of weight

COLONNADE

GRID OF POST-AND-LINTEL MODULES,
IN STONE
Many interior posts are needed to support
the stone lintels

GRID OF POST-AND-LINTEL
MODULES, WITH WOOD LINTELS
Fewer posts are needed, and longer
lintels are possible

2.35 Diagram Showing Post-and-Lintel Construction.

only a steep, claustrophobic tunnel inside that runs from the ground to the top. The small stone structure on top has thick walls with small doorways, a necessity given the weight of the roof above. However, since ancient times, people have made the aesthetic decision to have air and light in their buildings. The rest of this section looks at ways to open up structures and to make this possible.

Post-and-Lintel Construction

One ancient method of constructing walls, making openings, and supporting a roof is the **post-and-lintel system**. The basic module is two upright posts supporting a cross beam or **lintel** (Fig. 2.35). Posts can be either rectangular or cylindrical. Refined and decorated cylindrical posts are called **columns**, and a row of columns supporting lintels is called a **colonnade**. A grid of posts and lintels can support the roof of a large interior space (Fig. 2.35). This is **hypostyle** construction, marked by rooms filled with columns.

CONNECTION An example of a hypostyle hall is the *First Hypostyle Hall* at the Horus Temple at Edfu, Egypt (Fig. 8.35). The thick columns support a stone roof.

Post-and-lintel structures are often rectilinear, with prominent vertical and horizontal lines, as evident in *The Temple of Athena Nike*, on the Acropolis in Athens, Greece

2.36 MNESICLES. The *Temple of Athena Nike* (right) and the corner of *Propylaea* (left), 437–432 BCE. Athens.

The temple on the right shows post-and-lintel construction in its two porches, and load-bearing construction in the solid wall in between.

(Fig. 2.36). The side walls of the *Temple* are load bearing. The construction materials are important. Stone is durable, but heavy and brittle, so stone lintels need closely spaced supports. Wood, however, is light, flexible, and strong, and able to span great distances, so larger interior spaces can be opened up, and the posts can be thinned down. Of course, ancient wood buildings are long gone, while stone ones remain. The relative impermanence of wood and its ability to burn are its greatest drawbacks.

Important subcategories of post-and-lintel architecture are the Classical Greek and Roman architectural orders (Fig. 2.37). An order consists of a specifically designed column with a **base**, a **shaft**, a **capital**, and an **entablature**, all exhibiting standardized proportions and decorative ornamentation. The oldest is the **Doric Order**,

2.37, *below* Diagram of Greek and Roman Orders.

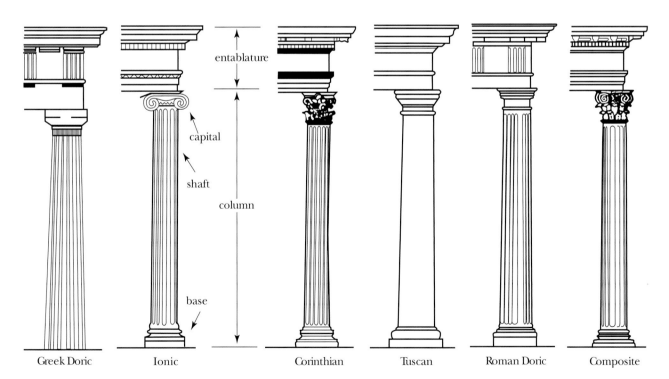

Greek Doric   Ionic   Corinthian   Tuscan   Roman Doric   Composite

2.38 Chinese wood frame structural system, showing brackets and cantilevers.

originating in the Greek Archaic period (650–500 BCE). The simple design is geometric, heavy, and relatively without ornamentation. Its column has no base, and its capital is a simple cushion. The ancient Greeks considered the Doric Order to exhibit masculine qualities. The temple porch on the *Propylaea*, to the left in Figure 2.36, is a Doric structure. The second order to appear was the **Ionic Order**, which is taller, more slender, and more decorative than the Doric, and was considered feminine. It has a stepped base and a scrolled, carved capital. It originated during the Greek Classical (Hellenic) period (500–323 BCE). *The Temple of Athena Nike* (Fig. 2.36 on the right) is Ionic. Later still was the **Corinthian Order**, which is the most complex and organic, with delicately carved acanthus leaves on its capital, dating from the Hellenistic period (323–100 BCE). Roman variations on those orders are Tuscan, Roman Doric, and Composite.

Wood Frame Construction

Wood frame architecture is very common in the East and the West. Wood frames have been used in the West,

especially for houses and small apartment buildings, and many feature load-bearing walls and trusses (see page 46).

The Chinese developed a distinctive wood frame architecture, based on the post-and-lintel model. This is the **complete frame system**, which contained these innovations: (1) totally non-load-bearing walls, (2) brackets, and (3) cantilevers. All the weight of the entire building was borne by large upright posts. Walls could be completely eliminated.

In the fifth century BCE, the Chinese developed **brackets**, which are clusters of interlocking pieces of wood shaped like inverted pyramids at the tops of upright posts, directly beneath the roof (Fig. 2.38). With brackets, fewer posts are needed, allowing for more spacious interiors. Two centuries later, the Chinese developed half-cylinder, overlapping roof tiles. Their considerable weight adds stability to the wood frame structure below, and they could be glazed in different colors.

Beginning in the eighth century CE, Chinese architects first used the **cantilever**, a horizontal beam anchored to and projecting out from an upright post (Fig. 2.38). Cantilevers support deep roof eaves and balconies. The roof design is often the most important and distinctive feature of significant historical Chinese buildings. Supported by cantilevers, the roofs often project far beyond the edges of the building proper, with shapes that incorporate very complex curves. Brackets are outlined and painted in bright colors.

Arches, Vaulting, and Domes

Stone would have limited use as a building material because of its weight and brittle nature were it not for the **arch** (Fig. 2.39), a structural innovation that dates back to ancient Egypt. The arch is made of wedge-shaped stones, or **voussoirs**, that are constructed from bottom to top, using a wooden scaffold for support. When the final **keystone** is placed in the center, the arch can support itself and the scaffolding can be removed. Arches can rest either on rectangular **piers** or on cylindrical columns, as we saw in the *Great Mosque of Cordoba* (Fig. 2.18).

2.39 Diagram Showing Arches, Arcades, Vaulting, Buttressing, and Domes.

voussoir
keystone
pier
round arch

arches
pointed arch

arcades

vaulting

barrel vault
groin vault

ribbed vault
with pointed arch

buttressing

arch with solid buttressing
flying buttresses
flying buttresses

dome

dome on a cylinder
dome on pendentives

Arches can be either round or pointed (Fig. 2.39). With a round arch, the distance between the supports determines the height of the arch, because the arch is a semicircle. A pointed arch is actually a round arch with some of the center removed. Builders can make a pointed arch higher or lower, regardless of the distance between its supports. A straight row of arches placed side by side is called an **arcade**.

Unlike post-and-lintel structures, in which the weight of the roof and lintel press down equally on all parts below, the weight of the arch is directed outward and then downward to the load-bearing columns or piers. There is no downward pressure over the void of the arch, and so higher and larger spaces can be spanned without the need for additional support posts. Arches can be constructed of stone, brick, or concrete. Arches, however, do have to

be supported from the outside to prevent lateral movement that would cause them to collapse. That support is called **buttressing** (Fig. 2.39), which is additional exterior masonry placed at key points to keep the arch stable. Buttresses can be solid masonry, or they may be opened up with their own internal arches, called **flying buttresses**.

Builders can expand and multiply the arch in several ways to create entire roofs made of stone. These stone roofs are called **vaults**, or **vaulting**, and are very durable and fireproof (Fig. 2.39). A **barrel vault** is an arch extended in depth from front to back, forming a tunnel-like structure. Barrel vaults have the disadvantage of creating rather dark interiors, as there are no windows in the vault area (Fig. 2.39). **Groin vaults**, sometimes called **cross vaults**, are barrel vaults positioned at ninety-degree angles to cross or intersect one another. This innovation allowed light to enter vaulted spaces and gave variation to the interior space, as seen in the *Cathedral of Dubrovnik: Nave Groin Vault* (Fig. 2.40).

A **ribbed vault** (see Fig. 2.39) is a variation of the groin vaulting system in which arches diagonally cross over the groin vault, forming skeletal ribs. Pointing the arch in the ribbed vault creates a **gothic vault**. Used commonly in the Gothic era in Europe, this innovation allowed builders to eliminate large wall areas under arches and to fill the resulting space with gleaming stained glass.

A **dome** theoretically is an arch rotated on its vertical axis to form a hemispheric vault. Domes can rest on a cylinder or a circular **drum**, or they can be placed on **pendentives**, which are the triangular concave sections created when a dome is placed on arches. Domes may also be placed on a square or a polygonal base, in which case the spaces created between the dome and its base are called **squinches**. Domes can be oval, as is visible at the top of Figure 2.40, the *Cathedral of Dubrovnik*. Domes can be ribbed and scalloped in shape, as seen in the Chapter Opener of the Great Mosque at Cordoba.

Vaulted or domed buildings are generally quite massive because of the material used to make them—stone, brick, or concrete. Vaults are very heavy structures and require thick supports. In many cases, architects disguise the massiveness of vaulted structures by placing buttresses on the exterior, out of sight of those enjoying the view of the interior. In the *Cathedral of Dubrovnik*, the plain, bright, airy vaults above contrast with the gray, heavy-looking arcade below.

2.40 Andrea Buffalini. *Cathedral of Dubrovnik: Nave Groin Vault.* Construction finished in 1713. Dubrovnik, Croatia.

Groin vaults cover the ceiling, except for the dome at the top of the page.

Recent Methods and Materials

Modern buildings differ from older structures in many ways. New materials, especially steel and steel-reinforced

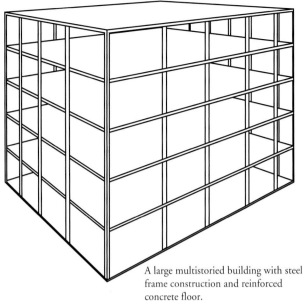

A large multistoried building with steel frame construction and reinforced concrete floor.

Diagram of reinforced concrete showing a metal bar embedded in concrete. This diagram shows a reinforced concrete floor with a cantilevered balcony.

2.41 Diagram of Steel Frame Construction and Reinforced Concrete.

2.42 *Seagram Building at Night*, 1954–1958. New York City. Steel frame construction made possible the gleaming modern skyscraper.

concrete, have resulted in structures taller than anything ever built before the nineteenth century. Like the human body, many modern buildings feature an internal skeletal support system. The outer surface of the wall is like a skin stretched over the bones.

Our expectations of basic comforts have changed, too, so now buildings have a variety of operating systems, such as heating and cooling systems, electricity, plumbing, and telephone and computer wiring, as well as appliances, intercoms, and surveillance systems. Two hundred years ago, this was all unknown.

Steel Frame Construction

High-strength structural steel was developed in the late nineteenth century and, with the invention of the elevator, made very tall buildings possible for the first time. **Steel frame construction** essentially expands the post-and-lintel grid vertically as well as laterally, with steel (instead of wood or stone), which can function as a skeleton that will support multistoried buildings (Fig. 2.41). Floors are usually poured concrete with embedded metal reinforcing bars.

At first, steel frame construction was disguised with stone facings so that buildings looked traditional, rugged, and durable. By 1900, however, the simple horizontal and vertical lines of steel frame construction were emphasized and apparent. Windows became big, reaching from framing member to framing member. Steel frame construction has been widely used ever since for all kinds of structures, but especially the high-rise office buildings that filled the downtowns of major cities all over the world from the mid- to late twentieth century, like the *Seagram Building at Night* (Fig. 2.42), designed by Ludwig Mies van der Rohe and completed in 1958. Called the **International Style**, these stripped-down, glass-covered, rectangular box buildings were enormously popular throughout the world. This image shows the Seagram Building nearing completion, and the appeal of the style is immediately apparent: the building is luminous and dramatic compared to the older structures around it. The skeletal structure is visible, and both horizontality and verticality are emphasized. International Style buildings generally had no ornamentation at all. Some critics have argued against the widespread, homogenizing use of the International Style in cities across the world, because many, many older structures were demolished, and they had given civic centers their distinct character.

Reinforced Concrete

Another building innovation that resulted from the development of high-strength structural steel was **reinforced concrete**, also known as ferroconcrete. Concrete was used by the Romans, but it is brittle and cracks easily. Ferroconcrete—steel reinforcing bars embedded in wet concrete—gives the concrete tensile strength, while the concrete provides a durable surface. Reinforced concrete was used for the floors of skyscrapers from their early days.

Gradually, architects began using reinforced concrete as an external building material for the finished surfaces of buildings. Concrete can be poured over steel reinforcing rods or mesh that can be shaped into any form the architect wishes. It makes possible free-form architecture, which places no limitations on the shape and mass of a structure.

CONNECTION Three famous examples of reinforced concrete structures appear in this book: Le Corbusier's *Notre Dame du Haut* (thumbnail, Fig. 8.29), the *Solomon R. Guggenheim Museum* (Fig. 15.5) and the *Sydney Opera House* (Fig. 15.4).

Truss and Geodesic Construction

Another skeletal structure, the **truss**, is based on a frame made of a series of triangles constructed in steel or wood (Fig. 2.43A). Trusses are very rigid because of the triangle and can be used to span great spaces or to support other structures. Steel trusses are common on railroad bridges, and wooden trusses can be found in the attics of most frame homes in the United States.

The geodesic dome (Fig. 2.43B) is a skeletal frame based on triangles that are grouped into very stable, strong polyhedrons. Polyhedrons are solid geometric figures

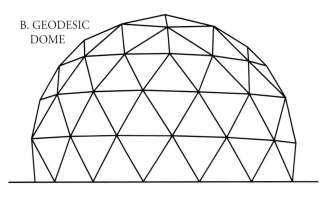

2.43 Truss (A) and Geodesic Dome (B) Structural Systems.

having many faces and are found in nature. Geodesic domes can be very large, and they require no interior supports. Builders can easily assemble the skeletal frame from prefabricated modular parts. The framework can be sheathed in glass, plastic, plywood, or a variety of other materials.

The triangles of truss or geodesic structures may be left visible when buildings are finished. In these cases, the buildings have a pronounced geometric appearance. The linear network of the truss skeleton thus becomes an important visual feature.

CONNECTION R. Buckminster Fuller's *U.S. Pavilion* (Fig. 6.37) was an enormous example of a geodesic dome.

Suspension and Tensile Construction

Suspension and tensile construction consists of steel cables attached to vertical pylons or masts that can support structures like bridges, exhibition tents, or sport arenas. The **Olympic Stadium**, Munich (Fig 2.44), designed by Gunter Behnisch with Otto Frei, was part of a vast sports complex with peaked roofs that recall the mountains of the nearby Alps. Computers were used to assist in designing roof shapes and supports and in determining how the structure would react in weather conditions. Nothing before had been undertaken at this scale, with this type of construction. In this case, a cable net attached to vertical masts holds up the PVC-coated polyester roof. Otto Frei was a pioneer in lightweight design.

2.44 Gunter Behnisch with Otto Frei. *Olympic Stadium, Munich,* 1972. Munich, Germany.

Suspended steel cables hold up the roof mesh, efficiently providing shade over a large area.

3.1 Nam June Paik. *Electronic Superhighway: Continental U.S., Alaska, Hawaii*, 1995. (Continental U.S. only.) 49-channel, closed-circuit video installation, neon, steel, and electronic components, 15′ ×40′ × 4′. Gift of the artist. Smithsonian American Art Museum, Washington, DC.

All kinds of media can be used to make art.

3

MEDIA

In the previous chapter we studied the elements and principles of art and architecture. Now we turn to the media used to make artworks. Media for drawing, painting, printmaking, sculpture, and craft-making has existed since prehistory. More recent media include film or digital imaging. The human body has always been used in artistic performance.

PREVIEW

A medium is the actual material substance used to make a work of art. This chapter covers various media within disciplines, which are the branches of art-making activity. We will start with the media used in drawing, painting, and printmaking, and then move to three-dimensional media and processes.

Media can be natural materials, such as stone, shell, straw, or clay. Synthetic art media include acrylics, fiberglass, or neon, as seen in Figure 3.1, Nam June Paik's Electronic Superhighway: Continental U.S., Alaska, Hawaii, *1995. As technology has progressed, photography, film, recordings, videos, and digital imaging have provided new media for artists.*

Going beyond the art supply store, artists also use materials from theater, industry, construction, or advertising. They can find materials in dumpsters and resale shops. They are free to use any media that best expresses their idea or subject matter.

In this chapter, we will see examples of artworks made from clay, bronze, natural fibers, found objects, wood, oil paint, acrylic paint, tempera, fresco, ink, charcoal, silverpoint, colored pencils, pastels, cloth, glass, gems, embroidery, photographs, neon lights, jade, steel, printmaking materials, human teeth, old tires, and more.

THE IMPORTANCE OF MATERIALS

It is easy to think that the idea is all that matters in a work of art, but in fact the physical embodiment of the idea is important as well. When artists choose the best medium to support their ideas, their art is stronger. The chapter opening image, Nam June Paik's *Electronic Superhighway: Continental U.S., Alaska, Hawaii*, 1995, is a large 49-channel, closed-circuit video installation, composed of neon, steel, and electronic components. All of those materials speak of advertising, signage, and televised imagery, which reinforce the idea that we know the United States in snippets, through bits of travelogues or passing scenes flashing through the car window. It would not be the same if Paik had made a painting of this idea.

Damien Hirst is an artist known for shocking or controversial works, an effect that is compounded by the materials

3.2 Damien Hirst. *For the Love of God*, 2007. Platinum life-size cast of a human skull, human teeth, and diamonds, 6.75″ × 5″ × 7.5″

The materials used to make this work of art add to its sensationalism.

he used in *For the Love of God* (Fig. 3.2), which is a platinum cast of an eighteenth-century human skull covered with 8,601 diamonds (1,106.18 carats) with the original human teeth. Skulls often symbolize mortality as well as *vanitas*, or the ultimate emptiness and impermanence of earthly things. In this case, there is an extreme contrast between the death skull and a lavish, rich lifestyle suggested by the diamonds. The asking price for this artwork was $50 million, a sensational price that is within the means only of the very wealthy, who are mortal as anyone else.

CONNECTION An example of a painting with a vanitas theme is Jan Davidsz. de Heem's *A Table of Desserts* (Figure 6.14).

We tend to think of media solely as the materials that the artist manipulates, but equally important is the **support**, which underlies the artwork. Figure 3.3, *Royal Profile*, from Egypt in the sixteenth–thirteenth centuries BCE, was drawn in paint on a fragment of limestone. Although the rock surface is rough and unforgiving, the artist rendered a clear and precise profile with pristine contour lines. Artists have made artwork on rocks, the earth, walls, paper, metal surfaces, and so on.

MEDIA IN TWO-DIMENSIONAL ART

Drawing

Drawing is one of the oldest disciplines in the history of art making, and it also seems to be innate. The first marks a toddler makes are scribbles, which are primary to the act of drawing. A wide range of materials are used in drawing.

Dry Media

Dry media for drawing often come in some kind of stick form. Pencil, sanguine chalk, pastel, and silverpoint are examples of dry media used in drawing.

One of the most common drawing tools is the **pencil**, a graphite rod in a wood or metal holder. The graphite comes in varying degrees of hardness, with the hardest creating thin, controlled lines. Robert Gober's *Untitled*, 1995 (Fig. 3.4), resembles a common, quick pencil sketch. His work deals with memory, childhood, religion, and sexuality. Pencils can also be used for large, incredibly detailed studies. Judith Baca's colored-pencil drawing, *Las Tres Marias*, 1976 (Fig. 3.5), contains two tightly rendered life-size drawings of women that look very much like a photograph. The drawings and the mirror in the middle invite viewers to "try on" different identities.

3.3, top left *Royal Profile*. Egypt, Ramesside period. Painted limestone. Louvre, Paris.

Ancient Egyptian artists did practice sketches on small pieces of rocks. Today, the support for drawing and painting is more often canvas or paper.

3.4, left ROBERT GOBER. *Untitled*, 1995. Pencil on paper, 8″ × 4 7/8″. Gift of Sarah-Ann and Werner H. Kramarsky. (159.1997). The Museum of Modern Art, New York.

The pencil is probably the most familiar art medium, and also one of the most versatile.

3.5, top right JUDITH BACA. *Las Tres Marias*, 1976. Colored pencil on paper mounted on panel with upholstery backing and mirror. Overall: 68 1/4″ × 50 1/4″ × 2 1/4″. Smithsonian American Art Museum, Washington, DC.

Pencil and colored pencil are capable of producing near-photographic detail, shown here in two life-sized drawings.

3.6 Douglas Schlesier. *Stone God Forbidden City*, 2002. Charcoal on paper with gold leaf and color, 25" × 38".

The rich blacks of charcoal create visual drama in this drawing.

3.7 Edgar Degas. *At the Milliner's* (ca. 1882). Pastel on paper, 27 5/8" × 27 3/4". Gift of Mrs. David M. Levy. The Museum of Modern Art, New York.

Pastels are sticks of almost pure pigment, and because of that, pastel drawings have an intensity that surpasses most other media.

Douglas Schlesier's *Stone God Forbidden City* (Fig. 3.6) was rendered in **charcoal**, a carbon stick created from burnt wood, with added touches of color and gold leaf. Charcoal is capable of producing rich, deep, dark areas and a range of lighter tones as well.

Chalk and **pastels** are colored materials held together by wax or glue and shaped into sticks. Sticks with more colored material and less wax produce soft, smudgy lines, whereas those with more wax or glue render precise,

3.8 Joseph Stella. *Marcel Duchamp* (c. 1920). Silverpoint on paper, 24 1/4" × 18 3/4". Katherine S. Dreier Bequest. (210.1953) The Museum of Modern Art, New York.

Silverpoint drawings are known for their delicacy and precise lines.

controlled lines. Pastels and chalks can be used both precisely and expressively. Edgar Degas was a master of pastel drawing, as seen in *At the Milliner* (Fig. 3.7), with expressive lines, colors, patterns, and textures.

A **silverpoint** drawing is produced by a thin stylus made of silver that leaves marks on paper or wood coated with layers of gesso as a ground. A **ground** is a fluid brushed onto a support to change the surface quality of the support. **Gesso** is a common ground made of very fine powdered white chalk suspended in glue (the traditional method) or acrylic medium (modern gesso). In this case, the gesso makes the paper better able to accept the silverpoint line. The metallic lines in silverpoint drawing will eventually tarnish and darken with age. This technique is seen in Joseph Stella's 1920 portrait of *Marcel Duchamp* (Fig. 3.8), an artist whose work was shown in Figure 2.26. Because silverpoint holds a point longer than other media, silverpoint drawings are distinguished by very delicate lines made with precision and control.

Wet Media

In drawing, wet media are in liquid form. Ink is the most common wet medium, and it can be used with either brush or pen. The combination of lines made by pen marks and washes applied by brush makes visually fluid imagery. This is seen in Mi Wanzhong's *Tree, Bamboo and Rock* (Fig. 3.9), with calligraphy by Chen Meng. Pen and brush each leave distinctive marks, with a wide range of effects resulting from diluting the ink. Drawing and painting overlap in artworks done in ink; *Tree, Bamboo and Rock* could be classified as a drawing or as a monochromatic painting.

Today, ink is most commonly found in felt-tipped pens and markers. Artists frequently grab any convenient writing tool for sketches. Yoshimoto Nara is a Japanese artist whose *Puffy girl/Screen memory*, from 1992–2000 (Fig. 3.10), is made with felt-tipped pens on a postcard.

3.9, *left* MI WANZHONG. *Tree, Bamboo and Rock.* Calligraphy by Chen Meng. Ink, 43 $^1/_3''$ × 14 $^1/_4''$. Musée National des Arts Asiatiques-Guimet, Paris.

Ink is a versatile medium. It can be applied to paper with a pen for controlled lines or with a brush for gray washes or bold, dramatic lines.

3.10, *below* YOSHITOMO NARA. *Puffy girl/Screen memory*, 1992–2000. Felt-tipped pen on postcard, 5 $^7/_8''$ × 4 $^1/_8''$ (14.9 (10.5 cm). Fractional and promised gift of David Teiger in honor of Agnes Gund. The Museum of Modern Art, New York.

When making sketches or drawings, artists frequently use whatever is available among their ordinary pens and pencils.

Nara is known for his drawings and seemingly quick, casual sketches of aggressive, angry children. Nara remarks that these are but small, irate beings surrounded by much larger, much more threatening adults.

Experimental Drawing Media and New Technologies

As mentioned in the Preview of this chapter, artists can choose from just about any material to use as a medium in their artwork. Cai Guo-Qiang's *Drawing for Transient Rainbow*, August 2003 (Fig. 3.11), is made with gunpowder on two pieces of paper. The sketch is related to the events he stages around the world, like *Black Rainbow* (Fig. 2.27).

Digital technologies have provided new ways for artists and architects to produce drawings. The architect Arata Isozaki's *Nara Convention Hall*, 1992 (Fig. 3.12), is a computer-generated print, created with the assistance of a computer-aided design program, which uses plots and mathematical formulas to produce vector drawings, three-dimensional solids, and surface modelers. Artists use computers with drawing and painting software to produce raster-based drawings, which are composed of many (millions of) dots of color rather than based on mathematical formulas.

Printmaking

Printmaking is the process of making multiple artworks or impressions, usually on paper, using a printing plate, woodblock, stone, or stencil. We will look at examples of relief, intaglio, lithography, and serigraphy printmaking. Monotype is a final category of printmaking that is closer to painting and produces a single impression.

Relief

In **relief** printing, areas not to be printed are cut away from the printing surface, so that the areas to be printed are left higher. Ink is applied to the higher areas, and the print surface is sent through a press or is hand rubbed to transfer the image to paper, as shown in Figure 3.13A.

Woodblock prints are examples of relief printmaking. The nineteenth-century print *The Printmaker's Workshop* (Fig. 3.14), from the School of Yokohama, began with an artist's drawing that served as a guide for the cutter. The cutter carved pieces of that image onto several wood blocks, one for each color. In our example, you can see the entire process of woodblock printmaking, including drawing the

3.11, top CAI GUO-QIANG. *Drawing for Transient Rainbow*, August 2003. Gunpowder on two sheets of paper, 179″ × 159 1/2″ (overall). Fractional and promised gift of Clarissa Alcock Bronfman. (508.2004). The Museum of Modern Art, New York.

Gunpowder is one of the more unusual media used to make a drawing.

3.12, bottom ARATA ISOZAKI. *Nara Convention Hall*, Nara, Japan, 1992. Computer-generated print, 21″ × 23″. Gift of the architect. (142.1993) The Museum of Modern Art, New York.

The computer is a very helpful tool for creating images of things that do not yet exist. Many artists use software that aids in design, animation, or drawing and painting.

negative areas
cut away

ink

paper

print

block

(A) Relief Printing

positive areas
cut into
surface

ink

paper

metal plate

wiped plate

(B) Intaglio

positive areas
drawn with crayon

acid fixer

water

ink

water

paper

stone

rewatered and
inked stone

(C) Lithography

frame   reverse mask

ink

squeegee

porous screen

paper

(D) Serigraphy

original design, cutting blocks, mixing colors, printing images, and drying the finished work on overhead lines.

Intaglio

Intaglio prints can have fine lines, a high level of detail, and rich, dark tones. The word *intaglio* comes from the Italian verb meaning "to cut into." Artists cut into a flat surface, usually a metal plate, to make the image or design. Ink is rubbed into the cutaway areas, and then paper and plate are put through a press to transfer the image to the paper (Fig. 3.13B). Several processes are used in making an intaglio print, including drypoint, engraving, etching, and aquatint.

To make a **drypoint** print, artists scratch a metal plate with a thin, pointed tool called a burin, or a graver. The ink is then rubbed into the scratches, and then the plate and paper are put through the press. The results can resemble a pencil drawing.

Engraving entails cutting or incising lines into a laminated woodblock or a polished metal plate. The ink

3.13, left Printmaking Diagram, showing the processes used for (A) Relief, (B) Intaglio, (C) Lithography, and (D) Serigraphy.

3.14, bottom *The Printmaker's Workshop*. Japan, Edo period, School of Yokohama, 19th century. Color woodblock print. Musée National des Arts Asiatiques-Guimet, Paris.

The woman in the upper-right corner is making the preliminary drawing for the print. Just left of her is the cutter who is carving the wood block. On the lower right, a woman is grinding inks, and left of her the actual printing is taking place. At the top in the middle, a standing woman is hanging finished prints to dry.

3.15 ALBRECHT DURER. *Knight, Death, and the Devil*, 1513. Engraving, 9 5/8" × 7 1/2". (24.5 × 19 cm). Musee du Petit Palais, Paris France. Bridgeman-Giraudon.

The amazing wealth of detail in this print is possible because fine tools were used to engrave thin lines into the printing plate.

which makes it adhere to the plate surface. Then the plate is placed in an acid bath, where the exposed areas are eaten away. Next, the plate is inked and printed in the same way as the other intaglio processes. With this technique, larger areas of flat tones and values can be created, whereas in the other printing processes these elements can only be achieved with linear hatching and crosshatching.

Lithography

Lithography starts with a drawing created with an oily crayon, pencil, or liquid on a limestone slab or a metal surface. Gum arabic, which is a water-based liquid, is applied to the entire surface, except where the oily marks resist it. The stone or plate is then inked with an oil-based ink, which adheres only to the greasy marks drawn on the surface (Fig. 3.13C). The plate or stone is then put through the press where the inked areas transfer to the paper.

3.16 PABLO PICASSO. *The Weeping Woman (La Femme qui pleure)*, 1937. Etching, aquatint, and drypoint; plate: 27 1/8" × 19 1/2"; sheet: 30 5/16" × 22 5/16". The Museum of Modern Art, New York.

Gray tones are produced by aquatint. Etching produces a variety of line qualities, while drypoint gives the finest lines.

is rubbed into the recessed lines, and the block or plate is put through the press. An example of a metal engraving is Albrecht Durer's *Knight, Death, and the Devil*, 1513 (Fig. 3.15). Engraving produces thin, precise lines that create both detail and rich values, as seen in this print. It is worth looking though a magnifying glass at an original Durer engraving to see the wealth of details unfold.

In an **etching**, a metal plate is coated with a sticky protective ground, into which the artist scratches a design. The plate is then placed in an acid bath, which eats away or etches the exposed metal surface. The etched areas hold the ink during the printing. An example of an etching that was combined with drypoint and aquatint is seen in Pablo Picasso's *The Weeping Woman* (Fig. 3.16). In this work, Picasso was able to achieve a rich variety of lines and values.

Aquatint is a process related to etching in which the metal plate is covered with a powder of acid-resistant resin. Heat is applied to the plate, which melts the resin,

3.17 KIKI SMITH. *Born*. 2002. Lithograph, composition and sheet: 68 1/16″ × 56 1/8″. Publisher and printer: Universal Limited Art Editions, West Islip, New York, West Islip, New York. Edition: 28. Gift of Emily Fisher Landau. (369.2002). The Museum of Modern Art, New York.

Lithography is the printmaking process that produces results that most resemble drawings.

Figure 3.17 shows Kiki Smith's lithograph, *Born*, from 2002. Smith's work often uses folk tales and mythologies as subject matter; life, death, and resurrection are frequent themes.

Serigraphy

Serigraphy, also called screen printing, is a process in which a stencil is attached over a piece of finely woven fabric stretched over a frame, which supports and gives strength to the stencil (Fig. 3.13D). Ink is then squeezed through the open areas of the stencil and deposited on the surface below, which could include sheets of paper, T-shirts, or cardboard boxes. **Photo silk screens** are variations on the regular screen printing process. Instead of using stencils, photographs are used with special chemicals to block the ink in certain areas from being squeezed through to the paper.

Andy Warhol popularized screen printing images with his multiple versions of celebrities like Jacqueline Kennedy or *Marilyn Monroe*, 1967 (Fig. 3.18), one of a portfolio of ten screen prints on paper. Repeating images in serigraphy is easy, and Warhol uses repetition to allude to mass production and commercialism.

Monotype

Unlike the previous printmaking processes we have looked at, this process makes only one impression of an image, hence the name **monotype**. On a sheet of plexiglass or metal, a drawing or painting is rendered in oil or a water-soluble paint. Paper is placed on top of the rendering and hand rubbed or put through a press to make the transfer.

3.18 ANDY WARHOL. *Marilyn Monroe*, 1967. One of a portfolio of ten screenprints on white paper, 36″ × 36″. Inv. 79-1970 a. Photo: Joerg P. Anders. © The Andy Warhol Foundation for the Visual Arts/ARS, NY. Kupferstichkabinett, Staatliche Museen, Berlin, Germany. Bildarchiv Preussischer Kulturbesitz.

With silkscreen it is possible to get broad areas of intense color.

3.19, *above* Paul Gauguin. *Two Marquesans*, 1902. Monotype, $12^1/_2'' \times 20''$. British Museum, London.

With monotypes, only one image can be produced from a single working of the plate. Some artists produce a second ghost image from an inked monotype plate, but usually the ghost image needs to be finished in some other medium.

3.20, *right* Natural pigments, similar to those used by the Navajo people to prepare ritual sand paintings. From left to right, the pigments are cornmeal, pulverized charcoal, brown sand, red ochre, ground gypsum, yellow ochre, gray sand, pollen, and brown clay.

Pigments in undiluted form can have amazing color intensity.

In Paul Gauguin's *Two Marquesans* (Fig. 3.19), we see the original and only print that looks like a combination of both drawing and painting.

Painting

Painting media generally consist of two basic components: pigment and binder. **Pigments** are intense colors in powder form, derived from animals, plants, minerals, and synthetic chemicals. The **binder** is the substance into which the pigment is blended and which holds the components together once it dries. Binders include egg yolk, wax, glue, drying oils, and acrylic liquid mediums, among others.

Although all paints contain colored material, some forms use no binders. Sand painting is a traditional art form in Navajo rituals, used especially for healing. Different natural elements, such as colored sand, crushed stone, charcoal, and pollen, are carefully sprinkled onto a clean, swept earthen floor. Artist priests chant and pray while they create their designs in sand. The sand paintings are then destroyed at the end of the ritual. Figure 3.20 shows a selection of dry natural pigments that can be carefully poured through the fingers onto the ground to create a sand painting.

Paintings are all made on some kind of support, usually stone, clay, plaster, wood panel, paper, fabric, and even found objects. We just saw that sand paintings use the earth itself as the support. Some of the oldest surviving paintings were made on clay vessels, as in the *Red Figure Kylix* by the Greek painter Douris, from the fifth century BCE (Fig. 3.21). **Slip**, a liquid clay, has been applied to the clay vessel before firing to create both the black background and the delicate black lines that add details to the figures. The red clay of the vessel shows through where no slip has been applied. Also, the human body is and has

3.21, *top* DOURIS. *Red Figure Kylix*, 490 BCE. Slip on clay, 13″ diameter. Kunsthistorisches Museum, Vienna.

The images produced with colored clays on Greek vases are the only record of Greek painting that has survived to the present day.

3.22, *bottom* A Chinese opera performer making up his face in front of a mirror.

The human body has always been used as a "canvas" for painting.

been a surface for painting. The Chinese opera performer in Figure 3.22 is painting his face in preparation for his character. His painted face, the text, costumes, music, and singing are all components of the genre.

3.23 JASPER JOHNS. *Flag*, 1954–1955. Encaustic, oil, and collage on fabric mounted on plywood, 42 1/4″ × 60 5/8″. Gift of Philip Johnson in honor of Alfred H. Barr Jr. The Museum of Modern Art/Licensed by SCALA / Art Resource, NY/© VAGA, NY

Encaustic paint is a mixture of wax and pigment, and it can be somewhat transparent if the ratio of wax to pigment is very high.

Encaustic

Encaustic is one of the most ancient forms of painting media. Because pigments are mixed into hot beeswax, the paints can be blended until they cool. Some encaustic paintings thousands of years old retain their colors and lustrous surfaces. The medium is still used today. The top layer of Jasper Johns's *Flag* (Fig. 3.23) is translucent encaustic over a layer of newspaper scraps and photographs, allowing the viewer to see the imagery embedded in the flag.

Fresco

Fresco is often used for large murals painted directly on walls. There are two kinds of fresco. In **fresco secco**, paint is applied to a dry plaster wall. In **buon fresco**, or true fresco, the plaster on the wall is wet, and wet pigment suspended in water is applied to and soaks into that surface, which results in a very durable painting. The artist must work quickly in small areas before the plaster dries. Buon fresco is remarkably durable, as evidenced by the *Glass*

Bowl with Fruit (Fig. 3.24), a Roman painting from the first century CE that survived 2,000 years despite being buried by the eruption of Mount Vesuvius in 79 CE.

Tempera, Gouache, and Watercolor

Tempera, gouache, and watercolor are three water-based paint media. Traditional **tempera** painting consists of pigments mixed with egg yolk, which is the binder. Egg tempera is a very strong, quick-drying medium that is excellent for rendering sharp lines and details. Figure 3.25 is Piero Della Francesca's *Portrait of Federico da Montefeltro, Duke of Urbino, and his wife Battista Sforza*, from approximately 1465. Even after 550 years, the colors and details remain clear and bright. Today, the term *tempera* may also refer to a completely different kind of paint, which is commercially available, uses synthetic binders, and is common as children's art materials.

Watercolors are pigments suspended in a gum arabic binder, which is a natural water-soluble glue. Watercolors are usually applied to paper in transparent layers of thin stains and are distinct because of their flowing quality. **Gouache** is watercolor with white chalk added to create an opaque paint. Its thicker consistency makes it easier to control. Gouache was often used for Persian miniatures, like *The Reader (frontispiece)* (Fig. 3.26), from the sixteenth century, because of the fine lines, great detail, and bright colors possible with the medium.

3.24 *Glass Bowl with Fruit*, Roman, 1st century, found in the Mt. Vesuvius region of Italy. Fresco wallpainting. Museo Archeologico Nazionale, Naples.

Fresco is a very durable painting medium, because the pigment is embedded in plaster.

3.26 *The Reader (frontispiece)*, Bukhara, Iran, first quarter of the 16th century. Gouache, gold highlights. Photo: Hervé Lewandowski. Louvre, Paris France.

Gouache is opaque watercolor that produces bright, matte color areas. When artists use fine brushes for gouache, they can make delicate lines and intricate details.

3.25 PIERO DELLA FRANCESCA. *Portrait of Federico da Montefeltro, Duke of Urbino, and his wife Battista Sforza* (ca. 1465). Tempera on wood each portrait 18.5″ x 13″. Uffizi, Florence, Italy.

Traditional tempera was made by grinding dry pigments into raw egg yolk, which, when dried, produces a tough and durable film.

Oil and Acrylic Paint

Both oil and acrylic paints are notable for their wide range of intense colors. They can be applied as **glazes**, which are nearly transparent layers of paint that leave a hint of color on the underpainting. Glazes can be built up, one layer over the other, to create a rich, subtle color effect. Oils and acrylics can be applied **alla prima** as well, a technique of painting in a direct style without layers, in which the painter often finishes a work in a single sitting. Both oil and acrylic paintings are most often executed on paper, wood, or stretched canvas. Usually, these supports have been coated with a gesso ground to keep the paint from soaking in and thus looking dull.

Oil paint has been in common use since the fifteenth century. The powdered pigments are ground into a slow-drying oil (usually linseed), usually on a support of wood or canvas, and are soluble in turpentine or mineral spirits. Slow-drying paint allows artists to easily blend colors and paint details. Glazing with oil paints can result in intense colors with lustrous, glowing surfaces, evident in Titian's *Venus of Urbino* (Fig. 3.28). Oil-based paints are also used for body painting, like that of the Chinese opera performer in Figure 3.22.

Acrylic paint is made with pigment that has been ground with a synthetic polymer liquid binder that quickly dries into a flexible film and can be applied to almost any support. David Hockney's *A Bigger Splash*, 1967 (Fig. 3.29), shows acrylic paint applied primarily alla prima, resulting in large areas of flat, bright color. Because acrylics are water-soluble, artists can also pour acrylic paint, glaze acrylics, or draw fine lines with it. All of these applications are evident in Margaret Lazzari's 2007 painting *Aqueous* (Fig. 3.30). Pouring gives a fluid quality to large areas of the background, while the center drawing, which is a radically enlarged copy of a Leonardo study of water movement, is done in thin, precise lines of acrylic paint. The rich color is the result of glazing.

Sprayed Paint

Thanks to current technology, paint can be sprayed in many ways. An **airbrush** is a small spray gun that is about the size of a pen. Compressed air is forced through the airbrush, which atomizes the liquid paint, allowing it to be sprayed onto a surface. An airbrush can render both large areas and fine details. Not only used for fine art, airbrushes also make their mark in illustration work, murals, signage, custom car finishes, and painting on the human body.

Spray paint is a commercial product in aerosol cans containing compressed air and quick-drying permanent

3.27 WANGECHI MUTU, *One Hundred Lavish Months of Bushwhack*, 2004. Cut-and-pasted printed paper with watercolor, synthetic polymer paint, and pressure-sensitive stickers on transparentized paper, irreg. 68 1/2″ × 42″. Fund for the Twenty-First Century. The Museum of Modern Art, New York.

Watercolor and gouache work well when combined with other media. Here, watercolor is combined with polymer paint and collaged printed papers.

Both watercolor and gouache are ideal for mixed-media work. Figure 3.27 is Kenyan artist Wangechi Mutu's *One Hundred Lavish Months of Bushwhack*, 2004, a collage and watercolor piece. The watercolor is evident in the red stains around the large woman's face. In Mutu's work, the seemingly aggressive, fantastic woman is actually injured and supported by the smaller person below. Mutu has said that women's bodies are "sensitivity charts," or "barometers, tracking the health, or more often the sickness, of any given society's own body politic." (quote from http://www.moma.org/collection/object.php?object_id=94766).

3.28 TITIAN (TIZIANO VECELLIO). *Venus of Urbino,* 1538. Oil on canvas, 4′ × 5′ 6″. Uffizi, Florence, Italy.

This oil painting started as an opaque monochrome underpainting, which then had many layers of jewel-like glazes applied to the surface.

3.29 DAVID HOCKNEY. *A Bigger Splash,* 1967. Acrylic on canvas, 8′ × 8′. Tate Gallery, London.

Acrylic paint can produce large areas of flat color, similar to the effect of latex wall paint.

3.30 MARGARET LAZZARI. *Aqueous,* 2007. Acrylic on canvas, 80″ × 75″. Collection of the artist.

Acrylics can be poured, glazed, or painted alla prima. They can be thinned and applied with a fine brush to produce lines.

3.31 Graffiti artist at work along the Brighton seafront. Spray paint is the medium of choice for most graffiti artists.

3.32 FAITH RINGGOLD. *The Bitter Nest, Part II: The Harlem Renaissance Party*, 1988. Acrylic on canvas with printed, dyed, and pieced fabric, 94″ × 83″. Smithsonian American Art Museum, Washington, DC.

Ringgold used quilting to tell stories of her childhood in Harlem.

paint, often used by graffiti artists (Fig. 3.31). Spray paint allows for broad areas of color and gradual transitions but will not do fine detail work. As a result, most graffiti artists work on a large scale.

Fabrics, Needlework, and Weaving

This category of art makes an ideal transition from the two-dimensional art disciplines and media we have just seen, to the upcoming discussion of three-dimensional works. It covers an enormous range of art objects, including tapestries, quilts, rugs, embroidery, and other woven objects. We will look at only a few examples here.

CONNECTION An example of a tapestry is *The Unicorn in Captivity*, Figure 14.03.

Faith Ringgold used the craft of quilting as an art medium to express her views on African American culture.

She did a series of quilts about her "tar beach," the tarred roof of the building she lived in as a child in New York City, and this quilt story became a famous children's book. In Figure 3.32, *The Bitter Nest, Part II: The Harlem Renaissance Party*, 1988, Ringgold creates a gathering of some of the luminaries of African American culture in the 1920s and 1930s.

The *Summer Robe* (Fig. 3.33), from the Qing Dynasty, is an example of incredibly intricate and detailed work, all executed in embroidery. Silk fabric forms the support for the needlework that contains complex designs such as the imperial dragon. The robe belonged to a eunuch of the court of the Empress Dowager, who reigned in the nineteenth century.

Moving further into three dimensions is *Sasa* (Fig. 3.34), from 2004, woven by Ghana artist El Anatsui from salvaged bits of copper wire and aluminum. The source for the aluminum is the metal foil wrapped around the necks of discarded liquor and wine bottles. El Anatsui has said that "Art grows out of each particular situation, and I believe that artists are better off working with whatever their environment throws up." Working with found or salvaged materials is something many artists do, as we will see in the next section when we turn in earnest to three-dimensional work. However, more than other found-object artists, this artist has managed to transform salvaged waste into an intricate, fabulous, and glowing object.

METHODS AND MEDIA IN THREE-DIMENSIONAL ART

Three-dimensional art ranges from traditional to new media, freestanding work, and relief sculpture. It can be site-specific and even kinetic. **Freestanding** sculptures are objects that are meant to be seen from all sides and

3.33, left *Summer Robe*. China, 19th century. Embroidered silk. Private collection.

Embroidery is an example of fabric and needlework art.

3.34, bottom EL ANATSUI. *Sasa*, 2004. Aluminum and copper wire, 21′ × 27.5′. Photo: Georges Meguerditchian. Musee National d'Art Moderne, Centre Georges Pompidou, ParisFrance.

Discarded strips of metal foil are woven into a sumptuous wall hanging.

could conceivably be placed in many different settings, like the *Monumental Heads* (Fig. 3.35), from the Easter Islands. A **relief** sculpture is meant to be seen only from the front, like the *Relief Carving* (Fig. 3.36) at Banteay Srei, from the latter part of the tenth century. Relief sculptures are usually carved out of a single face of a stone or wood block. An example of a **site-specific** sculpture is Richard Serra's *The Matter of Time*, 2005 (Fig. 3.37). Made of steel, this sculpture was specifically designed for that particular

3.35 *Monumental Heads*, Moai statue, c. 15th century. Volcanic tufa. Easter Island (Rapa Nui), Polynesia.

Freestanding sculptures can be seen from all sides.

3.36 *Relief Carving*. Second half of 10th century, Hindu. Banteay Srei, Cambodia. Detail of red sandstone carving.

Relief carvings are seen only from one side. Frequently, they are produced by carving into a flat surface plane of wood or stone.

3.37 RICHARD SERRA. *The Matter of Time*, 2005. Eight steel sheet sculptures, each 12 to 14 feet in height and weighing 44 to 276 tons. Guggenheim Museum, Bilbao, Spain.

This is a site-specific work, which means that it has been designed and arranged for this space in such a way that the space becomes part of the experience of the artwork.

room, creating passages throughout the space that alternate between spacious and tight or between compressed and elongated. The slightly tilting walls of the sculpture make the space seem to move. The title references in part the time required to move through and experience this large sculptural installation. In **kinetic** works, actual movement is part of the piece, as in Alexander Calder's "mobiles." *Crinkly* (Fig. 3.38), from 1970, is made of metal, wire, and paint and is suspended so it moves randomly in the natural airflow. Let us now look at media within specific sculptural disciplines.

Carving

One technique for creating three-dimensional work is **carving**, in which artists remove unwanted material from a large block of stone or wood or, more recently, synthetic products like Styrofoam. This is a **subtractive process**

3.38 ALEXANDER CALDER. *Crinkly*, 1970. Sheet metal, wire, and paint, 28″ × 65 ¹/₂″ × 12″. Private collection.

Kinetic artworks are designed to move, and that movement is part of the piece.

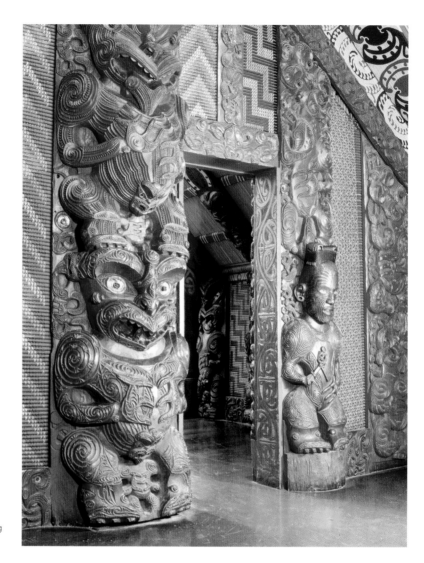

3.39 RAHARUHI RUKUPO AND OTHERS. Entrance doorway of a Maori meeting house called *Te Mana O Turanga,* opened 1883. Carved and painted wood. New Zealand.

A carved work starts from a large block of material. The artist cuts away what is extraneous to reveal the artwork. Wood, stone, Styrofoam, or other synthetic materials can be carved. See also Chapter 12 for more information on Maori meeting houses.

because the material is taken away. Stone sculpting goes back to the Paleolithic era and appears across cultures. We have just seen two examples of carving: in solidified volcanic ash, the *Monumental Heads* (Fig. 3.35), and in red sandstone, the *Relief Carving* (Fig. 3.36) from Banteay Srei.

Wood has been carved by artists over the centuries, but because it decays, wooden artworks are much newer than the oldest stone carvings. Wood has been used to carve representational sculptures, architectural decorations, furniture, and functional vessels. Figure 3.39 is the *Entrance doorway of a Maori meeting house called Te Mana O Turanga,* opened 1883, carved by Raharuhi Rukupo and others. Artists find wood to be a versatile medium for carving, allowing them to achieve deeply rounded forms and exact surface detail. In this case, the carving was done by a Maori ruler, and the details of the sculpture symbolize the clan's history.

Modeling

Sculptural forms can also be created by **modeling**, which is the pushing and pulling of a malleable substance, such as clay or wax. Modeling is often considered an **additive process**, because material is built up to create the final sculptural form. Clay is a common modeling material, which becomes hard and permanent after firing. Figure 3.40 shows an Aztec *Eagle Knight,* a ceramic sculpture of earthenware clay and plaster, from Mexico. As a sculptural material, clay is capable of extremely fine detail, as in Marilyn Levine's *Golf Bag* (Fig. 3.41), made of rolled and modeled clay slabs. The ceramic sculpture is an example of **trompe l'oeil** ("fool the eye") artwork, because it seems so convincing to be an actual leather bag. Viewers want to touch it in order to believe it is actually made out of clay.

Functional ceramics are also made with the additive sculptural process using clay. Functional pieces can be vessels, platters, cups, pitchers, and so on. Ceramics can be hand molded or pinched into their forms, fashioned out of coils or slabs of clay, or thrown on a potter's wheel. Figure 3.42 shows a pinched black-on-black *Bowl* made by Maria Martinez, a Native American from the San Idelfonso Pueblo in New Mexico. She and her son perfected this technique and design, which blends both

3.41 MARILYN LEVINE. *Golf Bag*, 1981. Ceramic, 34″ × 10 ³/₄″. Private collection.

A high degree of control over the surface and the details are possible with ceramic sculptures.

3.40 *Eagle Knight,* c. 15th century. Earthenware and plaster, 66 ⁷/₈″ × 46¹/₂″ × 21 ⁵/₈″. Aztec, Museo Templo Mayor, Mexico.

The artist shaped this sculpture by pushing and pulling clay until the final form was realized. Sometimes clay is also pressed into molds to create some forms.

3.42 MARIA MARTINEZ. *Bowl*, Undated. Blackware, 6 ³/₄″ × 9 ¹/₂″. Gift of International Business Machines Corporation. Smithsonian American Art Museum, Washington, DC.

Clay was pinched, smoothed, polished, and worked by hand to achieve the highly polished surface.

glossy and matte surfaces with decorative abstract symbols. This combination beautifully enhances the vessel's form.

Sometimes, a modeled sculpture is cast in bronze or plaster. Very small bronze sculptures are created using simple molds and end up as solid bronze pieces. But for larger bronze sculptures, artists use the **cire perdue** process (**lost wax** casting method). This method produces hollow metal sculpture with thin walls. As illustrated in Figure 3.43, a thin layer of wax is suspended between an interior and exterior mold. The wax is then melted out of the mold and replaced with molten metal. The **Classical** Greek sculpture of *The Marathon Boy* (Fig. 3.44) is a cast bronze work made using the lost wax method. Because of the cost and effort, only important artworks were created with the lost wax casting method.

Assembling

Assembled works are made of various parts that are then put together. Assembly in its most fundamental form can be seen in the elaborate neck gear of *Masai*

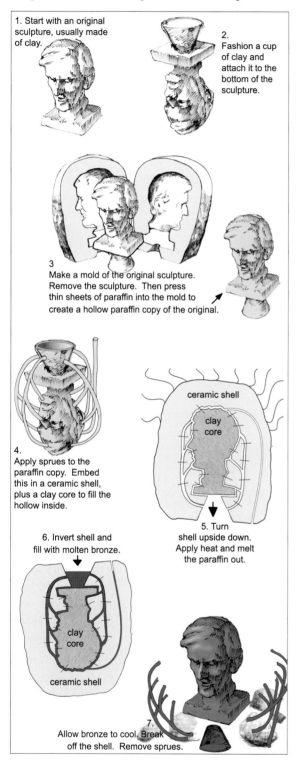

1. Start with an original sculpture, usually made of clay.

2. Fashion a cup of clay and attach it to the bottom of the sculpture.

3 Make a mold of the original sculpture. Remove the sculpture. Then press thin sheets of paraffin into the mold to create a hollow paraffin copy of the original.

4. Apply sprues to the paraffin copy. Embed this in a ceramic shell, plus a clay core to fill the hollow inside.

ceramic shell

clay core

5. Turn shell upside down. Apply heat and melt the paraffin out.

6. Invert shell and fill with molten bronze.

clay core

ceramic shell

7. Allow bronze to cool. Break off the shell. Remove sprues.

3.43 Cire Perdue, or Lost Wax, Casting Process.

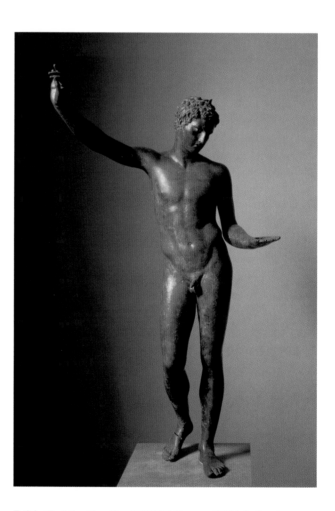

3.44 *The Marathon Boy*, 330 BCE. Bronze, 51″ high. Greek, Hellenistic period. National Archaeological Museum, Athens.

This is a hollow sculpture created using the lost wax (cire perdue) casting process.

Woman Wearing Beaded Necklace, Figure 3.45. The Masai women of Eastern Africa create elaborate beaded works to indicate their identity and position within their groups. Older beads were made from locally available materials like shells, bone, metals, and stones, but more recently the brightly colored imported beads have been favored.

Assembled artworks are often **mixed media**, which literally means mixing up the methods and their various media in a work. Mixed-media works may contain natural materials like stone or wood, but they may also use manufactured goods, photographs, industrial fixtures, and the like. Figure 3.46, *Nimba, Goddess of Fertility*, is an example of a sculpture in natural materials that has been carved and also assembled with the addition of the raffia skirt and shell ornamentation. When **found objects** or **ready-mades** (already existing objects) are incorporated into pieces, the resulting works are referred to as **assemblages**. Joseph Cornell created poetic, evocative assemblages in shallow boxes, with fragments of things that were

3.47, *above* Joseph Cornell. *Suzy's Sun (for Judy Tyler)*, 1957. 10 3/4″ × 15″ × 4″. North Carolina Museum of Art. The Joseph and Robert Cornell Memorial Foundation/VAGA, New York. North Carolina Museum of Art/CORBIS

This artist is well-known for his artworks that were assembled from cast-off materials. The worn quality of the elements adds to the overall feeling of things lost or remembered.

3.48, *left* Robert Rauschenberg. *First Landing Jump*, 1961. Combine painting: cloth, metal, leather, electric fixture, cable, and oil paint on composition board; overall, including automobile tire and wooden plank on floor, 7′ 5 1/8″ × 6′ × 8 7/8″. Gift of Philip Johnson. The Museum of Modern Art, New York. The Museum of Modern Art/Licensed by SCALA / Art Resource, NY

Combines are works that are both painting and sculpture.

once beautiful. In *Suzy's Sun (for Judy Tyler)* (Fig. 3.47), the sun, cut out from an antipasto tin, implies passing time and life cycles, along with a piece of driftwood and a spiraling seashell. The box is dedicated to a young actress who was killed in a car crash after filming *Jailhouse Rock* with Elvis Presley. In Figure 3.48, *First Landing Jump*, Robert Rauschenberg combined an oil painting with various found objects, including metal, leather, an electric fixture, cable, an automobile tire, and a wooden plank. The overall effect recalls the bold paint strokes of Abstract Expressionist paintings, but here, the strokes and marks are actual objects. Rauschenberg coined the term **combines** for works that are both painting and sculpture.

3.49 ANN PAGE. *petit homage – Stack VIII*, 2010. Mixed media:
Redwood cube with prototyped, infiltrated, gypsum modules, 14″
× 4.5″ × 4″.

The five modules in this sculpture were modeled using computer-
aided design software and were produced on a three-dimensional
printer.

Sculptures can be **fabricated** using industrial and commercial processes, such as welding or neon lighting. Nam June Paik's *Electronic Superhighway: Continental U.S., Alaska, Hawaii* (Fig. 3.1) is an example of a fabricated neon sculpture that is also a forty-nine-channel, closed-circuit, digital video installation. Richard Serra's *The Matter of Time* is an example of a work fabricated with industrial equipment designed to roll and shape sheet metal.

New Technologies

Artists can make sculptures from computer-aided design files and then "print" them on three-dimensional printers. For *petit Homage – Stack VIII* (Figure 3.49), from 2010, Ann Page created a digital model for the spiky, branching module and then had the printer make five exact copies by building up thin layer on top of thin layer of gypsum. She then stacked the modules vertically to recall both the austere geometry of minimalist art and also the growth patterns in plants. The redwood base has a similar tension between the organic and the geometric. Originally cut into a perfect cube, it has become distorted and more organic as it has aged and has been exposed to the weather. Again, the choice of media and materials supports the basic idea behind this artwork. The work is like a graft, where the perfection of machine-made objects meets the individual artist's touch.

Installation

Installations are usually mixed-media artworks designed for a specific interior or exterior space. In the Cornaro Chapel in the church of Santa Maria della Vittoria (Fig. 3.50), Gianlorenzo Bernini created a dramatic stage for his sculpture, the *Ecstacy of St. Teresa*. The 11′ 6″–high sculpture of St. Teresa and an angel is the centerpiece of the chapel. The work represents the mystical, religious rapture of St. Teresa as she is pierced by the angel's arrow of divine love. The figures appear to float in midair and are lit by heavenly rays. Bernini used the entire chapel space to amplify the ecstatic mood, blending architecture, sculpture, illusionistic painting, colored marble, bronze, and natural light. Even in the modern era, churches are often designed almost as installations that create a spiritual environment. The artist Henri Matisse designed the interior of the Chapel of the Rosary for the Sisters who

3.50 GIANLORENZO BERNINI. Cornaro Chapel with the *Ecstasy of St. Teresa,* 1645–1652, in the Church of Santa Maria della Vittoria, Rome. Marble, stucco, paint, natural light; central figures are marble, 11′ 6″ high. As illustrated by an anonymous 18th-century painting from the Italian School. The painting is located in the Staatliches Museum, Schwerin, Germany.

Installations transform the entire space of a room.

cared for him while he was ill. His cut-paper designs were translated into stained glass, as seen in Figure 3.51, *Tree of Life*, and were combined with a spare and light-colored interior.

Almost any material can be used in installations. In some instances, the same material can be used to create both freestanding sculptures and also installations. Dale Chihuly is a renown contemporary glass artist who

has created brilliantly colored sculptures in glass that resemble flowers, sea creatures, or patterns from Navajo weavings. He has created installations in glass that are far more ambitious than most undertakings by glass artists. His 2002 installation, *Seaform Pavilion* (Fig. 3.52), fills the ceiling on the Bridge of Glass in the Museum of Glass in Tacoma, Washington. Hundreds of individual pieces are combined to create a work that references the fantastic world of an undersea coral reef that seems to float overhead. When lit well, glass is a luminous medium that enhances the theme of this artwork.

Creating temporary exterior installations has been the life work of Christo and Jeanne-Claude. They install

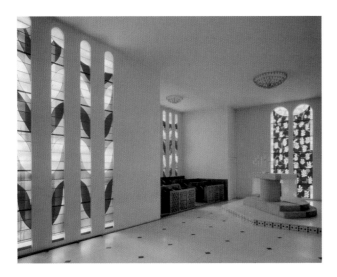

3.51, left HENRI MATISSE. *Tree of Life*, 1950–1951. Stained glass. Chapel of the Rosary, Vence, France.

Like installations, religious spaces are often carefully designed to transform the entire interior and, in this case, to provide a spiritual experience.

3.52, below DALE CHIHULY. *Seaform Pavilion*, 2002. Bridge of Glass at the Museum of Glass Tacoma, Washington.

This work is installed in the ceiling of a bridge between two buildings. The installation is composed of hundreds of individual pieces of blown glass.

3.53 CHRISTO AND JEANNE-CLAUDE. Running Fence, Sonoma and Marin Counties, California, 1972–76. Height: 18 feet. Length: 24 1/2 miles. 240,000 square yards of nylon fabric, steel poles, and steel cables. Copyright Christo, 1976/Photograph: Jeanne-Claude

The line of fabric transforms the landscape.

3.54 SUZANNE LACY AND LESLIE LABOWITZ. *In Mourning and in Rage.*

The human body is the prime element in performance art.

various materials at a specific site to enhance its natural beauty. In *Running Fence* (Fig. 3.53), fabric was stretched over the rolling countryside of Sonoma and Marin counties in California. The fabric fence visually emphasized the undulating contours of the land, especially when the sun was low and the land was dark, but the cloth reflected the warm-colored rays.

PERFORMANCE

Performance is a live-action event that is staged as an artwork. There are obvious similarities between performance art and theater, but in the sense that performance is art that occupies and transforms a space, it is related to installation. Other examples of performance art appear in Chapter 12, The Body, because performance art often requires the human body. We will look at only one example here. Figure 3.54 shows Suzanne Lacy and Leslie Labowitz in a feminist performance piece called *In Mourning and in Rage*. In this protest performance, ten women dressed in black drove in a hearse to a Los Angeles city council meeting. They were expressing both their grief and outrage for the ten victims of the Hillside strangler and for the overall violence against women that is sensationalized in the news media.

CONNECTION Ana Mendieta's *Arbol de la Vida, No. 294* (Fig. 12.36, at left) and Yoko Ono's *Cut Piece* (Fig. 12.37) are two other examples of Performance Art.

TECHNOLOGY-BASED MEDIA

Photography

In **photography**, a light-sensitive surface such as film is exposed to light through a lens, which creates an image from the environment on that surface. Multiple copies can be made of that original image on other light-sensitive surfaces. Early examples of monochromatic photographic processes are daguerreotype, platinum prints, and silver prints. *Frederick Douglass*, from 1855 (Fig. 3.55), is an example of a daguerreotype, the first commercially available photographic process. Daguerreotypes were quickly replaced by other photographic innovations, because their developing process required the use of toxic chemicals, and the end product was fairly delicate and had to be kept behind glass. Nevertheless, daguerreotypes are beautiful ghostly silver images of great clarity and detail, a medium that evokes a sense of poetry and lost history.

Photography has continued to evolve technologically. It is beyond the scope of this book to detail photographic

3.55 *Frederick Douglass* (ca. 1855). Daguerreotype, $2\,^3/_4'' \times 2\,^3/_{16}''$. The Rubel Collection, Partial and Promised Gift of William Rubel, 2001 (2001.756). The Metropolitan Museum of Art, New York.

This is an early form of photography and thus was precious, as indicated by the elaborate frame. The glass was necessary to protect the fragile surface.

3.56 ANDREAS GURSKY. *99 Cent, 1999*. Cibachrome print, 6′ 9 $^1/_2$″ × 11′. Inv.: AM 2000-96. Photo: Philippe Migeat. Musee National d'Art Moderne, Centre Georges Pompidou, Paris, France.

Photography has evolved so that very large, durable prints with near-permanent colors are possible.

history, but we will look at a cibachrome print by Andreas Gursky, entitled *99 Cent*, from 1999 (Fig. 3.56). Cibachrome is a photographic color-printing technology invented in the 1960s with vivid, fade-resistant colors and high detail, all on a print on a polyester base rather than paper. Gursky made these very large color prints of the vast interiors of 99-cent stores, in order to highlight the amount of low-cost, low-quality consumer goods available in the United States today.

Ever since photographs have become commonly available, artists have experimented with ways to alter or manipulate them. One example is **photomontage**, a collage or combination of many photographs to create a new image. Hannah Hoch very effectively used this technique in her political satirical work titled *Cut with the Kitchen Knife Dada through the Lost Weimar Beer Belly Cultural Epoch of Germany* (Fig. 3.57). As a Berlin **Dadaist** artist, Hoch promoted the idea of absurdity in this work by using cutouts of photos and words from magazines to create a sense of chaos and instability.

In addition to these older photographic technologies, artists today also have at their disposal digital cameras and a wide range of printers. Digital images can be easily manipulated with computer software. Output from digital images can be printed on hard copy, displayed on computer monitors, or projected onto a screen. In addition, all kinds of existing imagery can be scanned to become digital information.

The Moving Image

Artists have also worked in film and video, which are essentially photographs shot in sequence to give the illusion of movement. A film is a sequence of still photographs shot in rapid succession on a strip of film. When projected onto a screen, the progression of the still images gives an illusion of movement. Older video recorded both image and sound on magnetic videotape, which was displayed on television monitors. Video cameras first became accessible to the public and, thus, to artists in 1965.

The digital revolution has also transformed the moving image. We have already discussed the Chapter Opener, Nam June Paik's *Electronic Superhighway: Continental U.S., Alaska, Hawaii*. This is an example of a forty-nine-channel, closed-circuit, digital video installation. Lorna Simpson combines black-and-white film (which has been

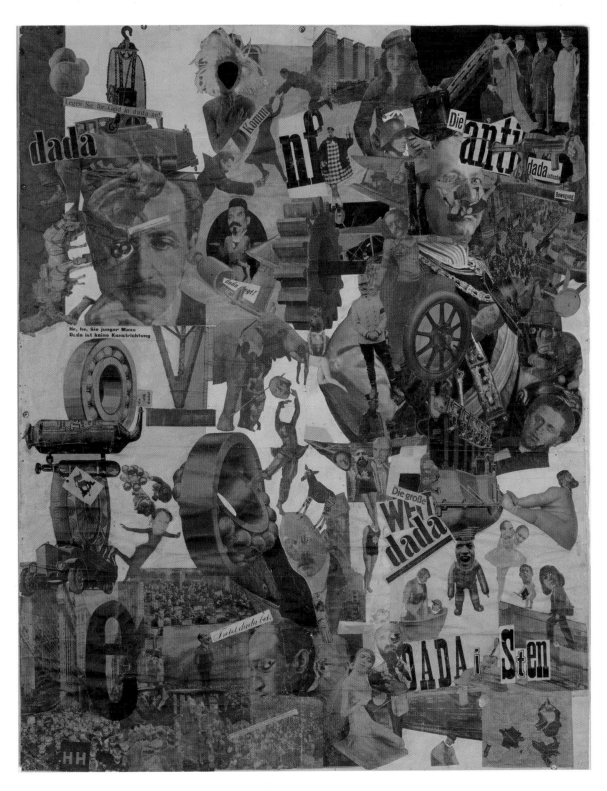

3.57 HANNAH HOCH. *Cut with the Kitchen Knife Dada through the Last Weimar Beer Belly Cultural Epoch of Germany*, 1919–1920. Photomontage, 3′ 9″ × 2′ 11″. Neue Nationalgalerie, Staatliche Museen, Berlin.

A collage of photographic images can have an absurd quality, because of disjunctions in the imagery and in the space.

3.58 LORNA SIMPSON. *Easy to Remember*, 2001. Still from 16 mm film transferred to DVD, sound; 2¹/₂ minutes.

Artists use new technologies for pieces combining imagery and sound.

3.59 TONY OURSLER. *Junk*, 2003. Fiberglass sculpture and DVD projection. Sculpture: 29″ × 39″ × 16″. Sarah Norton Goodyear Fund, 2003. Albright-Knox Art Gallery, Buffalo, New York.

The projected image animates the fiberglass sculpture.

digitized and now plays as a DVD) with an audio song in *Easy to Remember* (Fig. 3.58). The song is softly sung, which is intended to invoke memories of African American childhood. Tony Oursler's *Junk*, 2003 (Fig. 3.59), is a biomorphically shaped fiberglass sculpture with eerie images of rolling eyes and an incessantly speaking mouth projected onto it using a DVD projector. Oursler comments on the modern human condition of neediness, insecurity, and self-centeredness with a work that is funny and annoying at the same time.

4.1 *U.S. Capitol Building*, begun 1793, exterior last renovated in 1960. Frequently redesigned, expanded, and restored under architects William Thornton, Stephen H. Hallet, George Hadfield, James Hoban, Benjamin Henry Latrobe, Charles Bulfinch, Thomas U. Walter, Edward Clark, and J. George Stewart. Terracing by Frederick Law Olmstead.

The visual elements of this building have been carefully considered and arranged by the architects who designed it.

4

DERIVING MEANING

Art and architecture have meaning, but how do audiences understand the message? This chapter examines four basic areas in regard to meaning: (1) formal analysis; (2) content analysis; (3) the influence of historical context, physical surroundings, and method of encounter; and (4) writings about art.

PREVIEW

Art communicates complex ideas and emotions, and this chapter looks at the ways this is achieved. We begin with formal analysis, which examines the artist's use of the elements and principles that we saw in Chapter 2. Next is content analysis, dealing with subject matter and systems of symbols.

Historical context and physical surroundings are important in two ways. First, every work of art was created within its own historical, political, social, or religious context. Knowing about that context deepens our understanding of a work of art. Second, we now live in our own surroundings and historical context, and our situation today influences what we think about any art we see, both past and present.

Writings about art enrich our experience of it. We will look at several philosophical positions from which art has been analyzed. Sometimes, the writers contradict or add to each other's arguments, showing that the meaning of art is not fixed. New interpretations develop over time.

FORMAL ANALYSIS

Formal analysis is the integrated study of the elements and principles of art (see Chapter 2) and the way they are used in a specific artwork. Architecture can be formally analyzed as well. The arrangement of elements and principles in an artwork are called its **composition**.

Consider, for example, the *U.S. Capitol Building* in Washington, D.C. (Fig. 4.1, Chapter Opener). Formally, it is very wide compared to its height. It is symmetrical in relation to the central vertical axis. Horizontally, it is divided into five parts. The first, third, and fifth parts stand out and have vertical columns, with cast shadows that create strong lights and darks. The second and fourth areas are recessed, flat, and have low contrast. The central section of the building is most emphasized, because the dome creates a vertical emphasis and a strong focal point. The

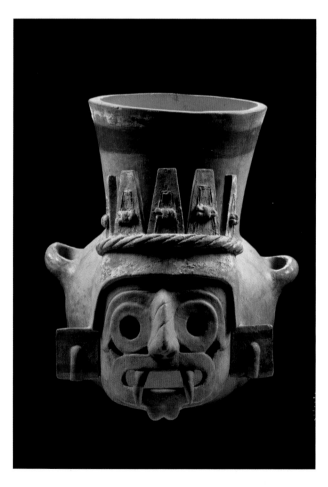

4.2 *Tlalco Vessel*, Aztec, ca. 1440–1469. Clay and pigment, 13″ × 13″ × 12.5″ Museo Templo Mayor, Mexico City, D.F., Mexico.
Michel Zabé/Art Resource, NY

Formally, this vessel is symmetrical and vertically oriented with several horizontal accents. The color scheme is predominantly blue and gray-brown.

building is very large and sits up high, with many steps in front. The structure is entirely white, which stands out strongly against the background. Of course, formal analysis can be limited to just the elements and their organization, but actually it goes beyond that. The formal elements make clear that this is an important building.

The formal qualities of any other artwork could be similarly analyzed, for example, the *Tlaloc Vessel*, 1440–1469 (Fig. 4.2), from Mexico. Without knowing anything about the work, we can see that it is frontal and symmetrical, the most formal of all compositions. The features of the face have been abstracted into simple geometric shapes. The emphasis in the vessel is more on the vertical than the horizontal, but there are some strong horizontal elements: (1) the red band near the top; (2) the two handles that align with the twisted braid; and (3) the large square earrings that align with the mouth. There are very few diagonal elements in this composition. The most prominent colors are blue and gray-brown.

Formal qualities add to an artwork because they are aesthetically satisfying. The elements in the *U.S. Capitol Building* are balanced. The size and relationship of one part to another have been carefully considered. In the *Tlaloc Vessel*, the integration of the face shape into the overall shape of the vessel is interesting, and the way the face has been simplified and made geometric is interesting to see as well. Looking at art is a very different experience from looking at the general environment, which is disjointed and disorganized. The formal qualities of artworks make them organized and satisfying visual experiences, adding considerably to the power of art.

CONTENT ANALYSIS

Content is an artwork's themes or messages. Content is conveyed primarily through the artwork's subject matter and through its symbolic or iconographic references.

Subject Matter

Subject matter is the substance of a work of art, in contrast to its form. Some aspects of subject matter are obvious just by looking at an artwork; for example, the *Tlaloc Vessel* is a ceramic pot that has a face on it. Other aspects must be learned; for example, the facts about Tlaloc, who was the Aztec god of rain. The Aztecs, rulers of large areas of Mexico from the fourteenth through sixteenth centuries, believed that Tlaloc sent rain to farmlands, and thus this deity's image often appears on drinking and water-carrying vessels. Tlaloc vessels were also used in Aztec religious rituals, when they would be filled with water and

4.3 Dona Schlesier. *Setting Cycles*, 2004. Mixed media on paper (oil pastel, handmade paper, papyrus, and thread), 30″ × 22″.

All works of art have both formal organization and subject matter, even abstract and nonobjective art.

4.4 Edward Hopper. *Nighthawks,* 1942. Oil on canvas, 33″ × 60″. Art Institute of Chicago.

There is obvious subject matter in this painting, as well as some concepts not immediately apparent.

broken in the temple, symbolically spilling the life-giving water onto the earth.

All works of art have subject matter, even abstract or nonobjective works (recall from Chapter 1 that abstract works are distortions or simplifications of some real-world entity, whereas nonobjective works have no real-world reference). In Dona Schlesier's 2004 mixed-media piece, *Setting Cycles* (Fig. 4.3), the subject matter is in the materials themselves and also in the dichotomies that she explores: smooth versus rough, organic versus mechanical, circular versus rectangular, colorful versus neutral,

empty versus dense, and so on. The round form may suggest the setting moon or the movements of planets, giving the viewer the option to interpret the work based on that name. Schlesier often uses ordinary materials, encouraging the viewer to think of dichotomies in everyday life. She made her own paper by shredding and soaking discarded paper of all kinds, and also made reference to ancient paper with the papyrus.

As part of their subject matter, artworks also have **subtext**, which are underlying ideas or messages. In Edward Hopper's 1942 oil painting, *Nighthawks* (Fig. 4.4), the obvious subject matter is of customers in a corner diner, late at night. Additionally, in many of his paintings, Hopper focused on the loneliness of city life, and indeed all four people in *Nighthawks* seem isolated from or unable to connect to others around them. The street outside is empty. A subtext in *Nighthawks* is a sense of impending doom or entrapment. There is no door shown to get in or out of the diner. The gloom captures the mood in the United States right after the attack on Pearl Harbor in 1941 plunged the country into World War II.

Iconography

Artists can use metaphors or symbols to convey content. A visual **metaphor** is an image or element that is descriptive of something else. In *Setting Cycles*, the handmade paper is just paper, but it acts as a visual metaphor for the passage of time as it is piled up one layer upon another, and some areas seem to be disintegrating with age.

A **symbol** is an image or element that stands for or represents some other entity or concept. Symbols are culturally determined and must be taught. For example, in the United States today, a dove is a symbol of peace. But people from other cultures would not know by observation alone to connect "dove" and "peace."

Iconography is a system of symbols that allows artists to refer to complex ideas. It literally means "image" (icono-) and "to write" (-graphy). Some cultures developed complex iconographic systems, for example, ancient Egypt, Byzantine art, medieval Europe, Buddhism, and Hinduism, to name only a few. In medieval Christian symbolism, the unicorn stands for both Jesus Christ and for a faithful husband in marriage (see Fig. 14.3). Mary, mother of Jesus, was often shown with flowers, symbolizing purity or sorrow.

Figure 4.5 is *Yama*, from Tibet around the mid-seventeenth or early eighteenth century. Once we become familiar with iconography, we would know that Yama is the Indian god of death, who later became the protector of the adherents of the Buddhist religion. Dressed in leopard skin and wearing a headdress of human skulls, Yama holds a thunderbolt chopper and skull, while standing on black lotus petals in a sea of blood. This fierce god fights against the inner demons such as hatred and lust. He tramples an agonized creature beneath his feet. Four buffalo-headed Yamas are located near the corners, and various holy figures hover above, while many skulls occupy the space below.

Iconography can be embedded in architecture. We already saw the *U.S. Capitol Building* (Fig. 4.1). Its design reflects Greek and Roman architecture, to visually connect the government of the United States to the idea of democracy (Greece) and power (the Roman Empire). The building has two wings, instantly conveying the idea of the two houses of Congress and physically containing them. The central dome symbolizes unity.

CONNECTION The *Maori Meeting House* (Fig. 3.39 and Fig. 10.17) contains political and religious iconography that is important to the native Maori people of New Zealand.

THE INFLUENCE OF HISTORICAL CONTEXT, PHYSICAL SURROUNDINGS, AND METHOD OF ENCOUNTER

In addition to analyzing form and content, it is important to also know the context in which an artwork was made, especially the historical, political, religious, and social conditions of the day. We have already seen that Edward Hopper was influenced by the horrific events at the beginning of World War II when he painted the lonely and isolated figures in *Nighthawks* (Fig. 4.4). Every artist and every artwork is similarly shaped by concurrent external circumstances.

Also, as we are viewing artwork today, we are also influenced by our own contemporary environment and society, which affects our ideas about artwork of the past, the present, and other cultures. In addition, the location and circumstances surrounding our encounter with art can change what we think about it.

Context for the Creation of the Artwork

Context consists of the external conditions that surround a work of art. Context includes a host of factors, such as historical events, economic trends, contemporary cultural developments, religious attitudes, social norms, other artworks of the time, and so on.

Historical context and geographic location had an enormous influence on Rembrandt van Rijn as he worked on the large painting, *The Company of Captain Frans*

4.5 *Yama*, Tibet, mid-17th to early 18th century. Distemper (pigments mixed with egg yolk, egg white, and/or size) on cloth, $72\,^3/_8''$ × $46\,^5/_8''$. The Metropolitan Museum of Art, New York.

This painting has a complex iconography, or system of symbols, that refer to religious beliefs of Buddhism.

4.6 REMBRANDT VAN RIJN. *The Company of Captain Frans Banning Cocq,* or *The Night Watch,* c.1642. Oil on canvas, 11′ 11″ × 14′ 4″. Rijksmuseum, Amsterdam, The Netherlands.

Historical circumstances influenced the artist in making this work. By showing members of the ordinary merchant class rather than nobles or popes, this artwork is indeed the product of a Protestant middle-class culture.

Banning Cocq (Fig. 4.6), also popularly called *The Night Watch*. During Rembrandt's lifetime, almost all countries in Europe were ruled by powerful kings or nobles, and all large paintings were made for royal palaces or for majestic Catholic churches. Yet Rembrandt and other Dutch artists worked for middle-class clients in the Netherlands, a republic run by city-dwelling manufacturers and merchants made prosperous by trade. No king or saint is depicted, only middle-class citizens assembling for a civil guard parade. This subject matter on a large scale never would have been commissioned if Rembrandt had lived under a seventeenth-century monarch. The painting hung in a banquet room in an Amsterdam militia hall, where

years of candle and fire soot darkened its varnish, resulting in the mistaken notion that this is a night scene.

Of course, context is just as important in artwork produced today. In the 1990s, Shirin Neshat produced a series of photographs called *Women of Allah*, one of which is *Speechless* (Fig. 4.7). Neshat was born in Iran and immigrated to the United States as a teenager, just as Iran was being transformed into an Islamic state led by clerics. Her subject is Islamic women and femininity in a country where women's actions and rights are limited by religious law. In her photographs, women's hands or faces emerge from beneath veils, often framed by guns or flowers. On the photos, Neshat wrote religious quotes or poetry in Farsi,

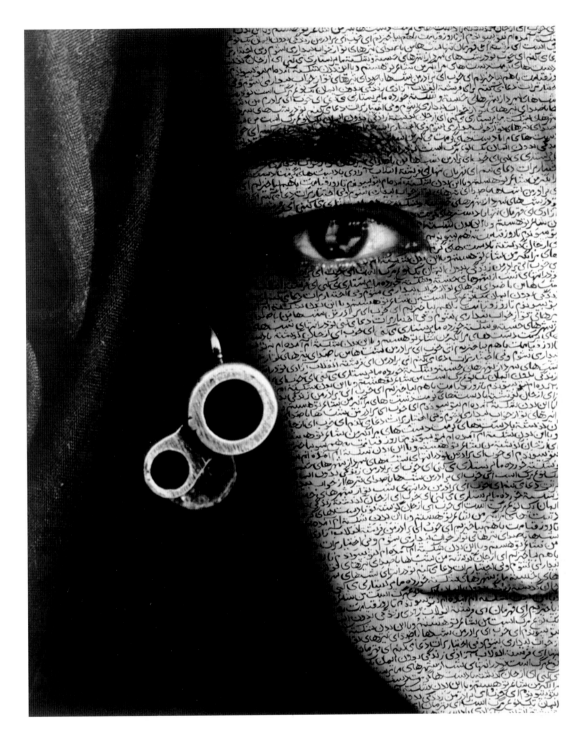

4.7 SHIRIN NESHAT. *Speechless*, 1996. Pen and ink over gelatin silver print, 49″ × 36″.

This photograph reflects aspects of being a woman in contemporary fundamental Islamic cultures.

the language of Iran. The context for Neshat's poignant photos is the political and social climate in fundamentalist Islamic cultures and Western reactions to that.

Physical Surroundings

The location of an artwork also affects its meaning. Many works of art can be moved physically from one location to another, but the location change might have a profound impact on the work. Historical events at a location can also change the meaning of an artwork.

An example of an artwork that takes its meaning from its site is *The New York City Waterfalls* (Fig. 4.8), 2008, on view for four months along the East River near Lower Manhattan. With the assistance of the Public Art Fund in New York, the artist Olafur Eliasson executed the four artificial waterfalls constructed of scaffolding and pumps, ranging from 90 to 120 feet high. While we commonly think of New York City as an enormous and dense urban mass, in reality it is situated in a mesh of waterways where fresh water meets salt water, an ideal habitat for wildlife. Eliasson wanted to dramatically integrate nature (the falling water) into the city space (the scaffolding), and to draw people back to the New York City waterfronts.

Another New York City sculpture was Alexander Calder's *Bent Propeller* from 1970 (Fig. 4.9). It was an imposing outdoor artwork that stood in the World Trade Center complex, and visitors before 2001 appreciated its large size and bold color in relation to its location, surrounded by skyscrapers that contained a huge economic and trading hub. Now it exists only in photographs, its name has a special irony, and its meaning is forever altered by the events of September 11, 2001.

Method of Encounter

We encounter art in all kinds of ways—in newspapers, in museums, out on the street, at religious sites, in public parks, in government or corporate buildings, in schools, at festivals, in malls, and so on. The nature of our encounter adds meaning to the artwork.

We know most works of art through photographs, which communicate only a fraction of the total experience

4.8, left OLAFUR ELIASSON. *The New York City Waterfalls*, 2008. Installation along the East River.

The meaning of this artwork comes in part from the location where it was situated.

4.9, below ALEXANDER CALDER. *Bent Propeller*, 1970. Sheet metal, bolts, and paint, 25' high. Destroyed on September 11, 2001, during the attack on the World Trade Center. World Trade Center, New York.

The historical events of September 11, 2001 affect how we think of this artwork.

4.10 *Potala Palace*, the former summer palace of the Tibetan Buddhist leader, the Dalai Lama. Lhasa, Tibet.

If you only know this famous palace through photographs, your experience of it is very limited.

4.11 *Drum*, Dong son Civilization, Vietnam, 3rd–1st BCE. Bronze, 24.5″ × 31″. From Tanh Hoa. Musee des Arts Asiatiques-Guimet, Paris, France.

In the museum, viewers are limited to visually studying this drum. In the culture for which it was originally made, it provided sound and visuals as part of a larger ritual.

of actually being in the presence of the art. The *Potala Palace* in Lhasa, Tibet (Fig. 4.10), begun in the seventeenth century, is an enormous structure situated high in the Himalaya mountains and the home of the Dalai Lama, the traditional spiritual and political leader of Tibet (the current Dalai Lama has lived in exile since the Chinese invaded in the 1950s). Looking at photographs at your leisure, you can study the entire palace, seeing it framed against majestic peaks or reflected in a nearby lake. Were you to actually approach and enter the palace, your experience would be quite different: physical exertion while climbing steep stairways, brisk mountain weather, partial glimpses of buildings rather than "the perfect shot," encounters with other pilgrims, tour buses at the base of the mountain, and so on.

Even for artworks that we actually encounter in life, the way we come in contact with them affects how we perceive them. To the people of the first millennium BCE Dong Son civilization (Vietnam), the bronze *Drum* (Fig. 4.11) with a resonating top plate was widely used in rituals related to the community, fertility, and dead warriors. The entirety of the rituals, plus the appearance of the drum and the sound it makes, was all part of the way the Dong Son people knew this artwork. Now, in a museum, we see only the isolated object, removed from its ritual context and mute. This is the same with every artwork we encounter. When we experience art as it is being used in life, we get a fuller and richer context for the work. In contrast, the museum preserves the work and removes it from the distracting environment.

WRITINGS ABOUT ART

Art writings help us understand the full meaning of artworks. There are three major groups who write about art: (1) art critics, who describe works of art (usually contemporary art) and then evaluate their significance; (2) art historians and academics, who primarily research art of the past and art of other cultures; and (3) curators, who write catalog essays, wall labels, and educational material for museum and gallery exhibitions.

The meaning of an artwork is not fixed and permanent from the moment it is made. Rather, each successive writer can add new interpretations to the same works of art. As an example, the writings about Georgia O'Keeffe do not all agree about her flower paintings, which view blooms up close and large, as in *Yellow Calla*, 1926 (Fig. 4.12). O'Keeffe connected such works to her love of nature. She wrote in one letter:

> There has been no rain since I came out but today a little came—enough to wet the sage and moisten the top of the dry soil—and make the world smell very fresh and fine—I drove up the canyon four or five miles when the sun was low and I wish I could send you a mariposa lily—and the smell of the damp sage—the odd dark and bright look that comes over my world in the low light after a little rain. (Cowart 1987:239)

Some writers believe that O'Keeffe's flower paintings represent female sexuality in a positive way, a notion that O'Keeffe rejected. Feminist writer and artist Judy Chicago wrote:

> [O'Keeffe] seemed to have made a considerable amount of work that was constructed around a center. . . . There also seemed to be an implied relationship between [her] own body and that centered image. . . . In her paintings, the flower suggests her own femininity, through which the mysteries of life could be revealed. (Chicago 1975:142)

Still other writers see a different feminist aspect to O'Keeffe's work, as in this quote by Ann Sutherland Harris and Linda Nochin:

> Her work since 1915 has been labeled "feminine" by many critics because of its association with the female body. But the wide range of her artistic language would seem to gainsay this simple description. Although O'Keeffe has rarely made a cause out of being a woman artist. . . . Her ability to go it alone has become a contemporary feminist model for freedom of thought and action. (Harris and Nochlin 1976:302)

The fact that there are contradictory interpretations of an artwork and of an artist's life is not a negative thing. Most

4.12 Georgia O'Keeffe. *Yellow Calla*, 1926. Oil on canvas, 9″ × 12³⁄₄″. Smithsonian American Art Museum, Washington, DC.

There is a lot of disagreement about whether the imagery in O'Keeffe's large flower paintings is sexual or not.

4.13 MORRIS LOUIS. *Blue Veil*, c. 1958–1959. Acrylic resin paint on canvas, 93.2″ × 158.5″.

Formalist critics praised paintings like this one because it does not depict recognizable subject matter, has no perceivable brushstrokes, and does not give the illusion of deep space.

great artwork contains complex messages that can be challenging, profound, or even conflicting.

Most art writers based their writings on a particular philosophical position. We will look briefly at several of these from the twentieth and early twenty-first centuries.

Modernist Criticisms

Modernist philosophical positions generally present master narratives that specify the correct way of analyzing any artwork. Inherent in modernism is the notion of progress, that previous art styles are preludes to the next significant step forward. Modernist philosophers seek the relationship between art and truth. Idealism and aesthetics are important, and as a result, fine art is emphasized as being far superior to popular culture.

The first modernist philosophical position is **formalist criticism**, emphasizing formal analysis. Formalism first appeared in England in the early twentieth century as a way to appreciate artworks from other cultures, in particular, the Japanese prints and African sculptures that were widely circulated in Europe. Although the European audience did not understand the subject matter and iconography of these artworks, they appreciate them as art from a formalist point of view.

After World War II, formalist criticism was associated with Modern Art in the United States. The critic Clement Greenberg promoted works such as Morris Louis's *Blue Veil* (Fig. 4.13), 1958–1959, because they were "self-critical," focusing on what was "unique to the nature of [their] medium," so that "art would be rendered 'pure'" (Greenberg 1961:13). *Blue Veil* was "pure" painting because it eliminated brushstrokes and emphasized the flatness of the painting surface. Recognizable imagery, symbolism, and narrative were eliminated as detrimental distractions. Painting was the medium that most thoroughly represented the ideas of formalist critics in the late 1940s and 1950s.

Ideological criticism, rooted in the writings of Karl Marx, deals with the political underpinnings of art. All art, according to this position, supports some particular political agenda, cultural structure, or economic/class hierarchy. Even artwork that may seem neutral is still political. For example, Serge Guilbaut researched the ways that the CIA promoted **Abstract Expressionist** artists, like Morris Louis or Jackson Pollock, in order to prove that the United States was culturally superior to Communist countries in the Cold War era after World War II. Other ideological theorists were Herbert Marcuse and Theodor Adorno.

Of course, some ideological writings do deal with art that is overtly political, and some artwork functions as ideological criticism. For example, the well-documented Mexican Muralist Movement of the mid-twentieth century promoted the rights and power of the indigenous Mexican people over the ruling class. The artist Juan O'Gorman produced murals that commemorated the struggle for Mexican Independence. *Panel of the Independence—Father Hidalgo (Retablo de la Independencia—Hidalgo)*, 1960–1961 (Fig. 4.14), shows atrocities committed against the indigenous people, as well as representing the church, the army, and major leaders in the struggle.

> **CONNECTION** Three other important leaders of the Mexican Muralist movement were Diego Rivera (see Fig. 9.25), José Orozco (see Fig 14.29), and David Siqueiros (see Fig. 11.7).

Psychoanalytic criticism holds that art should be studied as the product of individuals who are shaped by their pasts, their unconscious urges, and their social histories. Sigmund Freud wrote the first psychoanalytic criticism when he examined Leonardo da Vinci's work in light of Leonardo's presumed homosexuality and episodes from his early childhood. Psychoanalytic criticism seems appropriate for work that deals with strong emotional content, intuition, dream imagery, or fantasy, such as the 1941 painting *The Beautiful Bird Revealing the Unknown to a Pair of Lovers* (Fig. 4.15). The work of Joan Miró alludes to hallucination, fantasy, or dream. The artist developed a process of working that allowed him to switch between conscious and unconscious decisions as the image developed.

Structuralism holds that in order to understand a work of art, one must study the structure of art and the complex interrelationship of all its parts. Structure gives the meaning to an artwork, like a sentence determines the meaning of individual words within it. Structuralism was originally applied to the study of language, as was **semiotics**, the study of signs in verbal or written communication. Its systems of analysis were then applied to fields such as anthropology, architecture, and art. Although Structuralism is a modernist position, it influenced Post-Structuralist philosophies in the Postmodern era, which we will see next.

4.14 JUAN O'GORMAN. *Panel of the Independence—Father Hidalgo (Retablo de la Independencia—Hidalgo)*, 1960–1961. Mural. Museo Nacional de Historia, Castillo de Chapultepec, Mexico City.

Some artworks have overt political content. By painting such images, the artist ensures that this piece of history will not be forgotten, and he also promotes rights for the downtrodden everywhere by memorializing this uprising against an oppressive ruling class.

to protest latent Nazism in the German government. On October 18, she and two others were found dead in prison. Authorities declared the deaths suicides, but many factions suspected that the protestors were murdered by authorities. Richter's paintings represent a perfect post-structuralist moment. The unclear image evokes a young woman who appears open and friendly, totally discordant with the crimes she apparently planned. The blur also indicates the lack of closure and continuing controversy concerning what exactly happened to her and her cohort.

One post-structuralist, Jacques Derrida, introduced the idea of **deconstruction**, which holds that from the inside, any system looks natural and coherent, but that it is in fact filled with unseen contradictions, myths,

4.15, left JOAN MIRÓ. *The Beautiful Bird Revealing the Unknown to a Pair of Lovers,* 1941. Gouache and oil wash on paper, 18″ × 15″. The Museum of Modern Art, New York.

The imagery in this painting, as well as the surreal nature of the title, suggest a dreamlike quality.

4.16, below GERHARD RICHTER. *October 18, 1977,* 1988. One of fifteen paintings, oil on canvas. Installation variable. The Sidney and Harriet Janis Collection, gift of Philip Johnson, and acquired through the Lillie P. Bliss Bequest (all by exchange); Enid A. Haupt Fund; Nina and Gordon Bunshaft Bequest Fund; and gift of Emily Rauh Pulitzer. The Museum of Modern Art, New York.

This painting refers to highly publicized events in recent German history. The blurring refers to the controversies surrounding the deaths of three young radicals.

Postmodern Philosophical Positions

Postmodernism is not a continuation of Modernism, but rather a set of philosophical positions that question Modernism: "[P]ostmodernism endorses the modest proliferation of 'little narratives,' a bricolage of stories and images celebrating difference, plurality, and paradox" (Kearney and Rasmussen 2001:361). Where modernist philosophies stated certainties, postmodernism deals with subjectivity, nuances, and ambiguity. The following is a summary of several postmodern points of view.

Post-structuralism is a range of reactions against Structuralism, but it is not a homogeneous set of ideas. Although structure is important to study, post-structuralists believe that this will result not in one single meaning to an artwork, but rather in multiple meanings, because every viewer approaches the work with varying perspectives. Major post-structuralist writers include Jacques Derrida, Michel Foucault, and Julia Kristeva.

The artist Gerhard Richter's work reflects many post-structuralist ideas. In Figure 4.16, his black-and-white painting is one of a group of fifteen collectively entitled *October 18, 1977,* referring to the deaths of three leaders of the radical Baader-Meinhof group. Like an unclear news photo, Richter's painting is a blurred image of Gudrun Ensslin, who planned bombings and kidnappings or stereotypes. The collective self-portraits of Cindy Sherman seek to deconstruct stereotypes of woman in Western cultures. One self-portrait is *Untitled (Portrait of Marilyn Monroe)* (Fig. 4.17) from 1982; another is *Untitled Film Still #35* (Fig. 12.12), from 1979. Sherman produced many more self-portraits besides these two, and in them she photographs herself as in stereotypical roles often from movies, such as girl-next-door, the seductress, the trapped housewife, or the vulnerable hitchhiker. However, there is no "self" in these self-portraits. As the critic Douglas Crimp wrote,

4.17 CINDY SHERMAN. *Untitled (Self-Portrait of Marilyn Monroe)*, 1982. Ektachrome photo, 15.5″ × 9″. Museum of Fine Arts, Houston, Texas, USA.

The title of this artwork suggests that Cindy Sherman's self-portrait was modeled after a photograph of Marilyn Monroe, and that they were both playing socially defined roles rather than presenting images of their actual selves.

Sherman [as a person] is literally self-created in these works; her self is therefore understood as contingent upon the possibilities provided by the culture in which Sherman participates, not by some inner impulse. As such, her photographs reverse the terms of art and autobiography. They use art not to reveal the artist's true self, but to show the self as an imaginary construct. There is no real Cindy Sherman in these photographs; there is only the guises she assumes. And she does not create these guises; she simply chooses them in a way that any of us do. (Crimp 1989, reprinted in Risatti 1990:138–39)

Post-structuralist artists and critics in the late twentieth century often focused on the medium of photography, which easily copies existing things and can be produced in multiples for wide distribution. This fits the Postmodern idea that there is no original, no "real," only copies. In contrast, Modernist critics valued the original art object, unique and handmade by a gifted artist.

Feminist criticism is concerned with the oppression of groups (especially women) in a given society, along with the oppression of their belief systems. Feminism advocates equal social, political, and economic rights for all women and men. Some prominent feminist writers include Linda Nochlin and Griselda Pollock.

Feminists employ various strategies to achieve their goals. First, feminists have revised how we see historical artworks. For example, previous art historians treated nude women in paintings as simply part of the composition, whereas feminist writers analyze the work as having been made for the male gaze. (For more on the feminine body and the gaze, see Chapter 7). Feminists pointed out the large number of artworks made by men that feature female nudes in museums, while historically there are practically no male nudes painted by women.

 CONNECTION The Guerrilla Girls' 1986 poster *Do Women Have to Be Naked to Get into the Met. Museum?* (Fig. 13.1) is an example of an artwork functioning as feminist criticism.

Second, feminists have broken down the barriers encountered by women's artwork and the media they use. Modernist critics have denigrated pottery, weaving, and decorative work as minor arts. Now works such as the Navajo *Wearing Blanket* (Fig. 4.18), woven by a woman, are studied and featured in museums.

Finally, feminist critics and art historians have researched and publicized women artists who have been ignored in the past, such as the seventeenth-century Italian

4.18 *Wearing Blanket.* Navajo; Arizona, United States, 1860–1870. Wool, 67 1/2″ × 49″. Gift of Mrs. Russell Sage, 1910 (10.107.1).

Weaving was considered a minor art in the Modern era, but feminists have attempted to revise the perception of such media.

4.19 ARTEMISIA GENTILESCHI. *Judith and Holofernes,* 1612–1613. Oil on canvas, 62.5″ × 49.5″ Museo Nazionale di Capodimonte, Naples, Italy.

Feminist art historians have researched women artists in the past whose lives and works have been ignored, such as Artemisia Gentileschi.

artist, Artemisia Gentileschi, one of the most important painters of her era. Determined and skilled, she executed large historical paintings that were considered beyond the ability of women. After her death, she sank into obscurity, and her works, like *Judith and Holofernes,* 1612–1613 (Fig. 4.19), were attributed to her artist father. Herself a victim of rape and ill treatment from men, Gentileschi brought an immediacy to the beheading scene that is different from the idealized, sanitized way that male painters depicted the Biblical event.

Writings in **visual culture** attempt to integrate all of the visual components of contemporary culture. People in industrialized nations consume massive numbers of images every day, seeking information, meaning, or pleasure. To writers in visual culture, art is only part of this intense barrage of images and must be analyzed in relationship to film, advertisements, the Internet, television, and so on. People have become spectators rather than participants in their own lives, and the writers examine how we receive and use this diverse imagery. As Nicholas Mirzoeff wrote, "Visual culture . . . is not just part of your everyday life, it is your everyday life" (Mirzoeff 1998:3).

Obviously, visual culture covers an enormous amount of territory. However, it is helpful to look at just one example of visual culture analysis. Specifically, some writers have investigated the idea of the carnival and its relationship to artistic innovation. Vulgar, uninhibited, and anticlassical, carnivals gleefully undermine social order by celebrating the fabulous aspect of the grotesque, the temporary overturning of taboos, and excessive behaviors. Costumes decorate and enhance the body to create fantastic distortions and transformations. Carnivals are held throughout the world; a famous annual four-day carnival with all the glitter of the entertainment industry is held in Rio de Janeiro, Brazil, often in February, and in the United States there is New Orleans' Mardi Gras (Shohat and Stam 1998:34–37).

4.20 *Giant Puppet Parade.* Street Carnival in Olinda, Brazil, February 16, 2010.

Visual culture writers find associations between popular phenomenon and art making.

Figure 4.20 is an image from the carnival in Olinda, Brazil, which is known for its giant puppets that represent local and international celebrities and politicians. The fifteen-foot puppets are made of papier-mâché and are built and carried almost entirely by local anonymous people.

CONNECTION Chapter 15 deals with more aspects of visual culture. (See the discussion of Las Vegas on page 441, Figure 15.10.)

The final postmodernism philosophical position is **relational aesthetics**, which focuses on human relationships and social spaces, rather than emphasizing art objects in private galleries, homes, or museums. French art-critic Nicolas Bourriaud has written about relational aesthetics, and perhaps its most famous practitioner is the Brazilian-born Thai artist Rirkrit Tiravanija. Instead of displaying objects, Tiravanija's work in galleries has often consisted of cooking and serving Thai meals for gallery goers, which creates a climate for interaction between the artist and the viewers. Tiravanija also created a stainless steel Ping-Pong Table called *Untitled 2008 (the future will be chrome).* It is a beautiful and precious object, but rather than being hands-off, gallery goers play on it (Fig. 4.21). He has also created communal land projects in Thailand, for living, farming, and building.

Personal Interpretation

In the end, you may have your own meaning for a work of art. **Phenomenology** holds that you, the perceiving subject, engage with an artwork. Ultimately this interaction produces in you an intellectual and emotional response, based on your own ideas, personal tastes, experiences, and history. You might be immediately aware of some of these factors, while others lurk at the edges of your

consciousness. In studying art, you learn about yourself. Your interpretation may differ from everyone else's. Also, meaning may shift as you change, and a work of art may seem very different to you now than it did a few years ago.

4.21 Rirkrit Tiravanija. *Untitled, 2008 (the future will be chrome).* Polished stainless steel Ping Pong table, shown here with artists Jay Nelson, right, and Annie Wachmicki, obscured, playing Ping Pong during a NADA preview at the Ice Palace in Miami, Florida, on December 2, 2008.

Relational aesthetics promotes art practices that emphasize social interaction.

5.1 Imhotep. *Stepped Pyramid of Djoser (right) and Tomb Complex*, Saqqarah, Egypt, 2650–2631 BCE.

Works of art are the products of artistic vision and the cultural environment that fosters it.

5

MAKING ART, USING ART, AND PRESERVING ART

Who makes art? How do we use art once it is made? Why do we preserve art, or sometimes destroy it?

PREVIEW

This chapter begins with an in-depth look at artists and the roles they play in society, as well as the broader support structures around them. Artists make art, with the assistance of others who provide materials, support, training, professional assistance, technical expertise, and cultural standards.

It goes on to show how art is made both to be used and to serve a variety of functions, which is true for every work in this book. In addition, it will show that people keep art beyond its original functionality because it is meaningful to them. Governments keep art for its sacred or aesthetic qualities, for national pride, for enriching their cultural treasure, and for a stronger economy. Private and public art collections are great repositories of art. It will also discuss that keeping art is not a passive activity, for most of it must be actively cared for or managed. There are preservation and restoration challenges for ancient buildings as well as yesterday's computer art.

The chapter concludes with a discussion about works of art that are not preserved. Invading armies often destroy the art of those they vanquish. And some art is dynamically created, used, and then destroyed as part of rituals or performances.

ARTISTS

Before we begin discussing artists and their roles and the ways they make art, it is important to look at all the other people who contribute to the process of making art. Most artworks are the product of both the artist(s) and the broader culture that contributes to the making and the purpose of art. Let us break this down using the pyramids of ancient Egypt to see how the culture, the ruling class, the priest class, the artists/architects, and skilled laborers combined to create the conditions that allowed for the construction of this amazing funerary architecture.

The *Stepped Pyramid of Djoser and Tomb Complex* (Fig. 5.1, Chapter Opener) from 2650 BCE, obviously required more than one artist's effort to build. Thousands contributed to its physical construction, including engineers, skilled workers, and laborers, supervised by priests and architects. Funding necessary for all the pyramids ultimately came from the Egyptian economy, which was supported by the general population.

More people contributed to the pyramid concept. The pharaoh wanted to provide a fitting afterlife for himself. The design of the pyramid was the vision of one architect, Imhotep, who was considered a genius in his lifetime because he had the funerary structures built entirely of stone. He also found a way to stack these structures to reach a height that was unprecedented in Egyptian tomb design. Nevertheless, Imhotep's genius rested on a solid foundation provided by the Egyptian culture. All earlier Egyptian tombs were prototypes for his design; Imhotep's own design was later modified and refined for the *Great Pyramids* of Giza (see Fig. 9.4). Plus, the Egyptian priest class already had developed complex belief systems about the afterlife, and their rituals directed the design of temples and tombs. For example, to the left of the *Stepped Pyramid* in Figure 5.1, you can see several other structures used for the Heb Sed rituals during the pharaoh's lifetime and after death, which reinvigorated his strength. There were more structures in this complex, each serving a particular ritual purpose.

Other art forms—film, architecture, or any work of large scale—obviously require the active participation of many people to be realized. Even small-scale work, such as a student's oil painting, requires the input of teachers, past painters, and art critics to provide the necessary background of skills and ideas. The materials were developed by artists and scientists, and manufactured by art supply firms. The student probably has financial support, showing that parents, politicians, wealthy donors, or university administrators consider the study of painting to be important enough to pay for it.

Training Artists

Artists need to acquire skills, and traditionally, many started as apprentices in workshops to learn materials, manual skills, and styles from mature artists. There are examples of this system all around the world. For example, Leonardo da Vinci was trained as an apprentice of the artist Andrea del Verrocchio. Throughout Africa, artists traditionally were trained in the apprentice method, learning the tools and methods as well as aesthetic standards, as in the *Shrine of Shango* (Fig. 5.2). Among the Yoruba artists in modern Africa, "the final sharp cutting is best done by the master" while apprentices do the "mechanical aspects of the work, and as their skill increases, more and more is entrusted to them" (Fr. Kevin Carroll, quoted in Willett 1993:236).

In addition to apprentice systems, more structured institutions have existed for training artists. In medieval Europe, specialized societies called **guilds** preserved technical information for artists and regulated art making. Persian royalty from the thirteenth to seventeenth centuries sponsored the **kitab khana**, libraries and workshops of highly trained artists who produced fine illuminated manuscripts. Students learned from and later collaborated with senior artists. *Scribe and Painter at Work*, from the *Hadiqat Al-Haqiqat* (The Garden of Truth) by Hakim Sana'i (Fig. 5.3), shows the palace-like conditions where the best artists worked. The kitab khana was a precursor of art academies that were founded to provide systematized art instruction for young artists.

Academies in Europe appeared in the fifteenth century. One of the most famous was France's powerful Royal Academy (Académie Royale de Peinture et de Sculpture), founded in 1648 by King Louis XIV (Fig. 5.4). Through his ministers and the academy, the king controlled the decorative arts, architecture, painting, and landscape architecture for his enormous, lavish palace at Versailles and its surrounding gardens, as well as his other residences. Although art academies still exist in much-modified form, most artists in the United States today study in a college or university.

Some artists are self-taught, receiving no formal art training. Some work in isolation. For fourteen years in Washington, D.C., James Hampton worked on *The Throne of the Third Heaven of the Nations Millennium General*

5.2 *Shrine of Shango*, the Yoruba god of thunder, furnished with figures of women devotees, 20th century. Oroko wood, average 30″ high. Collection of Oba Laoye II, Temi of Ede, Nigeria.

Many cultures (for example, the Nigerian culture that produced these sculptures) use the apprentice system for training young artists.

5.3 JAGANATH. *Scribe and Painter at Work*, from the *Hadiqat Al-Haqiqat* (The Garden of Truth) by Hakim Sana'i, Mughal, 1599–1600. First Miniature, folio 15. Pen and ink on paper.

An early forerunner of art academies were *kitab khanas*, which were workshops and libraries that produced Islamic manuscripts.

5.4 NICOLAS RENE JOLLAIN THE ELDER. *Portrait of Louis XIV holding the plan for the Royal House at Saint-Cyr*, 1661–1715. Oil on canvas, 87″ × 65″. Chateaux de Versailles et de Trianon, Versailles, France.

King Louis XIV instituted the Royal Academy to set standards for artistic production in France.

5.5 JAMES HAMPTON. *The Throne of the Third Heaven of the Nations Millennium General Assembly*, c. 1950–1964. Gold and silver aluminum foil, Kraft paper, and plastic over wood furniture, paperboard, and glass, 180 pieces in all; overall configuration: $10^1/_2$′ $\times$ 27′ $\times$ $14^1/_2$′. Smithsonian American Art Museum, Washington, DC.

Some artists are untrained, as is the case with James Hampton, who produced this large sculpture in the evenings after working his day job.

Assembly (Fig. 5.5), laboring over it daily from the time he finished his day job as a janitor into the middle of the night. He dreamed of opening a storefront ministry after retirement. By the time he died, he had produced a heavenly vision with 180 pieces, made from inexpensive or cast-off materials.

Making the Art Object

In many cases, individual artists make their own artwork. Michelangelo Buonarroti did most of the painting on the colossal *Sistine Ceiling* because he was dissatisfied with the work that his collaborators did (see Fig. 8.21). Vincent van Gogh painted all his own paintings, because, as he wrote to his brother Theo, he valued the act of creation more than life itself. But sometimes, art objects are made by workshops, by the community, in collaborations, and so on.

We have already discussed apprentices in workshop situations in Italy and in Africa (Fig. 5.2), as well as the kitab khana of Persia (Fig. 5.3). Many prominent European artists maintained workshops from the fifteenth through the nineteenth centuries, staffed with many skilled professionals and apprentices and producing a large amount of artwork, all of which was credited to the master artist. Even today, some artists hire professionals to help build, assemble, paint, or produce their works of art.

CONNECTION Peter Paul Rubens maintained one of the largest and most prolific workshops in seventeenth-century Europe. See the *Abduction of the Daughters of Leucippus* (Fig. 13.9).

In community art making, large groups of people who are not normally considered artists contribute directly to the production of a work of art. In medieval Europe, many small, growing cities built impressive cathedrals that were symbols of community pride. Armies of craftsmen worked on these structures, but equally importantly, the townspeople, from the wealthy to the poor, also contributed their labor and often substantially paid for the church.

5.6 Displaying the *AIDS Memorial Quilt*, October 11, 1992. Washington, DC.

Ordinary people contributed to the making of this work of art, and also contributed to the funding for it and for AIDS research.

5.7 ANDO OR UTAGAWA HIROSHIGE. *Basket Ferry*, Kagowatashi, Hida Province, 19th century. Woodblock print, 13½" × 9". Leeds Museums and Galleries (City Art Gallery), United Kingdom.

Prints in 19th-century Japan were the products of collaborations among skilled professionals, including the artist, the block carver, the papermaker, and the printer.

The *AIDS Memorial Quilt*, begun in 1989 (Fig. 5.6; a different view is on page 262), provides another example of community art making. The *AIDS Memorial Quilt* is a composite of thousands of three-by-six-foot panels, each made by ordinary people to memorialize someone they lost to AIDS. It is a collection of individual remembrances, and each remembrance is an equal contribution to the fabric of the whole. The people who made the panels communicated their love and loss in ways that may be naive or may be sophisticated but collectively are very moving. The quilt is an ongoing effort of the Names Project, begun by gay activist Cleve Jones in San Francisco in the 1980s. It is also used as a fund-raising tool for AIDS research.

In many instances, art making is a collaborative activity among professionals of equal standing. The knowledge and skill of each collaborator are essential to the final art product. An example is traditional Japanese prints, like *Basket Ferry* (Fig. 5.7) by Ando or Utagawa Hiroshige, requiring the combined skills of many professionals all commissioned by a publisher. The artist made an original drawing, but the print itself was executed by a host of other professionals, including a papermaker, engraver, and printer, as illustrated in Figure 3.14.

CONNECTION Another example of artistic collaboration is John James Audubon's *Carolina Paroquet* from *Birds of America*. The book required the combined efforts of Audubon, a naturalist, and a professional engraver. (See Figure 14.25.)

The Role of the Artist in Various Cultures

Depending on the culture, artists may be considered ordinary people, skilled workers, priests, or people of special or prized skills.

Among the Hindu-Balinese people on the South Pacific island of Bali, almost everyone makes art, either visual art, dance, or music, although certain people are recognized as teachers or people of superior ability. Art, religion, and social institutions are completely intertwined. The visual arts alone consist of stone temples with relief carvings, wooden pagodas, wooden statues for smaller shrines, paintings, large decorated cremation towers used in funerals, items for personal adornment, masks for performances, textiles, sculptures made of baked dough, and food offerings for temples (see Fig. 8.16). Although simple offerings are made every day to deities, ancestors, and demons, Balinese women make large sculptures of fried, colored rice dough like the *Sarad offering* (Fig. 5.8) for temple festivals. Offerings like this exist but a short time and can be used only once, but the obvious care and skill that go into them indicate the significance of art in everyday life.

In some cases, making art is tied to gender roles. Among the Sepik peoples of Papua New Guinea, art making is men's work, and combined rituals and art create male solidarity within a tribe and protect their power from women or other hostile men. The *Male Spirit Mask* (Fig. 5.9) is worn by men in initiation rituals for boys, and it represents a water- or tree-dwelling male ancestor spirit. Individual men, with the help of a master artist, produce paintings and carvings that become vehicles by which an older man can pass his spirit to a younger man. By these means, the men's collective power and knowledge are preserved within their group.

> **CONNECTION** Read more on Sepik rituals and artworks in Chapter 13, page 373.

Artists may be considered anonymous skilled workers or laborers. For example, medieval artists and craftsmen who built the large cathedrals were not famous personalities but were more like skilled union members. In Communist China from the 1950s through the 1980s, artists were not to seek personal glory but to work anonymously making art for the common good. Among the Baule people of Western Africa (Ivory Coast), artists are skilled professionals, and the best earn prestige and high pay, but the artist's name is not associated with the sculptures they make. Rather, the owner of the piece performs rituals and develops the artwork's spiritual cult, like the *Baule Seated*

5.8 *Sarad offering* in Bali. Crafted of dyed rice dough, intricate sarad offerings are made during temple festivals by Balinese women. Photograph c. 1990. Bali, Indonesia.

In Bali, making art is tied with everyday rituals, and almost everyone participates.

Female Figure that represents a spirit wife (Fig. 5.10). A Baule ritual sculpture could be less effective if its human maker is emphasized.

Artists may also be considered to be people of special or prized skills. In particular, in Europe since the Renaissance, many European artists were considered to be creative geniuses. One such artist was Leonardo da Vinci, who also made contributions to the study of hydraulics, zoology, geology, optics, physics, botany, and anatomy, like the *Proportions of the Human Figure* (Fig. 5.11). To Leonardo, observation was essential to understanding the mechanics and the beauty of the world and, thus, the foundation of both science and art.

Art is often a vehicle for spirituality. The artist who makes spiritual art is sometimes also a holy person, priest, or shaman. In the Cook Islands in Polynesia, artists who carved ritual sculptures were specialists called *Ta'unga*,

5.9, *above* *Male Spirit Mask*, Middle Sepik, Papua New Guinea, possibly by the Arambak culture, 20th century. Cane, other plant fibers, cassoway feather, mud, and paint, $47'' \times 27'' \times 23^{1}/_{2}''$. Museum of Fine Arts, Houston, Texas, USA

In Papua New Guinea, making art is tied to gender; in this case, men make art as part of their rituals to protect themselves against enemies and the power of women.

5.10, *above right* *Baule Seated Female Figure*. Wood. Private collection.

Baule artists are not associated with the sculptures they produce; rather, the owners/commissioners of the artwork are associated with the artworks, because they perform the rituals that give the works their meaning.

5.11, *right* LEONARDO DA VINCI. *Proportions of the Human Figure (Vitruvian Man)*, c. 1492. Pen and ink on paper, $13^{1}/_{2}'' \times 9^{2}/_{3}''$. Galleria dell' Accademia, Venice.

Artists can be considered geniuses in some cultures and during some time periods, for example, Leonardo da Vinci, who was renowned for his artistic skills and contributions to science.

a word that also means "priest." They trained for a long time as apprentices, not only to attain art skills but also to acquire the spiritual power inherent in their tools and materials. Monks in monasteries produced medieval manuscripts, which were often handwritten and illustrated prayer books or Bibles. Men in several Native American tribes conducted ritual ceremonies that involved making art.

CONNECTIONS The sculpture *God Te Rongo and His Three Sons*, c. 1800–1900 (Fig. 7.5), carved by priest-artists, is a representation of a deity from the Cook Islands in Polynesia.

Hopi and Zuni men perform sacred ceremonies, part of which involves the distribution of Kachina dolls they made, like the *Ahola Kachina* at left (Fig. 8.19, page 208), with symbols that represent four directions as well as the heavens above and the nadir below.

Even in the twentieth century, some artists engage in practice that is considered shaman-like, for example, Joseph Beuys, who was known for creating work that he intended to help heal the traumatized human spirit after the horrors of World War II and to show a new way of living in the world. His 1969 work, *The Pack* (Fig. 5.12), is a conscious turning away from the industrialized modern state, represented by the van, to a more primitive human existence, represented by the sleds. Beuys equipped each sled with what humans need for this new journey: a flashlight for navigation, felt blankets for protection, and fat for sustenance. (http://www.tate.org.uk/modern/exhibitions/beuys/room6.shtm)

SUPPORT FOR ART MAKING

This section describes some of the common ways that artists have been financially supported to enable them to make their artwork.

Private Patronage

Throughout history, private patrons have contributed to the support of artists. Often, patrons are persons of power or wealth, who commissioned art for their homes or as monuments after their deaths. Louis XIV (Fig. 5.4) commissioned works to further his own glory. Other rulers and

5.12 JOSEPH BEUYS. *The Pack (das Rudel)*. 1969. Volkswagen bus made in 1961, 24 sleighs, each equipped with fat, felt blankets, belts, and torchlight. Staatliche Museen Kassel, Neue Galerie. 78″ × 157″ × 394″.

Artists can be spiritual leaders in their community.

powerful families have done the same. Religious groups have funded the creation of artworks that serve their beliefs, as evident in many of the images in Chapter 8, Deities and Places of Worship. Corporations in the United States have been major patrons of the arts. Many contemporary artists make their living as teachers in colleges and universities.

But also, ordinary people support art that is important to them. Japanese woodblock prints like *Basket Ferry* (Fig. 5.7) were made for the merchant class. Much of Baule sculpture, like the *Seated Female Figure* (Fig. 5.10), is commissioned by ordinary individuals for their personal shrines. The *AIDS Memorial Quilt* (Fig. 5.6) is funded by private donations.

The Market

Today, many artists create art on speculation, which involves making art that they later try to sell, either

5.13 Bunraku performance on stage, Japan, c. 20th century.

Taxes can be used to support artists. For example, artists working in traditional styles are supported by the Japanese Government because they are considered national treasures.

through their own efforts, through agents, or through galleries. This is the opposite of working on commission, when artists make specific works for patrons.

In the fine-art market, artists make works to sell through commercial galleries. Usually, gallery owners take a 50 percent commission on all artworks that they sell. In auction houses, art that has been in private collections may be resold. A few works of art have brought fabulous prices in auctions. For example, some van Gogh paintings have sold for tens of millions of dollars. Because auction houses usually resell art that was already in the hands of collectors or museums, artists do not directly benefit from auction house sales.

Traditional indigenous artworks sometimes are sold in commercial galleries or in tourist centers. These artworks are made specifically for foreign collectors, and the artists do not invest in them the meaning or the spiritual dimension of work made for their own culture. Such markets may help local art production to survive. For example, in Papua New Guinea, the making of ritual art like the *Male Spirit Mask* (Fig. 5.9) and the making of tourist

art are mutually dependent enterprises, each supporting and invigorating the other. On other, more remote islands, where there is little tourism and therefore little tourist trade, the visual arts are falling into a general decline (Lewis 1990:149–63).

Tax-Supported Art

Taxes support art either as direct payments to artists or as funding for major projects.

In Japan, taxes support traditional Japanese art forms. Traditional artists can be designated as Living National Treasures (*Ningen Kokuho*) because they are Bearers of Important Intangible Cultural Assets. Ningen Kokuho include musicians, dramatists, and visual artists, such as masters of Bunraku puppetry (Fig. 5.13), a serious form of puppet theater, also discussed in Chapter 15 on page 446. Some European countries, such as the United Kingdom, France, and Austria, set aside tax monies to support artists and art making. The Austrian government actively supports artists and also subsidizes galleries.

Almost all public monuments, government buildings, and palaces, including ancient Greek temples and Louis XIV's Versailles, were funded by tax revenues from ordinary people. Sometimes federal and local agencies combine their resources for major projects, like the *St. Louis*

5.14 EERO SAARINEN AND ASSOCIATES. St. Louis Gateway Arch, St. Louis, Missouri, constructed 1963–1965. Stainless steel exterior, 630' high.

Federal, state, and local taxes can be used to fund major art projects.

Gateway Arch (Fig. 5.14), designed by Eero Saarinen and Associates, and the Museum of Westward Expansion below it. Such works can become emblems of their city. In addition, many U.S. cities and counties have Percent for the Arts programs, in which a small percentage of the cost of any public building goes toward art for that building or for the area. Many Percent for the Arts programs apply to the construction of all public building as well as private ventures that receive tax abatements in redevelopment zones. Percent for the Arts program funding represents considerable income for some artists.

USING ART

As we saw in Chapter 1, art serves a function. Art is meant to be used, to enrich lives, to be spiritually potent, to educate, to support or protest existing power structures, to entertain, and so on. Kutlug Ataman's *Küba* (Fig. 5.15), from 2004, is a forty-channel video installation played on a classroom-like arrangement of cheap televisions and mismatched furniture. Upon first entering the space, the viewer encounters a room full of murmuring. But on all sets are recordings of individuals telling their stories of hardship and survival in the Istanbul neighborhood called Küba, with its community of marginalized people existing outside of social traditions, and where Ataman lived

intermittently for two years while developing this work. This is a poignant and life-affirming piece that is timely for the tensions and crises facing the world today. It functions to make apparent the impact of international politics on people, who speak directly (through the monitors) to tell other people their stories.

Studying art in books makes it difficult to imagine that almost all art was intended to be lived with in someone's home, or handled or worn in rituals, or used as part of life. Yet this is true, and it is part of your heritage as a human being to have real art as something you encounter regularly or live with every day.

KEEPING ART

Why do we hold on to art, often beyond its original usefulness? The answer involves many considerations, including its meaning and its economic value. We will also look at institutions designed for keeping art, and issues around preserving or restoring it.

National Pride and Glory

Nations keep art for several reasons. Consider the *Cathedral of St. Basil the Blessed* in Moscow (Fig. 5.16), built between 1555 and 1561. Aesthetically, St. Basil's is fantastic—tall,

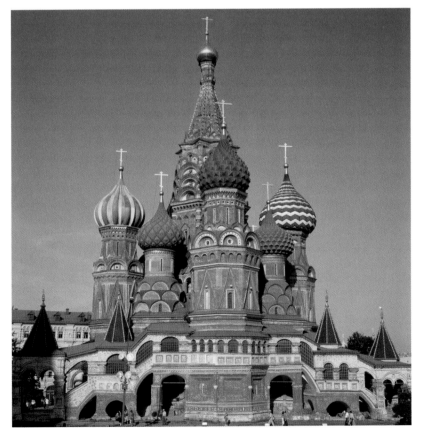

5.15, *above* Kutlug Ataman. *Küba*, 2004. 40-channel video installation with tables and chairs; color, sound. Commissioned by 2004–2005 Carnegie International, Carnegie Museum of Art, Pittsburgh, PA; Lehmann Maupin Gallery, New York; Thyssen-Bornemisza Art Contemporary (T-B A21), Vienna; and Theater der Welt, Stuttgart.

All art has a function at the time it was originally made. This work brings to Western audiences the stories of poor groups in Turkey.

5.16, *left* Exterior of the *Cathedral of St. Basil the Blessed*, Moscow, 1555–1561.

Originally, the function of this church was to glorify the Russian Orthodox church and the power of the Czar. It is now a secularized World Heritage site and a destination for tourists.

brightly colored, elaborately patterned, with nine domes, one over each chapel inside. It represented the strength of the Russian Orthodox Church and the power of the Czar, who commissioned the building of St. Basil's to celebrate his military victories over the Mongols. However, in 1918, the Czarist government was overthrown, and religions were discredited with the rise of the Communist regime in Russia. Because it represented both the Czar and Christianity, St. Basil's was closed, and by 1930, there were at least two serious proposals to tear it down to make more room for political parades in Red Square, where it is located. Because of the efforts of a few individuals (at least one went to prison over this), the church was spared.

Today, St. Basil's is the symbol for old Russia and a popular tourist attraction; it is difficult to believe that anyone in the Russian government today would propose its demolition. It has become part of the nation's pride and national glory. Almost every nation has distinctive artwork that it has claimed as particularly representative of itself, like the Statue of Liberty, Mount Rushmore, and the Capitol Building (see Fig. 4.1) for the United States.

In addition, nations keep art because it is good for the economy and for business. The presence of a major archeological, religious, or architectural site like St. Basil's stimulates the entire economy, attracts tourists, and generates thousands of local jobs. Cities with major museums attract millions in tourist monies. Major traveling exhibitions, like a show of Vincent van Gogh paintings, can be enormously beneficial economically to a city.

Nations also seize art treasures as a sign of domination over another people. This has happened historically and continues into the modern era. The last Aztec ruler, Moctezuma, gave his magnificent *Headdress* (Fig. 5.17) to the invading Spanish as a desperate measure to avoid his own demise. The Spanish conqueror Hernando Cortés accepted as tribute or took as plunder hundreds of Aztec works of art and sent them to the Spanish king, Charles V. The German artist Albrecht Dürer saw these objects in Brussels:

> A sun entirely of gold, a whole fathom broad; likewise, a moon, entirely of silver, just as big; likewise sundry curiosities from their weapons, armor, and missiles; . . . I saw among them amazing artistic objects, and I marveled over the subtle ingenuity of the men in these distant lands. (Miller 1986:202)

However, unlike Dürer, most Spaniards valued the gold used in Aztec art more than they valued the artworks. Among the objects Dürer saw, every one made of gold or silver was melted down for its precious metal.

Sometimes nations take foreign art to augment their own cultural treasures. Egypt in particular has suffered from having its art treasures hauled off by foreign invaders, including Ancient Romans, Napoleon's French troops, and British invaders. The British also removed considerable amounts of art from Greece in the early nineteenth century, such as the *Herakles or Dionysus* (Fig. 5.18) from the Parthenon in Athens, as well as many other sculptures that are currently housed in the British Museum.

5.17 *Feathered Headdress of Moctezuma*, Aztec, c. 1519. Quetzal and cotinga feathers, gold plaques, 45^1/$_2$" × 69". Kunsthistorisches Museum, Vienna, Austria.

Conquering armies often plunder and take the art of subjugated peoples.

5.18 *Herakles or Dionysus*, Athens, Greece, c. 447–432 BCE, from the east pediment of the Parthenon, Acropolis. Marble, approx. 3′ 6″. British Museum, London. (See also the text accompanying Figures 8.32 and 8.33.)

Art from ancient Greece was removed to Great Britain in the early 19th century. The Greek government has repeatedly demanded its return.

In World War II, the Nazis stole millions of works of art, and many are still missing or are in dispute. In addition, after World War II, Russia seized art from 325 German museums; many of those artworks had been taken by the Nazis from Jewish collectors in the 1930s. Attempts to have the stolen art returned have caused international uproars. Even more recently, U.S. and British troops invaded Iraq in 2003, and before security was established, the treasures of some Iraqi museums were stolen or hidden.

Museums and Private Collections

Museums and private collections are the repositories of much of the art in this book. Private collections are older than museums. Since ancient times, rulers, nobles, and priests have collected art and kept it in palaces or temples for aesthetic pleasure, personal or ritual use, or the display of power. In ancient Rome, art was displayed in baths, such as the *Baths of Caracalla* (see Fig. 15.7).

The word *museum* was used in fifteenth-century Europe to refer not to buildings but to collections consisting of paintings, sculptures, coins, curios, and natural objects such as ostrich eggs. The *Studiolo of Francesco I de' Medici* (Fig. 5.19), originally built between 1570 and 1572, is a chamber in Florence's Palazzo Vecchio, where Francesco I de' Medici, the Grand Duke of Tuscany, stored and

5.19 GIORGIO VASARI. *Studiolo of Francesco I de' Medici*. Studiolo, Palazzo Vecchio, Florence.

Private collections of curios and art objects were often housed in special rooms in palaces, which were precursors to museums.

experimented with his collection of rare and odd items. They were housed in twenty cabinets once located below the wall paintings, which were related thematically to the objects in the cabinets. These eclectic collections are like the many artworks, crafts, or exotic items that ordinary people display in their homes today. In the eighteenth century, industrialists, adventurers, and entrepreneurs joined the ranks of the nobility as private art collectors, accumulating works in vast numbers, encouraged by capitalism, which emphasizes ownership.

Museums as buildings became common in Europe in the nineteenth century. The development of museums as separate structures and institutions was fueled by the Enlightenment of the eighteenth century, which emphasized knowledge, reason, and cultural achievement, and by the Romantic movement of the early nineteenth century, with its fascination for the unknown, the sensual, and the exotic. Colonialism was another factor supporting the establishment of museums. It provided great wealth to Europeans, which made private art collections possible, many of which were eventually folded into the collections of European museums.

Museums often reflect the cultural milieu of their founding. *The British Museum* (Fig. 5.20) is a national museum, which is a large nationally funded institution with collections in many areas, like the Louvre Museum in Paris or the Smithsonian Institution in Washington D.C. Founded in 1753, the British Museum's first collections focused on ancient Greece and Rome and Renaissance Italy, cultures that Europeans then believed to have produced the highest achievements in art. The museum's Greco-Roman façade reflects that belief. More private collections were added, such as the Elgin Marbles, which are original sculptures from the Parthenon, including *Herakles or Dionysus* (Fig. 5.18). Later, the British Museum acquired large private collections of non-Western art, notably Chinese porcelain and sculptures from India accumulated through colonization. Some countries have demanded the return of their lost art heritage, like Greece, which wants the Parthenon sculptures returned. The British Museum has refused, claiming that it legally owns the works and that it saved them from damage and destruction.

Compare the British Museum to the *Guggenheim Bilbao* (Fig. 5.21) in Northern Spain, designed by Frank O. Gehry and completed in 1997. This is a contemporary art museum, and the design of its façade reflects the contemporary concept of art, just as the façade of the British Museum reflects the concept of art of its era. Resembling a contemporary sculpture, the building emphasizes abstract flowing form and monumental scale. All contemporary

5.20 Sir Robert Sidney Smirke. *The British Museum*, London, 1823–1847. Portico, south façade.

The façade of this museum reflects the attitudes of the era in which it was built. At that time, the British culture generally considered Greek art to be the highest artistic achievement of all time, and thus modeled their museum after the Greek temple design.

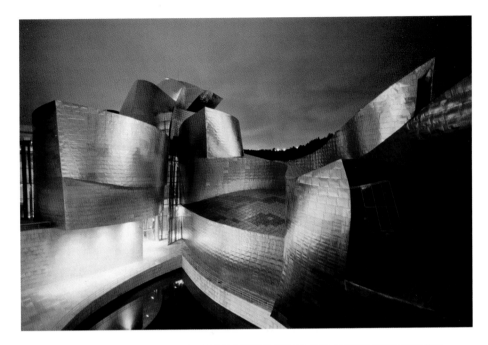

5.21 FRANK O. GEHRY. *Guggenheim Bilbao*. Bilbao, Spain 1997.

The façade of this museum also reflects attitudes about art from the era in which it was built. The sweeping forms and refined surfaces resemble modern abstract sculpture.

5.22 LEONARDO DA VINCI. *Mona Lisa*, Italy, c. 1503–1506; currently displayed behind bulletproof glass. Oil on wood, $30^1/_4'' \times 21''$. Louvre, Paris.

The mission of a museum is to preserve art, and at times the security measures make the art difficult to see.

art museums face a basic challenge: as time passes, their collection grows old and requires more of the museum's space, budget, time, and resources. This severely curtails the museum's ability to acquire new works, which can end its role as a contemporary museum.

Preservation and Restoration

Because art is valuable, enormous human effort and financial resources are devoted to preserving art from the ravages of time, the environment, industrial by-products, and even other human beings. Restoring works that are already damaged presents entirely different sets of problems, which we will examine.

Preservation

Small art objects are the easiest to preserve, because they can be kept where humidity, temperature, and light are controlled and where no one can touch them. Often, this causes art objects to become enshrined at a distance from the observer. It becomes difficult to remember that most artworks were made to be handled and used, and that few were ever designed specifically to be displayed in a museum.

For very famous works of art, the protective measures may become obstacles to seeing the work at all. For example, the curators of the Louvre Museum have surrounded Leonardo da Vinci's *Mona Lisa* (c. 1503–1506) with walls and bulletproof glass (Fig. 5.22). The lighting on the painting is very subdued to better preserve it. Large crowds make it even more difficult to see. Protective measures are necessary to deter vandals and political protesters who have tried to destroy many high-profile works for the symbolic significance of the act, using knives, hammers, rock, and axes. Recently, a woman tried to damage the *Mona Lisa* with a teacup because she had not been granted French citizenship.

If art does not fit into a climate-controlled building, preservation must counter (1) normal weather, which causes rust, fading, erosion, and cracks; (2) environmental pollution, such as smog and noise and vibrations; (3) wear and tear from tourists' feet, fingers, and breath; (4) damage by souvenir hunters, plunderers, adventurers, and vandals; and (5) damage from war.

Ancient paintings sealed in tombs or caves can deteriorate when they are exposed to air or humidity. Twenty-five years after their discovery, the caves at Lascaux, France (see Fig. 6.4), were closed to visitors because mold was destroying the images. In Spain, the *Hall of the Bison* (Fig. 5.23) likewise was closed to the public, and a replica of the cave was constructed nearby and opened in 2001. In 1994, more magnificent cave paintings were discovered at Chauvet, France. Only researchers are allowed inside, and even then for only four weeks per year for a few hours at a time, and they are provided with very little oxygen.

Exposure to regular weather erodes art, as can be seen on *Herakles or Dionysus* (Fig. 5.18), which was left in the open for centuries. Vibration from traffic is causing ancient ruins to crumble in Rome. Rain plus smog creates acidity that eats away stone. The threat is worldwide. In Mexico, air pollution is eating away at ancient Mayan temples in the Yucatán peninsula. In Athens, a thin layer of marble on ancient Greek temples is washed away with every downpour of acid rain. Many ancient Greek sculptures have been moved to climate-controlled buildings and have been replaced on-site with cast concrete copies.

New media—film, video, and computer art—present preservation problems. Older films were printed on material that gets gummy and brown and can spontaneously

5.23 *Hall of the Bison.* Paleolithic cave painting, Altamira Caves, Spain, 15,000–8,000 BCE.

Ancient paintings in caves can quickly deteriorate when the caves are rediscovered and reopened in modern times. Therefore, most cave paintings are not accessible to the general public.

5.24 *Army of the First Emperor of Qin* in pits next to his burial mound, Lintong, China, Qin Dynasty, c. 210 BCE. Painted terra-cotta, average figure 5′ 10″ high.

Restoring ancient damaged art requires research and careful handling, as well as some guesswork.

combust. Of all the U.S. films made before 1951, only half survive in any form. Old films can be copied onto newer materials, but that process takes an enormous amount of time and money, and many films have to be restored, as discussed on page 120. Videotape is also very fragile and can be easily damaged. A lot of old television and video art has been lost. Plus the equipment that played it is now obsolete. Kutlug Ataman's *Küba* (Fig. 5.15) requires hardware that will be outdated and replaced by newer technologies in a few years. How long will a museum have to maintain the technology to run the forty-channel video installation that was assembled in 2004? Computer art is equally vulnerable. Many computer prints fade. DVDs are current storage now, but they will be obsolete soon as well.

Restoration

The goal of art restoration is to return damaged or deteriorating art to its original condition, as much as possible. For older works that have been buried or weathered for centuries, restoration can be a massive effort. The enormous terra-cotta army surrounding the tomb of the first emperor of China, Shi Huangdi (Fig. 5.24), from 210 BCE, was rediscovered in 1974. Each soldier was once brightly

5.25 *Gone with the Wind,* 1939. MGM film starring Clark Gable as Rhett Butler and Vivien Leigh as Scarlett O'Hara. Copyright Metro Goldwyn Mayer.

Old films and videotapes are not on permanent archival materials, and often deterioration cannot be avoided.

painted with mineral colors, which have almost entirely worn away. Their weapons, iron farm tools, and objects of silk, bone, linen, leather, wood, and jade were badly disintegrated. It will take decades to excavate and restore Shi Huangdi's twenty-square-mile funeral complex. But how should artworks be restored when no one knows their original appearance?

Even modern artworks present difficulties in restoration. For older movies, various copies have to be located and spliced together to replace deteriorated parts. *Gone with the Wind* (Fig. 5.25), made in 1939, had its color and soundtrack enhanced during the 1998 restoration. Who is to say whether the enhancement really represents the original film version or merely reflects modern tastes for richer colors and fuller sound?

Questionable restoration practices continue to be used. Centuries-old temples in Southeast Asia, overgrown with tropical vegetation, have been scrubbed with modern detergents and sprayed with modern herbicides in efforts to clean off mold and fungus and to retard new plant growth. The enormous sculptures at Angkor Thom

in Cambodia (Fig. 5.26), for example, have been subjected to this treatment. Yet no one knows if the stones and carvings may have suffered long-term damage from the application of strong chemicals. In addition, many temples in Southeast Asia have been damaged by the wars of the last seventy years. At Coba, an ancient Mayan site in Mexico, most of the pyramids and other monuments are still engulfed in tropical jungle growth. How will they be restored so that future researchers can actually study what was left and tourists will be provided with a satisfying experience?

Cleaning paintings is equally tricky. Michelangelo's *Sistine Ceiling* was cleaned recently, removing layers of old varnish and candle soot that gave the work a brown, somewhat darkened appearance. For years, scholars had written that Michelangelo avoided using bright colors and favored defining forms through shading, as can be seen in the prerestoration detail of *The Libyan Sibyl* (Fig. 5.27). After cleaning, vivid greens, blues, and oranges appeared, as well as a rainbow of pastels. Cracks were filled or minimized. Many experts argued that the restorers went too far and removed Michelangelo's final layer of muted paint, and what we see now is the overly bright, hard-edged underpainting. Other scholars respond that the cleaning was well executed and requires a rethinking of Michelangelo's use of color (Fig. 5.28).

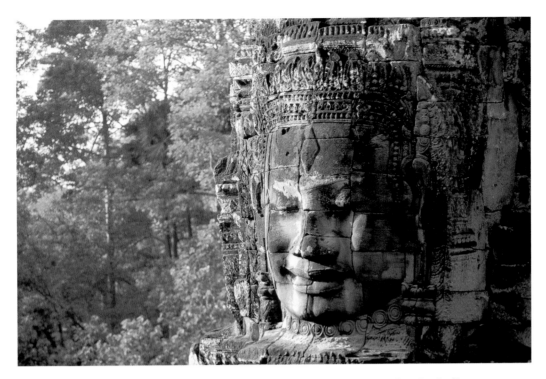

5.26 Buddha face carved in stone. Temple of Bayon, complex of Angkor Thom. Angkor, Cambodia.

Harsh chemicals have been used to clear forest growth off of ancient temples in tropical areas, but the potential for damage has not been sufficiently studied.

5.27 MICHELANGELO. *The Libyan Sibyl* (before restoration), Sistine Chapel, Vatican Palace, 1508–1512. Fresco. Detail of the *Sistine Ceiling.*

Years of grime and soot had darkened the paintings on the Sistine Ceiling.

5.28 MICHELANGELO. *The Libyan Sibyl* (after restoration completed in 1989), Sistine Chapel, Vatican Palace.

The most recent cleaning of the Sistine Ceiling revealed bright colors. Some experts said that the paintings were overcleaned.

WHEN ART IS NOT SAVED

Sometimes art is purposefully destroyed in conflicts when one culture or religion seeks to obliterate another. In other instances, art is destroyed as it serves its purpose in rituals. And some artists simply choose not to make enduring art objects.

Art Destroyed in Conflicts

In national, religious, or regional conflicts, art is often destroyed as a sign of dominance, as a result of negligence, or as part of ethnic cleansing.

Iconoclasm is the destruction of sacred images. The list of these occurrences is very long. For example, during the seventh and eighth centuries, many Christian icons in southern Europe and Asia Minor were destroyed because some Christian factions considered devotional religious images to be idolatry. Medieval Europeans destroyed many ancient Roman monuments. Much Aztec, Mayan, and Incan art and architecture were burned or demolished by the sixteenth-century Spanish conquerors, as discussed in reference to Moctezuma's *Headdress* (Fig. 5.17). Spanish missionaries ordered the destruction of all idols and books to eradicate the native religion, which represented a huge cultural loss. Hundreds of years ago, invading Moslems in Northern India destroyed the Hindu temples they found

there. During World War II, in an effort to wipe out Slavic cultures, German Nazis purposefully destroyed ancient Byzantine religious icons and many monuments during their occupation of western Russia. Iconoclasm continues today; for example, the former regime in Afghanistan, the Taliban, demolished the large fourth-century *Bamiyan Stone Buddha* in 2001, because the Koran forbids religious images (Figs. 5.29 and 5.30). Art continues to be lost in conflicts in Afghanistan and Iraq.

Sometimes older monuments are destroyed to make way for newer construction, such as the older *Temple of Quetzalcoatl and Tlaloc* (Fig. 5.31) at Teotihuacán, a pre-Aztec city in central Mexico. The temple was once covered with 366 painted sculptures representing the days of the year; now only a few remain at the bottom, because they were buried when the Teothuacanos used that part of the old temple for the foundation of the new temple constructed on top.

Art Used Dynamically in Rituals

Art can be lost or destroyed as part of rituals or dramatic performances. The Asmat men of New Guinea made *Bis or*

5.29, *left* *Bamiyan Stone Buddha*, Bamiya, Afghanistan, 4th or 5th century CE; demolished March 2001. 165′ high.

Artworks are often destroyed when they represent a culture or a set of religious beliefs that are in conflict with the current ruling government.

5.30, *below* Destruction of the large Buddha in March 2001. Bamiya, Afghanistan.

This ancient Buddha statue was destroyed by the Taliban government in Afghanistan because the Islamic fundamentalist government forbade religious images.

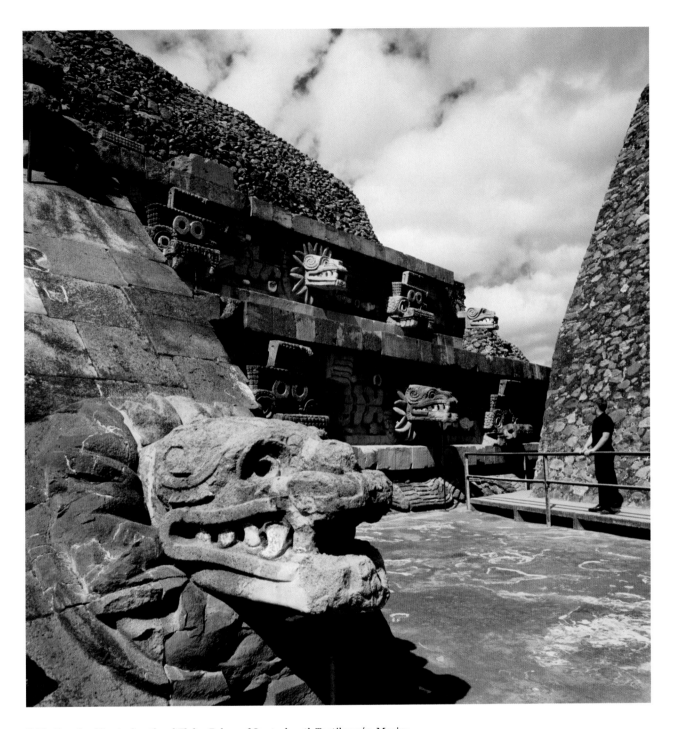

5.31 *Temple of Quetzalcoatl and Tlaloc*, Palace of Quetzalcoatl, Teotihuacán, Mexico.

This ancient temple was mostly destroyed centuries ago by the culture that built it, to serve as a foundation for a newer temple. Only the bottom parts were preserved, because they were buried under the new construction.

Bisj Poles, circa nineteenth to twentieth centuries, as part of rituals to promote male power, pass the spirits of the dead on to the living, and avenge the deaths of deceased clan members. Afterward, the poles were left to rot away among the sago palms, the Asmat's primary food source, to promote their fecundity. Thus, the deterioration of the art was an important part of rituals that redirected the human spirit after death. Nowadays, such poles are often

5.32 *Bis or Bisj Poles*, New Guinea, Irian Jaya; Asmat people, Omandesep, mid-20th century. The Michael C. Rockefeller Memorial Collection, Bequest of Nelson A. Rockefeller, 1979. Metropolitan Museum of Art, New York.

The Asmat people allow their artwork to be destroyed over time as part of their rituals. See Fig. 13.17 for a discussion of the rituals and meaning attached to the Bis or Bisj Poles.

5.33 ANDY GOLDSWORTHY. *Dandelion Line*, 2000. Storm King Sculpture Park, New York.

Some artists make work that is intended to be temporary, like this outdoor piece that lasted only a very short time.

preserved and may end up in museums across the world, as in Figure 5.32.

Navajo *Sand Paintings* are also destroyed to complete the ritual for which they are made. Navajo attitudes about beauty, art, and permanence are expressed in the following:

> A Navajo experiences beauty most poignantly in creating it and in expressing it, not in observing it or preserving it. The experience of beauty is dynamic; it flows to one and from one; it is not in things, but in relationships among things. Beauty is not to be preserved but to be continually renewed in oneself and expressed in one's daily life and activities. (Witherspoon 1977:178)

As is the case with the *Bisj Poles*, some museum curators, scholars, and tourists make efforts to preserve the art that the Navajos do not keep.

Nonobject Art

Some artists choose not to make permanent art objects. Andy Goldsworthy's *Dandelion Line* (Fig. 5.33) from 2000

was an outdoor installation with natural materials that rotted or blew away shortly after completion. Goldsworthy, however, does document his installations and sells those photographs through galleries. Another example comes from performance art, in which artists create an experience for people, rather than an object. Once the work is performed, it no longer exists in any material form, except for the photographs that document the event.

CONNECTION For examples of performance art, see Yoko Ono's *Cut Piece* (Fig. 12.37), Suzanne Lacy and Leslie Labowitz's *In Mourning and Rage* (Fig. 3.54), or James Luna's *The Artifact Piece* (Fig. 13.6).

II

WHY DO WE MAKE ART?

Art fulfills basic human pleasures and needs. It is functional and aesthetic. In the next ten chapters, we group the discussion of why humans make art into four sections:

SECTION 1   SURVIVAL AND BEYOND

Food depicted in art as glorious, sacred, or problematic

Domestic and commercial architecture based on climate, materials, and social preferences

Sexuality and the need for offspring

SECTION 2   RELIGION

The supernatural, as expressed in art

Memorials and tombs

SECTION 3   THE STATE

The power of the state made visible through portraiture, palaces, and fortifications

Glorifying war, documenting war, and memorializing peace

Art, protest, justice, and social criticism

SECTION 4   SELF AND SOCIETY

Our bodies and minds and the role of culture in shaping our perceptions of them

Social categories of race, gender, class, and clan

Art and our relationship to the natural world

The relationship among art, entertainment, and visual culture

Section 1 SURVIVAL AND BEYOND

Food, shelter, and reproduction are basic to human survival, regardless of how civilized or sophisticated we might be in the modern world. What role does art play in these? The major topics in the next two chapters are:

CHAPTER 6 FOOD AND SHELTER

Securing or glorifying food, and food's relationship to art, ritual, and sympathetic magic

Depicting food and eating in artwork

Investigating shelter for individual, group, and commercial use

CHAPTER 7 REPRODUCTION AND SEXUALITY

Representing fertility, primordial couples, lovemaking, and children in art

Exploring sexuality as seen through art

6.1 Excavations of ancient houses at Çatal Hüyük, Anatolia, Turkey, 7,500 BCE to 5,700 BCE.

6

FOOD AND SHELTER

Food and shelter are basic—without them, we die. In some cultures, art is used with rituals to help ensure these necessities. In others, the relationship among art, food, and shelter goes beyond survival: art is used to serve, store, and enjoy food, while structures are built not only to provide shelter but also to enhance and enrich lives through their aesthetic designs.

PREVIEW

This chapter begins with the History Focus, which covers Prehistory, when art aided in securing food and shelter. The earliest art we will see in Prehistory is linked to ritual and food. Later through time, we will see art that either glorifies or examines our relationship to food. Also discussed are several ancient and modern vessels that were used to store and serve food, which often had shapes and decorations that were meaningful to their users.

Further discussed is art about food that reveals broad social values and religious beliefs, that is, the significance of the way food is eaten at simple informal meals, or at feasts in religious ceremonies or major social events using elaborate art objects.

We will also see that shelter is essential for human life, but the design of shelter is not always limited to function, as many structures are works of art as well. Also studied is the wide range of styles in group living (for example, Çatal Hoyük, Fig. 6.1) or individual homes, which reflects broad social values, climate contrasts, and historical necessity. The chapter concludes with the evolution of commercial architecture from concrete to steel frame construction.

Connecting Art and History from
25,000–6,000 BCE

This chapter contains art dealing with food and shelter from ancient to contemporary times. Here, though, we focus just on prehistory, when food and shelter were immediate concerns and linked to art and ritual.

Human life began in Africa and then spread northward to Europe and Asia. Humans reached the Americas last, by crossing over the land bridge that likely existed long ago between Alaska and northeast Russia. Ancient sites of human habitation have been found all around the world. Our study begins in the **Paleolithic** era, or Old Stone Age, which began roughly 25,000 BCE.

Early people hunted wild animals and gathered berries, seeds, fruits, and plants for food. They lived in small, nomadic bands, moving on to find new food sources as needed. Three major accomplishments distinguished them. First, around 500,000 BCE, people began the controlled, regular use of fire for light, warmth, and cooking. Second, they began making stone tools at least 50,000 years ago, simple at first and then more advanced, and finally made tools from bone. They cleverly crafted axes, spearheads, fishing sinkers, beads, harpoons, and even needles for sewing. This was the

beginning of technology. And finally, art making began in the Old Stone Age and thus became an integral part of human existence.

The great majority of Paleolithic art is related to food and shelter. Accomplished paintings of wild animals were found in caves and rock shelters in southern Europe and Northern Africa (for example, the *Hall of Bulls*, Fig. 6.4). Small sculptures in bone or stone have been found much more broadly throughout Europe, Asia, and Africa (see Map 1). These small sculptures were made with primitive tools, but with remarkably lifelike results,

Map 1, *below* Prehistoric sites for carvings, rock paintings, or early settlements. This map shows sites in Asia Minor, northern Africa, and southern Europe. Still more sites exist around the world.

6.2 *Bison with Turned Head*, ca. 11,000 BCE. Reindeer antler, 4.2″ high. Photo by René-Gabriel Ojéda. Musée National de Préhistoire, Les Eyzies-de-Tayac-Sireuil, France.

This carving was part of a spear thrower. Its small size was necessary for nomadic people searching for food. Carvings like this were often found near the hearth, reinforcing the connection between art, ritual, food, shelter, and procreation.

whether they represented animals such as the *Bison with Turned Head* (Fig. 6.2) or were fertility figures like the *Venus of Willendorf* (see Fig. 7.3). Later on, people produced the first architecture when they built housing of mammoth bones covered with turf and skins.

Although the Paleolithic Era was long ago, some Stone Age cultures survived into the twentieth century.

An example is the Aboriginal people of Australia, hunters and gatherers whose mythology and paintings were intertwined, as in *Witchetty Grub Dreaming* (Fig. 6.5).

The **Mesolithic** Era, or Middle Stone Age, 10,000–7,000 BCE, saw the first experiments in raising crops and animals. Humans continued to live by hunting and gathering, but older

practices were intermingled with new during this time. The *African Rock Painting* (Fig. 6.3) shows people in hunting and herding scenes. There is no clear ending to the Old and Middle Stone Ages. The beginning of the **Neolithic** Period, or New Stone Age, is dated around 8,000 BCE, with expanded agricultural production and the beginnings of cities.

6.3 *African Rock Painting.* Cave painting of Tassili n'Ajjer, 2nd mill. BCE. Henri Lhote Collection. Musee de l'Homme, Paris, France.

Working women with children are herding cattle near their huts, which are represented by pale white ovals to the left.

World Art Map for Chapter 6

Jan Davidsz. de Heem.
A Table of Desserts.
Antwerp, Belgium.

NORTH AMERICA

Stan Wamiss. *Feast Dish.*

Tipi Cover.

Louis Sullivan. *Carson Pine Scott.*

Frank Lloyd Wright. *Falling Water.*

Judy Chicago. *Dinner Party.*

Pueblo Bonito.

Charles Moore. *Piazza d'Italia.*

Fuller. *US Pavillion.*
Safdie. *Habitat.*

Andy Warhol. *Heinz 57.*
Sue Coe. *There is No Escape.*
Edward Weston. *Artichoke.*
Wayne Thiebaud. *Pie Counter.*

Janine Antoni. *Gnaw.*
Duane Hanson. *Self Portrait with Model.*

EUROPE

Leonardo DaVinci. *The Last Supper.*
Hall of Bulls. Lascaux.
Bison with Turned Head. La Madeleine.

Andrea Palladio. *Villa Rotonda.*
Markets of Trajan. Rome.
House of Julius Polybius. Pompei.

Rock Painting.
Tassili n'Ajjer.

Tyi Wara Dancers.
Mali.

Basket (Pomo Tribe).
Northern California,
United States.

Dogon Cliff Dwellings.
Mali, Africa.

Afro-Portuguese Saltcellar

SOUTH AMERICA

**Silver representation
of a Maize plant (Incan).**
Chan-chan, Peru, South America.

N

0   1,000   2,000 Km.

0   1,000   2,000 Mi.

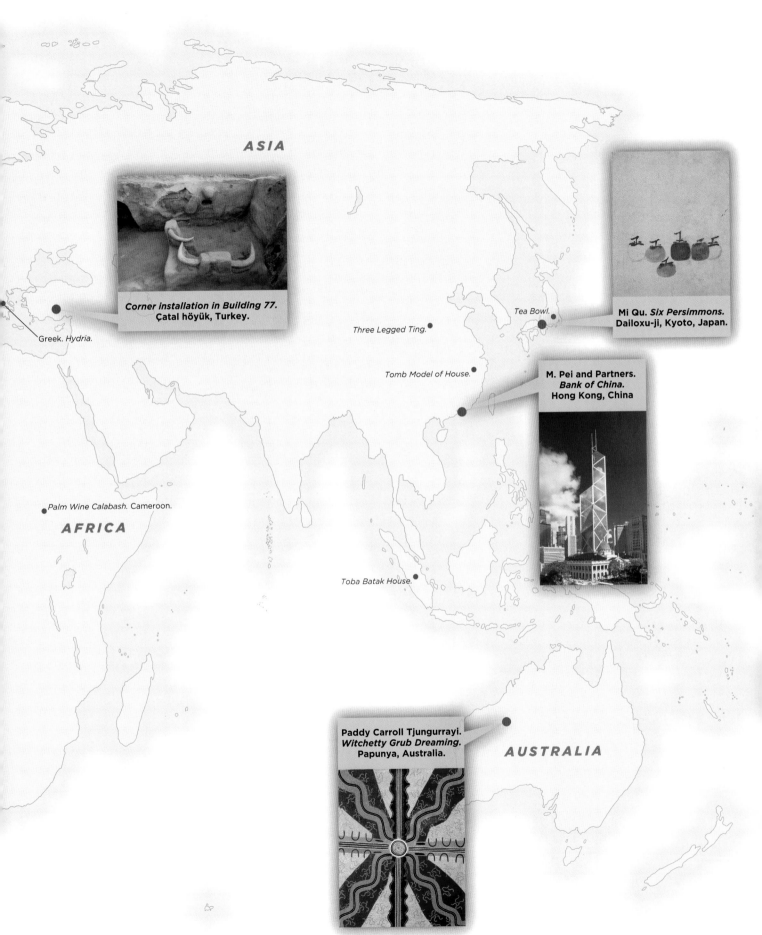

ASIA

Corner installation in Building 77. Çatal höyük, Turkey.

Greek. *Hydria.*

Three Legged Ting.

Tea Bowl.

Mi Qu. *Six Persimmons.* Dailoxu-ji, Kyoto, Japan.

Tomb Model of House.

M. Pei and Partners. *Bank of China.* Hong Kong, China

Palm Wine Calabash. Cameroon.

AFRICA

Toba Batak House.

Paddy Carroll Tjungurrayi. *Witchetty Grub Dreaming.* Papunya, Australia.

AUSTRALIA

25,000–6,000 BCE

BEFORE COMMON ERA (BCE)		
PALEOLTHIC ERA	**25,000 BCE**	

Above *Venus of Willendorf,* ca. 25,000–20,000 (7.3)

Cave Painting. *Hall of Bulls,* Lascaux, France, ca. 15,000–10,000

Bison with Turned Head, La Madeleine, France, ca. 12,000

MESOLITHIC ERA	**10,000**

Domestication of Sheep

NEOLITHIC ERA	**8,000**

Settlements in China and Chile

Birth of Agriculture in Mesopotamia and Mexico

Settlements in India	**7,000**
Domestication of Cattle	**6,000**

African Rock Painting, Tassili N'Ajjer, Algeria

Çatal Hüyük, Turkey, ca. 6,000–5,900

Unification of Egypt	**3,000**
Mesopotamia Civilizations	**2,000**
Irrigated Farming in the Andes	
SHANG DYNASTY, CHINA	**1,600**

Bronze Casting in China

ZHOU DYNASTY, CHINA (1046–221 BCE)

	500
ARCHAIC PERIOD, GREECE (600–480)	**600**
Greek Pottery	
HAN DYNASTY, CHINA (200 BCE– 200 CE)	
COMMON ERA (CE)	
Use of Arch and Concrete in Roman Architecture	**CE 1**
MOCHE CULTURE, PERU	**200**
MIDDLE AGES, EUROPE	**500**
EARLY BYZANTINE STYLE (527–726)	
Use of Cantilever in Chinese Architecture 800 (Fig. 2.38)	**800**
ANASAZI CULTURE, NEW MEXICO	**1000**
Spread of Chinese Culture to Japan	**1200**
AZTEC EMPIRE	**1300**
RENAISSANCE (1400–1600)	**1400**
INCA EMPIRE	
MING DYNASTY, CHINA	

Three-Legged Ting, Zhou Dynasty, China, 6th century BCE

Women at the Fountain House, 520–510 BCE

Above *Drum,* Vietnam (4.11)

House of Julius Polybius Pompeii, Italy, 62–79

Markets of Trajan, Rome, 100–112

Tomb Model of a House, Han Dynasty, China, 25–220

Pueblo Bonito, 1100

Dogon Cliff Dwellings with Granaries, Mali, 1200 to present

Mu-Qi. *Six Persimmons,* 1300 CE

Silver Representation of a Maize Plant, Peru, Inca, 1430–1532

Leonardo da Vinci. *Last Supper,* 1495–98

Palladio. *Villa Rotunda,*

MUGHAL DYNASTY, INDIA	**1500**	Italy, 1552		

MUGHAL DYNASTY, INDIA — **1500**

Italy, 1552

Saltcellar, Afro-Portuguese, 16th century

Tea Bowl, Japan, 17th century

1600 — *BAROQUE ERA (LATE 17TH CENTURY–18TH CENTURY)*

JAN DAVIDSZ. DE HEEM. *A Table of Desserts*, 1640

COLONIAL ERA — **1700**

INDUSTRIAL REVOLUTION — **1800**

Rise In Urban Population

Steel-Framed Structures

Tipi Cover, Sioux, USA, c. 1880

POMO. *Basket*, Native American, 1890–1910

Tyi Wara (or Chi Wara) Dance Headdresses, Late 19th century, Mali.

Palm Wine Calabash

Toba Batak House, 19–20th centuries

1900

SULLIVAN. *Carson Pirie Scott* building, Chicago, IL, 1904

World War I, 1914

World War II, 1939

WESTON. *Artichoke, Halved*, 1930

Above OPPENHEIM: *Object* (1.21)

Pop Art (1960) — **1960**

Food In Outer Space

WRIGHT. *Fallingwater*, Pennsylvania, 1936–1938

Above MARTINEZ. *Bowl*. 20th c. (3.42)

MODERNISM AND POSTMODERNISM (1975–PRESENT)

Above *Hunter and Kangaroo*, 20th c. (14.26)

THIEBAULD. *Pie Counter*, 1963

WARHOL. *Heinz 57 Tomato Ketchup*, USA, 1964

SAFDIE. *Habitat*, Canada, 1967

FULLER. *U.S. Pavilion*, Canada, 1967

1970 — JUDY CHICAGO. *The Dinner Party*, USA, 1974–1979

HANSON. *Self-Portrait with Model*, USA, 1979

MOORE. *Piazza d'Italia*, New Orleans, 1975–1980

1980 — TJUNGURRAYI. *Witchetty Grub Dreaming*, Australia, 1980

COE. *There Is No Escape*, Britain, 1987

PEI. *Bank of China*, Hong Kong, 1989

1990 — ANTONI. *Gnaw*, USA, 1992

World Population = 6 Billion — **2000** — WAMISS. *Halibut Feast Dish*, 2005

FOOD

Securing the Food Supply

In Prehistoric cultures, hunters, gatherers, and early farmers linked art and ritual to accomplish tasks like bringing rain for crops. This is "sympathetic magic," and the artist/shaman could attain great status in society, and in some cultures still does. Our focus figure is an example of this. Food, art, and ritual are likely linked in prehistoric cave drawings, like those in the *Hall of Bulls* at Lascaux in southern France, dated c. 15,000–10,000 BCE (Fig. 6.4), with huge woolly mammoths, horses, rhinos, aurochs (wild cattle), and reindeer. The paintings' exact purpose is unknown, but some anthropologists propose that rituals could be performed on the animals' likenesses to ensure a successful hunt. Spears and arrows were painted in or perhaps actually thrown at the image of the prey, ritualistically killing it. However, other scholars argue that the painted "arrows" are few and could be plant forms. They propose that these drawings were homage to earth and animal spirits. Either way, the current consensus is that these images had a ritual purpose linked to bounty in nature and the human food supply in the Paleolithic era.

The paintings, done from memory, were quite naturalistic, focusing on the animals' energy and movements and using the side view for easy recognition. Color came from naturally occurring materials, such as tar and charcoal for black, colored earth for yellow and brown, and rust for red. Dry pigment could be applied as powder or brushed on with animal fat. Given the crude materials and the rough stone walls, the drawings are especially amazing. Later, Paleolithic hunters and gatherers became Neolithic farmers, as shown in the *African Rock Painting* (Fig. 6.3) from Tassili n'Ajjer.

Across the world in Australia up to the present day, we see a similar phenomenon that links food, art, and ritual. Until recently, the Aboriginal people were a Stone Age culture that existed in the twentieth century. The "Ancestor Dreaming" of the Aboriginal people of Australia is a system of beliefs that accounted for the cosmos, from creation to death, and includes food gathering. Knowledge was passed along through song, chants, dance, and painting. For paintings in the past, Aboriginal artists applied colored dirt on the ground and destroyed the work at the

6.4 *Hall of Bulls*, c. 15000–10000 BCE. Cave painting, left wall, Lascaux, Dordogne, France. French Government Tourist Office.

These paintings may have been part of ancient rituals linked to the bounty of nature.

6.5 PADDY CARROLL TJUNGURRAYI. *Witchetty Grub Dreaming*, 1980. Paint on canvas. Australia, Aboriginal, from Papunya.

The patterns and symbols in this painting are part of the Aboriginal belief system of the origin of life and the sustenance of everyday existence.

6.6 *Tyi Wara (or Chi Wara) Dancers with Headdresses.* Bamana (or Bambara) people, Mali. Headdresses are generally made of wood, brass takcs, string, cowries shells, and iron, and are between 32″ and 38″ high.

Tyi Wara dancers are wearing headdresses of the mythic antelopes that brought agriculture to their community.

ritual's end. Aboriginal artists have made their paintings with more permanent materials since the 1970s.

Witchetty Grub Dreaming, by Paddy Carroll Tjungurrayi, from 1980 (Fig. 6.5), is a kind of contour map with symbols, indicating the location of precious food and water in arid central Australia. The work is strongly patterned, with alternating lights and darks and curving and straight lines, all radiating from a circle in the center point showing the source of the ancestor grub. The small, squiggled lines represent other grubs, an important food source, beneath the ground. Symmetry suggests the balance of the cosmos and the ancestors, providing sustenance for humans.

Another comparison can be seen in the Bamana people of Mali, who use masks, dance, and ritual to help ensure successful crops. The *Tyi Wara (or Chi Wara) Dance Headdresses*, from the late nineteenth or early twentieth century (Fig. 6.6), consist of male and female antelope masks, with the female bearing a baby antelope on her back. While the ground is being prepared for planting, young male dancers with masks and costumes

perform the leaping movement of the antelope dance, a ritual that causes the return of the mythical antelope who first gave humans the knowledge of agriculture. Plant life (crops), animal life (antelope), and humankind (ancestors) are united in this ritual. Pattern and rhythm are important visual elements in the headdresses, with interwoven negative and positive shapes.

 CONNECTION Many cultures have appealed to a deity spirit for food. One example, from Mesoamerica, is Xilonen, *Goddess of Young Corn* (Fig. 8.6, page 196).

In most industrial societies today, few people hunt and process the meat they eat, or gather food, or farm. Instead of religion, technology and business ensure the food supply. To clearly illustrate the change, look at British artist

6.7 SUE COE. *There Is No Escape*, Britain, 1987. Watercolor and graphite on paper, 22″ × 30″.

The stark black-and-white work is a critique of food industries in contemporary industrial societies.

Sue Coe's *There Is No Escape*, from 1987 (Fig. 6.7), which is unmistakably a harsh indictment of the contemporary meat industry. It is part of a large series entitled "Porkopolis," in which Coe shows living animals being transformed into packaged cuts of meat. Inside a slaughterhouse, Coe emphasizes the carnage and sympathizes with the pigs' fear, while the workers seem sadistic or subhuman. This emotional image is overall very dark, with a few lurid, glaring lights, but Coe wants us to see it as fact and to tie it to the contemporary meat-heavy Western diet.

Storing and Serving Food

The following are examples of the many kinds of vessels created around the world to hold food. They date from the Neolithic era to the twentieth century. Each combines utility with aesthetics and meaning.

Water is essential, so various peoples have developed inventive systems for storing liquids, using clay, leather, wood, and straw. Our focus figure for this section is the ceramic hydria, *Women at the Fountain House* (Fig. 6.8), dated 520–510 BCE from the **Archaic** Greek era, when

figure styles on pottery were evolving from stiff, simplified forms into more fluidly realized bodies. The hydria has a well-designed silhouette, with its body gracefully curving outward to the handles, which accentuate the widest part of the pot. From that point, the "shoulders" move inward dramatically, while the vessel's "neck" echoes but opposes the curves of the body. This is an example of black figure painting, in which a thin coating of black-firing clay covers the red clay of the vessel itself. Details are scratched in with a needle. Graceful women effortlessly collect water from the fountainhead, reiterating the purpose for the vessel. The scene is framed with floral and geometric designs.

While the Greeks used clay for water storage containers, the ancient Chinese made bronze vessels for storing liquids, such as ritual wine. These vessels may have been placed beside a shrine of deceased ancestors to receive blessings for a successful crop or good health. Some are elaborately and densely patterned over their entire surface, with monster faces at key locations, such as the handles, perhaps to keep away evil. Balance and harmony are important, visually expressing ancient Chinese philosophy and values. In our example (Fig. 6.9), we see a Zhou

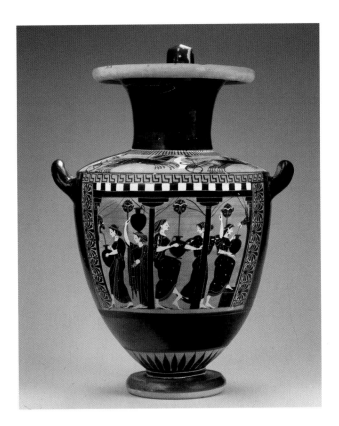

Three-Legged Ting with Cover, dated circa sixth century BCE. It has a simple shape with bands of patterns, supported by the three legs, or feet. Delicately incised abstract lines complement its overall form. Circles are repeated, even on the ting's cover, decorated with a **quatrefoil** pattern (like a four-leaf clover) and cleverly designed to be used as a serving bowl.

A well-woven container made of natural materials can hold liquid as well. Women of California and Pacific Northwest Coast tribes excelled at weaving baskets using willow and spruce twigs, pine needles, grapevines, and flax plants. The different colored materials in the basket wall resulted in geometric designs that were symbolic and often referred to nature, such as geese flying or sunlight breaking through stormy skies. These watertight baskets could be used for boiling acorns by placing hot rocks inside when

6.8 *Women at the Fountain House*, 520–510 BCE. Greek hydria. "AD" Painter. Ceramic, 20 3/4″ high. Museum of Fine Arts, Boston.

The images on this highly decorated vessel show women carrying water jugs very much like this very hydria.

6.9 *Three-Legged Ting with Cover*, Zhou Dynasty, China, c. 6th century BCE. Cast bronze, 5 3/4″ high.

The design of this bronze vessel, which was used in rituals to receive blessings from deceased ancestors, features circular details that complement the overall spherical form.

6.10, _above_ _Basket,_ 1890–1910. Clamshell disks, red woodpecker feathers, quail topknots, tree materials, 7″ diameter. Pomo tribe.

Intricate weaving, precious feathers, and beads mark this vessel, which was made by mothers and given to their daughters.

6.11, _right_ _Palm Wine Calabash,_ Bamileke people, Cameroon, Africa. Late 19th century. Beads on a cloth foundation, gourd, cowrie shells, 23 1/2″ h. Collection of The Newark Museum, Newark, New Jersey, U.S.A.

The shape of an ordinary gourd is evident beneath the beaded cloth, but the high quality of handwork and the decorative motifs mark this as an object for a ruler's use.

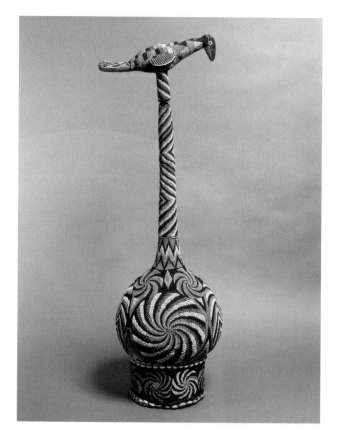

they are filled with water. The _Basket_ in Figure 6.10, dated 1890–1910, from the Pomo tribe, has been covered with feathers and shells over the basic woven design, adding layers of pattern. Mothers in California tribes made these special ceremonial gifts to mark significant moments in their daughters' lives, such as birth or puberty. Women treasured the baskets and were cremated with them at death. Though extremely delicate-looking, baskets such as this were used in everyday life and developed stains on the inside. The colored feathers represent the bravery and courage of the birds from which they came.

Another highly decorative vessel is the _Palm Wine Calabash_ (Fig. 6.11), from Cameroon. While gourds are basic containers for liquids in many traditional African cultures, this bead-covered gourd was for display, ritual and for royal use. It held palm wine, a common social drink in this area, but only the highest quality was stored here. Stoppers on such gourds were often an animal, for example, a leopard, an elephant, and, here, a bird.

Like water, salt is essential. At times, it has been a form of wealth. The European nobility used elaborate saltcellars as a status symbol, while medieval Europeans used salt to distinguish the status of guests: prestigious people sat "above the salt," while people of lower rank sat below. The ivory _Saltcellar_ from the sixteenth century (Fig.

6.12) was carved by African artists for export to Europe. The salt is held in the orb that is topped by an execution scene, showing a victim about to be sacrificed. Alligators serve as vertical supports below. The style reflects both African and Portuguese tastes, and both cultures valued the warmth and luster of ivory and used it for diplomatic gifts. The Portuguese likely drew the original design on paper, but African artists interpreted it, especially in the figure proportions, which echo African aesthetics with the large heads, simplified bodies, and short legs (see Chapter 13, The Body). The ivory has been worked very skillfully, with intricate patterning relieved by smooth areas, and with solid shapes punctuated by empty spaces.

> **CONNECTION** Can a dish design be an art form, or not? Read the discussion in Chapter 1, pages 12–16 on high art, popular culture, and craft.

So far in this section, the containers are one of a kind and expertly crafted. Andy Warhol's *Heinz 57 Tomato Ketchup* and *Del Monte Freestone Peach Halves*, dated 1964 (Fig. 6.13), are silk-screened wooden sculptures that look like mass-produced cardboard packing boxes for common grocery store items. In the United States, packaged foods

6.12, left *Saltcellar*, 16th century. Ivory, 17″ high. Afro-Portuguese, Sherbro Peninsula (Bulom), Sierra Leone.

This saltcellar was carved by African artists for export to Europe.

6.13, below ANDY WARHOL. *Heinz 57 Tomato Ketchup* and *Del Monte Freestone Peach Halves*, 1964. Silk screen on wood, 15″ × 12″ × 9 1/2″.

This work blurs the distinction between art and commercial packaging, and celebrates the simple colors, bold graphics, and clean layout of advertisements.

are often more familiar than food in its natural condition, and Warhol is celebrating this commercialism, indicating that most people enjoy it and are comfortable with it. To him, the design of a ketchup box is art and, therefore, as meritorious and meaningful as any other work of art. Its formal qualities are bright colors, large type, simple graphics, and an organized layout. Yet there is a sense of irony to the work, because whatever is merely comfortable eventually becomes hollow and meaningless. This work was created during the **Pop Art** movement, which was noted for glorifying popular culture items into art icons.

Art That Glorifies Food

In addition to sustaining us, food is beautiful. Food's shapes and textures are the subject of many sculptures and still life paintings, which also reflect cultural or religious values. Our examples date from the thirteenth century to the present.

Our focus figure is Jan Davidsz de Heem's *A Table of Desserts*, dated 1640 (Fig. 6.14), which reflects cultural and religious beliefs. In Europe, seventeenth-century still life paintings often were lavish displays boasting of wealth and abundance, in which food had become an aesthetic experience for refined taste. This was the **Baroque** era in art, known for exaggeration, artifice, and theatrics. Paintings of food take on almost a fetish quality, detailed and lovingly painted, like de Heem's sumptuous fruits and sweets on silver platters, laid on velvet. The food is not shown as a person standing or sitting at a table would see it, but is elevated to eye level, centralized and formally arranged, surrounded by heavy draperies and musical instruments. Oil paint makes deep, rich colors and textures possible. Yet, moral themes were part of *A Table of Desserts*. The tipping trays and half-eaten, soon-to-spoil food alludes to the idea of *vanitas*, that is, the impermanence of all earthly things and the inevitability of death.

In contrast to de Heem, look at U.S. artist Wayne Thiebaud's 1963 painting of desserts, *Pie Counter* (Fig. 6.15). It deals with food as a visual display and as a popular icon, rather than as nutrition for the body. *Pie Counter*

6.14 Jan Davidsz. de Heem. *A Table of Desserts,* Netherlands, 1640. Oil on canvas, 58 7/10″ × 79 9/10″. Louvre, Paris.

This glorious display of food has a subtheme about the impermanence of earthy life.

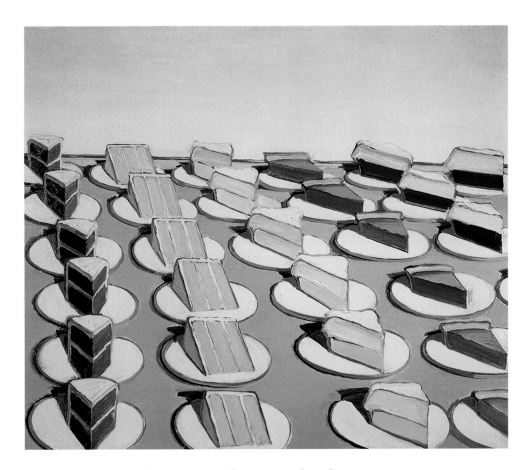

6.15 WAYNE THIEBAUD. *Pie Counter*, 1963. Oil on canvas, 30″ × 36″. © 2004 The Whitney Museum of American Art. © Wayne Thiebaud/Licensed by VAGA, New York, NY.

Reflecting modern cafeterias, this painting is a colorful display of standardized, mass-produced food.

shows the plentifulness, standardization, and bright colors in contemporary mass-produced cafeteria food, which is so appealing to many Americans. The thickly textured paint and bright colors are visually seductive and very different from de Heem's style. Thiebaud also alludes to the fact that for many, the abundance of fattening food has become something to resist rather than something to eat, while mass-media advertising pushes it. Interestingly, Thiebaud's painting and Warhol's *Heinz 57 Tomato Ketchup* (Fig. 6.13) are both from the same era of **Pop Art**.

In contrast to the sumptuousness of de Heem's and abundance of Thiebaud's paintings, Mu-Qi's *Six Persimmons*, dated circa 1269 (Fig. 6.16), reflects Zen Buddhism, which emphasized the importance of meditation and simplicity in life. This simple arrangement, with contrast between the plump fruits and the angular stems, and the spare richness of their color, is orderly yet irregular. Empty space is

6.16 MU-QI. *Six Persimmons*, Southern Song Dynasty, Dailoxu-ji, Kyoto, 13th century. Ink on paper, 14 1/4″ wide.

The simplicity of this still life reflects the philosophy of Zen Buddhism.

an important visual element. Many Zen masters chose to make ink paintings because of the form's spontaneity and simplicity, in contrast to the lushness of oil painting. But with ink, the strokes must be practiced for years to make them confidently, without erasing or correction.

Likewise, the *Silver Representation of a Maize Plant* (Fig. 6.17), 1430–1532, reflects the religious, political, and agricultural traditions of its culture, in this case, the Incan civilization of Peru. Maize was integral into Incan sacred and the mundane life. It was a food staple and was also used for making the most valued *chicha* (beer) that was consumed during religious festivals, such as the important eight-day celebration of the maize harvest. Incans were known to have made life-size replicas of plants and animals from gold and silver, arranging them into elaborate gardens. Both metals had symbolic significance: gold was believed to be the sun's sweat and silver the moon's tears. Food and feasting was also part of Incan political domination, as subservient peoples would provide food tribute to the Incan rulers and accept feasts from them as a sign of submission. This finely crafted piece is evidence of the key role that maize played in the Incan culture.

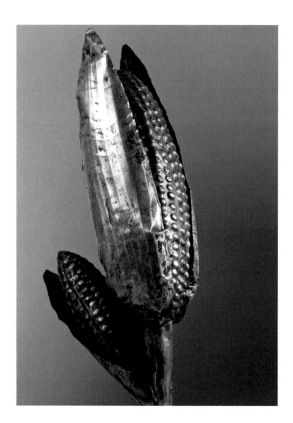

6.17 *Silver Representation of a Maize Plant*, Peru, Inca, 1430–1532. Ethnologisches Museum, Staatliche Museen, Berlin, Germany.

Maize was a food staple for the Incans and also was used to make beer, which was used in religious festivals. This silver replica glorifies the food so important to the Incans.

In Europe and the United States in the early twentieth century, photographs and paintings of food were often vehicles for abstraction and experimentation with media. In the early twentieth century, innovation in art and invention in industry were important, which is reflected in Edward Weston's *Artichoke, Halved*, 1930 (Fig. 6.18). Weston's photograph reveals the complex design and grace of natural forms, but it also shows off the technical achievement of photography, with the capacity to zoom in close and instantly capture minutely detailed images. There was little interest in food as sustenance or in its symbolic potential. An interesting comparison can be made with *Six Persimmons*, which reflects inner spiritual beauty, whereas *Artichoke, Halved* looks closely at structure and its inner physical beauty.

> **CONNECTION** Landscapes have also glorified food sources. See for example the lyrical depiction of *Apricot Blossoms* from China, Figure 14.17, and *Babur Supervising the Layout of the Garden of Fidelity* from Mughal India, Figure 14.18.

Art and the Act of Eating

We eat for nourishment, but how we eat is full of meaning. Some meals are very formal, like those involved in holiday celebrations or religious rituals. Some meals are very casual. In this section, we look at art that depicts formal or casual meals, as well as art objects associated with those meals.

Italian artist Leonardo da Vinci's *Last Supper*, 1495–1498 (Fig. 6.19), depicts the ritual meal as a religious ceremony. The composition is very formal and symmetrical, with the most important figure, Jesus, at the center, framed by the distant doorway. His hands, arms, and head form a triangle. Six followers are on each side, in groups of three. The perspective lines in the ceiling and wall radiate from Jesus' head. All are on one side of a long table like a head table; this seating arrangement implies that many witnesses, not shown, are also present at the meal, of which we as viewers are part. Leonardo's formula for depicting the *Last Supper* was so effective that this painting has become the standard.

> **CONNECTION** Review the discussion in Chapter 2 on linear perspective in relation to Leonardo's *Last Supper* (Fig. 2.20).

Another important ritual feast is the potlatch, from the Native Americans of the Northwest Coast. The potlatch was the formal mechanism for establishing social

6.18 EDWARD WESTON. *Artichoke, Halved*, 1930. Photograph. The Museum of Modern Art, New York.

The emphasis in this photograph is more on structure and form than on reflections of morality or philosophy.

6.19 LEONARDO DA VINCI. *Last Supper*, 1495–1498. Experimental paint on plaster, 14′ 5″ × 28′. Milan, Italy.

This image of a ritual meal is also a religious ceremony, and formally it deifies Jesus.

6.20 Stan Wamiss. *Halibut Feast Dish*, 2005. Yellow cedar or cypress, 25″ long × 13″ wide × 3 ¹/₂″ deep.

Certain animals would be symbols for a specific family. All details have been carved and then painted.

order among the people. The most powerful people gave the most lavish feasts and gifts, and the guests acknowledged that superior status by eating the food and by accepting the gifts. Some traditional serving dishes were as long as twenty feet and were prized possessions passed down through families. Stan Wamiss's *Halibut Feast Dish* (Fig. 6.20) is a contemporary serving dish for potlatches. Traditionally, carved animal forms were abstracted and rendered as geometric patterns, usually symmetrically around a vertical axis. Certain features, such as eyes, beaks, and claws, were emphasized, and black outlines establish the skeletal framework for the entire design. Contemporary pieces like this are brightly colored, because the artists used commercially available paints instead of natural dyes and pigments.

We can extend our comparisons to the Japanese tea ceremony, a formal, ritualized partaking of tea, influenced by Zen Buddhism, the philosophy behind *Six Persimmons* (Fig. 6.16). In Zen, personal meditation leading to enlightenment can include the most common of life's activities, including the making of tea. The host for a tea ceremony would carefully prepare the room, select vessels, and invite guests, guided by the idea that each gathering for a tea ceremony is a supremely intense and precious moment that can never be re-created. Tea bowls were unique, often imperfect in design, to convey the concepts of humility and of beauty embodied in humble things. The *Tea Bowl* (Fig. 6.21), from the seventeenth century, gracefully combines

a series of opposites: smooth glazes and textured glazes, round and square shapes, horizontals and diagonals and verticals.

Some artwork references a ritual meal, although no food is shown. *The Dinner Party*, 1974–1979 (Fig. 6.22), is the setting for an imaginary, formal meal to celebrate significant women in Western culture. For five years, many artists collaborated to produce the "women's-work" ceramics, china painting, and needlework, under the direction of U.S. artist Judy Chicago. Thirty-nine place settings each contain a painted porcelain plate and stitched runner with symbols and text that honor a woman in Western history. The triangle is a female symbol and the symbol of the ancient goddess thought to have brought forth all of life unaided. Each side of the triangle has thirteen settings, the number of men painted in renditions of the *Last Supper*. (Chicago thought the *Last Supper* was an interesting interpretation of the Passover Meal, which, in the Jewish tradition, cannot be held unless a woman is present.) The number 13 is also the number in a witches' coven. The "Heritage Floor," beneath the table, is covered with triangular tiles inscribed with the names of 999 significant women. The *Dinner Party* project also produced much scholarship on important women who had not been previously well known.

In contrast to the ritual meals just described, most meals are informal, everyday events. However, even the most casual meals reveal how people live and their social

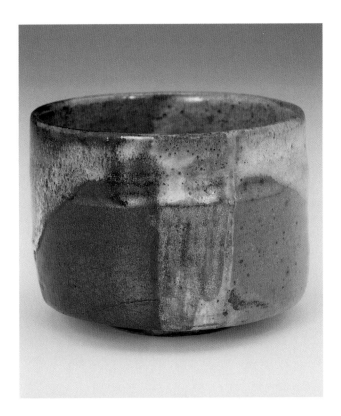

6.21, left *Tea Bowl*, Japan, 17th century. Ceramic, Satsuma ware, 4 2/5″ diameter at mouth.

Humble items often embody beauty, and their designs gracefully combine opposites.

6.22, below JUDY CHICAGO. *The Dinner Party*, 1974–1979. Painted porcelain and needlework, 48′ × 42′ × 36′.

The design of this dinner arrangement referenced Leonardo's *Last Supper* and reinterpreted it in feminist terms.

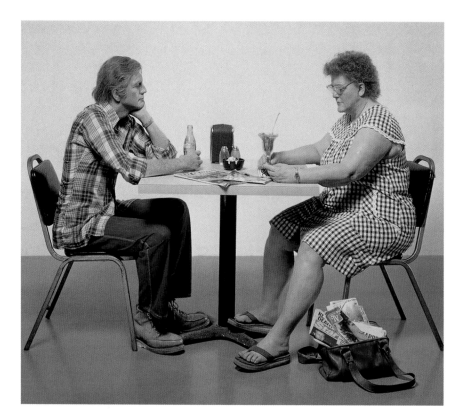

6.23 DUANE HANSON. *Self-Portrait with Model*, 1979. Painted polyester and mixed media, life-size. © Estate of Duane Hanson/Licensed by VAGA, New York, NY.

This realistically detailed sculpture often fools viewers into thinking they see actual people eating in a diner-like setting.

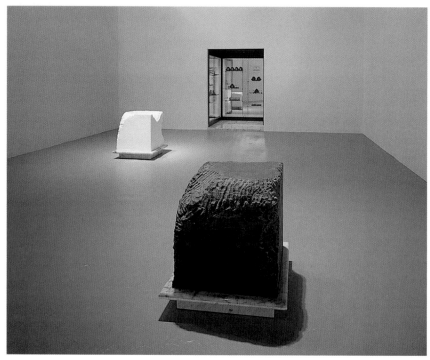

6.24 JANINE ANTONI. *Gnaw*, 1992. Three-part installation. Chocolate: 600 lbs. of chocolate gnawed by the artist; lard: 600 lbs. of lard gnawed by the artist; display: 130 lipsticks made with pigment, beeswax, and chewed lard removed from the lard cube; 27 heart-shaped packaging trays made from the chewed chocolate removed from the chocolate cube, dimensions variable.

This work is about the act of eating as a sculptural process.

habits. U.S. artist Duane Hanson's *Self-Portrait with Model*, 1979 (Fig. 6.23), presents the meal as a site for companionship. Yet there is more here. His life-size sculptures seem real at first. Hanson glorifies his subjects, but without idealizing them. The woman is very ordinary, and the artist is not an exalted genius but rather part of the sculpture, "breaking bread" with the model. The simple props—furniture, napkin holder, and salt and pepper shakers—suggest a greasy-spoon diner.

The last piece on the topic of eating is *Gnaw* (Fig. 6.24), dated 1992, by New York–based artist Janine Antoni, which began as a six-hundred-pound cube of chocolate and an equally large cube of lard. Throughout the run of the show, Antoni "sculpted" each block by biting and

6.25 MOSHE SAFDIE. *Habitat.* Designed for Expo '67 in Montreal, Canada.

This modern version of group living features stacked modular living units that open up onto gardens on the roofs of other units.

gnawing the edges. The chocolate was spat out and cast into the heart-shaped trays found inside candy boxes, turning the repulsive into sentimental prettiness. The lard she spat out was mixed with pigment and beeswax and cast into 130 lipsticks. The clean cubes of chocolate and lard became lumpy, gnawed masses, while the newly made trays and lipsticks were then shown in display cabinets, seen in the background of Figure 6.24. Replacing the traditional hammer and chisel with her mouth, Antoni transformed the act of eating into an artistic process. She was intimately relating to her creations: as babies put things into their mouths in order to know them, so, too, the artist consciously engaged in this experience. Using materials and objects that are socially defined as female fetishes, Antoni recast them in an art historical frame to raise questions about the position of women in art.

SHELTER

Domestic Architecture

Over the centuries, people have developed a wide range of houses, all serving the broad function of shelter, but done in amazingly different styles, due to the following factors:

- The need for protection from human foes, weather, animal predators, or insects
- Historical necessity, as some event required people to change their housing styles
- The availability of materials
- Aesthetic choice
- The desire to follow precedent, or to imitate a foreign style or a palace design
- Symbolic importance; the structure or decoration of houses may reflect important social values or religious beliefs
- Self-identity, as the house can be a reflection of its owner's beliefs or aspirations

Group Living

Group living is often essential for protection or for conservation of resources. Sometimes it is preferred for its greater access to social and commercial amenities. Our focus figure on group living is from the late twentieth century. As we compare it to past sites of group living, similar characteristics emerge.

In 1967, Israeli/Canadian architect Moshe Safdie created *Habitat* (Fig. 6.25) as an alternative to single-family urban sprawl housing, as well as the impersonal high-rise apartment. Safdie created low-cost housing that minimized land use and provided privacy and individualized living within a group setting. The prefabricated units are building blocks that can be stacked and arranged in many unique configurations, providing garden spaces on roofs. The structure was meant to be (1) energy efficient, due to compact design; (2) constructed of available natural resources; and (3) comfortable for many people living in a relatively small space.

Habitat is definitely a product of twentieth-century modernism, with the emphasis on simple geometric shapes, the lack of ornamentation, and the resemblance to abstract sculpture. However, aspects of *Habitat*'s design are taken from older examples of group living. Group living began as human beings tended to cluster together in communities for fortification against danger and to increase their chances of survival. The earliest examples of domestic architecture feature group living, which was begun as long ago as 25,000 BCE, with large circular or oval huts of animal hides covering a framework of light branches and accommodating several families.

6.26 Corner installation in Building 77, *Çatal höyük,* Anatolia, Turkey, 6,000–5,000 BCE.

An excavated interior room may have been a shrine, indicated by the installation of bull horns. Note the plastered walls.

6.27 *Pueblo Bonito,* Anasazi, New Mexico, 11th century.

This finely designed compound featured high-quality masonry work and originally had beamed ceilings.

The Neolithic town of *Çatal Hüyük* (Figures 6.1 and 6.26) in Anatolia was an early example of urban life. Its layout was likely an inspiration for Safdie's *Habitat.* The *Çatal Hüyük* era was notable for the beginning of agriculture, domesticated animals, flourishing crafts such as weaving, and copper and lead smelting. *Çatal Hüyük* consists of one-story, mud-brick and timber houses that were all connected and clustered around a few open courtyards placed near the center of the compound. The interior spaces had plastered and richly painted walls and floors. Intermingled among the houses were many shrines, roughly one for every three houses (Fig. 6.26). There were no streets and no ground-level doors (Fig. 6.1). Entrances were holes in the roofs, which also served as chimney vents. These houses were sturdier and more stable than

individual freestanding houses, and the solid exterior wall without openings was an effective defense against human or natural foes. The interior maze of spaces would also thwart invaders. Yet *Çatal Hüyük* was a peaceful town, as there is no evidence of weapons or fortification.

In creating *Habitat,* Safdie was also influenced by *Pueblo Bonito* at Chaco Canyon (Fig. 6.27), especially its energy efficiency, location near natural resources, and design for many residences. Around the eleventh century, it was constructed by the Anasazi people of New Mexico, North America, who were the ancestors of many native peoples of the Southwest United States. They were skilled farmers in a dry climate. *Pueblo Bonito* was a ceremonial fortress that may have been reserved for the Anasazi elite. It was built all in one piece over the rubble of previous

6.28 *Dogon Cliff Dwellings with Granaries*, Mali, Africa, 13th century.

These cliff dwellings have been in continuous use since the 13th century.

construction, with precisely aligned walls and doors. The structure has sweeping lines, contrasting with the rough vertical cliffs behind it. The walls cover four acres, with five-story structures and approximately 660 rooms surrounding dual plazas to accommodate perhaps 1,000 residents. Various clans occupied certain sections of the pueblo. The round, underground structures are kivas, centers for ceremony and contemplation.

Group living occurs also in the villages of the Dogon people in Mali, Africa, dating from 1200 and currently in active use. Clinging to steep cliffs that extend for 125 miles,

Dogon villages (Fig. 6.28) are dense collections of adobe houses, shrines, and granaries that are often irregular in shape and built on different levels to use all available space. Flat land is reserved for farming. Stone and mud walls make clusters for joint family households or compounds. The houses and granaries form an aesthetically pleasing pattern of vertical geometric shapes against the cliffs. Horizontal wooden beams project from the outer walls, providing footholds for maintenance as well as a distinctive pattern. Unused buildings deteriorate quickly and return to the earth.

6.29 *House of Julius Polybius,* Pompeii, Italy, First built in 2nd century BCE. Interior looking out into internal garden, reconstructed.

Airy courtyards, gardens, and artworks distinguished the villas of the wealthy in the ancient Roman Empire.

Individual Homes

The designs of individual homes embody climate concerns, aesthetic preferences, and cultural choices. Our focus figure is the *House of Julius Polybius,* in the excavated city of Pompeii (Fig. 6.29), a spacious and beautiful house for wealthy Romans in the first century CE. (In contrast, average Romans at this time lived in cramped, unheated, multistory apartment buildings with no sanitary facilities.) The villa's exteriors were rather plain, but inside, individual rooms opened onto courtyard spaces that brought fresh air and light into the center of the house. The front atrium in such houses often had a pool, called the impluvium, for collecting rainwater. Paintings and mosaics covered most interior walls and floors. Interior spaces flowed into the courtyard garden, usually furnished with marble tables and fountains. The Roman house was organized symmetrically around an axis that ran from the entrance to the back of the house, aligning a succession of lovely views and providing illumination throughout the dwelling.

CONNECTION An example of wall painting for a wealthy Roman residence is *Glass Bowl with Fruit* (Fig. 3.24).

It is interesting to compare the *House of Julius Polybius* with the *Villa Rotonda* (Fig. 6.30), a sixteenth-century Italian house influenced by Greek and Roman designs. This era was the **Renaissance**, known for the rebirth of learning in Europe from the fourteenth through sixteenth centuries and for the study of Greek and Roman culture. The designer, Andrea Palladio, was the chief architect of the Venetian Republic and wrote books promoting symmetry and stability as controlling elements of architectural design. Centuries later, his writings influenced Thomas Jefferson's design of his home, Monticello. Palladio's villa has a centralized plan, with thirty-two rooms and four identical porches, united by the central, dome-covered rotunda. The harmonious geometric shapes represent Renaissance philosophical principles of orderliness and hierarchy. Steep flights of stairs lead up to the structure, very much like a Roman temple on a platform.

In contrast, traditional Chinese house design reflects different cultural values and different responses to the environment than the houses we have just seen. Houses for the wealthy were modeled after the palaces of the first emperor of China, Shi Huangdi (ruled 221–206 BCE). No houses from the Han era have survived, but ceramic models of them were buried in tombs. A wealthy person's home typically had several stories, each slightly smaller than the one below it. Capping each level were wide eaves that were both functional and aesthetic, adding horizontal emphasis. Balconies encircled the house. Precious materials, such as gold and jade and bronze, were used for house ornamentation and accents. Inside, wall paintings would have illustrated Daoist fables and Confucian aphorisms with floral designs in brilliant colors. These features are evident on the relatively modest *Tomb Model of a House* (Fig. 6.31), dating between 25 and 220 CE. It may have served as a watchtower and probably had one or more courtyards, where chores were done. This timber frame house had non-load-bearing walls of compressed earth or mud that the wide eaves protected from rainfall. Elaborate brackets supported the roof.

6.30 Andrea Palladio. *Villa Rotonda*, Vicenza, Italy, 1552.

All parts of the *Villa Rotonda* are worked out in mathematical relationships to the whole.

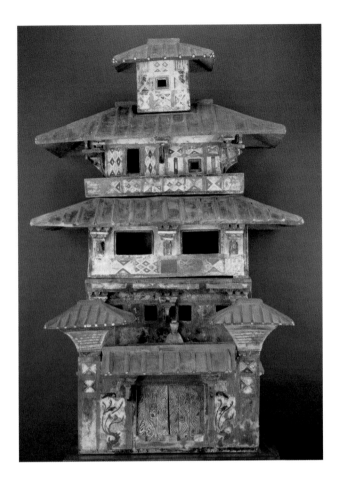

6.31 *Tomb Model of a House*, Eastern Han Dynasty, China, 25–220 CE. Ceramic, 52″ × 33″ × 27″. The Nelson–Atkins Museum of Art, Kansas City, Missouri.

The verticality and emphasis on roof design is apparent in this model of Han Dynasty house designs.

6.32 Decorated façade of *Toba Batak House*, Sumatra, Indonesia, c. 19th–20th centuries.

Traditional houses like this are still found in rural areas, but new housing in urban areas follows Western designs.

In Indonesia, distinctive wooden houses were designed in response to the tropical climate, with heavy rainfall, thick vegetation, heat, and insects. The *Toba Batak House* (Fig. 6.32) has a very steep roof that quickly sheds rain to keep it from soaking the thatch. Overhanging eaves shield the generous windows. When seen from the side, the roofline is highest at each end and curves downward at the center. The second and third levels have small sleeping and storage areas, so most people spent the day outdoors. Stilts raise the house to catch breezes, to protect the sleeping people from mosquitoes, and to provide security. Sometimes animals were kept on the ground level. Stilts are made of thick, hardwood tree trunks, necessary to support the heavy thatched roof, and soft wood was used for non-load-bearing walls. The entire house is pegged together instead of nailed, and the stilts sit on rocks, so that the structure flexes during earthquakes.

The parts of the *Toba Batak House* have symbolic meaning, with the internal spaces seen as maternal or womblike. The house is seen as a "transformer [that]

tames the terrifying vastness of the universe and at the same time inflates human concerns with cosmic grandeur" (Richter 1994:57). The house echoes the human body, with stilts as legs, the roof as the head, and the trapdoor entrance as the navel. From a cosmic perspective, the three levels are like the upper, lower, and middle worlds of the Indonesian universe; from a social perspective, the three levels of the house are likened to the social hierarchy separating slaves, commoners, and nobility (Dawson and Gillow 1994:14). This house, and others by this clan, is covered with painted patterns and guardian figures for fertility and protection.

Housing can also be shaped by historical necessity. For thousands of years, the Native Americans of Eastern and Central North America were stable populations who hunted and gathered food. With the coming of the Europeans, these peoples were displaced from their homelands and for a while lived on the Great Plains in movable houses, like the *Tipi*, circa 1880 (Fig. 6.33), originally a small tent used during hunting season. When later used as year-round housing, tipis were built as large as twenty-five feet high and were moved by horses. Animal skins, buffalo hide, or canvas covered the framework of slender poles. Adjustable flaps kept out wind or rain and ventilated smoke. Tipi covers and liners were often painted. Before the 1830s, the imagery consisted of stiff figures, whereas later ones often showed the tipi owner's personal adventures in nature or at war.

Our last house for comparison and contrast is *Fallingwater*, 1936–1938 (Fig. 6.34), arguably the most famous modern house in the United States. Frank Lloyd Wright designed it for the wealthy Kaufmann family from Pittsburgh as a weekend home in the woods to balance their urban lives. Wright believed that houses should be unified wholes that merge into their natural settings, using local materials. A large boulder is the base of the

house's central fireplace, while stones for walls came from nearby quarries. Geometric blocks, some vertical but most horizontal, sit low to the ground. There is no decoration, except the contrasting textures of stone and concrete. The house is arranged to allow maximum sunlight inside. Long, rectilinear windows frame views of the surrounding trees.

Fallingwater shows much influence from Japanese and Chinese architecture, especially in its cantilevered porches. Also, like much of the traditional domestic architecture of Asia, the walls in *Fallingwater* are not load bearing, but act as privacy screens. Also from Japan was the idea of a flowing interior space, with few walls and large windows.

CONNECTION Another Wright building is the *Solomon R. Guggenheim Museum* (Fig. 15.5).

Commercial Architecture

Commercial architecture provides shelter for the needs of business and trade. Here are a few examples considered to be important milestones in art. Our focus figure is again from the Roman Empire. The Markets of Trajan,

6.33 *Tipi cover*, North American Sioux, c. 1880. Decorated with images of tipis and equestrian warrior figures.

Tipis were portable housing that Native Americans of the Great Plains adopted once they were forced from their original homelands.

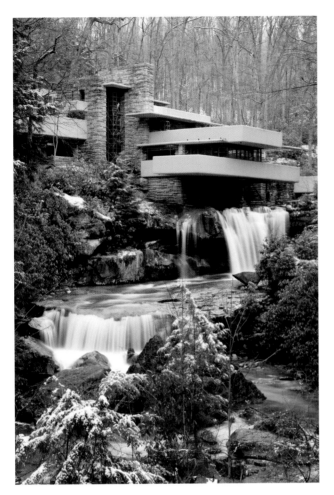

100–112 (Fig. 6.35), is a multistoried complex that held administrative offices and more than 150 shops. This large building on a very steep slope has a paved street cutting through at about mid-level. Its design was likely influenced by the enclosed markets of the Middle East called *souks* or *bazaars*, and it looks a lot like today's shopping malls. There were two levels of shops, called *taberna*, each with a wide doorway and attic storage accessible through a window on top. Although drab today, the interior was once quite decorative and enlivened with vendors, shoppers, and wares of all kinds. A terrible fire destroyed large sections of Rome in 64 CE, so newer construction like the *Markets* used concrete because it was cheap, flexible, and fireproof and could be covered with beautiful veneers of brick, marble, stucco, gilding, or mural paintings. Concrete construction made large, well-lit, multistoried projects feasible. Walls are load bearing, yet the arches channel the tremendous weight of the roof to massive piers, allowing large windows to pierce the walls. This was a tremendous accomplishment architecturally. The massive, muscular Roman style of architecture would have been impossible with only wood construction.

6.34 FRANK LLOYD WRIGHT. *Fallingwater*, 1936–1938. Kaufmann House, Connellsville vicinity, Pennsylvania.

Wright believed that houses should be unified wholes that merge into their natural settings.

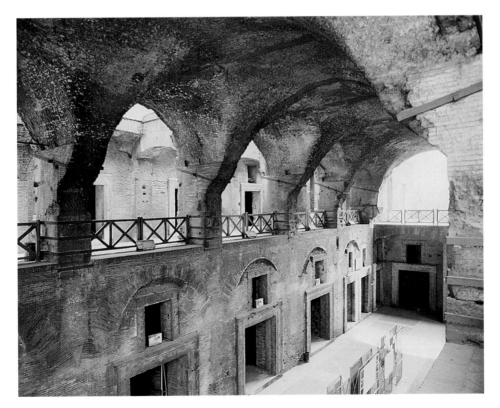

6.35 *Interior of Markets of Trajan*, Rome, 100–112 CE.

Concrete construction, arches, and vaults were exploited by the Romans to construct massive buildings.

CONNECTION Romans were known for their ambitious public buildings, such as the *Baths of Caracalla* (Fig. 15.7), the *Colosseum* at left (Fig. 15.11), and the *Pantheon* (Fig. 8.27).

In modern industrial nations today, stores and businesses are often located in high-rise buildings. The *Carson Pirie Scott* building, dated 1904 (Fig. 6.36), was one of the first innovative tall buildings in the twentieth century. The architect, Louis Sullivan, believed that "form follows function," meaning that buildings should not be shaped according to preconceived ideas, but should be an outgrowth of their function and of the materials used. He exploited the new design possibilities of steel frame construction, coupled with the invention of the elevator. Although iron and steel had been used in the past, those buildings were often sheathed in stone or brick or were novelties like the Eiffel Tower. Sullivan's buildings were supported by the steel framework with non-load-bearing walls stretched over it, much like the skin and muscles of the human body over the rigid skeleton. Height was emphasized more than horizontal elements.

On the ground floor, Sullivan introduced the large display windows that have become familiar fixtures in almost every retail store in the United States today. Sullivan saw these display windows as pictures, so he framed them with ornate cast ironwork with organic motifs referencing birth, flowering, decay, and rebirth. In contrast, the upper floors are plain with large horizontal windows that make evident the steel structure underneath. The curved corner provides vertical emphasis, with narrower, taller windows. The roof is de-emphasized, with no overhanging eaves or cornices. Rather, the building gives the impression that several more floors, similar in design, could be added right on top of the existing structure.

Late-Twentieth-Century Public Structures

Rome's architects were highly innovative in their designs and materials, and Louis Sullivan began the exploration of design possibilities in steel frame construction. A more recent innovator was R. Buckminster Fuller, an architectural engineer, inventor, designer, and mathematician with an interest in utopian design. He believed that well-guided technology would get maximum gain for minimum expenditure of energy, giving everyone more affordable shelter with more conveniences. His geodesic dome came to be a symbol for twentieth-century innovation and progress, while its emphasis on geometry and its use of the flexible

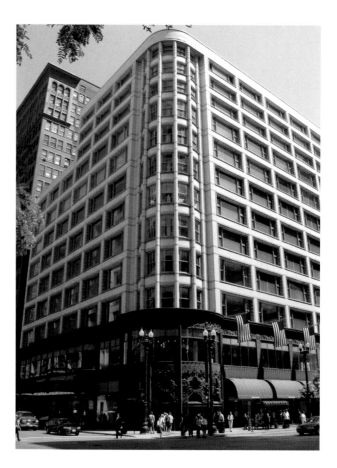

6.36 Louis H. Sullivan. *Carson Pirie Scott and Company*, 1904. Chicago, IL.

The upper floors of this office building reveal the steel skeleton that supports the entire structure.

metal framework made it continuous with the innovations of Sullivan's *Carson Pirie Scott* building. The domes are spherical networks of steel-frame tetrahedrons (a tetrahedron is a three-sided pyramid sitting on a triangular base). Depending on the number of modules used, the domes could be flat or tall and could be made to any size. (Fuller even proposed a three-mile-wide dome to enclose midtown Manhattan in a climate-controlled environment.) Domes enclose the largest internal volume within the least amount of wall surface, thus saving on materials. The framework of inexpensive, modular, linear elements could be assembled in a short time and could resist both internal and external pressures. The dome could be covered with a variety of materials, such as glass, plastic, cloth, wood, or paper.

Fuller's design for the *U.S. Pavilion* at Montreal's Expo '67 (Fig. 6.37) was built along with Safdie's *Habitat*. The nearly spherical dome, 250 feet in diameter, created a dramatic silhouette and glowed at night like an otherworldly orb. Because the dome is self-supporting, the interior can be configured in any way desired. Although

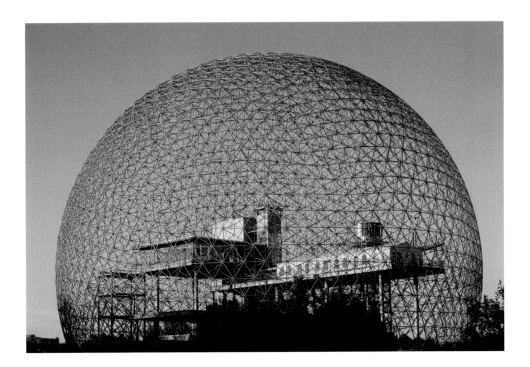

6.37, above R. BUCKMINSTER FULLER. *U.S. Pavilion*. Geodesic dome, diameter 250′. Expo '67, Montreal, Canada.

The geodesic dome is an architectural form that can be scaled to large size, can be distorted to be flat or tall, and can be covered with a variety of materials.

6.38, right I. M. PEI AND PARTNERS. *Bank of China*, 1989. Hong Kong.

Triangles form the basis of the visual design and physical structure of this building.

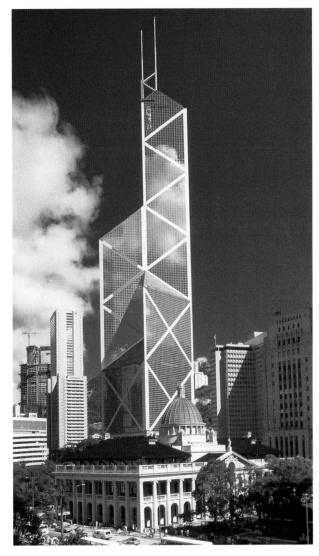

geodesic domes have been used as factories, greenhouses, mobile military living units, experimental biospheres, and research stations, they have yet to become popular for businesses or homes.

Generally, for mid-twentieth century office buildings, the rectangle dominated architectural design, which often emphasized spare, rectangular shafts of steel and glass devoid of ornamentation that rose from street-level plazas. This was called the **International Style** because of its global prevalence in large cities. One of the most influential architects of the International Style, Ludwig Mies van der Rohe, summarized this aesthetic with the phrase "less is more." The unadorned, simple, geometric style was seen as new, modern, heroic, and even utopian, as architects sought to transform urban centers with functional forms. See van der Rohe's *Seagram Building* (Fig. 2.42, page 52).

However, within a few decades, there arose a resistance to the International Style, which some saw as sterile and oppressive. The rectangle is dissolved into triangles and diagonals with the *Bank of China*, dated 1989 (Fig. 6.38), by the architectural firm of I. M. Pei and Partners. The base is subdivided into four equal triangular sections, and more triangles are created by the diagonal braces that stabilize the skeletal frame, a necessary addition because of earthquakes and high winds. Pei emphasized rather than hid the braces. The skeletal support for the building is innovative. At the corners are four massive columns. Beginning at the twenty-fifth floor, a fifth column at the center supports the load from the upper floors; that load is transmitted diagonally to the corner supports. The exterior of the *Bank of China* is gray anodized aluminum with reflective glass windows. The lower floors surround a twelve-story-high central atrium, while on top, dining and entertainment establishments boast spectacular views.

Other reactions against the International Style were more radical, like the *Piazza d'Italia* (Fig. 6.39) in New Orleans by Charles Moore with U.I.G. and Perez Associates. Moore believed that cities had lost much of their unique character because of new skyscrapers that all looked alike. He favored maintaining distinctness and the "presence of the past" in any location. The Postmodern architectural style of *Piazza d'Italia* emphasizes visual complexity, individuality, colorfulness, and even fun. **Postmodernism** is

6.39 CHARLES MOORE WITH U.I.G. AND PEREZ ASSOCIATES. *Piazza d'Italia*, 1975–1980. New Orleans, LA.

The many references to other styles of architecture make the *Piazza d'Italia* like an archeological site, where layer after layer of the past build up.

a late twentieth-century movement in which art forms were deconstructed to be analyzed and potentially reinterpreted and reconstructed. *Piazza d'Italia* is symbolically complicated as well, combining elements from the Roman Empire, the Italian Renaissance, and twentieth-century entertainment sites. To Postmodern architects, "less is a bore." A map of Sicily sits at the center of the plaza, connected to the larger map of Italy that joins the curved architectural fragments behind it. Like much of New Orleans, *Piazza d'Italia* suffered from the ravages of Hurricane Katrina in 2005.

Architecture continues to evolve past the Postmodern *Piazza d'Italia*. The past few years has seen the rise of **Deconstructivist** architecture, which rejects established conventions and seeks to shake the viewer's expectations. Deconstructivist buildings can be disorienting and irregular, and outside forms may give no clue to the space of their interiors. Many deconstructivist buildings resemble abstract sculptures more than traditional architecture.

CONNECTION Two examples of Deconstructivist architecture are Frank Gehry's *Guggenheim Bilbao* at left (Fig. 5.21, page 117) and his *Walt Disney Concert Hall* (Fig. 15.6, page 438).

7.1 HENRY MOORE. *Draped Reclining Mother and Baby*, 1983. Bronze, Length 104.5″. Fukuoka Art Museum, Fukuoka Prefecture, Japan.

Moore's work references both modern and ancient art that has sought to visually express the power of human reproduction.

7

REPRODUCTION AND SEXUALITY

In addition to food and shelter, human reproduction and sexuality are basic for the survival of the human race. In various cultures, art has aided and pictured human fertility, reproduction and sexuality, especially with charm-like figures, phallic symbols, fetishes, erotic images, and paintings and sculptures of marriage and children.

PREVIEW

This chapter begins with human reproduction by first examining early ritualistic fertility figures and murals and then comparing other more recent examples found in the Americas, Africa, and Oceania. It continues to look at sculptures, paintings, and images within their cultural contexts that have witnessed, documented, and commemorated the coupling and marrying of human beings, along with their lovemaking, birthing, and progeny. In addition, art reflecting sexual preferences and gender relationships will show various cultural attitudes, acceptances, and taboos.

We will see that this primal urge unites art throughout the ages, and even to the present day. The Chapter Opening image (Fig. 7.1) is Draped Reclining Mother and Baby *from 1983, an abstracted image that has captured the essence of that close relationship. The sculptor Henry Moore said "the Mother and Child . . . has been a universal theme from the beginning of time and some of the earliest sculptures we've found from the Neolithic Age are of a Mother and Child"* (Hedgecoe 1968: 61).

Connecting Art and History from
6000-2000 BCE

During the New Stone Age, which ended around 4000 BCE, groups of people around the world began to depend increasingly on agriculture for their food in addition to hunting. They began making stone tools and continued domesticating animals. All aspects of fertility were important concerns, from human reproduction to successful harvests.

In Chapter 6, we began the discussion of the city of Çatal Hüyük (8000–4000 BCE), located in present-day Turkey, an early farming and trading settlement with several thousand people. They were among the first to produce pottery and make metal and obsidian objects. They connected their houses for greater protection and built many shrines (see Fig. 6.1). The *Female Fertility Figure* (Fig. 7.2) shows a large, powerful, enthroned woman with attending lions. It is significant that this figure, with its highly accentuated breasts and belly, was found in a Çatal Hüyük grain bin.

Other cultures created female fertility figures as well, for example, in the Cycladic Islands off the mainland of Greece, where the *Idol from Amorgos* was found (Fig. 7.4), dated 2500–2300 BCE. She is also connected to fertility and was a probable descendant of the ancient mother goddesses of Greece.

Throughout this period until about 2000 BCE, we see the beginnings of civilizations around the world. The following factors influenced the growth of civilizations:

- Major rivers or bodies of water were necessary for the emergence of civilizations.
- Farming produced surplus food, which allowed for the development of cities and the division of labor within urban areas.

Map 2. The Development of Agriculture. Courtesy of Replogle Globes, Inc., Broadview, IL.

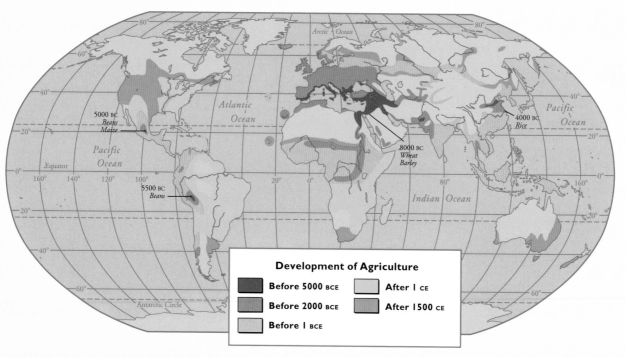

- Cities became political, economic, social, cultural, and religious centers.
- Trade became important among groups of people and between urban centers.
- Formal religions developed, often with many gods and with rulers as stewards of those gods.
- Political and social structures emerged, with hierarchical governments and sometimes bureaucracies. Society was organized around class systems, with priests, warriors, and the wealthy at the top.
- Writing developed in some areas.
- The military or warrior class emerged.
- Independent city-states were gradually merged into larger empires.
- Women were generally made subordinate to men.

In Mesopotamia, around 3000 BCE, several city-states arose along the Tigris and Euphrates rivers. They included Eridu, Ur, Uruk, Umma, and Lagash, and they were located in an area called Sumer. Surrounded by walls, these cities had political and economic control over the surrounding states. Here, people first scratched cuneiform symbols and other forms of writing into wet clay tablets. Here also is the first evidence of use of the wheel. Around 2300 BCE, the ruler Sargon united several of these city-states into the Akkadian Empire.

Many agricultural communities developed along the Nile River in Egypt. Travel along the Nile was swift and relatively easy, and the upper and lower areas of Egypt were united around 3100 BCE. A series of Egyptian dynasties ruled the area for hundreds of years, and the surrounding desert kept the land relatively free from foreign invasion. The Egyptians developed hieroglyphic writing. The Old Kingdom lasted from 2686 BCE to

7.2 *Female Fertility Figure,* found at Çatal Hüyük, Anatolia (modern Turkey), c. 6000 BCE. Terra-cotta, 7.9″ high.

This small, regal figure is enthroned and is attended by lions. She was found in a grain bin, suggesting her role in the success of her culture's fecundity.

2125 BCE, while the Middle Kingdom (2100–1700 BCE) saw increased contact with the outside world, especially in Africa and the Middle East.

South of Egypt, around 3500 BCE, the Nubian civilization emerged. At first, Nubia was a trading partner with Egypt, but later it came under Egyptian control.

Small centers of civilization emerged throughout the Americas. In 3000 BCE, skilled artisans around Lake Superior worked copper into jewelry and tools. Along the Supe River in Peru, the city of Caral flourished around 2600 BCE.

Around 6000 BCE, in the Indus River Valley (in present-day Pakistan), people began growing rice, bananas, sesame, wheat, barley, black pepper, and cotton. In 2500 BCE, the great city

of Mohenjo-Daro was established, with a population of 40,000. Many craft workers, sculptors, and potters lived in the city, which maintained a thriving trade in handcrafted and agricultural products.

In China along the Huang He (Yellow River) Valley, farmers used levees to control floods as early as 3000 BCE. Some researchers believe that as early as 2100 BCE, the Xia Dynasty brought centralized rule to a large region of China, although this has not been completely proven historically.

World Art Map for Chapter 7

Roger Van Der Weyden.
Virgin and Child in a Niche.
Flanders, Northern Europe.

Jan van Eyck. *Wedding Portrait.*

Henry Moore. *Draped Reclining Mother and Baby.*

NORTH AMERICA

Barbara Kruger. *Untitled (Your body is a battleground).*
Alice Neel. *Pregnant Woman.*

Jean Auguste Dominique Ingres. *Grande Odalisque.*
Edouard Manet. *Olympia.*
Louise Bourgeois. *Blind Man's Bluff.*

Venus of Willendorf.

Lynn Hershman. *Deep Contact.*

Mother and Nursing Child.

EUROPE

Georgia O'Keeffe. *Grey Line with Lavender and Yellow.*

Potawatomi Male Figure (Love Doll).
Crandon, Wisconsin.

Initiation Rites of Dionysos.
Oil Lamp with Love-Making Scene.

Catherine Opie. *Justin Bond.*

Aztec Marriage Couple.

Dogon Primordial Couple.

Kidder Figure.

Bamana Female Figure.
Mali, Africa.

Ashanti Akua'ba Doll.
Ghana, Africa.

Figure of a Deity: A'a Rurutu.
Austral Islands, Polynesia.

SOUTH AMERICA

Moche Pot Depicting a Woman Giving Birth Assisted by Midwives.
North Peruvian River Valley, South America.

N

0   1,000   2,000 Km.

0   1,000   2,000 Mi.

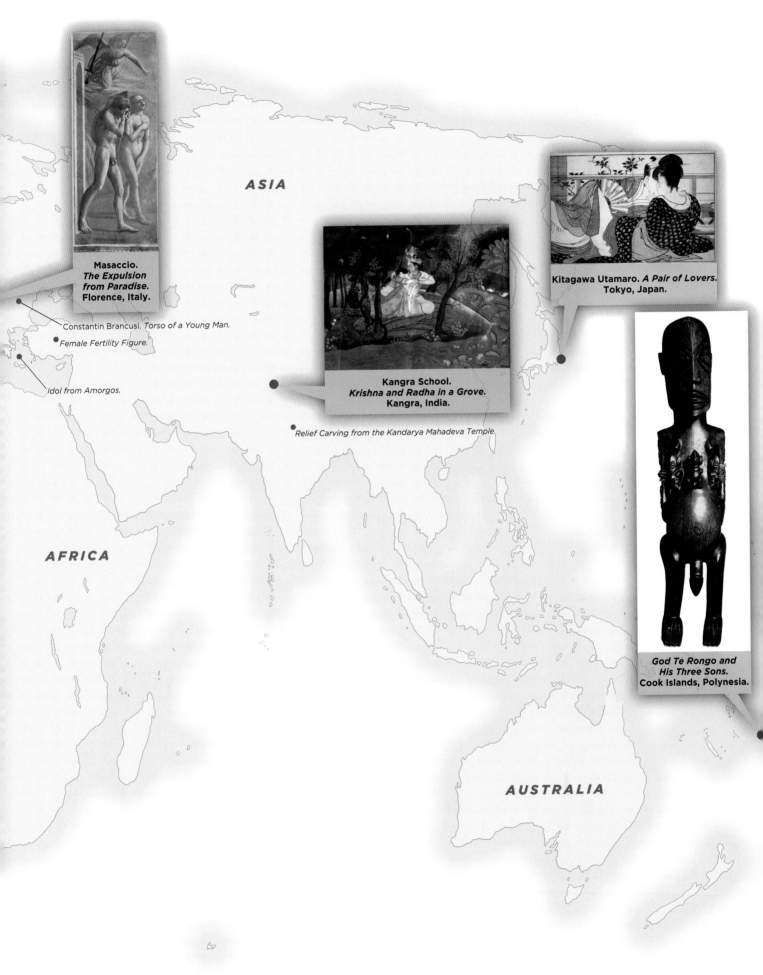

Masaccio.
*The Expulsion
from Paradise.*
Florence, Italy.

Constantin Brancusi. *Torso of a Young Man.*

Female Fertility Figure.

Idol from Amorgos.

ASIA

Kangra School.
Krishna and Radha in a Grove.
Kangra, India.

Relief Carving from the Kandarya Mahadeva Temple.

Kitagawa Utamaro. *A Pair of Lovers.*
Tokyo, Japan.

*God Te Rongo and
His Three Sons.*
Cook Islands, Polynesia.

AFRICA

AUSTRALIA

6000–2000 BCE

PALEOLITHIC ERA	**25,000 BCE**	*Venus of Willendorf*		**200**	*Kidder Figure*
MESOLITHIC ERA	**10,000**		**ROMAN EMPIRE**	**100**	
Settlements in China and Chile	**8000**				
Çatal Hüyük, Turkey					
NEOLITHIC ERA	**7000**				***Above*** *Laocoön and His Sons*, Hellenistic (12.18)
Settlements in India	**6000**				
		Female Fertility Figure at Çatal Hüyük		**CE 50**	*Initiation Rites of Dionysos, Villa of Mysteries*
Birth of Mesopotamia	**4000**		**MOCHE CIVILIZATION**		*Oil lamp with love-making scene*
Unification of Egypt	**3100**		*ROMANESQUE*	**1000**	*Moche Pottery Depicting Sexual Intercourse*
Old Kingdom	**2500**		**CAHOKIA CIVILIZATION**		*Mother and Nursing Child*
		Idol from Amorgos			
Civilizations in Crete					*Relief Carving from the Kandarya Mahadeva Temple*
Irrigated farming in Andes	**2000**				
SHANG DYNASTY —CHINA	**1600**		*GOTHIC*		*Moche Pottery Depicting a Woman Giving Birth Assisted by Midwives*

Above *Fowling Scene,* Egypt (9.6)

			RENAISSANCE	**1400**	
			AZTEC EMPIRE		VAN DER WEYDEN. *Virgin and Child in a Niche*
	1000		**MING DYNASTY —CHINA**		JAN VAN EYCK. *Wedding Portrait*
			MUGHAL DYNASTY —INDIA		MASACCIO. *Expulsion from Paradise*
					Aztec Marriage Couple
			BAROQUE	**1600**	
CHAVIN CULTURE			**BENIN KINGDOM —AFRICA**	**1700**	UTAMARO. *A Pair of Lovers*
			Captain Cook's voyages in Oceania		

Above *Sarcophagus with Reclining Couple,* Etruscan (9.8)

Radha and Krishna
in the Grove

U.S. Revolutionary War

French Revolution

ROMANTICISM   **1800**   God Te Rongo and
His Three Sons

REALISM   Figure of a Deity:
A'a Rurutu

Potawatomi Male Figure
(Love Doll)

INGRES. *Grande Odalisque*

MANET. *Olympia*

IMPRESSIONISM

POSTIMPRESSIONISM

Russian Revolution   **1900**   Dogon Primordial
Couple

World War I   **1915**   Ashanti Akua'mma dolls

O'KEEFFE. *Grey Line with
Lavender and Yellow*

BRANCUSI. *Torso of a
Young Man*

CUBISM, SURREALISM   **1925**

Above LANGE. *Migrant
Mother* (13.30)

World War II   **1939**

POSTWAR
EXPRESSIONISM   Bamana Female
Figure, Mali

Above MARISOL. *The
Family* (13.19)

1970   NEEL. *Pregnant Woman*

MODERNISM, POST   **1975**
MODERNISM

First observation of **1984**
Breast Cancer
Awareness Month

Desert Storm   **1990**

BOURGEOIS. *Blind
Man's Bluff*

KRUGER. *Untitled
(Your body is a
battleground)*

HERSHMAN. *Deep Contact*

OPIE. *Justin Bond*

2000

Above MUTU. *One
Hundred Lavish Months
of Bushwhack* (3.27)

THE PROMISE OF FERTILITY

As we have seen in the previous chapter, some art images and objects were created and used to secure food. Cave paintings, elaborate masks, wood carvings, and ceramic sculptures helped the hunter-gatherer and farmer to ensure the food supply. Also, art and art objects have functioned similarly to ensure human reproduction, again likely with "sympathetic magic" invoked through the art object.

Fertility Goddesses and Gods

Some of the earliest artifacts thought to relate to human fertility come from the Paleolithic and Neolithic periods of history. Some were small sculptures of female figures, depicted as abundantly fleshy and swollen, with their bellies, breasts, and thighs accentuated. They are called Fertility or Mother Goddesses, suggesting that they were part of a fertility ritual and cult.

Our first focus example is the *Venus of Willendorf* (Fig. 7.3), who is a well-rounded, abstracted female figure, only four inches high, carved from a found, egg-shaped piece of limestone and dating from around 25,000 BCE. The ancient artist-carver may have believed that the power of fertility was already contained in the natural egg shape of the stone even before it was carved. Its shape, along with the natural indentation that became the navel, may have been the reason the artist chose it. The figure was discovered near a hearth at an excavation site near the town of Willendorf, Austria, in 1908. The name "Venus" was given arbitrarily to the female figurines by the archaeologists who found them.

Although sometimes labeled as a fertility goddess, the figurine was likely more a charm or a fetish. The bulbous forms were carved and painted, giving repetition and pattern to the piece, emphasizing female qualities in the swelling forms. Even the head, perhaps covered with curls of hair or a headpiece of some sort, repeats the bulging, round bumps. Could this featureless head symbolize a budding bloom about to burst into flower?

Clearly, the figure does not realistically represent someone, but rather represents the physical essence of fertility, like the later example of a similar kind of sculpture that we have already seen, the *Female Fertility Figure* (Fig. 7.2). The *Venus of Willendorf* is small enough to hold in the palm of your hand, yet it appears to be large, strong, and robust. With her hands resting on her breasts, she suggests stability in addition to the power of fertility. People may have held the figurine for her power during childbirth, to ward off death, or to wish for good health. Whatever her function, she was likely a talisman for good fortune.

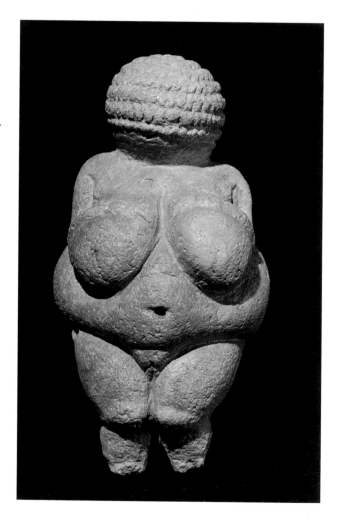

7.3 *Venus of Willendorf,* Austria, c. 25,000–20,000 BCE. Stone, 4 3/8" high.

This small but robust figure likely represented the power of female fertility, as seen in her bulbous anatomy. This sculpture may have aided reproductive rituals in the Paleolithic era.

Our first comparison figure is dated thousands of years later, where in the Cycladic Islands off mainland Greece was found a female figurine who likely is a descendant of the mother goddesses. Figure 7.4 is called the *Idol from Amorgos,* from 2500–2300 BCE, and is thirty inches high. Other figures like this range from a few inches to life-size and were found buried with the dead. The marble was carved with obsidian blades and polished with emery. Traces of paint were found on some figures, indicating that the eyes and jewelry (necklaces and bracelets) were accented in color. With her oval or egg-shaped head tilted back and her toes pointed, the *Idol of Amorgos* is thought to be a reclining figure. Slender and delicate, this abstract nude seems to emphasize feminine youth, in contrast to *Venus* and the *Female Fertility Figure.* Because these figures were found in burials, their purpose may have been to give new life to the dead, just as the young woman has the potential to give life. Sculpted very economically, the overall shapes are angular and wedge-shaped. However, the breasts, belly, and navel are subtly swelling on an otherwise stiff, planklike body (these figures are sometimes called "plank idols"). Incised lines indicate the neck fold, arms, pubic area, legs, and toes, and connect the geometric and organic forms.

CONNECTION *Goddesses dominated ancient rituals for thousands of years before gods came to prominence. For more on deities, read Chapter 8.*

Much later, in the nineteenth century, male fertility pieces were produced by Oceanic cultures. These figures show clear contrasts to the female figures discussed previously. Figure 7.5 shows the *God Te Rongo and His Three Sons* from Rarotonga, part of the Cook Islands in Polynesia. Carved of wood and standing more than twenty-seven inches high, he is balancing three small,

7.4 *Idol from Amorgos*, Cycladic Islands off mainland Greece, 2500–2300 BCE. Marble, 30″ high. The Ashmolean Museum, Oxford, UK.

This is one of several youthful female burial figures that were always slender and had pointed toes, as if reclining.

7.5 *God Te Rongo and His Three Sons*, Cook Islands, Polynesia, c. 1800–1900s. Wood, 27 ³/₈″ high. The British Museum, London.

This figurine of a male god depicts both his virility and divine lineage. It is cleanly carved in the frontal contained style.

human figures on his belly. Four more figures, in the same style but in low relief, are carved on his arm and forearm. The figure is endowed with a large penis in comparison to the rest of the figure, visually giving emphasis to the virility of *Te Rongo*. The exact character of this god is not known, as the European missionaries who collected such artworks were not interested in preserving the indigenous religion.

As we take a closer look at *Te Rongo,* we can see the precise, contained style of sculpture that is typical of works carved from a single block of wood. Careful planning was required to keep the proportion of the head equal to one-fourth of the body height. In addition, incorporating the small figures shows the artist's skill. The chest, a bit sunken in order to make room for the smaller figures, exaggerates the belly and penis, again suggesting reproduction. The oval shape of the head and the delineation of the facial features are repeated in the smaller figures, which clearly seem like infant images of the large figure. The surface of the wood is smooth and polished, keeping focus on the subject of the piece and less on its texture.

Male sculptures and art pieces such as *Te Rongo* were carved for religious rituals by specialists called *Ta'unga*, which is also the word for "priest." The specialist was trained through a long apprenticeship, during which he acquired the skill to control and attain the *mana* (power) in the materials and tools he used. In some cultures, the art object was created for one ceremony and then discarded, whereas in others, the object was meant to endure and be passed down from one generation to the next. The more the object was used in religious ceremony, the more mana it gained. These art objects became symbols of prestige and rank, and with them, their owners displayed their place in the hierarchical order of the gods, priests, monarchs, chiefs, and people. Taboos restricted their use to those of power and rank. When passed down through many generations, they also became objects of sacred information, such as the family lineage.

Some sculptures were figures representing an ancestor, who eventually, through generations of veneration, would become deified or elevated to the realm of the gods. This may have happened with *Figure of a Deity: A'a Rurutu* (Fig. 7.6), from the Austral Islands in central Polynesia. These specific ancestor deities were known as *Tangaroa* figures and represented a creator in the act of creating human beings. Family lineage was critically important in Oceanic cultures, and thus this godlike creator may well have been connected to a family ancestor. The figure is forty-four inches high and is carved from one block of wood. Like

7.6 *Figure of a Deity: A'a Rurutu,* Austral Islands, collected in 1820. Wood, 44″ high. The British Museum, London.

Here is another figure of a male deity carved in the contained style depicting the abundance of his progeny as seen clinging to his entire body.

Te Rongo, this deity sculpture is rendered in a contained style, compact and stiff. However, his body is covered with crawling, infantlike figures. Even the facial features are made up of the clinging little bodies. The back of the figure is hollowed out and contains additional small figures. We might be looking at the mythical creation of humankind in this figure or the creation of a specific ancestral line.

Fertility and Rituals

With the fertility figures we have just studied, the likely use of ritual and sympathetic magic has been discussed. The next works are examples of art that were definitely created for ritual.

7.7 *Initiation Rites of Dionysos*, Villa of Mysteries, Pompeii, Italy, c. CE 50. Fresco.

These murals decorate a room where the fertility rituals of Dionysos likely took place. The imagery combines architectural illusionism with three-dimensional realism within its pictorial space.

The focus example is the depiction of an ancient ritual that has been preserved in a group of wall paintings found in the Villa of Mysteries (Fig. 7.7), in Pompeii, Italy, dated from the middle of the first century. Pompeii was buried in volcanic ash when Mt. Vesuvius violently erupted in CE 79, which preserved the city and these mystical images for modern inquiry and appreciation. This cycle of paintings, which wrap around the four walls of a room, depict a solemn ritual of the mystery cult of Dionysos that may have been associated with sexual intercourse and fertility. In *Initiation Rites of Dionysos*, a young female novice is being prepared to join with Dionysos, the god of wine and fertility. The novice apparently is taking the role of Ariadne, his mythological mate, who is shown along with Dionysos and their accompanying entourage of mythological beings, witnessing the initiation. There is also an older woman who offers comfort to the frightened initiate, while nudes are dancing to the music played on a lute-like instrument. A priestess is ready to uncover and reveal the cult's draped sacred objects, which likely held the secrets of the mysteries of Dionysos and perhaps a concealed phallus. The event also includes a winged figure, who is whipping the young initiate.

The rite takes place in an illusionist **frieze** (a decorative horizontal band found in architecture), with the figures striking classic Greek poses against deep, rich, "Pompeian Red" panels. Evenly spaced columns subdivide the running narrative into scenes. The nearly life-size figures, with convincing volume and anatomy, move and turn in a shallow space, on a **trompe l'oeil** ("fool the eye") ledge. The frescoes in the Villa of Mysteries are excellent examples of Roman painting at that time. Walls were specially prepared with plaster mixed with marble dust, applied in several layers and polished to a marble-like finish, to enhance the frescoes' rich colors. It is significant that these paintings were located in a villa, or private home, in the country. The rituals reference sex and fertility, which are often home-based. In the case of the cult of Dionysos, the adherents were all women, who were housebound.

The next small sculpture is a Native American *Potawatomi Male Figure* (love doll) from Wisconsin, dated 1800–1860, and is nine inches tall (Fig. 7.8). It is carved in wood and partly adorned in wool fabric. These figure-like carvings, lacking arms, were used as "medicine" to control human behaviors and health. This type of figure could be used as a love charm to cast a spell on someone whose attentions were desired. Ethnologist Alanson Skinner reported: "It is often that the captor tires of his or her conquest, and leaves the victim, who is still under the spell of such a charm. Such a person will become frantic, and even go crazy, following the user of the charm everywhere" (Skinner 1923: 207). To have successful "medicine," the owners of the love dolls would have been spiritually prepared and, through dreams or visions, be given special powers by the spirits.

From the Bamana culture of Mali, Africa, the *Standing Female Figure* (Fig. 7.9) is made of wood and brass and is just over twenty inches high. Such figures were associated with a female fertility cult and were stored in special houses created for them. On occasion, such figures were brought out for public display or for elaborate rituals to aid women who were having difficulties in conceiving and childbearing. Figures such as this were also used in initiation rites for young men. This *Standing Female Figure* has sharp, angular planes and geometric forms. The head is also defined in clean curving planes. The hair is arranged in an abstract coiffure. Details in the face and hands are either completely eliminated or greatly simplified. The shoulders and chest are fairly squared until the protrusion of the conical breasts, which have been exaggerated. The elongated, erect torso has a slight swell at the navel down to where the abdomen connects to the short, bent legs. Beads adorn the ankles. Figures such as this often have geometric designs incised into the surface which may have represented scarification. Attention has been paid to the rich, shiny patina that causes finer details to show up well on the surface. Attention has been paid to the rich, shiny patina that causes finer details to show up well on the surface. The geometric forms are connected by lines, resulting in an aesthetically rich blend of the two- and three-dimensional elements in the piece.

In contemporary Africa, there are sets of rituals and art dealing with fertility. The twentieth-century *Akua'ba* (Fig. 7.10) from the Ashanti (Asante) culture in Ghana are fertility sculptures created solely for a ritual for women who are having difficulty in conceiving, and also to ensure a healthy and beautiful baby. *Akua* is the name of the first

7.8 *Potawatomi Male Figure* (love doll), Crandon, Wisconsin, 1800–1860. Wood and wool fabric, 9″ high.

This sculpture functioned as a "love doll" and was used as a charm to cast a spell on someone whose attentions were desired.

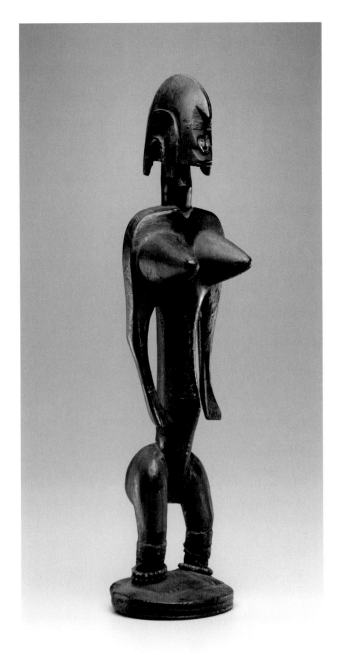

7.9 *Standing Female Figure,* Bamana, Mali, Africa, 19th- 20th centuries. Wood, copper, beads, and metal. 20.5″ high. Detroit Institute of Arts, USA.

This figure is used in elaborate rituals, including those that aid women who have difficulties in conceiving and childbearing.

7.10 *Ashanti Akua'ba Doll,* Ghana, Africa, c. 20th century. Wood, 13″ high. The British Museum, London.

This flattened abstracted figure is a ritual doll that is worn by women as an aid to conceive and to ensure a healthy, happy baby.

woman who used this ritual doll successfully and was able to conceive a baby. *Ba* (child) was added, hence, the dolls were called "Akua's child." *Akua'mma* is the plural form of the term. *Akua'mma* average about twelve to thirteen inches in height and are carved in wood.

To begin this ritual, a woman consults a priest, who advises her to have a doll carved. She would then adorn the doll in beads, care for it, and carry it wrapped on her back as mothers traditionally carry their actual babies. She would avoid gazing upon any deformity in a human or *Akua'ba* doll, so her baby would not be born with these traits. Instead, she was to gaze upon the well-carved *Akua'ba* that expressed the Ashanti ideal of beauty. If the ritual was successful, the woman might place the doll in a shrine in order to recognize the power of the priest she confided in, or she might give it to her child for a toy.

In these figures, we see the interpretation of beauty reduced to uncomplicated forms. The *Akua'ba* head, neck, arms, and torso are rendered in a circular disk and a series of cylinders. The figures are always female. The canon of beauty is suggested as a round face with a small mouth, a high forehead, and a long neck and torso. The linear facial features are cleanly carved in the lower half of the smooth facial disk, which is supported by a stack of disklike forms that suggest necklaces. The breasts and navel are minimal forms, but they clearly express the female gender.

ART DEPICTING PRIMORDIAL AND HUMAN COUPLES

Human couples have been depicted throughout the ages, some as primordial or first couple, the mother and father of humankind, and others as human couples representing the marriage ritual and its implications within cultural contexts. These depictions were rooted in the creation myths of many religions. They also come from marriage rituals that frame procreation in many cultures.

Primordial Couples

Our focus primordial couple is Adam and Eve, found in the Jewish, Christian, and Muslim religions and depicted widely in European art. In the Bible, Genesis 1:28, their creator commanded them to "be fruitful and multiply, fill the earth and conquer it." Later in Genesis, the Fall is described, and Adam and Eve are exiled from the Garden of Eden. It is this point in the story that a young Italian Early Renaissance artist named Masaccio painted in *The Expulsion from Paradise* (Fig. 7.11) on the wall of the Brancacci Chapel in the Church of Santa Maria del Carmine, in Florence, Italy, in 1427.

In *The Expulsion*, one can almost hear Eve's anguished cry and feel Adam's pain as they shamefully walk from the gate. Their movement is slow, every step more agonizing than the one before. Now God's commandment to "fill the earth" has become a painful burden. The artist paid particular attention to modeling the figures, using soft contrasts of values and color. Only essential details are included with Adam and Eve, specifically the gate to the Garden of Paradise and the angel with a sword barring their return.

Compare this anguish to the stately and formal couple in Figure 7.12, from the Dogon culture of Africa. This *Primordial Couple* is seated on an *imago mundi* (image of the world) stool supported by four figures. Stylistically, it is part of the Sudanese Group and carved with simple, nonferrous tools. Like the Oceanic figures, the sculptures are usually carved from one block of wood using the subtractive method. Sometimes, naturally occurring features in the wood block, such as a bend or a knot in the wood, are incorporated into the finished sculpture.

Seated in a frontal position, the *Primordial Couple* relate the harmony of the union of the first male and female, both of whom are equally exalted in the sculpture. The union also appears to represent their fertility as well as their roles in life. The male unites the figures with his arm embracing the female at her neck and his hand resting on the upper part of her breast. His other hand is resting on his penis, symbolizing their sexual union. They wear

7.11 MASACCIO. *The Expulsion from Paradise*, Brancacci Chapel, Santa Maria del Carmine, Florence, Italy, 1427. Fresco.

Adam and Eve are the first couple of the Jewish, Christian, and Muslim religions. This chapel mural depicts the beginning of their scriptures with the pair's exile from the Garden of Eden.

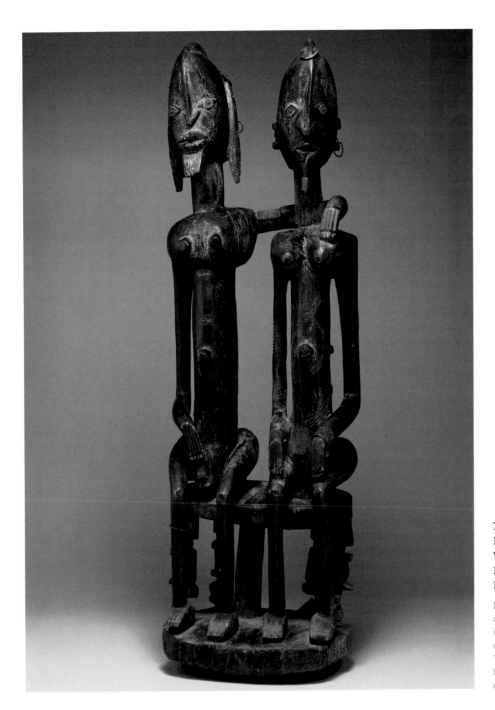

7.12 *Dogon Primordial Couple.*
Mali, Africa, c.19th–20th century.
Wood, 29″ high. Metropolitan
Museum of Art, New York, Gift of
Lester Wunderman, 1977.

Dogon's first male and female are
depicted in their defining roles
in life; on their backs he carries a
quiver, and she a babe in a sling.
Their fertility is gestured with his
left hand on her breast and his
other on his penis.

jewelry that symbolizes their sexual power. On their backs are carved representations of the roles they have in life. As hunter, warrior, and protector, he wears a quiver, while she has a child clinging to her.

Other details in the sculpture suggest their high position and perhaps their origin. She wears a mouth ornament called a "labret," and he wears a chin beard trimmed very much like the beards worn by Egyptian pharaohs. Their headgear is similar to that worn by the people of the Peul culture, who were enemies of the Dogon. This may represent Dogon domination or intermarriage between the two cultures. The piece is vertically emphasized by the two elongated figures and by the negative space we see throughout the figures. Visually there is a balance between the positive mass and the negative space in the sculpture. For the Dogon, a balanced design is a symbol for an ordered human culture (Roy 1985: 31).

Human Couples

The union of human couples is often documented in art across cultures. The focus example is *The Wedding*

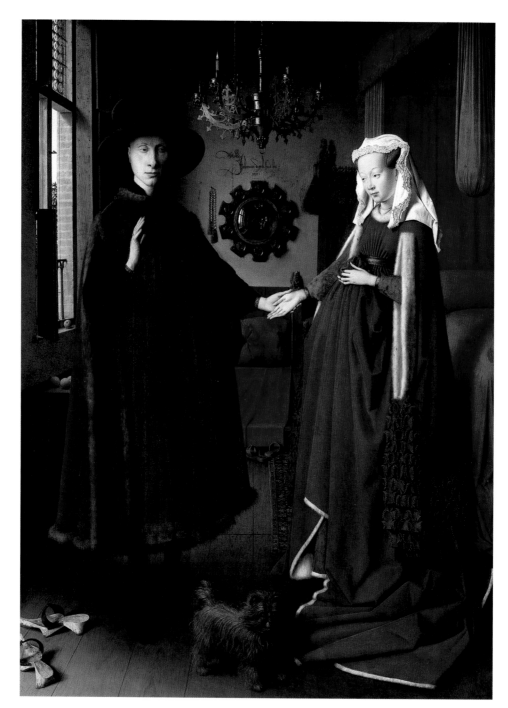

7.13 JAN VAN EYCK. *Wedding Portrait*, Flanders, Northern Europe, 1434. Oil on wood panel, 32″ × 25″. National Gallery Collection, London.

This early Renaissance oil painting visually certifies the wedding of an Italian businessman living in Bruges. The one-point perspective composition is full of both obvious and hidden symbolism giving meaning to this important event.

Portrait, or *Giovanni Arnolfini and His Bride*, from 1431 (Fig. 7.13), by Flemish artist Jan van Eyck, showing Giovanni Arnolfini, an Italian businessman living in the Flemish city of Bruges, and his betrothed. More than just a double portrait, this is a wedding certificate, with both obvious and hidden symbolism. The couple is shown in their bedroom chamber rather than in church. They are joining in marriage in the place where it will be consummated, suggesting the hope for many children. Indeed, the woman holds her clothing as if she expected to be pregnant soon. Less obvious symbols also fill the bedroom. In the chandelier, there is one candle burning although it is daytime, representing divine presence. The couple has removed their shoes, showing they are on holy ground. In the frame of the mirror appear medallions that depict the passion of Christ. On the chest and windowsill are oranges, the golden apples of the Hesperides, representing the conquest of death. There is a dog at the feet of the couple, symbolizing fidelity. Arnolfini raises his hand in a gesture of blessing. The prayer for fertility is also seen as the bed drapes are opened, and on the bedpost finial is a statuette of St. Margaret, the patron saint of childbirth. A

7.14 *Aztec Marriage Couple*, from the *Codex Mendoza*, Mexico, 1434. Bodleian Library, University of Oxford.

The Aztec marriage ritual literally "ties the knot" uniting the couple.

whisk broom is also hanging on the post, suggesting setting up a household.

To complete this document, van Eyck depicts official witnesses, including himself. In this one-point perspective rendering, the vanishing point is located above the mirror, where we see written in script, "Johannes de eyck fuit hic," which translates to "Jan van Eyck was here." And in the mirror, two figures appear, most likely the artist with a companion. Van Eyck was a pioneer in oil painting, and this work is approximately contemporaneous with Masaccio's *Expulsion*.

For a comparison, we will go to the Aztecs, where we also see poses and symbols indicating the union between the man and woman. Figure 7.14, *Aztec Marriage Couple*, from the fifteenth-century *Codex Mendoza*, depicts a man and woman seated on a mat, literally tying the knot. Aztec marriage ceremonies took place in the groom's home in front of the hearth. The codex tells us that this man is about twenty years of age, while the woman is fourteen or fifteen. It also provides details about a matchmaker and a soothsayer who studied the couple's birth signs in order to ensure their compatibility, and the parents' role in making the final selection. The bride's parents gave the

wedding banquet, which began at noon. At night, the bride, powdered with yellow earth and adorned in red feathers, was carried on the matchmaker's back to the groom's home. There the formal vows were performed by tying together their wedding garments, as seen in the illustration. Afterward, the bride and groom prayed for four days, then they were blessed by a priest and permitted to consummate their marriage. The man could marry additional wives (Townsend 1992: 188).

The *Aztec Marriage Couple* has outlined flat shapes, with color used decoratively. Clothing is depicted with simple flowing lines, which contrast with the angular pattern of the woven mat that surrounds the couple. The drawing of the hair provides more pattern in the image. While the *Wedding Portrait* is rendered in the dark, deep tones of oil paint, the *Aztec Marriage Couple* is bright and economically drawn to quickly convey essential ideas.

 CONNECTION *Menkaure and His Wife, Queen Khamerernebty*, Figure 10.3, page 272, are a couple from the Egyptian culture.

ART ABOUT LOVEMAKING

Lovemaking is essential in procreation. Sexuality is a libidinal urge that is gratifying, positive, and even energizing. We will look at five images from various cultures, each of which has its own way of defining and depicting this universal act.

Our first focus is the Roman *Oil Lamp with Love-making Scene,* dated to the first century BCE (Fig. 7.15). This clay oil lamp likely lighted a bedchamber in a home, rather than in a brothel where sexual imagery was found in graphic wall frescos. It depicts a couple in an intimate gaze while engaging in sexual intercourse on a fine bed. An inscription found in the ruins of Pompeii on a wall from an ordinary house reads "Hic Habit Felicitas" or "here lies happiness" (Mathieu 2003: 56), in a place where a lamplike our example would have been found. The relief figuresreflect ideal Classical Greek sculpture both in their artistic style and composure.

Another example depicting the act of lovemaking is the *Moche Pottery Depicting Sexual Intercourse* (Fig. 7.16). The tone of the Moche pottery is matter of fact, and shows some similarity to the figures on the Roman *Oil Lamp.* The Moche pot was probably created around 1000–1250, in the desert coast of Peru, in the thriving, artistically active civilization that preceded and was brought down by the Incas. The Moche custom was to bury ceramic pots with the dead that had naturalistic imagery recording their way of life and tribal customs, including lovemaking. The depictions of lovemaking were explicit and candid, and likely were made by the women of the culture, as they usually made the pottery. The figures are often lying on or under a blanket with a rolled pillow. Their faces exhibit no emotion. However, the variety of the sexual acts and the positions in which they are sculpted display a wide range of sexual pleasure and preference. Nothing was left to the imagination, as numerous sexual acts besides intercourse between a man and a woman appear. Such sculptures may have been designed as visual aids for sex education,

7.15 *Oil Lamp with Love-making Scene.* Roman, 1st century BCE. Ceramic. Museo Archeologico Nazionale, Naples.

This clay lamp depicts a couple engaged in sexual intercourse, suggesting that its place may have been on a bedside table or in a holder hanging on a wall in a bedchamber.

7.16 *Moche Pottery Depicting Sexual Intercourse,* Peru, c. 1000–1250. Ceramic. Museo Arqueologico Rafael Larco Herrera, Lima, Peru.

Incorporated onto a stirrup-handled pot, candid, explicit sexual intercourse is depicted. This pot was found in a burial along with others depicting life's daily activities in the Moche culture.

7.17 KITAGAWA UTAMARO. *A Pair of Lovers*, frontispiece from *Poem of the Pillow*, Japan, 1788. Wood block relief print, 9 3/4″ × 14 3/4″. Victoria & Albert Museum, London.

This is a "Shunga" print, which depicts lovers engaged in sexual intercourse. This is art depicting the "Floating World" (Ukiyo), which includes provocative, erotic subject matter.

illustrating not only human reproduction but perhaps birth control as well.

Our buff clay and slip-decorated piece was made by pressing clay into a mold. We are looking down on the top of the pot, where we can see the stirrup handle and spout at the right and the figures on the left. In addition to showing intercourse, the pot could certainly function very well as a vessel, probably to contain *chicha* (corn beer). The linked limbs of the figures create a circular shape that echoes the stirrup handle. The figures are shown economically, with a minimum of detail.

The next comparison comes from the hand of the famous Japanese printmaker Kitagawa Utamaro, one of the best of Japan's Golden Age (1780–1810) woodblock designers. Utamaro designed *A Pair of Lovers* (Fig. 7.17) as the frontispiece for the book *Poem of the Pillow*. The work reflects the *ukiyo* or "floating world" theme. Chinese and Korean Buddhist missionaries brought the printmaking technique to seventeenth-century Japan, as well as the notion of the "floating world," or the Buddhist concept of the transience of life. Non-samurai classes in Japan

translated that concept into the idea of prizing life's fleeting moments of pleasure—in other words: eat, drink, and be merry. These images often centered on female beauty, the theater, and entertainment, and these prints were produced and collected much like movie star posters or baseball cards are today.

A Pair of Lovers is a *shunga* print (translated as "spring pictures") and provocatively depicts erotica. *Poem of the Pillow* contained several prints considered to be Utamaro's finest shunga works. Gently and intimately erotic, this print captures a private moment in the closeness of these lovers. The exquisite interplay of pattern and line of the kimonos with the figures gives emphasis to the intertwining of their bodies as they make love. Even their heads and hands are eroticized, with the closeness of their faces and the strokes of their fingertips. This is a visual poem of line, pattern, and color that compose this floating world image of these lovers' pleasure.

CONNECTION *Komurasaki of the Tamaya Teahouse* (Figure 13.32, page 395) is a ukiyo-e print depicting a courtesan.

Images of ideal erotic sexuality were relatively common in India, and it is interesting to compare them to the idealized images from Pompeii and Japan, as well as to the blunt

7.18 *Kangra School. Radha and Krishna in the grove.* 1780. Kangra, India. Gouache on paper, 4.8″ × 6.75″. Victoria and Albert Museum, London, Great Britain.

An image of ideal sexuality, it depicts Krishna (an avatar of Vishnu) in a tender lovemaking scene with the shepherdess Radha.

Moche depictions. Erotic images in India appear as sculptures on Hindu temples and in miniature paintings from northern India from the seventeenth and eighteenth centuries. The miniature painting, *Radha and Krishna in a Grove*, dated circa 1780 (Fig. 7.18), shows Radha, a shepherdess, and Krishna, one of the incarnations of the god Vishnu, embracing in an ideal landscape. They sit on a bed of plantain leaves, near a stream filled with pink water lilies and surrounded by sheltering trees and blooms of all kinds. Krishna, wearing a crown, is conventionally depicted as blue. Both Krishna and Radha are graceful figures, bedecked in jewels or brilliantly colored cloth, outlined with flowing lines, and filled out with delicate details. They are placed in the center of the flower-filled grove, which emphasizes their forms against the blue-green background. Beautifully colored patterns and textures add to the visual delight of the painting.

Krishna is a deity, and the scene is highly idealized, even though there was an uneven status relationship between the two characters. The blending of their forms in a tender embrace was meant to be like the physical and spiritual

7.19 *Relief Carving from the Kandarya Mahadeva Temple*, Khajuraho, India, c. 1000.

Full-bodied figures are carved in relief depicting men and women in sexual union and masturbation, reflecting the open celebration of the blend of human sexuality with spirituality in Hindu beliefs. For more on the temple itself, see Figure 8.36.

union that all humans could experience through lovemaking. That union in lovemaking, by extension, was also like union with God. Such images as *Radha and Krishna in a Grove* were meant to be instructive, and the mythical sexual act was intended to be reincarnated regularly among living couples.

Also in India, we see men and women engaged in sexual union and masturbation in relief carvings on the *Kandarya Mahadeva* temple at Khajuraho (Fig. 7.19). Many of the carvings on the structure are openly erotic, with nude, sleek, full-bodied figures dancing, twisting, or writhing. Our example shows a scene with intertwined voluptuous bodies. The Hindu religion openly celebrates sexual love, as erotic coupling and self-pleasuring reflect the divine union with the Unbounded. To experience this carnal bliss is a virtue and a path that leads to redemption.

ART ABOUT SEXUALITY IN WESTERN CULTURE

Sexuality is not just focused on intimacy, love-making, and human reproduction. It is complicated in modern Western art because of the power relationship between men and women. Sexuality appears in mass media, sells products, and is part of political debates. Abstract works on sexuality capture the energy, but they often leave other specifics undefined.

The Feminine Body and the Gaze

How does sexuality work in an image when only a single figure is depicted? In Western culture, the meaning of such images depends on the subject of the picture, for whom it is made, and why.

7.20 JEAN-AUGUSTE-DOMINIQUE INGRES. *Grande Odalisque*, France, 1814. Oil on canvas, 35″ × 64″. Louvre, Paris.

The nude Turkish harem woman was intended to be an erotic image for European men in the 19th century.

Our beginning focus image here is the *Grande Odalisque* (Fig. 7.20), painted by Jean-Auguste-Dominique Ingres in 1814. It is a long, horizontal painting of a nude woman seen from behind. She is an odalisque, a member of a Turkish harem. Blue, gold, and cream tones predominate in the painting. The curve of the upper body echoes the curve of the hanging blue drapery. Accents occur at the woman's face and at her hand, holding the peacock-feather fan. Her back is extremely long, creating a sensual flow that complements the curves of her legs, arms, breast, and buttocks. Outline is emphasized, and the soft, flawless skin is delicately shaded. The smooth flesh contrasts with the patterned and textured cloth, feathers, and beads that surround and adorn the woman. Her pose is sensually relaxed.

Nineteenth-century female nudes in Europe and the United States were made for nineteenth-century men. They were the privileged audience for such pictures, as viewers whose gaze completed the sexual exchange implied in the painting. As critic Linda Nochlin wrote:

> As far as one knows, there simply exists no art, and certainly no high art, in the nineteenth century based on women's erotic need, wishes or fantasies. Whether the erotic object be breast or buttocks, shoes or corsets . . . , the imagery of sexual delight or provocation has always been created *about* women for men's enjoyment, by men. . . . Controlling both sex and art, [men] and [their] fantasies conditioned the world of erotic imagination. (Nochlin 1988: 138–139)

The fact that only the female is present in a sexual scene is significant. Without a lover in the scene, the odalisque is sexually available for the viewer—presumably the European male—who gazes upon her and "consumes" without being seen or consumed himself. The viewer took the place of the imagined Turkish sultan, with many women at his disposal.

For comparison, Edward Manet's *Olympia*, from 1863 (Fig. 7.21), is superficially similar to the *Grande Odalisque*. But *Olympia* scandalized the public, in part because her sexuality and nudity were not of a distant place and time. The woman, Victorine Meurant, also known as Olympia, was a famous Paris courtesan. This image is similar to a famous Italian Renaissance painting of Venus, a heavenly goddess. In nineteenth-century Europe, the concepts of prostitute, courtesan, and goddess were conflated. Mythological paintings of goddesses were an acceptably distant way to present the nude woman for the pleasure of the male viewer. Nineteenth-century wealthy men euphemized their "companions" as embodiments of beauty, like goddesses. Manet's painting shattered those illusions. Olympia's unromantic expression made clear that sex and money would be exchanged in her associations with wealthy men. Her gaze identifies and implicates a viewer, whereas in the *Grande Odalisque* the nature of the viewer is less explicit. The wealthy were horrified that their sexual dalliances could be seen in that light. Manet's painting

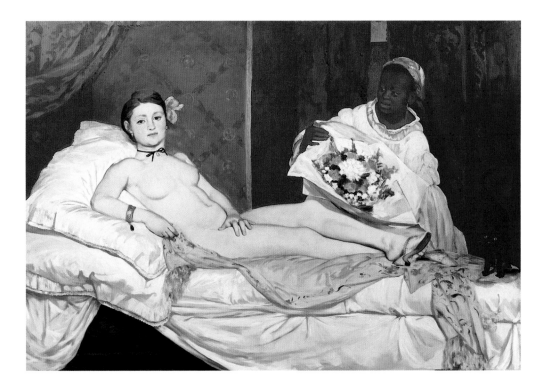

7.21 EDWARD MANET. *Olympia*, France, 1863. Oil on canvas, 51 $^{1}/_{4}$″ × 74 $^{3}/_{4}$″. Musée d'Orsay, Paris.

This painting of a courtesan scandalized the public, because it was not presented as a mythological or historical figure.

also reveals the social status accorded different races, with the African woman in the role of maid, the white woman as mistress.

> **CONNECTION** One of the inspirations for Manet's *Olympia* was the *Venus of Urbino* by Titian (Figure 3.28).

Although Manet's painting was attacked for its content, his defenders praised the work for its innovative paint quality. Manet painted thickly, directly on the white surface of the canvas ground, in a style called "alla prima" painting. His colors were flatter and brighter than the subdued tones of traditional academic painting. The body of Olympia is brightly lit. Light areas are separate from the dark, as distinct from most oil paintings since the Renaissance, where midtones predominate. Manet's personal style of brushwork led to many of the painterly concerns of twentieth-century artists, such as gestural mark making, flatness versus illusion of depth, and experiments in applying paint.

Sexuality, Politics, and Consumerism

In the computer-video installation *Deep Contact*, from 1990 (Fig. 7.22), the artist Lynn Hershman looks at the ways mass media uses sexuality in Western culture to

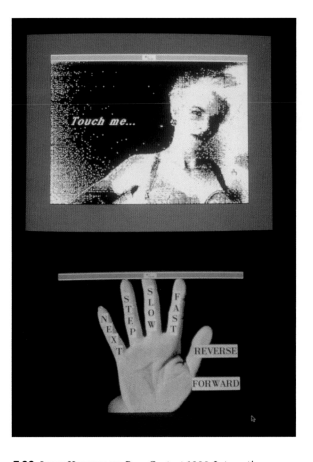

7.22 LYNN HERSHMAN. *Deep Contact*, 1990. Interactive computer-video installation at the Museum of Modern Art, San Francisco.

Sexuality is used to deliver a range of messages.

attract attention. At the beginning of the piece, the "guide" or hostess, Marion, dressed in sexually seductive clothing, knocks at the window-like surface of the touch screen and asks the viewer to touch her to begin the performance of the artwork. By touching different parts, the viewer can create interactive fictions, enter a paradise garden with various characters, or see video clips on reproductive technologies and women's bodies. Although not all of the content of *Deep Contact* is sexual, everything in the piece has been eroticized, including ideas about technology, self-awareness, and intimacy. The viewer of *Deep Contact* cannot be passive; if you do nothing, nothing happens. Thus, the viewer is dislodged from the position of anonymous, distant voyeur, and, at times, a nearby surveillance camera flashes the viewer's face on the screen in the midst of a performance.

Sexuality is also politicized, as we can see in *Untitled (Your body is a battleground)*, from 1989 (Fig. 7.23), which encapsulates both the shifting attitudes and the heated conflicts that surround women, sexuality, and reproduction. The artist, Barbara Kruger, took a political slogan from the 1960s and combined it with a photograph of a woman's face, split down the middle, positive image on one side and negative on the other. The woman looks like a model from a perfume or makeup ad in a fashion magazine. We viewers become part of the piece, as the staring woman makes us either identify with her or see her as opposite to ourselves. This poster was originally made about abortion rights, but it also alludes to other "battleground" body issues, such as race (black/white) or sexuality (homo/hetero).

CONNECTION Kruger's background is both in fine arts and in the mass media. In the 1980s, she was chief designer for the popular fashion magazine *Mademoiselle*. Her artwork pastes text over images, like magazine covers.. For more on the increasingly blurred relationships between fine art and the mass media, see the section "Categories of Visual Arts" in Chapter 1.

7.23 BARBARA KRUGER. *Untitled (Your body is a battleground)*, USA, 1989. Photographic silk screen on vinyl, 112″ × 112″. Eli Broad Family Foundation Collection, Los Angeles. Courtesy: Mary Boone Gallery, New York.

This photographic imagery deals with the shifting attitudes and conflicts that surround women, sexuality, and reproduction in Western culture.

7.24 CATHERINE OPIE. *Justin Bond*, USA, 1993. Chromogenic print, edition of eight, 20″ × 16″.

The artist's images of homosexuals, transsexuals, and dominatrixes expose the complexities of gender roles and sexuality.

7.25 GEORGIA O'KEEFFE. *Grey Line with Lavender and Yellow*, USA, 1923. Oil on canvas, 48″ × 30″. The Metropolitan Museum of Art

The image is derived from flower forms, but it visually suggests both female genitalia and sexuality.

To whom does "your" refer in Kruger's work—we the viewers or the staring woman? Kruger uses pronouns that are gender neutral, with no fixed subject, to imply that attitudes about sexuality (as well as race) are not fixed by nature. Kruger sees these categories as changing entities under social, political, and religious influence. Yet Kruger recognizes how harshly divided the rhetoric can be in these areas. The division down the middle, with black and white sides, indicates how polarized societies can be on these issues.

For a last comparison here we look at Catherine Opie's *Justin Bond*, 1993 (Fig. 7. 24). This is a photograph of a cross-dressing male whose attire and hair suggest both "good girl" and sexual potential. Opie's many photographs of homosexuals, transsexuals, and dominatrixes make apparent the complexities of gender and sexuality. She is interested in using photographs to catalog and archive the wide range of people and places around her. In addition,

the existence of such photographs complicates the idea of the privileged male viewer. *Justin Bond* meets the viewer's gaze with directness and confidence, challenging any attempt by the viewer to see his behavior as pathological. The image is distinct because of the rich colors, near-symmetry, and mixed messages.

Abstracted Sexual Imagery

Sexual imagery in art can be abstracted. Its forms may allude more or less to the human body, but humans themselves need not be represented.

Georgia O'Keeffe's *Grey Line with Lavender and Yellow*, from 1923 (Fig. 7.25), is an enlarged flower image. The simple, near-symmetrical composition is suffused with subtle color gradations interrupted by occasional lines. Throughout much of her life, O'Keeffe painted natural objects that verged on abstraction, with simplified forms and heightened color that increased a sense of beauty and desirability. She used these forms to express emotions rather than copying nature slavishly. The structure of her flower imagery resembles female genitalia (although she denied the association: see Chapter 4, page 96). Feminists have seen in her work a positive, female-based imagery that glorifies and beautifies female sexuality.

Figure 7.26, *Torso of a Young Man* (1924), by the twentieth-century Romanian sculptor Constantin Brancusi, abstracts forms of male sexuality. Influenced by the philosophy of the eleventh-century monk Milarepa, Brancusi sought to understand the universality of all life. With this inspiration, along with the Romanian folk art of his youth and the influence of African tribal art that so strongly affected many European artists, he created works that were intended to capture the essence and universality of pure form, working in related themes such as creation, birth, life, and death. He finished his pieces by hand to a precious perfection, leaving no visual signs of his handicraft, whether using marble, wood, or bronze. Some of his pieces look as if they have been machine tooled. As he developed an idea, his forms became more and more simplified. He is quoted as saying, "Simplicity is not an end in art, but one arrives at simplicity in spite of oneself, in approaching the real sense of things" (Janson 1995: 817). *Torso of a Young Man* is eighteen inches tall, with three cylindrical forms of highly polished bronze placed on a base composed of several geometric forms. One sculpture seems to be resting on another, contrasting the cylindrical "torso" with rectangular volumes. The simplified torso becomes an obvious phallic symbol.

Louise Bourgeois's abstracted imagery is much more explicitly sexual than are O'Keeffe's or Brancusi's. In *Blind Man's Bluff*, from 1984 (Fig. 7.27), the "body" is sexual, as the sculpture is like a large phallus covered with round, organic forms. The dichotomy of male versus female is blurred. In its appearance and name, *Blind Man's Bluff* invites touch. The marble at the center is polished to a silky finish, while the top and bottom are left roughly cut. The piece is fetishlike, suggesting a fixation on sexual body parts without necessarily any attachment to an individual as a whole. The plethora of organs has the quality of

7.26 CONSTANTIN BRANCUSI. *Torso of a Young Man*, Romania, 1924. Polished brass, 18″ high. Hirshhorn Museum, Smithsonian Institution, Washington, D.C.

Incorporating geometric forms in this work, the artist constructed a simplified torso that also represents a cylindrical phallus, the essence of male sexuality.

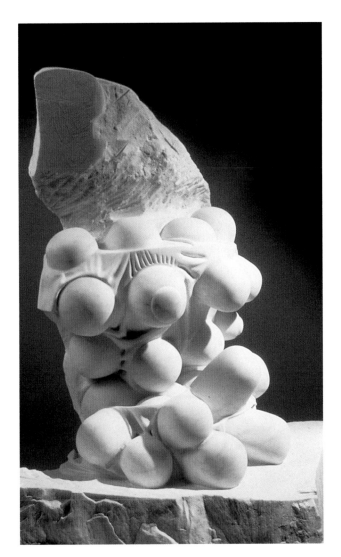

pleasure overload. Bourgeois's bulbous forms are ambiguous, as they are both breast-like and penis-like, or they may represent the sensitive nerves in the tongue or in genital organs. With Bourgeois's work, multiple interpretations of the forms are often possible and always subjective. Bourgeois's work stands in contrast to male-based heterosexual imagery like the *Grande Odalisque*.

IMAGES OF PREGNANCY, CHILDBIRTH, AND PROGENY

Images of childbirth are seen in many cultures and have existed for ages. Our first focus figure is a 1971 Western image by Alice Neel. Her 1971 painting *Pregnant Woman* (Fig. 7.28) shows us the physical effects of pregnancy on one woman's body and self. Her swollen belly and enlarged nipples contrast with her bony arm and ribs showing through the skin. Her pink, blood-flushed belly contrasts with the rest of her yellow flesh. Her facial expression seems wooden, passive, dazed, or fearful. The man's

7.27, left LOUISE BOURGEOIS. *Blind Man's Bluff*, USA, 1984. Marble 36″ × 35.5″ × 25″. Collection Cleveland Museum of Art.

Photo: Allan Finkelman Art © Louise Bourgeois Trust/Licensed by VAGA, New York, NY

The combination of male and female sexual imagery blurs genders as discrete categories in this work.

7.28, *below* ALICE NEEL. *Pregnant Woman*, USA, 1971. Oil on canvas, 40″ × 60″.

This painting depicts the physical effects of pregnancy on one woman's body and emotional self.

portrait behind her may suggest intimacy, distance, possession, or protection. Neel mostly painted portraits, often nude, creating a sense of drama with her unrelentingly realistic images. She captured subtleties of expression, as well as subtle color shifts, like the difference between yellow and pink flesh.

An interesting comparison is this ceramic figurine depicting pregnancy in the Guatemalan Maya culture dated between 250 BCE and CE 100 (Fig. 7.29). She is known as a *Kidder Figure* and is about ten inches high. The seated female has a babylike body, and she emphasizes her enlarged abdomen by gently resting her hands on it. The expression on her face seems to be one of contentment and joyous anticipation of the expected event. The Mayas likely identified small sculptures such as this with fertility cults. They linked general procreation with female maternity and fertility, and related it to the earth. The figures represent the bearers of human offspring as well as the mother of nature and the progenitor of plant life.

For another comparison we return to the Peruvian Moche culture to study a ceramic vessel that depicts childbirth in as straightforward a manner as their depiction of sexual intercourse in Figure 7.16. The *Moche Pot Depicting a Woman Giving Birth Assisted by Midwives* (Fig. 7.30) is another stirrup-handled vessel with small figures

7.29 *Kidder Figure*, Mayan, Guatemala, 250 BCE–CE 100. Ceramic vessel, 10″ × 7 1/2″ × 6 3/4″.

This youthful figure shows delight in her pregnancy. She is associated and identified with Mayan female fertility and maternity earth cults.

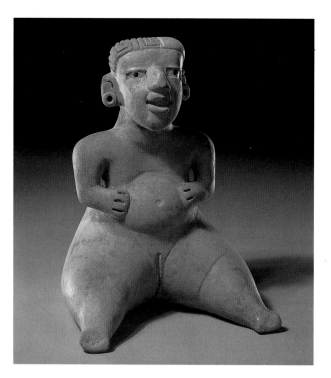

connecting the handle with the body of the pot. The figures clearly illustrate the act of childbirth. The mother giving birth shows a bit of a grimace, while the faces of the midwives seem expressionless. The scene seems to be clinically illustrating an event rather than capturing the moment of physical and emotional anticipation or even pain. It records the Moche birthing position and technique and may have taught expectant mothers and students of midwifery. Again, as in our other Moche example, the figures sit on top of the pot, compositionally well-integrated with the stirrup handle. The handle seems to function as the back support to the midwife, who holds the laboring woman. The bodies of those two women suggest a curving shape that turns down and concludes at the head of the midwife catching the emerging infant.

There are countless instances of mother and child imagery across many cultures, and we have already seen Henry Moore's archetypal sculpture of the *Draped Reclining Mother and Baby* (Fig. 7.1). Here we will look at two examples in depth. Interestingly, both have links to death despite depicting the presence of a new life.

Our focus mother and child image is a familiar Christian icon of Mary and Jesus. The example was painted by the northern Renaissance Flemish painter Rogier van der Weyden. A student of Jan van Eyck (Fig. 7.13), Rogier became the influential master painter of Brussels in 1436, and his work was often copied in the fifteenth century. Although he signed none of his work, his style is distinctive, with linear forms and brilliant color. *Virgin and Child in a Niche* was painted in 1432–1433 and is only seven inches by four inches (Fig. 7.31). Despite her size, Mary is majestically enthroned in a delicately carved architectural space, crowned as the Queen of Heaven. Yet she nurses the newborn redeemer, holding him tenderly. The Christian primordial couple, Adam and Eve (see Fig. 7.11), appear here as carvings on the niche. Adam, who has covered himself in shame, is about to be pushed off his pedestal by a hovering angel, expelling him from paradise. Eve holds the apple under the Tree of Knowledge, while the serpent looks down from the branches. In the center above, God the Father and the Holy Spirit as a dove observe the scene, completing the Trinity. The gentle and loving gaze of Mary upon her baby is calm, yet ominous in its understanding of the fulfillment of Old Testament prophecies.

The comparison piece is a ceramic human effigy vessel featuring a *Mother and Nursing Child* (Fig. 7.32) from the Mississippian Period (1200–1400), in an agricultural civilization located near the confluence of the Mississippi and Illinois rivers around Cahokia, Illinois. The Mississippians built large, truncated pyramid mounds topped with temples. Their religion strove to predict and control nature, with much attention paid to death. The *Mother and*

7.30, above *Moche Pot Depicting a Woman Giving Birth Assisted by Midwives*, Peru, c. 1000–1250. Ceramic. Museo Arqueologico Rafael Larco Herrera, Lima, Peru.

A stirrup-handled pot explicitly depicting the act of childbirth, which may have been a teaching aid to expectant mothers and students of midwifery.

7.31, right ROGIER VAN DER WEYDEN. *Virgin and Child in a Niche*, Flanders, Northern Europe, c. 1432–1433. Oil on panel, 7 1/4″ × 4 3/4″. Kunsthistorisches Museum, Vienna, Austria.

This painting depicts Christian beliefs in images that represent the potential of human progeny (Adam and Eve), and the birth of their Savior of Humankind (Virgin and Child).

Nursing Child was buried in a tomb that likely belonged to a high-ranking person. Tombs contained a quantity of elaborate naturalistic and fanciful funeral pottery, mostly effigies, which captured the spirit of the dead it honored. The *Mother and Nursing Child* expresses a graceful and serene image of a woman and her baby. A simple rendering, there is emphasis in the detail of the mother's face and in the nursing babe. Triangular shapes appear in the rest of the pose, as the mother's broad shoulders suggest an inverted triangle, and her folded legs suggest two other triangles. The simple, geometric form adds to the stability and calm of the figure. Representing a mother and her progeny in life, the effigy vessel may have ensured her potential to bear children in the afterlife.

7.32 *Mother and Nursing Child*, Cahokia, Illinois, USA, 1200–1400. Ceramic effigy vessel, Mississippian Period. St. Louis Science Center.

This is a burial figure that may have represented a mother and her progeny in life as well as her potential to bear children in the afterlife.

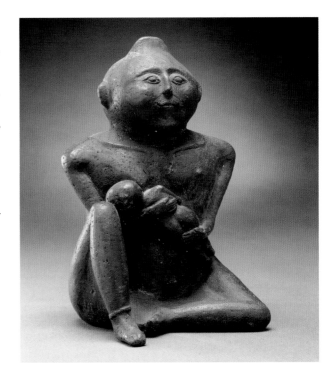

Section 2

RELIGION

The supernatural realm lies beyond our senses, yet in almost every age and culture, people have created diagrams, symbols, and pictures that express to some extent their understanding of divinity.

In the next two chapters, we will look at art from world cultures to see how humans make images of their gods and holy beings, as well as diagrams that account for the earth, humanity, the stars, and the cosmos. Also discussed are the places of worship humans have built, where they can feel a divine presence. Finally, we will see the kinds of art that have been made in reaction to—or in preparation for—death.

CHAPTER 8 DEITIES AND PLACES OF WORSHIP

Art that represents deities through images or symbols, and art that creates sacred spaces

CHAPTER 9 MORTALITY AND IMMORTALITY

Funerary art, commemorative art, and monuments.

8.1 *Transformation Mask*, Kwakiutl, British Columbia, 20th century. Painted wood.

Through rituals using masks like this one, the Kwakiutl people could access the spirit world.

8

DEITIES AND PLACES OF WORSHIP

By definition, the divine realm is beyond human ability to understand, but humans strive constantly to grasp this other world, to communicate with it or to be joined with it. Rituals, oral tradition, sacred writings, meditation, prayer, and music are but a few paths used by humans to connect to the Transcendent. Art is another.

PREVIEW

This chapter covers art that pertains to humanity's beliefs in the divine. It will look at how artists and architects have created images of the divine, holy beings, and places of worship. It will also show the use of naturalistic, geometric, animistic, and humanistic symbols and forms in religious imagery and sacred structures. We will see enormous richness and variety in the kinds of art used for rituals, sacred structures, and religious ceremonies. The image that opens our chapter, the Transformation Mask (Fig. 8.1), is but one example. We will see many more.

Connecting Art and History from
2000–500 BCE

This period saw major civilizations developing in complexity and flourishing all over the world. With them came some early images of deities and prophets, and also early places of worship.

Many civilizations in the Middle East continued to grow. Babylon was a center of religious worship, with tall ziggurats topped by temples, not unlike the earlier *Ziggurat at Ur* (Fig. 8.24). In Babylon between 1792 and 1750 BCE, Hammurabi recorded his Code of Law, covering the tax system, fair wages and prices, property rights

for women, and criminal punishment (Fig. 8.2). In 1350 BCE, the Assyrians conquered the Fertile Crescent, including Babylonia and, later, Egypt. They built extensive roads, developed a political system of provinces and governors, and established libraries of cuneiform tablets.

The Hebrew people went to Egypt in 1800 BCE because of drought in Canaan, and they were put into bondage. In 1250 BCE, Moses led the Exodus, and by 1000 BCE, the Hebrews conquered the people of Canaan and established Jerusalem. Their religion was

monotheistic and became the roots of Judaism, Christianity, and Islam.

The Persians lived east of the Crescent Valley from 550–330 BCE, with their capital at Persepolis. Their religion included the teachings of Zoroaster, which were written down in the book *Avesta*.

On the island of Crete, the Minoan civilization flourished through seafaring and trade. The Minoans produced many fertility figures and goddesses, like the *Snake Goddess* (Fig. 8.3). Around 1200 to 800 BCE, another maritime culture, the Phoenicians, prospered in small city-states in

MAP 3. The Middle East, Asia Minor and India, showing the locations of empires and the locations of the founding of the religions of Hinduism, Buddhism, and Judaism.

Empires and Major Religions

- Egypt 2600–650 BCE
- Babylon 2200–1600 BCE
- Assyria 1500–600 BCE
- Minoan 1900–1350 BCE
- Buddhism
- Hinduism
- Judaism

present-day Lebanon, with colonies in Carthage and North Africa and an active trade economy. They are also known for the phonetic alphabet, based on sounds of the human voice.

The long-lived Egyptians had three kingdoms. During the Old Kingdom, 2700–2200 BCE, the Great Pyramids and Sphinx were built. From 2100 to 1800 BCE, Egypt was ruled by invaders but later regained autonomy. In the New Kingdom, 1600–1100 BCE, remarkable temples were built that were similar in style to the later *Horus Temple at Edfu* (Figs. 8.34 and 8.35). The Egyptian religion was polytheistic. One goddess, Hathor, is represented as a cow as seen in Figure 8.5.

The Greek civilizations established city-states, the strongest being Athens and Sparta. The ancient Greeks are credited with developing the early forms of democracy. Around 500 BCE, the Golden Age of Greece began, producing great advances in philosophy, the arts (*Parthenon*, Fig. 8.32), architecture, writing, crafts, medicine, mathematics, and Olympic sports.

Between 750 and 500 BCE, the Etruscan people ruled Central Italy. Beginnning in 509 BCE, the Romans chipped away at their power, eventually drove them out and established the Roman Republic.

In India around 1500 BCE, nomadic peoples formed a new culture that incorporated Hinduism and the Sanskrit language. Later, the sacred text of the *Rig-Veda* was written. In 563 BCE, Siddhartha Gautama was born. He would later become the Buddha, the Enlightened One, founding the religion of Buddhism (see *Seated Buddha*, Fig. 8.9).

From 2000 to 1500 BCE, China was cultivating millet and wheat, using the potter's wheel to produce black pottery, and domesticating animals. Later, the Shang Dynasty (1500–1122 BCE) was known for developing

writing, cultivating silkworms, and producing white pottery, bronze works, and marble, jade, and ivory artworks. They practiced ancestor worship. Between 1123 and 256 BCE, the Chinese invented the crossbow and perfected lacquer.

In Africa, the Kush people lived in the Sudan between 2000 and 350 BCE. In 732 BCE, they conquered Egypt and ruled for one hundred years. In 600 BCE, they were conquered by the Assyrians.

On the American continent, the Olmec civilization existed on the coast of the Gulf of Mexico between 1200 and 400 BCE. They built great temples, pyramids, colossal heads, and monuments. They also invented

8.2, *above* *Hammurabi Stele*, Susa (modern Shush, Iran), 1792–1750 BCE. Detail showing the king standing before the sun god and god of justice Shamash, who commanded Hammurabi to record the law. Relief, 28" high.

an accurate calendar and a counting system. In northern Peru from 1000 to 200 BCE, the Chavin culture built temples with stone carvings and produced fine pottery and gold work. Mound builders, farmers, and potters lived in central North America.

Around 2000 BCE, Europe was still in the New Stone Age, with megalithic structures built over a widespread area. Religious rituals were mixed with astronomy and agriculture, as at *Stonehenge* (Fig. 8.26).

World Art Map for Chapter 8

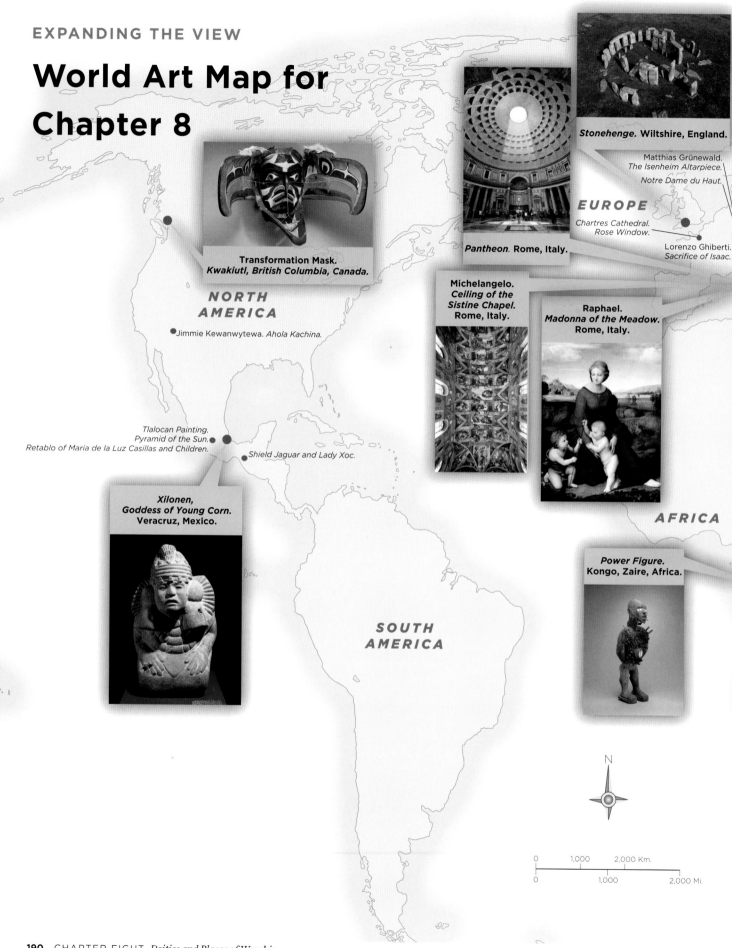

Stonehenge. Wiltshire, England.

Matthias Grünewald. *The Isenheim Altarpiece.*

Notre Dame du Haut.

EUROPE

Chartres Cathedral. Rose Window.

Lorenzo Ghiberti. *Sacrifice of Isaac.*

Pantheon. Rome, Italy.

Transformation Mask. *Kwakiutl, British Columbia, Canada.*

NORTH AMERICA

Jimmie Kewanwytewa. *Ahola Kachina.*

Michelangelo. *Ceiling of the Sistine Chapel.* Rome, Italy.

Raphael. *Madonna of the Meadow.* Rome, Italy.

Tlalocan Painting. Pyramid of the Sun. *Retablo of Maria de la Luz Casillas and Children.*

Shield Jaguar and Lady Xoc.

AFRICA

Xilonen, Goddess of Young Corn. Veracruz, Mexico.

Power Figure. Kongo, Zaire, Africa.

SOUTH AMERICA

N

0   1,000   2,000 Km.

0   1,000   2,000 Mi.

Zeus or Poseidon.
Athens, Greece.

Iktinos and Kallikrates. *Parthenon.*
Horsemen (Parthenon frieze).

Masjid-i-Shah
or Royal Mosque.
Isfahan, Iran.

ASIA

Round Hall from the
Temple of Heaven.
Beijing, China.

Dome of the Rock.
Jerusalem, Israel.

Snake Goddess.

Synagogue at
Dura-Europos.

Altar of Heaven.

Shrine to Vairocana Buddha.   Main Shrine at Ise (exterior).

The Water and Moon Guanyin Bodhisattva.

Mohammed's Ascent into Heaven.
Ziggurat at Ur (partially reconstructed).   Mandala of Samvara (Kharamukha Cakrasamvara Mandala).
Hammurabi Stele.   Shiva as Nataraja, or Lord of the Dance.

The Ark of the Covenant.   Kandarya Mahadeva Temple.
The Goddess Hathor and the Overseer of Sealers.   Seated Buddha.

First Hypostyle Hall, Horus Temple.

Great Stupa. Sanchi, India.

Great Pylon
of the Horus Temple at Edfu.
Edfu, Egypt.

Offering with Cili-Shaped Crown.

AUSTRALIA

2000–500 BCE

OLD KINGDOM—EGYPT	2700 BCE	
MIDDLE KINGDOM—EGYPT	2100	Ziggurat at Ur
BABYLON	2000	Stonehenge
EARLY GREEK CIVILIZATIONS		
NEOLITHIC EUROPE		
HEBREW CULTURE	1800	
Hammurabi's Code		
MINOAN CIVILIZATION	1700	
NEW KINGDOM—EGYPT	1600	Snake Goddess
INDIAN CIVILIZATION, HINDUISM AND SANSKRIT		
SHANG DYNASTY—CHINA		
	1400	
Assyrians Conquer the Fertile Crescent	1300	
Phoenician Civilization	1200	
Olmec Culture in Mexico		
CHAVIN CIVILIZATION—PERU	1000	
ETRUSCAN CIVILIZATION		
	700	
	600	The Goddess Hathor and the Overseer of Sealers, Psamtik
Birth of Buddha		
ROMAN REPUBLIC	500	
GOLDEN AGE OF GREECE		

PERSIAN EMPIRE		Zeus (or Poseidon)
		Parthenon
		Great Stupa
	400	

Above MNESICLES. *Temple of Athena and the Propylaea. Greece* (Fig. 2.36)

		Horus Temple
ROMAN EMPIRE	100	
		Pantheon
Birth of Jesus	4	
		Synagogue at Dura-Europos
	CE 200	Pyramid of the Sun
		Tlalocan Painting
		Ark of the Covenant mosaic
	400	

Above *Bamiyan Stone Buaddha, Afghanistan.* (Fig. 5.29)

	600	Seated Buddha
Founding of Islam		Main Shrine at Ise
		Dome of the Rock
	700	Kandarya Mahadeva Temple

900

Above EL CASTILLO. Chichen Itza, Mexico (2.34)

Shield Jaguar and Lady Xoc

1000

Shiva as Nataraja, or Lord of the Dance

Xilonen, Goddess of Young Corn

CRUSADES: WARS BETWEEN CHRISTIANS AND MUSLIMS FOR THE HOLY LAND

GOTHIC ERA—EUROPE **1100**

The Water and Moon Guanyin Bodhisattva

Chartres Cathedral

1200

MALI EMPIRE—AFRICA **1300**

Aztecs Build Tenochtitlan

1400

GHIBERTI. *Sacrifice of Abraham Tlaloc Vessel*

Above SANDRO BOTTICELLI. *The Birth of Venus*, Italy (1.4)

MARTIN LUTHER AND THE BEGINNING OF THE PROTESTANT REFORMATION, 1517 **1500**

RAPHAEL. *Madonna of the Meadow*

GRÜNEWALD. *Isenheim Altarpiece*

MICHELANGELO. *Ceiling of the Sistine Chapel*

COUNTER-REFORMATION

Mandala of Samvara

Altar of Heaven

Mohammed's Ascent into Heaven

HEIGHT OF THE ASHANTI EMPIRE—AFRICA **1600**

Masjid-i-Shah, or Royal Mosque

1700

AGE OF ENLIGHTENMENT

Above *Cheordez Prayer Rug*, Turkey (1.18)

1800

Power Figure

1900

Above *Nimba, Goddess of Fertility*, Guinea (3.46)

KEWANWYTEWA. *Ahola Kachina*

LE CORBUSIER. *Notre Dame du Haut*

DALAI LAMA EXILED FROM TIBET

Transformation Mask

Retablo of Maria de la Luz Casillas and Children

Offering with Cili-Shaped Crown

2000

RELIGIONS AND THEIR IMAGERY OF DEITIES AND HOLY BEINGS

For some religions, artists make images or sculptures of gods and goddesses and other holy beings to aid people in rituals. The faithful may believe that the deity is actually present in the artwork, or just represented by it.

Simple geometric shapes often symbolize God. The sphere and dome are significant in Islamic architecture, as they stand for the heavens and the oneness of God. In the Hindu religion, the circle can symbolize the unknowable Supreme Being. The triangle stands for the Christian Trinity. Words can also be symbols of God, such as in Islamic calligraphy. In many religions, light is a symbol for God.

Animal features or natural phenomena can represent, act as metaphors for, or symbolize deities (see Fig. 8.1). For example, the sun can be a symbol for God and, at other times, can actually be worshiped as a deity itself. In Christian art, Jesus is symbolized by a sacrificial lamb, and the Holy Spirit by a dove or by fire. Other religions are animistic, with natural elements or animals as deities or inhabited by spirits. The earth is often understood to be a female force because of its ability to generate life. Other religions depict God anthropomorphically—that is, with human attributes. Gods may be gendered and have humanlike personality traits.

In some religions, God is not pictured. Most African religions and the Hindu religion recognize a completely unknowable Supreme Being. In the Islamic religion, Allah is never depicted.

Let us now look at a few ways that deities and holy beings are depicted in artwork.

Animism

A basic belief found in our human legacy is **animism**. Its premise is that all the forces of nature are inhabited by spirits. Although there are no specific images of the spirits, a rock or tree can be carved into an image to bring out the natural force, as seen in the *Venus of Willendorf* (Fig. 7.3). The small egg-shaped stone was likely believed to contain the spiritual force of procreation, which would have been an important aid to ancient fertility rituals.

Polytheism

Polytheism is the belief in many gods with distinct and sometimes several functions. Likely the first of the polytheistic gods, the Earth Mother is the original deity in almost all areas of the globe—the giver of life and fertility and the carrier of death. In ancient myths of nomadic cultures—hunters and gatherers—the Goddess existed first. Later, she created her male counterpart, with whom she mated to produce the rest of Creation. As agriculture increasingly replaced hunting and gathering as the primary source of food, the importance of paternity increased,

8.3 *Snake Goddess*, Minoan, from the palace at Knossos, c. 1600 BCE. Glazed earthenware, 13 1/2″ high. Archeological Museum, Heraklion.

This goddess has likely evolved from the Earth Mother deity; she represents male and female regenerative powers of a snake shedding its skin.

and upraised arms energize this piece. She holds snakes, which may have represented male sexuality because of their shapes. Female fertility and regenerative powers may also have been connected to the snake's periodic shedding of its skin. The leopard-like animal on her head may have symbolized royalty. Her tiered dress and hairstyle likely represented Minoan fashion at that time.

> **CONNECTION** For more on early goddesses, see the sections on "Fertility Gods and Goddesses" and "Fertility Figures" in Chapter 7.

The ancient Greeks believed that the beginning of all life on earth was Gaia, the Earth Goddess. Her descendants, the Greek gods on Mount Olympus, had distinct personalities and formed alliances and enmities among themselves and with humans. They were responsible for many aspects of the natural world and human life, such as love, warfare, and the seasons. The Greek gods were always in human form, as the Greeks considered themselves superior to other religions that worshiped animals or mountains. The earliest images were stiff and frontal, without fluid movement, similar to Egyptian sculpture. Later Classic depictions had convincing anatomy and movement but were entirely idealized and flawless, conforming to Greek standards of beauty. Our focus example, *Zeus*, or possibly *Poseidon*, 460–450 BCE (Fig. 8.4), is from the Classic period. Zeus, chief among the Greek gods, is usually shown as a mature bearded male with an ideal, godlike physique. His right hand probably once held a thunderbolt, an attribute of Zeus, who is associated with the sky and storms (if the figure once held a trident, then he likely is Poseidon, God of the Sea). The over-life-size figure appears monumental, muscular, and ideally proportioned. It conveys a sense of action and energy and, at the same time, poise and dignity. Fully extended, Zeus's mighty body is balanced between the backward movement of his arm and its anticipated forward movement as he hurls a thunderbolt.

Now compare the deities of ancient Egyptian religion who were mostly personifications of natural forces, such as the daily rising of the sun, the ripening of crops, and the annual flooding of the Nile River. These divine beings required worship and sacrifice from humans, who appealed to them for special needs. Most were represented as animals or as animal-human combinations.

The goddess Hathor, associated with the sky, stars, love, mirth, and joy, was depicted as a cow or as a combination

8.4 *Zeus* or *Poseidon*, Greece, 460–450 BCE. Bronze, 6′ 10″ high. National Archeological Museum, Athens.

Greek gods appear in the ideal human form according to the Greek aesthetic rule of proportion.

along with land ownership, animal breeding, cities, and hierarchical classes. Powerful goddesses continued to be worshiped in many religions, but alongside important male gods.

We begin our focus with two artworks. The first, from an early polytheistic religion, is the *Snake Goddess*, 1600 BCE (Fig. 8.3), which probably evolved from the Earth Mother in the Minoan civilization on Crete from 2000 to 1200 BCE. The open bodice and prominent breasts tie this figure to early fertility goddesses. Her intense expression

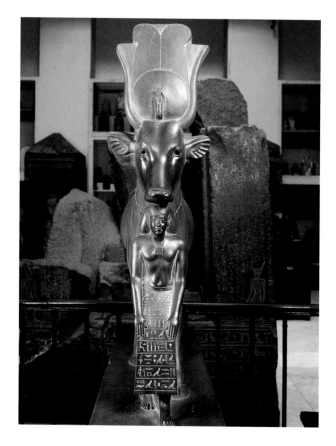

water was so essential and corn symbolically stood for all food. Having a special role as the protector of young corn plants, the maize goddess was called *Xilonen* (Fig. 8.6). In our image of her, dating from 1000–1200, the head is rounded, very humanlike, and grandly adorned. She wears a headdress with ornamental bands and ears of corn, a collar with sunrays, heavy ear pendants, and a jade necklace that symbolizes crop fertility. Also from Mesoamerica was Tlaloc, the rain deity who made crops flourish (see Fig. 8.45, another example can be seen in Fig. 4.2). The most worthy of the human dead were received into Tlaloc's heaven. Images of Tlaloc were common, as were temples dedicated to him. This god was traditionally shown with distinctive features: circular eyes, twisted serpent nose,

8.5, *left* *The Goddess Hathor and the Overseer of Sealers, Psamtik.* Saqqara, Egypt, Late 26th Dynasty, 6th century BCE. Gray stone; base: 11 1/2″ × 43 1/4″; height of cow to horns, 33″. Cairo Museum, Egypt.

Egyptian deities were usually personifications of natural forces or animal forms. This image is an offering to Hathor by an official, for her guidance in his duties.

8.6, *below* *Xilonen, Goddess of Young Corn.* Huastec. Tuxpan (Veracruz), Mexico, 1000–1200. Limestone, 33″ high.

This goddess's important function was to promote abundant growth of the corn crops.

of a woman and a cow. In *The Goddess Hathor and the Overseer of Sealers, Psamtik,* sixth century BCE (Fig. 8.5), she encompasses and hovers protectively over Psamtik, an Egyptian official. Her horns surround the head of a cobra, a sign of royalty, and the sun disk with a crown of feathers. Even in images of Hathor as a woman, her head is usually topped by the same combination of horns and sun disk, which symbolize royalty and divinity. The side view of this piece shows the entire length of the cow striding forward, with bone and muscle beautifully sculpted. In our front view of her calm, majestic face, we see more stylized features, such as the repeated ridges above the eyes and the radiating pattern in the ears. Psamtik keeps pace with Hathor. His standardized face and body show conventional divisions of breast, rib, and belly, while the arms and hands are presented frontally and symmetrically. His official duties are inscribed on his skirt. The work was likely commissioned by Psamtik as an offering that would have been placed in a temple to Hathor.

> **CONNECTION** In Chapter 9, a hawk representing Horus, the Egyptian Sky God, is on the coffin case of the Pharaoh Tutankhamen (Fig. 9.5, page 242).

Much later in time, the Mesoamerican cultures often linked the gods associated with corn and water, because

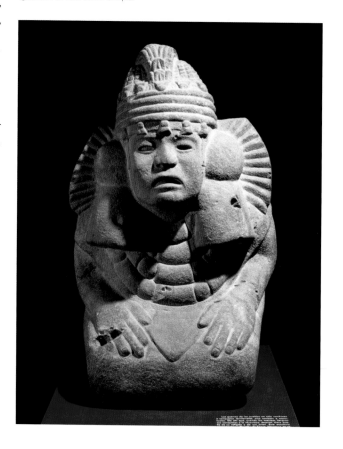

fanged mouth, headdress, large ear ornaments with pendants, and his face was flattened with features rendered as geometric shapes.

Compare how the Mesoamerican artists show the divine status of Tlaloc and Xilonen to the way that divinity is shown in Minoan and Greek gods. All are represented as human. Xilonen is shown naturalistically, yet grandly adorned to establish her divinity. Her staring eyes and down-turning mouth make her a remote, almost unapproachable goddess. The sculpture also has a monumental feel, which adds to the sense of distance. Tlaloc's face is abstractly human, making the deity seem more terrible, powerful, and removed from the experiences of everyday life.

> **CONNECTION** Look again at Figure 8.2, the *Hammurabi Stele*, which shows him standing before Shamash, the powerful Babylonian god of the sun and justice.

Pantheism

Pantheism is the belief that a divine spirit pervades all things in the universe.

Hinduism

Although the Hindu religion appears to have numerous gods, it is pantheism, rather than polytheism. This is because their "gods" are all manifestations, or "avatars," of a divine universal spirit, in this case, of *Brahman* the Unbounded. Brahman is one, pure being, pure intelligence, and pure delight, and is therefore unknowable. Although never pictured, Brahman can be partially known through the human senses, because all natural things, humans, and spiritual beings reflect Brahman.

The God Shiva, one of the primary avatars, is the source of good and evil, male and female. He is the unity in which all opposites meet. He is the destroyer of life, who also recreates it—terrible and, at the same time, mild. Since the tenth century, *Shiva* has often been depicted in Hindu art as *Nataraja, or the Lord of the Dance*, seen here in a sculpture from c. 1000 (Fig. 8.7). Shiva's body is shown as supple, sleek, and graceful. Cobra heads form the ends of his hair, and he stands in perfect balance. As the Lord of the unending dance, he is the embodiment of cosmic energy, yet the balanced pose also contains the concept of eternal stillness. The multiple arms tell of his power, and his divine wisdom is shown by the third eye in the middle of his forehead. His far right hand holds a small, hourglass-shaped drum, the beating of which stands for creation and the passing of time. The second right arm is coiled by a

8.7 *Shiva as Nataraja, or Lord of the Dance*. Naltunai Isvaram Temple, Punjai, India, c. 1000. Bronze.

Shiva is one of the primary avatars of Brahman, the Unbounded, the universal spirit of all things.

snake that symbolizes regeneration, while the hand forms a *mudra*, a symbolic gesture that here is a sign of protection. The far left hand balances a flame that symbolizes destruction, while the other left hand points to his feet. The left foot is elevated in the dance, indicating release from this earth, and the right foot crushes the personification of ignorance. The circle of fire that radiates around *Shiva* shows the unfolding and transformation of the universe and its destruction.

Buddhism

Rooted from Hinduism, the Buddhist religion follows the teachings of Siddhartha Gautama, a prince born in India near Nepal around 563 BCE. He fled from court life to become a homeless holy man and later achieved enlightenment, or Buddhahood. The Buddha, also known as Sakyamuni (meaning "the sage of the Sakya clan"), continued to teach for the next forty-five years until his death. Buddhists, like Hindus, hold that humans are perpetually reincarnated, most often into lives of suffering, based on the deeds of their past lives. By following the teachings of Sakyamuni, humans can overcome desires and the cycle of rebirth. Then they can attain nirvana, a transformation of their consciousness from the material world to the eternal realm.

For several hundred years after his death, Sakyamuni was represented by a set of symbols, but never as a human because he had achieved enlightenment. One symbol for Sakyamuni was the **stupa,** a sign of his death and attainment of nirvana. Originally, a stupa was a mound tomb. It eventually was transformed into a monument that contained the ashes or relics of a Buddha. An example of an early Buddhist stupa is the *Great Stupa* at Sanchi, third century BCE to CE first century (Fig. 8.8), a solid, dome-shaped mound of earth enclosed in brick or stone. The form of the mound represented the cosmos as the world

mountain, the dwelling place of the ancient gods and a sacred womb of the universe. The structure is encircled with a low balustrade wall containing four heraldic gates, all highly adorned with rich carvings. The gates, called **toranas**, are located at the four cardinal points in the circular wall. The balustrades are also densely carved. Pilgrims would come from all over the world to walk clockwise around the stupa and chant, meditate, and pray as they observed the special meanings of the carvings. The square enclosure on top of the dome symbolized the heavens, surmounted by the mast with umbrellas, called **chatras**, that united the world with the paradises above. The chatras signified the levels of human consciousness through which the human soul ascends to enlightenment. The stupa as a symbol of Buddhahood spread throughout Asia, although there were local variations in its design.

The eastern torana in front of the *Great Stupa* rises thirty-four feet. The gate contains many scenes showing episodes from the life of Sakyamuni, with Sakyamuni presented only by symbols, such as the empty throne, which represents Buddha's separation from his princely life; footprints, which represent the Buddha's spiritual journey; and the elephant, a bodily form assumed by the Buddha. Additionally, sensuous images of the nature deities have been retained from the early Vedic sculptural tradition. Small stupas carved on the gateway reliefs

8.8 *Great Stupa.* Sanchi, India, third century BCE–first century CE. Dome, 50′ high. Robert Harding Picture Library.

Siddhartha Gautama, whose early teachings founded Buddhism, is represented symbolically in this structure and carvings.

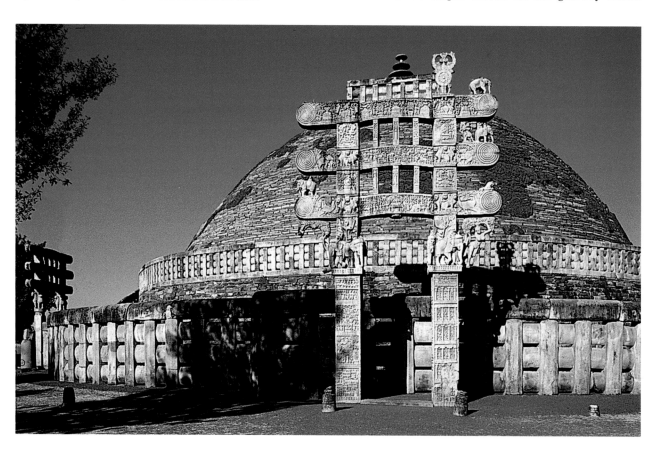

symbolize Sakyamuni in his attainment of Buddhahood; they look very much like the *Great Stupa*.

CONNECTION One of the carvings from the *Great Stupa* at Sanchi is the Yakshi (Figure 12.17, page 345).

As later sects emphasized a more personal Buddha, images of him in human form were produced, along with the traditional symbols. At first, these figurative sculptures were variations of older Hindu spirits, with certain Buddha-identifying attributes, such as the topknot of hair (a cranial bump indicating wisdom) and a circle between the eyebrows. Earlobes were long, since Sakyamuni was once a bejeweled prince.

In still later images, the emphasis was on the general serenity of Buddhahood. The red sandstone of the *Seated Buddha*, late fifth to early sixth centuries (Fig. 8.9), has been carved and polished to a smooth, flawless finish. The statue seems to represent a generalized holy being rather

8.9 *Seated Buddha*. Sarnath, Uttar Pradesh, India, late fifth–early sixth centuries. Sandstone, 63″ high. Sarnath Museum.

Later in Buddhism its founder is depicted as the Enlightened One, the Buddha.

than a specific person. The body seems almost weightless. The face is rendered as a perfect oval, and the torso and limbs are simplified into graceful lines and elegant shapes. Clothing is sheer and clinging, unworldly in its draping and its perfection. The tall arches of the brow, downcast eyes, and quiet but sensual mouth all speak of a transcendent serenity. The Buddha is seated in lotus position on a throne, under which are carved worshippers around the Wheel of the Law. Abstracted foliage above and around Sakyamuni represents the Tree of Enlightenment. His hands are posed in a preaching gesture.

Over the centuries, Buddhist beliefs became more complex. Bodhisattvas are living beings who have attained Buddhahood but have chosen to remain on earth to help others. While Buddhas in their serenity in nirvana may seem remote to struggling humans, the Bodhisattvas are immediate personal intercessors who give aid. *The Water and Moon Guanyin Bodhisattva*, c. 1100 (Fig. 8.10), is the most powerful Bodhisattva, with a great capacity for salvation. Depictions of *Guanyin* vary radically, with two to twelve arms, often crowned, sometimes with a muscular male body and sometimes with an effeminate body. In our example, the body is graceful and the face beautiful and serene. The elegance of the body and right hand, along

8.10 *The Water and Moon Guanyin Bodhisattva*, China, Song Dynasty, c. 1100. Painted wood, 7′ 11″ high. The Nelson-Atkins Museum of Art, Kansas City.

This image depicts a Buddhist living person who has attained Enlightenment, but has chosen to remain on earth to help others attain it.

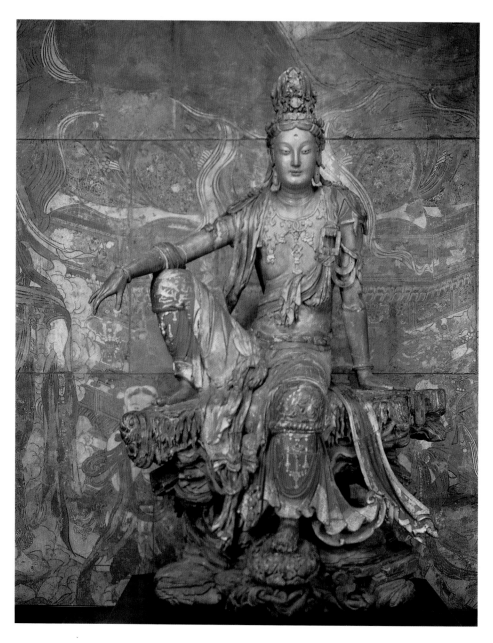

with the lavish carving and rich colors, make this sculpture sensually appealing. The diagonals of the figure's right leg and arm balance the verticals of the torso and the left limbs, while the flowing curves of the drapery unite all. Compare the similarities and differences of polytheistic imagery with those of the pantheistic religions.

Monotheism

Monotheism is the belief in one god and that there is no other.

Judaism

Judaism is one of the oldest monotheistic religions of the Western world and also the foundation of Christianity and Islam. The Jews consider themselves the Chosen People and have a special covenant with their God and Creator, Yahweh, who alone is to be worshiped and none other. It was thought by scholars that the making of art images in the Jewish faith was forbidden because of the Second Commandment. However, images have been found in scripture illumination and on the walls of ancient synagogues. In Figure 8.11, we see the interior of the *Synagogue at Dura-Europos*, dated CE 245–256, which is covered with paintings depicting Old Testament themes. Dura-Europos was an outpost in Syria and was probably founded around 323 BCE.

The *Synagogue at Dura-Europos*, originally a private home with a courtyard, was transformed into a place of worship in the second century CE. The paintings on the walls were didactic, illustrating stories found in the Hebrew Bible. The figures have stylized gestures, lack expression, mass, and depth, and, for the most part, stand in frontal rows, as a means to explain a concept or illustrate a story. Action was not depicted. Yahweh was shown as a hand emerging from the top of the panels. Evidently, this kind of image making was not forbidden for the Jews, but the worship of images was.

Christianity

Unlike Judaism, the traditions of **Christianity** have many kinds of images of God. Some Christians understand God as a single being, whereas others conceive of God as a Trinity, with three persons in one: the Father, Son, and Holy Spirit. The Father is usually depicted as an aged patriarch, wise, powerful, and judging. The Son was incarnated as Jesus and founded the Christian religion. He is believed by Christians to be the Savior of souls. Images

8.11 *Synagogue at Dura-Europos*, Syria, 245–256 CE. Interior, with wall paintings of biblical themes. National Museum, Damascus.

Images of the Hebrew deity Yahweh were forbidden; however, at times his hand appears in Old Testament paintings found on temple walls.

of Jesus range from a babe in arms to a young man in life, death, and resurrection. The Holy Spirit is represented as a symbol, either a dove or a flame of fire.

As an actual historical figure, Jesus is the most commonly depicted of the Trinity. In early images, he was a youthful, protecting shepherd, a comforting figure to early Christians, who were often persecuted by Romans. Once Christianity became the official state religion of the Roman Empire in the fourth century, Jesus was depicted as a royal ruler. Images of Jesus as miracle worker, judge, and teacher usually combine a narration of historical events with layers of symbolism.

In *Madonna of the Meadow* (Fig. 8.12) by Raphael Sanzio, c. 1505, Jesus is the robust, beautiful child in the center, with his cousin, St. John the Baptist, at the left, and Mary, his mother, who towers over both children. Although the children look youthful and sweet, their

solemn composure and the cross they hold portends their roles of savior and prophet. All figures are totally human, but their dignity and serenity seem divine. The blues, reds, and greens add to the sense of harmony. Mary and the two children fit into an implied triangle—a stable, symmetrical, sacred shape recalling the Trinity. Mary's silhouette completely contains the form of Jesus, attesting that she is Jesus' mother and establishing her as a symbol for the Christian church, through which Jesus remains present on earth. The large, sheltered body of water in the background implies a harbor, and Mary was known as the Port of Salvation.

In contrast, the *Crucifixion* from *The Isenheim Altarpiece*, c. 1510–1515 (Fig. 8.13), by Matthias Grünewald, shows Jesus at death, which for Christians is a moment both of annihilation and of redemption from sin. The dark, gloomy background obliterates all landscape detail. The

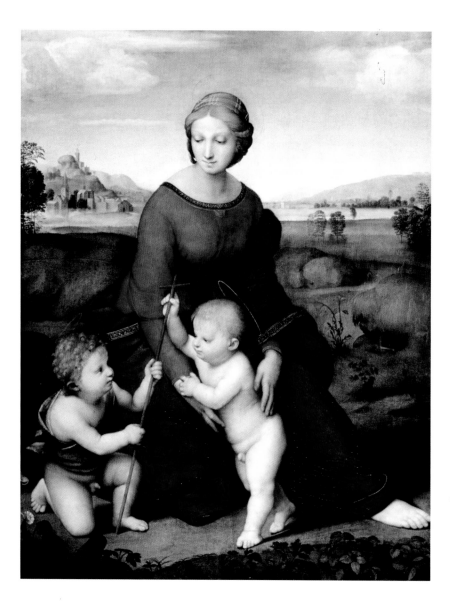

8.12 RAPHAEL. *Madonna of the Meadow*, Italy, c. 1505. Panel painting, 44 $\frac{1}{2}$″ × 34 $\frac{1}{4}$″. Kunsthistorisches Museum, Vienna.

Images of Christianity's deity can be depicted as one person or in three as in the Trinity. Jesus Christ is believed to be both divine and human, but is often presented in his human form, seen here as a baby.

grisly details of Jesus' sore-ridden and scraped skin, convulsed body, and drooping head are meant to be a realistic picture of a terrible death. At the same time, the *Isenheim Altarpiece* is a conceptual rather than a realistic representation. The bottom panel, which shows Jesus' body being placed in the tomb, would sit directly above the altar, where the body of Jesus is offered at Christian Eucharistic rituals in the form of bread and wine. The lamb in the *Crucifixion* panel, holding a cross and bleeding into a chalice, symbolizes animal sacrifices conducted by Jews in the past and the current offering of bread and wine. People who were present at the Crucifixion, such as Roman soldiers, are omitted from this painting, while St. John the Baptist is shown, although he had already died. Saints on side panels were associated with cures for the sick.

The painting was a form of consolation for patients in a hospital, for they could see the horrendous suffering of Christ and relate it to their own suffering. Also, the dark, suffering-filled *Crucifixion* panel opens in the center, and behind it are three joyful scenes from the life of Jesus—his conception, birth, and resurrection from the dead, all in brilliant colors.

CONNECTION For an example of a very early image of Jesus, see the *Catacomb of Sts. Peter and Marcellinus* (Fig. 9.17, page 253). Turn to *The Last Judgment* (Fig. 12.19, page 347) to see an image of Jesus as judge.

Islam

Islam was founded by Mohammed in seventh-century Arabia. Islam believes in complete submission to Allah, the same deity of the Jewish and Christian faiths. Islam's sacred scriptures, the Koran, contain its articles of faith. Whereas

8.13 MATTHIAS GRÜNEWALD. *The Isenheim Altarpiece*, Germany, c. 1510–1515. Oil on wood; center panel: *Crucifixion*, 9′ 9 1/2″ × 10′ 9″. Musée d'Unterlinden, Colmar, France.

Here the human Christ is depicted in his sacrificial crucifixion, which fulfilled the Christian prophecy of redemption as written in their scriptures.

8.14 *Mohammed's Ascent into Heaven.* From Nizami's *Khamsa (Five Poems)*, Tabriz, Iran, 1539–43. Ms. Or. 2265, fol. 195a. Made for Tahmasp. Safavid dynasty. British Library, London, Great Britain.

In a glorious array of fire and clouds, the veiled Mohammed ascends into heaven accompanied by angels.

images of Allah were forbidden, the Prophet Mohammed is sometimes shown in religious manuscript art. Figure 8.14 depicts *Mohammed's Ascent into Heaven,* a royal miniature that illustrates a copy of a collection of poems by the famous Persian poet Nizami Ganjavi. Mohammed's face is veiled, as was customary in such depictions, out of respect for the holy and for fear they could never be rightly portrayed. Prior to Mohammed's ascent into heaven, he embarked on a night journey on Buraq, a white winged horse that carried him through various stages of heaven, where he met several Jewish and Christian prophets, and also visited hell. Mohammed's night journey is important in Islamic thought, and is seen as symbolizing each man's spiritual journey. The saturated colors, elaborate details, and intricate renderings of clouds and flames mark this as a royal commission. In contrast to the rich center, the margins are covered with monochrome drawings of animals in surrounded by vegetation.

HUMANS RESPOND TO GOD

Humans use religious ceremonies, prayers, and rituals to acknowledge God and to request what they need for earthly or spiritual existence. Many religions require humans to make offerings to the gods, as outward signs of their devotion. Art frequently is part of this process.

Ceremonies

The Kwakiutl of the Pacific Northwest dwelled in two sites corresponding with summer food gathering and elaborate winter rituals, such as marriages, initiations, feasts, potlatches, and dramatic performances. Special houses were built for the winter ceremonies. Performers in full masquerade told their stories and became the supernatural beings of their masks.

Our example is the twentieth-century *Transformation Mask* (Fig. 8.1). During performance, its character changed from that of an earthly being to that of a supernatural being. At the critical moment in the story-drama, the dancer would turn and manipulate the mask with hidden strings and devices, and then turn back in a completely different mask. This surprising transformation might be the changing of a bear or a sea creature into one of the horrendous cannibal spirits. The intent of this magical event was to make humans fear the supernatural. Besides being superbly carved, the mask is exquisitely painted. Bright, bold colors in undulating shapes create overall harmonious compositions that complement the facial contours. This distinct aesthetic with its flowing curvilinear style is visible throughout Kwakiutl art forms, both past and present.

 CONNECTION Figure 6.20, page 144, shows a large *Halibut Feast Dish* used in a potlatch.

Offerings

In central Mexico, hundreds of believers leave small votive paintings called *retablos* at certain important religious shrines, as a form of prayer and thanks for a divine favor. Pictures with bright colors and text dramatically record emotional, miraculous events. These artworks also may contain holy cards, pictures of loved ones, diplomas, or legal papers.

Our focus figure here is the *Retablo of Maria de la Luz Casillas and Children* (Fig. 8.15). The translation reads:

> I give thanks to the Holiest Virgin of San Juan de los Lagos for having made me so great a miracle of saving me in a dangerous operation that was performed on me for the second time on the 9th day of October 1960, in Los Angeles, California. Which put me at the doors of death

8.15, *above* *Retablo of Maria de la Luz Casillas and Children,* Central Mexico, 1961. Oil on metal, 7″ × 10″.

This offering is a prayer of thanksgiving to the Virgin of San Juan.

but entrusted to so miraculous a Virgin I could recover my health, which I make apparent the present retablo: in sign of thanksgiving . . . (Durand and Massey 1995: 164)

The Virgin of San Juan de los Lagos is a small statue of Mary, the Mother of Jesus, in a shrine in the central Mexican state of Jalisco. Multiple scenes are common on retablos, and, in this example, we see Maria twice, both as a helpless and vulnerable patient on the operating table in a foreign land and as the supplicant with her children imploring the help of the Virgin. In the retablo, the Virgin looms large in the bleak, gray room, with golden rays, miraculously intervening in a fearful episode. Extraneous details are omitted to better emphasize the victim's helplessness and the Virgin's power.

Compare the retablo with the crafted offerings of the Balinese people. The Balinese have many days of religious observance, which they commemorate by giving handmade offerings. They regard these offerings as artworks and consider many of their people to be artists. Religion and art are integrated components of everyday life. Often, handmade offerings are modest, but on festival days, women make and carry to temples more elaborate offerings, such as the *Offering with Cili-Shaped Crown,* from the mid-1980s (Fig. 8.16). This intricate sculpture of fruit and flowers is cut and woven with palm leaves. An ancient symbol of wealth, fertility, and luck, the cili is a simplified

8.16, *right* *Offering with Cili-Shaped Crown,* Bali, c. 1985. Flowers, fruit, and palm leaves, approximately 24″ tall.

See also the text accompanying Figure 5.8 for more on art making in Bali. This intricately woven cili crown is an ancient symbol of wealth, fertility, and luck.

woman's head with a large, fanlike headdress radiating from it. In temple rituals, the gods accept the essence of the offering; afterward, any foodstuff that has not touched the ground is eaten in the temple or by the family making the offering. Offerings in the Balinese sense mean to give back in thanks and do not have the connotation of sacrificing something.

Sacrifices

History has shown that various forms of religious blood sacrifices have been practiced by humankind throughout the ages.

Judeo-Christian religions recognized the offering of foodstuffs and have a history of blood sacrifice. Cain offered farm produce to God; Abel offered an animal and animal fat; the priest Melchizedek prepared a ritual meal for an offering for Abraham. One famous story of sacrifice concerns Abraham, who prepared to kill his son Isaac at the command of God, but at the last minute he was allowed to substitute the slaughter of a ram. Our focus figure is a gilded bronze relief panel, *Sacrifice of Isaac* (Fig. 8.17), sculpted by Lorenzo Ghiberti in 1401–1402. It shows the emotionally intense moment when the youthful Isaac is bound on an altar of sacrifice, as his fierce-faced father Abraham holds the knife to his son's throat. The curves of their bodies echo each other, with Isaac pulling away as Abraham is poised to lunge forward. The nude body of Isaac is idealized and perfect, increasing the merit of the sacrifice. The intervention of an angel halted the sacrifice, and food, in the form of a ram (not visible in our detail), became an acceptable alternative offering. Although blood sacrifices are no longer offered in mainstream Christian religions, the Eucharistic offering of bread and wine may be celebrated, using many skillfully crafted art items.

In other cultures, human offerings to deities also entailed sacrifice, sometimes involving the spilling of human blood. In the various Mesoamerican cultures—Maya,

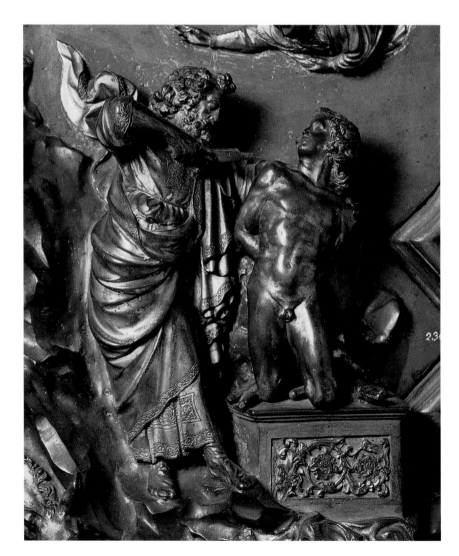

8.17 Lorenzo Ghiberti. *Sacrifice of Isaac* (detail), Florence, Italy, 1401–1402. Gilded bronze, 21″ × 17 1/2″. Museo Nazionale del Bargello, Florence.

This relief illustrates the ultimate test of faith in the Jewish and Christian religions.

8.18 *Shield Jaguar and Lady Xoc.* Classic Maya. From a palace at Yaxchilan, Chiapas, Mexico, c. 750. Relief.

This relief depicts a blood sacrifice that was required of the nobility in the Maya religion.

Toltec, Aztec, and others in Central America—the sun was believed to be ever thirsty for blood to stave off the power of the moon and was symbolized by a fiery tongue. In our comparison figure *Shield Jaguar and Lady Xoc*, dated c. 750 (Fig. 8.18), we see an example of a bloodletting ceremony, in which the Mayan ruler holds a torch over his principal wife as she pulls a thorny rope through a hole in her tongue. Those participating in blood sacrifices had to be high ranking, shown by their wrist bracelets, necklaces, crowns, and garb. Their flattened foreheads were signs of beauty, an unnatural effect created by binding boards on the soft skulls of very young children of the nobility. More extreme forms of blood sacrifice were practiced, such as cutting out the hearts of captured warriors or the captains of ball teams. Ballplayers were important members of society, and ball games were important religious rituals in which the ball itself and the opposing teams symbolized the terrible balance between the sun and the moon.

CONNECTION For more on the Mesoamerican ball games and their meaning, see the Mayan ball court in Figure 15.12, page 442.

Prayers

Prayer is a vehicle of communication between human beings and the gods, and it may take many forms. Our focus figure is from the Hopis of North America, who make small sculptures that act as a form of prayer. The Hopi believe that *kachinas,* or spirits of dead ancestors, dwell in their community for six months in winter and spring. Kachinas ensure the welfare of the community and sufficient moisture for crops. Male members of the Hopi community perform as kachinas during religious festivals.

Kachina performers also carve dolls that reproduce the costume of specific spirits. Our example, the *Ahola Kachina*, dated 1942, by Jimmie Kewanwytewa (Fig. 8.19), is the primary spirit at an important celebration. It is identifiable by the dome-shaped mask, yellow on one side and gray on the other, covered with small crosses. Other identifying attributes of the costume include the large, inverted black triangle on the face and the feathers from an eagle's tail that project from the head. The colors on the dolls, which reproduce the costumes, represent sacred directions: north is symbolized by blue or green; west by yellow; south by red; east by white; the heavens by multicolors; and the nadir by black. During ceremonies, children receive the dolls to educate them about the individual kachinas and the elaborate costumes and rituals. Women receive them as symbols of fertility. The dolls are hung from rafters in houses as blessings and as prayers for rain and good crops. Older dolls are stiffly posed, but newer ones are more naturally proportioned and often appear in active poses. Bright acrylic colors are now used, and feathers are often carved, as certain birds become endangered.

A comparative example of an art object used as a form of prayer is the African *Power Figure*, such as the sculpture in

Figure 8.20, which would be used to counter the evil influence of enemies, whether human, animal, or spiritual. This example is dated c. 1875–1900. Sculptors carve the power figure with an open mouth, indicating that the sculpture will "speak out" on behalf of anyone who is beset by evil. Shamans activate them, first by ritually placing medicines in cavities in the figure's abdomen or in the back or head. Then they release the figure's power by driving in one metal nail or blade for each request for help. Once effective, the exact nail representing a particular request must be removed. This *Power Figure* is visually dramatic, with its compact form, expressive face, and bristling nails. Power figures are rarely used now, as African religious practices are evolving, and rituals may be abandoned or amalgamated into other beliefs.

The Cosmos

Artists in various religious traditions have created artworks that map the cosmos, showing the origin of the world, the structure of the universe, spiritual beings, the place of humans in relation to the gods, or a diagram of time.

The images on the *Ceiling of the Sistine Chapel* is our focus figure, painted by Michelangelo (Fig. 8.21) from 1508 to 1512, which present the origin of the universe, of human

8.19 Jimmie Kewanwytewa. *Ahola Kachina*, Hopi, Third Mesa, Oraibi, 1942. Cottonwood, paint, feathers, wool, 13″ high. Museum of Northern Arizona.

These doll figures act as a form of prayer for the welfare of the community and as a teaching aid for the young.

8.20 *Power Figure (Nkisi n'kondi)*, Kongo, Zaire, 1998. Wood, nails, blades, medicinal material with cowrie shell, 46 ¼″ high. Detroit Museum of Art.

This figure is used as a form of prayer for protection against evil influences from enemies.

8.21 MICHELANGELO. *Ceiling of the Sistine Chapel*, The Vatican, Rome, Italy, 1508–1512. Fresco, approximately 128′ × 45′.

These Christian scenes present the origins of the universe, human beings and sin.

8.22 *Mandala of Samvara* (*Kharamukha Cakrasamvara Mandala*), Tibet, c. 16th century. Water-based pigments on cotton cloth. 23″ high, 18″ wide.

This image diagrams a map of the structure and relationships of all entities of the universe.

beings, and of sin. Pope Julius II commissioned the work; more accurately, the pontiff's strong will triumphed and Michelangelo reluctantly acquiesced. The artist felt that he was a sculptor and that painting was a less noble art form. Originally, the work was to consist only of the twelve apostles with some other ornamentation. But as Michelangelo proceeded, he changed the imagery from the apostles to nine scenes from Genesis, along with seven prophets and five sibyls. Illusionistic marble frames subdivide the broad expanse of the ceiling.

At the center bottom of Figure 8.21 is a panel showing God as a powerful-bodied, older man in pink robes, separating the light in the lower right from the darkness in the upper left. Next, God creates the sun and the moon and then separates the water from land. Following are the creation of Adam, then Eve, and original sin, in which Adam and Eve break God's commandment and are expelled from Paradise. The three center panels at the top are concerned with stories of Noah, the patriarch of the human race after a devastating flood destroyed most life on earth. These cosmic moments are depicted in bright, clear colors against plain backgrounds, emphasizing the bodies' dramatic shapes.

Our comparative example, a mandala, is a radially balanced, geometric diagram augmented by images of deities, humans, and symbols of the universe. Together, they form a map of the structure and relationships among all entities of the cosmos, in accordance with Hindu or Buddhist beliefs. By meditating on the mandala, people can begin to grasp these cosmic relations and understand their place within them.

The mandala begins with a circle, which symbolizes the void before all creation. Into this emptiness the image of the God will appear. In our example, the *Mandala of Samvara*, dated c. sixteenth century from Tibet (Fig. 8.22), the deity Samvara (also referred to in this work as Cakrasamvara, who rules and sets into motion the universe) erotically embraces his female Buddha consort, Vajravarahi. Samvara, an angry emanation of the Absolute Being, is shown with blue skin and multiple arms, symbols of his power and divinity. He is pictured here with a donkey face, because those meditating on this image learn the illusory nature of the physical body. Radiating from this center are eight paths, which terminate at the sides or corners of a square. These paths refer to rays of light, the cardinal directions, and elements, such as fire, water, wind, and earth. Other fierce deities, combinations of animal and human forms, occupy these paths.

While the inner circles contain deities, the large outer circle encloses charnel fields, where vultures, wild dogs, or cremation fires consume the bodies of the dead (there are generally no graveyards in Southeast Asia). The details are both gruesome and gleeful, vividly depicting harmful forces. Immediately outside the ring of the charnel fields are eight auspicious signs, such as a lotus blossom and a white conch shell, which represent divine gifts offered to Buddha. The outermost areas of the mandala are populated with images of monks, mystics, and more deities.

The underlying geometry makes the mandala both simple and complex. During meditation, it can be followed from the outside inward to the center circle, indicating stages of increasing enlightenment. In reverse, the mandala represents the emanation of the creative force responsible for all life, which originates from Samvara. The mandala reinforces the belief that the cosmos, including the physical and spiritual worlds, is an uninterrupted whole of continually fluctuating energy states. Red is a common color of Tibetan mandalas and predominates here. The brilliant blue comes from lapis lazuli, an expensive pigment derived from grinding semiprecious stones. Thus, the work was probably commissioned by a wealthy patron.

PLACES OF WORSHIP AND THEIR GENERAL CHARACTERISTICS

Since prehistory, people have set aside special places for religious worship. All of them, from simple to grand, are designed to reveal something of the spiritual realm and to provide an experience beyond the normal and mundane. Across cultures and religions, places of worship may:

- Shelter a congregation
- House sacred objects
- Incorporate elements of nature
- Incorporate symbolic geometry in their dimensions or the determination of their location
- Be sites of sacred ceremonies and pilgrimages

Regarding the first point, it is sufficient to say that places of worship were often designed to house a large group of people, all of whom are participating at the same time in ritual observances. The other four characteristics are explained more fully here.

Housing Sacred Objects

Many places of worship were built specifically to house a sacred image, text, or artifact of a religion. Temples, cathedrals, churches, shrines, and altars may contain a sacred object. For example, in the Jewish religion, the most holy structure is called the *Ark of the Covenant*. It is a special tabernacle that held these sacred objects, as depicted in Figure 8.23. Moses constructed the Ark according to instructions from Yahweh, so that the prophet could communicate with and receive revelations from him during the exodus from Egypt. Our image is a mosaic from the fourth century CE, which depicts the *Ark* in the center of

8.23 The *Ark of the Covenant* and sanctuary implements. Hammath, near Tiberias, 4th century. Mosaic. Israel Antiquities Authority, Jerusalem.

This is the image of the tabernacle (enclosure) that houses the Hebrew sacred scriptures of the Torah.

the composition. Sanctuary implements, including elaborate seven-branched candelabra, flank the tabernacle.

Other religions also house sacred objects in their places of worship, as we shall see later in this chapter. Often, these are specially constructed buildings, such as temples or churches. In many cases, however, formal structures are not necessary. For example, among many African religions, shrines that hold sacred objects are part of ordinary houses. This is an important aspect of many African religions, as they weave spiritual forces with everyday life.

Incorporating Elements of Nature

Places of worship can be natural sites: mountains, springs, and sacred trees or groves. Mountains have been meeting places between heaven and earth or dwelling places of divine beings. Rocks can be seen as containers or symbols for spirits and deities. The earth and water are the sources or sustainers of life. Trees may be seen as sources of truth and symbols of the cosmos, existing simultaneously in the underworld, the earth, and the heavens. Fire, light, and the sun are divine symbols or sometimes spirits themselves.

The focus figure is the *Ziggurat at Ur* (Fig. 8.24), dated c. 2150–2050 BCE. It is a sacred artificial mountain erected by the Sumerians of the city of Ur to honor their special deity from among the Sumerian pantheon of gods. Its corners point toward the four points of the compass, reflecting the movement of the sun. The word *ziggurat* means "mountain" or "pinnacle." Surrounded by flat land, this terraced tower of rubble and brick seemed to reach into the heavens. The *Ziggurat at Ur* has three broad staircases,

each with one hundred steps, leading to a temple-shrine forty feet above the ground, dedicated to protective gods and goddesses and attended to by special orders of priests and priestesses.

The Shinto religion in Japan teaches that forests and enormous stones are sacred dwellings of the gods of nature, who are called the **Kami**, all connected to growth and renewal. Our comparison example, the *Main Shrine at Ise* (Fig. 8.25), is located in a forest, on a holy site. Only the roof is visible above a high, protecting fence. Through ritual, the Kami are prevailed upon to enter the shrine, where their powers are worshiped and their aid solicited. A mirror placed inside facilitates their coming into the shrine.

The *Main Shrine at Ise* is made of natural materials, primarily wood and thatch. It is rebuilt every twenty years to exactly the same specifications, so what we see in Figure 8.25 is both a new building and a structure that dates from c. 685. With each rebuilding, the builders observe careful rituals and express gratitude as they take wood from the forest. Boards taken from the same tree are placed together in the building of the shrine. The wood is left plain and unpainted to retain its natural character, and it is carefully fitted and joined with pegs. Nails are not used. The golden color of the wood and the simple but striking geometry are dramatic and impressive.

8.24 *Ziggurat at Ur* (partially reconstructed), Third Dynasty of Ur, Iraq, c. 2150–2050 BCE.

This structure was built to house and honor the Sumerian deity of the ancient city of Ur.

8.25, *above* *Main Shrine at Ise* (roofline), Japan, c. 685, rebuilt every twenty years.

Careful rituals are observed as this structure is ritually rebuilt.

CONNECTION Compare the basic design of the Shinto shrine to the *Toba Batak House*, Figure 6.32, page 151

Using Geometry Symbolically

Many cultures use geometry and symmetry to symbolize divinity, all-encompassing totality, perfection, and time-lessness. Such geometry may determine the placement or orientation of religious sites, or a building's plan, layout, or elevation.

Our focus is on *Stonehenge*, dated c. 2000 BCE (Fig. 8.26), located in Wiltshire, England. It was built at a time when religion and science were not separate but were a single unified means of understanding natural forces. Thus, *Stonehenge* is likely an altar for religious rituals as well as an astronomical device that maps solar and planetary movement upon the earth. The stone arrangement marks the midsummer solstice, essential to an agrarian civilization dependent on successful crop planting.

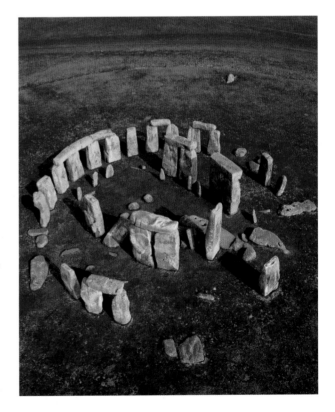

8.26 *Stonehenge*, Wiltshire, England, c. 2000 BCE. Diameter: 97'; upright stones with lintel, approximately 24' high.

It is likely that the stone arrangement marks the midsummer solstice, needed for planting cycles.

Other Neolithic stone arrangements in the area align with *Stonehenge*, creating a larger network that may have mapped force fields within the earth.

The first building phase of *Stonehenge* was a gigantic circular ditch, with rubble piled to create an outer bank. The later core of *Stonehenge* consists of a ninety-seven-foot-diameter ring of colossal sarsen stones, twenty-four feet high with their capping lintel. An inner ring of bluestones in turn surrounds a horseshoe-shaped stone arrangement and, finally, an altar stone in the center. A heel stone, separate from the circle, marks the solstice. Builders dragged the stones twenty-four miles, pounded and rubbed them to shape, and likely set them in place using ropes and earthen ramps. *Stonehenge* includes several large rings of holes dug into the ground that conceptually connect the center stones to the surrounding earth.

For comparison, we see centuries later how simple geometric shapes formed the basis of a Roman building that alluded to divine qualities of perfection and completion. The *Pantheon*, 118–125 (Fig. 8.27), is a shrine to the chief deities of the Roman Empire. A 142-foot-diameter sphere fits into the interior space, making the width of the building equal to its height. The dome, a perfect hemisphere, is the top half of that sphere. A thirty-foot circular opening at top (the **oculus**, or eye) creates a shaft of sunlight that dramatically illuminates the interior. Squares are inscribed in the dome and wall surfaces and are the

8.27 *Pantheon*, Rome, Italy, 118–125. Concrete and marble; 142′ from floor to opening in dome. © Sylvain Sonnet/Corbis

This structure was designed using geometric shapes to which the Romans attributed divine qualities of perfection and completion.

8.28 *Shrine to Vairocana Buddha.* Longmen, Luoyang, Valley of the Yellow River, China, c. 600–650. Natural rock carving, 50′ high.

This colossal statue represents the universal principle dominating all life and phenomena.

basis of the pattern on the marble inlay floor. The entire structure is symmetrical, both inside and out, and creates the impression of loftiness, simplicity, and balance.

In fact, throughout this chapter, we will see the circle and square and verticality in many religious structures, and geometry was important for their placement and orientation.

Providing Sites for Sacred Ceremonies and Pilgrimages

Places of worship can be sites where sacred ceremonies are performed and destinations for pilgrimages. Sometimes there is no special architecture, only the use of the arts— music, dance, singing, literature, or the visual arts. In the Southwest United States, the making of sand paintings has constituted an essential part of Navajo religious ceremonies for centuries. These impermanent paintings are made directly on clean-swept floors of houses and are destroyed in the course of the ceremony. Very few have ever been photographed or documented; however, the rituals are fixed, and certain symbols must be repeated each time. To cure illness, ensure success in hunting, or promote fertility, the artist-priest chants and prays while making the painting using the natural elements of colored sand, crushed stones, charcoal, and pollen. The person in need sits in the center of the painting to receive the supernatural power. Sometimes ceremonies are performed for the earth itself.

> **CONNECTION** The cave paintings at Lascaux and Aboriginal paintings were essential parts of rituals (see Fig. 6.3, page 129 , and Fig. 6.4, page 134).

A pilgrimage is a journey to a shrine or sacred place for believers hoping to receive special blessings or deepening of faith. The concept of journey is both metaphoric and actual, as the soul's spiritual search for understanding has been likened to a physical journey. Almost all major religions incorporate the concept of pilgrimages into their belief systems, and so Muslims journey to Mecca, Jews to Jerusalem, Catholics to various sites such as Lourdes, Hindus to shrines dedicated to various deities, and so on.

Our first example is from the Longmen Caves in China, a huge complex of cave-shrines housing thousands of sacred statues, which is a Buddhist pilgrimage destination. At Longmen, 1,352 caves have been carved into the limestone mountains, with more than 97,000 statues and 3,600 inscriptions dedicated to Buddha. The largest of these is the monumental *Shrine to Vairocana Buddha*, dated c. 600–650 (Fig. 8.28), who is the universal principle dominating all life and all phenomena. He is attended by

8.29 Le Corbusier. *Notre Dame du Haut*, Ronchamps, France, 1950–1955.

The church's design recalls praying hands, dove wings, and a boat hull, Christian symbols of divine generosity.

demons and lesser buddhas who govern their own worlds, a model used by tyrant emperors in China to justify their rule. In fact, the carvings at the Longmen caves were supported by imperial patronage. The Buddha at the center is serene, massive, and volumetric, with drapery defined with a few simple curves, to enhance the colossal scale of the carving.

Another pilgrimage destination is the small church *of Notre Dame du Haut* (Fig. 8.29), a Catholic chapel in the Vosges Mountains of France, built between 1950 and 1955. The design recalls praying hands, the wings of a dove, and the shape of a boat, all Christian symbols of divine generosity to humans. The shape of the structure resembles sculpture. To accommodate very large crowds on holy days, the church was fitted with an outdoor altar and pulpit (visible toward the right in this photograph), so that services could be conducted for twelve thousand pilgrims on the lawn. Then, the building's exterior becomes a monumental sculptural backdrop for the religious event. The interior of *Notre Dame du Haut* is a relatively small space with limited seating, almost mystically dark and cavelike, with deep-set, square, colored-glass windows piercing the walls.

Another site for comparison is the *Dome of the Rock* shrine, which was built in Jerusalem in 687–692 (Fig. 8.30). This historic place is a sacred pilgrimage for Jews, Christians, and Muslims. This oldest example of great Islamic architecture was built by the caliph Abd al-Malik as a monument to the triumph of Islam over the land of the Jews and Christians in 638. Built on a rock platform,

8.30 *Dome of the Rock*, Jerusalem, 687–692.

This pilgrimage shrine marks the site of the triumph of Islam in Jerusalem.

it occupies the site believed to be the burial place of Adam, the altar upon which Abraham's son Isaac was saved by the angel, the Hebrew Temple at Jerusalem destroyed by the Roman Emperor Titus in 70, and finally the stone from which Mohammed ascended to heaven and thereafter returned to his home in Mecca. The monumental shrine's design was influenced by the geometric characteristics of Roman and Byzantine architecture. Its structure is a highly ornamented octagonal platform topped with a gilded dome.

TEMPLE COMPLEXES AND LARGE-SCALE SACRED ARCHITECTURE

Some religious sites are more grand, extensive, and complex than what we have already seen. They are some of the most famous works of art in the world. They all incorporate the general characteristics of sacred sites that we saw at the beginning of this chapter. But we will see that they do much more than that. When a religion has become firmly established and tied to political power, these expensive, labor-intensive, long-term projects are possible. Thus, grand places of worship are expressions of temporal power, religious power, and broad cultural values. With imposing size and lavish detail, these structures are spectacles, amazing to see. In ceremonies, the individual is reduced to spectator, part of the throng that adds to the religious importance of the site.

First, compare the plans of six of the seven major sites we will study (Fig. 8.31). All are drawn to the same scale. Even the smallest, the *Kandarya Mahadeva Temple*, is imposing with its 130-foot height. The largest, the *Pyramid of the Sun* in Central Mexico, is truly enormous. The plans also reveal how important geometry is in these designs

A. HORUS TEMPLE
pylon facade 118' high

pylon

courtyard

pylon

hypostyle hall

B. ACROPOLIS
Parthenon approximately 60' high

to marketplace

Parthenon

slopes of the plateau

C. CHARTRES CATHEDRAL
north tower 377' high

tower

west facade

nave

apse

tower

transept

0   100   200   300
                    FEET

8.31 Comparison of the plans of various places of worship. Notice that all plans are drawn to the same scale and vary tremendously in size. Heights vary tremendously also; they are indicated next to each plan. A. *Horus Temple* (top left), B. *Acropolis* (middle left), C. *Chartres Cathedral* (lower left), D. *Pyramid of the Sun* (top center), E. *Kandarya Mahadeva Temple* (right), F. *Masjid-i-Shah* (lower center).

See Figure 8.36 for the plan of the Buddhist temple compound, the *Altar of Heaven,* which is too large to be shown to scale here.

to suggest perfection, completion, balance, and formality. Symmetry is an excellent visual metaphor for political power and divinity.

The plan of the seventh major site, the Buddhist *Altar of Heaven,* is shown in Figure 8.36. The temple compound is integrated into the design of a quarter-mile-wide park and will be discussed in that context. Let us begin our

study of religious compounds and large-scale sacred architecture with the Greeks.

The Greek Temple

In studying Greek temple design, we will use the Parthenon in Athens as our focus example. Athens is situated on

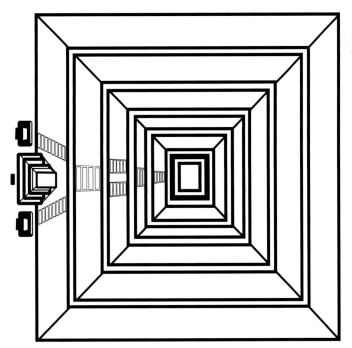

D. PYRAMID OF THE SUN
215' high

womb chamber   assembly hall

E. KANDARYA MAHADEVA TEMPLE
130' high

main plaza of Isfahan

polo goalposts

main portal of mosque

courtyard

lesser courtyard   lesser courtyard

F. MASJID-I-SHAH
minarets 110' high

0   100   200   300
FEET

a plain surrounded by mountains, with a high plateau in the center dedicated to the city's patroness, Athena. This plateau, the Acropolis, forms a dramatic setting for temples and is a mountain to climb in the pilgrimage journey. Smaller buildings, clustered along the steep approach, contrast dramatically with the large temples and open space at the top (see plan). It is visually impressive from many surrounding viewpoints.

8.32 IKTINOS AND KALLIKRATES. *Parthenon*, Athens, Greece, 447–432 BCE. Pentelic marble; columns 34′ high, dimensions of structure 228′ × 104′.

This structure is the standard Classical Greek temple using the post-and-lintel construction and the Doric Order.

Temple Design

The *Parthenon* (Fig. 8.32) is a good example of a standard Classical Greek temple. Following a three-hundred-year precedent, it is a two-room structure with pediments above the short sides and a colonnaded porch all around. It is more graceful and refined than older temples, but, like them, was covered using the post-and-lintel system. This particular style (or "order") of temple was called Doric and could be easily identified by its column. The Doric column had no base, a simple cushion capital, and a shaft that was fluted, or carved from top to bottom with thin, vertical channels. High-quality marble blocks were carefully stacked and finished so that the columns originally appeared seamless.

In designing the *Parthenon*, the architects Iktinos and Kallikrates often treated it more like a piece of sculpture than architecture. Like a pedestal, the steps form the base for the structure. They are higher at the middle of each side and lower at the corners, to counteract the illusion of sagging in the middle. Thus, the *Parthenon* contains optical illusions. The corner columns are thicker and placed closer to neighboring columns to compensate for the glaring bright sky behind them that would make them seem thinner. Outer columns lean slightly toward the middle of the building to make the *Parthenon* more visually cohesive. The shaft of the Doric column swells slightly at the middle, called *entasis*, to give the column a feeling of organic flexing.

 CONNECTION Near the Parthenon are the Propylaea and the Temple of Athena Nike (Fig. 2.36, page 48). See also Figure 2.37, page 48, for diagrams of the Doric, Ionic, and Corinthian orders.

Sculpture and Relief Carving

The *Parthenon* had two interior rooms for housing sacred objects, rooms that only a few priests entered. Religious ceremonies took place outside, so originally the exterior was richly adorned with sculpture and brightly painted. Large sculptures of the gods stood in the pediment and near the roof, and a long band of sculpture (three feet six inches high, 524 feet long), called a **frieze,** girded the top outside walls of the *Parthenon*'s two inner chambers.

8.33 *Horsemen* (from the Parthenon frieze), Athens, Greece, c. 440 BCE. Marble, 42″ high.

These images are carved in an upper band around the structure, representing part of the participants in the Panathenic Festival procession.

Carved c. 440 BCE, the frieze shows a long procession of Greek worshipers climbing up to the *Parthenon*, including marshals, youths, maidens, musicians, jar carriers, horsemen, and charioteers, some bringing animals for sacrifice. At the beginning of the procession, the worshipers are raucous and unorganized, like our *Horsemen* (Fig. 8.33). Gradually, the worshipers become solemn and orderly as they approach the gods. This is a depiction of the special Panathenaic Festival procession, which occurred only once every four years to bring a new ceremonial tunic to robe an ancient wooden statue of Athena.

The carving on the sculptural frieze is very high quality, an especially amazing feat given that the sculpture is almost twice the length of a football field and was completed in less than a decade. Overlapping, crisscrossing diagonals—horses legs, waving hands, drapery—communicate the bustle early on. Gods and humans are similarly rendered as rounded and lifelike, with carefully carved muscles. They are dignified, composed, well-proportioned, and idealized. The frieze is carved more deeply at the top and more shallowly at the bottom to make it clearer to viewers below.

Mathematical Proportions and Greek Philosophy

In their science, geometry, art, religion, and philosophy, the Greeks were engaged in a search for perfection. For example, they believed that certain geometric ratios and certain musical intervals resonated with the cosmic order and were in tune with the heavens. Thus, builders used a consistent set of proportions to determine the length and width of parts within the *Parthenon*, and they balanced horizontal and vertical elements to give the structure a quality of self-containment. By not being overwhelming in size, the *Parthenon* also reflects the Greek idea of the value of the individual. Now compare this Classic Greek temple with the following examples of worship places.

The Egyptian Temple

Egyptian temple design remained relatively constant for three thousand years, and so the study of one will illustrate the qualities of many.

Setting and History

Protected by the desert, life in ancient Egypt was unusually stable. Natural cycles, such as night and day and the annual flooding of the Nile River, provided powerful symbols for the Egyptian religion. The Egyptians used

8.34 *Great Pylon of the Horus Temple at Edfu*, Egypt, c. 237–57 BCE. The pylons are 118′ high and the façade is 230′ wide. Unlike most Egyptian cult temples, this one is located on the west side of the Nile River.

These "geometric" mountains flank the entrance to the temple, functioning both as a gate and a social barrier blocking the lower classes from entry.

symbolic geometry to demarcate sacred alignments in the landscape. East-west marked the path of the sun god, Re, symbolizing life, death, and resurrection. The north-south axis paralleled the Nile River. Generally, cult temples, which were used to worship gods, were located on the east bank of the Nile, like the rising sun, while funerary temples were on the west. Cult temples were often parts of large sacred cities. Successive pharaohs would add new temples to the complex or expand existing ones.

> **CONNECTIONS** Other than cult temples, much Egyptian architecture, such as the *Mortuary Temple of Hatshepsut* (Figure 9.7, page 244), consists of tombs and funerary temples.

Temple Design

The *Horus Temple at Edfu* housed the sacred cult image of the sun falcon, Horus. Because cult temples were believed to be the actual dwellings of the gods, they were modeled after the residences of nobles and pharaohs (see plan, Fig. 8.31). Courtyards and halls were like reception rooms, leading to the sanctuary that corresponds to the private family bedrooms. For purity, amulets protected the temple's foundations, and its outer edges were walled.

The *Great Pylon of the Horus Temple at Edfu*, built c. 237–57 BCE (Fig. 8.34), is a temple front entrance, with two large, symmetrical, geometric "mountains" flanking the large doorway. The image may have been derived from the Nile River flowing between cliffs. Visually, the pylons both define the entrance and act as barriers; indeed, the lower classes of the Egyptian population were forbidden to enter. Statues and carvings animated the great surfaces, and they were painted to make the temple facade very colorful. The four vertical niches once held tall poles with flying banners.

All doorways and open areas were aligned to create a straight-line path that continues throughout the temple, suggesting the flow of the Nile River and echoing the Egyptians' sanctified experience of nature. The temple floor was painted to depict a river, and the ceiling was decorated with sun rays and the stars of the night sky. Two covered rooms are located beyond the entrance courtyard at Edfu (see plan). They were hypostyle halls, with parallel rows of columns that supported the ceiling. In the *First Hypostyle Hall* at Edfu (Fig. 8.35), the columns are huge and closely spaced, clogging the interior space. The stone roof necessitated closely spaced supports. The concept of the passageway is again emphasized, as the space is not really usable as a room. The shapes of the columns and capitals were probably derived from the bundles of reeds used to build the very early Egyptian buildings. To express divine permanence and power, Egyptians translated that original organic material into massive and monumental granite and limestone. The stone capitals often resemble lotus buds, blossoms, or palm fronds. The shafts of the

8.35 *First Hypostyle Hall, Horus Temple at Edfu*, Egypt, c. 237–57 BCE. The roof slabs are 50′ from the floor.

These huge closely spaced supporting columns resemble lotus buds, blossoms, or palm fronds.

columns swell like the flexing of organic materials. At Edfu, the columns of the hypostyle hall are fifty feet tall; at another temple site, Karnak, the central columns in the hypostyle hall are sixty-six feet high, and the capitals at the top are twenty-two feet in diameter, large enough to hold one hundred people. The massive stones are held in place solely by their tremendous weight.

The temple became darker with each succeeding room, and rooms became smaller, with lower ceilings. To help protect its purity, the sacred image of Horus was kept in the sanctuary at the very back, sealed by heavy doors covered with bronze or silver and decorated with precious stones. The holiest areas were opened only on special occasions and could be approached only by a very few. The sacred image of Horus did not always reside in darkness, however. On certain special feast days, such statues were taken out and rejoined with the sun to recover their vigor.

The Hindu Temple

Theology and Temple Design

Hinduism is based on two belief systems. The first is nature-based and venerates the various spirits responsible for the incredible abundance of plant and animal life in India. From this came the concept of reincarnation, an infinitely repeating cycle of death and life. Around 1500 BCE, invaders brought the second belief system—an understanding of the cosmos in symbolic, geometric terms. For them, the circle stood for the totality of the universe; the square was that divine force made physical in life on earth; a vertical pole was the pillar between heaven and earth, a link that also ensured their separation. A good person would eventually break the cycle of rebirth and death and move into a changeless, timeless union with the Supreme Consciousness, Brahman.

Temple architecture gives form to these spiritual beliefs. The earliest temples were cave temples carved into mountains, like opening the earth's womb to find the divinity enshrined inside. Other temples were freestanding, thick-walled cubes, containing a womb-chamber that housed the cult image or symbol of the deity. A heavy tower, like an abstract mountain, covered it, and a few relief sculptures adorned the exterior. Worshipers brought offerings, meditated, and made sacrifices individually, but remained outside. Priests tended to the deities housed inside and acted as intermediaries for the worshipers. Thus, the Hindu temple was more like sculpture with a small interior. There is no collective service in the Hindu religion, and the temple is the dwelling of the deity.

Later Hindu temples and precincts became much more elaborate, but the same basic formula of womb-chamber and mountain remains. In now-deserted Khajuraho, an important political capital in the tenth and eleventh centuries, was a grouping of thirty temples, symbolizing abundance and proliferation. One was the *Kandarya Mahadeva Temple* (Fig. 8.36), dedicated to Shiva in his manifestation as Mahadeva, who maintains all living things. The *Kandarya Mahadeva Temple* is still an artificial mountain that surmounts the small, dark womb-chamber. The basic shapes are symbols of male and female sexuality,

8.36 *Kandarya Mahadeva Temple*, Khajuraho, India, 10th–11th centuries. This is one of thirty temples at this site, dedicated to Shiva, Vishnu, or Mahavira. Main tower is 130′ high.

This temple is dedicated to Shiva, and is seen as an artificial mountain that surmounts a small dark womb-like chamber.

representing sexual energy and the procreative urge. Then, almost lifelike, they break down into multiplying, cascading forms that are fantastic in their variety and number. Several attached porches and a front assembly hall add to the proliferating forms.

Despite the multiplicity of forms, visual unity is maintained because of the basic mountain-like form and because of the simple umbrella shape (which represents the Unbounded) that surmounts the tallest tower, above the womb-chamber. Thus, the temple exterior was an instrument of meditation on reincarnation. Up close, the relief carvings become more readable, with images of deities and of smaller shrines. Many are openly erotic, because the Hindu religion believes that carnal bliss reflects divine union with the Unbounded.

CONNECTION Figure 7.19, page 177, shows an erotic scene from the *Kandarya Mahadeva Temple*.

Geometry and its Significance

The plan of the temple (Fig. 8.31) is a mandala, a geometric drawing that symbolizes the universe, which we saw in Figure 8.22. Four porches on the temple pointing in the cardinal directions mark the four sides. Then the squares and circles, which have cosmic meaning, are repeated, rotated, and overlaid, and then expanded into space, to create the fantastic compilation of shapes proliferating to become the outer layer of the temple, which still relates to the inner sanctum.

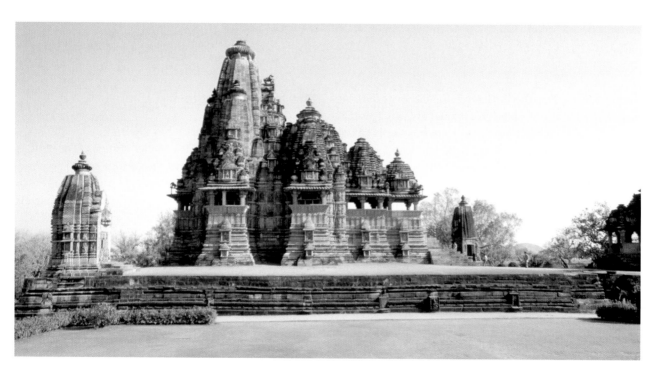

The Buddhist Temple

Distinct versions of Buddhist temples sprang up in India, Southeast Asia, Indonesia, China, Japan, and Korea. For now, we will confine our discussion to just one Buddhist temple compound from China, the *Altar of Heaven*, and to one temple within it, the *Temple of Heaven*.

The *Altar of Heaven* (Fig. 8.37), constructed over the fifteenth and sixteenth centuries, is a large, tree-filled temple compound located in Beijing, south of the palace core. Surrounded by a four-mile wall, the compound is square at its southern end and semicircular at its northern end. To the Chinese, the round shape symbolized the heavens, while the square represented the earth.

The major structures and roadways of the complex are laid out on a north-south axis. Altars and temples face south, the source of temperate weather and abundance, while the north was the source of evil influences. Temple complexes were also carefully sited relative to the forces of wind and water (*fengshui* means "wind and water"), because wind disperses the breath of life and must be stopped by water. All structures are symmetrical and enclosed by walls, railings, terraces, or gates, expressing the Chinese values of seclusion and order.

Design of a Pagoda

Three or four times a year, the emperor used the *Temple of Heaven* (Fig. 8.38), built in 1420 and restored in 1754,

1/4 mile

The Altar of Heaven, Beijing
A Altar of Heaven
B Imperial Lofty Throne
C Temple of Heaven
D Palace of Fasting

8.37 *Altar of Heaven*, Beijing, China, 15th–16th centuries. Plan and artist rendering.

This illustration show the grounds of the altar and temple complex.

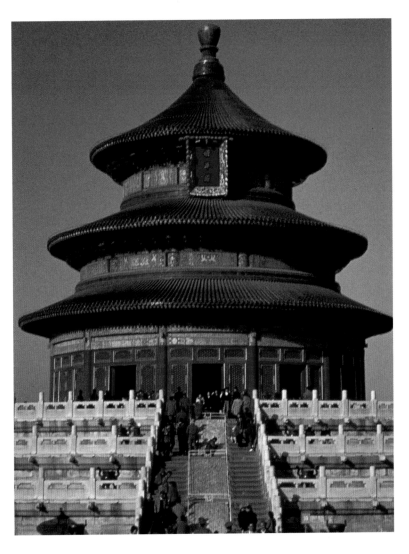

8.38 Round Hall from the *Temple of Heaven*, Beijing, China, begun 1420, restored 1754. Wood with tile roof.

This is a three-tiered pagoda where the Emperor officiated religious and political ceremonies outside of the Forbidden City.

to officiate at religious-political ceremonies, mostly dedicated to the earth and crops. The temple is a lofty, three-tiered pagoda, a cone-shaped structure distinguished by its layers of eaves and gilded orb on top. Its shape is a geometrically simplified mountain form, like the Hindu temple. The entire structure is 125 feet high and nearly 100 feet across. The wide eaves provide shelter from bright sun and rain. The colors and patterns in this wooden building are brilliant. It has a gently curving, violet-blue tile roof, similar to the color of a dark blue sky. The outside walls are deep red, offset with bands of gleaming gold. The interior is red lacquer with foliage patterns in gold and blue and contains green and white beams. Twenty-eight tall posts on the interior entirely support the roof. There are no walls, only doorlike partitions pierced with latticework. The four central posts represent the four seasons, while other columns represent months of the year and the division of day and night. In the center of the stone floor is a marble slab with a design incorporating the dragon and phoenix, symbols of the emperor and empress.

The *Temple of Heaven* sits atop three terraces surrounded by richly carved, lacelike, white marble balustrades. Worshipers circumnavigate the round structure at different levels to symbolize the achievement of wisdom. The temple's symmetry and order contrast strikingly with expanses of wooded areas.

The Hebrew Temple

Because the ancient Hebrew peoples seldom had a permanent homeland in the early years of their history, a tent was likely their early place of worship as well as a temporary temple. In approximately 957 BCE, King Solomon built the first Temple in Jerusalem, a grand structure that replaced the portable sanctuary of old. It was destroyed in 586 BCE, and the second temple was begun and dedicated in 515 BCE. Today the Wailing Wall in Jerusalem is believed to have been a part of the remaining ruins of that temple and is now the site where Jews from all over the world still go to pray. The wall is one of the foundations for the platform of the *Dome of the Rock* (Fig. 8.30). In more recent centuries, the synagogue has evolved for Jews as a community house of worship, assembly, and study, and they house their sacred objects: an Ark, scrolls of the Law, an eternal flame, and candelabra. This modern temple may be designed in various architectural styles.

> **CONNECTION** Earlier in this chapter, we saw examples of art from Hebrew places of worship. Review the wall painting at the Synagogue at *Dura-Europus* (Fig. 8.11) and the *Ark of the Covenant Mosaic* (Fig. 8.23).

The Gothic Cathedral

The imposing, mystical **Gothic** cathedral is one of the most famous forms of a Catholic church. Christians believed that the body and earth were profane and sinful, while the soul was sacred. They saw the church building as the heavenly Jerusalem on earth. Abbot Suger, a leading cleric during this era, remarked upon entering a Gothic church, "I see myself existing on some level . . . beyond our earthly one, neither completely in the slime of earth nor completely in the purity of Heaven." Gothic cathedrals were all funded by and built in cities, indicating the rise of cities and monarchies and a decline in feudalism. The modern humanist view that values the individual was beginning to develop at this time. Gothic churches are remarkable human achievements. While they evoke the spiritual realm, they do so by giving pleasure to the senses.

> **CONNECTION** The early Christians worshiped in homes or catacombs. An example of a catacomb, the *Catacomb of Sts. Peter and Marcellinus*, can be seen in Figure 9.17, page 253.

Plan and Design

Gothic cathedrals towered over the towns around them, which is evident with *Chartres Cathedral* (Fig. 8.39), built between 1194 and 1220. The spires symbolized the church's role linking heaven and earth. Flat, blank walls are almost nonexistent. Large windows are filled with tracery, a lacy stone framework that holds sections of glass in place. Blank spaces are covered with figurative sculptures or decorative carvings, showing Jesus, saints, rulers, and sometimes demons. Flying buttresses create a visual pattern of forms that jog in and out, as can be seen in Figure 8.39. Towers, arches, buttresses, and arcades create vertical lines that continue from ground to roof. The plan of *Chartres* is symmetrical, while its shape (Fig. 8.31) is a cross, symbolizing Jesus'

8.39 *Chartres Cathedral*. Chartres, France. Although parts of the west front date from 1145–1170, most of the exterior of this structure was built between 1194 and 1220. South tower 344′ high, north tower 377′ high; the cathedral itself is 427′ long. A rose window is visible at the middle of the church.

The tall vertical design emphasized by its spires symbolize the Roman Catholic Church's role of linking heaven and earth.

crucifixion as the act of salvation that redeemed sinful humanity.

The emphasis on verticality continues inside. Long lines rise from the floor, up the piers, and between the windows, and flow gracefully up the pointed groin vaults. The vaults seem to billow overhead rather than being stone structures that weigh tons. There is also a strong horizontal pull toward the altar, with the large windows at the apse end that are like bright beacons.

Window Design

The large stained-glass windows were not only incredible technical achievements but also powerful symbols of heavenly radiance. Previously, churches tended to be very dark, but these windows fill the Gothic church with muted light. The flying buttresses on the outside make the enormous windows possible, because the buttresses and not the walls are holding up the vaults above.

8.40 *Rose Window.* From the north transept of *Chartres Cathedral.* Chartres, France, 1233.

The stained glass filled the church with light. In the center are Mary and Jesus, surrounded by Old Testament prophets.

The *Rose Window*, from 1233, on the north transept of Chartres (Fig. 8.40), shows rings of Old Testament prophets and kings surrounding Mary with her child Jesus. This illustrates the Christian concept that the Old Testament culminated in the birth of Christ. Mary's central location indicates the raised status of women. (In fact, the church is dedicated to Mary.) The female model was now Mary, mother of the savior Jesus, rather than sinful Eve. Geometry was used to locate the various small scenes in this window by inscribing and rotating squares within a circle. The window is shaped like a blooming rose, a symbol of Mary.

CONNECTION For an example of the English style of Gothic architecture, see the *Chapel of Henry VII*, Figure 9.19, page 255.

The Islamic Mosque

The religion of Islam requires that its adherents pray five times a day while bowing toward Mecca, the birthplace of the prophet Mohammed. On Friday, men are required to attend collective prayer services in mosques, a word derived from the Arabic **masjid**, which means "prostration." The faithful ritually cleanse themselves and then assemble on beautifully patterned rugs facing Mecca for prayer, sermons, and readings from the Quran (or Koran), the Islamic book of sacred texts.

It is thought that the plan of Mohammed's house in Medina influenced the design of early mosques, which were simple courtyards with shaded areas. On the wall facing Mecca was the **mihrab**, a special marker niche. A stepped pulpit called the **minbar** was usually located next to the mihrab. The tall minarets could be seen from afar, giving hope to weary travelers. There are no icons, statues, or images in Islamic worship or in mosques.

Later Developments in Mosque Design

One of the most beautiful mosques ever constructed is located in ancient Persia, or present-day Iran. Shah Abbas I (the Great) sought to make Persia an important center and undertook an ambitious urban renewal program in the capital city, Isfahan. With the *Masjid-i-Shah*, or *Royal Mosque* (Fig. 8.41), dated 1612–1637, the individual parts of the mosque became elaborate and were given separate identity. The portals, for example, became separate, large structures distinguished by elaborate decoration and pattern to awe and draw in the viewer. The once-simple courtyard evolved into a two-story arcade covered with blue-patterned tiles, with four huge, porch-like portals, where schools of Islamic theology could be assembled. The covered prayer hall is physically and conceptually separate from the open courtyard. Worshipers move through a series of interlocking areas to leave the profane world and enter the sacred realm. The single minaret has multiplied to four.

The *Masjid-i-Shah* has a very rough exterior finish, contrasting with the lavishly decorated interior. The spaciousness and symmetry of the mosque represent the infinity and completeness of Allah.

Pattern

Ornamentation is profuse and serves several purposes: (1) it symbolizes Allah in its suggestion of infinity and

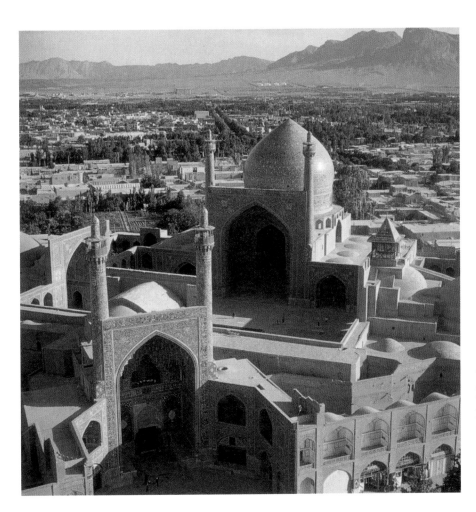

8.41 *Masjid-i-Shah,* or *Royal Mosque*, Isfahan, Iran, 1612–1637. The arch of the main portal, to the left in this picture, is 90′ high; the minarets are 110′ high.

The design of the mosque featured various spaces that worshippers moved through to leave the profane world and enter the sacred realm.

8.42 *Masjid-i-Shah,* or *Royal Mosque* (detail of the main portal), Isfahan, Iran, 1612–1637.

This photo shows the intricate ornamentation of pattern and calligraphy meant to draw in and awe the viewer.

pools are common, and this mosque has one in the court-yard. Seen reflected in pools, the buildings seem smaller but more beautiful. Disturb the water, and the image vanishes. Text passages on mosque walls are a favored form of decoration. Calligraphic lettering was stylized to become very elegant and, in some instances, almost indistinguishable from geometric or foliage patterns. The panels on either side of the doorway in Figure 8.42 resemble Persian weavings and tapestries. In the Islamic world, weavings serve utilitarian functions in the home, palace, and mosque, but they are also high aesthetic achievements and signs of favor. As treasured portable objects, they recall the early nomadic Arabs and the founding of Islam. The **mukarnas (muqarnas)**, or vaults, in the upper left in Figure 8.42, are also pattern elements. The hanging quarter-domes break up the structure and disguise the mass of the building.

The entire complex is unified by the enormous, patterned turquoise dome that dominates the Isfahan skyline. The circular dome stands for the heavens and symbolizes the oneness of Allah.

> **CONNECTION** The *Taj Mahal,* Figure 9.20, page 256, is an Islamic funerary structure decorated with carved and inlaid stones.

The Mesoamerican Temple

Mesoamerican temples often took the form of a pyramid with a small structure on top. Indeed, the pyramid or the mound was a frequent holy site throughout the Americas, from Illinois to Peru.

History and Setting

Thirty miles north of today's Mexico City, the Teotihuacá-nos, a pre-Aztec people, built a vast religious center in a large city high on a plateau surrounded by mountains, a center that reached its peak from 100 to 400 CE. Teotihuacán, or "Place of the Gods," had 200,000 residents, enormous temples, and numerous and lavish palaces, and governed a wide area. Unlike in previous rambling Mesoamerican cities, the streets of Teotihuacán were rigidly laid out on a grid oriented to north, south, east, and west, and even a river through the town was channeled to conform to that grid. The main north-south corridor, the *Avenue of the Dead,* formed the religious center of the city, with more than one hundred temples in two miles. The incredible scale of the Avenue of the Dead dwarfs any of the places of worship we have seen so far. Still, the style of architecture is remarkably consistent throughout, and the overall design

creation; (2) it enhances the sacred character of the mosque; (3) it identifies and makes visually distinct the various parts of the mosque, so that portals, porches, windows, domes, and the mihrab are easily recognizable; and (4) the ornamentation disguises the mosque's mass, although not the form. The mosque walls seem to be merely thin screens of incredible color and delicate pattern, rather than thick, heavy, massive brick walls.

Other elements add more pattern. Windows are covered with decorative screens that break up the light into patterns as it reflects off the patterned tiles. Reflecting emphasizes both space and mass: the pyramids as solid mass, with plazas as voids that were often the same size as the bases of the pyramids. Ball courts were also included.

The very building and growth of Teotihuacán directly led to its decline, as forests were leveled to fire plaster kilns, resulting in soil erosion, along with the failure of rains and the decline of the city.

Temple Designs

In the middle of the Avenue of the Dead was the *Pyramid of the Sun*, begun before 150 CE (Fig. 8.43) and probably dedicated to sun worship. It was aligned east-west and along the rising of the star cluster Pleiades on the days of the equinox and once had a temple atop it. The pyramid is quite simply staggering in size, covering 7.5 acres and rising 215 feet. The Teotihuacános did not use the wheel and had no beasts of burden, so people carried the 2.5 million tons of earth, stone, and rubble to the site. Probably

three thousand laborers worked thirty years to complete the pyramid. The ledges, tiers, vertical insets, and square corners visually separate the pyramid from the rounded mountains that surround it. To prevent erosion, it was built with a relatively low profile, with embedded stone walls set perpendicular to the outer face. The design features **talud** and **tablero** construction, alternating slopes and inset platforms.

The entire earthen mound was once covered with huge clay bricks faced with stone, and finished with a coat of smooth, white, polished lime plaster. It must have looked like a gleaming white mountain, with certain parts painted in color. Ceremonies with splendid pageantry were likely held on the steps and ledges.

> **CONNECTION** There are many similarities between the *Pyramid of the Sun* and the *Ziggurat at Ur* (Fig. 8.24, page 212), seen earlier in this chapter.

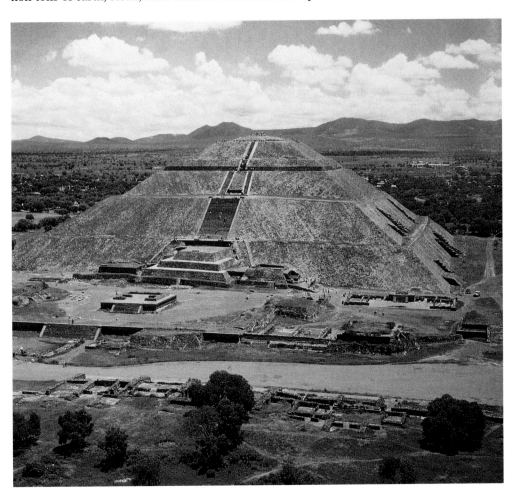

8.43 *Pyramid of the Sun,* with the *Avenue of the Dead* in the foreground. Teotihuacán, Mexico, begun before 150 CE. Pyramid is 768' along one side of the base.

This huge pyramidal temple is part of an expansive complex of temples and courtyards.

8.44 *Tlalocan Painting*. From Tepantitla compound, Teotihuacán, Mexico. Copy by Agustin Villagra. Original: pigment on stucco.

This frontal image represents the water god with water droplets springing from her hands

Temple Painting

Early temples had sculptural ornamentation, but after the third century, paintings were used, like the restored copy of the *Tlalocan Painting* (Fig. 8.44), from a palace in Teotihuacán. A large frontal figure at the center is a water god with green water droplets springing from her hands. Plants populated with butterflies and spiders grow from her head, while two priests, shown symmetrically and smaller in scale, attend and make offerings. The colors in this restored version are bright, with an especially intense red background. The deity is distinguished by her larger size, frontality, and the profusion of symmetrical patterns that ornament her. In fact, the entire piece shows the Teotihuacános' fondness for elaborate symmetrical patterns, both in framing and in depicting characters.

9.1 KANE KWEL. Coca Pod Coffin, Ghana, Africa, 1970s. Wood and enamel paint, 92″ long.

This is a coffin crafted for a coca tree farmer, which memorialized the life's work of the deceased.

9

MORTALITY AND IMMORTALITY

We opened this book with the observation that creating art is strictly a human phenomenon. Our awareness of our mortality and the quest for immortality seem to be two other strictly human phenomena. Life, death, and the afterlife have always been and will continue to be intertwined in the human experience of art-making.

PREVIEW

In this chapter we see that from ancient times to the present, the living make both tombs and commemorative art to serve various purposes. These purposes may (1) express the cultures' ideas and values about death and the afterlife; (2) closely tie religion to ritual burials; (3) promote political and social intentions; (4) visually establish power; and (5) guarantee honor, fame and/or glory. The artwork covered here ranges from the awesome grandeur and ambition of the Pyramids to the bright and personal quality of the Coca Pod Coffin by Kane Kwei (Fig. 9.1).

Connecting Art and History from
500 BCE—500 CE

Major civilizations and empires flourished around the world at this time (see Map 4). The great wealth and power of these empires produced elite classes who commissioned amazing works of art, among which were monumental tombs and funerary art that preserved their fame.

In Greece, which consisted of independent city-states, 500–338 BCE is considered the Classical Age. In Athens, artworks reflected Greek humanism with their idealized yet naturalistic representations of the human figure, as seen in the *Grave*

Stele of Hegeso (Fig. 9.15). Athens also developed an early but short-lived form of democracy. In the fourth century BCE, the Macedonians conquered the Greeks and, under Alexander the Great, invaded Persia and defeated King Darius. Alexander's empire, stretching as far as India and the Middle East, further spread Greek influence.

The Etruscan civilization, consisting of city-states, occupied much of central Italy. Much of what we know about Etruria comes from excavations of their tombs and funerary art. Tomb paintings of lively people engaged in feasts, dancing, or enjoying outdoor sports are common, as in the *Banqueters and Musicians* from Tomb of the

Leopards (Fig. 9.9). The *Sarcophagus with Reclining Couple* (Fig. 9.8) indicates that Etruscan women enjoyed considerable independence. They attended symposia and sporting events, were equals at banquets with their husbands, owned property independently, and likely had a high rate of literacy. Beginning in 509 BCE, the Romans began chipping away at Etruria and completely overwhelmed the Etruscans by 273 BCE.

Rome was founded as a city in 753 BCE, but by 100 CE its influence had spread into Europe, Asia Minor, and North Africa. At first a republic, Rome became an empire in 27 BCE when Caesar Augustus came to power. His reign was the beginning of the Pax Romana (Roman Peace), which lasted

Map 4. The Assyrian and Persian Empires. Courtesy of Replogle Globes, Inc., Broadview, IL.

for two hundred years and saw the construction of many amazing Roman monuments, including the *Pantheon* (Fig. 8.27), the *Colosseum* (Fig. 15.11), and the *Ara Pacis* (Fig. 10.33). In Rome, an individual's or a family's pedigree was important, evidenced by the many busts of ancestors or funerary monuments, as in the *Statue of Togato Barberini* (Fig. 13.13) or *Funerary Relief of a Circus Official* (Fig. 9.16).

Jesus Christ was born during Augustus's reign. Early Christian art, such as the *Good Shepherd* from the *Catacomb of Sts. Peter and Marcellinus* (Fig. 9.17), developed within the influence of Roman art, although Christians were subject to periodic persecutions. In 312, Emperor Constantine made Christianity legal, and eventually it became the religion of the empire. The fragments of the *Colossal Statue of Constantine* (Fig. 9.2) clearly indicate that he was a powerful ruler, but others found it difficult to hold the huge expanse of the empire together, and it was subdivided periodically. Nomadic tribes from northern Europe overran the western part of the Roman Empire by 476 CE. The eastern portion survived for another thousand years as the Byzantine Empire.

In India, the Mauryan Empire united most of the country with a central government between 321 and 185 BCE. The major rulers were Chandragupta and Asoka. The empire included northern and central India (modern Pakistan and part of Afghanistan). The Golden Age of India occurred between 330 and 500 CE during the Gupta Empire, begun by Chandragupta I. During this time, India prospered, and the arts were highly developed (see the *Lion Capital*, Fig. 2.15).

In China during the Zhou Dynasty, which ended in 256 BCE, Confucianism and Daoism were practiced, and the art of lacquering was developed. From 221 to 206 BCE, Shi Huangdi destroyed rival states and unified China, establishing the Qin Dynasty. To consolidate his power, he had all historical books burned and scholars burned or buried alive to eradicate old traditions. He established a civil service and bureaucratic government that continued for centuries in China. He built the Great Wall (see Fig. 10.22), highways, and canals, and standardized weights, measurements, axle widths, currency, and script styles for trade. The life-size ceramic army, the *Soldiers from Pit 1* (Fig. 9.10), that guarded his extravagant tomb is an eloquent visual monument to a ruthlessly ambitious ruler.

Shi Huangdi's dynasty ended quickly after his death and was succeeded by the Han Dynasty (202 BCE to 222 CE). Arts included wall painting and sculpture. There was a major expansion of both domestic and foreign trade.

During this period, Egypt was dominated by foreign powers, but their funerary art practices continued. Further south in Africa, the Great Empire of Ghana was established in 300. The Ghanaians set up trade routes

9.2 *Colossal Statue of Constantine*, fragments. Palazzo dei Conservatori, Rome, c. 330 CE.

Constantine was the first Roman emperor to legalize Christianity in the Empire.

and controlled trade in gold and salt. South of Egypt, the independent state of Kush thrived as a result of vigorous trade. In 400, the Bantu people settled in South Africa.

In Mesoamerica, the Maya developed writing, a calendar, sophisticated architecture, painting, and sculpture between 250 and 900. In Peru, the Chavin culture flourished between 1000 BCE and 200 CE and developed agriculture and art. Later, the Moche, whose culture dates from 200 to 800, built pyramids, buried their dead in elaborate tombs, and made fine pottery (see Fig. 7.30). Their leaders were warrior-priests whose regalia likely inspired awe and fear (see the artifacts from the *Royal Tomb of Sipán* in Figure 9.12 and the *Peanut Necklace* in Figure 9.13).

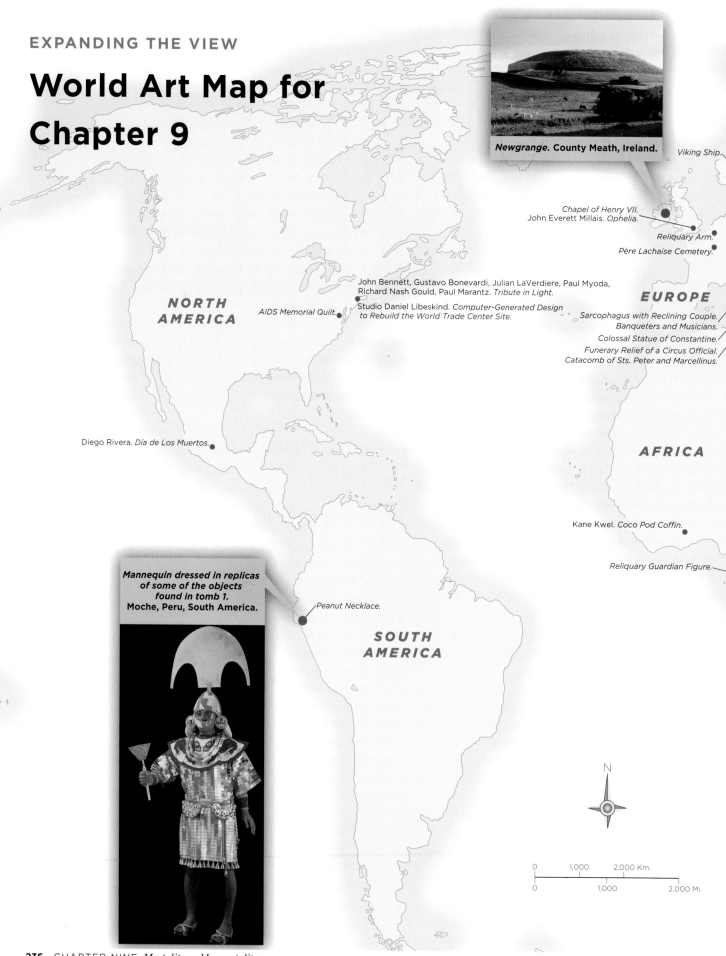

World Art Map for Chapter 9

Newgrange. County Meath, Ireland.

Viking Ship.

Chapel of Henry VII.
John Everett Millais. *Ophelia.*

Reliquary Arm.

Père Lachaise Cemetery.

John Bennett, Gustavo Bonevardi, Julian LaVerdiere, Paul Myoda, Richard Nash Gould, Paul Marantz. *Tribute in Light.*

EUROPE

AIDS Memorial Quilt.

Studio Daniel Libeskind. *Computer-Generated Design to Rebuild the World Trade Center Site.*

Sarcophagus with Reclining Couple. Banqueters and Musicians.

Colossal Statue of Constantine.

Funerary Relief of a Circus Official.
Catacomb of Sts. Peter and Marcellinus.

NORTH AMERICA

AFRICA

Diego Rivera. *Día de Los Muertos.*

Kane Kwel. *Coco Pod Coffin.*

Reliquary Guardian Figure.

Mannequin dressed in replicas of some of the objects found in tomb 1. Moche, Peru, South America.

Peanut Necklace.

SOUTH AMERICA

N

0	1,000	2,000 Km.

0	1,000	2,000 Mi.

ASIA

Gianlorenzo Bernini. *Baldacchino.* **Rome, Italy.**

Warrior. Shaanxi, China.

Mausoleum of Mao Zedong.

Grave Stele of Hegeso.

Soldiers from Pit 1.

Great Pyramids.

Innermost Coffin of Tutankhamen. Thebes, Egypt.

Fowling Scene.

Mortuary Temple of Hatshepsut.

Taj Mahal. Agra, India.

Helmet Mask (Tatuana). New Ireland, Papua New Guinea, Oceania.

AUSTRALIA

500 BCE-500 CE

| UNIFICATION OF EGYPT | 4000 BCE | Newgrange burials |
| OLD KINGDOM – EGYPT | 3000 | Great Pyramids at Gizeh |

Above Pyramid of Djoser (5.1)

MIDDLE KINGDOM – EGYPT		
NEW KINGDOM – EGYPT	2000	Mortuary Temple of Hatshepsut
		Coffin of Tutankhamen
CHAVIN CULTURE— PERU	1000	
ETRUSCAN CIVILIZATION		

Above Royal Profile (3.3)

Sarcophagus with Reclining Couple

Banqueters and Musicians

| GOLDEN AGE OF GREECE | 500 | Grave Stele of Hegeso |

CHAVIN CULTURE IN PERU CONTINUES FROM 1000 BCE

PERICLES' GOLDEN AGE OF GREECE		
Parthenon restored		
ROME ESTABLISHED FIRST REPUBLIC		
Peloponnesian War		
Alexander invaded Persia	400	Soldiers from Pit 1 Warrior
Birth of Jesus Christ	CE	
ROMAN EMPIRE	100	Funerary Relief of a Roman Circus Official
MOCHE CIVILIZATION—PERU		Royal Tomb of Sipán
FIRST EMPEROR— CHINA QIN DYNASTY		
ZHOU DYNASTY	200	
Daoism and Confusium		
Constantine Legalized Christianity	300	Catacomb of Sts. Peter and Marcellinus ceiling painting
GOLDEN AGE OF INDIA-GUPTA EMPIRE		
GREAT AFRICAN EMPIRE OF GHANA		
BYZANTINE EMPIRE	500	
Islam Religion founded		Viking Ship
GOTHIC ERA	1000	Reliquary Arm
MALI EMPIRE AT HEIGHT		

Above GHIBERTI: Sacrifice of Isaac (Fig. 8.17)

RENAISSANCE BEGINS	**1500**	*Chapel of Henry VII*
BAROQUE ERA BEGINS	**1600**	
		Bernini: *Baldacchino*
		Taj Mahal
AGE OF ENLIGHTENMENT	**1700**	
Colonization of the Americas and Africa		
Industrial	**1750**	

Above *Ceremonial Mask, Zaire (1.6)*

Revolution		
American Revolution		
French Revolution		
South American Revolution		
ROMANTICISM	**1800**	*Père Lachaise Cemetery*
Mexican Independence from Spain		
Mexican Revolution	**1850**	Millais: *Ophelia*

Russian Revolution	**1900**	
World War I		Rivera: *Día de Los Muertos*
World War II		
PEOPLE'S REPUBLIC OF CHINA		
Vietnam War	**1950**	*Reliquary Guardian Figure*
Death of Mao Zedong		*Mausoleum of Mao Zedong*
Desert Storm		*AIDS Memorial Quilt*

Above Hockney. *A Bigger Splash (3.29)*

September 11 Terrorist Attacks	**2000**	

Above Smith: *Born (3.17)*

	2002	*Tribute in Light*

EARLY TOMBS: MOUNDS AND MOUNTAINS

The very earliest tombs in many cultures are shaped like hills or mountains. The Egyptians built pyramids, which were geometric mountains. Others built funeral mounds that look like naturally occurring grass-covered hills, some small and others quite large. They contain hidden burial chambers, usually for elite members of a society. Some were lavishly furnished. The locations of mound graves were often tied to a natural phenomenon, such as the movement of the sun. Mound graves can be found in Europe, Asia, the Middle East, and the Americas.

Ancient Burials

Funerary practices, religion, agriculture, and astronomy were often interrelated among early peoples. Among the oldest tombs are the late Stone Age mounds in western Europe. In Ireland, the late Stone Age tomb of *Newgrange* (Fig. 9.3), from 3200 BCE, is part of a complex of tombs and monolithic rock structures. It contains 220,000 tons of loose stone with a white quartz rock facing on one side. Inside a long passageway leads to a cross-shaped interior

chamber with five burials. The passageway has forty-ton stones, some decorated with spirals and geometric patterns, perhaps indicating stars and planets. It is sealed to prevent water seepage. *Newgrange* is oriented so that for about two weeks around the winter solstice, a burst of brilliant morning sunlight radiates down through the entire passage, illuminating one patterned stone in the burial chamber. Over time, like other mounds, *Newgrange* eroded and blended into the natural landscape. After the fourth century, *Newgrange* was an abandoned and undisturbed site until 1699, when it was rediscovered by men quarrying for building stone.

CONNECTION *Stonehenge* (Fig. 8.26) is an example of a monolithic rock structure, dating from the same era as *Newgrange*.

9.3 *Newgrange*, County Meath, Ireland, 3200 BCE. Neolithic.

This ancient mound is oriented so that during the winter solstice, sunlight radiates through a passage that illuminates a patterned stone.

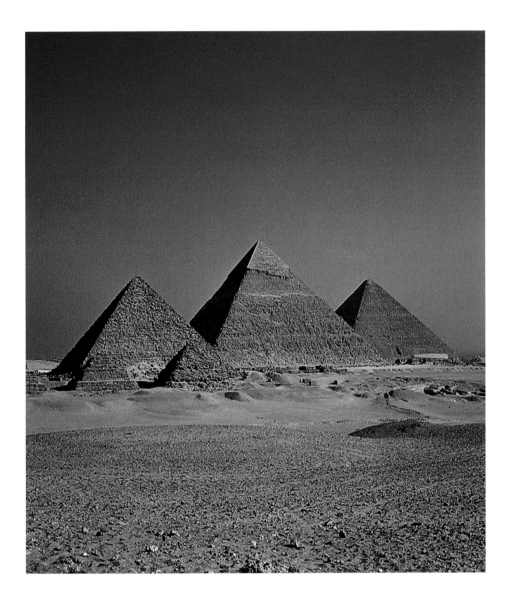

9.4 *Great Pyramids*, Gizeh, Egypt. From left, *Menkaure*, c. 2525–2475 BCE; *Khafre*, c. 2575–2525 BCE; *Khufu*, c. 2600–2550 BCE.

Oriented to the sun, these are the pharaohs' tombs, who were believed to be sons of the sun god Re.

The *Great Pyramids of Egypt* are perhaps the most famous ancient burial sites, and they serve as the focus figures for this section. Like *Newgrange*, the *Great Pyramids* are very old, very large, very influential in style, and oriented to the sun. They are the tombs of the pharaohs, the rulers of Egypt who were believed to be the sons of the most powerful of all the gods, Re, the Sun God. The pyramids, standing dramatically on the edge of the Sahara Desert, are artificial mountains on a flat, artificial plane. They are part of a necropolis, composed of tombs and mortuary temples, that extends for fifty miles on the west bank of the Nile. The pyramids of pharaohs *Menkaure*, c. 2525–2475 BCE, *Khafre*, c. 2575–2525 BCE, and *Khufu*, c. 2600–2550 BCE (Fig. 9.4), are the largest among all the pyramids.

The numbers associated with the very largest, the pyramid of *Khufu*, are often recited but still inspire awe: 775 feet along one side of the base; 450 feet high; 2.3 million stone blocks; average weight of each block, 2.5 tons.

> **CONNECTION** An earlier version of Egyptian pyramids can be seen in the *Stepped Pyramid of Djoser* (Fig. 5.1).

The *Great Pyramids* have interior chambers that are quite small and, when opened in modern times, contained only empty stone crypts. The tombs may have contained provisions, but they were robbed shortly after they were sealed. In an effort to thwart grave robbing, which was rampant in ancient Egypt, later pharaohs stopped building enormous, expensive, ostentatious tombs like the pyramids. Instead, later rulers were buried in less-costly chambers cut deep into the sides of mountains, with hidden entrances (see *Tutankhamen*, Fig. 9.5).

FURNISHED TOMBS

Many cultures believed that the afterlife was similar to this life and that the dead continued to "live" in the tomb and needed furnishings like those used when they were alive, such as furniture, clothing, utensils, and precious items.

Egyptian Tombs and Mortuary Temples

One thousand years after the *Great Pyramids*, the Egyptians provide the supreme examples of furnished tombs, which were the meeting place between earthly life and eternity. According to Egyptian beliefs, a human soul possessed both a **ba** and a **ka.** The *ba* is part of the soul whose seat was the heart or abdomen in the body. It is depicted as a human-headed bird. When humans take their last breath, the *ba* flies from the body. After the body has been mummified seventy days later, the *ba* returns, hungry and thirsty. A well-prepared tomb is filled with provisions to satisfy the needs of the *ba* in the afterlife, including water, wine, grains, dates, cakes, and even dehydrated beef and fowl.

The *ka* is the mental aspect of the human's soul. It is symbolized by two outstretched arms or by an attendant figure that represents the double of the personality. The *ka* dwells in a lifelike statue of the deceased, which is placed in the tomb. It was important for both the statue and the sarcophagus to have a strong likeness of the dead person, so that both the *ba* and *ka* could easily recognize their destinations. The *ba* and the *ka* were thought to enter the tombs through a small chimney or an air vent. Provisions for the *ka* would include chairs, beds, chariots, models of servants, kitchen utensils, dishes, and simulated food (unlike the real food the *ba* required). Combs, hairpins, and ointments were also included, along with games for entertainment. Rich treasures of gold and silver as well as carriages and boats for the *ka*'s journey to heaven have also been found in the more elaborate tombs.

These richly furnished tombs have been targets for robbers since early times. Despite later pharaohs' efforts to hide their tombs, almost all were robbed long ago, except that of King Tutankhamen, which was only partly plundered. Ironically, while stealing treasures from a nearby tomb, robbers happened to heap more debris on the entrance to Tutankhamen's tomb, so it remained undisturbed until 1922. Among the amazing treasures

9.5 *Innermost Coffin of Tutankhamen*, Thebes, Egypt, c. 1325 BCE. Gold inlaid with enamel and semiprecious stones, 6′ 1″ long. Egyptian Museum, Cairo.

Unlike many of the pharaohs' tombs, this one was only partly plundered, leaving a vast amount of funerary treasure.

9.6 *Fowling Scene*, Thebes, Egypt, c. 1400–1350 BCE. Paint on dry plaster, approx. 32″ high. Wall painting from the tomb of Nebamun. The British Museum, London.

This is a depiction of an Egyptian noble in the afterlife hunting in the abundant Nile River.

found in Tutankhamen's tomb was his *Innermost Coffin*, dated c. 1325 BCE, in Figure 9.5. It is beaten gold, weighing nearly three-quarters of a ton, and is inlaid with semiprecious stones. Two other, larger coffin cases of gold fit over it, and together they encased the mummy. To preserve bodies and make them recognizable, they were mummified with **natron**, a mineral mixture found in the desert. Portraits also were placed in the tomb as substitute spirit receptacles in case something happened to the mummy. Pharaohs had several stone statues or effigies in gold, like the *Innermost Coffin*. The wings of the god Horus protectively encircle the coffin, and Tutankhamen holds insignia of his rank. Certain features are standard on Tutankhamen's face: the distinctive eye makeup; the false beard, a symbol of power; the striped head-cloth; the cobra head to frighten enemies. Nevertheless, it is indeed a portrait of Tutankhamen.

The tomb also contained inlaid chests, gilt chairs, and other wooden items covered with gold; carved watchdogs; life-size guardian statues; jewels; and so on. To provide for the comfort of those of high rank, clay statues of servants were included in the tombs. Because Tutankhamen died unexpectedly before the age of twenty, there was little time to prepare his tomb, as mummification, funerary rites, and burial had to be completed in seventy days. Archeologists believe that his tomb was surely less lavishly furnished than those of pharaohs with long reigns. It is small and its walls were painted, whereas other rulers' tombs were large, barrel-vaulted chambers with relief carvings.

In Egyptian tombs, wall paintings and carvings recreated the pleasures and labors of earthly existence. The *Fowling Scene*, a wall painting from the tomb of Nebamun, c. 1400–1350 BCE (Fig. 9.6), shows an Egyptian noble hunting in the marshes along the Nile River. The air is filled with birds that are painted with care and distinction, and the water is thick with fish. Pattern is important, as seen in the water ripples and the repeated image of birds in the nobleman's hand. The marsh grasses fan out in a beautiful but rigid decoration. Depth is rarely shown in ancient Egyptian paintings, so everything is distributed vertically or horizontally. Pattern elements are visual metaphors for the seasonal cycles of the Nile, the unchanging culture, and the vast desert that surrounds the river valley.

In this wall painting, humans dominate the scene. The noble is shown in the formal manner reserved for exalted persons: head, shoulders, legs, and feet in profile; eyes and shoulders frontal. Size was an important indicator of rank, so the nobleman is larger than his wife and daughter, indicating their lower status.

When high-ranking Egyptians began to hide tombs in hillsides, the funerary temples that formerly were appendages to pyramids were enlarged and emphasized. The *Mortuary Temple of Hatshepsut*, c. 1490–1460 BCE (Fig. 9.7), of the Eighteenth Dynasty, shows this later development. The temple was the monument to her greatness. It once housed two hundred statues of her and many brightly painted reliefs showing her divine birth, coronation, military victories, and other exploits. In the years after her

9.7 *Mortuary Temple of Hatshepsut*, Deir el-Bahri, Egypt, c. 1490–1460 BCE.

This funerary temple was a monument to the greatness of Egypt's woman pharaoh.

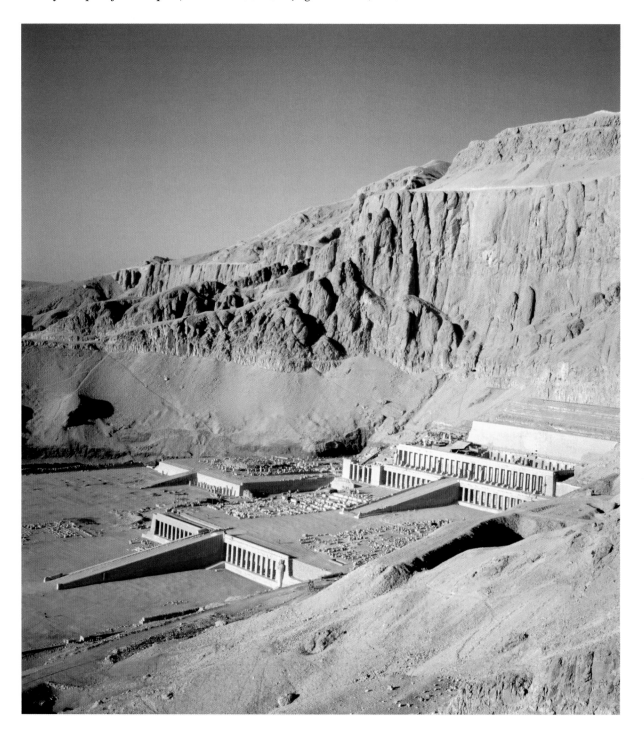

death, Hatshepsut's portraits were defaced, and records of her rule were obscured until they were rediscovered in the nineteenth century.

This large temple has an open, light design, without the mass and weightiness of the earlier pyramids. The simple vertical columns echo the cliff's rock formations. A quarter-mile-long forecourt contained a garden with a pool and papyrus and with rows of frankincense trees. The garden was a pleasure in Egyptian life and, thus, was prominent in their afterlife imagery. An inscription from another tomb says: "May I wander around my pool each day for evermore; may my soul sit on the branches of the grave garden I have prepared for myself; may I refresh myself each day under my sycamore."

Etruscan Tombs

It is interesting to compare Egyptian funerary practices with those of other cultures. The Etruscans were another ancient people who buried their dead in earthen mounds furnished for the afterlife. The Etruscan civilization was a loose band of city-states in west-central Italy. It developed in the eighth and seventh centuries BCE, flourished, and then was overtaken by the expanding Roman Empire in the fifth and fourth centuries BCE. Around the city of Cerveteri, the Etruscans buried their dead under row after row of earthen mounds arranged along "streets" in a necropolis. The Etruscan tombs often had several modest-sized rooms, laid out much like houses. These tomb chambers were carved directly out of the soft bedrock, called **tufa**. Furnishings, such as chairs and beds and utensils, were sometimes carved in relief on the underground rock surfaces. They simulated a domestic interior. In contrast to those of other civilizations, the Etruscan tombs are not grand monuments to powerful rulers, but reminders of a society that emphasized sociability and the pleasures of living.

The freestanding terra-cotta sculpture *Sarcophagus with Reclining Couple*, c. 520 BCE (Fig. 9.8), comes from a tomb in Cerveteri. The clay sarcophagus, with life-size figures, was molded in four pieces. The wife and husband are

9.8 *Sarcophagus with Reclining Couple*, Etruria (Italy), c. 520 BCE. Painted terra-cotta, 45 1/2″ tall. From a cemetery near Cerveteri. Museo Nationale di Villa Giulia, Rome.

A couple enjoys a banquet on their coffin in this freestanding sculpture.

shown at the same scale, reclining together at a banquet, sharing the same couch. This reflects the fact that Etruscan women had more rights than women in most other cultures. The facial features are similar and standardized on both figures, and their hair is represented as a geometric pattern. Their bodies are somewhat flattened and unformed from the waist down. Despite these unnatural features, the wife and husband still give the impression of alert liveliness, health, and vigor. Their gestures are very animated.

Etruscan tomb art emphasizes pleasure. In tombs carved into cliffs near the Etruscan city of Tarquinia, the walls were often covered with paintings. One example is *Banqueters and Musicians*, from the Tomb of the Leopards, c. 480–470 BCE (Fig. 9.9), so named for the leopards painted on the wall near the ceiling. To the left, banqueters recline on couches while servants bring them food and drink. The women are shown with light skin and men with dark, according to conventions of representation at that time. One man holds an egg, a symbol of rebirth. To the right, musicians dance across the wall. Gestures are lively and animated and are made more visible by the oversized hands. Golds, reds, and greens predominate, and the circle and checkerboard patterns on the ceiling add to the general colorfulness of the scene.

Funeral Complex of Shi Huangdi

Our next comparison shows one of the most extensive tombs ever constructed. At age thirteen, Ying Cheng became the ruler of the Qin state in 259 BCE. By 221 BCE, he had subdued the rival neighboring states to unify China and found the Qin Dynasty. A brutal ruler, he assumed the title *Shi Huangdi*, the "First Emperor." Shi Huangdi accumulated amazing power, ruthlessly homogenizing Chinese culture and eradicating all opposition to his rule (see *History Focus* on page 235). Shi Huangdi built for

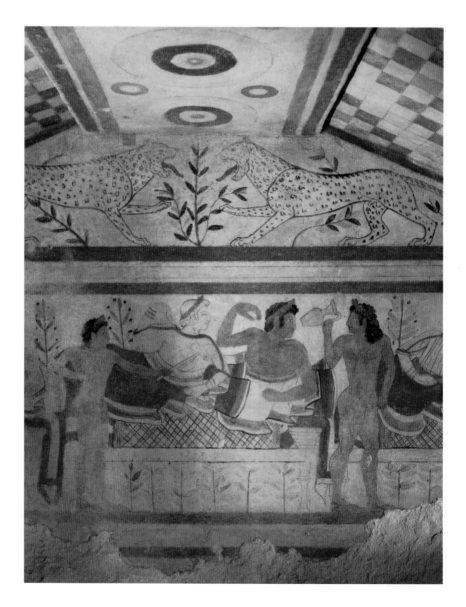

9.9 *Banqueters and Musicians*, Etruria (Italy), c. 480–470 BCE. Mural painting from the Tomb of the Leopards in a cemetery near Tarquinia.

The pleasures of Etruscan life included feasting, music, and dancing.

9.10, _above_ _Soldiers from Pit 1_, Shaanxi, China, 221–206 BCE. Painted ceramic; average figure height, 5′ 9″. Near the tomb of Shi Huangdi.

This terracotta army is only part of the funerary complex built for the First Emperor of China.

9.11, _right_ _Warrior_, Shaanxi, China, 221–206 BCE. Painted ceramic, lifesize. From the tomb of Shi Huangdi. Cultural Relics Publishing House, Beijing.

Each of the warriors is made from a combination of standardized and hand-crafted parts.

himself a large, lavish underground funeral palace. In 1974, peasants digging a well uncovered pieces of a huge, buried army of 6,000 life-size clay soldiers guarding the afterlife palace complex. Since then, archeologists have concentrated on excavating and restoring the terra-cotta army only; the tomb is mostly untouched.

The _Soldiers from Pit 1_ (Fig. 9.10), from 221–206 BCE, are arranged in eleven columns, with four soldiers abreast in nine of the columns. In this image, only a small percentage of the life-size sculptures are visible! The torsos are hollow, while the solid legs provide a weighty bottom for support and balance. The bodies are standardized: frontal, stiff, and anatomically simplified. Certain features, such as hands, were mass-produced in molds. However, every face is different and sculpted with great skill and sensitivity, like the _Warrior_ (Fig. 9.11). He is one of four kinds of soldiers, including cavalry, archers, lancers, and hand-to-hand fighters, all sculpted at least four inches shorter than the commanders. The hair is shown with detailed, individualized knotting and braiding, typical of Chinese infantry of the time.

The clay soldiers were outfitted with bronze spears, swords, crossbows, or all three and were originally painted in vivid colors. The army stood on brick "streets" that were fifteen to twenty feet below ground level. Separating the columns were rows of pounded earth that supported wood beams that once covered the entire pit. Fiber mats and plaster were placed over the beams to seal the pits and prevent water seepage. All were hidden under a low, flat mound of dirt.

Royal Tombs of the Moche Civilization

From 150 to 800 CE, the Moche civilization extended for more than four hundred miles along the Pacific Ocean in modern Peru (see *History Focus* page 235). Moche society was stratified from rich to poor, which is reflected in their burials, ranging from simple shallow pits to elaborate burial chambers on pyramids. Warrior-priests apparently ruled the Moche civilization, judging by their richly furnished graves. The primary reason for warfare in Moche society was to capture prisoners for sacrificial ceremonies. A class of skilled artisans worked full time to create gold and silver metalwork for elite burials, as well as pottery for all classes.

For our next comparative tomb complex, we look at the *Royal Tomb of Sipán* from c. 300 (recently discovered in 1980). Similar to the treasures found in the tombs we have looked at, this one also contained several sets of warrior-priest ceremonial gear, including many layers of jewelry, breastplates, weapons, and ornamental feathers. The mannequin in Figure 9.12 is dressed in a small portion of the objects found in the tomb. He is wearing a cloth covered with gilded platelets, shell beads over his wrists and shoulders, and a truly striking helmet on his head. A nose plate is suspended from a hole in the nasal septum. This one is plain gold; others are elaborately decorated. From his waist hang crescent-shaped bells that would have jangled with every step. Figure 9.13 shows the magnificent *Peanut Necklace*, with ten gold and ten silver "beads." The peanut may have been a ceremonial food or a food of honor. The Moche used gold and silver symmetrically. An

identical pair of weapons was found in one tomb, one in gold and one in silver. In another tomb, a gold ingot was found in the deceased's right hand and a silver one in the left. Some nose plates are symmetrically half gold and half silver.

 CONNECTION Like the Moche people, the Inca represented a treasured food in silver. See *Silver Representation of a Maize Plant* (Fig. 6.17), page 142.

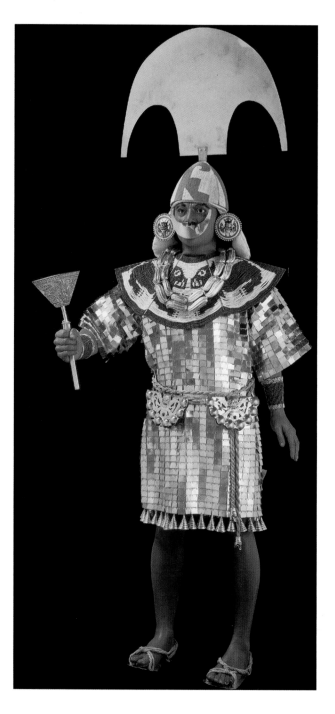

9.12 Mannequin dressed in replicas of some of the objects found in tomb 1, Moche Civilization, Peru, c. 300. The Fowler Museum of Cultural Heritage, University of California at Los Angeles.

This figure shows the elaborate gear worn by a warrior priest.

9.13 *Peanut Necklace*, Moche Civilization, Peru, c. 300. Gold and silver necklace from the *Royal Tomb of Sipán*, 20″ diameter. Museo Archeológico Nacional Bruning de Lambayeque, Peru.

This fine necklace was worn in life by a warrior priest and later buried with him.

Viking Ship Burial

The Vikings were maritime raiders from Scandinavia with settlements in Iceland, England, northern France, and Russia in the ninth and tenth centuries. Their tombs reflect how important sea travel was to their civilization. The *Oseberg* ship burial, located under a mound approximately 20 feet high and 130 feet long and excavated in 1904 near Oslo, Norway, was the tomb of a high-ranking Viking woman. The ninth-century tomb had been robbed centuries ago, but large wooden items were left behind. Our last comparison is *The Viking Ship* (Fig. 9.14), which was probably the private vessel of a wealthy family, intended for use near the coast and on inland waterways. It had a mast and sail plus rowlocks for thirty oarsmen. The graceful curves of the low, wide ship culminate in tall spiral posts at stem and stern; the one at the front is carved like a coiled snake. Rising up each post are relief carvings of elongated animal forms interlocked in complex, lace-like patterns. In these intricate carvings, each animal is composed of a layered network of crisscross lines. Other wooden objects were found in the burial, including beds, carts, and sledges, with carvings of imaginary birds or totally unidentifiable beasts. All convey a feeling of wild agitation, firmly contained within the margins of the carving.

DEVELOPMENT OF CEMETERIES AND GRAVE MONUMENTS

During the first millennium BCE, mound tombs were gradually replaced by other funerary art and architecture.

9.14 *Viking Ship*, Norway, early 9th century. Oak, 65′ long. From the Oseberg ship burial, Viking Ship Museum, Oslo. Photo from the University Museum of National Antiquities, Oslo, Norway.

This ship burial was the tomb of a high-ranking princess.

Tombs became commemorative structures instead of furnished homes for the afterlife.

The ancient Greeks developed the earliest commemorative funerary architecture in Europe and the Middle East. Although large, magnificent mausoleums were the privilege of the wealthy, cemeteries near Greek (and, later, Roman) cities were laid out for the burial of the merchant and working classes. As populations in cities grew, cemeteries with small plots marked by upright monuments became practical. In ancient Greece, the most common monuments were (1) small columns that supported vases, urns, or small statues; (2) life-size freestanding figures of young men or women; or (3) relief carvings on stone slabs, like the *Grave Stele of Hegeso*, c. 410–400 BCE (Fig. 9.15), which is our focus figure. Hegeso is the seated woman, whose servant has brought her jewelry. Quiet, everyday moments were often depicted on Greek grave markers. A simple architectural frame encloses the scene. Its straight edges contrast with the curve of the chair and complex drapery folds. The bodies are rounded and naturalistic, but they also are idealized in their proportions and in their serenity and composure. Grave markers such as this were once colorfully painted. *Hegeso*'s combination of idealism and naturalism echoes the Greeks' emphasis on humanism, as seen in the *History Focus* (page 234).

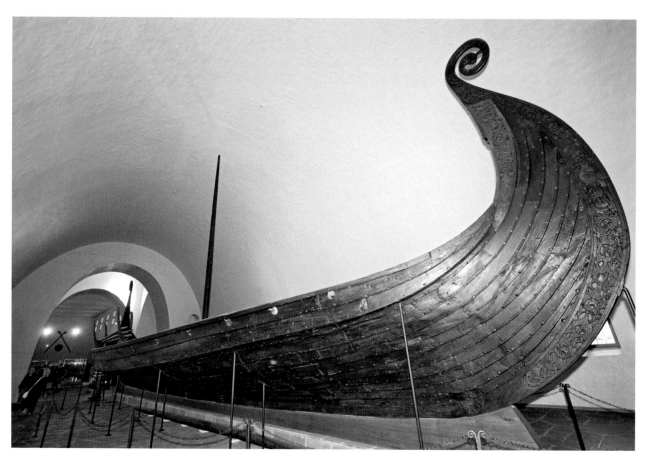

In ancient Rome, the dead were buried outside the city walls, along roadways entering the city, in highly visible funerary monuments to preserve an individual's fame, family honor, and standing in society. The tomb was the

9.15 *Grave Stele of Hegeso*, Athens, Greece, c. 410–400 BCE. Marble relief, 5′ 2″ high. From the Dipylon cemetery. National Archeological Museum, Athens.

This stele depicts the deceased woman with a servant bringing her jewelry.

meeting place for the living and the departed, and families would hold feasts at the tomb, putting out food and drink for the dead to enjoy.

Roman family tombs and mausoleums were built in several styles: altar-tombs, towers, modified Greek temples, diminutive Egyptian pyramids, or combinations of these. Almost all featured inscriptions and relief carvings that announced the fame of the individual or family interred there. Tombs of the wealthy had lavish sculpture in

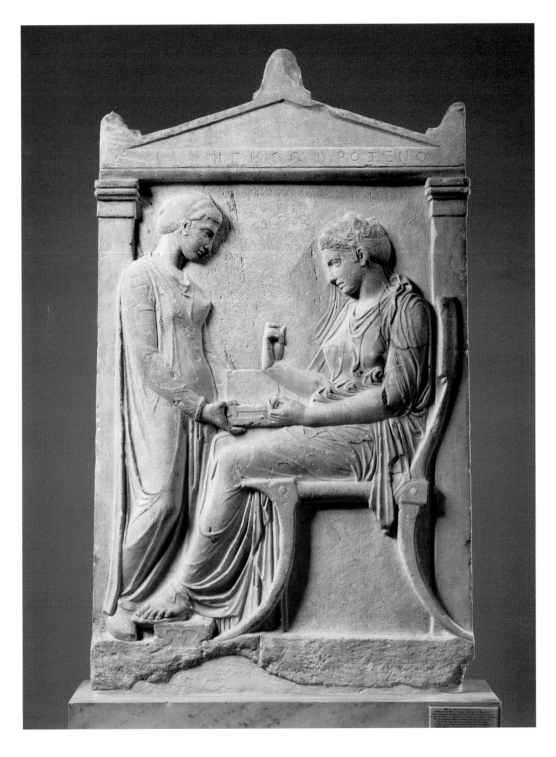

dignified, idealized Greek styles. In contrast, the *Funerary Relief of a Circus Official*, dated 110–130 CE (Fig. 9.16), was produced for a working-class person's tomb and is very cramped in style, is full of details, and has numerous characters. The largest figure is the official himself, holding hands with his wife at the far left. In Roman art, the handshake symbolized marriage. The wife is smaller, as she is of lesser status, and she stands on a pedestal as a sign that she died before him. The faces of the official and his wife are frank, unflattering portraits. The Romans often produced nonidealized likenesses—in this case, with forehead wrinkles, protruding ears, and a drooping nose and mouth. The official and his wife are crowded to the side to give space for the Circus Maximus. Only one team of horses is shown, but their leaping stance communicates the speed and competitiveness of all the chariot races. The racecourse is tilted up and diminished in size behind the chariot, while the charioteer is shown twice, once driving the team and again holding a palm branch of victory. The deceased may be a race official, or he may be the charioteer himself, shown in his younger days.

9.16 *Funerary Relief of a Circus Official*, Ostia, 110–130. Marble relief, approx. 20″ high. Vatican Museum, Rome.

Details crowd together in this relief depicting a working-class man at his job, with his family.

CONNECTION Realistic portraiture was important because respected ancestors raised the status of the living Romans, as discussed in *History Focus,* page 235. For an example of nonidealized Roman portraiture, see *Statue of Togato Barberini* (Fig. 13.13).

BURIAL IN PLACES OF WORSHIP

In some cultures, a preference arose for being buried in holy sites. This practice could be either a sign of religious devotion or the desire for prestige. The most sanctified places for burial were reserved for those with the greatest wealth, power, or religious standing.

Christian Burials

Early Christians buried their dead rather than cremating them because they believed the body would be resurrected and rejoin the soul at the end of time. Around Rome, vast underground networks called *catacombs* were dug out of **tufa**, as were the Etruscan burial chambers. They were used from the second through the fourth centuries,

9.17 *Catacomb of Sts. Peter and Marcellinus*, Rome, early 4th century. Ceiling painting from a cubiculum, fresco.

The center circle shows Jesus as the Good Shepherd; surrounding half-circles show scenes from the biblical story of Jonah and the Whale.

and some were five levels deep. From floor to ceiling, passageways were lined with openings for bodies, which were sealed after burial and decorated with painted plaster or carvings (an unsealed opening is visible in Figure 9.17). The catacombs became sanctified places during times of persecution from 249–251 and 303–306: martyrs were buried there, fugitives hid from the Romans, and, occasionally, worship services were conducted. Christians refused to recognize the divinity of the emperor or pay token tribute to Roman gods; therefore, the Romans considered them destabilizing to civil order.

Periodically in the catacomb passageways, small rooms were carved out to be used as mortuary chapels. They were often plastered and painted, like the ceiling in the fourth-century mortuary chapel (Fig. 9.17) from the *Catacomb of Sts. Peter and Marcellinus*, in Rome. We will begin our focus here. The style and imagery are very similar to Roman secular painting in which pastoral scenes were common. But here, lambs take on the symbolic meaning of the Christian "flock" of followers protected by Jesus, the Good Shepherd, who is shown in the central

circle of the ceiling painting. Decorative motifs of birds, foliage, little angels, and images of the seasons also come from Roman secular painting. The background was usually white, for better visibility in the dark tunnels, with red and green lines dividing scenes. Lively and energetic figures, rendered in quick brushstrokes, occupy the shallow space.

CONNECTION Later Christian art became much more formalized, rigid in design and awe-inspiring in size, as seen in the detail of the *Deesis Mosaic* from the Hagia Sophia in Istanbul (Fig. 2.16).

Eventually, Christianity became accepted and legalized in 313, and, under the emperor Constantine, it became the official religion of Rome (see *History Focus, page 235*). During his lifetime, Constantine funded the construction of lavish churches over the tombs of famous martyrs, one of which was Old St. Peter's in Rome. St. Peter's tomb lay in the ground but was marked by six twisting marble columns and four brass candelabra, each ten feet tall and finished in silver. By the sixteenth century, Old St. Peter's, a deteriorating timber church, was no longer a fitting symbol for the expanded Catholic Church, and so a newer, grander St. Peter's was constructed in stone.

9.18 GIANLORENZO BERNINI. *Baldacchino*, St. Peter's, Rome, Italy, 1624–1633. Gilded bronze, 100' high.

This tall canopy is mounted over the tomb of St. Peter.

The saint's tomb continued to be the focal point of the new church, marked by a new canopy in bronze, called a *Baldacchino* (Fig. 9.18), designed by Gianlorenzo Bernini between 1624 and 1633. This grand, lavish structure, taller than an eight-story building, recalls the cloth canopies that originally covered tombs of early martyrs, and its curving columns recall those that Constantine placed in Old St. Peter's. The vine-covered, twisting columns seem to leap up and support the canopy as if it were weightless, instead of tons of bronze, which was stripped from the nearby *Pantheon* (see Fig. 8.27) and melted to make the *Baldacchino*. Compare the grandeur of the *Baldacchino* with the modest size and simple imagery of the Catacomb painting. That comparison makes evident the growth of the Catholic Church from an outlawed fourth-century sect to a major religious and political power in the sixteenth century.

Over the centuries, Christian church burials were periodically banned, as tombs rapidly overtook church interiors. However, the rich and powerful continued to enjoy church burials, partly because many churches depended on the donations that accompanied the burial. (The poor and working classes were buried outside in cemeteries and in rural churchyards.) The *Chapel of Henry VII*, dated 1503–1519 (Fig. 9.19), is a large chapel, almost a separate church on the back of London's Westminster Abbey, built to house the tomb of Henry VII and his wife and to honor his deceased uncle, Henry VI. To help atone for his acts of war and royal intrigue, Henry VII donated to various charities and gave funding to Westminster Abbey, where the monks had lobbied heavily for the royal burial, along with its generous endowments. The tomb established the abbey's fame, making it a destination for pilgrims.

The chapel is built in the **English Perpendicular** style, a variation of the **Gothic** style. The ceiling seems to rise up on slender piers between the windows and then fan out gracefully and drape downward into lacy vaults. Window tracery and carvings add to the overall effect. Sculptures of saints fill the remaining wall space. The height and delicate patterning make a fitting symbol of royal power at the end of the age of chivalry. A carved wooden screen encloses the tombs of Henry VII and his wife, Elizabeth of York, which have bronze effigies atop them. The tombs are directly behind the altar, the most venerable location in the chapel. Westminster Abbey continued to be used for royal burials until the eighteenth century, and it houses tombs of illustrious statesmen, military leaders, artists, and poets as well.

CONNECTION Compare the French Gothic cathedral emphasis on verticality with the elaborate Perpendicular style of the *Chapel of Henry VII*. See *Chartres Cathedral* (Figs. 8.39–8.40, pages 227–228).

Islamic Mausoleums

The wealthy and powerful among Islamic societies were sometimes buried in mausoleums adjoining mosques. For example, Shah Abbas the Great, a seventeenth-century Persian ruler, was buried in a mausoleum attached to the *Masjid-i-Shah* (see Figs. 8.41 and 8.42).

Possibly the most famous Islamic mausoleum is the *Taj Mahal*, the final resting place of Mumtaz Mahal and a monument to the greatness of her husband, Shah Jahan, ruler of the Mughal Empire in India. The emperor apparently loved her dearly; she may have been his trusted

9.19 *Chapel of Henry VII*, Westminster Abbey, London, England, 1503–1519. Interior, toward east.

Built in the English Perpendicular style, this chapel houses the tombs of royalty.

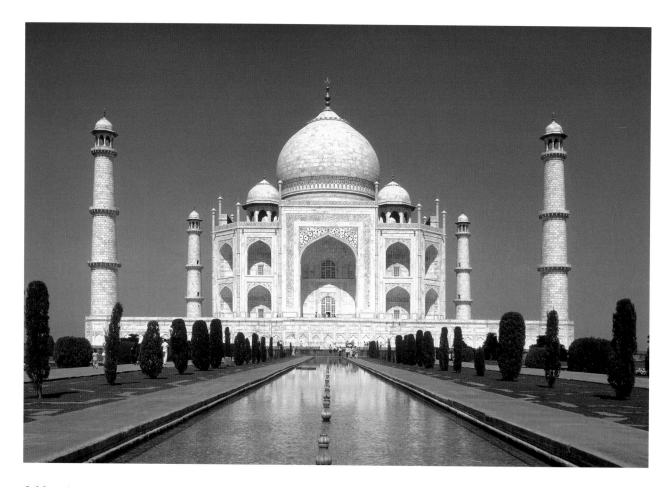

9.20 *Taj Mahal*, Agra, India, 1632–1654.

This famous Islamic shrine is a memorial to the wife of a great Shah.

advisor. The *Taj Mahal* (Fig. 9.20), built between 1632 and 1654, is an imposing and impressive structure, comparable in ambition to the *Baldacchino* in St. Peter's and the *Chapel of Henry VII*. The *Taj Mahal* sits at the north end of an expansive walled and gated garden, like some in Turkey and Iran. Such gardens symbolized Paradise and were earthly re-creations of it. Canals divide the thirty-five-acre garden into four equal squares, with a large reflecting pool in the center. Those four squares are further subdivided into fours. The canals symbolize the four rivers of Paradise, from the Quran. An inscription on the garden's main gate reinforces the link between the garden and Paradise:

> But O thou soul at peace,
> Return thou to the Lord, well-pleased, and well-pleasing
>   unto Him.
> Enter thou among my servants,
> And enter thou My Paradise.

> (The Quran Sura 89)

CONNECTION In the manuscript painting *Babur Supervising the Layout of the Garden of Fidelity* (Fig. 14.18, page 415), we see an example of a walled garden from Persia.

The *Taj Mahal* symbolizes the throne of Allah, a celestial flowering rising above the Paradise garden, buffered from the outside world. A red sandstone mosque and guesthouse flank the white mausoleum. The *Taj Mahal* is a compact, symmetrical, centrally planned structure, on a raised platform and surrounded by four minarets. The huge dome dominates and unites the entire building, but the various parts, from arched portals to windows to porches, maintain their own identity. The *Taj Mahal* seems billowing and light, and, combined with its reflection in the pool, it seems to float. The walls throughout the *Taj Mahal* are decorated lavishly with inlaid or carved floral designs, with onyx, red sandstone, agate, jasper, cornelian, lapis, coral, jade, amethyst, green beryl, and other semiprecious stones.

RELIQUARIES

In some religions, bones, tissues, and possessions of deceased holy persons are kept and venerated. Since the time of the Roman Empire, Christians have sought out the relics of saints and martyrs as they prayed to God. The practice continued in medieval Europe, where pilgrims would visit prominent medieval churches to ask special favors in the presence of a saint's relics. Fragments of clothing or body parts were kept in *reliquaries*, small precious shrines like the *Reliquary Arm*, c. 1230 (Fig. 9.21).

9.21 *Reliquary Arm*, Mosan (Belgium), c. 1230. Silver over oak; hand: bronze-gilt; appliqué plaques: silver-gilt, niello, and cabochon stones; 25 1/2″ × 6 1/2″ × 4″. The Metropolitan Museum of Art, The Cloisters Collection.

Reliquaries contained items or body parts of Christian holy people, in this case, an arm bone fragment.

Frequently, these shrines were sculptures in the shape of the body part contained within. Our focus example was built to hold pieces of arm bone from an unknown holy person. Clergy used it to bless the faithful or heal the ill. Reliquaries were expensive to produce, as was appropriate because relics were precious. In addition to decorations in silver, gold, and gemstones, this reliquary has scenes from the lives of Saints Peter and Paul. Reliquaries were related as much to the jeweler's craft as to sculpture.

In contrast, reliquaries from Africa often held the remains of venerated ancestors. Most African religions honor ancestors through ritual and sculptures because they are believed to affect the welfare of the living in many ways. *Mbulu Ngulu (Reliquary Guardian Figure)* (Fig. 9.22), from Gabon in west-central Africa, was placed on a

9.22 *Mbulu Ngulu (Reliquary Guardian Figure)*, from the Kota region of Gabon, Africa. Likely 19th–20th century. Wood, metal.

This sculpture was placed over a container with the skulls and long bones of ancestors that founded a clan.

bag or basket that contained the skulls and long bones of the ancestors who founded a clan. The guardian protected relics from evil and helped obtain food, health, or fertility from these ancestors. The sculpture, combined with the relics, was considered the image of the spirits of those dead ancestors. Offerings were made to them.

This *Mbulu Ngulu (Reliquary Guardian Figure)* and others like it were constructed over flat wooden armatures and then covered with sheets and wires of brass or copper. The faces were oval and usually concave, with projections to show the elaborate hairstyles traditionally worn in the area. The guardian figure probably evolved from figurative sculptures with hollow torsos in which bones were originally placed, a practice that became impractical as more bones were accumulated. In their present form, these figures could also be used in dances. These sculptures were extremely influential in the development of twentieth-century European modern art.

> **CONNECTION** Pablo Picasso was influenced by African sculpture. See *Les Demoiselles d'Avignon* (Fig. 1.5).

9.23 *Père Lachaise Cemetery*, Paris, France, opened 1804.

This cemetery's design was influenced by Romanticism, an art style popular in Europe in the 19th century.

MODERN COMMEMORATIVE ART

Commemorative art from the past two centuries is varied and includes monuments that deal with personal loss, memorials for groups, and monuments for important political leaders. They express loss, preserve memory, or transform the experience of death. Elements are drawn from fine art, architecture, popular culture, folk art, and craft.

Modern Cemeteries

From the middle of the eighteenth century and into the nineteenth century, cemeteries within cities in Europe reached a crisis point. Expanding cities began to overtake neglected churchyards, which were overcrowded with graves that were seen as unhealthy and sources of pollution. As a result, civil authorities gradually removed control of burial practices from the churches and established new, large, suburban cemeteries that buried the deceased who followed any (or no) religion.

In Italy, the new cemeteries were rigidly organized in tight grids. In contrast we will focus on the northern Europeans, who favored the picturesque cemetery, like the *Père Lachaise Cemetery*, opened in 1804 (Fig. 9.23), originally on the outskirts of Paris. Its design was influenced by **Romanticism**, a major art and cultural movement of the nineteenth century that emphasized a return to a simpler, rural way of life, just as the Industrial Revolution was creating increasingly packed cities, greater pollution, and mechanization of life. The cemetery was laid out with meandering paths on a hilly site, with massive trees overhead. As families could own plots in perpetuity, they often constructed elaborate and fantastic structures, running the gamut from Egyptian, Greek, Roman, Byzantine, and Gothic to modern art nouveau styles. Urns, columns, and obelisks abound. Their exotic qualities are further manifestations of Romanticism. The famous and the obscure are buried together here, making the cemetery a national tourist attraction, like many burial places in this chapter.

Now compare *Ophelia* (Fig. 9.24), painted by John Everett Millais in 1852, which is contemporary with some of the monuments in *Père Lachaise Cemetery*. Ophelia, a character in the Shakespearean play *Hamlet*, becomes incapacitated from grief and later drowns. This painting exhibits the same feeling toward picturesque nature that is apparent in *Père Lachaise Cemetery*, with deep color, lushness, accurate detail, and extraordinary delicacy. *Ophelia*'s pose and flower-strewn dress already suggest the casket. The whole scene is lacking in the grisly details of

9.24 JOHN EVERETT MILLAIS. *Ophelia*, England, 1852. Oil on canvas, 30″ × 44″.

This painting depicts a romantic image of death in repose within a picturesque scene.

madness and death by drowning, but rather is permeated with tragedy and poetic feeling. At *Père Lachaise Cemetery*, many monuments echo the sensibilities expressed in this painting, with sculptures of family members reaching for each other or lying together in death.

Contemporary Memorial Art and Practices

Today's art and rituals of death serve a broad array of social, political, and personal needs. On the personal end of the spectrum is Kane Kwei's *Coca Pod Coffin* (Fig. 9.1), which we saw at the beginning of this chapter. Kwei's workshop has produced personalized coffins primarily for Ghana locals but also for people all around the world. His coffins are designed to reflect the life work and values of the deceased. The bright colors and almost startling design honors the deceased, whose body would be placed in the long pod. The horizontal ridges echo the horizontal axis of the pod, which is balanced by the vertical diminutive tree to the left.

While the *Coca Pod Coffin* celebrates the life work of a person, the rest of the art we see in this section has a more social dimension to the funerary structures and traditions. One famous tradition is the Day of the Dead, a popular celebration mixing Christian and Aztec beliefs. It is celebrated in Mexico and parts of the United States with

9.25 DIEGO RIVERA. *Día de Los Muertos*, Mexico, 1923. Fresco, detail showing the city fiesta. South wall, Court of the Fiestas, Ministry of Education, Mexico City.

Christian and Aztec beliefs are mixed together in Mexican celebrations of the dead.

local variations. Marketplaces become sites for parades and spirited celebrations. In private homes, altars commemorate the family's dead, with burning incense and pictures of the departed placed next to their favorite foods to welcome their returning spirits. Families may spend the night at the graveyard with the deceased, decorating the gravesites and burning hundreds of candles.

Diego Rivera depicted this important ritual celebration in a series of murals about Mexican history and culture in the Ministry of Education building in Mexico City, which is our focus figure here. The painting *Día de Los Muertos*, executed in 1923 (Fig. 9.25), shows the urban observance of the feast day; two other panels depict more traditional rural observances. Great crowds fill the marketplace in a raucous celebration. In the foreground are food vendors and children in skull masks. Hanging under the awning in the background are satirical skulls and skeletons of various characters, including a priest, a general, a capitalist, and a laborer. In Mexico, the carnival atmosphere of Day of the Dead invites political satire and commentary. Rivera painted his figures in a simplified, rounded, monumental style. He insightfully recorded different individuals' personalities, and he captured the crush and excitement of the crowd and the spirit of the event.

For comparison we go to northeast of Australia to New Ireland and nearby islands, where villagers hold memorial festivals to commemorate recently deceased clan members. Both the festivals and the sculptures carved for the occasions are called *malanggan*. Planning takes several months, as special crops must be planted, pigs raised for the feast, and sculptures carved for the occasion. Honoring the dead requires a great expenditure of effort and wealth, which stimulates the local economy and creates stronger alliances among villages and clans. *Malanggan* also include initiation rites for young men. Although they have evolved as a result of foreign influence, *malanggan* rituals continue to be enacted.

Some *malanggan* carvings are narrative sculptures with intricate openwork carving. Humans and various animals transform into one another or merge ambiguously, but the exact meanings are clan secrets. Less complex is the *Helmet Mask* or *Tatanua*, shown in Figure 9.26,

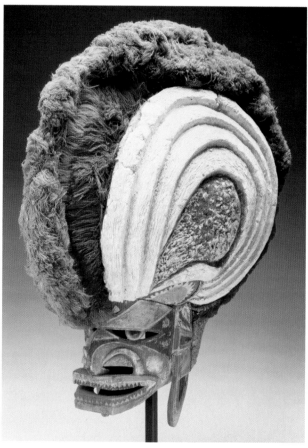

9.26 *Helmet Mask (Tatanua)*, Oceania, 19th century. Northern New Ireland, Papua New Guinea. Wood, paint, natural fibers, and opercula shells. 15 1/4″ × 9 1/2″ × 12″. Museum of Fine Arts, Houston, Texas, USA.

Great feasts were prepared and many carvings made for malanggan rituals, which commemorated recently deceased clan members.

which is used most frequently in dances. Combined with rituals, the fierce and dramatic masks provide an opportunity for spirits to be present in the villages. They are made of painted wood, vegetable fibers, and shells, and the top crest resembles men's traditional hairstyles. The traditional colors for *malanggan* are red, black, white, and yellow, which have symbolic meaning; for example, red usually means danger.

The Day of the Dead and *malanggan* rituals commemorate the dead as well as serve social needs. Our next work functions commemoratively and politically. The *Mausoleum of Mao Zedong* (Fig. 9.27) not only houses the body of the leader of the Communist revolution in China but also asserts the authority of the Communist government after centuries of imperial rule. Mao's historical accomplishments included helping to restore Chinese independence and redistributing land to the peasants.

The major axis of Beijing, the Chinese capital, runs north-south, and official buildings, palaces, public grounds, and city gates were placed along this axis, along with the Forbidden City and the Imperial Palace. This alignment signifies the authority of the imperial dynasties. In front of the Forbidden City is Tiananmen Square, a large, important ceremonial space. The *Mausoleum of Mao Zedong* is deliberately located in the square, on the north-south axis, as the Communist leaders claim to be rightful successors to the emperors.

CONNECTION See the discussion of the elaborate Forbidden City and the *Imperial Throne Room* in the Hall of Supreme Harmony in Chapter 10 (Fig. 10.13).

CONNECTION Like the tomb of Mao Zedong, the *Vietnam Veterans Memorial* (Fig. 10.30) stands on politically significant ground, the Mall in Washington, D.C.

9.27 *Mausoleum of Mao Zedong*, Tiananmen Square, Beijing, China, latter half of the 20th century.

This is a monument to both the power of Communism and its leader.

Another powerful art project to compare is the *AIDS Memorial Quilt*, shown here in 1996 (Fig. 9.28), a commemorative work with a personal and political impact. The quilt is composed of thousands of individual three-by-six-foot panels, approximately the size of a twin-bed blanket, which would cover the body of one person who died from AIDS. Friends or family make each panel and decorate it, sometimes only with initials, but often more elaborately, with photographs, memorabilia, or details of a life story. The work is organized by a group called the Names Project in San Francisco, and most people contributing quilt pieces have no art training. The format of a quilt is especially appropriate for this collaborative, grassroots product of loving remembrance. After only a few years, the *AIDS Memorial Quilt* has become a vast public spectacle, which communicates the enormity of the epidemic and its toll in the United States alone. The quilt changes every time it is displayed. In Figure 9.28, its proximity to the White

House and government buildings means that the disease was recognized publicly as a crisis and a tragedy by the U.S. government.

The tragedies of September 11, 2001, have been memorialized in several ways. For one month in 2002, *Tribute in Light* (Fig. 9.29), designed by three architects and two artists, projected two powerful beams of light into the night sky where the twin towers of the World Trade Center once stood. *Tribute in Light* has been recreated each year since for the anniversary of the attacks. These temporary "towers" of light appeared architectonic, because each was composed of forty-four high-powered lamps that, combined, resembled a three-dimensional column with fluting. As light, the beams referenced hope and aspiration, but because they were immaterial, they also recalled the transitory nature and vulnerability of earthly things.

Studio Daniel Libeskind has developed models for new construction on the World Trade Center location, as

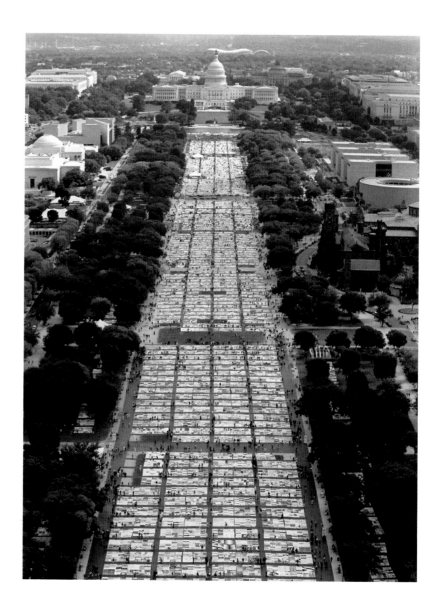

9.28 *AIDS Memorial Quilt.* Displayed on the Mall in Washington, D.C., October 11, 1996. Organized by the Names Project, San Francisco.

This huge, collaborative work commemorates the loss of loved ones to a deadly disease.

9.29 JOHN BENNETT, GUSTAVO BONEVARDI, RICHARD NASH GOULD, PAUL MYODA, JULIAN LAVERDIERE, AND PAUL MARANTZ. *Tribute in Light*, New York City, 2002. High-power lamps. World Trade Center Memorial at Ground Zero.

Two vertical beams, composed of 88 search lights, are lit in memory of the 911 tragedy.

shown in the *Computer-Generated Design to Rebuild the World Trade Center Site*, 2003 (Fig. 9.30).The proposal includes a ring of lower office buildings and one large Freedom Tower, a tapering, twisting seventy-story sky-scraper, topped by an openwork cable superstructure and a spire. The Freedom Tower will be 1,776 feet tall, com-memorating the year of the Declaration of Independence. The goal of the architect and design teams is to have the tower symbolize the spirit of the United States, while being extremely safe and secure and not competing with the design of the old World Trade Center.

The area in the middle of the ring of buildings will be left open for a tree-covered plaza and permanent memorial to those who died at the site on September 11, 2001. Michael Arad and Peter Walker's design has been chosen for that permanent memorial, *Reflecting Absence* (Fig. 9.30), con-sisting of two sunken reflecting pools. Access areas beneath the pools feature walls with the victims' names inscribed, a meditation room, and a site for leaving mementos. The sunken pools mark the footprints of the old towers.

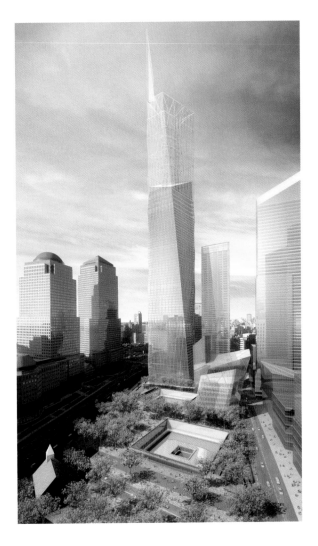

9.30 STUDIO DANIEL LIBESKIND. *Computer-Generated Design to Rebuild the World Trade Center Site.* Selected design for World Trade Center Site Memorial—*Reflecting Absence* by Michael Arad and Peter Walker, copyright 2004 LMDC. Rendering by dbox. Courtesy of Lower Manhattan Development Corp.

A group of five towers, plus a sunken memorial in the middle, contain symbolic attributes that recall the spirit of the United States as well as memorialize the September 11 attacks.

Section 3

THE STATE

Rulers and governments use art to celebrate and spread their earthly power. Art is also used in war, either in creating weapons and armor for it or in making images that promote it. It also gives us images of peacemaking and monuments for peace.

Art can be an equally strong voice of protest against a government or against a social practice. People who are not in power can use art to affirm their ideas and to protest against warfare, oppression, or political policy.

CHAPTER 10 POWER, POLITICS, AND GLORY

Art made in the service of political rulers, or as records of war or peace.

CHAPTER 11 SOCIAL PROTEST/AFFIRMATION

Art as a vehicle for affirming the rights of oppressed groups or protesting injustice

10.1 *Imperial Palace*, Forbidden City, Beijing, China.

This is an enormous palace compound that once had 9,999 rooms and was a city unto itself for the ruling emperor and nobility.

10

POWER, POLITICS, AND GLORY

Throughout human history, a vast amount of artwork has promoted, popularized, or propagandized governments as well as those who lead them. Art has depicted war and helped shape our reaction to it. Art has also celebrated peace.

PREVIEW

This chapter will show how art has played a tremendous role in promoting and glorifying the state and its rulers' authority, prestige, and achievements. Portraits, sculptures, paintings and special objects denote glory, supremacy, and status. The state also is made magnificent in art, especially in monuments, seats of government, and palaces, as in the Imperial Palace (Fig. 10.1).

We will also see how art can glorify war and document its impact on those involved. A warrior's paraphernalia raises the owner's status, and artistry enhances the spirit and function of the weapon. War scenes can exalt the drama, give alternate views of battle, or emphasize its horror. War memorials may evoke deep patriotism or private mourning and contemplation. Peace itself is given an image in painting, and beautifully crafted art objects may become peace offerings. Peace memorials may glorify the abundance possible when there is no war.

Connecting Art and History from
500–1300 CE

World history from 500–1300 witnessed the rise and fall of many kingdoms, with rulers using art to increase their prestige. Civilization centers flourished throughout the Americas. The Moche civilization (200–800) of coastal Peru produced great temples of sun brick and had elaborate burials filled with metal, jewels, and ceramic treasures. The Inca civilization in the Andes Mountains was shortly to emerge. North American centers included the Mississippian culture (c. 800) and the Anasazi (1000–1300), who built the famous cliff dwellings in the southwest United States.

Map 5 The Expansion of Islam, the Byzantine Empire, and the Migration of Germanic People into Southern Europe. Courtesy of Replogle Globes, Inc., Broadview, IL.

Central America saw the succession of many great empires with ambitious architecture and advances in learning, especially in mathematics and astronomy. All were hierarchical societies, governed by a supreme ruler with warrior and priest classes. Teotihuacán reached its height around 600. The old Maya Empire in the Yucatan Peninsula thrived until around 900, with grand temples and palaces, like the *Palace at Palenque* (Fig. 10.12). From the Toltec culture (900–1200) around Veracruz came the *Tula Warrior Columns* (Fig. 10.20). Beginning in the thirteenth century, the Aztec built a powerful empire in central Mexico, with engineering feats that included irrigation and drainage systems and road building.

During this period, the Byzantine Empire and the expansion of Islam dominated Eastern Europe, the Middle East, central Asia, and northern Africa. One of the great rulers of the Christian Byzantine Empire (476–1453) was Justinian, whose notable churches featured mosaics such as the *Emperor Justinian and His Attendants* (Fig. 10.4). Wealthy Byzantium had many centers for learning and for preservation of ancient knowledge. It began to decline around 1100, due to warfare with Muslims.

The prophet Mohammad founded the Islamic religion in the early seventh century. Islam spread quickly, often openly accepted and sometimes through warfare. Muslim armies conquered northern Africa, Spain, and the Middle East within one hundred years and advanced on India beginning in 1000. Important Muslim kingdoms were established in today's Spain, Iraq, and Turkey. The Muslims were known for their accomplishments in algebra,

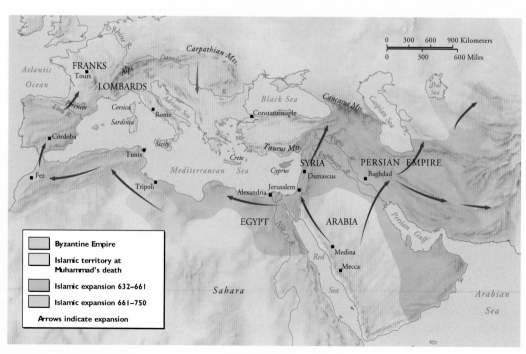

geometry, astronomy, optics, and literature, as well as for the creation of great universities and libraries.

This was the Middle Ages in Europe, beginning with the dissolution of the Western Roman Empire and concluding with the early forms of the modern European nation-states. Until 600, Europe experienced upheaval as Germanic peoples migrated south and east. Once they settled, they founded Christian kingdoms with architecture and art influenced by Rome and Byzantium. Large monasteries and the Catholic Church in Rome were more powerful than any other European government. Almost all art was religious. The Crusades (1095–1291), a series of wars for control of the Holy Land, brought the Germanic Europeans in further contact with Byzantium and the Muslim Empire. Feudalism was the main form of social and economic organization. The Black Death (1347–1351) ravaged Europe, killing one-third of the population. By 1200, a distinctive art form, Gothic, developed in Northern Europe.

Africa also saw the emergence of several early empires. Northern empires were Islamic, while southern empires followed native African religions. Powerful and wealthy Ghana (c. 700–1200) controlled the area's trade in salt and gold. Its ironworks produced powerful weapons. Later in the same area, Mali became a large Islamic empire. Farther south, in Ife, the twelfth century saw the founding of the Yoruba civilization, with its famous *Crowned Head of an Oni* (Fig. 10.5). Also in the south, the Zanj people thrived on trade with China, Arabia, and India from 1200 to 1500, and the kingdom of Zimbabwe flourished, with its great stone buildings.

India experienced a resurgence of Hinduism beginning in the sixth century, and many huge temple complexes were constructed. After 1000, Muslims invaded and established the Mughal Empire in northern India. In the south,

10.2 YAN LIBEN. *Portraits of the Emperors* (detail), China, 7th century. Ink and colors on silk, 17.5″ high.

Chinese emperors were believed to be Sons of Heaven. Their lavish attire, serene expression, and relatively large size all attested to their brilliance.

strong Hindu dynasties continued, with ambitious building programs. Indian art and architecture spread to Southeast Asia and Indonesia throughout this period. In Cambodia, the Khmer people developed a culture noted for its amazing architecture and sculpture, like *Jayavarman VII* (Fig. 10.6).

The imperial court in China promoted the arts throughout this era, with accomplishments in poetry, literature, music, ceramics, and painting, like the *Portraits of the Emperors* (Fig. 10.2). The dynasties were the Tang (618–906), Song (960–1279), and Yuan (1279–1368). The Yuan was founded by invading Mongolians under Kublai Khan. Inventions included the magnetic compass, paper money, book printing, and gunpowder. After 1368, the Ming Dynasty began an ambitious building program, which included

the structures in the Forbidden City (Fig. 10.13 and Fig. 10.1) and the *Great Wall* (Fig. 10.22), and China became an international naval power.

Japanese recorded history begins around the year 600, when the Japanese culture changed as a result of foreign influences. It imported the Buddhist religion, mathematics, architecture, the arts, and agricultural methods from the Chinese but eventually modified them. Shinto is the native Japanese religion. Japan produced the world's first novel, The *Tale of the Genji*, by Lady Murasaki Shikibu, illustrated in the handscroll, *Heiji Monogatari* (Fig. 10.24). From the eighth through the nineteenth centuries, Japan was essentially a feudal state, with a hierarchy of military leaders under the shogun, and it experienced periods of internal strife.

World Art Map for Chapter 10

**Red Horse. *Battle of Little Big Horn*.
Crow Agency, United States.**

Presentation Pipe Tomahawk.

Mesquakie Bear Claw Necklace.

NORTH AMERICA

Edward Hicks. *The Peaceable Kingdom*.

Felix W. Weldon. *USA Marine Corps War Memorial*.
Maya Ying Lin. *Vietnam Veterans Memorial*.

Mathew B. Brady (or staff).
Dead Confederate Soldier with Gun.

Triumph of the Will.

Charles Barry and A. W. N. Pugin. *Houses of Parliament*.

Jules Hardouin-Mansart and Charles Le Brun. *Hall of Mirrors*.

Andrea del Verrocchio. *Equestrian Monument of Bartolomeo Colleoni*.

Emperor Justinian and His Attendants.

EUROPE

Arch of Titus.
Ara Pacis Augustae.

Pablo Picasso. *Guernica*. Madrid, Spain.

Cloak and Feather Hat.

Moctezuma's Headdress.

**Palace at Palenque.
Chiapas, Mexico.**

**Tula Warrior Columns.
Hidalgo, Mexico.**

Olowe of Ise. *Palace Sculpture*.
Crowned Head of an Oni.
Plaque with *Warrior and Attendants*.

SOUTH AMERICA

N

| 0 | 1,000 | 2,000 Km. |
| 0 | 1,000 | 2,000 Mi. |

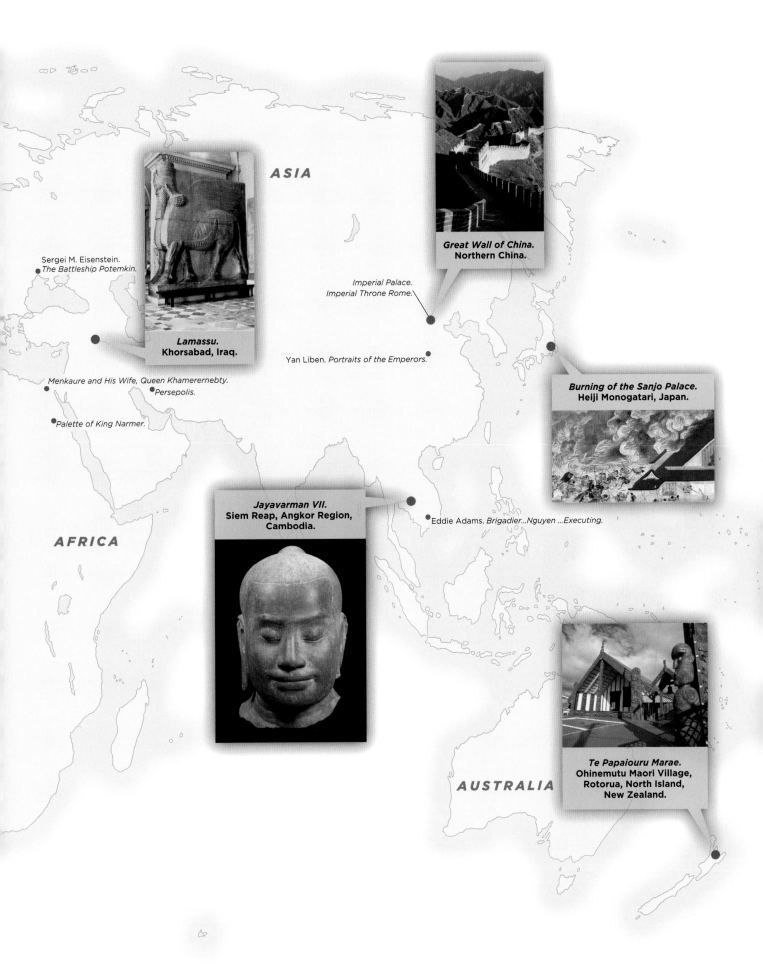

ASIA

Sergei M. Eisenstein.
The Battleship Potemkin.

Lamassu.
Khorsabad, Iraq.

Menkaure and His Wife, Queen Khamerernebty.
Persepolis.

Palette of King Narmer.

Great Wall of China.
Northern China.

Imperial Palace.
Imperial Throne Rome.

Yan Liben. *Portraits of the Emperors.*

Burning of the Sanjo Palace.
Heiji Monogatari, Japan.

Jayavarman VII.
**Siem Reap, Angkor Region,
Cambodia.**

Eddie Adams. *Brigadier...Nguyen ...Executing.*

AFRICA

AUSTRALIA

Te Papaiouru Marae.
**Ohinemutu Maori Village,
Rotorua, North Island,
New Zealand.**

500–1300 CE

PALEOLITHIC AGE	**15,000 BCE**	
UNIFICATION OF EGYPT	**3200 BCE**	

Above *Hall of the Bison,* Altamira (5.23) 15000 BCE

Palette of King Narmer

Menkaure and His Wife, Queen Khamerernebty

	1500
ASSYRIAN EMPIRE	**1000**
ACHAEMENID PERSIA	**500**

Lamassu

Persepolis

ROMAN REPUBLIC *The Great Wall*

Above *Colosseum* (15.11)

	100
ROMAN EMPIRE	

Ara Pacis Augustae

Arch of Titus

TEOTIHUACÁN	**200 CE**
German Migration in Europe	**400**
BYZANTINE EMPIRE BEGINS	**500**

Emperor Justinian and His Attendants

Palace at Palenque

TANG DYNASTY— CHINA	**600**

ISLAM FOUNDED		
JAPAN—HISTORIC ERA		
	700	
	800	
	900	
YORUBA CULTURE FOUNDED		
MAYA—TOLTEC CULTURE		
SONG DYNASTY— CHINA		
ROMANESQUE Era	**1000**	*Tula Warrior Columns*
ANASAZI CULTURE		*Crowned Head of an Oni*
	1100	

Above *Angkor Wat,* Cambodia (2.31)

Jayavarman VII

	1200	
GOTHIC Era		
YUAN DYNASTY— CHINA	**1300**	*Burning of the Sanjo Palace*
		Moctezuma's Headdress
AZTEC EMPIRE		
Black Death		
INCAN EMPIRE	**1400**	
RENAISSANCE IN EUROPE		
MING DYNASTY— CHINA		VERROCCHIO: *Equestrian Monument of Bartolomeo Colleoni*

MUGHAL DYNASTY— INDIA

Above *Taj Mahal (9.20)*

Forbidden City Begun   **1500**   *Imperial Throne Room*

BAROQUE STYLE   **1600**

BENIN KINGDOM— AFRICA   **1700**   *Hall of Mirrors*

Cloak and Feather Hat Plaque with Warrior and Attendants

U.S. Revolutionary War

French Revolution   **1800**   *Mesquakie Bear Claw Necklace*

ROMANTICISM

REALISM   *Te Papaiouru Marae, a Maori Meeting House*

Presentation Pipe Tomahawk

HICKS: *The Peaceable Kingdom*

BARRY AND PUGIN: *Houses of Parliament*

BRADY (OR STAFF): *Dead Confederate Soldier with Gun*

IMPRESSIONISM   RED HORSE: *Battle of Little Big Horn*

POSTIMPRESSIONISM

Russian Revolution   **1900**

Above *Grand Mosque, Djenne (1.23)*

World War I

CUBISM

SURREALISM

World War II

1950

MODERNISM

1960

POSTMODERNISM

Vietnam War

Fall of the Berlin Wall

2000

War in Afghanistan

War in Iraq

EISENSTEIN: *The Battleship Potemkin*

RIEFENSTAHL: *Triumph of the Will*

PICASSO: *Guernica*

Hiroshima Peace Memorial Park

WELDON: *USA Marine Corps War Memorial*

ADAMS: *Brigadier General . . . executing . . .*

Above SAARINEN, St. Louis Gateway Arch (5.14)

LIN: *Vietnam Veterans Memorial*

Above HAACKE: *MetroMobiltan (11.15)*

THE GLORY OF THE RULER

The following artistic devices are often used to glorify a ruler's image:

- *The idealized image*: the ruler's face and/or body are depicted without flaw and often with youthful vigor; the idealized image often includes a wise or dignified demeanor
- *Symbols*: details are included that indicate omnipotence, authority, or divine blessing; some symbols show military or religious power
- *Compositional devices*: the ruler often occupies the center of a picture and may be shown larger than attendants or other figures; the ruler's clothing may attract attention

Divine Rulers, Royalty, and Secular/Religious Leaders

Many heads of state throughout history have considered themselves not only royalty but also religious leaders or members of a divine or mythic family. Images helped them to spread and communicate that idea.

We begin our focus here with an early example of a royal portrait, the Egyptian royal couple, *Menkaure and His Wife, Queen Khamerernebty*, dated c. 2600 BCE (Fig. 10.3). They stand side by side, united by the queen's embrace, placing the same foot forward. Young, strong, and confident, they display the Egyptian ideal of beauty and maturity. Khamerernebty is shown as large as Menkaure, as pharaonic succession was traced through the female line. The compact pose makes the sculpture more durable and permanent, befitting the pharaohs as divine descendants of the Sun God, Re.

The sculpture was carved from a block of slate, a very hard stone. One view was likely sketched on each side, according to the Egyptian canon of proportions, and then carved inward until all four views met. Traces of paint were found on the piece. Menkaure was the pharaoh who built the third and smallest of the *Great Pyramids* at Gizeh (see Fig. 9.4). This shrine-like statue was found in his valley temple.

> **CONNECTION** Chinese emperors were considered to be divine Sons of Heaven. See the detail of Yan Liben's *Portraits of the Emperors* in the *History Focus* Figure 10.2.

Our comparisons begin with another royal portrait, *Emperor Justinian and His Attendants*, from the Church of San Vitale in Ravenna, Italy, built in the sixth century (Fig. 10.4). Justinian dominates this image, just as he dominated the Byzantine Empire, an outgrowth of the old Roman Empire that grew in power from the sixth century onward (see the *History Focus* on page 266). A devout Christian, he occupies the center spot between clergy to the right and military and state leaders to the left. As emperor-priest, Justinian wears a purple cloak and a magnificent jeweled crown and carries a golden bowl with bread used in Christian ritual. The solar disk or halo behind his head indicates divine status, a device used in Egyptian, Persian, and late Roman art. The emperor

10.3 *Menkaure and His Wife, Queen Khamerernebty*, Gizeh, Egypt, Fourth Dynasty, c. 2600 BCE. Slate, approximately 4′ 6 ½″ high.

This early portrait of the royal couple displays the equal status of Menkaure's wife Khamerernebty, who passes on the Pharaonic succession through her offspring.

10.4 *Emperor Justinian and His Attendants*, Church of San Vitale, Ravenna, Italy, c. 547. Mosaic on the north wall of the apse. Canali Photobank.

This devout Christian Emperor dominates the center of the composition, which represents his power over both the military and the Church.

is flanked by twelve figures, alluding to Christ and the twelve apostles. The clergy hold sacred objects: the crucifix, the book of Gospels, and the incense burner. Even a soldier's shield displays the **Chi-Rho**, an ancient symbol of Christ. A similar mosaic (not pictured here), *Empress Theodora and Her Attendants*, faces the Justinian mosaic in the church's sanctuary. Theodora, Justinian's wife, was an able and effective co-ruler, and her image indicates her equal rank and power.

In the next comparison, the head alone carries the exalted qualities of a ruler. In west-central Africa, several superb portrait heads were made in the twelfth to fifteenth centuries, each very much like the *Crowned Head of an Oni* (Fig. 10.5). This head represents a ruler in one of the many early empires emerging in Africa at this time

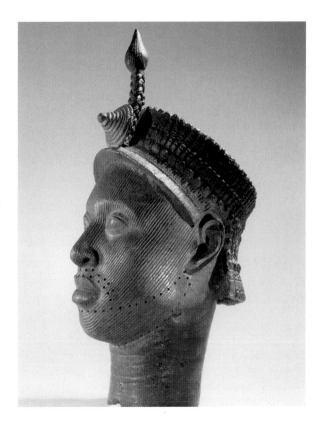

10.5 *Crowned Head of an Oni,* Wunmonije Compound, Ife, Nigeria, 12th–15th centuries. Yoruba. Zinc, brass; smaller than life size. Museum of the Ife Antiquities, Ife, Nigeria.

This delicately detailed portrait of an early African ruler expresses a sense of calm, security, and poise.

(see *History Focus* on page 267). The delicately detailed portrait is in a naturalistic style that contrasts with the more abstracted art from much of Africa. The face has a remarkable sense of calm and serenity, with beautiful flowing features, making it an outstanding example of an idealized royal portrait. Scholars still debate the exact identity and use of these portrait heads, but many believe each head represents a Yoruba or Benin ruler, who traced their rule back to the mythic first human ancestor. The crown was likely a royal insignia. The lines on the face may indicate scarification or perhaps strings of a beaded veil. Also visible are neck rings that are similar to those worn today among the Yoruba.

CONNECTION To see the range of styles in African art, contrast the naturalistic quality of the *Crowned Head of an Oni* with the more abstracted style of the *Reliquary Guardian Figure* (Fig. 9.22, page 257).

CONNECTION Yoruba leaders today are identified by such headgear as the *Great Beaded Crown of the Orangun-lla*, in Figure 13.26, (page 389). These contemporary crowns are ancient forms that may date back to those worn by the early onis.

Also from the twelfth century is the portrait head of *Jayavarman VII* (Fig. 10.6), the last great king of the Angkor Empire of the highly civilized Khmer people (in present-day Cambodia). He was a mighty military leader who conquered invaders and fought back rival states; one campaign lasted twenty years. Jayavarman VII was also well known for his amazing building projects, including the great *Temple of Bayon* at Angkor Wat that boasts fifty towers, each side with a large face of Buddha. Yet in this portrait, Jayavarman chose to be represented almost as a mystic, and in fact his own conversion from Hinduism to Buddhism spread that religion in the area. His face is softly modeled with eyes downturned in meditation, and his gentle smile became famous in Khmer art.

CONNECTION Jayavarman's likeness may have been the model for the Buddha faces on the *Temple of Bayon at Angkor Wat* (Fig. 5.26, page 121).

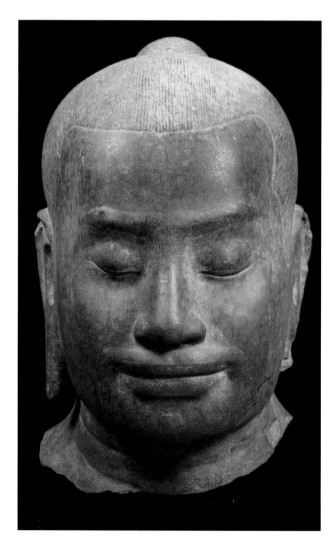

10.6 *Jayavarman VII*, Cambodia, province of Siemreap, Angkor region, late 12th or early 13th century CE. Bayon style. Sandstone head, 16″ × 9″ × 12″. Musée des Arts Asiatiques-Guimet, Paris, France.

The portrait of the last and most powerful King of the Angkor Empire and the Khmer people displays his contemplative mysticism after his conversion from Hinduism to Buddhism. His turned-down eyes and gentle smile became known in Khmer art.

10.7 *Cloak and Feather Hat*, Hawaii, 18th century. Museo de America, Madrid, Spain.

Only monarchs were allowed to wear the woven red and gold feathers that represented royalty and prosperity.

Many royal portraits from various cultures use similar attributes that convey an exalted quality: the idealized face/body, the symbolic details, centralized composition, and dignified demeanor.

Objects of Royalty and Prestige

Royalty have been exalted with elaborate thrones, garments, dazzling jewelry, or objects of power. We have three examples here to compare.

Hawaiian royal objects were made of materials that were taboo to all others in the society, unlike the gold and gems in a European crown, which any wealthy individual could possess. Hawaiians considered feathers sacred and connected with the gods, so only royalty could own or wear them. The *Cloak and Feather Hat* (Fig. 10.7) is magnificent apparel made of red and gold feathers. Although feather work is common in many Pacific islands, the Hawaiian work is the most developed and intricate. Colors have symbolic value, with red representing royalty, while yellow signifies a prosperous future. Hawaiian royalty also enjoyed large, elaborate feathered fly whisks called *kahili*, which were common objects transformed into luxury items and used for special occasions.

> **CONNECTION** See *Moctezuma's Headdress* in Figure 10.34 (page 296) to compare Hawaiian and Aztec feather work.

Among the Mesquakie people around Tama, Iowa, in the mid-1800s, grizzly bear claws were signs of high status, just as diamonds and pearls might be of value in other cultures. The prairie grizzly's nails—over three inches in length—were difficult to acquire and were considered a great trophy. The *Mesquakie Bear Claw Necklace* (Fig. 10.8) represented the strength and tenacity of the bear, which added to the dignity of the owner. The unassembled materials—claws, colored glass beads, otter pelts, and silk ribbons—would be given to those who owned the rights to create the neckpiece. The striking repetition of delicate curves suggests the lethal potential of each claw. The decorated otter pelt is attached to the necklace to become an elegant train.

Contemporary Political Leaders

Images of contemporary political leaders are fundamentally different from those of the past, just as the concept of "ruler" has evolved. Today, almost no rulers openly consider themselves to be of divine descent, and many are not royalty. And with photography, pictures of rulers come to us not as artworks, but as a flood of newspaper or television images. There is a great difference between images that are produced under the ruler's direction and those over which the ruler has little or no control. In 1934, Adolf Hitler commissioned the film *Triumph of the Will* (Fig. 10.9), directed by Leni Riefenstahl, to glorify his rule, his military strength, and the Nazi order of Aryan supremacy. A work of brilliant propaganda, Riefenstahl's film established Hitler as the first media hero of the modern age.

Given unlimited funding by Hitler, Riefenstahl had a staff of more than 130 people, sixteen cameras, four sound trucks, and cranes and dollies for dramatic shots. Skillfully edited into the film were speeches, parades, cheering crowds, and the lush music of the popular German composer Richard Wagner. Although the film was a documentary covering a six-day rally celebrating Hitler at Nuremberg, the imagery was entirely staged. Of course, all film and photographic content can be manipulated when shot, as well as retouched and altered later. In this case, Riefenstahl carefully set the scene so that Hitler is presented to and worshipped by the masses as Germany's savior. In close-ups of Hitler's smiling face, his charisma is evident. At the end of the film, we see an aerial shot of massive military power in rigid formation under Hitler's control (Fig. 10.9). This utopian image of harmony and strength appealed to those whose lives were in disorder, and human history experienced one of its most horrendous episodes.

One can wonder about Riefenstahl's motivation. Perhaps she was a devout believer in Hitler and Nazi dogma,

10.8 *Mesquakie Bear Claw Necklace*, Tama, Iowa, USA, c. 1860. Otter pelt, grizzly claws, glass beads, silk ribbon, 16 1/4″ long, 14 1/4″ wide, 3″ high. Photo archive of the National Museum of the American Indian.

This prestigious adornment represented the strength and tenacity of the grizzly bear, which added to the dignity of its owner.

10.9 Leni Riefenstahl. *Triumph of the Will*, Germany, 1934. Film. Kobal Collection.

Adolf Hitler commissioned this film in order to glorify his rule, military strength, and the Nazi order of Aryan Supremacy.

or perhaps she was seduced by the opportunity to work in a new art medium with unlimited funds. Whatever the case, Riefenstahl's prototype in film would affect future campaigns for political elections as well as lay the foundation for consumer advertising.

THE POWER OF THE STATE

Palaces, government buildings, and monuments can make the state and the ruler seem powerful and glorious.

Palaces

As official residences of kings, emperors, and religious leaders, palaces visually represent the state's power. Often palaces are seats of government. Palaces frequently have the following qualities:

- Their grand size distinguishes them from ordinary residences.
- They are usually lavishly ornamented.
- Height is often an important element.
- They feature art prominently, often adding symbolic content.

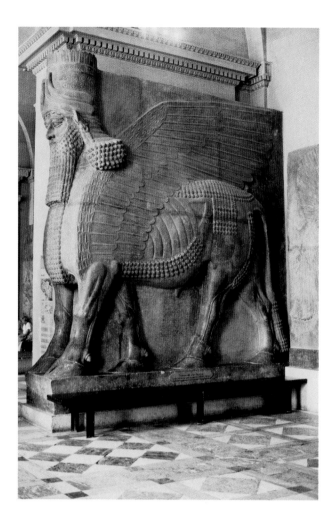

10.10 *Lamassu*, Khorsabad, Iraq, 720 BCE. Limestone, 14' high.

Two of these huge sculptures dominated the palace gate to Khorsabad, the Assyrian capital. It was meant to terrify and intimidate all those who entered.

CONNECTION We will look at other fantastic animals, and the reasons humans invented them, in Chapter 14, Nature, Knowledge, and Technology.

Our focus figure is an outstanding early example of a palace that comes from the Achaemenid civilization in ancient Persia, which produced a body of monumental art of outstanding splendor. The palace of *Persepolis*, begun by Darius I in 518 BCE and destroyed by Alexander the Great in 331 BCE, took fifty years to build (Fig. 10.11). The heavily fortified palace citadel was located on a terraced platform measuring 1,500 feet by 900 feet, with mud walls reaching sixty feet high and sometimes faced with carved stone slabs and glazed brick. Interior spaces were large, wide **hypostyle** halls, with many carved columns supporting the roofs. The windows were made of solid blocks of stone with cutout openings. Stairs were also chiseled from stone blocks and then fitted into place.

The Royal Audience Hall was two hundred feet square and sixty feet high and may have held up to 10,000 people. One hundred tall columns (some visible in the left background of Fig. 10.11) supported a massive wood-beam ceiling. On top were elaborate capitals with curving scrolls and foreparts of bulls or lions. Some had human heads. A grand staircase, cut directly from natural rock formations, was covered with reliefs depicting subjects presenting tribute to the king. Gates at Persepolis had guardian figures like the *Lamassu* (Fig. 10.10).

Like the Persians, the Mayans of Central America created large palaces with high platforms and relief sculpture. Occupied from 514 to 784, but abandoned before the Spanish conquest, Palenque remained completely hidden by tropical flora until it was rediscovered in modern times. Palenque was the center of one of several successive empires in Central America (see *History Focus* on page 266). It had the living quarters for the Mayan royalty, a center for religious rites, facilities for astronomical studies, and an administrative precinct.

The *Palace at Palenque* (Fig. 10.12) featured four courts, each surrounded with rooms and galleries, likely used for administrative purposes. Several thrones were found within the galleries. Built on a thirty-foot-high platform, the complex measures 250 feet long by 200 feet wide. Large, painted stucco masks of human faces once adorned the ends of the terraces. Nearby, a vaulted underground aqueduct brought water to the *Palace*. The seventy-two-foot-high tower adds important verticality to the horizontal design. Large tower windows facing the four cardinal points may have had both astronomical and defensive uses. The profusely decorated interior was covered by parallel rows of **corbel** vaults and arches. This allowed for thin inner walls and airy rooms that countered the fierce tropical heat. The outer walls were pierced with T-shaped

Our introduction to palace art is the mighty *Lamassu* (Fig. 10.10), from 720 BCE, an enormous sculpture from Khorsabad, capital of the Assyrian Empire. The Assyrians, known for their ruthlessness and brutality, dominated the Near East for more than three hundred years. With enormous size and glaring stare, two large *Lamassu* guarded the palace gate, to terrify and intimidate all who entered. A form of a divine genie, the winged creature is part lion or bull, with the head of a human being. The horned crown symbolizes the king's divine power. Carved from one large block of stone, the *Lamassu* has five legs to show movement and stability at the same time. From the side, the *Lamassu* appears to be striding forward. The front view, however, shows the beast at a stalwart standstill, blocking the viewer's forward movement. Stylized and natural elements are combined, with hair and wings depicted with linear and repetitive patterns, while the strong, muscular legs and facial features are more naturally rendered.

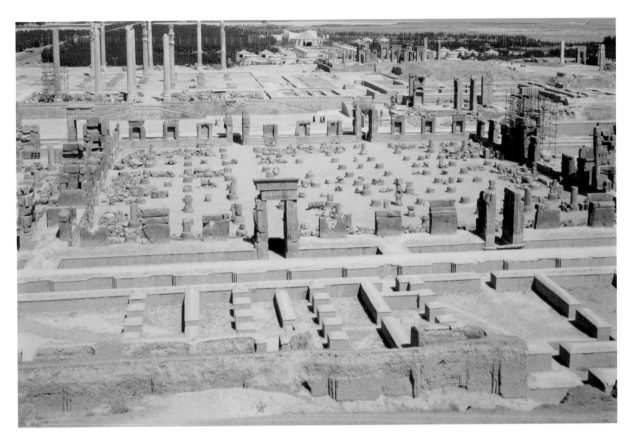

10.11 *Persepolis*, general view, Persia (Iran), 559–330 BCE.

This awesome palace complex consisted of many structures, including hypostyle halls. These halls contained many carved columns that supported their roofs.

10.12 *Palace at Palenque*, Chiapas, Mexico, 514–784. Maya.

This complex featured four courts, each surrounded by rooms and galleries, which were likely used for administrative purposes.

windows and doorways. The thin walls and airy rooms countered the fierce tropical heat.

Chinese royal architecture helped sustain the emperor's rule, because its magnificence supported his claim to be Son of Heaven, father of the people, and the one who maintained Heaven on Earth. Compare now the Forbidden City, an enormous palace compound that once had 9,999 rooms, which resembles a city unto itself within Beijing. No commoners were allowed to enter. The major structures have gleaming yellow tile roofs and rich vermilion walls. Pure white marble staircases connect one courtyard after another. There were also mansions of princes and dignitaries, lush gardens, artificial lakes, theaters, and a library, laid out in a symmetrical plan. The city's major axis is north-south, with most structures facing south, the source of

fruitfulness (north brought evil influences). The *Imperial Throne Room* (Fig. 10.13), part of the Imperial Palace shown in Figure 10.1, is one example of the interior decoration. The majestically high ceiling is covered with elaborate patterns subdivided by grids. The focus of the room, the throne, is framed by columns and elevated on a stepped platform.

CONNECTION Other Chinese examples of ambitious royal building projects are the *Soldiers from Pit 1* (Fig. 9.10 and 9.11, page 247) from the tomb of Qin emperor Shi Huangdi, and the *Great Wall* of China (Fig. 10.22, page 288).

Like the Forbidden City, the palace complex at Versailles was both a sign of power and an instrument for maintaining that power. It was built by King Louis XIV of France, the Sun

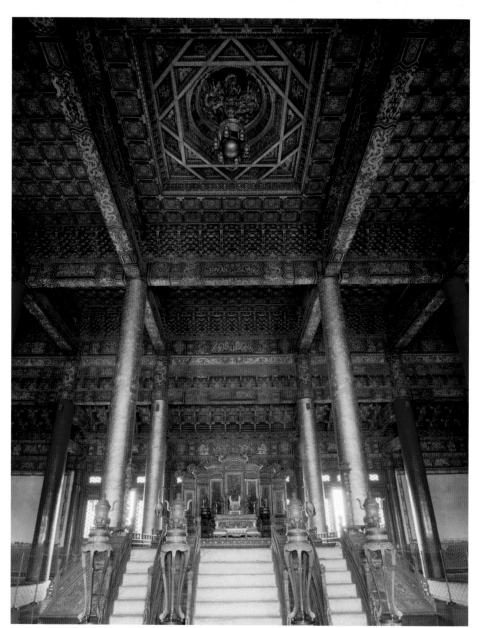

10.13 *Imperial Throne Room,* in Hall of Supreme Harmony, Forbidden City, Beijing, China.

The grandeur of this royal room helped sustain the emperor's rule, because its magnificence supported his claim to be the Son of Heaven and the father of the people.

10.14 Jules Hardouin Mansart and Charles le Brun. *Hall of Mirrors,* Versailles, France, c. 1680.

The grand spaces, dramatic embellishments, and theatrical display of this palace were signs of Louis XIV's power.

King who identified himself with Apollo. Louis moved his entire court from Paris to Versailles in 1682 in order to better control them. Originally Louis's grandfather's hunting lodge, Versailles was extensively enlarged and remodeled. Approximately 36,000 workers took twenty years to complete it to Louis's liking, with grand spaces, dramatic embellishment, and theatrical display in the **Classical Baroque** style. The connected buildings measure 2,000 feet wide and are surrounded by seven square miles of parks. More than four million tulip bulbs were planted in the parks' flower beds.

Inside, the *Hall of Mirrors* (Fig. 10.14), 240 feet long, connects the royal apartments with the chapel. The ceilings were covered with marvelous frescoes, and the long, mirrored room was embellished with gilded bronze capitals, sparkling candelabra, and bejeweled trees. Just as Louis XIV dominated the French church, nobility, and peasants, he also controlled the arts, fashion, and manners. He established the French Royal Academy of Painting and Sculpture to ensure a steady supply of works that would glorify his person and reign (see Fig. 5.4).

CONNECTION At Versailles, Louis XIV stripped the nobility of their power, so they occupied their time in games of romance and intrigue, as in Fragonard's *The Swing* (Fig. 13.25, page 388).

The Palace at Ikere, the residence of a Nigerian ruler, provides another example for comparison of artwork that symbolizes kingly power. Olowe of Ise carved the *Palace Sculpture* (Fig. 10.15) showing the senior wife, the queen, standing behind the enthroned king. Women are revered for their procreative power, so the royal female towers over the king while crowning him, because she is the source of his power. His conical crown is topped by a bird, a symbol for the reproductive power of mothers, female ancestors, and deities. The interlocking forms of king and queen visually convey monumentality and elegance. Details, such as the pattern of body scarification, add authenticity to the sculpture. Yoruba aesthetic values are evident: "clarity, straightness, balance, youthfulness, luminosity and character" (Blier 1998:85).

Yoruba kings would seek the best artists to make artwork for their palaces, as a way to increase their prestige. Olowe of Ise spent four years (1910–1914) at Ikere producing around thirty pieces (see Fig. 1.2 for another example). Songs or poems of praise (**oriki**) were composed about him:

> *Handsome among his friends.*
> *Outstanding among his peers.*
> *One who carves the hard wood of the iroko*
> *tree as though it were as soft as a calabash.*
> *One who achieves fame with the proceeds of his carving.*

> (Blier 1998:85)

Thus, across several continents and several centuries, we have seen palaces built with certain distinguishing features: large size, height, and terraces and/or platforms, embellished with decorated interiors and symbolic sculptures.

Seats of Government

Social and political pressures help determine which styles of architecture are used in government buildings, as seen in the designing of England's *Houses of Parliament* (Fig. 10.16), our focus figure. In 1836, the old Houses of Parliament burned. A new design was sought that would reinforce England's desires to create a "national identity" and express patriotic spirit. Architect Charles Barry designed the general plan in the **Gothic Revival** style,

10.15 OLOWE OF ISE. *Palace Sculpture*, Ikere, Nigeria, 1910–1914. Yoruba. Wood and pigment, 60″ × 13 1/4″.

The senior wife stands behind the enthroned king, giving her high status for her procreative power.

10.16 CHARLES BARRY AND A. W. N. PUGIN. *Houses of Parliament*, London, 1840–1860. 940' long.

This seat of government structure was designed in the Gothic Revival style, breaking away from the popular Neoclassical style at the time.

while A. W. N. Pugin was responsible for suitable ornamentation. They felt that the style of the soaring medieval cathedrals appropriately represented a Christian nation. New building materials, such as cast iron, enabled the Gothic Revival style to flourish on a grand scale.

Pugin and Barry were hotly criticized for breaking away from **Neoclassic** architecture, which was widely used for public and government buildings in western Europe and the United States, like the U.S. Capitol Building (Fig. 4.1). The painter John Constable argued that the new Gothic Revival design of Parliament was a "vain endeavor to reanimate deceased art, in which the utmost that can be accomplished will be to reproduce a body without a soul" (Honour and Fleming 1995:621). Pugin, however, felt that Gothic art never died or lost its soul. He believed that Gothic was a principle rather than a style, "as eternally valid as the teaching of the Roman Church" (1995:621). He also reasoned that contemporary Greek temples were mere imitations and had no integrity.

The long, horizontal buildings are topped with Victoria Tower on one end, while the famous clock tower, with Big Ben, is on the other. Ironically, the building's plan is clearly symmetrical with repetitive ornamentation, qualities of Classical architecture. However, the building resembles a medieval church or a castle-fortress, visually housing Parliament in a metaphor of the church's strength and the government's power.

> **CONNECTION** *Chartres Cathedral* (Figs. 8.39–8.40, pages 227–228) and the *Chapel of Henry VII* in Westminster Abbey (Fig. 9.19, page 255) are two examples of Gothic architecture, which inspired the design of the Houses of Parliament.

Just as a new architectural style was developed for the *Houses of Parliament*, a new form of architecture evolved on New Zealand in response to political and social needs. In the nineteenth century, the Maori nation was undergoing tremendous change as a result of European

10.17 *Te Papaiouru Marae*, Maori Meeting House, Ohinemutu Maori Village, Rotorua, North Island, New Zealand, late 19th century.

This important structure was an elaborate version of the chief's house and a site for reaffirming tribal values and clan ties.

colonization. The Maori Meeting House, like *Te Papaiouru Marae* (Fig. 10.17) in Ohinemutu, was an elaborate version of a chief's home and a site for reaffirming old tribal values and clan ties. It represented the body of a powerful ancestor, and, once inside, the living became one with their ancestor. The porch is considered to be the ancestor's brain, the **bargeboards** are the ancestor's arms and hands, and the roof's ridgepole represents the ancestor's backbone, terminating at the front with a face mask. Inside, the rafters and wall slabs represent the ancestor's ribs and are covered with carved and painted vines that symbolize the clan's generations.

The sculptures on Maori meeting houses are visually overwhelming. These profuse carvings, swirls, lines, and frightening imagery empower clan members, while intimidating any outsiders. The carvings represent mythical first parents and the tribe's history, in this case, Tamatekapua, who was the captain of the canoe that first brought the tribe's ancestors to New Zealand. Inspirational stories about clan heroes, told in the presence of these images, pass on clan history, traditions, and values to the young.

Monuments

A final category of government art is the commemorative monument. These structures are often very large, with architectural elements, sculpture, and inscriptions. Although we are looking at only one monument in this section, later in this chapter are examples that relate to war and peace. In addition, you can find many monuments in cities around the world that commemorate past events, civic leaders, and military heroes.

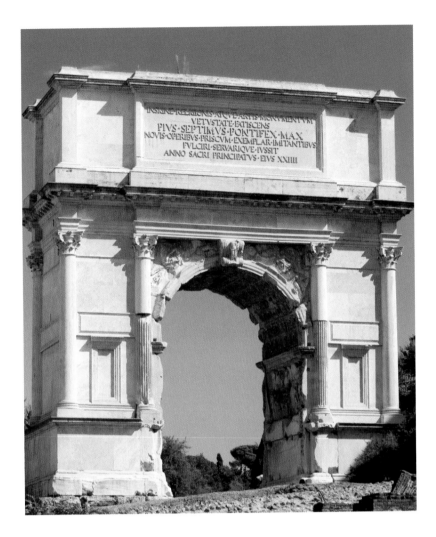

10.18 *Arch of Titus*, Rome, Italy, 81 CE. Marble on concrete, 50' high, 40' wide.

This structure both illustrates and commemorates Titus's victories and his apotheosis (becoming a god).

CONNECTION The *Portrait of George* (Fig. 11.30, page 326) is a monument to slain San Francisco mayor George Moscone. Another example is the *Monumental Heads* from the Easter Islands (Fig. 3.35, page 72).

Roman triumphal arches commemorate military victories or major building projects. The *Arch of Titus* (Fig. 10.18) was built along the Via Sacra (the Holy Road) in Rome, by Titus's brother Domitian, to record Titus's **apotheosis.** The inscription at the top reads roughly, "... dedicate this arch to the god Titus, son of the god Vespasian."

This single-passageway arch (others have two or three) is a mini–**barrel vault**. Engaged columns have both Ionic and Corinthian elements, a Roman synthesis of Greek **orders**. The **attic** is the uppermost section with the inscription. "Winged victories" in the **spandrels** symbolize Titus's military successes. Under the vault, one relief depicts Titus being carried up to heaven on the back of an eagle, giving a visual image of his deification. Other relief carvings show his military victories.

WAR

War is part of the history of most civilizations and cultures, and it is part of the story of power, politics, and glory.

Warriors, Weapons, and Fortifications

Warriors have been depicted in art since 8000 BCE. Warrior images can be found in almost every culture since then. Frequently, fierceness is shown in the following ways:

- Large size of warriors
- Emphasis on armor, weapons, or regalia of power
- Menacing or aloof facial expressions

Our focus figure is a soldier mounted on his horse. Before the modern era, the warrior on horseback was greatly feared. Andrea del Verrocchio's colossal bronze

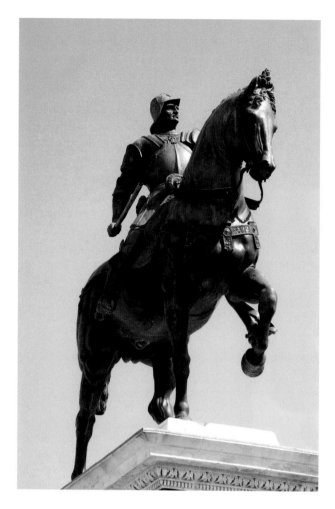

10.19 Andrea del Verrocchio. *Equestrian Monument of Bartolomeo Colleoni*, Italy, c. 1483–1488. Bronze, 15′ high. Campo Ss. Giovanni e Paolo, Venice.

The statue of this warrior mounted on horseback represents his fearsome victorious power.

Equestrian Monument of Bartolomeo Colleoni (Fig. 10.19) joins the horse's power with the rider's strength and determination. Colleoni was a **condottiere,** or mercenary soldier, who fought many campaigns for the city-state of Venice during the fifteenth century. The fifteen-foot-tall statue is raised on a high pedestal, so that viewers are vulnerably placed under the horse's raised hoof. The animal's tense, bulging muscles, Colleoni's twisted pose, and his scowling face are the very embodiment of aggression.

For contrast, we see in the Toltec city of Tula in central Mexico, colossal *Tula Warrior Columns* (Fig. 10.20), which stand on a temple platform atop a pyramid dating between 900 and 1000. These sixteen- to twenty-foot-tall figures once held up the temple roof; figuratively, they "supported" the religion. Stiff, blocky, and frontal, they are carved in low relief from four basalt drums attached with dowels

10.20 *Tula Warrior Columns*, Mexico, 900–1000. Toltec. 16′ to 20′ high.

These tall and stable totem-like guardian figures supported the roof on an elevated temple base.

and originally painted in bright colors. They wear Toltec garb with elaborate headdresses, and each held **atlatls**— spear-throwers—at their side. Thus, the warriors' attire is more than functional; it is also aesthetic to increase their power and prestige. The warriors' uniformity gives the impression of a formidable army that could crush anything. Stylized butterflies, carved on their chests, were the souls of past warriors.

CONNECTION Compare the *Equestrian Statue of Marcus Aurelius* (Fig. 1.3) for a nonwarrior image of a ruler on horseback

Another comparative example here is a brass *Plaque with Warrior and Attendants* (Fig. 10.21), which depicts an impassive Nigerian warrior king from the seventeenth or early eighteenth century. Larger than his two attendants, the king displays classic African figurative proportion, approximately three heads high. His apron and shield have leopard imagery, a regal symbol made more important because of the artistic attention given to it. Dominating the composition are the warrior's spear, helmet, and shield. Often, armor and weapons were protection for both the body and the spirit. The frontal, symmetrical composition of the *Plaque* conveys absolute authority, power, and strength; the face is aloof. These plaques were documents of kings, warriors, and famous events and were displayed prominently in Benin palaces. The plaques represented the king's power and literally were his image among his people, because he rarely appeared in public except to wage war and to officiate at religious ceremonies.

And finally, outstanding among war architecture is the *Great Wall* of China (Fig. 10.22). Begun in 206 BCE during the Qin Dynasty, with major additions during the Ming Dynasty (1368–1644 CE), this 1,500-mile-long wall

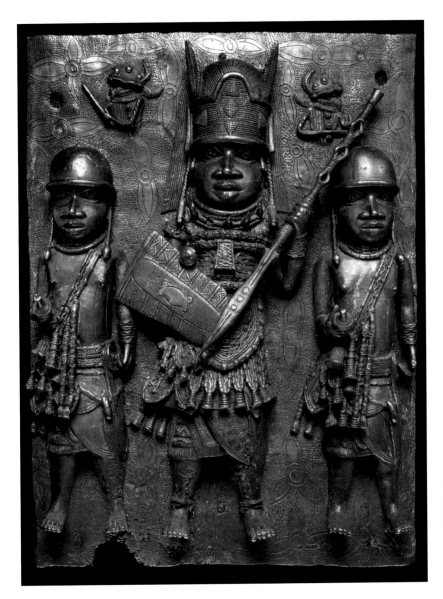

10.21 *Plaque with Warrior and Attendants*, Nigeria, 17th or early 18th century. Benin. Brass, 19 1/4″ high.

In the center of this plaque is an impassive warrior king, flanked by his two attendants. It conveys his absolute authority, power, and strength.

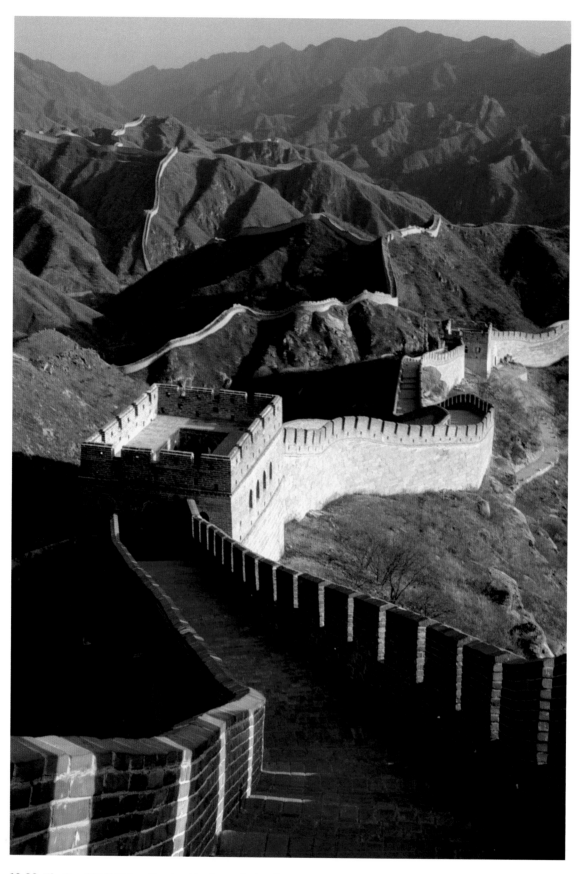

10.22 *The Great Wall*, China. Construction began during the Qin Dynasty in 206 BCE, with major work occurring during the Ming Dynasty, 1368–1644 CE. Brick faced, average height 25′, 1,500 miles long.

This enduring war fortification is considered a "wonder of the world."

10.23 *Palette of King Narmer*, Egypt, c. 3000 BCE. Slate, 25″ high.

The relief carvings both depict and commemorate the unification of Upper and Lower Egypt, and the glory of its victorious pharaoh.

is a "wonder of the world." New pieces of it are still being discovered, and the section near Beijing has been restored. The brick-faced wall averages twenty-five feet in height and width, and it creates a light-colored, undulating line on the brown and green hills. Strategically placed watchtowers provide points of visual emphasis. The towers contained embrasures for cannons and were used as signal stations, with smoke by day and fires by night.

War Scenes

Art can present war as a memorable, even glorious, action-filled event. Or art can document battles from various points of view. Finally, art can emphasize the horrors of war.

Glorifying War

Here we begin our focus in Egypt with the *Palette of King Narmer* (Fig. 10.23), from 3000 BCE, which was used for mixing black eye makeup worn by ancient Egyptian men and women. The carving records the forceful unification of Egypt, when Narmer (also called Menes), king of Upper Egypt, was victorious in war over Lower Egypt. At top center, the horizontal fish above a vertical chisel are pictographs for "Narmer." Flanking Narmer's name are two images of Hathor, the cow goddess of beauty, love, and fertility, who was the king's protector. Like *Menkaure* (Fig. 10.3), Narmer is shown in the formal, standardized pose typical of Egyptian art, but here he is larger than those around him because of his status. Horizontal divisions (or **registers**) separate scenes.

On the right, a large King Narmer, wearing the tall white crown of Upper Egypt, is about to administer a deadly blow to the enemy he grasps by the hair. Behind him is a servant who is carrying his sandals, his bare feet suggesting that this is a divinely predisposed event. The falcon represents Horus, the god of Upper Egypt, standing triumphantly on a head and papyrus, both representing Lower Egypt. In the bottom register are dead prisoners.

On the left, the triumphant Narmer wears the cobra crown of Lower Egypt. Preceded by standard-bearers, he inspects the beheaded enemies lined up in rows with their heads tucked between their feet. The intertwined necks of beasts may represent unification of Egypt.

Compare the battle depictions in the *Palette of King Narmer* with a painting of a battle that occurred during the Kamakura era in medieval Japan. The country was convulsed by civil war and two invasions by the Mongol emperor Kublai Khan (see the *History Focus* on page 267). Warfare and artistry were particularly interwoven at this time. The martial arts were elevated to a precise art form, and literature featured long tales of war and battle, unlike the courtly love tales from the period immediately preceding. The *Heiji Monogatari* is an illustrated scroll nearly twenty-three feet long, telling the tale of two feuding clans in the twelfth century. It was to be unrolled one scene at a time and viewed by two or three people. One scene, the *Burning of the Sanjo Palace* (Fig. 10.24), shows the tumult and disorder of warfare. As flames and smoke erupt dramatically, the raiders dash away to the left, trampling their victims or leaving them trapped in the burning rubble. Strong visual contrasts heighten the sense of chaos. Jumbled shapes differ from the clean lines of the palace roof. Groups are juxtaposed with single figures to build and then diffuse dramatic moments.

Nineteenth-Century Battle Scenes

In the preceding examples, the artists had license to exaggerate or even fantasize about the battles and warriors. The nineteenth-century invention of the camera changed that. Along with romanticized photographs of war heroes came horrific battlefield scenes, such as *Dead Confederate Soldier with Gun* (Fig. 10.25), by Mathew B. Brady (or staff), from 1865. We begin our focus here. The first to photograph war, Brady made 3,500 photographs covering both sides of the U.S. Civil War. Brady often arranged props, such as the rifles, to enhance both the composition and the sense of tragedy. Rough textures fill the image, except for the smooth planes of the soldier's face and rifle stock. The fallen tree forms a horizontal barrier separating the dead soldier from the living. His fallen body parallels the guns and rubble in the background behind him.

Compare here another point of view in the *Battle of Little Big Horn* (Fig. 10.26), painted in 1880 by the Sioux artist Red Horse, which presents the Native American's version of Custer's last stand. The Sioux had been given

10.24 *Burning of the Sanjo Palace*, from the *Heiji Monogatari*, hand scroll (detail), Japan, Kamakura period, late 13th century. Ink and color on paper, 16 ¼″ high, 22′ 9″ long.

This long scroll tells the tale of two feuding clans in medieval Japan.

10.25 MATHEW B. BRADY (OR STAFF). *Dead Confederate Soldier with Gun,* USA, 1865. Civil War photograph.

This photograph is one image of many taken during the Civil War in North America, the first war to be photo documented in world history.

10.26 RED HORSE. *Battle of Little Big Horn*, USA, 1880. Sioux. National Anthropological Archives, Smithsonian Institution, Washington, D.C.

The depiction is a Native American's version of this historic battle.

land in a treaty with the U.S. government, but gold prospectors, settlers, and the railroads wanted it revoked. The flamboyant Lt. Col. George Custer attacked the Sioux and their leader, Sitting Bull, thinking this would help Custer to be elected U.S. president. As the painting illustrates, Sioux warriors advance from the right in their last victory as a nation. Custer was defeated, and the dead and wounded from both sides occupy the bottom of the image. Red Horse stacked figures above each other to show both the chaos and the detail of battle.

Twentieth-Century Images of War

Although war is still glorified in twentieth-century art, as we saw in Riefenstahl's *Triumph of the Will* (Fig. 10.9), more and more images present the horrific side.

After the revolution of 1917 in Russia, Communist leader Vladimir Lenin saw the advantages of film as a new medium. Sergei M. Eisenstein was commissioned to glorify the collective heroism and martyrdom of the Soviet people in his masterpiece film, *The Battleship Potemkin*, made in 1925 (Fig. 10.27). A great admirer of U.S. filmmaker D. W. Griffith, Eisenstein used many cinematic devices: full views; extreme close-ups; panned shots; iris (blurred edges); traveling (moving from front to back or back to front); flashbacks; and crosscutting (two events interwoven for dramatic effect).

Eisenstein's strength, however, was his editing. He used a rapid form of **montage** that allowed the viewers to piece together the narrative from fleeting images. The Odessa Steps Massacre sequence in *The Battleship Potemkin* shows the horrendous conclusion of a failed 1905 uprising. It lasts four minutes and twenty seconds, but contains 155 separate shots, all from different camera angles, showing Czarist soldiers firing on unarmed people, a mother holding a dead child, the bloodied face of a beaten woman, a baby in a carriage that careens down the steps, a horrified student, and the dreadful aftermath of the dead lying on the stairs of the port. The quick-cut images capture the feeling of terror, panic, and chaos.

Compare now one of the greatest twentieth-century paintings, *Guernica* (Fig. 10.28), by Pablo Picasso, which dramatized the 1937 destruction of the Basque capital during the Spanish Civil War. German Nazi planes bombarded the city, which burned for three days and left more than 1,000 people dead. In Paris, shocked and outraged, Picasso immediately set down sketches for the painting, blending the nightmarish aspects of **Surrealism** with his own style of **Cubism**. The bull represents Fascist Spain, doomed to be tortured and suffer a slow, inevitable death. The gored, dying horse is the Spanish Republic, while the fallen soldier holding the broken sword represents the spirit of resistance

10.27 Sergei M. Eisenstein. *The Battleship Potemkin*, Russia, 1925. Film stills.

This film was commissioned to show the collective heroism and martyrdom of the Soviet people after the Russian revolution of 1917.

10.28 PABLO PICASSO. *Guernica*, Spain, 1937. Oil on canvas, 11′ × 28′ 8″. Prado Museum, Madrid. Institut Amatller d'Art Hispanic

This work dramatized the destruction of the Basque capital by Nazi fire bombs during the Spanish Civil War in 1937.

against tyranny. Other heads represent shocked witnesses to the suffering and carnage. The electric light bulb shaped like an eye suggests that the world is being shown its inhumanity. A sense of agony pervades. Picasso experienced a conversion after Guernica. In earlier work, he was more concerned with the formalistic elements in art. Subsequently, he said, "Painting is not done to decorate apartments. It is an instrument of war for attack and defense against the enemy."

> **CONNECTION** Turn to Chapter 11 for examples of protest art against war.

War Memorials

An entire book could be devoted to monumental art dedicated to war victories, battles, and the dying. In this chapter, we have already seen the *Arch of Titus* (Fig. 10.18), which both enhanced the emperor's fame and memorialized his battle victories.

The *USA Marine Corps War Memorial* (Fig. 10.29), sculpted by Felix W. Weldon and dedicated in 1956, commemorates the 6,800 U.S. soldiers who died in the

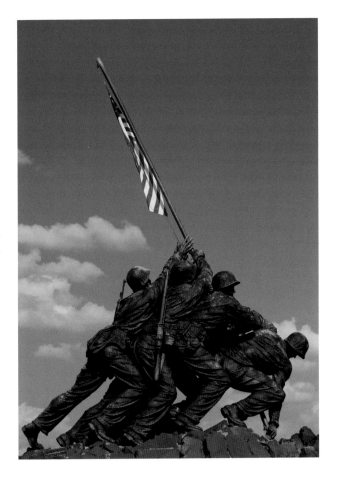

10.29 FELIX W. WELDON. *USA Marine Corps War Memorial*, Arlington, Virginia, USA, 1954. Cast bronze, over life-size.

These statues commemorate the soldiers who died during the battle for Iwo Jima in World War II.

10.30 MAYA YING LIN. *Vietnam Veterans Memorial*, Washington, D.C., USA, 1982. Black granite, 492′ long; height of wall at center, 10′ 1″.

A reverent and quiet space, the shrine wall contains the names of 58,000 men and women who died in the Vietnam War.

victorious battle for Iwo Jima Island in World War II. This sculpture is a copy of an Associated Press photograph that captured the recreation of the flag raising after the Marines' charged up Iwo Jima's Mt. Suribachi. Weldon's bronze sculpture is larger than life-size, grand, and dramatic. The soldiers form a triangle to indicate strength and solidity, while the numerous diagonals suggest tumbling haste. The past blends with the present, as every day, a real flag is raised and lowered on the memorial.

For contrast in design we look at another commemoration for Americans lost in war. The *Vietnam Veterans Memorial*, 1982, by Maya Lin (Fig. 10.30) is located on the Mall in Washington, D.C. The names of nearly 58,000 men and women who died in the Vietnam War, from 1959 until 1975, are carved in chronological order on its black granite face. Its polished surface reflects the faces of the living and superimposes them on the names of the dead, which forces a personal connection between the two. Family and friends make rubbings of the names and leave all kinds of

remembrances, such as poems or childhood mementos. Visitors meditate or mourn rather than celebrate. This lack of glory made the *Memorial* very controversial, so figurative sculptures of heroic soldiers and nurses were added later near the site. Taken all together, these monuments create a powerful memorial to the Vietnam War.

The long, V-shaped memorial is set into the ground with one end pointing to the Washington Monument, a symbol of national unity, and the other end pointing to the Lincoln Memorial, remembering a nation divided by civil war. This reflects the national anguish over soldiers who died in a war about which the general population was ambivalent. Magazine and newspaper coverage had brought the blunt realities of the war into U.S. homes, as evident in *Brigadier General Nguyen Ngoc Loan summarily executing the suspected leader of a Vietcong commando unit* (Fig. 10.31), a war photograph from 1968 by Eddie Adams. Its harshness contrasts severely with romanticized images of war.

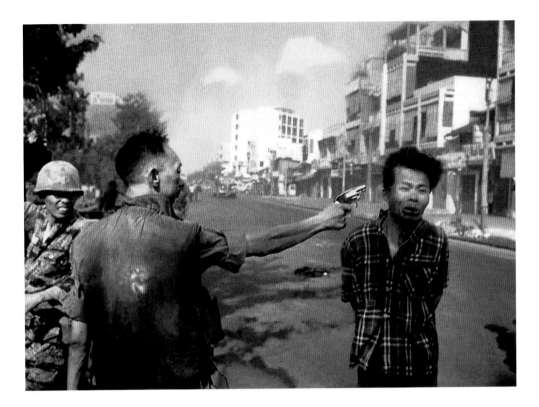

10.31 EDDIE ADAMS. *Brigadier General Nguyen Ngoc Loan summarily executing the suspected leader of a Vietcong commando unit*, Saigon, South Vietnam, February 1, 1968.

This brutal and blunt photo showed a reality of the Vietnam War in U.S. publications.

PEACE

Winged allegorical figures, doves, women, and pastoral landscapes have symbolized peace in Western art. Gardens, bells, and temples serve as monuments to peace in Asia, Europe, and the Americas.

CONNECTION Ambrogio Lorenzetti's *Allegory of Good Government* (Fig. 11.20 page 318) contains a personification of peace and shows the prosperity that comes with peace.

Art about Peace

Edward Hicks's *The Peaceable Kingdom* (Fig. 10.32), painted between 1830 and 1840, is based on the following biblical passage:

> The wolf also shall dwell with the lamb, and the leopard shall lie down with the kid; and the calf and the young lion and the fatling together; and a little child shall lead them. (Isaiah 11)

Hicks was also inspired by the Quaker William Penn and his treaty with the Indians, which is visible in the background as a copied detail from a famous painting by U.S. artist Benjamin West. This moment came to signify a utopian new world. Hicks's visual metaphors have become standard language for expressing the concept of peace. A luminous sky glows in the background, while lush vegetation frames the foreground figures. The animals are rendered in a flat, decorative, imaginative style. There is a feeling of innocence and peace, without strife and turmoil.

Peace Monuments and Peace Offerings

An example of a peace monument is the *Ara Pacis Augustae* (Fig. 10.33), from 13–9 BCE, built to commemorate Emperor Augustus's stopping of the civil wars between Spain and France. It sits on a podium with twelve steps, enclosed by walls covered with reliefs of the Earth Mother,

10.32 EDWARD HICKS. *The Peaceable Kingdom*, USA, 1830–1840. Oil on canvas. 17 ⁷/₁₆″ × 23 ⁹/₁₆″. Brooklyn Museum of Art.

A passage from the Bible (Isaiah 11) inspired the Quaker artist to express a message of peace in this work.

Tellus; Aeneas, the legendary founder of Rome; and two long processions led by Augustus. Carved foliage and fruit garlands symbolize the golden age of plenty as well as fecundity, ripeness, and peace, all under the rule of Augustus. Sacrificial offerings of animals and humans are indicated. The whole piece was probably brightly painted. Although the *Ara Pacis* celebrates the peace of the Roman Empire, it can also be seen as a victory monument that glorifies the emperor Augustus.

When peace treaties are signed, art and gifts are often exchanged to seal the agreement. Precious objects might also be offered to show submission or to avoid further confrontation. *Moctezuma's Headdress* (Fig. 10.34) is believed to have belonged to the last Aztec ruler, Moctezuma, who may have given it to the Spanish leader Cortés as a peace

offering or as a desperate last measure to avoid his own demise. Objects made of feathers are frail, and not many survive long periods. This one is exceptional. The four-foot-high headdress features iridescent green feathers from the quetzal bird's tail and has blue feathers from the cotinga interwoven with small gold disks. Three hundred workers staffed the royal aviaries that produced these feathers. Moctezuma's wives and concubines probably made the piece.

Native Americans created tomahawks and pipes used exclusively for peaceful exchange. The *Presentation Pipe Tomahawk* (Fig. 10.35) is an aesthetically beautiful work meant to be presented as a ritual peace offering. It is made of hickory wood, silver, iron, and lead. The name "Ottokee," a member of the Great Lakes Ottawa tribe in 1820, is engraved in silver inlay on the handle, along with

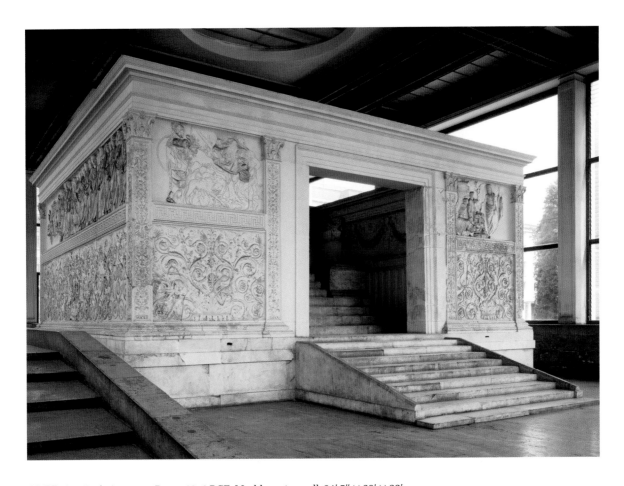

10.33 *Ara Pacis Augustae*, Rome, 13–9 BCE. Marble; outer wall, 34' 5" × 38' × 23'.

This structure was built to commemorate Emperor Augustus's stopping the war between Spain and France.

10.34 *Moctezuma's Headdress*, Mexico, c. 1319. Aztec. Quetzal and cotinga feathers, gold plaques. Kunsthistorisches Museum, Vienna.

This object was believed to be given to Hermán Cortés by the Aztec ruler as a last resort for peace before his own demise.

naturalistic fish and an abstract curvilinear pattern. On the head and blade of the tomahawk are engraved an acorn, a heart, and a half moon. The style of the engravings suggests European influences. The pipe tomahawk may have been crafted by European, American, or Ottawan metalsmiths.

Recently in the twentieth century, memorials to peace were constructed in Hiroshima, Japan, and in Los Angeles, California. These peace parks, not shown here, were built to heal wounds of war. It is hoped that such memorials will become a more prominent part of human history.

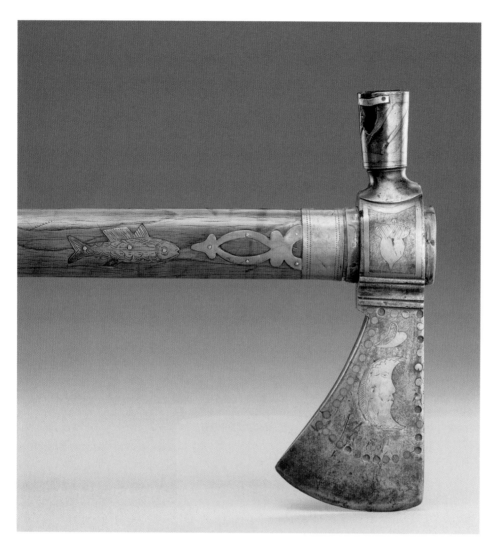

10.35 *Presentation Pipe Tomahawk*, USA, c. 1820. Ottawa. Wood, inlaid metal. 23 1/2″ × 8″.

Ironically, this weapon was superbly crafted only to be given as a peace offering, never for use in battle.

11.1 Cildo Meireles. *Insertions into Ideological Circuits: Coca-Cola Project*, Brazil, 1970. Screen print on Coca-Cola bottles.

This work was created as a response to Brazil's military government in 1970, which supported itself by "selling" the country to foreign investors, including the United States.

11

SOCIAL PROTEST/ AFFIRMATION

Many artists protest injustice with their artwork. They identify villains, honor heroes, and promote causes with emotional and visual impact unequaled by the written word. Protest art is a form of affirmation, because it is based on respect for human dignity and the belief that change is possible. Two other chapters contain related images. Chapter 10 has artworks about war. Chapter 13 contains art that examines race and gender.

PREVIEW

This chapter begins with art that depicts the cruelty and destruction of war and exposes cynical military leaders. All forms and styles, ranging from realism and abstraction to conceptual, can express the human struggle for liberty against totalitarian forces.

We will also see how artists have protested many forms of oppression, such as the exploitation of laborers, acts of betrayal, or repressive governments. They have used all kinds of media, as with the modified Coke bottles in Figure 11.1. Their art has been used to protest colonization and pollution as well as to affirm indigenous values. "Normal" conditions are reexamined by artists and, in many cases, found wanting. Half-truths, stultifying bureaucracies, police states, and upper-class greed and mindlessness are all targets for artistic critique. Other artists look at consumerism, oppressive patriarchy, the status of women, and institutionalized discrimination.

Connecting Art and History from
1300–1550 CE

The world in 1300 was still a patchwork of relatively autonomous, relatively isolated regions. Two hundred fifty years later, much of that had changed. Many conditions in the modern world have their roots in this era.

Many areas of the world were ruled by strong centralized governments. China during this period was ruled by two dynasties: the Yuan dynasty of the Mongolian invaders, which ended in the mid-1300s, and the native Ming dynasty, known for its territorial expansion as well as its amazing building program, which included rebuilding the Great Wall and constructing the Forbidden

City. Wealth was distributed to lower classes through the Civil Service and land ownership. This was a period of stability, prosperity, religious tolerance, and a high standard of living. Chinese ships traveled to India and Africa, and the Portuguese landed at China's ports in 1514.

Islam continued to expand in Asia, Africa, and southeastern Europe. Around 1280, the mighty Ottoman Empire was established with Turkey as its center, and it expanded its territories in North Africa and the Middle East. Many Ottoman rulers were art patrons, great builders, and conquerors. They generally tolerated

other religions. Likewise, the Mughal Empire in India was known for its ambitious building program, its humane rulers, and its illuminated manuscripts. The Safavids ruled Persia after 1500.

At this time, Europe saw the end of the Middle Ages and the beginning of the Renaissance. The rise of Christian humanism in the fourteenth and fifteenth centuries brought an emphasis on reason, human abilities, and intellectual achievement, as exemplified by scholars and leaders such as *Jean de Dinteville and Georges de Selve ('The Ambassadors')* (Fig. 11.21). This humanistic tradition has

Map 6 Patterns of World Trade. Courtesy of Replogle Globes, Inc., Broadview, IL.

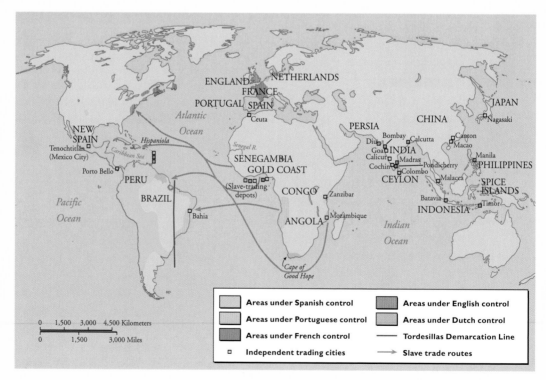

continued to grow, and, because it promotes the inherent worth and dignity of all human beings, it is the basis for much social protest art. Small areas of Italy had republican governments, notably Florence and Siena, as shown with the *Allegory of Good Government* (Fig. 11.20). In Italy, the era brought increased prosperity and the rediscovery of Greco-Roman culture.

Beginning in 1300, the secular power of the Catholic Church slowly declined in Europe. The Church's religious authority was challenged in the 1500s when the Protestant Reformation divided European Christians between the Protestants and Catholics.

This was the beginning of the age of exploration and expansion. European sailors undertook amazing voyages of discovery, most notably in the Americas in 1492. Advanced civilizations had flourished earlier in Central America, especially the Maya/Toltec culture, with hieroglyphics, ball courts, and palaces. In 1500, the Aztecs dominated central Mexico and had a complex society with accomplishments in painting, architecture, astronomy, and cosmology. The Aztec *Coatlicue* (Fig. 11.2) is a colossal freestanding sculpture of a deity representing sacrificial death as well as the potential for new life. The *Codex Borbonicus* (Fig. 11.22) is an example of Aztec bookmaking and painting accomplishments that also shows the culture's calendar system. In 1519, the Spaniards conquered the Aztecs and attempted to wipe out their culture; later, they also conquered the Incas of Peru and established a large colonial empire in America.

Other adventurers circled the globe, visiting ports in Asia and India. Trade expanded greatly in the 1500s and reached many parts of the world. For Europe, the spice trade with Southeast Asia and the slave trade with

Africa were important. Other traded commodities included fur, fish, timber, tobacco, rice, silver, gold, sugar, cacao, coffee, diamonds, tea, silk, cotton, and ivory.

The Kingdom of Zimbabwe flourished from 1300 to 1450 in Africa. Other central areas of Africa remained free of Europeans, but African slaves from coastal areas were brought to Europe and the Americas beginning in the 1500s. England, Portugal, and France as well as Spain established American colonies. Spain and Portugal divided South America along the Tordesillas Demarcation line. In still-isolated Australia, the Aboriginal peoples were growing in population and developing long-distance trading among themselves.

11.2 *Coatlicue*, Tenochtitlán, Mexico, c. 1487–1520. Aztec. Andesite, 11′ 6″ high. Museo Nacional de Antropología, Mexico City.

This freestanding colossal statue is an example of the art style of the Aztecs of Central America. It depicts a deity who represents sacrificial death as well as the potential for new life.

Thus we have seen the beginnings of slavery, the expansion of Islam, and European colonization taking hold as long as 700 years ago. The injustices and conflicts resulting from the slave trade are still the subject of contemporary artworks, such as Yinka Shonibare's *Mr. and Mrs. Andrews Without Their Heads* (Fig. 11.18), Kara Walker's *"They Waz Nice White Folks While They Lasted"* (Fig. 11.19), and William Kentridge's *Drawing from Mine* (Fig. 11.31).

World Art Map for Chapter 11

NORTH
AMERICA

Kara Walker. *They Waz Nice White Folks While They Lasted.*

Ester Hernández. *Sun Mad.*
Robert Arneson. *Portrait of George.*

Edward Kienholz. *The State Hospital.*

Ben Shahn.
***The Passion of
Sacco and Vanzetti.***
**Massachusetts,
United States.**

Leon Golub. *Mercenaries I.*

Robert Motherwell. *Elegy to the Spanish Republic XXXIV.*

Lewis Hine. *Leo, 48 Inches High, 8 Years Old, Picks Up Bobbins at 15¢ a Day.*

Jenny Holzer. *Untitled (Selected Writings).*

Hans Haacke. *Metromobiltan.*

Jacob Lawrence. *No. 36: During the Truce Toussaint Is Deceived
and Arrested by LeClerc. LeClerc Led Toussaint to Believe
That He Was Sincere, Believing That When Toussaint
Was Out of the Way, the Blacks Would Surrender.*

David Alfaro Siqueiros. *Echo of a Scream.*
Codex Borbonicus.
Coatlicue.

Eugène Delacroix.
Liberty Leading the People.
Paris, France.

Yinka Shonibare. *Mr. and Mrs. Andrews
Without Their Heads.*
William Hogarth. *Breakfast Scene.*

Honoré Daumier. *The Legislative Belly.*

EUROPE

Hans Holbein the Younger.
Sir Thomas More.

George Grosz. *Fit for Active Service.*
John Heartfield. *Goering the Executioner.*
Käthe Kollwitz. *The Outbreak ("Losbruch").*

Francisco Goya.
The Executions of May 3, 1808.
Prado, Spain.

Pepón Osorio.
The Scene of the Crime (Whose Crime).
Puerto Rico.

Miguel Antonio Bonilla. *The Knot.*
El Salvador, Central America.

SOUTH
AMERICA

Cildo Meireles.
Insertions into Ideological Circuits: Coca-Cola Project.

N

| 0 | 1,000 | 2,000 Km. |
| 0 | 1,000 | 2,000 Mi. |

ASIA

Magdalena Abakanowicz. *Backs.*

Ambrogio Lorenzetti. *Allegory of Good Government:
The Effects of Good Government in the City and in the Country.*

Mona Hatoum.
Light Sentence. Palestine.

Shomei Tomatsu.
Woman with Keloidal Scars.
Nagasaki, Japan.

AFRICA

Paddy Dhatangu, David Malangi,
George Milpurrurru, Jimmy Wululu,
and other artists from Ramingining.
The Aboriginal Memorial.
Canberra, Australia.

AUSTRALIA

William Kentridge.
Drawing from Mine, South Africa.
Johannesburg, South Africa.

1300–1550 CE

ROMANESQUE ERA	**CE 1000**		

Above *Zen Stone Garden*, Daitokuji (1.8)

Slave trade begins: Africa, Europe, and the Americas

Spice trade— Dutch East Indies and Southeast Asia

MUGHAL EMPIRE IN INDIA — **1600 / 1612** — *BAROQUE ERA*

Above ARTEMISIA GENTILESCHI. *Judith and Holofernes* (4.19)

KAMAKURA PERIOD—JAPAN — **1192** — Temple, Kyoto, 1192.

GOTHIC ERA — **1200**

CHOLA KINGDOM— INDIA

YUAN DYNASTY— CHINA

MAYA/TOLTEC CULTURE IN MESOAMERICA

ROCOCO style — **1700**

Japan closed to Westerners

Rise of merchant class in Japan

HOGARTH: *Breakfast Scene*

1300 — LORENZETTI: *Allegory of Good Government*

Black Death in Europe

MING DYNASTY— CHINA

Great Wall of China rebuilt

RENAISSANCE in Europe — **1400**

OTTOMAN EMPIRE IN TURKEY, NORTH AFRICA, AND MIDDLE EAST

Christopher Columbus

1500 — *Coatlicue*

Codex Borbonicus

1550 — HOLBEIN: *The Ambassadors*

GOYA: *The Executions of May 3, 1808* — **1800**

DAUMIER: *The Legislative Belly*

ROMANTICISM

Displacement of Native Americans from Western U.S. — **1819**

Above THEODORE GERICAULT. *The Raft of Medusa*, (1.12)

DELACROIX: *Liberty Leading the People*

Aboriginal decline in Australia

REALISM — **1850**

Colonial rule established in Africa

Civil War, U.S.

End of slavery in U.S.

Portuguese arrive in China

Spanish conquest of the Aztecs and Incas

Martin Luther and the Reformation

European colonies in the Americas

Above Frederick Douglass (3.55)

IMPRESSIONISM	
POST IMPRESSIONISM	**1875**
FAUVISM, CUBISM, FUTURISM, DADA	**1900**
SURREALISM, FANTASY, SUPREMATISM	**1907**
	1910
World War I	**1914**
Harlem Renaissance	**1920**
Great Depression	**1930**
Stalin and the U.S.S.R.	
Spanish Civil War	
World War II	
POST-WAR EXPRESSIONISM	**1940**
U.N. Universal Declaration of Human Rights	**1948**
ABSTRACT EXPRSSIONISM	**1950**
PEOPLE'S REPUBLIC OF CHINA	
Cold War, 1950–1990	
Civil Rights Movement, U.S.	**1960**

KOLLWITZ: *The Outbreak ("Losbruch")*

HINE: *Leo, 48 Inches High …*

SHAHN: *The Passion of Sacco and Vanzetti*

GROSZ: *Fit for Active Service*

HEARTFIELD: *Goering the Executioner*

LAWRENCE: *No. 36: During the Truce Toussaint Is Deceived . . .*

SIQUEIROS: *Echo of a Scream*

MOTHERWELL: *Elegy to the Spanish Republic XXXIV*

Above HAMPTON: *Throne of the Third Heaven . . .* (5.15)

Cesar Chavez and the United Farm Workers	
Six-Day War—Israel	
MODERNISM	
POSTMODERNISM	
Islamic Revolution in Iran	
Nicaraguan Civil War	
Iraqi invasion of Kuwait	
Apartheid ends— South Africa	
World Conference on Global Warming	
USA Patriot Act	

Above AIDS Memorial Quilt (9.28)

TOMATSU: *Woman with Keloidal Scars*	
KIENHOLZ: *The State Hospital*	
GOLUB: *Mercenaries I*	**1970**
MEIRELES: *Insertions into Ideological Circuits*	**1975**
ABAKANOWICZ: *Backs*	
HERNANDEZ: *Sun Mad*	**1980**
HAACKE: *Metromobiltan*	
ARNESON: *Portrait of George*	
The Aboriginal Memorial	
HOLZER: *Untitled (Selected Writings)*	
	1990
	1993
SHONIBARE: *Mr. and Mrs. Andrews Without Their Heads*	
KENTRIDGE: *Drawing from Mine*	
HATOUM: *Light Sentence*	
BONILLA: *The Knot*	
OSORIO: *The Scene of the Crime (Whose Crime?)*	
	2001
Walker: *"They Waz Nice White Folks"*	

PROTESTS AGAINST MILITARY ACTION

For thousands of years, artists have depicted war, sometimes glorifying the victors, sometimes showing the defeated and those killed or wounded. Not until two hundred years ago, however, did artists begin to make art that protests a particular war or the idea of warfare altogether. One likely reason is that a sizable percentage of past art was made for victorious political or religious leaders. Warfare was one means to gain power, and art was a way to display that power. Especially since World War II, however, growing numbers of artworks have protested full-blown war, police actions, covert operations, and guerrilla activity.

Our beginning focus is on a pivotal piece in the history of protest art: *The Executions of May 3, 1808* (Fig. 11.3), from 1814. The artist, Francisco Goya, based his painting on sketches he had made of the actual event as it happened six years earlier. The citizens of Madrid unsuccessfully rose up against Napoleon Bonaparte's occupational army in 1808. The soldiers captured many of the rioters and executed them a short distance outside the city. Goya individualized the Spaniards trembling, praying, or protesting as they face the firing line, so that we identify with their horror. We particularly focus on the man in white with outstretched arms who is posed like the crucified Jesus, surrounded with light colors against the pervasive gloom. In contrast, Goya has dehumanized the soldiers, with repeated poses and hidden faces. The barrels of their pointing rifles are rigidly organized, like a war machine. Goya's painting goes beyond partisanship and could stand for any mass execution.

We have several examples to compare, beginning with Käthe Kollwitz. This artist dedicated her work to ending war and poverty. She lived in Germany through the two world wars, losing a son and a grandson in the fighting. In her artwork, however, she frequently turned to past conflicts to show the destructive energy of war. *The Outbreak ("Losbruch")*, dated 1903 (Fig. 11.4), is the fifth in a series of seven prints that tell of the Peasant War in Germany in the early sixteenth century. In the first four prints in the series, we see the causes for the peasant revolt: abuse by the ruling class, poverty, crushingly hard work, rape of the women. In the fifth image, *The Outbreak ("Losbruch")*, the peasants revolt, propelled by their wretched living conditions.

11.3 FRANCISCO GOYA. *The Executions of May 3, 1808*, Spain, 1814. Oil on canvas, 104 $^3/_4$″ × 135 $^3/_4$″. Prado, Madrid.

Painted from sketches the artist made at the actual event, this work was a pivotal protest against Napoleon's occupational army in 1808 Madrid.

11.4 KÄTHE KOLLWITZ. *The Outbreak ("Losbruch")*, Germany, 1903. Etching, 20″ × 23¼″.

This work depicts an uprising in the 16th-century Peasant War in Germany, one of seven prints etched by the artist to show the destructive energy of war.

The composition of the work is remarkable. The peasants group at the right, while already at the left they rush at deadly speed to attack their oppressors with crude weapons and farm tools. The dark woman in front becomes the leader and the conscience for the group. Her upraised arms incite them to action, while her bony, twisted hands and arms are documents to the incredible harshness of the peasants' life. Stark blacks and whites flash across the image, visually conveying the emotional moment.

Kollwitz shows a woman leading the revolt, breaking old stereotypes about women's passivity. This also attests to the misery of the peasants' lives—in the end, the women rose up. The uprising was unsuccessful, as the forces of the ruling class suppressed the peasants with brutality. The last two prints of the *Peasant War* series show a mother searching for her dead son among piles of bodies, and peasant prisoners bound together awaiting execution.

11.5 GEORGE GROSZ. *Fit for Active Service*, Germany, 1918. Pen and ink, 14½″ × 13½″. The Museum of Modern Art, New York.

Digital Image © The Museum of Modern Art/Licensed by Scala/Art Resource, NY, 243.1947, Art © Estate of George Grosz/Licensed by VAGA, NY

In this drawing the artist exposes well-fed doctors and self-absorbed officers who send elderly, sick, and very young men to the front lines to fight for Germany near the end of World War I.

Fit for Active Service (Fig. 11.5), a 1918 pen-and-ink drawing by George Grosz, exposed the bloated doctors and self-absorbed officers, secure in their bureaucratic assignments, who sent elderly, sick, or very young men to the front lines to fight for Germany near the end of World War

I. (All able-bodied men had been sent out much earlier.) With grim wit, the artist's pen outlines the smug, laughing faces of the officers in the foreground. Farther back, two mute soldiers stand at attention. The seams in their uniforms line up with the floor and the window frames. They are conformists subsumed into the structure, without independent conscience. The doctor at the center seems almost happy, since he has found another body for the front lines. Outside, factories contentedly belch out the machinery of war. In contrast to the spare and flattened manner in which the other figures are portrayed, the skeleton seems the most human, as it is rounded, detailed, and adorned with rotting organs and tufts of hair.

John Heartfield dedicated much of his art to exposing and condemning the horrors of Nazi Germany. He was born in Germany as Helmut Herzfelde but later anglicized his name. *Goering the Executioner*, dated 1933 (Fig. 11.6), is a **photomontage**, in which news photographs are combined and manipulated with drawing. It

11.6 JOHN HEARTFIELD. *Goering the Executioner*, Germany, 1933. Photomontage cover for AIZ magazine. Reproduced from John Heartfield by Wieland Herzfelde (Dresden: Veb Verlag dur Kunst, 1964).

The artist depicts the Nazi Field Marshal as a butcher to forewarn the public of the party's bloodshed that was to come in Germany during World War II.

appeared on the front page of the Prague newspaper *AIZ* (*Arbeiter-Illustrierte-Zeitung*). The subject is Field Marshal Hermann Goering, one of the major leaders of the Nazi party. Heartfield pulled Goering's head forward, increasing the thickness of the neck and emphasizing the aggressiveness of his bullying face. Behind him burns the Reichstag, the German parliament building, destroyed in 1933 by an act of terrorism that was likely perpetrated by the Nazis but officially blamed on Communists. The Nazis used this excuse to seize absolute power and end any democratic government. Black-and-white elements give the image an unvarnished, blunt quality. Goering's meat cleaver and stained apron have the quality of factual truth, even though the artist added those props. Heartfield's warnings of Nazi bloodshed proved to be prophetically true. Heartfield was forced to leave Germany and spent much of the 1930s and 1940s in England.

In the mid-1930s, Spain was engulfed in a civil war that in many ways was a prelude to World War II. In 1937, David Alfaro Siqueiros painted *Echo of a Scream* (Fig. 11.7) in response to the horror of the Spanish Civil War. Siqueiros symbolized all of humanity with the screaming, helpless, pained child sitting amid the debris and destruction of modern warfare. The sky is filled by the large, detached head—the child's head repeated—a massive cry that symbolizes the combined pain of all the victims we do not see. The dark tones and blue-gray colors of the painting add a somber note to the ugly surroundings. The painting also alludes to urbanization and industrialization, and to the endless piles of waste that are the result of "progress" and "innovation." Siqueiros knew his subject matter firsthand. He was a Mexican citizen who fought in Spain in the International Brigade, composed of volunteers from fifty countries who fought for the Spanish Republic against the Fascists and their German Nazi backers. He was also a political activist and social reformer.

CONNECTION See Pablo Picasso's *Guernica* (Fig. 10.28, page 293) for another artwork that deals with the Spanish Civil War.

Later, Robert Motherwell painted the *Elegy to the Spanish Republic XXXIV*, between 1953 and 1954 (Fig. 11.8), part of a series of more than 150 paintings that mourned the loss of liberty in Spain after the Fascist forces were victorious. Although the paintings do not tell a story, Motherwell believed that abstraction communicated, in universal terms, the struggle between life and death and between freedom and oppression. The large size of the painting makes these struggles seem monumental. Motherwell was influenced by **Surrealism**'s process of expression called **Automatism**, which incorporates intuition, spontaneity, and the accidental when creating artworks, similar to **Abstract Expressionism**'s style. His black-and-white forms suggest several Spanish motifs, according to Robert Hughes (1997:496). They are bull's testicles, the patent leather berets of the Guardia Civil, and living forms (represented by the large, ovoid shapes) being crushed by the black bands.

11.7, left DAVID ALFARO SIQUEIROS. *Echo of a Scream*, Mexico, 1937. Enamel on wood, 48″ × 36″. Gift of Edward M. M. Warburg (633.1939). The Museum of Modern Art, New York, NY.

Digital Image © The Museum of Modern Art/Licensed by SCALA/Art Resource, NY © Estate of David Alfaro Siqueiros/SOMAAP, Mexico City/VAGA, New York.

Painted in response to the horrors of the Spanish Civil War, this work symbolizing all of human suffering through the screaming pained child sitting amid the debris of modern warfare.

11.8, below ROBERT MOTHERWELL. *Elegy to the Spanish Republic XXXIV*, USA, 1953–1954. Oil on canvas, 80″ × 100″.

Albright-Knox Art Gallery, Buffalo, NY © Dedalus Foundation / Licensed by VAGA, New York, NY.

This work was part of a series that contained 150 paintings in which the artist expresses his mourning over the loss of liberty in Spain after the Fascist forces were victorious during their Civil War.

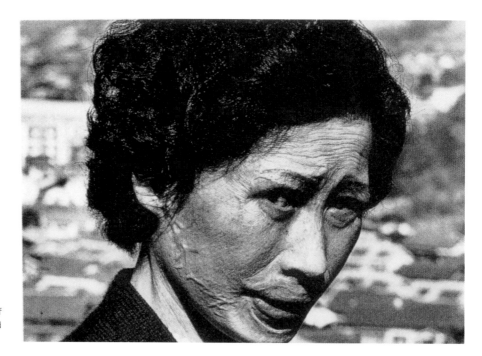

11.9 SHOMEI TOMATSU. *Woman with Keloidal Scars* (from the series *11:02 – Nagasaki*), Japan, 1966. Gelatin silver print, 11.5″ × 16″.

This powerfully disturbing photograph is one of a series that exposes the mutilation of victims who survived the atomic bombing of Nagasaki, Japan, at the end of World War II.

From the other side of the world, Tomatsu Shomei's *Woman with Keloidal Scars* (Fig. 11.9) is one of a series of photographs of victims of the atomic bombing of Nagasaki, Japan, at the end of World War II. The blast was so powerful that it vaporized the victims who were nearest the center of impact. Those farther away suffered terrible injuries and deformities. Tomatsu's photograph is technically beautiful, with a full range of deep blacks and silvery grays, but the lacy texture is excessive fibrous tissue stretched over the woman's skull. With her pained, fearful expression, her psychological and physical injuries still seem fresh, although inflicted long ago. Yet there is a strange sense of normalcy, as if she were out sightseeing. Tomatsu made this series to document past horrors and to protest against U.S. troops stationed in Japan for decades. Since World War II, some Japanese have pushed for complete, permanent demilitarization of the country.

Leon Golub's painting, *Mercenaries I* (Fig. 11.10), from 1976, shows two "guns for hire" dangling a bound victim between them, using brute power to bolster a repressive government. These professional fighters are devoid of any ideological stance; they are simply paid thugs. The mercenaries are flattened figures against the flat background. They are pushed aggressively to the foreground, and we, the viewers, are dwarfed by the nearly eleven-foot height of the painting. Looking up, we share the same view as the

11.10 LEON GOLUB. *Mercenaries I*, USA, 1976. Acrylic on canvas, 116″ × 186 1/2″.

The Broad Art Foundation. © Leon Golub / Licensed by VAGA, New York, NY Courtesy Ronald Feldman Fine Arts.

This work shows two "guns for hire," exposing thugs who use brute force to bolter a repressive government.

victim, who has no identifying traits and could be anyone, even us. The paint, applied thickly at first, has been scraped repeatedly so that the surface seems raw and nasty. The flesh looks particularly repulsive, both on the cruel faces of the mercenaries and on the tortured victim. The colors are jarring and acidic.

Golub worked from news photographs and insisted that his images realistically report atrocities occurring regularly in the world. His images have an immediacy to them because of the news and because of entangled global politics and economies.

FIGHTING FOR THE OPPRESSED

Artists who fight for the rights and affirm the values of economically or politically repressed peoples use several strategies to make their points most forcefully. These include beauty, illustration, narrative, humor, and shock. Most social protest works are designed generally to affect public consciousness, rather than to prescribe specific changes.

Strategies for Protesting Oppression

Interestingly, beauty and excitement can be very effective elements in protest art, as our focus figure displays. In Eugène Delacroix's *Liberty Leading the People*, painted in 1830 (Fig. 11.11), Liberty has been personified as a partially nude woman—apparently flesh and blood—but reminiscent of a Greek goddess in her profile and in her idealized body. Energized and oblivious to danger, she carries a rifle and the flag of the French Revolution. She forms the peak of a triangle made up of merchants, students, laborers, soldiers, and even young boys who emerge from the smoke, debris, and dead bodies to move toward the light that surrounds Liberty.

The lower and middle classes revolted many times against European ruling classes in the late eighteenth and early nineteenth centuries. This painting is an homage to the Paris revolt in 1830. Delacroix's painting mixes realistic, idealistic, and romantic elements. Realistic are the faces of the men, who look like Parisians of the day, and the details of the clothing, weapons, and the Paris skyline

11.11 Eugène Delacroix. *Liberty Leading the People*, France, 1830. Oil on canvas, approximately 8′ 6″ × 10′ 8″. Louvre, Paris.

This is an homage to the 1830 Paris Revolt in France in which the artist personifies liberty's fight against oppression of the people.

in the background. Idealistic elements include the glowing, goddess-like figure of Liberty, and the belief that revolution will lead to a better way of life. The work is romantic in its portrayal of fighting as thrilling, dangerous, and liberating. Compare this work to Siqueiros's *Echo of a Scream* (Fig. 11.7), where warfare is not romanticized.

We again have several figures for comparison here. One of the most direct ways to make social protest art is to illustrate the oppressive situation. At the beginning of the twentieth century, sociologist and artist Lewis Hine photographed miserable labor conditions and slum housing in the United States. He was particularly known for exposing child labor in mines and textile mills, where children were doing the lowest-paying, most tedious jobs. *Leo, 48 Inches High, 8 Years Old, Picks Up Bobbins at 15¢ a Day*, from 1910 (Fig. 11.12), shows a young boy who dodges under textile looms to pick up loose thread spools. Children in these jobs ran the risk of injury or death from moving machinery. They typically worked ten- to twelve-hour shifts in the mills, six days a week, making schooling impossible. Child laborers were destined to remain illiterate, poor, and overworked. Hine fully documented the youthfulness of the child laborers by giving his photos long titles, yet in some ways, they were unnecessary. Hine's composition emphasizes the large scale of the weaving machines—their great length and height—that dwarf the child. Leo seems very young and apprehensive. The factory is gloomy, littered, and staffed by women, another underpaid group. Hine's pictures are more difficult to forget than wordy ideological arguments, pro or con, on labor conditions.

Hine worked with the National Child Labor Committee, a private group dedicated to protecting working children, and the loosely organized Progressive Movement of the early twentieth century, which sought reform for many problems resulting from urbanization and industrialization. He lectured and his images were published in magazines, making his work unusually successful in changing both public opinion and public policy. Child labor was eventually outlawed in the 1930s.

Ben Shahn used narrative as a protest strategy in *The Passion of Sacco and Vanzetti*, dated 1931–1932 (Fig. 11.13), to tell the story of Nicola Sacco and Bartolomeo Vanzetti, Italian immigrants who were active in labor organizations, avoided the draft in World War I, and were political anarchists. They were arrested and convicted for robbery and murder, despite several witnesses who testified that they were elsewhere at the time of the crime. Many claimed that Sacco and Vanzetti were convicted because of their politics, as the judge allowed the prosecution to make inflammatory statements about their political beliefs during the trial. In his painting, Shahn collapses time, showing simultaneously the courthouse steps, the framed portrait of the judge who presided over the original trial, and the ashen faces of Sacco and Vanzetti as they lie in their coffins. Prominent in the middle are three commissioners who declared the trial to have been legal, thus allowing the executions to take place. The commissioners are dour and righteous, bolstered by institutional rigidity. The harsh colors express Shahn's distress at the death of the two men, whom Shahn and many others felt were heroes.

11.12 LEWIS HINE. *Leo, 48 Inches High, 8 Years Old, Picks Up Bobbins at 15¢ a Day*, USA, 1910. Photograph, 8 1/2″ × 11″. University of Maryland Library, College Park, Maryland.

This artist was known for exposing child labor in mines and textile mills, where children were working at the most tedious, dangerous, lowest-paying jobs, as seen in this photo.

Jacob Lawrence also used narrative to recount the accomplishments, challenges, and oppressions of the African community uprooted to the Western Hemisphere by slavery. He made thirty-one paintings about Harriet Tubman and twenty-two about John Brown. The paintings reconstruct the past with lengthy, narrative titles to make the story clearer and to inspire African Americans today. Our example is *No. 36: During the Truce Toussaint Is Deceived and Arrested by LeClerc. LeClerc Led Toussaint to Believe That He Was Sincere, Believing That When Toussaint Was Out of the Way, the Blacks Would Surrender* (Fig. 11.14). It is one of forty-one paintings made from 1937 to 1941 about François-Dominique Toussaint-L'Ouverture (or "Louverture"), a slave who led a revolt in Haiti that resulted in the abolition of slavery there in 1794. Toussaint then established a semiautonomous black government,

11.13, *left* BEN SHAHN. *The Passion of Sacco and Vanzetti*, USA (Lithuanian-born), 1931–1932. Tempera on canvas, 84 ¹/₂″ × 48″.
The Whitney Museum of American Art.

This painting tells the story of the unjust conviction and execution (for robbery and murder) of Italian immigrants who were active in labor organizations, avoided the draft in World War I, and were political anarchists.

11.14, *below* JACOB LAWRENCE. *No. 36: During the Truce Toussaint Is Deceived and Arrested by LeClerc. LeClerc Led Toussaint to Believe That He Was Sincere, Believing That When Toussaint Was Out of the Way, the Blacks Would Surrender*, USA, 1937–1938. Tempera on paper, 11″ × 19″.

This work is one of forty-one paintings about a slave who led a revolt to abolish slavery in Haiti.

resisting French, English, and Spanish attempts to control Haiti. He was eventually captured by French forces and died a year later in a French prison. Haiti finally overcame the French in 1804 and became the first black-governed country in the Western Hemisphere.

Lawrence completed forty-one preliminary drawings and then worked on all of the paintings simultaneously, so that the series has formal cohesion with its bold, flat, simplified style. Colors are limited, with black and white punctuating the images, giving them strength and starkness. *No. 36* shows the French soldiers' crossed swords that pin Toussaint in the center. The floor tilts up, and the walls of the room trap him at the intersection of colors. The black chair reads like bars of a prison. Broad sections of yellow and green in the background unify the image, while the center, with its greatest density of detail, provides a forceful focal point. In his use of space and color choices, Lawrence was influenced by Cubism as well as the bright patterns of handmade rugs.

CONNECTION Lawrence trained in Harlem during the Harlem Renaissance and was influenced by the vibrant community of artists, writers, and performers, as shown in Faith Ringgold's *The Bitter Nest, Part II: The Harlem Renaissance* Party (Fig. 3.32, page 70). An example of a Cubist work is Pablo Picasso's *Guernica* (Fig. 10.28, page 293).

Hans Haacke's *MetroMobiltan* (Fig. 11.15), 1985, is art designed to raise social consciousness. Haacke was advocating for native Africans in South Africa who were politically and economically repressed under *apartheid*, a system of legal racial separation. In the 1980s, many nations, including the United States, denounced apartheid. Less known, however, were corporate profits from apartheid enforcement, including those of U.S.-based oil company, Mobil, which sold supplies to the South African police and military. To counter negative publicity, Mobil provided major financial backing to the Metropolitan Museum in New York City to mount a blockbuster exhibition, "Treasures of Ancient Nigeria." MetroMobiltan raises awareness of the often-hidden ways that one country's culture and economy can profit from an unjust situation half-way around the world.

Formally, *MetroMobiltan* is like a stately altar. The elaborate frieze echoes the Metropolitan Museum facade, but the inscription is from the museum's 1980s pamphlet advising corporations to sponsor museum shows as "creative and cost effective answers" if the corporation is experiencing difficulties in "international, government or consumer relations." The three silk banners indicate Mobil's policies. Hidden behind is a black-and-white photomural of a funeral procession for black South Africans shot by police. *MetroMobiltan* links the museum, the oil company, and apartheid, but the layering shows that people might be unknowingly involved in an oppressive situation that they condemn.

11.15 HANS HAACKE. *MetroMobiltan.* 1985. Glass fiber, fabric, photograph, 140″ × 240″ × 60″. Photo: Philippe Migeat. Musee National d'Art Moderne, Centre Georges Pompidou, Paris, France.

Haacke showed that three apparently different phenomena are actually intertwined: the oppressive policies of apartheid in South Africa, the profits of an oil company, and artwork shown at a major museum.

11.16 EDWARD KIENHOLZ. *The State Hospital* (detail), USA, 1966. Mixed media, 8′ × 12′ × 10′. Moderna Museet, Stockholm.

To protest against society's treatment of people it deems incompetent, the artist made this installation that exposes the neglect and filth he found in a state mental hospital.

> **CONNECTION** Compare *MetroMobiltan* to works that memorialize past events, like the *USA Marine Corps War Memorial* (Fig. 10.29, page 293). Both have monumental presences and realistic elements. However *MetroMobiltan* combines different points of view about a situation, while the *War Memorial* represents a single perspective.

Shocking ugliness can be used in the service of protest art. In *The State Hospital*, from 1966 (Fig. 11.16), artist Edward Kienholz criticizes the way society deals with people it deems incompetent. The outside of this work, not shown here, is a grim, boxlike cell with a locked, grimy door. Inside, a naked mental patient is strapped to his bed. His mattress is filthy, and the bedpan is streaked with excrement. His head is replaced by a fish bowl with two black fish swimming aimlessly inside. Encircled in neon is the cartoon balloon above his head that shows another image of himself. The patient is completely isolated and has no life beyond this room. Kienholz's props are actual institutional objects: the bed frame, the urinal, the rolling

table (barely visible at left). The strongest impact, however, comes from the pathetic body of the patient—his bony knees; his sagging, exposed genitals; his leathery skin. The realism makes the sculpture seem more immediate to the viewer.

To look inside, one has to peer through a barred window, which makes everyone on the outside part of "normal" society that supports such institutions in which the powerless are mistreated. Looking through the window, viewers take on the role of guards or surveillance cameras. Kienholz drew on his experiences as an employee in a mental hospital, where he saw, for example, a staff member repeatedly hit a patient in the stomach with a soap bar wrapped in a towel, so there would be no surface bruises.

Cildo Meireles made *Insertions into Ideological Circuits: Coca-Cola Project* (Fig. 11.1) in the 1970s in response to Brazil's military government, which supported itself by "selling" the country to foreign investors, mostly from the United States. Much of the natural environment, as well as the cultures of indigenous peoples in Brazil, was being destroyed because of such policies. Meireles and others wanted to affirm Brazil's autonomy and resist becoming a market for foreign goods, but art that was openly critical of the government was repressed. So Meireles took empty Coca-Cola bottles, screen-printed subversive messages on them, and then returned them for refilling. The added writing on the bottles is almost invisible when they are empty. Only the person holding the bottle close while drinking the soda can easily read the message. Using Coca-Cola bottles as vehicles for political messages was clever in many ways: first, because Coca-Cola is everywhere; second, because Meireles took advantage of the already-existing system of reusing bottles; and third, because Coca-Cola is a popular symbol for U.S. culture.

> **CONNECTION** Some would say that printing "Yankees go home!" on Coca-Cola bottles is not art. Others would argue that an artist's job is to increase the viewer's awareness. For more on this topic, see Chapter 4, Deriving Meaning.

Humor is another strategy for effective protest. In *Sun Mad*, dated 1981 (Fig. 11.17), Ester Hernandez takes familiar imagery from popular, commercial culture and subverts it. For decades, the raisin growers around Hernandez's hometown heavily used insecticides that contaminated the groundwater the local population used for drinking and bathing. Hernandez took the packaging of the best-known raisin producer, Sun Maid, and changed the usual image of healthy eating into a message of death. Her grimly humorous work is effective because the raisin industry advertising is so successful and we know the original image.

Hernandez chose an art form that allows her to reach many people, just as advertising does. This work is a color screen print that has been reproduced and widely disseminated on T-shirts and postcards. Even though Hernandez was reacting to a specific instance of contamination, her work reaches out to everyone who ingests pesticide residue or to farm workers who were sprayed with pesticides while working in the fields.

Yinka Shonibare uses historical quotes, clothing, and humor to protest the colonial past and to show the complexity of world trade and culture in his *Mr. and Mrs. Andrews Without Their Heads*, 1998 (Fig. 11.18). A contemporary British artist of Nigerian origin (Nigeria was a British colony), Shonibare has created a three-dimensional parody of the famous eighteenth-century painting in which the landed gentry show off their estate. In his version, Shonibare has beheaded the aristocrats, recalling the fate of the ruling class during the French Revolution. The most complex aspect of the piece, however, is the printed cotton cloth, the kind associated with idealized African culture, which Mr. and Mrs. Andrews are wearing. The cloth is not African at all, but is made in the batik method that the Dutch and English manufacturers learned in Indonesia and then sold in West Africa. Shonibare shows that all cultures are intertwined and hybridized, and although many people may like the idea of cultural purity, it does not exist.

11.17 ESTER HERNANDEZ. *Sun Mad*, USA, 1981. Color serigraph, 22" × 17".

This work exposes the dangerous chemical pesticides that are used in vineyards to grow grapes that eventually become raisins. These poisons leach into the public drinking water.

> **CONNECTION** Shonibare based his sculpture on the eighteenth-century painting by British artist Thomas Gainsborough, *Mr. and Mrs. Andrews* (Fig. 2.11).

Some art dealing with past injustices and oppressions is met with mixed responses, even art by those who are descendants of the oppressed. Kara Walker is an African American artist who creates life-size, cutout silhouette figures based on racist imagery of the slave era in the United States. Petticoated plantation mistresses, slaves with their masters' heads under their skirts, bastard children, black women squeezing out multiple babies between their legs, slaves being tortured or murdered—all are depicted as elegant flat shapes, both humorous and shocking. The imagery is based on fact and fantasy, primarily from pulp fiction sources dealing with subjugation and titillation. In works like *"They Waz Nice White Folks While They Lasted" (Says One Gal to Another)*, from 2001 (Fig. 11.19), Walker's cutouts are enhanced with projections in darkened galleries,

11.18 YINKA SHONIBARE. *Mr. and Mrs. Andrews Without Their Heads*, Courtesy Stephen Freidman Galleries, London. Collection of the National Gallery of Canada, Ottowa. 1998. Wax-print cotton costumes on mannequins, dog mannequin, painted metal bench and rifles, 65″ × 224″ × 100″.

Historical quotation, clothing, and humor are used here to protest the colonial past and to show the complexity of world trade and culture.

11.19 KARA WALKER. *"They Waz Nice White Folks While They Lasted" (Says One Gal to Another)*, USA, 2001. Cut paper and projections on wall, 14′ × 20′.

The cutout life-size figures of images based on literature about the slave era in the United States has had both positive and negative responses.

so that viewers participate in the action by casting their own shadows on the wall, joining the animated and raucous silhouettes hung there. Walker has received many letters of protest from black people who believe that she should refrain from presenting negative images of African Americans. Walker responds that she makes these images because they are controversial and should be discussed.

Affirming the Values of the Oppressed

When a group of people is oppressed, their way of life tends to be discounted or ridiculed. Art is an especially effective tool for affirming the lifestyles and values of downtrodden groups.

We begin our focus art figure in Italy. When Ambrogio Lorenzetti painted the fresco *Allegory of Good Government: The Effects of Good Government in the City and in the Country*, dated 1338–1339 (Fig. 11.20), Italy was a patchwork of city-states regularly thrown into turmoil by civil strife, unstable governments, and petty tyrants. In contrast, Lorenzetti showed how common citizens prosper when Justice, Prudence, Temperance, and Fortitude reign, represented by hovering allegorical figures (one is partly visible at upper right). In our detail here, businesses flourish and culture thrives in the secure city. Not shown here is the rest of the mural to the right, which depicts fruitful farms. This late-Gothic painting is full of delightful details of everyday life in fourteenth-century Italy. The sweeping panorama was a remarkable achievement in Italian painting of the era.

Likewise in Northern Europe, power was concentrated in religious and secular rulers, but their absolute authority was being questioned (see *History Focus,* page 300), while the idea developed of the worth of the ordinary individual. In 1533, Hans Holbein the Younger painted the portraits of *Jean de Dinteville and Georges de Selve ("The Ambassadors")* (Fig. 11.21). De Dinteville was a political leader and de Selve a religious leader, but both were fervent humanists, as indicated in the various items on the table between them, reflecting their worldly interests in culture, arts, mathematics, astronomy, and so on. The emphasis on learning, rather than authority, is very significant, and Holbein paints the two men with intelligent eyes and gravitas that go beyond the pomp of their robes. However, symbols of discord are present, with a broken lute string alluding to tensions between church and secular authorities, as well as the long, stretched shape at the bottom that becomes a skull, or symbol of death, when viewed from a severe oblique angle. This painting is famous for its fine detail, monumental figures, and rich colors.

In contrast, a different form of art can affirm the history and culture of a people even as that culture is being attacked and eradicated. The Aztec *Codex Borbonicus* (Fig. 11.22) is a religious calendar that was made during the period of the Spanish conquest, either just before or just after the fall of the Aztec empire (see Connecting Art and

11.20 AMBROGIO LORENZETTI. *Allegory of Good Government: The Effects of Good Government in the City and in the Country* (detail), Italy, 1338–1339. Fresco. Sala della Pace, Palazzo Publico, Siena, Italy.

In this work the artist shows how common citizens prosper when Justice, Prudence, Temperance, and Fortitude reign

11.21, *left* HANS HOLBEIN THE YOUNGER. *Jean de Dinteville and Georges de Selve ("The Ambassadors"),* 1533. Oil on oak, 81.5″ × 82.5″. National Gallery, London, Great Britain

At left is de Dinteville, a French nobleman serving as ambassador to London, and his friend, Bishop de Selve, at right. They exemplifying the humanistic influence in active and contemplative life.

History, page 301). The *Codex Borbonicus* and the handful of other manuscripts that have survived from this era preserve the pre-Columbian culture. This image depicts calendar **glyphs** surrounding the large image of two gods, Quetzalcoatl (light and sun) and Tezcatlipoca (moon and destruction), who are devouring a man. Traces of Aztec culture survive in Central America to the present day.

We can also see how Aboriginal artists have used art to affirm their cultural values, which have been suppressed by Australians of European descent. Because of colonization, many Aborigines lost their land or were killed. While the rest of the country was celebrating the two-hundredth anniversary of Captain Cook's "discovery" of Australia, the Aboriginal population commemorated Invasion Day.

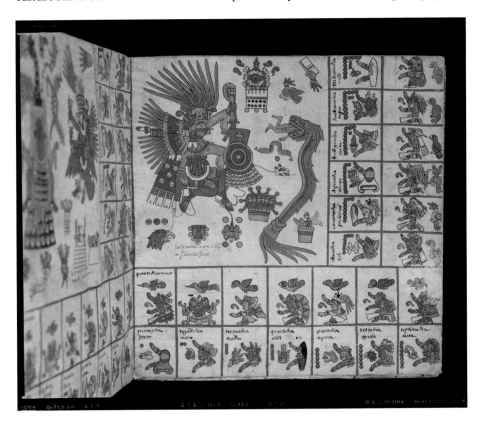

11.22 *Codex Borbonicus,* early 16th century. Detail depicting Quetzalcoatl and Texcatlipoca. Paint on vellum, 39 cm × 40 cm. Aztec.

This religious calendar was made close to the Spanish conquest in Mexico. Its preservation affirms the history and culture of the Aztec people.

Fighting for the Oppressed **319**

Forty-three artists collaborated to make *The Aboriginal Memorial*, installed in 1988 (Fig. 11.23). The work is composed of two hundred logs, one for each year of settlement, hollowed out as traditional Aboriginal coffins. They are memorials to all the native peoples who died as a result of European settlement and were never given proper Aboriginal mortuary rites. Artists painted the logs with their important clan **Dreamtime** symbols, affirming traditional Aboriginal culture, which was undermined and, at times, outlawed. Poles reach as high as ten feet and seem like living growths springing up with vibrating patterns and vigorous animal imagery (Caruana 1993:206).

CONNECTIONS For more on Aboriginal culture and Dreamtime imagery, see *Witchetty Grub Dreaming*, Figure 6.5 (page 135). Like the Australian Aboriginal artists, many contemporary Native American artists continue to reference traditional imagery and art processes in the work they produce today, as in the late-twentieth-century *Bowl* by Maria Martinez (see Figure 3.42, page 75).

Puerto Rican–born Pepón Osorio's mixed-media installation, *The Scene of the Crime (Whose Crime?)*, 1993–1999 (Fig. 11.24), affirms the worth of Puerto Rican culture in New York, while protesting how the people are depicted in mass media. He has re-created a typical Puerto Rican house, cluttered with kitsch statuettes, inexpensive religious objects, plastic plants, sentimental family photos, trophies, covers of *TV Guide*, and so on. Police tape and bright lights indicate a crime has happened, and a mannequin corpse lies face down at the back of the installation, but everything is remote and no details are given. A welcome mat in front reads: "Only if you can understand that it has taken years of pain to gather into our homes our most valuable possessions; but the greater pain is to see how in the movies others make fun of the way we live." Because much is obscure or just out of sight, viewers' reactions are based on stereotypes or narratives from mass media, including assumptions of drugs and crime in the culture, or class-based condemnations of the décor. Like Kara Walker (see Fig. 11.19), Osorio at times has received negative responses, some from Latino viewers who want to distance themselves from these cultural stereotypes.

Mona Hatoum is an artist of Palestinian descent who has lived in London since 1975, when she was forced to flee the fighting in Beirut. Her work deals poetically with personal identity, the body, surveillance, and control. *Light Sentence*, 1992 (Fig. 11.25), is an installation of wire mesh

11.23 Paddy Dhatangu, David Malangi, George Milpurrurru, Jimmy Wululu, and Other Artists from Ramingining. *The Aboriginal Memorial*, Australia, 1988. Natural pigments on 200 logs; heights: 16″ to 128″. National Gallery of Art, Canberra.

This installation affirms the survival of the Aboriginal culture and commemorates the dead after the impact of the Europeans in Australia on Invasion Day, the two-hundredth anniversary of Captain Cook's "discovery" of the continent.

11.24 Pepón Osorio. *The Scene of the Crime (Whose Crime?)*, Puerto Rico/USA, 1993–1999. Mixed-media installation, dimensions variable. Bronx Museum of the Arts, New York.

In this installation, the artist affirms the worth of Puerto Rican culture in New York, while protesting how the people are depicted in mass media.

11.25 Mona Hatoum. *Light Sentence*, Palestine/England, 1992. Mixed media, dimensions variable. Musée National d'Art Moderne, Centre Georges Pompidou, Paris.

This artist's work deals poetically with personal identity, the body, surveillance, and control. The swinging light alludes to the instability that those without power endure.

lockers in a dark room, stacked to human height. In the middle, a bare light bulb swings around, casting wildly rocking shadows so that the cell-like room seems to sway. The swinging bulb is like a sometimes-blinding prison searchlight, implying surveillance. Lockers should hold private possessions safely, but here everything is exposed. The piece suggests animal cages in an experimental laboratory and connotes the oppressively uniform high-rise housing for low-income people. *Light Sentence* reveals the instability that those without power endure.

QUESTIONING THE STATUS QUO

The status quo is the existing state of affairs, which appears natural or inevitable instead of constructed and evolving.

In this section, artists take a critical look at the "normal," at all those underlying and ingrained systems, beliefs, and ways of operating within a culture.

The Social Environment

Our focus here begins with artist William Hogarth. He satirized the English upper classes in a series of six paintings called *Marriage à la Mode*, dated c. 1745, a comedy mixed with criticism and condemnation. In the second of the six images, *Breakfast Scene* (Fig. 11.26), the wall clock indicates past noon, but the couple is just meeting over the breakfast table in their lavish mansion. The disheveled, bored husband has been out all night. The puppy sniffs at his pocket where another woman's

11.26 WILLIAM HOGARTH. *Breakfast Scene* (from the series *Marriage à la Mode*), England, c. 1745. Oil on canvas, 28″ × 36″. National Gallery, London.

In a series of comedic paintings, this artist satirized the English upper classes in the 18th century.

11.27 MAGDALENA ABAKANOWICZ. *Backs*, Poland, 1976–1982. Eighty pieces, burlap and glue, each over life-size.

The artist suggests in this installation the modern malaise of uniformity and the loss of self and individuality.

lingerie hangs. The young wife stretches after a night of cards and music at home. The overturned chairs indicate that the evening became a bit raucous. The paintings on the walls indicate a taste for sexual intrigues, despite the presence of classical busts and religious images for propriety. At left, a servant rolls his eyes, clutching unpaid bills.

The young man is a penniless nobleman whose father arranged this marriage to the daughter of a wealthy merchant. For her part, the arranged marriage brings status and a title, Lady Squanderfield. She casts a flirting glance at her husband, but he is completely unresponsive. A vacuum of unconcern separates them. The series ends miserably with infidelity, scandal, and death by duel. Hogarth's paintings were turned into inexpensive prints that were enormously popular and received widespread distribution among the English middle class.

Compare now Magdalena Abakanowicz's *Backs*, dated 1976 to 1982 (Fig. 11.27). Her composition consists of eighty slumping, hollow backs that are more than life-size, but without legs, heads, and hands. They hunch forward, immobile, in lines all facing the same direction. *Backs* alludes to the human condition in times of great distress. Abakanowicz lived in Poland during World War II, saw her mother's arm shot off at the shoulder, and witnessed death, pain, and destruction. In postwar Soviet-dominated Poland, she encountered many hardships in her struggle to make artwork.

Backs suggests the modern malaise of uniformity and of loss of self and of individuality. Organic fibers were pressed into the same plaster mold to make all eighty backs, so that each is very similar to the others. However, small degrees of individuality emerge in the twist of the fiber and in the slight variations created as each back was removed from the mold. The thick, matted fibers resemble wrinkled skin, knotted muscles, and visceral tissue. Their organic quality emphasizes our physicality and our ties to the natural world. The weary backs also suggest endurance, strength, and survival.

Contrast now another installation installation, this one by Jenny Holzer, who focused on the mass of implicit beliefs that are widely accepted in the United States today, in *Untitled (Selected Writings)*, dated 1989 (Fig. 11.28). Holzer wrapped electronic signs around the spiral interior of the Solomon R. Guggenheim Museum in New York City and placed a circle of red granite benches below. The stream of words jumps out from the darkened interior of the museum, starting at the bottom, and then swirling up until they disappear at the top of the spiral. The phrases seem familiar, but as a whole, they sound contradictory or even a little idiotic. As Holzer herself says, "They're about how we drive ourselves crazy with a million possibilities that are half correct" (Auping 1992:55). "A sincere effort is all you can ask" is countered with "Enjoy yourself because you can't change anything anyway." Another example is, "Protect me from what I

11.28 JENNY HOLZER. *Untitled (Selected Writings)*, USA, 1989. Extended helical LED electronic signboard, with selected writings; 17 Indian Red granite benches. Installation view at Solomon R. Guggenheim Museum.

Holzer's work focuses on the mass of implicit beliefs that are widely accepted in the United States today. The quickly flashing words show how a million possibilities of half-truths contradict each other and can drive us crazy.

LE VENTRE LÉGISLATIF.

Aspect des bancs ministériels de la chambre improstituée de 1834.

11.29 HONORÉ DAUMIER. *The Legislative Belly*, France, 1834. Lithograph; image: 11 1/8″ × 17 1/8″; sheet: 13 11/16″ × 20 3/16″. Bibliothèque Nationale de France, Paris.

Daumier was particularly known for his political cartoons with his pointedly satirical caricatures in 19th-century France. Today this is commonplace in newspaper and magazines.

want," written in a culture where money can buy almost anything. The electronic signs flash words like a mass-media attack, and then they quickly slip away almost before we can grasp them. In contrast, the words carved in the stone benches below are permanent, but just as conflicting. The sheer number of phrases, the speed at which we see them, and their contradictory messages destroy thought, although we normally think of words as the carriers of meaning.

Art Versus Politics

In Chapter 10, Power, Politics, and Glory, we saw art that promoted the personal glory of a ruler or the power of a state. In this section, we will see art that pokes at the political status quo.

The political cartoon has a long history of challenging politics and society in Western nations. In France, Honoré Daumier was especially known for his pointedly satirical **caricatures,** until an 1835 government crackdown outlawed works like our focus figure, *The Legislative Belly* (Fig. 11.29), from 1834. Here, members of the French legislature are mean-spirited, sleeping, or arrogant. The curving walls echo their fat bellies. Although Daumier depicted specific politicians (who would have been recognized by the French public at that time), his great composition and caricatures are an indictment to corrupt lawmakers at any time, in any place.

Portrait of George, dated 1981 (Fig. 11.30), by Robert Arneson, is a bust portrait of George Moscone, a popular mayor of San Francisco in the late 1970s. Moscone's smiling face is distinct and lively, animated by splattered colors. The bust sits on a column casually covered, graffiti-like, with phrases recalling Moscone's background, some of his more memorable sayings, and events from his life and death. Moscone and Harvey Milk were assassinated in 1978 by a disgruntled San Francisco city supervisor named Dan White, who had disagreed with Moscone on most political points, including issues concerning homosexuals.

The bust was made for a new civic center in San Francisco. Arneson's *Portrait of George* departs from the status quo of bland, bronze portrait heads of political leaders that are common in parks and in lobbies of public buildings. This sculpture is irreverent, colorful, and very large. Marks that suggest bullet holes pierce the pedestal, and a yellow, phallic Twinkies snack cake is prominent. At his trial, Dan White received a light sentence for his crimes, because his lawyers argued that he was unbalanced at the time of the shooting from eating too many Twinkies. Many San Franciscans protested the sentence, and there was a night of rioting. Because Arneson's sculpture was a vivid reminder of the murder and riots, *Portrait of George* was officially removed from the civic center after one week because the pedestal was deemed crude and inappropriate. The work was later sold to a private collector.

In South Africa for many years, the economic and political status quo was based on apartheid, a system of laws and social standards that repressed the native population. William Kentridge created charcoal drawings and film animations based on the causes and injustices of apartheid. Kentridge's work, however, goes beyond the specifics of the South African situation. The *Drawing from Mine*, from 1991 (Fig. 11.31), shows the white businessman with tangled financial tapes wrapped around sculptural heads of Africans, very much like the *Crowned Head of an Oni* (Fig. 10.5). Kentridge's art points out the moral difficulties that attend all instances of power, ownership, and oppression on a grand scale. This charcoal drawing and others were photographed repeatedly, while Kentridge drew and erased, to create the short film sequence called *Mine*.

Our last example of protest art is from contemporary El Salvador, with Miguel Antonio Bonilla's *The Knot* (Fig. 11.32), from 1994. The two ominous figures represent the country's police and politicians, who conspired in the

11.30 ROBERT ARNESON. *Portrait of George*, USA, 1981. Glazed ceramic, 94″ × 29″ × 29″. Private Collection. Estate of Robert Arneson/VAGA New York NY. Courtesy of George Adams Gallery New York.

This piece is a memorial to San Francisco's mayor, who was assassinated in 1978 by a disgruntled city supervisor who disagreed with most of his political points, including homosexuality.

11.31 WILLIAM KENTRIDGE. *Drawing from Mine*, South Africa, 1991. *Mine* is a 5-minute, 49-second film. Charcoal.

This artist created drawings and film animations based on the causes and injustices of apartheid in South Africa.

1980s to create an oppressive regime in El Salvador. The knot that connects them seems to be made of two extended, elongated phalluses. In this way, Bonilla referred to the chauvinism in his culture that allows factions to oppress others and also causes domestic violence. Bonilla took a

political risk in this painting because of its criticism of the political status quo. He also took artistic risks, making the painting purposefully ugly and shocking. The style of this work was contrary to prevailing Salvadoran aesthetics for painting at that time.

11.32 MIGUEL ANTONIO BONILLA. *The Knot*, El Salvador, 1994. Acrylic on canvas, 51″ × 78″.

The two ominous figures represent the country's police and politicians that conspired in the 1980s to create an oppressive regime in El Salvador.

Section 4

SELF AND SOCIETY

Self and society include our physical bodies, our minds, and the larger world we inhabit. Art is a great mirror that we hold up to see ourselves and to help understand our surroundings.

CHAPTER 12 MIND AND BODY

The nature of humans in general and individuals in particular, as seen through art

CHAPTER 13 RACE, GENDER, CLAN, AND CLASS

Art that reflects the larger social structures within which each person operates

CHAPTER 14 NATURE, KNOWLEDGE, AND TECHNOLOGY

Art that reveals the shifting relationship of humans to animals, to the land, and to the knowledge systems and technology that we create

CHAPTER 15 ENTERTAINMENT AND VISUAL CULTURE

The examination of the visual components of some forms of entertainment, and the way that art relates to these forms

12.1 *Nobles at the Court of Shah Abbas*, Chehel Sotun, Isfahan, Iran. Persian School, Safavid Dynasty, Reign of Abbas I. 1588–1629. Detail of a fresco wall painting.

This palace wall painting shows idealized human forms from 17th-century Persia.

12

MIND AND BODY

The body is very personal: this is my body, this is me. The body is very social: we study each other; we use our bodies to communicate attitudes; the ways we dress and walk are meaningful to the group. Mind and body are completely intertwined. Through art that deals with the mind and with the body, different cultures show their concept of the individual, as well as human nature in general and larger social trends.

PREVIEW

The chapter begins with portraiture, which might be (1) an intimate encounter with the mind and spirit of a unique individual; or (2) a face that represents an idea or set of ideas or a historical moment, rather than revealing the inner being of a person.

In this chapter, we see art that idealizes the human face and form. Just one example is Nobles at the Court of Shah Abbas *(Fig. 12.1). We will see that sometimes idealized bodies allude to a range of notions about human nature. Other artwork emphasizes the tragic or the debased in human nature. In yet other examples, the body is measured and studied like a machine.*

Increasingly, humans include themselves as part of the larger physical, spiritual, and technological world, which is reflected in art. Physical and psychological pressures can distort the body and affect the mind. In artwork that deals with sickness and death, the horrible and the beautiful often are mixed. Art can represent states of mind, including transcendent states, fantasy, nightmares, or surreal dreams. Art can also be psychologically active and influence the people who use or display it.

Finally, in this chapter we see that the body can be either art material or art tool. It is malleable and can be scarred, sculpted, or painted. It is a primary element in performance art. It is the most wonderful art-making tool we have.

Connecting Art and History from
1550–1750 CE

Cogito ergo sum. "I think, therefore I am" wrote René Descartes, French philosopher and mathematician, at the beginning of the Enlightenment in Europe (roughly 1640–1789). This period saw advances in philosophy, science, literature, and human rights. Increasingly, learned people believed that men were entitled to life, liberty, the pursuit of happiness, property ownership, and individual rights.

Interest in the human mind and body was strong during this period. The founding principle of the Enlightenment was that human reason was the primary authority in science and in politics. Anatomies of the human body were written or republished across Europe, as well as examples from Japan and Persia (see the *Persian Anatomical Illustration*, Fig. 12.22; another example is by Andrea Vesalius, Fig. 14.24). The emphasis on reason also eventually fostered an interest in its opposite, as seen metaphorically in Giovanni Battista Piranesi's fantastic *Prison* series (Fig. 12.31).

In some areas of the globe, the rising support for human rights in time led to the curtailing of the power of kings. The beliefs of the Enlightenment contributed to the power and prosperity of the Dutch middle class during this period, which Rembrandt depicted in many paintings (Fig. 12.10). The Netherlands were Calvinist Protestant, a religion that believed industriousness and spirituality were the measure of an individual. Humanist philosophy flourished in leading Dutch universities, and learning was valued in upper and middle classes. Power in the country was distributed among wealthy bourgeois families, rather than concentrated in a monarchy. In addition to the political situation in the Netherlands, Enlightenment principles contributed to the American Revolution in 1776 and the French Revolution in 1789 in the forty years immediately following this period.

However, across most of the world, this era saw the increased development of centralized states with powerful leaders. Suleyman the Magnificent (or Suleiman) (Fig. 12.2) ruled during the Golden Age of the Ottoman Empire (centered in modern Turkey), when it was the greatest power in the world. During his reign of 1520–1566, the arts flourished, including painting, ceramics, poetry, and architecture, and he supported expanded education and reformed the law for greater justice

MAP 7 The Ottoman Empire, the Safavid Empire, the Mughal Empire, and the Qing Dynasty, in 1650.

Empires around 1650 BCE
- Ottoman Empire
- Safavid Empire
- Mughal Empire
- Qing Dynasty

0   1,000   2,000 Km.
0   1,000   2,000 Mi.

for all, including lower classes and non-Muslims. Militarily adept, he conquered areas of Eastern Europe and dominated the Middle East.

Shah Abbas I led Persia's rise in power, and that country became a rival to the Ottoman Empire in the late 1500s. Abbas excelled at both war and diplomacy, and patronized the arts, especially in Isfahan, his new capital, which he undertook to make into one of the most beautiful cities in the world. *Nobles at the Court of Shah Abbas* (Fig. 12.1) is a detail from a series of large paintings from one of his palaces. He also funded the construction of the famous *Masjid-i-Shah* (Fig. 8.41 and 8.42).

The Mughal Empire continued in India, and Akbar (1556–1605) oversaw a period of humane rule, peace, and prosperity. Mughal artists excelled at miniature painting (for example, Akbar's grandfather is shown in *Babur Supervising the Layout of the Garden of Fidelity*, Fig. 14.18). The empire subsequently weakened throughout the eighteenth century.

Turning to Asia, after a long peasant uprising ended in 1644, China also saw a period of remarkable tolerance, prosperity, and unity, especially under the reign of Kangxi (1661–1722). Japan continued to be ruled by local warlords until 1603, when Tokugawa Ieyasu unified Japan under his command and closed the country to foreigners. The Japanese merchant class grew in number and wealth for the next few hundred years. Japanese art was distinguished by painted scrolls, screens, and gardens.

Europe had already embarked on a period of global expansion. With the exception of limited access to a few ports, Europeans were kept out of China, Japan, and India. However, the English, French, and Spanish quickly divided the Americas into colonies. Spanish rule was the most extensive, covering western North America, Central America, and most of South America, except for Portuguese

Brazil. Latin American societies were multiracial, reflecting intermarriage among native populations, Europeans, and Africans since the 1500s. Because Latin America was more remote, European rulers exercised less direct control, and large, local landowners developed extensive power. In contrast, the population in the English colonies continued to be mostly European, both racially and culturally.

Africa's heartlands continued to be self-ruling and relatively isolated, although the coastal regions were engaged in the slave trade with Europe. The Asante Kingdom was established in western Africa in 1680. Likewise, in Southeast Asia, Dutch and English traders continued in the lucrative spice trade, but the inland areas were generally unaffected and self-ruled.

In Europe, 1560–1650 was a period of crisis because of religious wars between Catholics and Protestants, competition for colonial lands, and hardship caused by crop failures. In response to the unrest, new centralized powers emerged after 1650. In some cases, these were absolute rulers who governed all aspects of their country with tight control—for example, Louis

12.2 Nigari, Ra'is Haydar. *The sultan Suleyman the Magnificent as an old man with two dignataries.* Ottoman miniature, c. 1560. H. 2134, fol. 8. Topkapi Palace Museum, Istanbul, Turkey

Suleyman was the greatest leader of the Ottoman Empire, which was the strongest world power of its time.

XIV of France, Peter the Great of Russia, and the rulers of Prussia. The Habsburgs ruled Austria, but the nobility maintained considerable power. England developed a constitutional monarchy. The Baroque style of art dominated European art at this time. One strong influence on the Baroque era was the heroic sculptures and paintings of Michelangelo, as seen in *David* (Fig. 12.20).

Also, beginning in 1700, the world population grew dramatically for four reasons: (1) better immunity to diseases that had been spread by the first explorers, (2) a period of climate warming, which improved agricultural conditions, (3) new food sources through trade, and (4) the invention of gunpowder, which allowed rulers to control larger areas with their armies and to create more stability.

World Art Map for Chapter 12

Edvard Munch. *The Scream.*

Rembrandt van Rijn. *Self-Portrait.*

Eadweard Muybridge. *Handspring, A Flying Pigeon Interfering.*

Lucian Freud. *Leigh under the Skylight.*

Richard Hamilton. *Just What Is It That Makes Today's Homes So Different, So Appealing?*

Mask of the Swan and White Whale. Alaska, Northwest Pacific.

Chuck Close. *Fanny (Fingerpainting).*

Vincent van Gogh. *Portrait of Dr. Gachet. Portrait of Dr. Gachet.*

Gislebertus. *The Last Judgment.*

Umberto Boccioni. *Unique Forms of Continuity in Space.*

NORTH AMERICA

EUROPE

Giovanni Battista Piranesi. *Prison.*

Michelangelo Buonarroti. *David.*

Agesander, Athenodorus, and Polydorus of Rhodes. *Laocoön and His Sons.*

Bill Viola. *Dolorosa (Production Stills from the Video Installation).*

Cindy Sherman. *Untitled Film Still.*

Hannah Wilke. *Intra-Venus.*

Mark Rothko. *Green, Red, Blue.*

Jackson Pollock. *Lucifer.*

Andres Serrano. *The Morgue (Hacked to Death II).*

Nancy Burson. *Untitled Image from Faces.*

Ana Mendieta. *Arbol de la Vida.*

Head from the Tomb of the Temple of Inscriptions.

Kahlo. *Self-Portrait with Monkey.* Coyoacán, Mexico.

Ngere Girl Prepared for a Festival.

Double Mask.

Male Torso, Ghana, Africa.

SOUTH AMERICA

Matta-Echaurren. *Listen to the Living.* Santiago, Chile, South America.

0   1,000   2,000 Km.

0   1,000   2,000 Mi.

ASIA

Nobles from the Court
of Shah Abbas I.
Isfahan, Iran.

Suleiman the Magnificent.

Polykleitos. *Doryphoros (Spear-bearer)*.

Nefertiti.

Torso.

Persian Anatomical Illustration.
Anonymous Drawing from the Tibb al-Akbar (Akbar's Medicine).

Yoko Ono. *Cut Piece*.

Mori. *Star Doll*.
Tokyo, Japan.

Shimomura Kanzan.
Study for the Portrait of Okakura Tenshin.

AFRICA

Yakshi. Sanchi, India.

AUSTRALIA

Tomika te Mutu.
Motuhoa Island,
New Zealand.

1550–1750 CE

INDUS RIVER CIVILIZATIONS	**3000 BCE**	*Torso (Harappa)*
	1350	

Above Innermost Coffin of Tutankhamen (9.5)

Bust of Nefertiti

EGYPT, EIGHTEENTH DYNASTY		
OLMEC CIVILIZATIONS	**900**	

Above Emperor Justinian and Attendants (10.4)

CLASSICAL ART— GREECE	**400**	POLYKLEITOS: *Doryphoros*
HELLENISTIC ART— GREECE		
MAURYAN DYNASTY FOUNDED IN INDIA		

Above Warrior, Tomb of Shi-Huangdi (9.11)

Laocoön and His Sons

Yakshi

	100 CE	
EARLY CHRISTIAN art	**350**	

MAYAN CIVILIZATION	**600 CE**	*Head from the Tomb of the Temple of Inscriptions*
ROMANESQUE ART	**1100**	GISLEBERTUS: *The Last Judgment*
GOTHIC ART	**1200**	
RENAISSANCE ART	**1400**	
	1500	
REIGN OF AKBAR— INDIA		MICHELANGELO: *David*
		HAYDAR: *The sultan Suleyman the Magnificent as an old man with two dignataries.*
TOKUGAWA SHOGUNATE— JAPAN	**1600**	*Nobles at the Court of Shah Abbas*
BAROQUE ART		
Thirty Years' War— Europe, 1618–1648		
Louis XIV of France	**1650**	REMBRANDT: *Self-Portrait*
Kangxi of China		
Enlightenment		PERSIAN: *Anatomical Illustrations*
ROCOCO ART	**1700**	Piranesi. *Prison no. XIV*
ROMANTIC ART	**1750**	
Latin American Independence Movement	**1800**	
VICTORIAN ERA— ENGLAND	**1850**	

Above Wearing Blanket, Navajo (4.18)

IMPRESSIONISM	**1875**		
POST-IMPRESSIONISM			
		Tomika Te Mutu	
Freud and Psychoanalysis		MUYBRIDGE: *Handspring*	
	1890		
		VAN GOGH: *Portrait of Dr. Gachet*	
		MUNCH: *The Scream Double Mask*	
FAUVISM, CUBISM, FUTURISM, DADA	**1900**	*Male Torso* (Ancestor figure), Baule	
World War I	**1914**	*Mask of the Swan and White Whale*	
END OF THE OTTOMAN EMPIRE		BOCCIONI: *Unique Forms of Continuity in Space*	
SURREALISM, FANTASY, SUPREMATISM	**1917**		
	1922	KANZAN: *Study for the Portrait of Okakura Tenshin*	
	1938	KAHLO: *Self-Portrait with Monkey*	
World War II	**1940**		
POST-WAR EXPRESSIONISM			
		POLLOCK: *Lucifer*	
		MATTA: *Listen to the Living*	
ABSTRACT EXPRESSIONISM, MINIMALISM, POP ART	**1950**	ROTHKO: *Green, Red, Blue*	
Death of Stalin			
KHRUSHCHEV ERA— SOVIET UNION			
	1960	HAMILTON: *Just What Is It ... ?*	
FLUXUS		ONO: *Cut Piece*	

Death of Mao Zedong—China	**1970**	MENDIETA: *Arbol de la Vida, No. 294*	
MODERNISM	**1975**		
POSTMODERNISM			
	1980	SHERMAN: *Untitled Film Still #35*	
		CLOSE: *Fanny (Fingerpainting)*	
		Ngere Girl Prepared for a Festival	
Tiananmen Square Uprising—Beijing			
REUNIFICATION OF GERMANY	**1990**	BURSON: Untitled image from *Faces*	
CREATION OF THE EUROPEAN UNION			
		FREUD: *Leigh under the Skylight*	
		WILKE: *Intra-Venus*	
		SERRANO: The Morgue (*Hacked to Death II*)	
Digital Video, Digital Imaging			
		MORI: *Star Doll*	
Mandela becomes president of South Africa			
	2000	VIOLA: *Dolorosa*	

OURSLER. *Junk* (3.59)

DEPICTING THE BODY

We start by examining portraits and self-portraits. Beyond the likeness of an individual, some portraits represent inner mental states and some represent social preferences or political issues. Following that is a section on the physical body and the ways that artworks reflect social ideals as well as concepts about human nature in general.

Portraits

In art, a successful portrait goes beyond simply creating a likeness. First we see portraits that show individuals in ways that mirror their sociopolitical milieu. Second, we look at portraits that reveal character or inner state of mind.

Our focus figure for portraits that mirror the sociopolitical milieu is the famous bust of Queen Nefertiti, from the Egyptian New Kingdom's Eighteenth Dynasty (Fig. 12.3), likely sculpted by the artist Thutmose c. 1350 BCE. Her features are definitely individualized but also idealized, with a perfectly symmetrical face, long nose, full lips, flat ears, and graceful neck, all below the tall royal crown. Beyond her likeness, however, *Nefertiti* displays the new aesthetic canon, which is eased, flowing, naturalistic, and elegant, different from the rigid, more abstract style found

in prior Egyptian art. This canon, called the Armana style, was begun by Amenhotep III, Nefertiti's father-in-law. She was married to Akhenaten, the pharaoh who broke with Egyptian tradition and started a short-lived monotheistic religion.

Nefertiti's beauty as rendered in this painted limestone portrait has influenced the Western aesthetic of feminine beauty, in both the past and the present. Her name reflects this, as it translates to "The Beautiful One has come."

> **CONNECTION** Another ancient head modeled with refined, portrait-like sensitivity is the *Jayavarman VII* (Fig. 10.6, page 274).

Compare Nefertiti with Suleyman the Magnificient, whose likeness we have already seen in Figure 12.2. Both are idealized portraits. Both have a presence and composure that is emblematic of their political status.

In contrast, the *Study for the Portrait of Okakura Tenshin*, painted in 1922 (Fig. 12.4), records a face that emphasizes inner character and reveals a shrewd, intelligent individual. Additionally, the portrait mirrors the social, political, and aesthetic controversies in Japan during his time. Okakura (1862–1913) was a writer, aesthete, educator, and art curator who lived when rulers of Japan were ending three hundred years of isolation and embarking on a period of rapid Westernization. Eastern-influenced music, literature, religion, and medicine were suppressed and Western modes were introduced. The one exception was the visual arts, in which traditional and Western styles—and mixtures of the two—flourished. Traditional Japanese paintings and prints were popular and sold well not only in Japan but also in the West. They influenced many Western artists, such as Vincent van Gogh (see Fig. 12.5).

Okakura and a U.S. scholar, Ernest Fenollosa, wrote the first Western-style history of Japanese art and established a Japanese museum, an academy of art, and art appreciation societies, which were essentially Western cultural institutions. Before this, the Japanese aesthetic tradition did not include these concepts and institutions. Later, Okakura wrote *The Ideals of the East*, in which he created the concept of Asia as the East in contrast to the West. Eventually, he moved to the United States and

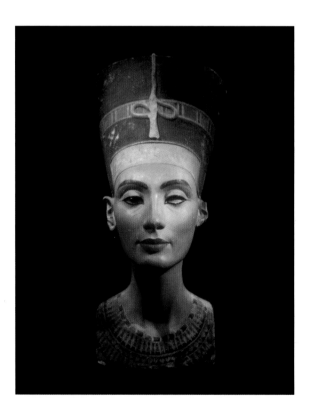

12.3 *Nefertiti*, Egypt, c. 1350 BCE. Portrait bust, approximately 1′ 8″ high. Aegyptisches Museum, Staatliche Museen zu Berlin, Berlin, Germany.

An idealized portrait, Nefertiti embodies the ancient Egyptian concept of female beauty.

became an assistant curator in the Japanese and Chinese Department of the Boston Museum of Fine Arts.

The very style of *Study for the Portrait of Okakura Tenshin* reflects much of the controversy that raged around Japanese art during his time. Japanese-style contour lines and flat shapes are apparent here, especially in Okakura's left hand and sleeve, but the face and hat are rendered with Western chiaroscuro—that is, by dark and light shading. Okakura smokes a Western cigarette while wearing traditional Japanese garb. Okakura believed that only the combination of modernism and tradition meant progress in art. His face is the focal point of the composition, sitting atop

the triangular shape of his body, and his features make a great study of shrewdness, toughness, and perception.

CONNECTION For an example of a face rendered in traditional Japanese style, with outlines only, see *Komurasaki of the Tamaya Teahouse* (Fig. 13.32, page 395).

Next, we see an extreme example of a portrait that focuses on a person's inner mental and emotional state, yet even here there are also social dimensions to the image. In the *Portrait of Dr. Gachet*, dated 1890 (Fig. 12.5), Vincent van Gogh painted a free-thinking, eccentric, homeopathic doctor with the foxglove flower to symbolize his profession. With a melancholy face and pose, Gachet leans on

12.4, left SHIMOMURA KANZAN. *Study for the Portrait of Okakura Tenshin*, Japan, 1922. Pigment on paper, 53 1/2″ × 26″. Art Museum, Tokyo National University of Fine Arts and Music.

This drawing combines Japanese and Western art styles. It was made at the historical moment when both Japanese art and European art were profoundly influenced by each other.

12.5, below VINCENT VAN GOGH. *Portrait of Dr. Gachet*, Netherlands, 1890. Oil on canvas, 26 1/4″ × 22″.

Portraits can be visual records of inner emotional states.

two nineteenth-century novels about tragic and degenerate life in Paris.

Gachet's portrait is also a vehicle for van Gogh to make observations about modern urban life in general, which van Gogh found to be full of suffering. In this case, the artist may have revealed as much about himself as he did about his subject. Van Gogh found life in Paris to be unhealthy and miserable, and he took refuge in his art, in the countryside, and in medical help. At this time, van Gogh was painting at a feverish pace, but he was less than two months away from his own suicide. Thick paint animates the entire surface, with emphatic dashes and tight swirls that model form, increase color saturation, and indicate van Gogh's own agitation and intensity. Thus, Gachet's likeness was both an image of Gachet and a reflection of van Gogh's own inner state.

In *Fanny (Fingerpainting)*, dated 1985 (Fig. 12.6), artist Chuck Close has used the portrait not so much to reveal inner personality, but more to create an amazingly detailed record of the structure, ridges, pores, and wrinkles of an elderly woman's head. The scale is enormous. Her head is more than nine feet high. Her face fills the foreground space of the painting, pushing toward us her lizard-like eyelids, her watery eyes and cracked lips, and the sagging skin of her neck. With this painting, we can stare curiously at a person's face, an action considered impolite in U.S. culture.

The pose is ordinary, like that on a driver's license. Her nonidealized features are lit unflatteringly from both sides, leaving darker shadows at the center of her face. But the scale and surface make her face forceful and imposing. Copying his photographic sources, Close has the painting in sharp focus in certain areas, such as the tip of the nose, and soft focus in more distant points, such as the hair, base of the neck, and shoulders. The expression on the woman's face also makes evident the photographic source: her eyes are focused on the camera that is close to her nose, and she seems both tolerant of and slightly affronted by it.

In the 1992 series called *Faces*, Nancy Burson also gave us the opportunity to indulge our curiosity about

12.6 CHUCK CLOSE. *Fanny (Fingerpainting)*, USA, 1985. Oil on canvas, 120″ × 84″. National Gallery of Art, Washington, D.C., donation of Lila Acheson Wallace.

This is a large portrait with an amazing amount of textural detail.

other people's faces. She used a cheap plastic camera to make grainy, fuzzy photographs of children with unusual faces due to genetic conditions, accident, or disease. The low-quality lens produced surprisingly beautiful images, with blurred edges, softened highlights, and grainy but luminous shadows. Burson's photographs reveal some aspects of the children's personalities, such as friendliness, dreaminess, caution, concern, curiosity, and boldness. Our untitled example (Fig. 12.7) shows the boy at the left obligingly posing and encouraging the other to do so also, while the other boy remains reluctant and suspicious of manipulation. Framing makes the child at the left seem to be moving, while the other appears more pinned at the center.

Burson's photographs act as a mirror to the viewers, who reveal themselves in their reactions to the images. Burson noted that people who dwell on disaster see these children as disasters, whereas others react to them as they would to other children. Thus, degrees of normal and abnormal are more the viewers' judgments than objective standards.

We now compare full-body portraits, which often reveal more about the sitter's personality than just a face rendering. *Leigh under the Skylight*, painted in 1994 (Fig. 12.8), is one of Lucian Freud's many full-body portraits. During the long process of sitting for a painting in Freud's

12.7 NANCY BURSON. Untitled image from *Faces*, USA, 1992. Silver gelatin print, 15″ × 15″. Twin Palms Publishers, Santa Fe, New Mexico.

The artist used a cheap camera with a bad lens to create a blurry but evocative double portrait.

12.8 LUCIAN FREUD. *Leigh under the Skylight*, Britain, 1994. Oil on canvas, 90″ × 48″. Acquavella Contemporary Art, New York.

Freud's portraits are known for their amazing range of paint applications and for revealing the inner being of his sitters.

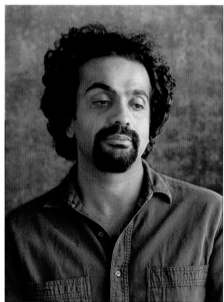

12.9 BILL VIOLA. *Dolorosa* (production stills from the video installation), USA, 2000. Courtesy of the Artist.

This work is high-resolution video replayed slowly, so that the viewers have a chance to study the intense emotions presented on the screen.

studio, the sitters unintentionally reveal clues about their most intimate selves, primarily through their poses and facial expressions. The figure of Leigh is massive, and from the low point of view assumed by the artist, he appears to be almost gigantic. Yet the flesh is soft. The crossed legs, deeply lined face, and furrowed brow communicate a sense of tightness. The figure appears almost stuffed up against the space of the skylight, wary and exposed. The paint is thick and buttery below the knees and the top of the belly, but congealed and clotted around the jaw, nipples, navel, and genitals. The excess of texture is both fascinating and repulsive. This full-size nude is definitely a portrait of an individual man, in contrast to the full-size nude *Doryphoros* (see Fig. 12.14), which is a depiction of "Man."

Video allows artists to make moving portraits. Bill Viola's *Dolorosa* (Fig. 12.9) consists of two flat-panel monitors arranged like a diptych or a double-frame portrait showing a weeping man and woman. At first glance, the videos look like paintings, because the color is so saturated, the picture so sharp, and the movement so excruciatingly slow. Only after a few minutes of study do we see the subtle changes in their faces, expressing a deep, almost unbearable sorrow. Viola made this study of emotional states and more than twenty others in a series titled *The Passions*, based on **Renaissance** and **Baroque** paintings of figures in sorrow, ecstasy, or astonishment. Rather than restage the old paintings, Viola sought to expand their emotional and spiritual dimensions. Viewers can study faces as never before.

Self-Portraits

We will look at four artists who have made many pictures of themselves. Rembrandt van Rijn made at least sixty-two self-portraits. Frida Kahlo painted herself fifty-five times, which represents almost one-third of the artwork she did in her entire lifetime. Cindy Sherman has photographed herself hundreds of times in various guises and settings. Likewise, Mariko Mori has made multiple images of herself that cross the boundaries between fine art, consumer culture, and kitsch.

Our focus figure is by Rembrandt van Rijn, who recorded his face as strong, vulnerable, cloddish, or sophisticated, and ranging from youth through old age. The paintings are emotional barometers as well, showing happiness, worry, sorrow, humor, or resignation. In *Self-Portrait*, painted in 1669 (Fig. 12.10), Rembrandt records both a human face and a human soul. His lit face emerges from the void of the background. Light seems both to reflect off the surface of his face and to emanate from inside his head. His dark, piercing eyes express gentleness, pain, and knowledge. The left side of his face is in soft shadow, a fitting visual metaphor for a man of wisdom facing his own death. In fact, Rembrandt died later that year. Earth tones, blacks, dull reds, and luminous yellows predominate in this painting. The paint surface is rich and thick. Rembrandt studied himself in a country where both religion and the state promoted individualism (see *History Focus* on page 330).

Compare the subtle emotions of Rembrandt's face with the fiercely unblinking expression in our next example. In her fifty-five self-portraits, Frida Kahlo conducted a long inquiry into her inner and her outer being, as well as the broader social and political forces that had influenced her life. Yet her face stays almost the same in all her paintings: distinctive and unemotional, with an unrelenting gaze that looks back at the viewer. She surrounds herself

12.10 REMBRANDT VAN RIJN. *Self-Portrait*, Netherlands, 1669. Oil on canvas, 23 1/4″ × 20″. The Hague, Mauritshuis.

Rembrandt's self-portraits, produced over many decades of his life, are a moving record of the pleasures and sorrows in the life of this man.

with signs and images of the different factors that shaped her very self, such as her ancestry, her physical body, her nearly fatal accident and chronic pain, the indigenous Mexican culture, the landscape, the Christian religion, and her relationship with Diego Rivera, a prominent Mexican artist. In *Self-Portrait with Monkey*, painted in 1938 (Fig. 12.11), Kahlo's face is central, studying us as we study her. Her long hair is braided and pulled on top of her head in traditional Mexican style, to show her identification with the peasant culture. Lush foliage from the Mexican landscape surrounds her head. For Kahlo, the monkey was her animal alter ego. In other self-portraits, Kahlo uses such symbols as hummingbirds, which stood for the souls of dead Mayan warriors, and blood, which alludes to the crippling injuries she suffered in a bus accident, to Mayan bloodletting ceremonies, and to the Christian crown of thorns.

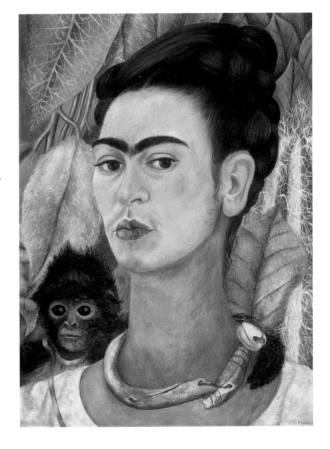

12.11 FRIDA KAHLO. *Self-Portrait with Monkey*, Mexico, 1938. Oil on masonite, 16″ × 12″. Albright-Knox Art Gallery, Buffalo, NY.

Kahlo painted her face many times, almost always with the same impassive expression. She surrounded her image with symbols of her personal history and of Mexican history that were significant in her life.

CONNECTIONS For an example of a work by Kahlo's husband, Diego Rivera, see *Día de Los Muertos* (Fig. 9.25, page 260). A Mayan relief depicting a bloodletting ritual, *Shield Jaguar and Lady Xoc*, appears in Figure 8.18, page 207.

Kahlo's and Rembrandt's self-portraits show the inner self of a unique, deeply feeling person. In contrast, Cindy Sherman photographed herself hundreds of times, but the cumulative effect is one of fragmentation, not of piecing together a unique individual. Each image of Sherman reflects a socially prescribed or media-disseminated role. Our example, *Untitled Film Still #35* (Fig. 12.12), is one of a series of sixty-nine fake film stills she made between 1977 and 1980. They were all black and white, eight by ten inches, the exact format of B-movie stills. She wears a wide range of costumes and poses in all kinds of settings, with a vast array of props, as if unaware of the camera. Sherman often reveals the mechanics of her self-portraiture; in this picture, the shutter release cable that Sherman operates is visible on the floor at the left.

In the photos, Sherman is sometimes almost unrecognizable as she reenacts roles for women that are given to us by the media, such as the sweetheart next door, the housewife, the girl left behind, or the vulnerable hitchhiker from a slasher film. In *Untitled Film Still #35*, Sherman appears as a poor woman who is hardened, trapped, sullen, and sexy. The grimy setting and costumes seem to be taken from the 1930s. The kick marks on the door allude to an atmosphere of violence. This image is the reversal of the independent, single, working girl who becomes the happy homemaker. Sherman suggests that we have no built-in sense of identity, but rather compose ourselves from pieces of popular culture. The *Film Still* self-portraits are collectively a portrait of familiar female stereotypes, as represented through the media.

CONNECTIONS To read what critics have said about Sherman's work, turn to pages 99–100 and Fig. 4.17.

Japanese-born Mariko Mori is an artist and a former fashion model and fashion designer living in both New York and Tokyo. She creates photographs and performances starring herself in various roles, such as geisha or cyberchick, which she sees as total fabrications. Embracing the commercial world that uses models to sell messages, she sees her artwork as part of pop culture and wants to connect art with movies and fashions. In *Birth of a Star*, she

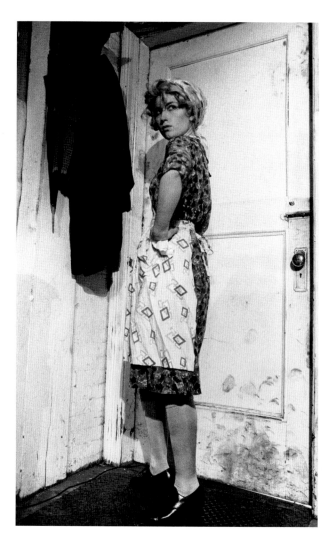

12.12 CINDY SHERMAN. *Untitled Film Still #35*, USA, 1979. Gelatin silver print, 8 × 10. Collection of Eli and Edythe Broad, Los Angeles.

Sherman's work asks the question of whether a person's very self emanates from inner impulses or is molded from culturally given models.

photographed herself as a teen rock star in a shiny, plastic, plaid skirt and spiked purple hair, surrounded by computer-manipulated floating bubbles. Afterward, she translated that same image into *Star Doll*, 1998 (Fig. 12.13), an edition of ninety-nine dolls. Because her identity is a totally fabricated hybrid, her work raises the question, "What is 'self'?" Mori's work collapses distinctions among the categories of art, toy, fashion, kitsch, frivolity, and serious inquiry.

The Physical Body

Artists use the body to address ideas about the essence of humanity as well as cultural ideals.

12.13, above MARIKO MORI. *Star Doll*, 1998 (edition for Parket 54, 1998–1999). Multiple of doll, 10 $\frac{1}{4}$″ × 3″ × 1 $\frac{9}{16}$″ (irregular). Publisher: Parkett, Zurich and New York. Manufacturer: Marmit, Tokyo. Edition: 99.

Mori's self-portrait is a commercially packaged version of herself as artist, model, and fashion designer.

12.14, right POLYKLEITOS. *Doryphoros (Spear-bearer)*, Rome, c. 450–440 BCE. Marble after a bronze original, 6′ 11″ high. Museo Nazionale, Naples.

Polykleitos developed a canon of proportions, in which each part of the ideal body was in carefully controlled proportion to all other parts.

The Idealized Body

Our first examples present the human body in ideal terms, although that varies from culture to culture. Protagoras said, "Of all things, the measure is man," and the ancient Greeks had a great respect for the human mind and body, esteeming the arts, sciences, philosophy, and athletics. The democratic government, although limited, meant that individuals were self-governing. Athlete, philosopher, scientist, statesman, playwright, and warrior were all ideal occupations for men. The Greeks believed that humans were capable of near perfection, defined as a fit body guided by a keen mind. Emotions were generally

considered less important than the intellect and should be properly contained. Nudity was common in art and in athletic events, both of which glorified the unclothed, idealized human form. The focus figure for this section is *Doryphoros*, or "Spear-bearer," dated 450–440 BCE (Fig. 12.14). This sculpture by Polykleitos is a slightly larger-than-life-size nude male that reflects the Greeks' deep appreciation of the human body. The figure is idealized in several ways: (1) in the balanced pose; (2) in the internal proportions; (3) in the restrained emotions; and (4) in the roles depicted—youth, athlete, and warrior. This work was executed in the Greek **Classical** art style.

The pose is simple, balanced, and understated. The statue's straight leg and arm create a vertical line on the left, balanced by the bent leg and arm on the right. Balance is also expressed across the body. The straight leg and bent arm are tensed, versus the hanging arm and flexed leg, which are relaxed. The action is minimal and at the same time complex in its subtleties, with small twists, stretches, and compressions. This **contrapposto** (counterbalanced) stance is the way many people stand, so the sculpture re-creates an image of a living, flexing body.

Polykleitos invented and applied a now-lost system of mathematical and geometric proportions, called the Canon, which harmonized one body part with another in his sculptures. *Doryphoros* was originally conceived as a sculpture that would illustrate and demonstrate the Canon. A few of the simpler proportions of the Canon are still known; for example, the length of the longest finger equaled the length of the palm of the hand, and together they were used as a measure for the length of the arm. The breast nipples are one head-length below the chin, and the navel is another head-length below the nipples. This system also determined the placement of all the muscles. Polykleitos and the Greeks of his era believed that mathematical proportions resulted in a harmonious figure that was morally and aesthetically good. (In fact, the body is blocky, the result of the application of the Canon.) Polykleitos' total combination of balance, proportion, restraint, and youthful heroism made *Doryphoros* one of the most famous nudes of its time as well as the Roman era and the Italian Renaissance.

> **CONNECTIONS** See *Zeus* or *Poseidon* (Fig. 8.4, page 195) to compare the similarity between images of gods and humans in Greek Classical art.
>
> The original *Doryphoros* was executed in bronze, using the lost wax process. For more information, Fig. 3.43, page 76.

It is interesting to compare *Doryphoros* with the *Male Torso* (Ancestor figure) in Figure 12.15, which was likely carved in the twentieth century in the Baule area of Africa. Internal proportions, idealized character, harmony of parts, and restraint are important elements here as in *Doryphoros*, but the visual result is very different. In most traditional African sculpture, the front view of the human figure was sculpted symmetrically; arms are in parallel positions, legs both on the ground, head facing forward.

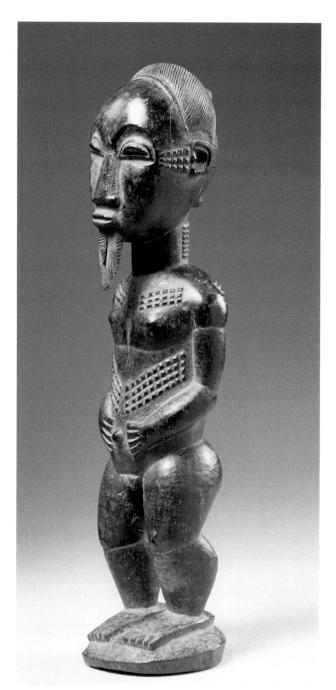

12.15 *Male Torso* (Ancestor figure), Africa, c. 19th–20th century. Wood, 20 1/2" high. Baule. The British Museum, London.

In African art, ideal proportions for the human body were usually divided vertically, with one-third for the head, one-third for the torso, and one-third for the legs.

This formal, frontal pose contributes to the dignified, almost solemn aspect of the sculpture. In contrast, the side view features counterbalanced curves: the abdomen and knees project forward, balanced by the buttocks to the back. The straight neck and back interrupt the curves. The distinctive silhouette of the head is the focus for the entire work. This sculpture is likely the depiction of an ancestor.

In some African traditions, the head and neck were considered the most important parts of the body, and thus were apportioned one-third the height of the entire figure. The torso occupied another third, and the legs the last third. The sculptor's first cuts set these proportions. The major forms were sculpted next, and, finally, decorative patterns enlivened the surface. The patterns represent scarification and carefully combed, braided, twisted, or beaded hair. The pattern elements are all confidently carved without mistakes or reworking, because African sculptors generally were well trained as apprentices. The *Male Torso* combines naturalistic and abstracted features; for example, the chest and arms are relatively naturalistic compared to the stylized hands. This echoes tendencies in African sculpture as a whole, which runs the gamut from realistic to very abstract.

We continue with our comparisons of ideal figures by turning to two examples from ancient India. *Torso*, dated c. 3000 BCE (Fig. 12.16), is a carving from the ancient Harappan civilization that was centered on the Indus River in what is now Pakistan. The sculpture is an idealized version of the human body, with a supple, rounded form. The arm sockets suggest that the figure originally included several arms, possibly representing a youthful deity. The somewhat distended stomach suggests a yogic breathing posture. The stone has been so sensitively shaped that it gives the impression of living flesh, smooth muscle, and a little pad of fat. In contrast to the crisply articulated forms in *Doryphorus* and in the *Male Torso* from Baule, here the outlines and forms are smooth and curving, suggesting grace, flexibility, sensuality, and even vulnerability.

Yakshi, dating from the first century BCE in India (Fig. 12.17), continued the rounded form and sensuality of the *Torso*. Yakshi is a nature spirit who represents fertility; her breasts are exaggerated to emphasize her powers—her touch caused trees to flower. Her nearly nude body is curving and rounded and can be seen through her transparent skirt with the hemline draping across her shin. *Yakshi* twists with incredible flexibility, looking natural in a pose that would leave a human totally off balance. Jewelry adorns her lower arms and legs, giving interest to the less-curving features of her body. Her belt visually emphasizes her broad hips in contrast to her small waist. For the next several centuries, India produced an enormous amount of splendid figurative sculpture, and the twisting pose and voluptuous form appear often. Thus, in India, sensuality is an important and central characteristic of human nature.

12.16 *Torso*, India (Harappa, Pakistan), c. 3000 BCE. Red sandstone, 3 1/2″ high. National Museum, New Delhi.

In ancient India, the ideal body had a soft, supple, fluid quality.

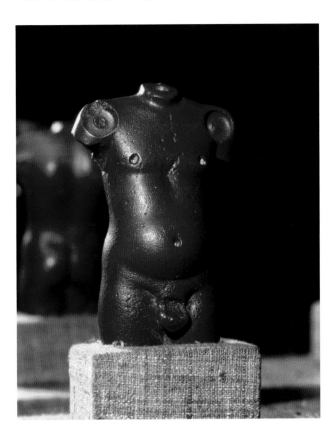

12.17 *Yakshi* (detail of East Gate, Great Stupa), Sanchi, India, early Andhra period, 1st century BCE. Sandstone, approx. 5′ high.

The ideal female body in ancient India was very well rounded and remarkably limber.

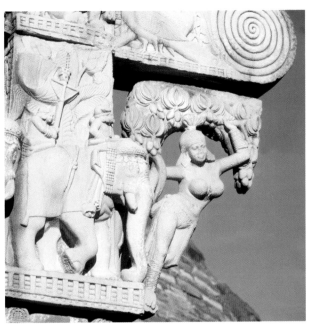

Many cultures do not have a tradition of depicting nudes in art, yet even these cultures have representations of ideal human forms. Return to the Chapter Opener, Figure 12.1, *Nobles at the Court of Shah Abbas*. Note the graceful tilt of the head, the elegant hands, the serene facial expression, and the relaxed pose. This beautiful couple represents ideal qualities of youth in early-seventeenth-century Persia.

Flawed Humanity

Having looked at idealized human forms, we turn now to art in which human flaws are part of the content of the work.

At first glance, our focus figure seems to completely fit into the category of art that shows idealized human bodies. But *Laocoön and His Sons*, dated 300 to 100 BCE (Fig. 12.18), was created during the centuries that followed the idealized image of *Doryphoros*, when Greek art turned to depicting humans engaged in violent action, vulnerable to age, injured, diseased, and subject to feelings of pain, terror, or despair. Two cults were particularly influential in this era known as Hellenistic Greece: *Stoicism*, in which individuals were urged to endure nobly their fate and state in life; and *Epicureanism*, which advocated intelligent pleasure seeking in life because death was the end of existence. Both philosophies imply a kind of resigned acceptance of fate and a withdrawal from the Classic Greek ideal of the

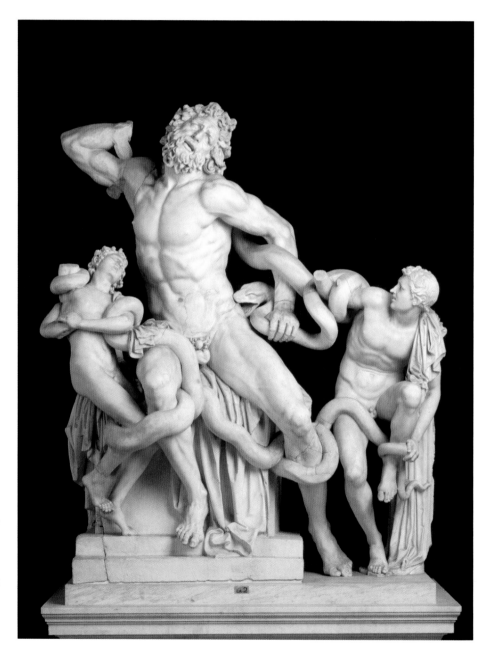

12.18 Agesander, Athenodorus, and Polydorus of Rhodes. *Laocoön and His Sons*, Greece, late 2nd–early 1st century BCE. Marble, 7′ 10″ high. Hellenistic (Roman patronage). Vatican Museums, Rome.

The dramatic display of emotion in this sculpture stands in contrast to *Doryphorus*, which represents a balance between mind and body and emphasized restrained emotions.

active, heroic, involved person. The **Hellenistic** Greek art style then emerged.

Laocoön and His Sons shows these changing concepts of the human body and human nature. In *Laocoön*, the human bodies are impressively muscular, an inheritance of the Classical Greeks, but the balance of mind and body, and the contained emotion, has here burst apart in a scene of high drama and sensationalism. Laocoön was a Trojan priest who tried to warn his fellow citizens against accepting the Trojan Horse as an apparent token of surrender from the Greeks who had been warring against them. Greek warriors hid in the horse, and they overcame the Trojan forces once the horse was inside the fortifications. The gods, who sided with the Greeks against the Trojans, sent sea serpents to strangle and kill Laocoön and his sons, even as they were making offerings at an altar. The story seems to be one of great injustice, as a virtuous man helping his fellow citizens is cruelly crushed by the gods. Human vulnerability and lack of control of one's fate are well demonstrated.

The figures are like a group of actors on a stage, all facing forward as if performing for an unseen audience (which is common of Hellenistic sculpture). Their struggles are theatrical. Their bodies are idealized, but the father's is overdeveloped and muscle-bound, more spectacular than heroic. Emotionality is increased by the deeply cut sculpture and Laocoön's dramatic reach into the surrounding space. The textures and surfaces vary from skin to hair, and cloth to serpent.

Compare now a representation of the body when human nature was held in low esteem. In Europe, medieval Christians saw a great split between the purity of God's divine realm and the natural world, a transitory place of sin and corruption. The mortal body was given over to appetites and lusts that led humans into sin and endangered their immortal souls. Salvation with God was possible only through the Church. In *The Last Judgment* (sculpted in the **Romanesque** style), dated c. 1130 (Fig. 12.19), from the main entrance of the Church of St. Lazare, we have another example of art depicting flawed humanity.

12.19 GISLEBERTUS. *The Last Judgment*, France, c. 1130. Stone carving, 21′ wide, 12′ high. West tympanum of the Church of St. Lazare, Autun, France.

The bottom band shows humans raised from the dead on the last day, while Heaven is shown at center left, and the scales of Judgment and Hell are at center right. Body styles differentiate between holy and evil characters.

Unlike the muscular body of *Laocoön*, here the human bodies are depicted as miserable, frail, and pitifully unattractive. The scene illustrates the end of time, when every person rises from the ground to be judged forever as worthy of heaven or condemned to hell. In the lower section of this carving, the cowering humans rise from their box-like graves and huddle in line until a pair of large hands, like oversized pliers, clamps around their heads. All are then plucked up and deposited on the scales of Judgment, where they risk being snatched by demons and stuffed in hell for eternity. The saved souls clutch fearfully at the robes of the angels.

Because human nature was considered so base, the idealized Greek nude was inconceivable, and the concept of a naturalistic body as beautiful and good had long since disappeared. The body in medieval art was distorted to communicate moral status. Thus, naked humans are puny. Good angels are elongated and serene, their anatomical distortions emphasizing their distance from earthly beings. The demons, however, seem to have been modeled on a flayed human corpse, with the exposed ribs and muscles of a tortured body, while their faces grimace horribly. Their claw feet are beastlike, and indeed the human body was associated with animals, which were seen as even more distant from God. Jesus is depicted in a grand manner reigning over heaven and earth, frontal and symmetrical, and much larger than all others.

It is interesting to compare the Medieval depiction of the human form with an example from the Renaissance. Attitudes about human nature had shifted again. Humanistic philosophy of this time celebrated the glory of humanity: Italian philosopher Giovanni Pico della Mirandola declared in the fifteenth century, "There is nothing to be seen more wonderful than man," reflecting an attitude very similar to the Greeks'. Michelangelo Buonarroti, the famous painter, sculptor, and architect of the Italian **Renaissance**, believed that the human form was the most perfect and important subject to depict. He believed that his work was an echo of God's divine creation of humanity. Like most other Italian artists of that time, he was strongly influenced by Hellenistic and Roman sculptures that were being excavated in central Italy, for example, *Laocoön and His Sons* (Fig. 12.18). The nude as an ideal form became popular again.

But Renaissance nudes were different from the Classical nudes. On the one hand, the body was seen now as a work of God and deserving of respect and honor. Yet the medieval beliefs persisted regarding the enduring soul versus the corruptible body. *David*, dated 1501 to 1504 (Fig. 12.20), represents the Israelite youth who

12.20 MICHELANGELO BUONARROTI. *David*, Italy, 1501–1504. Marble, 14′ 3″ high. Galleria dell'Accademia, Florence.

The youthfulness of David is expressed in the oversized hands and in the tension on his face.

fought the giant warrior, Goliath, saved his people, and later became the greatest king of the Old Testament. Michelangelo chose the moment that the young David first faces Goliath. Tension is apparent in his frown, tensed muscles, and protruding veins. The sculpture is not self-contained, in contrast to *Doryphoros* (Fig. 12.14);

the turning figure of David is "completed" by the unseen Goliath. The head and hands are oversized, indicating youthful potential still maturing and a greater potential violence, all attributes that differ from the restrained, relaxed *Doryphoros*. David's inner tension speaks of the core of being, the soul, that is separate from the body. The body is ennobled and emphasized, but only as a vehicle for expressing the soul.

David reflects some broad trends. During the Renaissance, there was also a growing interest in scientific inquiry and the study of human anatomy. Michelangelo, Leonardo da Vinci, and other Italian artists performed dissections to assist them in rendering muscles. Also, David versus Goliath was a popular story in the republic of Florence, the city-state in central Italy for which this sculpture was made. Florence was ruled by a group of wealthy families rather than by a single leader, and Florentines saw themselves as much more self-determining than citizens of other areas that were ruled by tyrants.

Our final comparison within the category of less-than-perfect humanity is the 1956 collage by Richard Hamilton, *Just What Is It That Makes Today's Homes So Different, So Appealing?* (Fig. 12.21). In an era of consumerism, people often gauge their worth by the purchases they can make, not by character, deeds, fate, or karma. Body shape becomes something that can be bought, too. In this **Pop Art** collage, we see the aestheticized body ideals of the late twentieth century: the buff, muscular man of amazing

sexual prowess (the Tootsie pop) and a super-thin, sexy woman with a fashion-model pout on her face. The faces and bodies have been molded through implants, plastic surgery, and the latest abdominal workout machine. In addition, the couple's attractiveness is enhanced by their acquisition of trendy props, which in the 1950s included modern furniture, the latest appliances, and new media products. Hamilton took his imagery from popular magazines and billboards. The rug is a designer version of a Jackson Pollock action painting, which we will see at the end of this chapter. The cluttered composition, with all things new and chic, makes everything seem arbitrary and faddish. Hamilton's lampoon of modern consumer culture reveals the effectiveness and ridiculousness of advertising, because it projects ideal body images that are so extreme, images to which we can never (but must always try to) measure up.

> **CONNECTION** Hamilton's work is fine art with mass-media imagery, and he is critical of both. For more, see "Fine Art, Popular Culture, and Kitsch," in Chapter 1.

The Body as the Subject of Scientific Study

Starting with the Renaissance and moving toward the modern era, religious models for human nature held less sway in Europe and were increasingly challenged and displaced by concepts of humans based on scientific inquiry, whether physical anatomy, medicine, or psychiatry. This shift was also apparent in artwork.

In the discussion of *David*, Figure 12.20, and also in the *History Focus* section (page 331), we have mentioned that anatomical studies were written or republished in many parts of the world throughout the second millennium, most for medical or artistic reasons. This growing interest in anatomy resulted in body depictions that differ from those designed to reveal religious truths, philosophical positions, or inner emotions. The *Persian Anatomical*

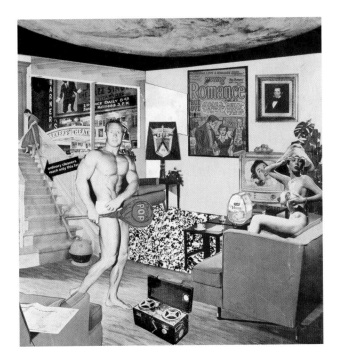

12.21 RICHARD HAMILTON. *Just What Is It That Makes Today's Homes So Different, So Appealing?* England, 1956. Collage, 10 1/4" × 9 3/4". Kunsthalle Tubingen, Germany.

This work mocks the notion that status can be acquired by purchasing consumer products, or by manufacturing an ideal body type for oneself.

Illustration (Fig. 12.22) from Iran or Pakistan around 1680–1750, shows a pregnant female. She draws back the skin of her chest and abdomen to reveal inner organs, including her heart, stomach, and uterus. Around her are detailed drawings of other organs, including two hearts and lungs. She holds a plant in her hand, which may have been symbolic of her fruitfulness.

CONNECTION Another famous anatomical study is Andreas Vesalius's *De Humani Corporis Fabrica*. His *Fourth Plate of Muscles* (Fig. 14.24, page 419) is an example of European Renaissance scientific studies of anatomy.

12.22 *Persian Anatomical Illustration,* anonymous drawing from the *Tibb al-Akbar (Akbar's Medicine)* by Muhammad Akbar, known as Muhammad Arzani. Iran or Pakistan, c. 1680–1750. Ink and pigment on paper.

The body has been the subject of scientific study in many cultures around the world.

Moving closer to our present era, new technologies changed the understanding of the human body. For artists, the invention of photography meant that human movement could be stopped and examined as never before. *Handspring, a flying pigeon interfering, June 26, 1885* (Fig. 12.23) is a study of the human body in action made by Eadweard Muybridge and subsequently published with other such studies in the book *Animal Locomotion.* Muybridge invented a special camera shutter and then placed twelve cameras so outfitted in a row. When the athlete performed the handstand, his movements broke the series of strings stretched across his path, thus progressively triggering each of the twelve cameras.

For Muybridge, the human body was an object of detached, scientific study and not a powerful presence like *David* or the *Male Torso* from Baule. With Muybridge, the concept of the human body was altered and was recognized as being modified by time and space. Muybridge made similar studies for all kinds of human and animal movement. He also developed a cylindrical device that allowed his images to be mounted, rotated, and viewed to give the illusion of motion. In this respect, his work was a precursor of cinema.

The Limits of the Self

Is the individual person a discrete entity? What are the boundaries between the self and the environment, between the self and the spiritual realm, or between the self and technology?

Many Oceanic cultures of the South Pacific conceive of the person as an amalgam of life forces, physical substances, and ritual knowledge that come from many sources. That amalgam, which is at this moment a particular person, is in fact constantly changing and transforming and also in danger of coming apart.

Ritual tattooing was one way of strengthening the individual and was used throughout the more eastern islands of the South Pacific. Extra eyes, for example, gave the tattooed person more power and decreased vulnerability. Tattooing is often part of initiation rites that gradually harden the human body for adulthood. Extensive tattooing subjected a person to severe pain for a long time, but the result was generally seen as a kind of ritual empowerment. On the Marquesas Islands, the entire body was tattooed, while tattooing was confined to the buttocks and thighs of the women of Fiji and of the men of Samoa, Tahiti, and Tonga.

The tattoos of *Tomika Te Mutu of Coromandel* (Fig. 12.24), a nineteenth-century Maori tribal chief, were seen as an extra protective shell and a new ritual skin. Tattooing

12.23 EADWEARD MUYBRIDGE. *Handspring, a flying pigeon interfering, June 26, 1885,* England/Scotland/USA, 1887. Print from an original master negative, Plate 365 of *Animal Locomotion.* International Museum of Photography at George Eastman House, Rochester, New York.

The photograph allows artists and scientists to study the mechanics of human movement.

was effective in war, as it distracted and confused opponents. The tattoos also identified the individual. Among the Maori, facial tattoos were often considered more memorable than the person's natural features, which is true of Tomika Te Mutu. The chiseled whorls emphasize his scowl, piercing vision, hot breath, and fierce mouth. Traditional Maori tattooing is done with chisels, which gouge deep grooves in the skin. Curves and spirals are similar to the patterns in Maori woodcarving.

CONNECTION Turn to Figure 10.17, page 284, to see Maori woodcarving on a traditional meeting house.

If ritual beliefs can shape the concept of the human being, then scientific discoveries and technological advances can also do so. A vast range of environmental factors

12.24 *Tomika Te Mutu of Coromandel,* New Zealand, 19th century. Maori chief.

Tattoos applied to the body were believed to provide a ritual protective skin to rulers of the Maori people.

12.25 UMBERTO BOCCIONI. *Unique Forms of Continuity in Space*, Italy, 1913. Bronze (cast 1931), approx. 43″ high. The Museum of Modern Art, New York; acquired through the Lillie P. Bliss Bequest.

This artwork presents the human figure distorted by external forces, and thus continuous with all other forms and energy in space.

influence the living body. The human being is seen now as permeable and as an integrated part of the total world.

In *Unique Forms of Continuity in Space* (Fig. 12.25), cast in 1931, the artist Umberto Boccioni dissolves the conventional belief that the skin layer defines the body's outer edge. To him, the body is a mass of wave energy defined by its movement through a fluid atmospheric medium. Significantly, the body is considered less as a human and more as a form that is continuous with others in space. Muscle and bulk are implied, but the sculpture resembles a map of aerodynamic turbulence and the distorting effects of air currents on forms. Boccioni was part of an art

movement called **Futurism**, which celebrated violence, speed, energy, motion, force, and change, which reflected his contemporary world.

Sickness and Death

Humans become ill and die, topics which are also addressed in art. *Intra-Venus*, dated from 1992 to 1993, is a series of large-scale photographs that the artist, Hannah Wilke, made with her husband, Donald Goddard, as she struggled with and eventually succumbed to cancer. In this series, both cancer and its medical cures transform and ravage Wilke's body. The frequently larger-than-life photographs present her body to us as it weakened, bloated, and bled. The size makes the physical reality of sickness apparent; it is "in your face." In one bust-length portrait, we see her bald scalp, mottled skin, and bleeding, pus-filled tongue, all resulting from her cancer treatment. Yet many of the images show that her body possessed a kind of monumental beauty and that Wilke was still a person of humor and strength.

In three panels from *Intra-Venus* (Fig. 12.26), Wilke assumes three poses derived from images of sexually attractive nudes taken from fine art and from magazines, such as *Playboy*. Her glance implies the presence of a sexual partner, as she poses herself as the object of voyeurism. Her posture speaks of narcissistic pleasure. She is Venus, the goddess of love and beauty, even with the ravages of disease and surgery. Wilke reclaims sexuality for herself in sickness and, thus, challenges conventional ideas of attractiveness. In doing so, her last work continued her earlier art. Before the onset of cancer, her body conformed to "fashion model" looks, and she frequently used her body in her artwork to undermine or critique how female beauty is currently defined and consumed in the United States.

CONNECTION For more about the sexual meaning of gaze and gender roles in images, see *Olympia* by Edward Manet (Fig. 7.21, page 179).

The Morgue (Hacked to Death II), dated 1992 (Fig. 12.27), is one of a series of twenty large-scale photographs by

12.26 HANNAH WILKE. *Intra-Venus*, USA, 1992–1993. Chromogenic supergloss photographic prints (13); each panel: 26″ × 39 ½″.

This artist examines the beauty of her body even when ravaged by disease.

12.27 ANDRES SERRANO. *The Morgue (Hacked to Death II)*, USA, 1992. Cibachrome, 49 ¹/₂″ × 60″. Musée d'Art Contemporain de Montréal. Courtesy Paula Cooper Gallery, New York.

This photograph is an intimate look at violent death.

Andres Serrano, showing close-up details of the bodies of people in morgues who have died as a result of accidents, violence, or disease. The location is not important, however, as Serrano's images block out the surroundings. In some images, it is not clear if the person is lying on the side of a road or asleep in bed. No body is shown in entirety, so the individuals have no identity. They are close and intimate to the viewer.

The Morgue (Hacked to Death II) is a disturbing image, not only for its content, but because it is impossible to see this death as distant, as one would see a death on the evening news. We can see each hair as it grows out of the person's pores, study the dirt ground into the skin, trace the blood where it flowed and congealed. We cannot miss the dull, unfocused eye in dead center of the image. Serrano's framing, focusing, and manipulation of tones is artful and aesthetic; the refinement and beauty of the image jar with its content.

> **CONNECTION** Compare this image of death with those from war, such as Mathew Brady's *Dead Confederate Soldier with Gun* (Fig. 10.25, page 291).

THE PSYCHOLOGICAL DIMENSION IN ART

Much art is related to the mental or emotional state of humans. We have already seen this in some portraits in the beginning of this chapter. Now we turn to work that functions psychologically in one of three ways. First, we see an example of art in which the body is affected by a host of internal emotional and mental forces. Second, we see two works that are intended to be psychologically potent and

12.28 EDVARD MUNCH. *The Scream*, Norway, 1893. Oil painting, 35 ³/₄″ × 29″. National Gallery, Oslo, Norway.

Inner emotional forces have distorted and deformed the head into almost a skull-like form.

affect the mental states of those who view or use the art. Finally, we will examine three example of art that act as records of a mental or emotional state.

Illustrating the first kind of art is our focus figure, *The Scream* (Fig. 12.28), painted by Norwegian artist Edvard Munch in 1893. In this work, the distorted body is the vehicle for expressing inner terror, anxieties, and pressures. Realism has been abandoned to give form to these internal emotions. At this time, Sigmund Freud had propagated his theories of repression and neurosis as both social and personal ills, which influenced Munch and other artists. The central character glances back at distant figures, but it is unclear whether they are part of the scene or disinterested bystanders. Whatever the situation, the foreground figure is overcome by fear that has twisted the body and reduced the face to a near skull. The figure stands in complete physical and emotional isolation, cupping its hands over its ears and screaming at a pitch that reverberates in the landscape and in the sky. The colors are emotionally distorted and heightened.

Let us turn now to art that is intended to be psychologically active when used, worn, or displayed. The *Double Mask* (Fig. 12.29), from the Ejagham people of the Cross River area of Cameroon, is an example of masks that in many African cultures are intended to be psychologically potent, either by giving the wearer extra power, or by intimidating the audience witnessing a performance with the mask. This *Double Mask*, which is just one example of the great variety of African masks, was carved and then covered with fresh antelope hide, which when dried gives the mask a startlingly life-like finish. The masks were used by associations whose members had achieved notable feats or had mastered important skills. The masks were used in rituals and celebrations that promoted group cohesion. People of rank within the associations had the right to wear the masks. The double face looking forward and backward likely suggested heightened spiritual powers.

Compare the *Double Mask* with the *Mask of the Swan and the White Whale* (Fig. 12.30), from the North American Inuit (Eskimo) culture. In Inuit beliefs, the swan leads the white whale to the hunter. Traditionally, the Inuit culture has depended on whale hunting to provide many necessities, so during rituals the wearer of this mask would receive added powers in whale hunting. The mask is visually striking. It is asymmmetrical and eccentric, with a grinning half-face. Its shape suggests whale fins, and it is adorned with bird feathers. This mask was produced by the Yup'ik people of Western Alaska, who created masks that are noteworthy for their amazing inventiveness.

12.30 *Mask of the Swan and the White Whale*, Inuit, early 20th century. Wood, 19.25 high. Musée du Quai Branly, Paris.

The Inuit people of Alaska are known for their inventive masks that are intended to increase the power of those who wear them in rituals.

12.29 *Double mask*, Ejagham People, Cross River, Cameroon, 19th–early 20th century CE. Wood, hide, pigment, rope, beads; height: 13.75″. Ethnologisches Museum, Staatliche Museen, Berlin.

This artwork is intended to be psychologically potent for those who use it.

In our final category of art in this section, we look at works that are meant to be records of an inner emotional state. Italian artist Giovanni Battista Piranesi's *Prison* (Fig. 12.31), from 1745, does not focus on the human form like Munch's *Scream*, but the complicated, dreary spaces of the dungeon act as a metaphor for the darker, twisted side of the human mind. The fantastic gloominess of this prison is pervaded by hopelessness and a lack of meaning, and exit seems impossible. Small humans are dwarfed as they move through the oppressive space. These complex, dark chambers are the exact opposite of sunny landscapes, but each can be seen as a metaphor for a human state of mind.

Our next example is Chilean artist Roberto Matta-Echaurren's 1941 painting, *Listen to Living* (Fig. 12.32). His work is an example of **Surrealism**, a movement that

12.31, *left* GIOVANNI BATTISTA PIRANESI. *Prison*, 1745, from Le Carceri, No. XIV (first state). Etching.

Although this image shows a gloomy architectural interior, it is a visual metaphor for the dark side of the human mind.

12.32, *below* ROBERTO MATTA-ECHAURREN. *Listen to Living*, 1941. Oil on canvas, 29 1/2″ × 37 7/8″. Inter-American Fund.

Surrealist paintings like this one are often intended to be reflections of the unconscious mind and to allude to cosmic forces in life, such as creation and destruction.

emphasized absurd or dream states. Matta's paintings are called "inscapes," as he sought to create in pictorial space an image of the workings of the human mind. His work is marked by vivid colors, luminous patterns, and bold lines, all against a vague, unspecific background. Although he does not depict realistic scenes, Matta's work is often preoccupied with primordial creation and cycles of destruction. During and after World War II, his surrealistic abstractions also reflected the horrors of war. His painting technique was marked by spontaneity, smearing and splotching the paint on the canvas until he arrived at shapes that resonated with the unconscious.

Our last example of an artwork meant to record a mental state is by U.S. artist Mark Rothko, who started as a figurative painter but eventually abandoned imagery that depicted the physical world for abstractions that hint at a sublime moment or transcendent state of being. He created a series of paintings that contained large rectangles, sometimes only vaguely defined, against a field of other colors. Shapes and background emerge, float, and glow, as in *Green, Red, Blue*, 1955 (Fig. 12.33). Rothko first applied thin "veils" of paint that soaked into and stained the canvas. He then applied many layers on top to create shapes that seem present and yet hard to define, hovering in a space that is real and yet not wholly knowable.

12.33 MARK ROTHKO. *Green, Red, Blue*, USA, 1955. Oil on canvas, 81 1/2" × 77 3/4". Milwaukee Art Museum.

By painting glowing colors and hovering shapes, the artist hoped to allude to a sublime, transcendent state of being.

Rothko used abstraction as a means to address these broad and fundamental feelings and ideas, because figurative or narrative imagery was too specific and too limiting. In addition, Rothko's abstractions were meant to provide a kind of direct physical experience to the body.

THE BODY IN ART AND AS ART

The body is not only depicted in art; it is used in making art, or it is transformed to become artwork.

The Body as Art Material

The human body is material for art making. It can be painted or sculpted, or it can be part of a performance or spectacle. In all of these instances, the living body energizes, personalizes, or adds emotional content to the artwork. We have already seen an example of body art in the tattooed face of *Tomika Te Mutu* (see Fig. 12.24), where his skin is the canvas on which the artwork is made. The marks on the face of the *Male Torso* (Ancestor figure) from Baule (see Fig. 12.15) may be like the scarification patterns that the Baule people created on their own bodies. In both cases, the body art has great cultural significance.

Modifying the living human body has a long history. The Mayan *Head from the Tomb of the Temple of Inscriptions* from Mexico (Fig. 12.34), dated mid- to late seventh century, shows how the human body is plastic and moldable, a kind of raw material from which works of art can be made. To the Mayans, a flat, sloping forehead was beautiful and aesthetically pleasing, so they bound and compressed infants' heads to deform the shape as they were growing. Hair was bluntly cut at different levels and woven with jade ornaments, cotton threads, and flowers. The stair-step cut on the sides and the top plume of hair were common designs. The resulting human head was a living artistic creation, the image of which is reproduced in this stucco sculpture in the round, which was once brightly painted. This portrait sculpture of a ruler known as Shield II (or Pacal II in Mayan) was found next to his tomb.

Body ornamentation is an art form in many traditional African cultures, as we have seen, where rituals are the supremely important events for the community, governing all aspects of life, death, everyday survival, and interaction with the spirit world. But not all body art involves scarification. In many of these cultures, body painting is equivalent to wearing masks or costumes. Among the Ngere people in the late twentieth century, girls paint their torsos white and their faces in brilliant colors after initiation, as in *Ngere Girl Prepared for a Festival* (Fig. 12.35). The patterns of color are similar to the way the face can be

12.34 *Head from the Tomb of the Temple of Inscriptions*, Mexico, mid–late 7th century. Maya. Stucco, 17″ high. Palenque, Chiapas, Mexico. Museo Nacional de Antropología, Mexico City.

The human body is malleable and can be changed for aesthetic purposes. Mayan rulers often flattened the foreheads of their offspring and hair was cut and sculpted in a dramatic way.

12.35 *Ngere Girl Prepared for a Festival*, Africa, late 20th century. Body painting.

Body painting is an important art form among some African people.

12.36 ANA MENDIETA. *Arbol de la Vida, No. 294*, Cuba/USA, 1977. From the series *Arbol de la Vida/Silueta* (Tree of Life/Silhouette). Color photograph documenting the earth/body sculpture with artist, tree trunk, and mud, at Old Man's Creek, Iowa City, Iowa. Collection Ignacio C. Mendieta.

This artist covered her body in mud and assumed distinct poses to represent primal female forces with her own personal body.

abstracted and broken down into parts in sculpture, while the parallel lines in the white paint echo both chisel marks and sculptural hair patterns. Body painting, like tattooing, makes the living body into a work of art, expands its power and its protection, announcing the status of the person in the community—in this case, an initiated girl.

Cuban artist Ana Mendieta created several outdoor performances that dealt with her body directly or the trace of her body on the earth. Individual works in the series, called *Silueta* (Silhouette), were performed in Iowa and in Mexico from 1973 until 1980 and exist now only as documentary photographs. In *Arbol de la Vida, No. 294*, dated 1977 (Fig. 12.36), Mendieta made herself into a body sculpture covered with mud and straw. She posed against a tree in a manner reminiscent of ancient fertility

12.37 YOKO ONO. *Cut Piece*, Japan/USA, 1964. Photo documentation of performance at Yamaichi Concert Hall, Kyoto.

The human body is often a primary element in performance art.

goddesses, leaving traces of mud on the bark. The site of her performance was very dramatic, with a massive tree growing at the edge of a deeply cut creek bed. In other works in the *Silueta* series, Mendieta sculpted the mud or used stones or flowers to trace the outline of her body on the earth. It was important to use her living body in these performances, because they became like rituals in which the energy of her living being was joined with that of the earth, which she believed was a force that was omnipresent and female.

CONNECTION Review the discussion of ancient fertility goddesses, such as *Idol from Amorgos* (Fig. 7.4, page 165).

Contemporary performance art almost always involves the body. Japanese-born artist Yoko Ono wrote scripts that set up situations for artworks, but the exact outcome of the pieces was determined by chance or by spontaneous audience participation. In a 1964 performance of *Cut Piece* (Fig. 12.37), Yoko Ono entered an empty stage clothed in a black dress and sat/knelt in a traditional position for Japanese women. She held aloft scissors and then placed them in front of herself, as if preparing for *seppuku* (ritual suicide). She then invited and encouraged audience members to cut away her clothing. As the performance proceeded, she sat without showing emotion. Long pauses occurred during the performance. Ono was influenced by John Cage, a composer who believed that the silences between sounds were as important as the music.

12.38 JACKSON POLLOCK. *Lucifer*, USA, 1947. Oil, aluminum paint, and enamel on canvas, approx. 3′ 5″ × 8′ 9″. Collection of Harry Ward and Mary Margaret Anderson.

The poured and dripped paint is a permanent record of the actions of the artist's body as he bent his back, lunged forward, and swung his arm to make this painting.

More and more skin showed until she was nearly nude and bare-chested, and the performance ended as she gasped and covered herself.

Cut Piece alludes to several ideas: the traditional male sexual prerogative over the female body; the display of the body for the consuming gaze; violation and control; and the herd mentality among humans. Roles are confused in the piece: Ono, apparently the violated, also set up the situation. Yet the audience members acted freely, as it was beyond her control to dictate what they did. The artist's body and the actions of the audience are the art piece, not the photo document we see in this book. The physical presence of real bodies, the quality of spectacle, the uncertainty, and the palpable experience of time passing are potent elements that still photography cannot convey.

Ono was part of the **Fluxus** movement in New York, which sought to create a kind of anti-art or non-art. In Fluxus, art was conceived as an artist-initiated experience rather than an object, like a painting or sculpture. For both Ono's and Mendieta's work, photo documentation is all that remains.

The Body as an Art Tool

The first and most important tools of artists are their bodies: their fingers, hands, and arms, guided by their minds. In making works of art, artists continually touch the entire surface of their works. This is obvious with sculptors who model clay with their hands, but even painters work the entire surface of their images with sensitive brushes and often adjust or finish their work with their fingertips. Although the touch of photographers and computer artists may leave no mark on their works, their hands are nonetheless essential and present. In *Fanny (Fingerpainting)*, which we saw in Figure 12.6, artist Chuck Close created the woman's enormous head in detail, showing the texture of her hair, skin wrinkles, her watery eyes, and the cloth of her dress. The entire work was painted with the artist's hand and fingerprints. Although it looks like a photograph, the face in fact is a mass of finger smudges, a record of everywhere the artist touched. The mark of the hand relates to fossils and the handprints in prehistoric cave paintings and to the first marks we made as children.

When Jackson Pollock painted *Lucifer* (Fig. 12.38) in 1947, the motion of his entire body was very significant. This style of painting is called "gestural abstraction" or **action painting.** The "action" came from the movement of the artist. The canvas was laid down on the ground, and Pollock poured, dripped, and flung paint upon it as he stood at the edges or walked across the surface. He lunged and swirled about in furious outbursts, which were followed by periods of reflection. His body movements were fixed and recorded in the paint surface, which is a rhythmic mesh of drips, congealed blobs, and looping swirls.

12.39 Jackson Pollock at work in his Long Island Studio, 1950.

Pollock's act of painting and the painting itself were frequently described in quasi-combat terms. He saw the canvas on the ground as a plane of action, but when hanging on the wall in front of the viewer, it became a plane of confrontation. Pollock believed his spontaneous, energetic painting style fit the mood of the United States immediately after World War II. He also believed that the power of his unconscious mind was being released in action painting and that his painting style was a burst of primal energy and a release from civilized constraints. The action painter was seen as being an isolated genius, almost always male, whose work had no moral message and no narrative, just pure paint and pure body action.

CONNECTION For another example of an artist who uses his body as art material, see James Luna's *The Artifact Piece* (Fig. 13.6).

Do women have to be naked to get into the Met. Museum?

Less than 5% of the artists in the Modern Art sections are women, but 85% of the nudes are female.

GUERRILLA GIRLS CONSCIENCE OF THE ART WORLD
www.guerrillagirls.com

13.1 GUERRILLA GIRLS. *Do women have to be naked to get into the Met. Museum?* USA, 1986. Street poster. Courtesy www.guerrillagirls.com.

Art can point out inequities between genders within a culture.

13

RACE, GENDER, CLAN, AND CLASS

All persons are born with race and gender characteristics, class standing, and genealogy that will affect their lives. These characteristics contribute to personal identity, but on the downside, they may also trigger prejudice and discrimination. Art reflects these issues.

PREVIEW

This chapter shows how art can forge racial identity and preserve the history and values of an ethnic group. Other examples show art that exposes racial oppression.

Gender roles are reinforced or challenged in artworks. Some works are intended to strengthen the status quo in the gender relationships. Other art in this chapter protests inequality, such as our chapter opener, Do women have to be naked to get into the Met. Museum? *(Fig. 13.1), by the Guerrilla Girls. We also see art in which gender is tied to ideas of beauty or heroism within a culture.*

Artwork preserves clan identity and traditions, and it documents clan history. Some clans place great importance on venerated ancestors, and art helps to maintain the presence of the ancestors. Art also reflects the way some cultures are organized around clans and some around the nuclear family. Art can show us the attachments within the nuclear family or the shifting definitions of family.

Art from various cultures show the ways that social classes live. Often, class rank and distinction is evidenced by the size of the architecture and the quality of art objects used by the wealthy versus those used by the poor. Classes also develop their own styles of artwork. In this chapter, we see images in which poverty mark the figures from the lowest classes, while middle and upper classes enjoy leisure and comfort.

Connecting Art and History from
1750–1850 CE

The period 1750–1850 brought major changes in the history of humankind. In 1760, the Industrial Revolution was beginning in Europe—power machinery replaced hand labor, and steam engines replaced water wheels and spinning mills. Many important inventions were developed in the late eighteenth and early nineteenth centuries, including the steam engine (1775), the cotton gin (1793), the telegraph (1836), and the sewing machine (1844). Workers formed the first trade unions to fight for their rights, and Karl Marx and Friedrich Engels wrote the *Communist Manifesto*, published in 1848. People moved to the cities to work in factories, and a middle class grew and gained power while working classes struggled for rights. This was also the Age of Enlightenment, which fostered ideas of personal liberty. All of this tremendously affected ideas of race, gender, class, and clan.

The middle of Africa during the 1700s remained mostly isolated, although Europeans established trading ports on the coast. During the 1800s, the need for raw materials to

Map 8   Independence Movements in North and South America

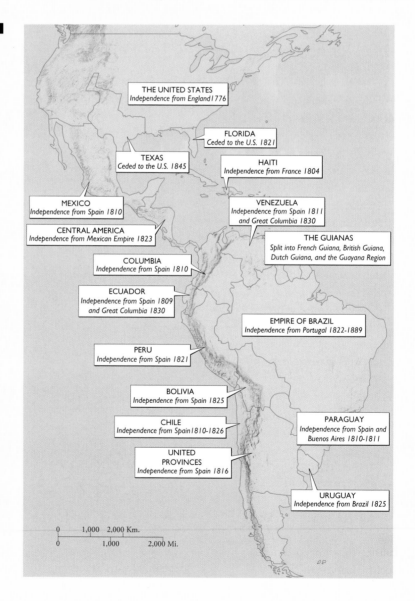

fuel the Industrial Revolution drove the Dutch, Portuguese, English, and other Europeans to colonize the entire continent. Toward the latter part of this period, the empires of Zimbabwe and Asante came to an end.

Europeans also divided the entire Americas through colonization. The French claimed land from Canada through the Great Lakes and down the Mississippi River. Britain controlled the thirteen colonies, and Spain claimed Florida, Texas, New Mexico, Arizona, and California as well as vast territories in Central and South America. In India, Great Britain set up colonial rule, and, later, Queen Victoria would become the Empress of India. The British also claimed eastern Australia in 1770.

Also during this time, Japan saw the continued rise of its merchant class, and color woodblock prints called *ukiyo-e* were made that appealed to their tastes and financial means. One example is *Komurasaki of the Tamaya Teahouse* (Fig. 13.32). The Japanese middle class also developed theatrical forms that were distinct from those of the ruling class. Japan was ruled by the Tokugawa Shogunate, which held military power, whereas the emperor was the political and religious leader.

The Qing (or Manchu) Dynasty ruled in China during this period, reaching its height throughout the 1700s. China continued to be ruled through the bureaucratic system of government. Emblems were worn on robes to distinguish members of the enormous Chinese court, like the *Rank Badge with Peacock* (Fig. 13.2). Wars, internal unrest, natural disasters, and an outdated bureaucracy eventually led to the Qing dynasty decline in the mid-nineteenth century. Between 1839 and 1842, the Opium Wars broke out between China and Britain. Britain had smuggled opium from India into China, causing mass addiction to the drug, which in turn greatly affected

13.2 *Rank Badge with Peacock*, China, late 18th–early 19th century. Qing Dynasty. Silk, metallic thread on silk, 12 1/8″ × 12 1/8″. The Metropolitan Museum of Art, New York.

Richly embroidered badges distinguished among groups in the Chinese court. The Imperial Family badges had dragons and phoenixes, while those of military officers featured lions or tigers, and civil officials wore birds. Peacocks were worn by civil officials who had attained the third rank among nine possible ranks.

China's economy. Britain won the war and gained Hong Kong plus five ports in China for trade.

A series of political revolutions occurred during this era that had enormous impact on the modern world. In 1775, the thirteen colonies began a revolution against England, which eventually resulted in an independent United States (see Map 8). George Washington became the first president of the United States in 1789. In France, the nobility enjoyed great wealth and leisure, exemplified by the frivolity in *The Swing* (Fig. 13.25). Eventually, the disparity in wealth and lifestyles between the rich and the poor led to the French Revolution in 1789, in which the monarchy was overthrown. Many French, both aristocrats and citizens, were executed on the guillotine during the Reign of Terror following the uprising. In art, the revolutionary spirit was presented in **Neoclassical** terms, as seen in

Oath of the Horatii (Fig. 13.10). In 1804, Napoleon took control of France and conquered a vast but short-lived empire. In 1812, in South America, revolutionary leaders such as Simón Bolívar of Venezuela and José de San Martín of Argentina fought for independence from Spain. By 1825, all of the Spanish colonies in South American had thrown off colonial rule (see Map 8).

World Art Map for Chapter 13

EUROPE

Jan Vermeer Van Delft. *The Kitchen Maid.*

Arthur Shaughnessy. *Interior House Post.*
Examples of formline design in Northwest Coast art.

Georges Seurat. *La Grande Jatte.* Paris, France.

Jacques-Louis David. *Oath of the Horatii.*
Jean-Honoré Fragonard. *The Swing.*

NORTH AMERICA

General Idea. *Baby Makes 3.*

Peter Paul Rubens. *Abduction of the Daughters of Leucippus.*

Diego Velazquez. *Las Meninas.*

François de Cuvilliés. *Hall of Mirrors.*
Statue of Togato Barberini.

Elizabeth Murray. *Sail Baby.*
Dorothea Lange. *Migrant Mother, Nipomo Valley.*
Betye Saar. *The Liberation of Aunt Jemima.*

James Vanderzee. *Society Ladies.*
Guerrilla Girls. *Do women have to be naked to get into the Met. Museum?*

James Luna. *The Artifact Piece.*

Simon Rodia. *Watts Towers.* Los Angeles, California, United States.

Marisol. *The Family.*

Bamgboye of Odo-Owa. *Epa Headdress called "Orangun."*

Portrait Heads from Tomb 6. Oaxaca, Mexico.

Adesina Family, Great Beaded Crown. Ila Orangun, Nigeria, Africa.

SOUTH AMERICA

N

0   1,000   2,000 Km.

0   1,000   2,000 Mi.

Marc Chagall. *Over Vitebsk.*

ASIA

**Zhang Zeduan,
Spring Festival Along the River.
Beijing, China.**

***Uji Bridge.* Tokyo, Japan.**

Rank Badge with Peacock.
Hung Liu. *Trauma.*
Paik. *Buddha Duchamp Beuys.*
Kitagawa Utamaro. *Komurasaki of the Tamaya Teahouse.*

Seated Scribe.

**Temple of Ramses II.
Abu Simbel, Egypt.**

AFRICA

**Painting from a Cult House.
Sepik Region, Papua,
New Guinea.**

***Bisj Poles.*
Buepis Village,
New Guinea.**

AUSTRALIA

1750–1850 CE

OLD KINGDOM, EGYPT	**2700 BCE**		
	2500	*Seated Scribe*	
	2000	*Temple of Ramses II*	
ACHAEMENID CIVILIZATION	**500**		

1617	Rubens: *Abduction of the Daughters of Leucippus*	
1656	Velazquez: *Las Meninas*	
1660	Vermeer: *The Kitchen Maid*	
1700		

Age of Enlightenment

ROCOCO STYLE

England, France, Spain colonize the Americas

Dutch and Portuguese establish trading ports in Africa

Above Persepolis (10.11)

ROMAN EMPIRE	**100**
	75 *Statue of Togato Barberini*
TANG DYNASTY— CHINA	**600 CE**

1734	De Cuvilliès: *Hall of Mirrors*
1750	
1760	Fragonard: *The Swing*

Industrial Revolution

HISTORIC ERA—JAPAN

American Revolution — **1775**

Teotihuacán—Mexico	**640**	*Portrait Heads from Tomb 6*
	700	

1776	David: *Oath of the Horatii*

French Revolution — **1789**

ROMANESQUE ERA	**1000**	Zhang Zeduan: *Spring Festival Along the River*
GOTHIC ERA	**1200**	
RENAISSANCE BEGINS	**1400**	
	1500	
BAROQUE Era	**1600**	

Above Utamaro: *A Pair of Lovers* (7.17)

1794	Utamaro: *Komurasaki of the Tamaya Teahouse*

South American Revolutions — **1800**

First trade unions established

Britain colonizes India

Above Hall of Mirrors, Versailles (10.14)

Opium Wars between Britain and China — **1839**

Communist Manifesto	**1848**		Feminist Movement	**1962**	Marisol: *The Family*
	1850				Adesina Family: *Great Beaded Crown of the Orangun-Ila*
				1972	Saar: *The Liberation of Aunt Jemima*

Above Summer Robe, China (3.33)

IMPRESSIONISM	**1875**				
POST-IMPRESSIONISM					
Women's suffrage movement begins	**1884**	Seurat: *La Grande Jatte*			
POINTILLISM					
FAUVISM, CUBISM, FUTURISM, DADA	**1900**		POSTMODERNISM	**1974**	Bamgboye of Odo-Owa: *Epa Headdress called "Orangun"*
		Bisj Poles		**1975**	
SURREALISM,	**1907**	Shaughnessy: *Interior House Post*			
FANTASY,					
SUPREMATISM					
	1908				
World War I	**1914**	*Painting from a Cult House*			
		Chagall: *Over Vitebsk*			
	1921	Rodia: *Watts Towers*			

Above Baca: *Las Tres Marias* (3.5)

Harlem Renaissance	**1927**	VanDerZee: *Society Ladies*		**1979**	
	1936	Lange: *Migrant Mother, Nipomo Valley*		**1983**	Murray: *Sail Baby*
				1984	General Idea: *Baby Makes 3*
				1986	Luna: *The Artifact Piece*
					Guerrilla Girls: *Do women have to be naked to get into the Met. Museum?*
					Paik: *Buddha Duchamp Beuys*

Above Kahlo: *Self-Portrait with Monkey* (12.11)

				1989	Hung Liu: *Trauma*
World War II	**1940**				
POST-WAR	**1950**		End of Apartheid in South Africa	**1991**	
EXPRESSIONISM					

RACE AND ART

This section contains several artworks that deal with race. Some help form a cohesive identity for a racial group, whereas others challenge negative attitudes.

Art That Promotes Ethnic History and Values

These works of art examine or illustrate the history or values of a certain ethnic group. Our focus figure originates in Russia in the 1800s and early 1900, where Jews were considered outsiders because of laws and traditions originated and maintained both by the Jews and by the Russians. Jews were allowed to live only in certain areas and were restricted from attending universities. That separateness was often passively accepted, but at times Jews suffered from anti-Semitic terrorism. Even so, Russian Jews were often cultural innovators and, in many cases, were known throughout Europe as artists, musicians, and writers.

Marc Chagall was a prominent Jewish artist who grew up in Russia but spent most of his long life in Paris, France. Many of his paintings imaginatively re-created Jewish village life at the turn of the twentieth century in Russia, which was in fact disintegrating as a result of political, religious, and economic pressures. Chagall's imagery was a personal, sometimes incoherent, reordering of bits and pieces of his experience, including folktales, festivals, marriages, funeral practices, and suffering and death caused by anti-Semitism. In *Over Vitebsk*, dated 1915–1920 (Fig. 13.3), Chagall painted a large, solitary figure floating over his own village, representing thousands of Eastern European Jewish refugees who fled to Russia, displaced by World War I. In Yiddish, "passing through" is expressed as wandering "over the village," which Chagall painted literally by means of the floating figure, the refugee. A sense of being rootless and upheaval pervades the picture. The space in the foreground of the picture appears fractured, which Chagall devised from **Cubism** to represent instability. The colors are from **Fauvism**, an art movement that originated in Paris in which color was exaggerated in paintings for greater power and expression.

Compare Chagall's lyrical scene with the frank, forthright portraiture of James VanDerZee, a commercial studio photographer whose works are a record of the Black Renaissance of Harlem, generally dating from 1919–1929 (he continued to photograph the Harlem residents through the 1940s). VanDerZee's photographs contrast strongly with the two kinds of images of African

13.3 Marc Chagall. *Over Vitebsk* (after a painting of 1914), Russia/France, 1915–1920. Oil on canvas, 26 1/2″ × 36 1/2″. The Museum of Modern Art, New York. Acquired through the Lillian P. Bliss Bequest, 1949.

Chagall's painting re-creates and memorializes the experiences of Jewish people in Russia at the end of the 19th century.

Americans from that time. The most common were crude racial caricatures of African Americans from postcards, comics, magazines, picture books, and greeting cards. On the other hand, a few photographers depicted African Americans as helpless victims of racism and their situation as a problem to be solved.

In contrast, VanDerZee's African Americans are autonomous, healthy, and self-aware. They were the black middle class, like the women pictured in *Society Ladies,* photographed in 1927 (Fig. 13.4). His subjects were intellectuals, merchants, and writers who demanded full participation for blacks in U.S. politics and culture. The furniture and trappings of comfort surround his well-dressed sitters. Their poses convey a variety of emotions, including confidence, humor, directness, and dreamy wistfulness. VanDerZee was influenced by movies of the 1920s and 1930s and encouraged sitters to take poses from the films. At times, VanDerZee provided costumes and props that allowed his sitters to expand their personalities.

CONNECTION Another artist of the Harlem Renaissance, Jacob Lawrence, painted the history of African Americans in the Western Hemisphere. For more, see *No. 36, During the Truce Toussaint . . .* (Fig. 11.14, page 313).

Art That Criticizes Racism

Unflattering images of African Americans have been common in popular culture over the past 150 years—for example, the pickaninny, Little Black Sambo, and Uncle Tom. Another is Aunt Jemima, a domestic servant whose title of "aunt" was a commonly used term of subordination for African American domestic servants, nannies, and maids. Aunt Jemima is a caricatured jolly, fat woman who has been used recently to sell commercially prepared pancake mix. In the 1972 mixed-media piece *The Liberation of Aunt*

13.4 JAMES VANDERZEE. *Society Ladies*, USA, 1927. Black-and-white photograph. Donna Mussenden VanDerZee.

Art can promote the status and create a positive perception of a racial group. In this case, the portraits show the confident, affluent people of the Harlem Renaissance in the United States.

Jemima (Fig. 13.5), Betye Saar uses three versions of Aunt Jemima to question and turn around such images. The oldest version is the small image at the center, in which a cartooned Jemima hitches up a squalling child on her hip. In the background, the modern version shows a thinner Jemima with lighter skin, deemphasizing her Negroid features. The older one makes Jemima a caricature, while the new one implies she is more attractive if she appears less black.

The middle Jemima is the largest figure and the most emphasized. Her patterned clothing is very bright and colorful. Her black skin makes her white eyes and teeth look like dots and checks, too. This Jemima holds a rifle and pistol as well as a broom. A black-power fist makes a strong silhouette shape in front of all the figures, introducing militant power to the image. The idea of Aunt Jemima, in any of its forms, can no longer seem innocuous. Saar enshrined these images in a shallow glass display box to

13.5 BETYE SAAR. *The Liberation of Aunt Jemima*, USA, 1972. Mixed media, 11 3/4″ × 8″ × 2 3/4″. University Art Museum, University of California, Berkeley. Purchased with the aid of National Endowment for the Arts funds.

This work illustrates, and therefore protests, the ways that African Americans were often depicted in folk art and in commercial imagery.

make them venerable. Symmetry and pattern are strong visual elements.

In *The Artifact Piece,* performed in 1986 (Fig. 13.6), Native American artist James Luna challenged the way contemporary American culture and museums have presented his race as essentially extinct and vanished. In this performance piece, Luna "installed" himself in an exhibition case in the San Diego Museum of Man in a section on the Kumeyaay Indians, who once inhabited San Diego County. All around were other exhibition areas with mannequins and props showing the long-lost Kumeyaay way of life. Among them, Luna posed himself, living and breathing, dressed only in a leather cloth. Various personal items were displayed in a glass case, including contemporary ritual objects used currently on the La Jolla reservation where Luna lives, recordings by the Rolling Stones and Jimi Hendrix, shoes, political buttons, and other cultural artifacts. Around Luna are labels pointing out his scars

from wounds suffered when drunk and fighting. The mixture of elements revealed a living culture.

In this striking piece, Luna challenged the viewer to reconsider what museums teach about cultures and what constitutes a cultural artifact. Museum artifacts may be simply the things that, by chance, happened to survive. In other cases, some objects are kept, whereas others are ignored or destroyed. Thus, we learn less about Native American culture than we learn about the current culture's ideas about Native American cultures. In addition, museums and museum visitors often discount living cultures of today and are only interested in preconceived idea of "cultural purity." "Authentic Indians" are those who are long dead. Native Americans who are alive today are less interesting to museums, because they are cultural mixtures who may wear athletic shoes rather than moccasins. Luna sees himself in a new way. Although he still considers himself a warrior, he is a new one who uses art and the legal system to fight for Native Americans. In *The Artifact Piece,* Luna also touches on the effects of alcohol on Native Americans.

Who Is Looking at Whom?

In the United States, hundreds of images are produced every day dealing with other cultures, so we develop ideas

13.6 JAMES LUNA. *The Artifact Piece,* USA, 1986. Installation/performance at the San Diego Museum of Man. Museum of Man, San Diego.

The purpose of art is often to make simple stereotypes more nuanced and accurate. Luna's work is intended to debunk a simplistic image of Native Americans.

about foreign or ethnic groups from the mass-media images we consume. But who makes those images of others, and why? Are the viewers in a privileged position because they "consume" the images of others without directly interacting with them? Chapter 7 covered the gaze in reference to sexuality. Now we return to it to see how art can both reflect and undermine racial relationships in the world.

Look back to *Society Ladies* (13.4) and *The Artifact Piece* (13.6). In both, the viewer is made self-conscious of looking, rather than enjoying it from an isolated, privileged position. In *Society Ladies,* the older woman gazes out with an appraising look, which makes the viewers aware of their own gaze. This kind of frank return of the gaze also marks the work of Frida Kahlo (see Figure 12.11), whose work affirms and identifies with indigenous people in Mexico, especially the underclass. In *The Artifact Piece,* the sheer presence of a living being in a museum display interrupts the viewers' unself-conscious gaze and their consumption of easy, stereotypical ideas about a long-ago culture.

In his 1989 video installation, *Buddha Duchamp Beuys* (Figure 13.7), Nam June Paik takes on the gaze in relation to East and West. The title, the Buddha statue, and the television reference various parts of the world and the consumption of culture through media, without direct contact. This seems to reinforce the detached, privileged viewer, but what is interesting here is that viewer lives in cultures other than Western industrialized nations, undermining Western domination. In addition, Paik's artworks generally emphasize collaboration, humor, and the new world models coming from cultural interaction. Paik had collaborated on projects with Joseph Beuys, mentioned in the title (see Figure 5.12; Figure 2.26 shows a work by Duchamp). So Paik turns around cultural dominance and replaces it with a potentially confusing but also open playing field of cultures meeting cultures. The

13.7 NAM JUNE PAIK. *Buddha Duchamp Beuys.* 1989. Video installation with Buddha sculpture, as seen in the exhibition held at the Kunst Palast Museum in Duesseldorf, Germany, September 2010.

Paik's work brings together opposites, sometimes humorously, in ways that suggest new potentials for cultural interaction.

13.8 *Painting from a Cult House*, Slei, Middle Sepik Region, Papua New Guinea, c. 20th century. Palm leaves on a bamboo frame, painted with earth pigments, 44″ × 61 1/2″. Museum der Kulturen, Basel, Switzerland.

Within the Sepik culture, art is used along with rituals to pass male power on to the next generation.

video camera loops images, suggesting that we are only meeting ourselves.

GENDER ISSUES

Every culture sets up standards that define and limit acceptable behavior for women and for men. Artwork from different eras and cultures often gives us clues about those social restrictions and, in some cases, is actually part of making them.

Art and Ritual Perpetuating Gender Roles

In the early twentieth century, before the disruption of foreign influences, men dominated women among the Sepik people of Papua New Guinea, and art and rituals reinforced and dramatized this relationship. Sepik art also made men powerful in war.

The rituals, called "Tambaran," took place in large, decorated cult houses. Men saw their rituals as creating men from infants, usurping women's procreative power. Unlike the Western notion that an individual exists from birth, many South Pacific peoples believed that a person's

very being was built through a lifetime of ritual experiences. Men invested their vigor into the paintings and carvings that hung in the cult house, in order to pass their spirits on to younger men at lower stages of initiation. *Painting from a Cult House* at Slei (Fig. 13.8) is an artwork associated with Tambaran rituals from the early twentieth century. The curvilinear design create multiple faces, with gaping, tooth-filled mouths, large noses, and numerous eyes. Faces can be read stacked or superimposed on each other. The curves and spirals fill the triangular shape of the painting—cramped and small at the edges, swelling into large, aggressive forms in the middle. The colors—black, red, and off-white—are bold, with high contrast from dark to light. Major forms, such as mouths and eyes, are outlined repeatedly in alternating black and white lines, resulting in vibrating patterns that express the idea of fearsome vigor.

Gender Reflected in Art and Architecture

Gender roles are often revealed in art and are reflected in architecture and fashion. Our focus figure, *Abduction of the Daughters of Leucippus*, painted by Peter Paul Rubens

13.9 Peter Paul Rubens. *Abduction of the Daughters of Leucippus*, Flanders, 1617. Oil on canvas, 7′ 3″ × 6′ 10″. Alte Pinakothek, Munich.

Rubens' painting reflects his culture's ideals about femininity and masculinity,

in 1617 (Fig. 13.9), is another example of European painting dealing with sexual exotica, like the *Grande Odalisque*, which we saw in Chapter 7 (Fig. 7.20). The scene comes from Greek mythology. Castor and Pollux, twin sons of Zeus, capture a philosopher's two daughters as they were out horseback riding. Aided by Cupids, the two immortals lower the women, who resist with dramatic but ineffective, fluttering gestures. Interestingly, this painting is also commonly referred to as *Rape of the Daughters of Leucippus*, as an old meaning of *rape* was "the carrying away of someone by force."

Blue skies, shimmering cloth, and a variety of textures add to the rich surface and the sensual color harmonies. The composition places all figures in a compact diamond shape, which suggests movement because of its instability. On the left, dark tones act as a foil to the lighter areas in the center. Various textures, such as armor, satin, flesh, and hair, are all expertly painted.

The painting indicates what was considered masculine and feminine during that era. All figures represent ideal body types. The women's voluptuous, soft fleshiness was considered sexually attractive and a sign of health and wealth. Outdoor activity was appropriate for the darker-skinned, muscular men versus the pale women who occupy the domestic interiors. The painting also represents current ideas of gender behavior. Men had privilege over women's bodies. Women learned to be helpless, and they relied on social structures to protect their virtue. The expressions of the men are subdued and determined, while the women are much more emotional. The men are at least partially clothed—one is in armor—while the women are unclothed and displayed. Western art history has numerous examples of the female nude providing pleasure for male viewers, legitimized because it was "art."

All kinds of trappings can serve as indicators of masculinity or femininity. In *Oath of the Horatii*, painted in 1784

13.10 Jacques-Louis David. *Oath of the Horatii*, France, 1784. Oil on canvas, 10′ 10″ × 14′. Louvre, Paris.

While this painting illustrates an event from Roman history, it also shows the kinds of behavior that reflected femininity and masculinity in eighteenth century France. The Neoclassical architecture was associated with masculinity and revolution.

(Fig. 13.10), Jacques-Louis David represents a scene from the early history of ancient Rome, in which three brothers vow to represent the Roman army in a fight to the death against three representatives of an opposing army. Their father hands them their swords, reminding them of the manly virtues of courage and patriotism, while their sisters and wives swoon at the right, in dread and sorrow at the anticipated killing (one of the sisters was to marry a representative of the opposing army). Heroic actions are a mark of masculinity, reinforced by the women's passivity. In a moment of male bonding, forged in the face of danger, the three brothers become a single force, a part of each other, and each willing to die for the others and for an external cause.

There are other gender indicators. The male dress is rendered in angular lines that contrast with the soft curves of the female attire. The men hold weapons as their job is war, while women's jobs are concerned with children. The architecture's symmetry and the composition's overall balance suggest the orderliness of this world. The images both reflect the "reality" of gender roles and create that "reality." They spring to some extent from existing social conditions, but they also entrench those conditions and make them seem natural, not just social conventions.

In this painting, one indicator of masculinity is the background of classical architecture, which was popular during the French Revolutionary era when this painting was executed. The use of classical elements in art and architecture at this time formed a style called **Neoclassicism**, which was a revival of Greek and Roman aesthetics after the ruins of Pompeii were discovered. Also at this time, French citizens were about to overthrow the oppressive, parasitic French monarchy and aristocracy. The nobility favored decorative architecture called **Rococo**, such as

13.11 François de Cuvilliès. *Hall of Mirrors*, Germany, 1734–1739. Amalienburg, Nymphenburg Park, Munich.

The Rococo architectural style was associated with the aristocracy and also thought to have feminine qualities.

that seen in the *Hall of Mirrors* at the Amalienburg hunting lodge in Munich, Germany, dated 1734–1739 (Fig. 13.11), by François de Cuvilliès. Rococo architecture was seen as female, with its emphasis on delicate, curving, colorful decoration. Square walls and ceilings dissolve in curves, and these curves dissolve under the abundance of nature-based decoration and the reflecting mirrors, crystal, and silver. The ceiling appears to be an open sky, with birds flying from branch to branch of gold-leafed stucco trees. All elements—the architectural shell, the precious materials, the detailed, graceful decorations—contribute to the entire exquisite effect. The French middle class, on the verge of revolt, chose the clean, simple, austere, Roman-inspired architecture that we see in the background of *Oath of the Horatii* to distinguish themselves from the aristocracy and to serve as an appropriate symbol for their ideas.

Indeed, in Western culture, architecture is gendered; that is, different styles come to be associated with certain qualities, and those qualities in turn are associated with masculinity or femininity. This goes back at least as far as the ancient Greeks, who saw the Doric order as masculine and the Ionic as feminine. Although the architecture behind the *Horatii* was considered manly, while the *Hall of Mirrors* was considered feminine and elegant, nothing inherent in these styles requires them to be understood in this way. In another situation, the *Horatii* background might be seen as bare and oppressive and the *Hall of Mirrors* considered uplifting and stirring to the imagination. The gendered associations of Western architectural styles continue, as writers commonly associate the modern, bare, high-rise skyscrapers of the late 1960s and 1970s with masculinity.

CONNECTION The Doric and Ionic orders are illustrated in Figure 2.37. *The Swing* (Fig. 13.25, page 388) is a **Rococo** painting by Jean-Honoré Fragonard and reflects the same sensibilities as the *Hall of Mirrors*.

Critiquing Gender Roles

Gender roles are often widely accepted and seem quite natural within a culture at any one time, but when there are deep political or social changes, the roles can become very controversial.

People change their bodies to enhance their femininity or masculinity, usually by dieting, plastic surgery, implants, scarification, and various bindings that mold body parts. In her work, artist Hung Liu has examined foot binding, practiced in China from the Song Dynasty (960–1279) until the beginning of the twentieth century. Many Chinese women's feet were bound from birth to artificially confine their growth, distorting them into small, twisted fists that were sexually attractive to men. With bound feet, walking was extremely difficult, but the mincing steps were considered delicate and lovely. Bound feet left women handicapped, which also ensured that they remained subservient. When imperial rule ended in China and the Communist government came to power and mandated physical labor for all able-bodied people, many foot-bound women resorted to prostitution.

Liu ties oppressive gender practices to broader political repression. In *Trauma*, dated 1989 (Fig. 13.12), the woman at the center publicly shows her bound feet. Although bound feet were considered erotic in private, public exposure was a shameful act. Below her is an image of a dead Chinese student, killed by Chinese government forces when they violently crushed the demonstrations for freedom in 1989 in Tiananmen Square. Liu sees the killings in Tiananmen Square as a shameful event for China. Behind the woman's head, the outline map of China is upside down, whereas its reflection below, cut out of red felt, becomes a bloodstain on the floor below the student. The bowl on the floor is a vessel often emptied and filled, but never in exactly the same way. Poetically, the empty bowl represents China and the artist herself, emptied and then refilled by the cycles of history. Because of their long history, the Chinese commonly make associations between contemporary events and events of the distant past, a habit of thought that is evident in Liu's work.

The next work, the Guerrilla Girls' *Do women have to be naked to get into the Met. Museum?* (Chapter Opener, Fig. 13.1) seeks to correct a specific kind of gender discrimination. In 1986, when the poster was made, high-profile art exhibitions in prestigious museums often included very few women artists. In other words, a naked woman painted by a man might be shown in a museum, but a painting by a woman artist was not likely to be. On the poster, the woman's body is that of the *Grande Odalisque* (see Fig. 7.20 in Chapter 7, Reproduction and Sexuality), whose aesthetically pleasing elongated torso reclines on cushions, on

13.12 Hung Liu. *Trauma*, China/USA, 1989. Ink on plywood cutouts, acrylic on wall, felt cutout, and wooden bowl, 108″ × 52″ × 26″. Courtesy of the Artist.

Footbinding, a tradition from Imperial China, is here associated with a massacre of student protestors that happened in 1989 in Beijing.

display for male viewers to enjoy and "consume." However, her head has been obscured by a gorilla mask, like those the Guerrilla Girls wore in public appearances to maintain their anonymity and to liken themselves to revolutionary guerrillas who seek to overthrow a dominant power.

The Guerrilla Girls is a collective of anonymous women artists and arts professionals whose mass-produced, inexpensive posters feature text, image, and humor combined with strong graphics. They protest the fewer exhibitions, fewer jobs, and lower pay for women artists, and the underexposure of their work. The Guerrilla Girls in masks showed up at galleries and museums hosting high-profile art events where women were underrepresented. The purpose of their work is to cause exposure, embarrassment, and, eventually, change. Later Guerrilla Girls posters have been concerned with racial imbalances in the art world.

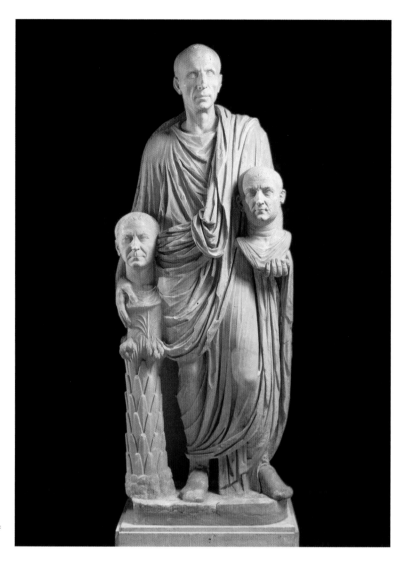

13.13 *Statue of Togato Barberini*, Rome, Italy, Early 1st Century CE. Marble, 65″ high. Palazzo Barberini, Rome.

Genealogy was important to the ancient Romans, and people of rank were expected to display busts of their ancestors.

CLAN

A clan is a group of people joined by blood or marriage ties. It could be as small as two people or extend to groups of families who share a common ancestor and recognize one member as leader.

The Extended Family

Art helps solidify extended families in three ways: (1) art makes major ancestors available to the living clan members; (2) art depicts important events in the clan's history; and (3) art is an important element in rituals that bring the entire clan together.

Ancestors

For many, the founding members of a clan have a major impact on the prestige of the living people and on their ability to function with power and authority. Our focus figure is from ancient Rome, whose people believed their ancestry was tremendously important. They preserved portraits of their ancestors and venerated their memory, as a way of establishing their own importance as they went about the business of living. At first, these ancestor portraits were simply death masks, made by pressing soft wax on the face of a deceased family member shortly after death. However, the wax masks deteriorated after a few years and looked like death, with sagging tissue and sunken eyes. Around the first century BCE, affluent Romans began having copies of the death masks made in marble for permanence, and so the face could be sculpted to appear energetic or even monumental.

The *Statue of Togata Barberini* (Fig. 13.13) is an excellent example of Roman portrait sculpture made to worship an ancestor and to glorify the lineage. Here, Togata Barberini is holding portrait busts that boast of his lineage. All three faces

13.14 *Portrait Heads from Tomb 6*, Lambityeco, Oaxaca, Mexico, 640–755. Stucco, each head 10 $1/2''$ × 11 $1/2''$.

Ancestors provide legitimacy for rulers in this ancient culture and were consulted on difficult matters.

are factual, unflattering records of appearance. Personality also comes through in the expressions. Ancestor portraits were treated with respect and were frequently copied for various family members; having a unique art object was not important. For large sculptures like this, the portraits were individually made and often were inserted into mass-produced and standardized marble bodies, echoing the process for making the ceramic *Army of the First Emperor of Qin* (Fig. 5.24). Prominent Romans kept sculptures and busts in a shrine in the family home and brought them out at funerals and family ceremonies as status symbols.

Compare the Roman busts with the *Portrait Heads from Tomb 6* (Fig. 13.14). Among the Zapotec people of Oaxaca in southern Mexico, ancestors were so important that the living interred the dead in tomb chambers under their houses and consulted them on pressing problems. By displaying their ancestors' leg bones, the rulers ensured their right to rule. These underground tombs were lavishly decorated, houselike crypts, with sculpture and

painting to make ancestors available to the living. Tombs were reopened when a clan leader died, and important rituals were held there to transfer that leader's power, wealth, and energy to the living. Figure 13.14 shows two *Portrait Heads* from a tomb in the town of Lambityeco, in Oaxaca. They are life-size heads sculpted in stucco that date from 640–755. The heads seem very lively and create a strong presence. The male head on the left has a goatee, a beaded necklace, and earrings, and his hair is pulled up and tied in a bun above his forehead. Lines through his eyebrows and below his eyes are ancient symbols or glyphs that identify him. The wife's head, to the right, is lined with age. Her hair is styled with ribbons very much like that of Zapotec women today. The faces have individualized features and are definitely portraits. They likely represent the founding parents of a clan. Both were important as lineage was traced through the male and female sides. These portrait heads are located on the lintel above the tomb entrance and may represent the first ones buried within.

CONNECTION Among the present-day Zapotec, belief in the power of the dead continues. They celebrate *Día de Los Muertos*, as in Diego Rivera's painting (Fig. 9.25, page 260).

Clan History

Art is also instrumental in preserving clan history, which helps ensure clan cohesion and thus increases its power.

The *Interior House Post*, dated c. 1907, in Figure 13.15, is our focus figure for this section. It was one of four posts carved by Arthur Shaughnessy for the Raven House of the John Scow clan of the Northwest Coast of North America. The Raven House was a lineage house; such structures were built when a new lineage was being founded because of death or marriage. When first opened, these houses were used for festivities when the new leader assumed his ceremonial name. Guests would be invited to several-day celebrations called potlatches, with elaborate singing and masquerades. Later, the interior was subdivided to create living quarters for several clan families.

The carvings in lineage houses were visual aids that accompanied the telling of clan legends and history and were concentrated in significant areas, specifically around doorways, on interior posts, and on exterior totem poles. The intention of the Northwest Coast artist is not to invent new forms, but to re-create old ones invested with new life and energy. The carvings might represent specific ancestors (like animals in European family crests) or important deities, or a human in animal form. House posts both physically support the house and symbolically represent

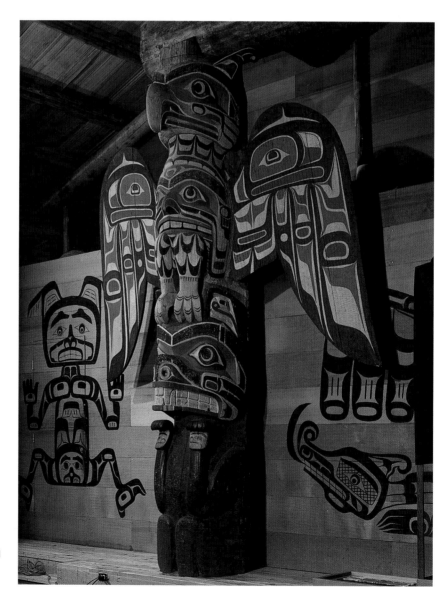

13.15 ARTHUR SHAUGHNESSY. *Interior House Post*, Gilford Island, British Columbia, Canada, c. 1907. Kwakiutl. Carved and painted red cedar, 180″ × 132″ × 34″. Seattle Art Museum.

Art is a vehicle for clan cohesion. Sculptures like these were featured in lineage houses and were prominent in ritual feasts when the leadership of the clan changed.

the spiritual and mythical foundation of the clan. The top of our *Interior House Post* has a mythical thunderbird with imposing, spread wings, representing a chief. Its powerful curved beak and curved ears suggest supernatural powers. Extra eyes are placed on the wings and torso, again to imply power. The feathers are examples of formline design, typical of much Northwest Coast art. The formline (Fig. 13.16) divides and merges, creating a continuous flowing grid that beautifully unifies the overall decoration. The ovoid is always convex on its upper side with the lower side slightly concave; the shape possibly was inspired by the elliptical spots on a ray fish. We also see two examples of the "U form" (Holm 1995:29, 37–41). Black emphasizes the major shapes, while red, white, green, and yellow are added for brightness and high contrast. For this *Interior House Post*, Shaughnessy used newly available commercial paint for brighter colors. Older works were painted with natural pigments, so their color is less saturated.

The figure below the thunderbird is a bear, a common figure on family crests, often associated with an elder or a high-ranking person. It has bared teeth, an upturned nose with circular nostrils, and compact arms and legs. Bodies were usually compressed, but heads were oversized, often one-third the total figure. Essential features were emphasized in a highly stylized manner, whereas less important features were understated or even omitted. In this example, the bear's claws are given prominence—an extra face is painted on each paw—while the torso is generalized, without musculature or surface detail. The claws and muzzle were separate pieces added to the trunk, again increasing the dynamism of the carving.

CONNECTION For more on Northwest Coast rituals, see *Halibut Feast Dish* by Stan Wamiss (Fig. 6.20, page 144).

Art Used in Clan Rituals

Clan ties are strengthened through rituals, and art is often an essential part of those rituals. Among the Asmat people of Irian Jaya, of Western New Guinea, the living engaged in elaborate rituals to pass on the life force of the deceased clansmen to the rest of the group. They carved and erected tall poles called *Bis* or *Bisj Poles* (Fig. 13.17), up to sixteen

13.16, *above* Examples of formline design in Northwest Coast art. A: ovoid form; B: typical U complex with semiangular curves; C: split U with outline (after diagrams by Bill Holm).

This diagram illustrates the kinds of outlines that are basic to the design of Pacific Northwest art.

13.17, *right* *Bisj Poles*, Buepis Village, Fajit River, southwest New Guinea, c. 19th–20th century. Asmat. Wood and paint, approx. 16' high.

Large sculptures such as these are associated with rituals that enhance male power and fertility.

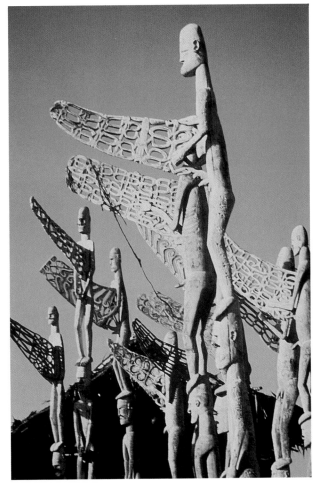

feet high, which were named and which represented the deceased clansmen, now called ancestors. The large openwork projections on the top figures are penises, representing power in warfare and in fertility. The height and intricate carving make the poles impressive. The negative and positive shapes and grim faces speak of bristling warlike energy. Sometimes poles were painted in high-contrast colors. As recently as the 1950s, the Asmat were headhunters, and part of their rituals involved avenging a clansman's death, as they believed that death is not natural, but caused by enemy warfare or magic. After the men carved and painted the *Bisj* poles, the ritual feast prepared them for actual headhunting. Warriors stood before the poles and bragged about their power and received the strength

of the ancestors for success in headhunting. These rituals were also tied to fertility, as successful warriors were rewarded with sexual favors. After the rituals, the poles were traditionally left to rot in groves of sago palms, where they would pass their vitality on to the plants that provide a staple food for the Asmat.

Art, ritual, and clan identity are intertwined among the Yoruba people of west-central Africa. The Epa Festival is held every other year for three days in March to promote fertility and the well-being of the community. The *Epa Headdress called "Orangun"* (Fig. 13.18), sculpted by Bamgboye of Odo-Owa, was used in masquerades to honor the family. The base of an Epa headdress is a helmet that fits on top of the performer's head, and it is carved with

13.18 BAMGBOYE OF ODO-OWA. *Epa Headdress called "Orangun,"* Erinmope, Nigeria, 1974. Yoruba. Wood and paint.

The Epa Headdress contains an image of the founder of the clan and is used in rituals to promote fertility and the well-being of the community.

grotesque Janus-like faces, front and back. Above the helmet is a large structure with an equestrian figure, the nomad warrior chief who founded several towns. Other characters represent important members of the household. Although such masks weigh more than fifty pounds, young dancers would perform athletically in them.

13.19 MARISOL. *The Family*, Venezuela, 1962. Painted wood and other materials in three sections; overall, 6′ 10″ × 65 1/2″ × 15 1/2″. Advisory Committee Fund (231.1962.a–c), The Museum of Modern Art, New York. The Museum of Modern Art, New York/Art Resource, NY. Art . Marisol Escobar/ Licensed by VAGA, New York, NY.

The relationships between members of a nuclear family are investigated in this sculpture.

The Nuclear Family

In highly industrialized societies, where individuals have great mobility, the extended family has lost much of its strength, and the clan has dwindled to the nuclear family. These artworks about the nuclear family do not emphasize unifying rituals or shared ancestors, in contrast to the art for large clans that we have just seen. Rather, artists examine the nuclear family to find its strengths, its changes, and its points of tension.

Our focus figure, *The Family*, dated 1962 (Fig. 13.19), by Marisol, presents us with a mother and her children arranged as if sitting for a photographer. Feelings of both mutual affection and personal awkwardness emanate from the three older children, as they present themselves to the world as family members and as individuals. The

13.20 ELIZABETH MURRAY. *Sail Baby*, USA, 1983. Oil on three canvases, 126″ × 135″. Walker Art Center, Minneapolis, Minnesota.

The formal elements of this painting allude in an abstract way to bouncy, energetic children.

mother in the center is dignified, solid, and thoughtful, but not elegant. She links all the figures and elements. The doors and decoration behind suggest the domestic setting, but they seem generally poor. Marisol's figures are blocks of wood, drawn on and minimally carved, each maintaining its own separateness while interlocking with the group. The shoes and doors are real, found objects that Marisol incorporated into her work. *The Family* contrasts with the uniformity and affluence of the nuclear family as it was commonly presented on U.S. television in 1962, with shows like *Leave It to Beaver* and *Father Knows Best*.

Compare the literal representation of Marisol's *The Family* with *Sail Baby*, dated 1983 (Fig. 13.20), by Elizabeth Murray, which is an abstract painting about family life. Three rounded canvases suggest the bouncy, energetic bodies of infants or children. The bright colors recall the palette of childhood. The yellow shape becomes a cup, referring to the role of parents, the domestic sphere, and feeding. The grouping of the three shapes suggests the closeness of siblings, all with similarities and, at the same time, each a unique individual. The ribbon of green reflects their relatedness and the intimacy of their lives. The artist, in fact, has said that this painting is about her own siblings and her children. Other of her abstract paintings refer to different family relationships, such as mother-daughter and husband-wife.

As the twentieth century drew to a close, the definition of family had been expanded. *Baby Makes 3* (Fig. 13.21),

13.21 GENERAL IDEA. *Baby Makes 3*, Canada, 1984–1989. Lacquer on vinyl, 78 ³/₄″ × 63″. By permission of General Idea.

The nuclear family is reconfigured in this artwork.

from the late 1980s, is by General Idea, the Canadian collective of three artists, A. A. Bronson, Felix Partz, and Jorge Zontal, who had been working together since 1968. General Idea presented a homosexual approach to the nuclear family, showing three men in bed in the clouds, looking tranquil and impish. The work both pokes fun at the idea of the happy nuclear family and also shows how gays and lesbians re-create such family and social structures. *Baby Makes 3* also alludes to recent discoveries in science that suggest methods other than heterosexual reproduction to generate a biological family. The image appeared on the cover of *File*, which was General Idea's parody of *Life* magazine. General Idea critiqued many aspects of popular culture that so heavily promote the heterosexual nuclear family. They created their own versions of TV dinners, postage stamps, boutique items, videos with commercials, and so on.

CLASS

A group of people sharing the same economic, social, or ruling status comprises a class. Class boundaries are rigid in some cultures, whereas in others, people can easily move up or down the social ladder. Class becomes like a very large extended family, where individuals often find their identity and their social circle.

Art and class structure can be linked in several ways: (1) members of different classes may be depicted with distinctive body styles and poses; (2) artwork can show the environment, accoutrements, and activities that mark members of a certain class; and (3) a work of art can be a status item, the possession of which indicates the class of the owner.

Class Status and Body Styles

Our focus figure is from ancient Egypt, where the human body was sculpted in different ways, depending on the person's class. Upper classes, consisting of the pharaoh and his family, the nobility, and the priests, were depicted in formal, highly standardized ways that indicated immediately their importance in the social hierarchy. The four gigantic statues at the *Temple of Ramses II* at Abu Simbel, dated c. 1275–1225 BCE (Fig. 13.22), are examples of official

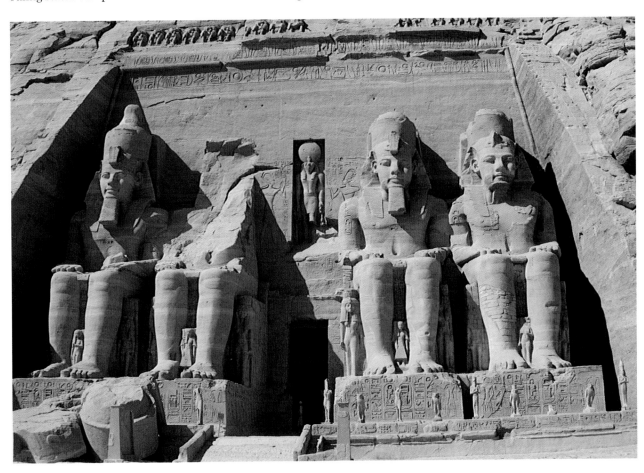

13.22 *Temple of Ramses II*, Egypt, 19th Dynasty, c. 1275–1225 BCE. Abu Simbel (now relocated). Each colossal statue is 65' high. John P. Stevens/Ronald Sheridan Ancient Art & Architecture Library.

In ancient Egypt, members of the ruling class were depicted in art in a formal, compact, frontal, idealized way.

images of the pharaoh. Befitting his semidivine status, he is enormous. The repetition of the image reinforces the idea of his imposing grandeur and divinity. Another eight standing statues of Ramses II are just inside the doorway, each standardized, each thirty-two feet high. The seated pose is frontal, composed, and symmetrical, according to the Egyptian aesthetic, with few breakable parts. The expressionless face and staring eyes look outward in timeless serenity. The body of Ramses II is well developed and flawless, frozen forever in idealized, youthful prime. Smaller figures at Ramses' knees and feet are members of his family, their smaller size indicative of their lesser rank. Enormous projects of this kind were very costly and demanded the skills of the best carvers, reinforcing the status of the very highest classes.

The colossal statues of Ramses II were intended to be permanent memorials to him, as befitting his rank. In 1968, the statues were moved to higher ground and affixed to artificial cliffs to avoid their being submerged in the back pools of the new Aswan Dam. Their permanence remains.

By contrast, the *Seated Scribe*, dated c. 2500–2400 BCE (Fig. 13.23), is a portrait of an Egyptian court official of much lesser rank than the pharaoh. The sculpture is limestone, a relatively soft, inexpensive stone considered to have an unattractive finish, so the work was painted. The result is more lifelike and thus less eternal and permanent than the monumental stone image of Ramses II at Abu Simbel. As befitting those of lower class, there is much less formality and idealization in the portrait of the scribe. His pose is more relaxed, and the figure is cut away from all backing stone. His face is expressive and personalized, rather than eternally calm and divine. He seems intelligent, alert, and aware. His body shows the effects of age, with sagging chest muscles and a potbelly, attributes that would be considered disrespectful in a portrait of a pharaoh.

CONNECTION The Egyptians were not the only people to create idealized images of their leaders. See images of rulers in Chapter 10, such as *Emperor Justinian and His Attendants* (Fig. 10.4, page 273).

Class Activities and Lifestyles

Art records not only the lifestyles of the rich and famous but also the more mundane existence of the lower classes. We will look at a cross-cultural selection of images that reflect class activities and class lifestyles. It is important to remember that the great majority of these images are made by the ruling class or middle class, often of themselves but also of classes below them.

The Ruling Class

In many cultures, art is used to define people of high rank. In Europe in the last millennium, portraits were often records of those in high positions, as only the wealthy could afford to commission or own an oil painting.

Our focus figure is *Las Meninas* (Fig. 13.24), painted by Diego Velazquez in 1656. The title means "Maids of Honor," which by itself marks the upper class. At the center of the composition is the blond Infanta Margarita, the daughter of King Philip IV and Queen Mariana of Spain, the focus of considerable attention and energy. She is shown almost casually in the painter's studio. This informal image was not meant for public display but for the king's private office. Although the Infanta is not painted in a throne room or with a crown, we can understand her exalted position through many elements in the painting. Her location at the center of the picture, the light that floods her, and her glowing white dress all mark her as the most

13.23 *Seated Scribe*, Egypt, 5th Dynasty, c. 2500–2400 BCE. Painted limestone, approx. 21″ high. From a mastaba tomb at Saqqara. Louvre, Paris.

Members of the Egyptian lower classes were depicted more naturally than were the members of the ruling class.

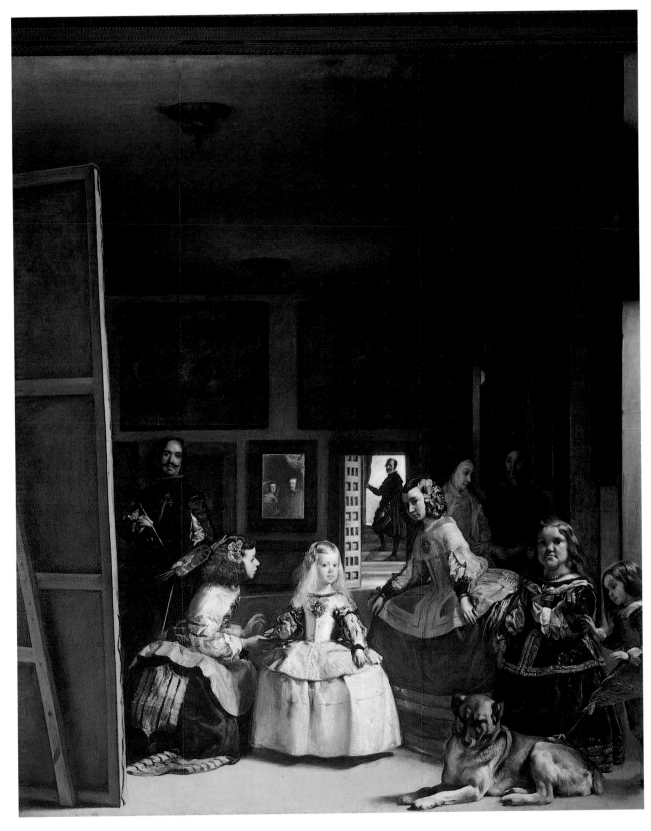

13.24 DIEGO VELAZQUEZ. *Las Meninas*, Spain, 1656. Oil on canvas, approx. 10′ 5″ × 9′. Museo Nacional del Prado, Madrid. Institut Amatller d'Art Hispanic.

This painting depicts the family of the Spanish monarch. In addition, because the painting is a large and costly item, possessing it is another indicator of status.

important figure. As the presence of servants is also a sign of rank, she is attended by two young ladies in waiting, two dwarfs, and two adult chaperones, male and female, in the shadowy right background. Her royal parents are reflected in the mirror against the back wall; presumably, they are standing where the viewer of the painting would be.

The space of the painting is majestic: light floods the foreground; the room is grand; the deep space extends back in the distance. The space is also made complex by mirrors. One we see but the other we cannot, although its presence is implied by the fact that Velazquez peers outward, presumably into a mirror, to paint himself. Velazquez is the standing figure at the left of the painting, working on a large canvas, perhaps this very picture.

Size is important. This painting is ten and one-half feet by nine feet. A physical object this large is a sign of rank and a mark of distinction, as well as is owning, possessing, or commissioning such an artwork. Diego Velazquez was a celebrated and famous artist. His prestige is an important addition to the royal commissions.

Sometimes class was indicated by its members' activities. *The Swing* (Fig. 13.25), painted by Jean-Honoré Fragonard in 1766, shows the frivolous sexual escapades

13.25 JEAN-HONORÉ FRAGONARD. *The Swing*, France, 1766. Oil on canvas, 35″ × 32″. Photo Wallace Collection, London.

In a pre-French Revolution painting, the upper class is engaged in frivolity.

of the French aristocratic class in the mid-eighteenth century. During that period, they enjoyed tremendous wealth and privilege and had few responsibilities, as most of their power had been assimilated by the French king and most of their duties assumed by an ever-growing middle class. The aristocracy was effectively transformed into a leisure class, with little to do but become embroiled in their own intrigues.

In *The Swing*, a young, aristocratic woman enjoys a moment of swinging, assisted by the bishop in the shadows who pulls the ropes. Hidden among the bushes in the lower left is a young nobleman, enjoying a peek up the woman's skirt as she playfully kicks off her pink shoe at a statue of Cupid. All details speak of the wealth and the lack of purpose of the aristocracy: the lush parks of their beautiful estates sprinkled with statuary, their rich clothing, the complete frivolity of their days' activities, and their interest in sexual intrigues. Fragonard's rich colors, delicate details, and sensual textures lend sweetness to the scene, and a sense of fragility. In fact, the aristocratic class was shortly to be brutally eliminated by the French Revolution, which began in 1789 (see *History Focus*, page 363).

Dress and other paraphernalia are often a sign of rank, as already illustrated with the *Rank Badge with Peacock* (Fig. 13.2), and also seen in the attire of nobility above. (Members of the military and even the Boy or Girl Scouts today dress to show rank. Priests of most religions also dress distinctively to show their status.) Here we will focus on one example, the *Great Beaded Crown of the Orangun-Ila* (Fig. 13.26), from the Yoruba people of Nigeria in Africa.

13.26 BEADWORKERS OF THE ADESINA FAMILY OF EFON-ALAYE. *Great Beaded Crown of the Orangun-Ila*, Ila Orangun, Nigeria, 20th century. Yoruba.

Rulers in many cultures are often distinguished by crowns and elaborate dress.

The image shows not only the crown but also the robe and staff that are signs of rank. Crowns such as this one are worn by high-ranking territorial chiefs and are similar to the headgear worn by priests and the supreme ruler. Rank is made apparent through dress in a number of ways: (1) the shape of the clothing or headgear, (2) the materials used, and (3) the meaning of the decorative symbols. The conical shape of the crown is a highly significant Yoruba symbol. It represents the inner self, which, in the case of those of rank, is connected with the spirit world. The cone shape is repeated in the umbrella that protects the chief from the sun and in the peaked-roofed verandas where he sits while functioning as the ruler. Beads have been used in Yoruba crowns at least since the 1550s and likely even earlier. The birds on the chief's crown and robe represent generative power, closely associated with women's reproductive abilities and the life-giving, stabilizing structure of Yoruba society. The long, white feathers at the top of the crown are from the Okin, called the royal bird by the Yoruba people.

CONNECTION For an example of the conical shape crown in Yoruban art, see the *Palace Sculpture* by Olowe of Ise (Fig. 10.15, page 282).

The Working Class and Middle Class

In cities, dense populations provide opportunities for commercialization and specialization for merchants, skilled workers, laborers, restaurateurs, entertainers, household workers, and others. This new class was distinct from the nobility and from traditional farm laborers.

We begin our discussion with *The Kitchen Maid* (Fig. 13.27), painted by Jan Vermeer in 1660, showing a maid in a modest home in the Netherlands of the seventeenth century. In this painting, the working class is elevated in dignity. The mundane tasks of pouring milk and arranging

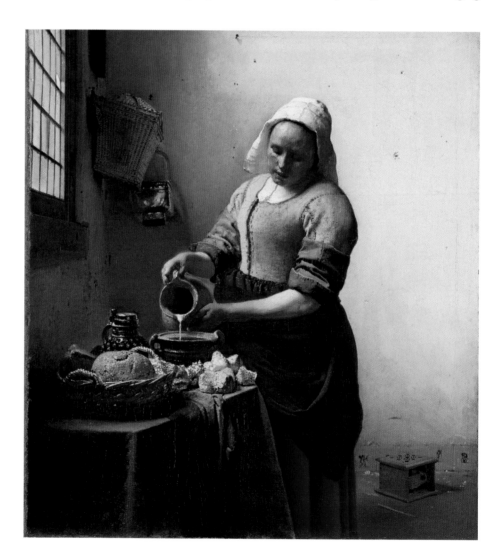

13.27 Jan Vermeer van Delft. *The Kitchen Maid*, Netherlands, 1660. Oil on canvas, approx. 17″ × 15″. The Rijksmuseum, Amsterdam.

She is only pouring milk, but this working-class woman appears dignified within a glowing space.

bread seem almost sacred. The gentle light bathes, outlines, and gives a strong sense of the physical presence of a humble woman, an image with such simplicity and directness that she almost personifies virtue. Her work seems healthy and life sustaining. The woven basket, the crust of the bread, the earthen jug, and the texture of the wall seem glowing and burnished with age. The color harmonies of cream, gold, and rust are earthen versions of the strong primary colors red and yellow.

Vermeer often painted ordinary scenes from everyday life, a category of paintings called **genre painting**. This was part of an overall tendency in the Netherlands of the seventeenth century to emphasize and elevate middle-class domestic life, where music, reading, and culture flourished and basic needs were met. The maid, from an even lower social level, is treated with the same respect. The sphere of women was the home, and *The Kitchen Maid* reflects the ideals of womanhood at that time: virtue, modesty, hard work. As a middle-class country without a king or an aristocracy, the Netherlands focused on the family

and family life and the individual. Portraits were common, as were moralizing genre scenes that criticized such vices as laziness, drunkenness, and lust.

> **CONNECTION** *The Self-Portrait* (Fig. 12.10, page 341) by Rembrandt van Rijn reflects the same sense of individual worth and the sacredness of a modest life as does Vermeer's *Kitchen Maid*.

Compare the quiet of *The Kitchen Maid* with the bustle of our next image. Kaifeng, the longtime capital of China, had 260,000 households in the year 1105. Scenes of its urban culture are recorded in the scroll painting, *Spring Festival Along the River* (Fig. 13.28), by Zhang Zeduan, from the late eleventh or early twelfth century. A painting this size was undoubtedly commissioned by a member of the aristocracy, and so this image represents an upper-class concept of ideal middle-class life, animated with crowded, bustling activity. Details show merchants selling goods in booths, people eating in restaurants, farmers delivering

13.28 Zhang Zeduan. *Spring Festival Along the River* (detail), China, late 11th–early 12th centuries. Handscroll, ink on silk, 10″ high × 207″ long. The Palace Museum, Beijing.

The wealth of details speaks of the bustle and hard work of the merchant class in China.

produce, and so on. Friendly neighbors were helpful and involved with each other. For example, onlookers shout advice and gesture from the bridge and banks as boatmen steer their vessel under the Rainbow Bridge. Each small scene is rendered with the same amount of detail and similar color, and the accumulated scenes give a picture of busy, contented, unassuming middle-class life.

A later painting records the increased affluence and leisure of the middle class in Western countries. Georges Seurat's *La Grande Jatte*, dated 1884–1886 (Fig. 13.29), is a park scene. In an era of increasing industrialization, the very creation of parks was the result of the affluent middle class's desire to reintroduce nature into increasingly crowded cities. The painting shows a collection of strangers outdoors on a modern holiday. Unlike villagers attending a local festival, the groups do not know each other. The figures are proper, composed, and orderly. Details of middle-class dress are carefully recorded. Almost all figures are shown rigidly from the side, front, or back. Diagonals are reserved for the left side of the painting and are stopped by the orderly verticals on the right. Shadows mass in the foreground, and light in the back.

The painting reflects the growing emphasis on and awareness of science. The woman in the right foreground holds a monkey on a leash, and the similarity between the monkey's curved back and the bustle on her dress shows an awareness of Charles Darwin's theories of evolution and the resulting social Darwinism, which placed women closer on a continuum to the rest of nature than men were placed. Also, Seurat was influenced by the science of color and optics, especially the works of the scientist Eugène Chevreul, as he painted with small dots of intense colors laid side by side in a style called **Pointillism**. Chevreul theorized that contrasting colors applied that way could intensify each other. The dots of bright colors eliminated muddy mixtures, and, in fact, this painting up close is a somewhat dizzying and disorienting mass of small colorful dots. So labor-intensive was this process that it took Seurat more than two years to complete the work.

The Poor

Art provides us a record of the poor, their way of life and their struggles. Art itself, however, is sometimes an upper- or middle-class luxury, so in some cases artworks

13.29 Georges Seurat. *La Grande Jatte* (also called *A Sunday on La Grande Jatte—1884*), France, 1884–1886. Oil on canvas, approx. 6′ 9″ × 10′. The Art Institute of Chicago.

Art shows that the middle class enjoyed increased leisure time in Europe at the end of the 19th century.

represent how the more affluent classes saw the very destitute.

CONNECTION Turn to Chapter 11 for art that protests oppression of lower classes by those in power. Two examples are Kathe Kollwitz's *Outbreak* (Fig. 11.4) and Lewis Hine's *Leo, 48 Inches High. . .* (Fig. 11.12)

Migrant Mother, Nipomo Valley (Fig. 13.30), photographed by Dorothea Lange, is one of many workers who were starving at a migrant camp Lange visited in 1936. Lange's field notes tell us about the woman: "Camped on the edge of a pea field where the crop had failed in a freeze. The tires had just been sold from under the car to buy food. She was 32 years old with seven children." The woman's face and pose express both strength and desperation. Skin, clothes, and hair show signs of poverty and hard times. Fear and uncertainty permeate the scene, made more acute because we also see the emotional ties of the family and the fear of the children. *Migrant Mother, Nipomo Valley* is an example of documentary photography, which purports to record facts objectively and in a straightforward manner. In reality, we know that this family posed for Lange, that she made several exposures of them, and that she edited her prints for the most effective image. Nevertheless, it is important that we understand the photograph to be factual, whether or not it was staged or manipulated.

Lange was a New York commercial photographer who was hired by California and federal agencies to document migrant farm workers during the Great Depression in the United States. Her photographs were especially effective because she made her subjects so human and so immediate. Her photographs were credited with improving conditions for migrant workers in California. The black-and-white photograph was an especially effective medium to use to express conditions of poverty, to concentrate on the facial expression, and to lend the aura of truth.

CONNECTION Many other U.S. artists took up the cause of the poor or laboring classes throughout the nineteenth and twentieth centuries. Turn to Ester Hernandez's memorable print, *Sun Mad* (Fig. 11.17, page 316).

13.30 DOROTHEA LANGE. *Migrant Mother, Nipomo Valley*, USA, 1936. Gelatin silver print. From the Collections of the Library of Congress.

One of the most famous images of the Great Depression, this photograph appeared originally in a San Francisco newspaper and created an outpouring of food donations for the migrant workers.

Art Objects That Indicate Class Status

Finally, different kinds of art are often indicators of class. Art objects are made for and reflect the needs and tastes of specific classes. We could have chosen from many examples to illustrate this concept, but we will focus first on two from the era of the Tokugawa Shogunate (1573–1868) in Japan. We will conclude with an example from the United States of the twentieth century.

Historically in Japan, classes were kept rigidly distinct. The ruling class consisted of the imperial family and the warriors, who divided the land and were its feudal rulers, led by the shogun. The very poorest class consisted of the peasants, who farmed the land that belonged to the warrior class. In addition, a middle class of urban dwellers began to emerge, starting in the mid-1600s and continuing into the twentieth century. This class was composed primarily of merchants, manufacturers, and laborers, and the largest concentration of them was in the city of Edo, known today as Tokyo. As each group was kept separate and distinct, they all developed their own cultural spheres, and different art styles developed for each class.

The warrior-rulers, (or **samurai**), built for themselves splendid stone castles that were both fortresses and self-aggrandizing monuments. Because of the stone construction, rooms in these castles were large, gray, and dimly lit. The warrior-rulers commissioned large screens, sliding doors, and wall paintings to lighten and decorate the dark, drab interiors. For example, *Uji Bridge*, from the sixteenth or seventeenth century (Fig. 13.31), is a large screen more than five feet tall. The bridge arcs across the top of the screen, partly obscured by mists. In the foreground, the river rolls past a water wheel. Dramatic willow branches contrast with budding leaves. The dark branches stand in stark contrast to the golds and reds of the background. The painting expresses qualities of simplicity and beauty, perishable with the passing of the moment. The gold leaf background reflected light in the dim castle interior.

The artwork of the middle class was often the *ukiyo-e* print (see *History Focus*, page 363). These prints were modest in size and produced in large numbers, so that the cost of each was within the reach of the middle-class merchant. They were kept in drawers and therefore did not require a castle to house them. The *ukiyo-e* prints were eclectic in style, combining Japanese, Chinese, and, later, Western styles. Because they were inexpensive to produce, the artist who drew the original design was able to be innovative. For lavish screens like the *Uji Bridge*, artists had much less latitude in the designs they produced.

Ukiyo-e prints showed generally one of three subjects: famous Kabuki actors, beautiful young women, and landscapes. *Komurasaki of the Tamaya Teahouse* (Fig. 13.32), designed by Kitagawa Utamaro in 1794, is an example

13.31 *Uji Bridge*, Japan, Momoyama period, 16th–17th centuries. Six-fold screen, color on paper, 62″ high. Tokyo National Museum.

Large golden screens were used to decorate the castles of warrior-rulers in Japan.

13.32 Kitagawa Utamaro. *Komurasaki of the Tamaya Teahouse*, Japan, 1794. Multicolor woodblock print from the series "A Collection of Reigning Beauties," 15″ × 10″. Tokyo National Museum.

Color woodblock prints were a favored art form of the Japanese merchant class.

of the beautiful woman theme, showing the courtesan Komurasaki. The woman is charming, but human existence is fleeting and transitory; thus, the beautiful can add a melancholy note, making humans ache all the more for life's passing. This wistfulness is a quality of many Japanese images, as we saw even with the *Uji Bridge* screen. The colors are exceedingly delicate, with yellow ochres, olive tones, dull reds, grays, and blacks—not blazingly bright. The line quality of the prints was splendid—elegant, fine, curving and graceful here (or, in the case of prints of the energetic Kabuki actors, vigorous and even wild). The lines in the face and hair are especially refined, while the folds of the drapery are expressed in bold marks

and curves. Geishas and courtesans were depicted in ways that would make them outlets for male desires; the market for these pictures was married men, who would see in these women for hire a fleeting beauty and an erotic perfection that they desired. Especially famous courtesans and geishas would be depicted in popular prints, and their images circulated and collected.

CONNECTION You can read more about Japanese prints with *A Pair of Lovers* (Fig. 7.17, page 175). The production of such prints is discussed in Chapter 3, Media, on page 61 and with Figure 3.14.

Our last example, *Watts Towers* (Fig. 13.33), was made by a working-class man for a working-class neighborhood in Los Angeles. Beginning in the 1920s when he was in his late forties, Simon Rodilla (also called Simon or Sam Rodia) labored for more than thirty years in his backyard to erect a nine-part sculpture, more than one hundred feet high. It was an amazing artistic and physical effort. The tower forms rise dramatically against the sky, while the openwork pattern adds an element of rhythm. The *Watts Towers* are constructed of rods and bars shaped into openwork sculptures. The concrete coating on the *Towers* was encrusted with ceramic pieces, tiles, glass, seashells, mirror pieces, and other shiny or broken castoffs, creating a glittering mosaic-like surface. An immigrant from Italy, Rodia wanted to construct a monument to pay tribute to his adopted land.

Rodia was not academically trained as an artist, and his work does not reflect the major art trends of his day. His work was not made for an upper-class audience. As a result, many critics place *Watts Towers* in categories outside of fine art. It has been variously described as folk art, outsider art, or naive art. The dense and shimmering surfaces have caused some to relate his work to crafts and decorative arts. Some have even called it "kook" art, claiming that Rodia was trying to make a transmitter to contact aliens. Some of these descriptors ("naive," "kook," "decorative," etc.) have more or less pejorative connotations, while "folk" suggests an art category of less value than fine art. But there is no denying the visual power of the *Watts Towers*.

CONNECTION Another work of "folk art" is the *Retablo of Maria de la Luz Casillas and Children* (Fig. 8.15, page 205). Read about that work and then review the discussion of "Fine Art, Popular Culture, and Kitsch" in Chapter 1 pages 11–16.

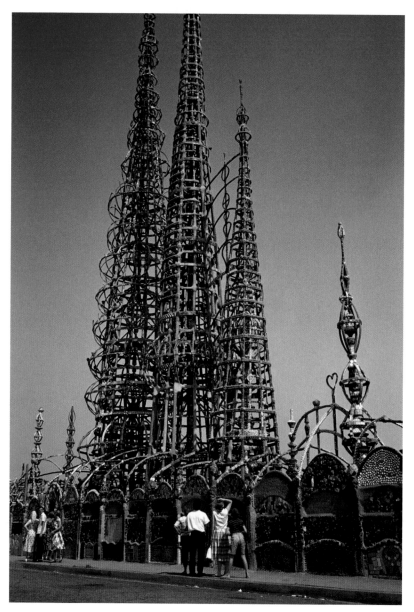

13.33 SIMON RODIA. *Watts Towers*, USA, 1921–1954. Reinforced concrete with mixed media and found materials, 100' high. Los Angeles, California.

These towers were built by a working-class man in his spare time, over a span of 33 years.

14.1 *Shaman's Amulet*, Alaska/British Columbia, c. 1820–1850. Sperm whale tooth, 6 1/2″ long. Tlingit. Indiana University Art Museum, Bloomington.

Animal and human forms combine in this artwork to increase the power of the shaman.

14

NATURE, KNOWLEDGE, AND TECHNOLOGY

Art can imitate, praise, or criticize the world around us. That world consists of animals, plants, and the earth. It also contains the things that humans build, such as knowledge systems, technology, and cities.

PREVIEW

This chapter examines art with themes related to the world around us. The first artworks we see look at animals, to find out what humans consider to be ideal or powerful in nature and how art with animals reflects desirable or despicable qualities in humans. The chapter opener, Shaman's Amulet *(Fig. 14.1), is just one example of animals depicted in combinations with each other and with human forms to indicate superhuman powers. We will also look at the various meanings behind landscape imagery.*

The next artworks either promote or spread human knowledge about the world, or critique human knowledge as insufficient for understanding either human nature or everything around us. Finally, we will see that artists examine technology to see how it is helping us or hurting us.

Connecting Art and History from
1850–1950 CE

Three major trends marked this period: industrialism, modernization, and nationalism. Before we begin that discussion, it is important to note that even at this time, many areas of the world remained unindustrialized. For example, in central Australia, artists in the Aboriginal culture produced works such as *Hunter and Kangaroo* (Fig. 14.26). Within industrialized nations, artworks such as Ansel Adams' *Clearing Winter Storm, Yosemite National Park, California, 1944* (Fig. 14.15) glorified the beauty of untouched nature.

Nevertheless, industrialism was transforming the world. Western European nations continued to build their colonial empires in Africa and Asia. The years from 1850 to 1914 marked the high point of colonialism, even with increased resistance and colonial independence movements. Because they generally had more undeveloped land, the colonies provided raw material for industrialized nations. The Industrial Revolution, which had already begun in Great Britain, spread to other areas of western Europe and the United States. The Industrial Revolution brought amazing advances in technology as well as profound social changes, including the development of a large middle class and an industrial working class, the creation of factories, great increases in population, and mass migration into urban areas, as reflected in Fernand Léger's *The City* (Fig. 14.31). Scientific advances were important, especially in medicine and physics. Science also influenced art, especially Impressionism and Futurism. Claude Monet's style of painting in *Water Lily Pool* (Fig. 14.14) is based in part on optics.

The newly powerful middle class enjoyed greater educational opportunities and leisure time. Many new leisure activities took place in nature, as seen in Renoir's *The Luncheon of the Boating Party* (Fig. 14.2). The working class continued to suffer with poverty, long hours, and political oppression. Karl Marx coauthored the *Communist Manifesto* in 1848, and the labor movement was agitating for fair wages, safe working conditions, and reasonable hours for workers. Civil

Map 9 World map showing colonial empires.

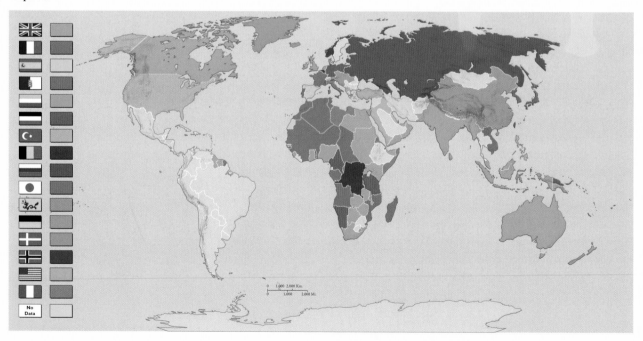

rights movements for racial and gender equality grew in power throughout this period.

Nationalism is devotion to one's country, especially promoting that country's interests and culture above all others. Nationalistic fervor saw the formation of modern nations in South America, central Europe, and the Balkans. In the United States, the Civil War (1861–1865) both split and then reinforced the national identity.

In Japan, this was a period of nationalization, industrialization, and modernization. In 1868, the old shogun rulers of Japan were overthrown. Emperor Meiji rose to power and began the rapid industrialization of Japan and modernization of its society. In 1874, Japan began a period of expansion in Asia, following the model of Western colonial empires. Japan envisioned itself as the dominant power in Asia.

The Great War (World War I) broke out in 1914 and lasted until 1918. Its causes were many, including increased friction among European nation-states, entangling alliances, internal conflicts caused by ethnic groups that had not yet achieved nationhood, and competition for colonies and trade. The war and the terms of the peace treaty embittered Germany, one of the losing nations. Art movements such as Dada and Surrealism developed in response to the horrors of World War I, the crumbling social order, and increased industrialization, as seen in Salvador Dalí's *The Persistence of Memory* (Fig. 14.28). Other artworks were more pointedly critical, like José Clemente Orozco's *Gods of the Modern World* (Fig. 14.29).

Imperial rule was beginning to crumble. The 1912 revolution in China ended centuries of dynastic rule. The Russian Revolution of 1917 created

14.2 Pierre Auguste Renoir. *The Luncheon of the Boating Party*, France, 1881. Oil on canvas, 51″ × 68″. The Phillips Collection, Washington, D.C.

The European middle class enjoyed greater leisure time in the late 19th century, including pleasurable outings in nature.

a Communist state and ended the rule of the czars. The centuries-old Ottoman Empire, centered in Turkey, was broken up in 1919. Unfortunately, totalitarianism in other forms was on the rise. In Stalinist Russia and Nazi Germany in the 1930s, the state had absolute power, and dictatorships arose in Latin America. Fascism dominated in Spain and Italy as well.

The 1930s and 1940s were periods of great hardship and destruction. The Great Depression was a decade of severe financial difficulty for industrialized nations, and many people suffered. The depression's unemployment and homelessness, coupled with extreme nationalism and the rise of totalitarian regimes, led to World War II. A bloody prelude to that war was the Spanish Civil War, waged by Fascists and Republicans/ Communists from 1936–1939, each side heavily aided by foreign countries. Beginning in 1931, Japan, Italy, and Germany began seizing lands around them, until war was declared in Europe in 1939 and in the Pacific in 1941. When the horrendous destruction of World

War II finally ended in 1945, at least 17 million soldiers and perhaps as many as 40 million civilians were dead, including the millions who died in German concentration camps.

The years immediately following World War II saw the founding of the United Nations, the destruction of old European colonial empires, and the establishment of Communist China (1948). Also established was the modern state of Israel, which displaced the Palestinians.

Thus, many issues that we see in today's world had their roots back a century or more, as the foundations were laid for the global economy, global trade and resources, and global political entanglements.

World Art Map for Chapter 14

Shaman's Amulet.
Alaska/British Columbia,
Northwest Pacific.

NORTH
AMERICA

Robert Smithson. *Spiral Jetty.*

Ansel Adams.
Clearing Winter Storm, Yosemite National Park.

David Smith. *Cubi XXVI.*

Mierle Laderman Ukeles. *The Social Mirror.*

Serpent (or Snake) Mound.

John James Audubon. *Carolina Paroquet.*

Walter de Maria. *The Lightning Field.*

Relief.

José Clemente Orozco. *Gods of the Modern World.*

Vessel in the Form of a Monkey.
Veracruz, Mexico.

Anselm Kiefer. *Breaking of the Vessels.*

Andreas Vesalius of Brussels. *The Fourth Plate of Muscles.*
Jan Bruegel. *A Stoneware Vase of Flowers.*
The Unicorn in Captivity.

John Constable. *The Haywain.*

Bridget Riley. *Current.*
Chris Ofili. *Monkey Magic—Sex, Money and Drugs.*
Joseph Mallord William Turner.
The Fighting Temeraire Tugged to Her Last Berth to Be Broken Up.

Pierre Auguste Renoir. *The Luncheon of the Boating Party.*
Claude Monet. *Water Lily Pool.*
Fernand Léger. *The City.*

EUROPE

Salvador Dalí. *The Persistence of Memory.*

Jean Tinguely.
Homage to New York: A Self-Constructing, Self-Destructing Work of Art.

Rock Art.
Acacus Mountains, Libya.

SOUTH
AMERICA

Nazca Spider.
Nazca, Peru, South America.

N

| 0 | 1,000 | 2,000 Km. |
| 0 | 1,000 | 2,000 Mi. |

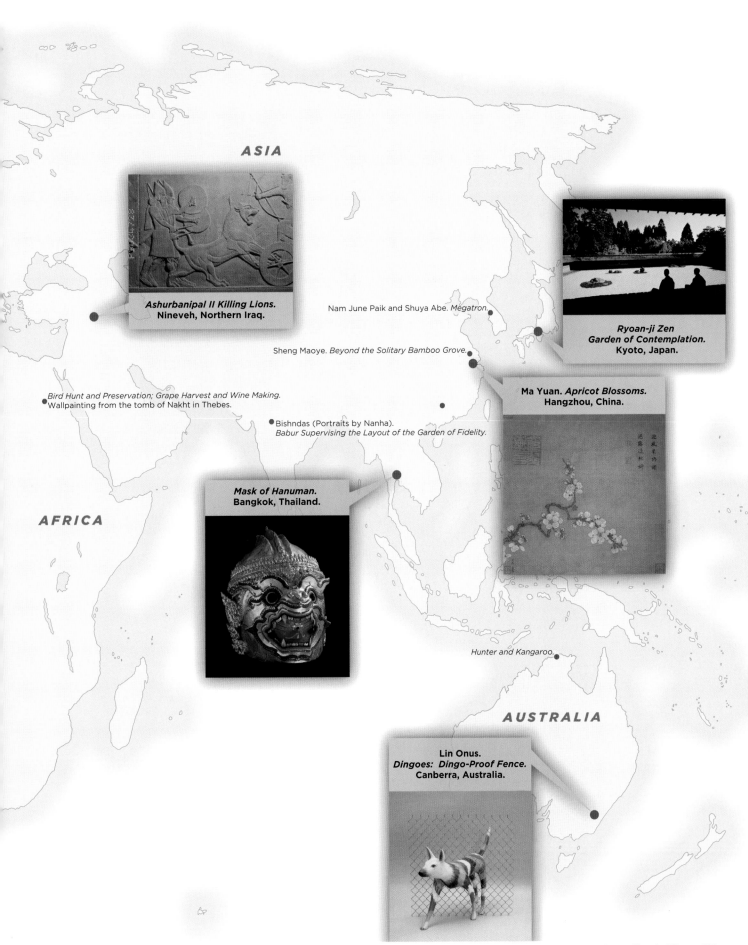

ASIA

Ashurbanipal II Killing Lions.
Nineveh, Northern Iraq.

Nam June Paik and Shuya Abe. *Megatron.*

Ryoan-ji Zen
Garden of Contemplation.
Kyoto, Japan.

Sheng Maoye. *Beyond the Solitary Bamboo Grove.*

Ma Yuan. *Apricot Blossoms.*
Hangzhou, China.

Bird Hunt and Preservation; Grape Harvest and Wine Making.
Wallpainting from the tomb of Nakht in Thebes.

Bishndas (Portraits by Nanha).
Babur Supervising the Layout of the Garden of Fidelity.

AFRICA

Mask of Hanuman.
Bangkok, Thailand.

Hunter and Kangaroo.

AUSTRALIA

Lin Onus.
Dingoes: Dingo-Proof Fence.
Canberra, Australia.

1850–1950 CE

Domestication of horse and camel	**10,000 BCE** — Rock Art, Libya
	3500
Wheel appears— Mesopotamia	
Bronze casting in Sumeria	
	2000
First library in Sumeria	Bird hunt and preservation; grape harvest and wine making. Wallpainting from the tomb of Nakht in Thebes
First libraries in China	**1700**
	Ashurbanipal II Killing Lions
China: The Silk Trade	**600** — Relief (Olmec)
	300
Library at Alexandria	
Paper first used in China	**100 CE**
Elephants first used in warfare	
Printing invented in China	**200**
Islamic libraries established	Spider (Nazca)
Temple libraries in Japan	
	Industrial Revolution begins
	800 — Vessel in the Form of a Monkey
ROMANESQUE Era	

Above Relief Carving, Cambodia (3.36)

1000	Serpent (or Snake) Mound
Moslem paper mills in Spain	
GOTHIC Era	
Medieval universities	
1300	Ma Yuan: *Apricot Blossoms*
RENAISSANCE IN EUROPE	**1400** — The Unicorn in Captivity

Above Eagle Knight, Aztec (3.40)

Gutenberg's press	
1500	Ryoanji Zen Garden of Contemplation
	Vesalius: *The Fourth Plate of Muscles*
1600	Sheng Maoye: *Beyond the Solitary Bamboo Grove*
BAROQUE ERA	Bruegel: *A Stoneware Vase of Flowers*
	Bishndas: *Babur Supervising the Layout of the Garden of Fidelity*

Steam locomotive—Europe	**1800**

Above RUKUPU, *Entrance Doorway for a Maori Meeting House* (3.39)

Shaman's Amulet

1821	CONSTABLE: *The Haywain*
1827	AUDUBON: *Carolina Paroquet*
1838	
1840	TURNER: *The Fighting Temeraire*

Early experiments in photography

Invention of dynamite

Edison and the light bulb

Labor Movement

IMPRESSIONISM

POST-IMPRESSIONISM

Above HINE. *Leo, 48 Inches High* (11.12)

Women's Rights Movement

First flight, Wright Brothers	**1900**

Above CEZANNE. *Landscape at Aix, Mount Sainte-Victoire* (1.13)

World War I	1919	LÉGER: *The City*
	1932	DALÍ: *The Persistence of Memory*
	1934	OROZCO: *Gods of the Modern World*

Great Depression

Early experiments with computers

	1940	ADAMS: *Clearing Winter Storm, Yosemite National Park, California, 1944*

World War II

Establishment of Communist China

1950
1960

Above UTZON: *Opera House, Sydney, Australia* (15.4)

POP ART		TINGUELY: *Homage to New York*
	1964	RILEY: *Current*
	1965	SMITH: *Cubi XXVI*
	1970	
		SMITHSON: *Spiral Jetty*
	1971	DE MARIA: *The Lightning Field*
Desktop publishing	1980	UKELES: *The Social Mirror*
POST-MODERNISM		
Digital imaging	1989	ONUS: *Dingoes: Dingo-Proof Fence*
The Internet	1990	KIEFER: *Breaking of the Vessels*
Reunification of Germany		
	1995	PAIK: *Megatron*
	1999	OFILI: *Monkey Magic, Money and Drugs*

NATURE

Our natural world consists of the earth and its flora and fauna. The relationship of humans and animals is very complex. We hunt them, love them, and eat them. They are part of industry, as we breed some and extinguish others. We identify with animals and project our highest aspirations and deepest fears onto them. Likewise, humans use landscape imagery, both the wild and the cultivated, to project their own ideals.

Animals

Animals appear in art in every culture, in forms both real and imagined. Animals were likely the subjects of humans' first drawings. They figure in myths and religious narratives, such as "Noah and the Ark" and the *Ramayana*. Humans have recorded animal likenesses and have invented bizarre creatures from parts of other living beings.

 CONNECTION The cave drawings at Lascaux (Fig. 6.4, page 134) are among the oldest existing drawings made by humans.

Fantastic Creatures

Fantastic creatures are the product of human imagination, fear, and desire. Because they really do not exist, their human creators can assign a meaning and purpose to them.

The ancient Greeks invented several fantastic creatures that usually were threats to humans or represented degraded human nature. Harpies were woman-headed birds who lured and fed on men. Centaurs were man-headed horses known for their lustfulness. Satyrs were men with goat or horse attributes and were prone to drunkenness and sexual excess. Medieval Europeans were especially interested in fantastic animals, like the satyrs and centaurs from antiquity, and made up several of their own. Medieval beasts, however, often acted like humans in narratives that had a moralizing purpose, or were demons in warnings about hell. Fantastic creatures still feed popular imagination today, as mermaids, giant insects, vampires, and werewolves thrive in film and popular fiction.

Our focus figure for this section is *The Unicorn in Captivity*, dated late fifteenth century (Fig. 14.3). The unicorn is a horse with some goat features and a long, single horn projecting from its forehead. Ancient Greeks and Romans first described it, but it was very popular in late medieval literature. "Unicorn" horns were expensive,

prized possessions (they were actually the spiral tusk of a narwhal, an arctic whale) that could purify water and remove poison. Another common belief was that the unicorn could elude all hunters. However, when it saw a virgin, it put its head on her lap and could easily be caught.

The Unicorn in Captivity is the last image in six Netherlandish tapestries. Our example shows the unicorn as a brilliant white horse captured in a paradise garden, surrounded by an abundance of decorative flowers and plants distributed in a flat pattern that fills the space from top to bottom. The unicorn has a lively and soulful expression on its face. It is surrounded by a fence, wears a jeweled collar, and is chained to a pomegranate tree. There are two different sets of meanings for the unicorn in these tapestries. One is that of Jesus, believed to be the source of spiritual life, who was hunted by men, was brutally killed, and then rose back to life. Or, the image may represent true love in the Age of Chivalry, with the unicorn (man) enduring terrible ordeals to win his beloved. The collar represents a chain of love, mentioned in medieval allegories as a sign that a gentleman submits to his lady's will. The pomegranates dripping red juice onto the unicorn may symbolize Christ's sacrifice or human fertility. Multiple meanings were common in the medieval era, as a way to acknowledge the complexity of life.

Fantastic creatures can express various forms of power. The limestone *Relief*, dated sixth century BCE (Fig. 14.4), comes from the Olmec culture of ancient Mexico, which produced many instances of animal imagery that combine natural and fantastic elements. Here, a warrior or priest is seated and wearing an elaborate jaguar-serpent helmet with the extended jaw of the creature forming the chinstrap. Towering over him is a large serpent with heavy brows and a crest like some sort of imaginary bird. Undoubtedly, the animal attributes protect the man as well as combine with him to create heightened powers.

Compare the *Relief* with the *Shaman's Amulet*, dated c. 1820–1850 (Chapter Opener, Fig. 14.1). Like the *Relief*, the *Amulet* shows the combination of animal forms as a source of power and protection, here among the peoples of the Northwest Coast of North America. A shaman was a person with supernatural powers, believed to be a bridge among the human, animal, and spirit worlds. The amulet was a visible sign of the shaman's power, and it extended that power. The most prominent animal is the sea serpent, whose head is to the right, swallowing a human. This indicated that the shaman could take on the forms of certain animals and could operate in both the animal and human realms. Other animals include a bear, for its strength, and a bird, for its ability to fly. The smooth, arching outline is echoed in interior details such as the folded arms, lines

14.3, _above_ *The Unicorn in Captivity*, South Netherlandish, 1495–1505. Wool warp, wool, silk, silver, and gilt wefts, 12′ 1″ × 8′ 3″. Gift of John D. Rockefeller Jr., 1937. The Metropolitan Museum of Art, New York, Cloister Collection.

The unicorn had various symbolic meanings for Medieval Europeans.

14.4, _right_ *Relief*, La Venta (Mexico), 6th century BCE. Basalt, 38 ¹/₂″ high. Olmec. Museo Nacional de Antropología, Mexico City. The Metropolitan Museum of Art, New York.

The combination of animal features protected the man and perhaps extended his power.

of feathers, and the serpent's mouth. A dark patina gives depth to the work.

Another example of fantastic creatures comes from Thailand, a country with monsoon rains, thick jungles, and abundant animal life. Plants, birds, and beasts abound in traditional Thai art and are associated with forces in nature. Most images have more than one meaning. Monkeys, for example, are common wild animals in Thailand, and they are metaphors for humans, who aspire to be gods. In many Hindu and Buddhist tales, they also indulge in behavior unfit for humans or gods, such as lust and drunkenness, and thus present the realistic side of human nature in contrast to the idealized.

Mask of Hanuman (Fig. 14.5) is a headpiece representing the white monkey-hero and loyal follower of the deity Rama in the Thai story *Ramakien* (called the *Ramayana* in India). Performers wear this mask when representing this fantastic creature, a divine monkey with white fur, jeweled teeth, and a white crest of hair that shone like diamonds. His heroic exploits were many, including helping rescue Rama's wife from a demon and bringing a mountain of medicinal plants to cure the wounded in battle. The *Mask of Hanuman* is equally fantastic, covered with gleaming metal and enamel. Red, black, and green dramatically

14.5 *Mask of Hanuman.* Enamel inlay, gilt, gems, and other materials; fits over a human head. National Museum of Bangkok, Thailand.

This mask represents a mythical monkey who seems even more fantastic because of the rich materials and exaggerated facial features.

outline his facial features. His bulging eyes and snarling mouth are visually arresting, alert, and ferocious. Gold serpents curl at his ears. Hanuman is modeled from an actual monkey, the leaf-eating langur from India (Taylor 1994:35–38).

Compare the Thai monkey with that in the contemporary painting by Chris Ofili, *Monkey Magic—Sex, Money and Drugs,* 1999 (Fig. 14.6). The monkey is again a stand-in for human behavior, and here it holds an empty turquoise vessel and tries to capture three powerful elements of life: sex, money, and drugs, represented by three clumps of dried elephant dung attached to the canvas. The surface is colorful and shiny with thick beads of paint and layers of glitter, which emphasizes the imagined rather than the real. A British artist of Nigerian descent, Ofili uses dried elephant dung to reference the African ritual use of it. His paintings often rest on balls of dung, seeming to come up from the earth rather than hang on the wall.

In some cases, a group of people feel such an affinity with an animal that they use it to represent themselves

14.6 CHRIS OFILI. *Monkey Magic—Sex, Money and Drugs*, Great Britain/Nigeria, 1999. Acrylic, collage, glitter, resin, pencil, map pins, and elephant dung on canvas, 96″ × 72″. Museum of Contemporary Art, Los Angeles.

Animals act as stand-ins for humans, as this monkey reaches for sex, money, and drugs.

and their interests, as in Lin Onus' *Dingoes: Dingo-Proof Fence* (Fig. 14.7). The fantastic dingo of this sculpture is a wild dog that has a coat in colors representing the native Aboriginal people and has the ability to pass through fences. This work upholds the wild animals' right to the land in Australia, as well as supports the aboriginal way of life that leaves the natural environment intact. It protests the fencing, farming, and grazing of Australian land, a practice brought by European settlers that aggressively altered the land. In this artwork, the dingo-proof fence turned out to be ineffective against natural forces.

 CONNECTION Examples of fantastic creatures appear in previous chapters. They include human-headed winged bulls, at left (*Lamassu*, Fig. 10.10, page 278), serpents (*Laocoön and His Sons*, Fig. 12.18, page 346), and totem animals (*Interior House Post*, Fig. 13.15, page 380).

Observed Animals

Animals are magnificent creatures, and, in many instances, their likenesses—without embellishment—are sufficient justification for a work of art.

Our focus figure shows that from very earliest times, humans have recorded the likenesses of animals they encountered. Figure 14.8 is one of hundreds of ancient rock art images from the Acacus Mountains in western

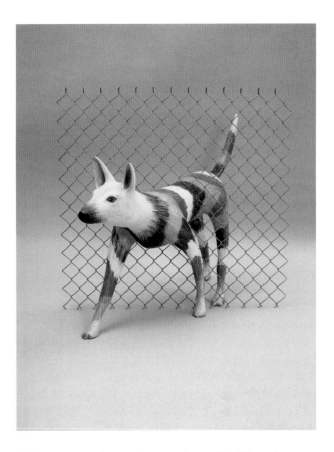

14.7 LIN ONUS. *Dingoes: Dingo Proof Fence* (detail from the series *Dingoes*), Aboriginal, Australia, 1989. Synthetic polymer on fiberglass, wire, metal, 37 1/2″ high. National Gallery of Australia, Canberra.

The dingo, a wild dog in Australia, is here shown as able to walk right through fences constructed by humans.

14.8 *Rock Art* from the Acacus Mountains, Western Libya, c. 10,000 BCE.

This is an ancient rendering of an elephant scratched into a rock that is graceful, beautiful, and accurate.

Libya, in what is now the Sahara Desert. However, at the beginning of the Holocene Era around 10,000 BCE, the area supported vegetation and large animals, like the elephant shown in our example. There are also paintings and carvings of humans, giraffes, antelopes, and domesticated animals. This *Rock Art* drawing depicted the elephant with great accuracy and sensitivity, in a work that is memorable even for our modern eyes.

Compare the *Rock Art* with the next work, a relief that was part of extensive carvings from a palace in Ancient Assyria that shows how people admire animals and, at the same time, desire to destroy them. In the detail entitled *Ashurbanipal II Killing Lions*, c. 650 BCE (Fig. 14.9), the lion's muscles, veins, and bones show its tremendous strength, fierceness, and agility. Although they greatly admired the beauty of the living lion, the Assyrian elite slaughtered the animals in a public spectacle, the royal lion hunt. Lions in cages were released in an enclosed arena, where the king, Ashurbanipal, accompanied by bowmen and spearmen, would face them to show his courage. Other scenes show a large number of lion carcasses piled behind the king, or wounded lions slowly dying. Assyrians believed that the longer a man or beast took to die, the higher the layer of heaven that was attained in the afterlife. The Assyrians made many such relief carvings to cover the mud-brick palace walls. They boasted the king's power not only in lion hunts but also in battle campaigns and in accompanying the gods.

Contrast the degree of detail in the Assyrian *Lions* with the large animal drawings produced by the Nazca culture, a pre-Incan civilization in southwestern Peru. The drawings are located on a rocky, arid plain, with no wind and essentially no rainfall. A casual footprint or scrap of litter will remain undisturbed for years. The Nazca drawings were made at least 1,400 years ago by scraping the brown surface of the desert floor, revealing lighter-colored sand beneath. The earliest drawings were of animals, such as birds, whales, monkeys, or dogs. Our example, *Spider* (Fig. 14.10), dates from around 200–600. Later drawings consisted of large geometric shapes, spirals, and long, straight lines that extend for miles or radiate from center points. Many drawings were made right on top of previous ones.

The Nazca drawings are remarkable for their regularity and simplicity. All lines are a standard width and executed as a continuous path. The Nazca people probably used rudimentary surveying instruments and string to plot the paths. The drawings are so large and the plain so flat that most drawings can only be seen from the air.

14.9 *Ashurbanipal II Killing Lions*, Assyria, c. 650 BCE. Limestone relief, approx. 60″ high. From the Palace of Ashurbanipal, Nineveh (northern Iraq). The British Museum, London.

By fighting and killing fierce lions, Assyrian rulers affirmed their own bravery and fitness to rule.

14.10, *above* *Spider*, Nazca, Peru, c. 200–600. Henri Stierlin.

This large drawing was created when brown surface rocks were scraped away to reveal yellowish surface below. The humans who made the drawing never saw the entire work because of its huge size.

14.11, *right* *Vessel in the Form of a Monkey*, Veracruz, Mexico, late Classic period, 800–900. Clay, 8 ¹/₂″ high. Indiana University Art Museum, Bloomington.

When shaken, the cup makes a rattling noise like the chattering of monkeys.

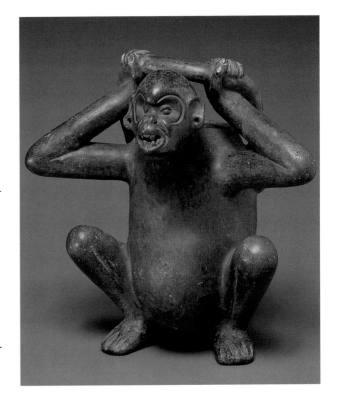

Some long, straight lines may have been used for astronomical sightings, while others may have been paths that connected the plain's various shrines. In this arid area, the animal drawings may have been messages or offerings to water gods residing in mountains. Even today in areas of Peru and Bolivia, the spider is highly regarded because it predicts weather changes and may foretell rainfall.

Another instance of carefully observed animals can be seen in the *Vessel in the Form of a Monkey* (Fig. 14.11), made between 800 and 900 in the pre-Columbian Veracruz culture in Mexico. Animal-shaped vessels were common in many Mesoamerican and South American cultures. The monkey's squatting pose, with its arms overhead grasping its own tail, and its facial structure are so convincingly naturalistic that its species can be identified: it is a spider monkey. The artist has captured the animated expressions and energy of the animal. In addition, small rocks sealed inside in hollow pockets rattle when the vessel is shaken, mimicking the monkey's chatter. Monkeys were kept as pets and were featured in Mesoamerican mythology. They were also linked to dancers, because of their quick, agile movements, or to uninhibited sexuality (Pelrine 1996:75). The monkey in this example has pierced ears, like humans. On the formal side, the vessel can be enjoyed for its design: the vessel is formed by the monkey's belly in front and the expanded back. The opening is behind the monkey's head. The rounded belly contrasts with angular forms of the arms, as do the concentrated facial details with the smooth abdomen. Protruding forms, negative spaces, and dark hollows all add to the vessel's visual richness.

The Land

This section contains landscapes, flowers and gardens, and earthworks, which are gigantic sculptures using the earth as their base.

Landscape Imagery

A landscape image is different from the actual outdoors. Landscape images are carefully created translations of reality that often have deeper social or religious meanings. Landscape paintings were particularly common in the United States and in Europe in the nineteenth century. Landscapes tended to have a nationalistic look. For example, German landscapes sometimes were marked by melancholy or morbidity. English landscapes, however, tended to emphasize the open-air expansiveness of farm scenes. Our focus figure for this section is John Constable's *The Haywain*, from 1821 (Fig. 14.12), which shows a broad

14.12 JOHN CONSTABLE. *The Haywain*, England, 1821. Oil on canvas, 4′ 3″ × 6′ 2″. The National Gallery, London.

This scene of the broad English countryside emphasized an open-air quality, but the painting was made in the studio from sketches the artist had executed outdoors.

meadow in the distance, with a farm scene in front. The composition seems casual, direct, natural, and unstudied, but Constable carefully observed everything, especially the clouds. Tranquility pervades all, as a warm mellow light washes over the land, and brilliant clouds play against the blue sky.

Constable's work appealed especially to Europeans who had migrated in large numbers to industrial cities and missed contact with nature. Before painting large canvases, Constable made numerous outdoor studies that he saw as being scientific (meteorology was his avocation). His work also grew from **Romanticism**, which elevated nature and immediate experience. In his works, he used stippling, in which small dabs of bright color and white are applied to reproduce shimmering light. His method was important later to **Impressionism.**

Compare Constable's landscape with Sheng Maoye's *Beyond the Solitary Bamboo Grove* (Fig. 14.13), from the seventeenth century, both of which were a reaction to city life. In China and Japan, landscape paintings were especially popular among upper- and middle-class urban populations, especially in noisy and polluted areas. The booming city of Suchou, wealthy from the European silk trade and tourists, had one park that was so overcrowded that a local artist called it "squalid," with "visitors [who] flock there like flies swarming on meat" (Cahill 1966:87). Paintings like *Beyond the Solitary Bamboo Grove* made pristine nature once again available. Landscapes were displayed in homes on large, hanging silk scrolls; fans or smaller albums were made for private viewing. Our example shows the soft blur of misty mountains, an isolated hut, and the distinctive silhouettes of various trees, all rendered by subtle washes of ink and light color. Inspiration for paintings often came from poetry or the beliefs of Daoism (or Taoism), which held that nature was a visible manifestation of the Absolute Dao, the ultimate substratum from which all things come. Nature also reflected Daoism in its rhythms, changes, and transformations. Chinese landscapes are carefully composed imaginary scenes. Artists practiced their brushwork for years to achieve a sense of effortlessness and spontaneity, qualities valued in Daoism.

In comparison, the Impressionist landscape painter Claude Monet was motivated by a desire to capture the subtle qualities of light and reflection. Unlike Constable

14.13 SHENG MAOYE. *Beyond the Solitary Bamboo Grove*, China, c. 1625–1640. Ink and color on silk, 11 1/4″ × 12″. From an album of six leaves; landscapes inspired by Tang poems. The Metropolitan Museum of Art, New York.

This landscape painting has a quality of poetic reverie.

or Maoye, Monet executed his finished paintings almost exclusively outdoors. In his later years he planted his own water garden at his home in Giverny, France, to provide himself with inspiration close at hand. In *Water Lily Pool* (Fig. 14.14), from 1900, the colors are dazzling; by mixing vivid strokes of pure color, Monet achieved the effect of sunlight upon water. In Monet's later career, his paintings approached abstraction, as brushstrokes became more important than imagery. The Impressionists' emphasis on observation paralleled the ideas of scientists and philosophers of the day, who posited that reality was only that which could be sensed, measured, and analyzed.

These three landscape paintings all depict the actual or implied presence of humans. In contrast, painters and photographers in the United States produced more images of pristine, untouched nature, where one could imagine that humans had never been. Ansel Adams was particularly well known for grand and romantic photographs of remote landscapes, like *Clearing Winter Storm, Yosemite National Park, California, 1944* (Fig. 14.15). In our example, the mist- and cloud-covered mountains are the focal point, while the texture of clouds and trees balance each other. The center seems to recede into infinite space.

Adams worked very hard exploring, studying, and waiting for just the right moment for his shot. In this case, the light caught the waterfall while the surrounding cliff was in dark shadow. Finally, Adams manipulated his prints in the darkroom to achieve the full range of tones, from brilliant white to darkest black. His splendid photographs raised public support for national parks and for the environmental movement in general.

Flowers and Gardens

Art gives us framed, composed, distilled, and transcendent images of flowers. And gardens are living sculptures, exotic refuges arranged for human enjoyment. Water is frequently a central motif in a garden of any size. Paintings of gardens attempt to capture that same sense of pleasure and release.

Flowers are sources of beauty and are often used symbolically. This section's focus figure is Jan Bruegel's *A Stoneware Vase of Flowers*, 1607–8 (Fig. 14.16). This joyful display of vitality is filled not only with the fresh flowers but also with insects that abound. Bruegel layered his paint to create bright, subtle mixtures that captured the silkiness and translucency of petals. He claimed that they were lovelier than gold and gems, proving it with rings and jewels at the lower right. Bruegel's flower arrangements never existed in real life. He combined local meadow flowers and

14.14 CLAUDE MONET. *Water Lily Pool*, France, 1900. Oil on canvas, 35″ × 39 ³/₄″. The Art Institute of Chicago.

Monet worked outdoors on his paintings in an effort to capture the color and brilliance of natural light.

14.15 ANSEL ADAMS. *Clearing Winter Storm, Yosemite National Park, California, 1944*, USA.

Landscapes can imply the presence of humans or can suggest a pristine space where no one has been before, as with this photograph.

exotic varieties in a single vase and included specimens that bloom in different climates and in different seasons. Yet he painted only from life, using a magnifying glass, sometimes waiting months for a certain bloom. Bruegel's flower paintings are like little pictures of paradise. Since medieval times, flowers had been sacred symbols: the iris, for example, represented Jesus, while the rose stood for Mary. The symbolism may have enriched the meaning of the painting for Bruegel's patrons.

Flower paintings were particularly popular in both China and Japan. (In fact, in Japan, flower arranging is considered an important art form, on the level of painting, calligraphy, and pottery.) An example from China is *Apricot Blossoms*, dated early thirteenth century

14.16 JAN BRUEGEL. *A Stoneware Vase of Flowers*, c.1607–8. Oil on Panel, 23.75″ × 16.5″. Fitzwilliam Museum, University of Cambridge, UK/The Bridgeman Art Library

This bouquet is realistic in detail but not in the grouping of flowers, because the blossoms shown here come from various places and bloom in different seasons.

(Fig. 14.17), by Ma Yuan, a lyric painting with lines of poetry by Empress Yang, which read: "They greet the wind with artful charm;/Boasting pink beauty moist with dew." Ma Yuan's brushwork is refined. The blossoms are outlined in elegant curves, while the ink strokes that make the branch are crisp and angular. The twisting branches bend and display themselves in an off-balance, irregular composition that captures the unexpected forms in nature. Branch and poem both seem to be suspended in the space. The rich golden background and the delicate blossoms contrast with the dark branch. The beauty of the blossoms is simple and timeless, but the flowers last only a short time.

Ma Yuan was a professional court painter who collaborated with Empress Yang on other works as well. Such painters produced many small works, with poems penned by the emperor or his circle, to be given away as gifts and favors. Both poetry and painting were believed to have the capacity to express ineffable beauty. Ink wash paintings look simple, but they require long practice. Also, artists

had to know how to paint the essence of apricot blossoms, to suggest the whole experience of the short-lived blooms, including their smell and their movement in the wind. It is interesting to compare the kinds of painting skills required of Ma Yuan and Jan Bruegel, as each composed their works.

Gardens also often carry symbolic and philosophical meaning, just as paintings of flowers do. For example, gardens were very popular among the ruling classes of Persia, central Asia, and Mughal India, all areas under Islamic rulers (these areas are modern-day Iraq, Iran, Afghanistan, Pakistan, and northern India). The painting, *Babur Supervising the Layout of the Garden of Fidelity*, c. 1590 (Fig. 14.18), illustrates many key concepts of Islamic gardens that represent Paradise. Water is channeled in four directions, representing the rivers of Paradise. The four resulting squares can be repeated or subdivided and yet maintain the integrity of the original layout. The proliferation of squares represents the abundance of Allah's

14.17 MA YUAN. *Apricot Blossoms*, China, Southern Song Dynasty, early 13th century. Album leaf with ink and color on silk, 10′ high. National Palace Museum, Taiwan.

This painting was not done from direct observation, but from memory after the artist had repeatedly practiced the necessary brushstrokes.

14.18 BISHNDAS (PORTRAITS BY NANHA). *Babur Supervising the Layout of the Garden of Fidelity*, India, c. 1590. Manuscript painting, gold and gouache on paper, 8 ³/₄″ × 5 ³/₄″. Mughal. Victoria and Albert Museum, London.

Mughal gardens have great religious and political symbolism.

creation. The outer wall provides privacy and protects the trees and birds from surrounding desert. The English word *paradise* comes originally from ancient Persian words for "walled garden."

Babur Supervising the Layout of the Garden of Fidelity is a book illumination from the memoirs of Emperor Babur, a botanist who took great interest in planning many gardens throughout the lands that he ruled. Here, he is dressed in gold and is directing engineers and workmen. For Babur, the gardens helped establish his identity and secure his power. Originally a minor prince, he conquered much of central Asia and northern India, claimed to descend from Genghis Khan and Tamerlane (Timur), and established gardens, which was a prerogative of princes. In

addition, Babur believed his rule created order out of the chaos, and the garden's symmetry was a sign of that.

CONNECTION Review the discussion of the Taj Mahal (Fig. 9.20, page 256) for more on Islamic gardens symbolizing Paradise.

In comparison, the Japanese have different traditions for gardens. One kind of Japanese garden is planned around a pond or lake, and features rocks, winding paths, and bridges to delight the viewers with ever-changing vistas. A second tradition is exemplified in the *Ryoanji*

Zen Garden of Contemplation, c. 1488–1499 (Fig. 14.19), in a courtyard of a Buddhist temple in Kyoto. The rock garden reflects Zen Buddhist beliefs that the world is full of change and disorder, but meditation can lead to an understanding of the oneness of the universe. Visitors do not walk through the garden, but sit along the edge meditating on the raked quartz gravel that represents the void both of the universe and of the mind, while the dark rocks represent material substances and worldly events that float through those voids. The garden also represents an ocean journey, with gravel raked to signify waves and boulders now standing for mountains. The fifteen large rocks, each of a distinctive shape and outline, are arranged such that visitors can see only fourteen at once from any angle. The fifteenth can be seen through the mind's eye after spiritual enlightenment. The *Ryoanji Zen Garden of Contemplation* is small, but because the largest boulder is at the front and the smaller at the back, there is an optical illusion of greater depth.

Earthworks and Site Pieces

The earth itself and natural phenomena can become sculptural materials. *The Lightning Field*, 1971–1977 (Fig. 14.20), by Walter De Maria, is this section's focus figure. The work consists of a large, flat plain surrounded by mountains in New Mexico, and four hundred stainless steel poles arranged in a rectangular grid measuring one kilometer by one mile. *The Lightning Field* requires some effort and endurance on the part of viewers. It is remotely located, and to see it, a visitor must get permission from the Dia Foundation, which commissioned the work. Once on-site, the viewer waits for whatever happens. On clear days, the shiny, pointed poles catch the sun and glow against the natural vegetation. On stormy days, an occasional bolt of lightning may strike a pole, creating a fleeting, but dramatic, visual effect. *The Lightning Field* is better known through photographs that document it in different conditions than it is by actual experience. In this respect, the work is also a conceptual piece, existing primarily in the mind of the viewer, who contemplates the contrast between constructed and natural elements, the slow passage of time in the desolate environment, and the imagined experience of the work as known through various photographs.

Contemporary **earthworks** are large-scale environmental pieces in which the earth is an important component. Earthwork artists not only use natural materials but also are responsive to their sites. The monumental scale of their work is an attribute of both ancient and modern art. There is a minimalist emphasis on simple shapes. Robert Smithson's *Spiral Jetty*, 1970 (Fig. 14.21), was made

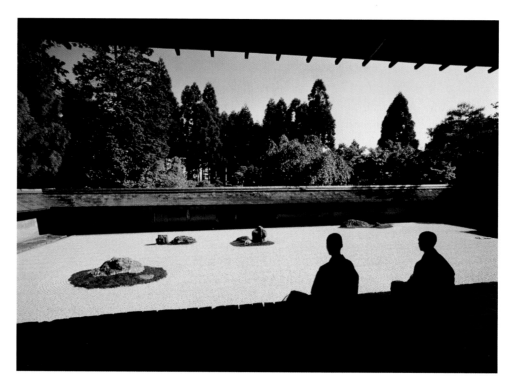

14.19 *Ryoanji Zen Garden of Contemplation*, Japan, c. 1488–1499. Walled garden, 99′ wide × 33′ deep. Daijuin Monastery, Kyoto.

This garden is not meant to be entered, but to be contemplated from the side.

14.20 WALTER DE MARIA. *The Lightning Field*, USA, 1971–1977. Four hundred stainless steel poles, average height: 20′ 7″; land area: 1 mile × 1 kilometer in New Mexico.

This work of art incorporates the ground, the sky, and weather activity.

of rocks, dirt, salt, and water, extending into the flat, still surface of the Great Salt Lake. Smithson thought the spiral suggested an incredible potential force, like a dormant earthquake or a raging cyclone immobilized. Located in a remote site, *Spiral Jetty* was seen by few people and now is often invisible because of the rising lake level.

Smithson was interested in moving his art outside of the gallery and away from traditional art materials. He saw his earthworks as unifying art and nature. Human design is, of course, evident in this work. Less evident is what went into making the piece, which involved heavy earth-moving equipment, engineering skills, and many workers.

Smithson was also influenced by the mound builders of native North American cultures, who used dirt to construct large ceremonial sites. Mounds and pyramids were relatively common in the ancient world, but the North

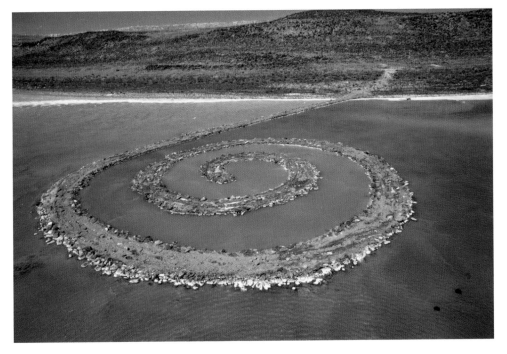

14.21 ROBERT SMITHSON. *Spiral Jetty*, USA, 1970. Earthwork; black rocks, salt crystals, earth, red water (algae), 1,500′ long × 15′ wide × 3 1/2′ high. Great Salt Lake, Utah.

Courtesy James Cohan Gallery, New York. Art . Estate of Robert Smithson/Licensed by VAGA, New York.

Rocks were moved and dirt shaped to create this massive earthwork.

American mounds are unique in being animal-shaped, like the *Serpent* (or *Snake*) *Mound*, c. 900–1300 (Fig. 14.22), in Ohio. The serpent's body follows a natural ridge near a small river. The distended jaw of the 1,400-foot-long serpent is pointing to the upper right. Its body is rhythmically curved and ends with its spiraling tail. In 1846, the snake's body was five feet high and thirty feet wide, but it has since eroded to four feet by twenty feet. An oval shape inside the serpent's jaw, measuring almost 79 by 158 feet, encircles a plateau topped with what may have been a stone altar. The builders must have had a great admiration for the snake to stamp its form so dramatically on their landscape, especially since they never enjoyed an aerial view of it. Like Smithson's *Spiral Jetty*, the *Serpent Mound* required the labor of many workers to dig and carry earth to the site.

Ecological Concerns

Artists who deal with the land and with landscape often have ecological concerns as part of their motivation to make art. We already saw this with Ansel Adams' *Clearing Winter Storm, Yosemite National Park, California, 1944* (Fig. 14.19). And very possibly the creators of the *Serpent Mound* (Fig. 14.22) believed that the land was sacred.

Today, however, ecological concerns are clearly political and social issues. *The Social Mirror*, 1983 (Fig. 14.23), by Mierle Laderman Ukeles, focuses on the problem of waste caused by growing populations and consumerism. Ukeles had a clean New York City garbage truck fitted with gleaming mirrors, which transform it into a piece of sculpture. *The Social Mirror* also has a performance element, as in this photograph taken when the truck was part of a parade. The mirrors reflect the faces of the public, making them aware that they make trash and are responsible for its impact. The mirrors also glamorize the garbage truck and raise the status of sanitation workers, whose labor is not respected but is absolutely necessary. All of Ukeles's work since the mid-1970s has focused on ecological issues of maintenance, recycling, waste management, and landfill reclamation.

KNOWLEDGE

Humans systematically study and examine the world in an attempt to understand (and often control) its course. Although all art is a kind of knowing, this section focuses on art that deals directly with a body of knowledge. The first group consists of informative images, in which art helps explain a specific body of learning. The second group

14.22 *Serpent* (or *Snake*) *Mound*, near Locust Grove, Ohio, c. 900–1300. Earthen sculpture, 1,400' long. Native American.

Ancient earthworks were either mounds or in this case were shaped into animal forms.

14.23 MIERLE LADERMAN UKELES. *The Social Mirror*, USA, 1983. A 20-cubic-yard New York City garbage collection truck fitted with hand-tempered glass mirror with additional strips of mirrored acrylic. The New York City Department of Sanitation.

This garbage truck reflects back to the people the image of themselves, to make them aware that they generate the trash of New York City.

provides glimpses into areas of intuited knowing. Finally, art critiques what we consider knowledge.

These same ideas—scientific knowledge, intuited knowledge, or critiqued knowledge—are found in other fields of knowledge and artistic disciplines. And like artists, many in these fields came to question the use of knowledge for destructive purposes after the horrible wars of the twentieth century (see *History Focus*, page 399).

Informative Images

There are numerous examples of art that illustrate a specific body of knowledge. Our focus figure is from the Low Countries in 1543. There, Andreas Vesalius of Brussels published *De Humani Corporis Fabrica*, a study of bones, muscles, and internal organs based on the dissection of human bodies, which is considered the beginning of modern science. Before that time, Western knowledge of the human body was based on ancient Greek, Roman, and medieval Arabic writings. Vesalius's studies corrected errors in old sources and added a tremendous amount of new knowledge. Important here, however, is that Vesalius created a major work of Western science and art.

The Fourth Plate of Muscles, dated 1543 (Fig. 14.24), shows that Vesalius gradually stripped the cadaver's outer

14.24 ANDREAS VESALIUS OF BRUSSELS. *The Fourth Plate of Muscles*, Flanders, published in 1543. Engraving from *De Humani Corporis Fabrica*.

This is a work of anatomical science and a work of art. It also reflects attitudes about human nature that were prevalent at that time.

muscles, but left them partly attached to make clear their relationship to deeper muscles just exposed. Nonetheless, the body is standing as if alive and turning on one leg, because Vesalius wanted to show the living, moving body instead of the separated parts of the dead. Altogether, eight plates of muscles make a lurid and fascinating narrative of dismemberment. In *The First Plate of Muscles*, the body stands like a classic statue, with an aura of grandeur mixed with a sense of pathos. Our *Fourth Plate* is both fascinating and horrible. By the time we arrive at the seventh and eighth plates, the disjointed cadaver is dangling on ropes. The works comment both on the wonder of the human body and on its inevitable disintegration.

De Humani Corporis Fabrica is a collaborative work. Vesalius created sketches and notes, which other artists polished. An unknown artist drew the landscape backgrounds, and an unknown professional made the engravings. Another famous illustrated study, also a collaborative work, is John James Audubon's *Birds of America*, a very large book that contained 435 plates. Robert Havell Jr. made most of the printing plates from Audubon's original watercolor studies.

Birds of America is an outstanding work, both artistically and scientifically. *Carolina Paroquet*, 1827–1838 (Fig. 14.25), shows several birds in scientific detail, with all the markings and in their habitat. Audubon eliminated the background to emphasize the birds' defining silhouettes. The birds are arranged in two arcs, one that echoes and one that opposes the direction of the main branch. The entire work is a decorative pattern that is enhanced by the bright colors.

Drawings in the service of science continue to be made. Even though photography might seem to be an adequate substitute for them, artist drawings can emphasize details that either do not stand out in photographs or become lost in the wealth of detail. Medical books are still enhanced with drawings, and medical illustrations are essential aids for study. Drawings also are used in studies of plants and insects and for very small items.

For comparison, look at a painting that is meant to be an educational aid. *Hunter and Kangaroo*, c. twentieth century (Fig. 14.26), is from the Aboriginal people of Australia. The painting on bark shows the instant that the hunter's spear is about to enter the animal. The animal is shown in x-ray style, meaning that both external silhouette and internal organs are evident, to assist the hunter with the kill. We can see the kangaroo's backbone, heart, and intestines. The kangaroo is larger than the hunter, because it is the subject of the painting. This work, and others like it on bark and on the walls of cave shelters, was meant to be

14.25 JOHN JAMES AUDUBON. *Carolina Paroquet*, USA, 1827–1838. Watercolor, 29 $\frac{1}{2}$″ × 21 $\frac{1}{4}$″. Original for Plate #26 of *Birds of America*. North Carolina Museum of Art.

Audubon's work on birds in North America is still a valuable research resource today.

educational and, perhaps, ritually powerful. The hunter's body implies movement and energy. The specific form of cross-hatching associated paintings with individual clans and endowed the painted objects with spiritual force.

CONNECTION Other Aboriginal paintings transmit knowledge from one clan member to another, as we saw in Paddy Carroll Tjungurrayi's *Witchetty Grub Dreaming* (Fig. 6.5, page 135).

Some works of art are experiential in a way that is both conceptually interesting and educational. For example, the Optical Art (or **Op Art**) style was popular in the United States and Europe in the 1960s. Bridget Riley's *Current*, 1964 (Fig. 14.27), is a precisely painted pattern of undulating lines that affect our visual perception. The work seems to pulsate and flicker, similar to experiments by psychologists who test the limits of visual perception to better

14.26 *Hunter and Kangaroo*, Australia, c. 20th century. Paint on bark, 51″ × 32″. Aboriginal. Oenpelli, Arnhemland. Private collection, Prague.

This is a work of art as well as an educational diagram about kangaroo anatomy.

14.27 BRIDGET RILEY. *Current*, Great Britain, 1964. Synthetic polymer paint on composition board, approx. 58 ¹/₂″ × 58 ¹/₂″. The Museum of Modern Art, New York.

This pattern reveals aspects of how the human eye works.

 CONNECTION Georges Seurat also relied on the science of optics in his work *La Grande Jatte* (Fig. 13.29, page 392).

understand how our vision works. The painting is also related to mathematics, as each line is a sinusoidal curve, in which the interval between each dip increases as your eyes move away from the central horizontal axis. *Current* makes evident that our vision is physiological, because our eyes tire and hurt if we stare at the image too long. Its large size means that, up close, the work encompasses our entire visual field, both the sharp foveal vision at the center and our peripheral vision at the edges.

Art and Intuited Knowledge

For humans, the world consists not only of the external environment but also of the internal realm of the mind and the metaphysical world. Art also deals with knowledge that humans can intuitively grasp without necessarily being able to articulate it. This kind of knowing is the product of dreams, visions, and speculative guessing. It is not necessarily systematic, organized, or scientific.

Surrealism was an early-twentieth-century art movement in Europe and the United States that explored the unconscious, especially through dream imagery. Surrealism developed in part as a reaction to increased industrialization and to the horrors of World War I (see *History Focus*, page 399). Surrealists posited that this unconscious or dream world is at least as real as, and probably more important than, the ordered and regimented external world in which humans function. This is evident in our focus figure, *The Persistence of Memory*,

1931 (Fig. 14.28), by Salvador Dalí. For example, watches are devices of knowing and a means of maintaining external order. However, here the watches are limp and useless. The landscape stretches out, vast and empty. The sky glows in splendid blues and golds, while the still water reflects the sun-bathed cliffs like a flawless mirror. Nothing makes sense, but Dalí has painted everything with rigorous detail and convincing realism so that book-learned knowledge fades in importance, and we enter the eerie scene with a kind of intuited knowing. Swarming ants and a fly allude to the horror dimension in dreams.

CONNECTION For more on artwork that is inspired by mental and emotional states of mind, see Chapter 12, *Body and Mind*, especially the sections on Portraits and Self-Portraits (pages 336–346), as well as The Psychological Dimension in Art (pages 353–356).

The Critique of Learning

Gods of the Modern World, 1932–1934 (Fig. 14.29), painted by José Clemente Orozco, is the focus figure for this

14.28 SALVADOR DALÍ. *The Persistence of Memory*, Spain, 1931. Oil on canvas, 9 1/2" × 13". Museum of Modern Art, New York.

Surrealism presents dreams, intuition, and visions as a kind of knowledge.

14.29 JOSÉ CLEMENTE OROZCO. *Gods of the Modern World*, Mexico, 1932–1934. Fresco, 126" × 176". Twelfth panel in a cycle of murals entitled *An Epic of American Civilization*. Baker Memorial Library, Dartmouth College, Hanover, New Hampshire.

The artist Orozco presents the argument against the pursuit of sterile knowledge.

section on art that looks critically at human knowledge. This painting is a warning against the academic who is completely occupied with sterile research or learning that has no value outside of academia. The black-clad university scholars line up like midwives to watch a skeleton give birth to miniature scholar-skeletons and stacks of obscure books. Orozco believed that sterile education passes for knowledge, but it actually keeps the young busy without giving them any real wisdom or understanding. The lurid red background suggests urgency, as if the world is on fire, but no guidance or concern can be found among the learned. Their posture is aloof, frontal, stiff, and unresponsive. The style of the work is very striking. The rhythm of the lines is strong, from the verticals of the academic robes, to the black and white of the skeleton's ribs, to the swaying parade of book spines below. Significantly, this painting is in the library of a prestigious U.S. college, to be seen by all students and professors.

Compare Orozco's painting with *Breaking of the Vessels*, 1990 (Fig. 14.30), through which artist Anselm Kiefer looks at knowledge on many different levels. The piece consists of a three-tiered bookshelf filled with massive volumes whose pages are made of sheets of lead. The books sag perilously, some about to fall from the shelf. Glass shards from the books have fallen, and their shattering has covered the floor all around. Above, written on a half-circle of glass, are the Hebrew words *Ain Soph*, meaning "the Infinite." Dangling copper wires connect thick stumps projecting from the sides. The piece is seventeen feet high and weighs more than seven tons. The shattered glass covers several square yards of floor all around.

The piece contrasts the infinity and clarity of the spiritual realm with the thick, dull, ponderous containers of human knowledge. Human knowledge, as contained in and symbolized by the books, is limited and sagging under its own weight. Visually, the heavy lead pages are like the blackened pages of burned books. The knowledge contained within them seems inaccessible to most people; the book format hides knowledge rather than exposes it. The books seem as though they might even be rotting away, ready to crash to the floor. The sheer mass of the sculpture becomes a metaphor for the accumulated struggles to acquire and preserve human knowledge, but books and their contents disintegrate. The work alludes to the fact that all human endeavor is cyclical like nature; it is subject to periods of decline and entropy that eventually lead to regeneration.

The title *Breaking of the Vessels* refers to mystical Hebrew writings (the Kabbalah) that tell of the awesome, uncontainable Divine essence whose power filled and shattered the fragile vessels of the universe upon Creation.

14.30 Anselm Kiefer. *Breaking of the Vessels*, Germany, 1990. Lead, iron, glass, copper wire, charcoal, and aquatec, 17' high. St. Louis Art Museum.

Old books are not always storehouses of knowledge. They may make knowledge inaccessible, or they may rot and fall apart.

The title symbolizes the introduction of evil into the world. It also refers to the atrocities of *Kristallnacht* (the Night of Crystal or the Night of Broken Glass), when the Nazis vandalized and terrorized Jewish neighborhoods in Germany and Austria in November 1938.

14.31 FERNAND LÉGER. *The City*, France, 1919. Oil on canvas, 91″ × 117 1/2″. Philadelphia Museum of Art.

Industrialism and modernism has produced forms and shapes that artists have found exciting and innovative.

TECHNOLOGY

Technology is the last component of the outside world in this chapter. First we will see three artworks regard technological advances as good, healthy, exciting, and even aesthetically pleasing. The next group of three artworks evaluates our constructed world for both its positive and negative impacts.

Technological Advances

When considering technology today, we most likely think of the world since the Industrial Revolution of the nineteenth century and more recent developments in transportation, manufacturing, and communication. Technology advanced rapidly in the early twentieth century, causing cities to expand and producing structures in shapes and sizes never seen before. Particularly striking were bridges, factories, skyscrapers, ocean liners, and fast trains. Our focus figure is *The City*, dated 1919 (Fig. 14.31), by Fernand Léger, an artist who was influenced by **Cubism**. This painting suggests the newness and excitement of geometric industrial structures and the precision and efficiency of machines, all of which struck Léger as forms of beauty. The city of Léger's painting is rendered in abstract forms but speaks of its concrete, steel, electrical power, and transportation systems. The repetition of colors and shapes suggests the staccato of city sounds. Letterforms refer to

billboard advertisements. The colors are bright and artificial. Other shapes resemble a jumble of roofs and walls, bridge trestles, or factory smokestacks. Even humans are robotlike, as their bodies are composed of geometric volumes. The space seems shallow, as all forms are compressed and pushed forward, in contrast to the open horizon and distant spaces in paintings of rural scenes.

Yet technology has long been part of human history and has often made life easier, as we can see in comparing *Bird Hunt and Preservation; Grape Harvest and Winemaking,* a series of wall paintings from the Tomb of Nakht at Thebes, Egypt (Fig. 14.32). Nets, wine presses, and ceramic jugs, all the product of ancient technologies, help in the processing of food and creating the sense of plenty pervading these scenes. Figures are arranged in an orderly fashion, using their handcrafted tools, giving a sense of cooperation arising from human labor, human technology, and nature. Paintings from all over the world record similar scenes. Two examples from Japan alone that we have already seen in this book are *Uji Bridge* (Fig. 13.31), with the water wheel in the foreground, and *The Printmaker's Workshop* (Fig. 3.14), showing women producing woodblock prints using cutters, rollers, and other tools.

David Smith's *Cubi XXVI*, 1965 (Fig. 14.33), is abstract art imitating some qualities of machines. Smith used industrial fabrication to create this stainless steel sculpture and others in this series. He learned this technology as a factory worker. His works are marked by a machine

14.32 *Bird hunt and preservation; grape harvest and wine making.* Wallpainting from the tomb of Nakht in Thebes, Egypt; 18th dynasty (1540–1300 BCE). Copy by Francis Sydney Unwin, 1915. Photo: Knud Petersen. Location: Tomb of Nakht, Sheikh Abd el-Qurna, Tombs of the Nobles, Thebes, Egypt

Simple technologies have long been part of human life.

14.33 DAVID SMITH. *Cubi XXVI*, USA, 1965. Steel, approx. 10′ × 12′ 6″ × 2′ 3″. Alisa Mellon Bruce Fund. Image © National Gallery of Art, Washington, D.C. Art . David Smith/Licensed by VAGA, New York, NY.

The materials and processes of industry were used to make this geometric sculpture.

14.34 Joseph Mallord William Turner. *The Fighting Temeraire Tugged to Her Last Berth to Be Broken Up*, England, 1838. Oil on canvas, 35 1/4″ × 48″. The National Gallery, London.

New technology regularly replaces the old, but the artist asks whether this represents actual progress or mere innovation.

aesthetic, and thus his processes and materials are the same as those that would be used to make a locomotive. The large, geometric shapes of stainless steel cubes, rectangles, and cylinders look machine-manufactured, with clean edges, flawless welding, and precise fits. They resemble mass-produced items. The structure, unsoftened, is bluntly emphasized. Strong, balanced forms seem to defy their weight. The metal surfaces, however, were abraded to give them a spiral pattern that seems to dissolve the solidity of the volumes. Smith emphasized gesture, so that the sculpture seems to be striding along, like an animated stick figure of a walking person. The forms suggest vectors in space, some in opposition to others. The work also suggests forces suspended and in movement, like components of a machine.

Evaluating the Constructed World

We have already seen Ukeles's *Social Mirror*, which dealt with consumerism and its impact on the land. The following artists present technology to us in a way that makes clear its mixed impact.

The focus figure is *The Fighting Temeraire Tugged to Her Last Berth to Be Broken Up*, 1838 (Fig. 14.34). In it, Joseph Mallord William Turner distinguishes between innovation and progress. He painted the tall, shimmering, white form of the elegant sailing vessel against the new powerful tugboat, which is squat, dark, and smoky. By this time, sailing vessels were obsolete for war or commerce, superseded by more modern technology. Turner marked the *Temeraire*'s passing by the splendid glowing sunset (marred by the tug's smoke!)—both ship and sunset were soon to be lost forever. Turner was famous for his facility with paint; thick blobs become an array of golden clouds, brushy strokes blend where mist meets blue sky. The scene is a conflict between light and darkness, and light is just about to be eclipsed.

Without a doubt, Turner was romanticizing archaic technology, responding to the latest innovation that seemed ugly to him. He painted this work in his old age, as a sign of his own life drawing to a close. The beautiful colors and expressive handling of the paint convey the poignant feeling of beauty and loss, transforming an otherwise nondescript harbor scene along the Thames River in London into a picture of poetic beauty.

Compare Turner's sense of loss with the humor and absurdity of Jean Tinguely's *Homage to New York*, 1960 (Fig. 14.35). The work looked like a whimsical machine. Tinguely constructed it with the help of an engineer, using junkyard machine parts. It was designed to destroy itself

14.35 JEAN TINGUELY. *Homage to New York: A Self-Constructing, Self-Destructing Work of Art*, Switzerland, 1960. Mixed-media sculpture. Photograph of the work as it self-destroyed in New York City on March 17, 1960.

To Tinguely, machines have a comic dimension. They never perform exactly as expected, and their use always has unintended consequences.

in one evening in the gardens of the Museum of Modern Art in New York City, which it did, but not according to plan. A fire in some parts necessitated the unscheduled participation of the New York City Fire Department. Tinguely was mocking the machine, and yet celebrating it for qualities very different from Léger's *The City*. To Tinguely, the machine was not magnificent because of its clean design or its efficiency, but for its unexpected results. Machines never work in exactly the way that we expect them to, nor can we anticipate all the results of using them. Tinguely's satirical work references the frenzy of the machine age and, by extension, the city of New York at that time, which in some ways could be seen as a large machine, absurd in its size, complexity, haphazard workings, and entertainment value.

> **CONNECTION** *Homage to New York* was both an environmental sculpture and a happening. For more on such works, see the sections "Engaging All the Senses" and "Chance/Improvisation/Spontaneity" in Chapter 2.

For us now, technology includes computers and televisions. For nearly forty years, artist Nam June Paik has been exploring what that means and its impact on us as humans. *Megatron*, 1995 (Fig. 14.36), is composed of more than two hundred video screens divided into two groups, displaying video clips, digital distortions, and animation sequences. Paik's images are from high and popular culture, from East and West, and include scenes from the Olympic Games, experimental art events, rock concerts, and Korean rituals as well as sexual images, scenes of aggression, and, sometimes, simply a wall of white screens or a display of national flags. Visually, the piece is very dense, as images are juxtaposed or tumble one after another. Pictures are even nested inside each other, as can be seen in the upper left, in which the large shape of a flying bird is composed of smaller images. *Megatron*'s visual assault is matched by the cacophonous sound track. Yet over time, the piece may have a lulling or perhaps hypnotic effect.

The viewer is restricted to the role of spectator, dwarfed and essentially silenced by the forceful presence of *Megatron*. The accumulation of screens and the large size of *Megatron* speak of the imposing presence of the mass media in everyday life, a feature in the home, in business, in sports, in entertainment, in commerce, and so on, where again the viewer is a spectator only. The making of *Megatron* was a technological feat, as images are fed by laser disc players and controlled by seven computers in such a way that sequences rarely repeat. In this way, the piece reflects our everyday lives, in which we are bombarded by disjointed but familiar images while flipping through television channels, zipping past freeway billboards at sixty-five miles per hour, or surfing the Internet.

This piece and others by Paik are about the act of perception, how reality is presented, and how we as viewers reintegrate the random images. To Paik, the recombinations and dislocations of images are potentially playful and constructive. He sees his pieces as creative ways of thinking about the reshaping of our lives and becoming engaged in the diversity and variety in contemporary culture.

14.36 NAM JUNE PAIK, in collaboration with Shuya Abe. *Megatron* (three views), Korea, 1995. Eight-channel video and two-channel sound installation in two parts, overall size 12′ × 33′ × 2′. Courtesy Holly Solomon Gallery, New York.

Technology provides us with a nonstop barrage of information, music, and image snippets, which can be recombined and experienced in infinite numbers of arrangements.

15

ENTERTAINMENT AND VISUAL CULTURE

The art in this chapter is intertwined with the performing arts, popular culture, and entertainment. Historically, the overlap among those categories has been common. Today, the field of Visual Culture studies them together.

PREVIEW

This chapter begins by examining buildings designed to enhance the enjoyment of leisure activities, such as concerts, sporting events, and exhibitions. Next are art objects that depict musical performers, dancers, or athletes. Then we look at the many ways that art is interwoven with theatrical productions. Afterward, we turn our attention to artworks that are props or instruments in theater, music, or dance performances.

The chapter concludes with a look at the premises of **Visual Culture***, the academic field that examines areas of culture that rely on visual images. This provides the opportunity to consider some issues at the intersection of contemporary art, television, comics, video games, movies, and video art. Computer technology especially has blurred the boundaries among all categories of visual images. Also, an artwork may borrow some qualities from movies or amusement parks, evident in the immersive aspects of the museum installation in Figure 15.1, which shows one scene from Pipilotti Rist's sixteen-minute-long looping video,* Pour Your Body Out (7354 Cubic Meters), *from 2008–2009. Popular culture also borrows from and is influenced by art.*

Art and History in Context,
1950 CE–PRESENT

The contemporary era is marked by international tensions that create great rifts in the world fabric, while at the same time advances in information technology begin to make a global community possible.

At the end of World War II, the United States and the Soviet Union emerged as competing superpowers. The Cold War (1950–1991) saw a massive arms buildup, pitting the United States and western Europe against the Soviet Union and its eastern European satellites. Communist China was the third major force. Tensions among the major powers spawned protracted regional wars in Korea and Vietnam. Television brought these world conflicts directly into people's homes in industrialized nations.

Cold war competition also centered on technology and culture. Technological superiority was sought in the arms race and the race for space (moon landings, satellites, and space stations). The United States emphasized art of individual self-expression over art made in service of the state, such as the social realism of the Soviet bloc and China. Some key qualities in U.S. art at this time can be seen in Barnett Newman's *Broken Obelisk* (Fig. 15.2), with its abstraction, simplified form, grand scale, and tension in balance that seems so perfect and at the same time so precarious.

With its oil riches, ethnic conflicts, and religious wars, the Middle East has been another major source of global unrest (see Map 10). The Arab-Israeli conflict is ongoing, dating from 1947. The independence of Hindu India and the creation of Moslem Pakistan produced tensions that are still present. An Islamic revival and resistance to Western culture have resulted in the mixing of religion and civil government, seen, for example, in the fundamentalist revolution in Iran. The unrest has spread, causing such events as the destruction of the World Trade Center, bombings and violence in Indonesia, and the wars in Iraq and Afghanistan.

The 1950s and 1960s brought big political changes to Africa and Latin America. In Latin America, dictatorships were common throughout the 1950s and 1960s; some were replaced later with democracies. Revolutions, coups, and civil wars occurred in many countries, including Cuba, Chile, El Salvador, and

Map 10, Location of the world's oil reserves.

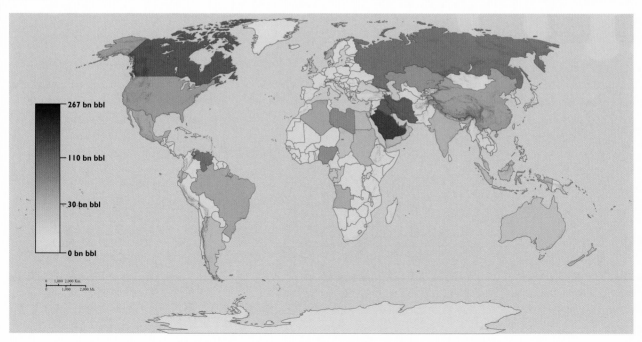

267 bn bbl

110 bn bbl

30 bn bbl

0 bn bbl

Argentina. The 1960s saw the founding of modern African states.

This era also brought economic changes. In 1975, China began a program to become a major manufacturer of goods and electronics and became an important economic force in the world. Meanwhile, after 1991, the Soviet bloc disintegrated, and the Communist system was discarded or modified. Elsewhere, open trade agreements, such as the European Union and the North American Free Trade Agreement (NAFTA), exist in many areas. The World Trade Organization (WTO), created in 1994, is an international body that enforces trade treaties and laws. The global trade community has created opportunities as well as conflicts, economic hardships, and environmental problems.

For nations like the United States, this is the postindustrial era. While most traditional industrial production is overseas, other forms of capitalism,

like the entertainment industry, are growing in importance, starting as long ago as early movies as well as television productions like *I Love Lucy* (Fig. 15.30). Tourism supports many art, cultural, and entertainment sites around the world. *Las Vegas, Nevada* (Figure 15.10) perhaps panders most blatantly to tourists.

The trend toward globalism continues, with events in one part of the world often having profound effects everywhere. Culture now can be and is exported globally, as with Miyazaki's *Spirited Away* (Fig. 15.32). By 1980, anthropologists could find no group of people on the entire planet who did not listen to radio. Nevertheless, older art forms continue, although modified, as with the *Asmat Hand Drum* (Fig. 15.25), Locke's *Open Circle Dance* (Fig. 15.26), and the *Kanaga Masked Dancers* (Fig. 15.27). In fact, older art forms often influence newer productions, such as the Broadway play *The Lion King* (Fig.

15.2 BARNETT NEWMAN. Broken Obelisk, 1963–1969. Cor-Ten steel, 24′ 10″ × 10′ 11″ × 10′ 11″ (749.9 × 318.8 × 318.8 cm). Given anonymously. The Museum of Modern Art, New York.

This is an example of the large, bold artworks produced in the United States during the Cold War era. The theme of this work is the balance between life and death forces, which is symbolically expressed through the pyramid and the obelisk.

15.21). Blockbuster exhibitions have brought the superstar phenomenon to art. Communication and computing technologies are converging. Digital technologies are the basis for writing, information access, sound-mixing, video editing, and still-image manipulation.

The global culture has brought changes to the natural world. AIDS and other new, quick-spreading diseases have caused alarm. With melting ice caps and destruction of rain forests and coastal habitats, the earth's environment is changing.

World Art Map for Chapter 15

Toulouse-Lautrec.
Jane Avril. Paris, France.

Judith Leyster.
Boy Playing a Flute.

Kevin Locke. *Open Circle Dance.*
South Dakota, United States.

NORTH AMERICA

Frank King. *Gasoline Alley.*

Pipilotti Rist. *Pour Your Body Out (7354 Cubic Meters).*

Morton Feldman, Merce Cunningham,
Robert Rauschenberg, and John Cage. *Summerspace.*

Matthew Barney. *Cremaster 1: The Goodyear Chorus.*

Barnett Newman. *Broken Obelisk.*
Frank Lloyd Wright. *Solomon R. Guggenheim Museum.*
Frederick Law Olmsted and Calvert Vaux. *Central Park.*
Julie Taymor. *Scene from The Lion King.*
Allan Kaprow. *Household, May 1964.*

EUROPE

Baths of Caracalla.

Adam Jones. *Las Vegas, 2004.*

I Love Lucy.
Frank Gehry. *Walt Disney Concert Hall.*

Colosseum.
Polykleitos. *Theater at Epidauros.*

Ball Players.

Great Ball Court.
Chichén Itzá, Mexico.

Maria Candelaria.

*Kanaga
Masked Dancers.*
Mali, Africa.

Acrobat.
Mexico City, Mexico.

SOUTH AMERICA

N

| 0 | 1,000 | 2,000 Km. |
| 0 | 1,000 | 2,000 Mi. |

Harp Player. Cycladic Islands, Greece.

Bull Jumping.

Lyre. Ur, Iraq.

Musicians and Dancers. Thebes, Egypt.

ASIA

Hayao Miyazaki. *Spirited Away.* Tokyo, Japan.

Bunraku.

Hakone Open Air Museum. Hakone National Park, Japan.

AFRICA

Asmat Hand Drum. Southwest Asmat Coast, Indonesia.

AUSTRALIA

Jörn Utzon. *Sydney Opera House.* Sydney, Australia

1950 CE–PRESENT

2685 BCE	Lyre
2500	Harp Player

Pipes and chimes in Chinese tombs

Bull Jumping

1400	Musicians and Dancers
1000	Acrobat

Above Lamassu, Assyria (10.10)

CLASSICAL GREEK ERA | **400** | POLYKLEITOS: *Theater at Epidauros*

Early museum— Alexandria

100

Three orchestras/ 829 members— Han Dynasty

70 CE	Colosseum
100	
200	Baths of Caracalla

Roman art placed in baths, temples, gardens, villas, and forums

Early theater in India based on Sanskrit epics

Chinese Opera in the Tang Dynasty

900

GOTHIC ERA

Noh theater—Japan

RENAISSANCE

Shakespeare, the Globe

Precolonial masquerades in Africa

BAROQUE ERA

Bunraku and Kabuki theater—Japan

Beginnings of modern museums

Opera at high point in Europe

Peking Opera

Zoetrope— precursor to film

Telegraph invented

First art museums in West

IMPRESSIONISM

POST-IMPRESSIONISM

Telephone lines installed in New England

First film screenings

SURREALISM

Hollywood—film capital

First commercial radio broadcast

1200	The Great Ball Court
	Ball Players
1600	LEYSTER: *Boy Playing a Flute*

Above FRAGONARD: The Swing (13.25)

1800	
1850	OLMSTED AND VAUX: *Central Park*
1870	
	TOULOUSE-LAUTREC: *Jane Avril*
1900	
1920	

Left timeline

Beginning of global music culture

KING: *Gasoline Alley*

1940

WRIGHT: *Solomon R. Guggenheim Museum*

Maria Candelaria (Xochimilco)

Television broadcasting begins

Cold war **1950** *Asmat Hand Drum*

ABSTRACT EXPRESSIONISM

Color television and color movies

Korean War

Space programs begin in U.S. and U.S.S.R. *I Love Lucy*

1960

End of European Colonies in Africa

MINIMALISM

NEWMAN: *Broken Obelisk*

UTZON: *Opera House,* Sydney

Hakone Open-Air Museum

FELDMAN, CUNNINGHAM, AND RAUSCHENBERG: *Summerspace*

FLUXUS KAPROW: *Household*

Kanaga Masked Dancers

Above Fuller: *U.S. Pavilion, Expo' 67* (6.37)

Vietnam War

Right timeline

POSTMODERNISM **1970**

Technological and Industrial Revolution—China **1980**

Above Lin: *Vietnam Veterans Memorial* (10.30)

TAYMOR: *The Lion King* **1990**

Operation Desert Storm

Above OLDENBURG, BRUGGEN, GEHRY. *Binocular Entrance— Chiat Building* (2.33)

Above ISOZAKI. *Nara Convention Hall* (3.12)

Expansion of the Las Vegas strip

Digital video

Internet BARNEY: *Cremaster 1: The Goodyear Chorus*

LOCKE: *Open Circle Dance*

War on terrorism **2000**

iPod introduced GEHRY: *Walt Disney Concert Hall*

MIYAZAKI: *Spirited Away*

RIST: *Pour Your Body Out*

ARCHITECTURE FOR ENTERTAINMENT

Art and architecture give visual form to cultural, athletic, and entertainment events. Structures must function well and comfortably accommodate their audiences. In addition, these spaces must meet the aesthetics, expectations, and values of the audience for the activities that happen inside. Sports, arts, and entertainment often have political or religious implications, or have meaning beyond one of simple leisure or game playing. Often, the structures that house them make these meanings clear.

"Houses" for the Arts

Our focus figure for this section is also the oldest, because it contains precedents for all auditoriums and **amphitheaters** that follow. Ancient Greek comedies and tragedies were originally part of ritual festivals dedicated to the deity Dionysos. They were first performed in natural settings, in the hollows of hills. Eventually, magnificent theaters were designed to add visual significance to these dramas, like the *Theater at Epidauros* (Fig. 15.3), designed by Polykleitos the Younger around 350 BCE. It is a theater of great size (387 feet in diameter) and formal grandeur that suggests the Classical Greek ideal shape, the circle. The *theatron*, or seating area, could accommodate 12,000 spectators on its fifty-five tiers of stone benches, which rise at a high angle for clear views and good acoustics for all. Stairs connect each section for easy access. At the very center was the orchestra platform, a circle in which the chorus would dance near or around the altar of Dionysos. Behind the orchestra is a long, rectangular structure used for the stage, backed by the **skene**, a building that provided a backdrop for the plays and contained dressing rooms and scenery. These ritual plays included music and dance, with actors wearing elaborate costumes with oversized masks to emphasize the characters' emotions and amplify their voices through megaphone-like mouths.

The stage and audience structure of the *Theater at Epidauros* continues to be used for the interior design of Western houses of the performing arts through the ages. However, the outside structure of these buildings reflects the values of their eras. Nineteenth-century houses for the arts often had ornate exteriors to emphasize their importance or to link them to the Classical heritage. Today, houses for the arts often reflect modern values of innovation, bold movement, or future potential. The *Opera House* (Fig. 15.4) in Sydney, Australia, stands on the harbor's edge to greet visitors arriving by air, land, or sea. The Danish architect Joern Utzon thought of it as "functional sculpture." Called **organic architecture**, this style was rooted in the work of Frank Lloyd Wright (see Fig. 15.5). Utzon was also influenced by the platform architecture of Mesoamerica. The cascading vaults suggest the billowing of the sailboats in Sydney Harbor, and they are faced with gleaming ceramic tile, adding jewel-like reflections to the fluid forms. Windows are covered by two laminated layers of amber glass, creating a quiet interior with spectacular views of the surrounding harbor. The concert halls, theaters, auditoriums, and recording studio are all lined with rich natural woods, both for aesthetics and acoustics.

15.3 POLYKLEITOS. *Theater at Epidauros*, Greece, c. 350 BCE. Hellenic Ministry of Culture.

The arrangement of the stage and the audience's seating has set the standard for most Western theaters and auditoriums.

15.4 JOERN UTZON. *Opera House*, Sydney, Australia, 1959–1972. Reinforced concrete; highest shell 200′ high.

The structure resembles billowing sails, like the ships in Sydney Harbor.

CONNECTION *The British Museum* (Fig. 5.20, page 116) is an example of a nineteenth-century house for the arts built to resemble a Greek temple.

Frank Lloyd Wright's *Solomon R. Guggenheim Museum* (Fig. 15.5) is another example of organic architecture, here designed to exhibit art. Its rounded form encloses a ramp that spirals around an empty center that is ninety feet wide. Certainly the museum creates a striking visual image. The viewer takes an elevator to the top and then walks down past individual bays with paintings, allowing closer focus on small groups of artworks. Yet, critics point out that this space does not work well for showing paintings and sculptures. Artwork can be seen only up close or from all the way across the central open well. There is no in-between vantage point, and some works suffer. Rather than choosing their own course, viewers must see the works in the predetermined order. Because the floor slopes, the exhibition space does not work well for sculptures, and paintings appear askew against the curved wall.

15.5 FRANK LLOYD WRIGHT. *Solomon R. Guggenheim Museum*, New York City, USA, design begun in 1943, structure completed in 1959.

This museum resembles a modern, abstract sculpture.

15.6 FRANK GEHRY. *Walt Disney Concert Hall*, USA, 2003. Los Angeles, California.

There is no single focal point in this concert hall design.

CONNECTION For a view of the inside of the Solomon R. Guggenheim Museum, see Jenny Holzer's installation *Untitled (Selected Writings)* in Figure 11.28, page 324.

Frank Gehry's *Walt Disney Concert Hall* (Fig. 15.6), 2003, in Los Angeles, is a recent entry among world-class music centers. Trained as a sculptor, Gehry creates buildings that are often irregular, colliding, sculptural, and perhaps even disorienting, because they are asymmetrical or have no apparent central point. The concert hall's structural systems are disguised under the curving stainless-steel surface. Gehry has said, "I approach each building as a sculptural object, a spatial container, a space with light and air, a response to context and appropriateness of feeling and spirit. To this container, this sculpture, the user brings his baggage, his program, and interacts with it to accommodate his needs. If he can't do that, I've failed" (www.pritzkerprize.com). Such architecture is called **Deconstructivist** because of its many unique viewpoints that do not coalesce into a unified whole. It is also **Neo-Modernist**, with its emphasis on abstract form.

Other Visual and Performing Art Environments

Throughout the ages, art spaces have been combined with structures that serve other uses. Ancient Greeks had art galleries near their temple complexes. In medieval churches in Europe, treasuries held precious artworks from nearby and far-off lands. Today, government buildings all over the world may contain galleries highlighting the artwork of the nation.

In the Roman Empire, many rulers spent public funds to build bathhouses, theaters, amphitheaters, circuses, arenas, and stadiums for the pleasure of their subjects, and they adorned those structures with art. At one time, Rome had more than nine hundred bathhouses, ranging from imperial baths to no-frills public baths, where Romans improved their health and socialized. Features included workout rooms, steam rooms, massage rooms, swimming pools, and warm, hot, and cold baths. Imperial baths boasted libraries, art galleries, restaurants, bars, gymnasiums, and shady walkways, and offered theater performances, public lectures, athletic contests, and so on. Excavations of bathhouse sites have revealed much ancient sculpture.

Our focus figure for this section is the *Baths of Caracalla* (Fig. 15.7), built between 211 and 217 by the emperor of the same name, which could serve 1,600 clients. Once covering fifty acres, even its ruins are still amazingly impressive. The baths had brick-faced concrete walls 140 feet high supporting the huge vaulted ceiling. It was an imperial bath, so the interior was palatial, decorated lavishly with stucco ceilings, marble facing, mosaic floors, and colossal statuary. The water for the baths came from the aqueduct, another brilliant Roman invention. Heated air circulated through hollow floors and walls to warm the rooms.

CONNECTION In the sixteenth century, the Greek sculpture *Laocoön and His Sons* (Fig. 12.18, page 344) was discovered buried in the ruins of an imperial Roman bath.

In the United States from the nineteenth century to today, the large city park offers a variety of diversions. *Central Park* (Fig. 15.8), in the middle of Manhattan, is a retreat from bustling New York City. With its artwork, performing spaces, and green setting, it is like the Roman *Baths of Caracalla*, but without the spa. The long, narrow park is considered an outstanding example of landscape architecture, and in 1965 it was declared a National Historic Landmark. Designers Frederick Law Olmsted and Calvert Vaux worked with the natural setting rather than completely reshaping it. Hog farms, open sewers, and hovels had to be removed before millions of flowers, trees, and shrubs could be planted. Trails, roads, and bridges

15.7, left *Baths of Caracalla*. As reconstructed in the hand-colored engraving of a 19th-century illustration, *Citizens of ancient Rome enjoying the Baths of Caracalla.*

This lavish and grand structure was the site for many relaxing, sporting, and cultural activities.

15.8, below Frederick Law Olmsted and Calvert Vaux. *Central Park*, New York City, USA, 1857–1887.

The visual arts, performing arts, and other leisure activities find a home in this oasis in the middle of the dense city.

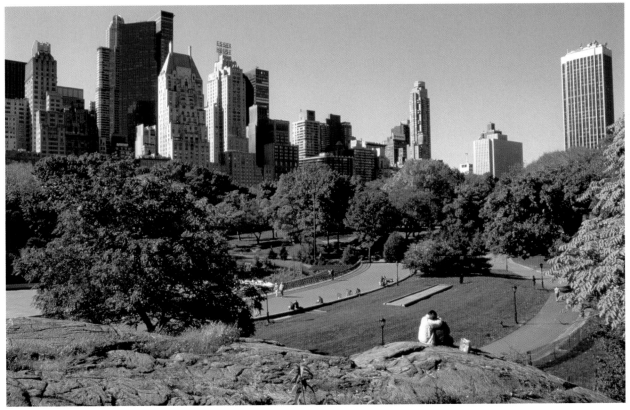

were added within the natural rolling terrain. The park today features all kinds of entertaining places and events:

- The Metropolitan Museum of Art
- Sheep Meadow, now used for free musical concerts
- Delacorte Shakespeare Theater (free)
- The Ramble (wilderness area trails)
- Zoo and the Children's Zoo
- Wollman Rink and Lasker Rink and Pool
- Chess and Checker Pavilion
- The Harlem Meer, a small lake with a boathouse
- Fort Fish and Fort Clinton, blockhouses from the Revolutionary War and the War of 1812
- Sculptures honoring statesmen, writers, children, animals, birds, and military events
- Tennis courts, baseball diamonds, football and soccer fields, children's playgrounds, a cafeteria, bike and bridle paths, and many gardens

> **CONNECTION** The formal gardens that surrounded European palaces like *Versailles* (10.14) and *Nymphenburg* (13.11) were one inspiration for large urban parks in the United States.

The Hakone Open-Air Museum (Fig. 15.9), opened in 1969, is a museum set in nature, located in Japan's scenic Hakone National Park. Like the *Baths of Caracalla*, it is a special environment for appreciating the arts. The exquisitely manicured lawns, woods, and gardens complement the many contemporary outdoor sculptures displayed there, all against the breathtaking beauty of the Hakone Mountains. Indoor galleries feature sculptures and paintings by famous twentieth-century Japanese and European artists.

The mixed-use features of the *Baths of Caracalla* can be seen again in *Las Vegas*, Nevada (Fig. 15.10), where art mixes with gambling, tourism, sports, and entertainment. The casino areas of Las Vegas are dense with reproductions, including Paris's Eiffel Tower, the Sphinx and pyramids of Egypt, the Venetian waterfront, the New York City skyline with the Statue of Liberty, a medieval castle, and so on. Original and copied art are featured in galleries and in the casinos. Major boxing events are held here. Neon art and illuminated signs glow throughout the night. A huge visual spectacle, Las Vegas is a site of tourists' fantasies and desires for glamour and wealth, often satisfied through copies and representations, through the act of looking and being looked at.

Sports Arenas

Architecture provides a framework and an appropriate setting for the drama and spectacle of sports events. Our focus figure for this section is again from Rome. In its original condition, the *Colosseum*, or the Flavian Amphitheater (Fig. 15.11), was a feast for the eyes. This huge structure covering six acres was faced with rich veneers of marble, tile, plaster, and bronze. The 160-foot-high outer wall is encircled by four horizontal bands, three with arches flanked by Greek Classical columns—a monumental celebration of Greco-Roman architecture. Emperors who

15.9 *The Hakone Open-Air Museum*, Hakone National Park, Japan, opened in 1969.

Cultural treasures and natural treasures mix in this park-museum.

succeeded the infamous tyrant Nero built it between 70 and 82 CE, on the site of an artificial lake in Nero's private park, where his colossal statue stood (hence, the name *Colosseum*).

Inside, a complex design of ramps, arcades, vaults, and passageways efficiently moved more than 50,000 spectators. Admission was always free to all; however, the seating was reserved by rank. The hot sun was blocked by a huge cloth canopy managed by a special detachment of the navy. The center area could be covered with sand for hunting sports and gladiator games, or filled with water to enact mock sea battles. Complex underground passages, rooms, and elevators were added later so that animals, scenery, and prisoners could make dramatic entrances to the spectacles. The *Colosseum* was dedicated to blood sports, and thousands of humans and animals perished in the gruesome games, which continued until 523.

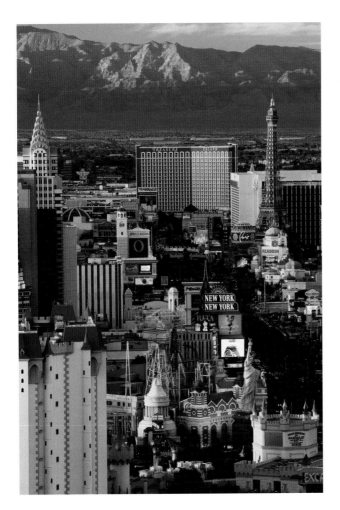

15.10, *left* *Las Vegas*, 2004. Sunset, elevated view.

The casinos are lavish visual experiences of brilliant lights, historical replicas, and original art.

15.11, *below* *Colosseum*, Rome, 70–82 CE.

This sport site was lavishing decorated and ambitiously engineered, in part because of the political importance of the building and the events staged in it.

15.12 *The Great Ball Court*, Chichén Itzá, Mexico, 11th–13th centuries. Stone, 567' × 228', I-shaped. Maya-Toltec.

This large, imposing structure housed games that had great ritual significance.

On the North American continent, the Maya culture developed a ball sport that was a form of ritualistic entertainment. *The Great Ball Court* in Chichén Itzá, Mexico (Fig. 15.12), from the eleventh to thirteenth centuries, measures 567 feet by 228 feet. Compared to the *Colosseum*, its basic shape is an I-shaped court rather than an oval amphitheater. However, both the *Colosseum* and the *Great Ball Court* have an architectural grandeur because they were ritually or politically important. The *Great Ball Court* has twenty-seven-foot-high walls with two stone rings mounted near the top. Similar to contemporary soccer, the players had to use their heads and bodies to project the hard ball, which took much strength and skill through the long, arduous game. The Mayan people saw the ball game as a metaphor for the epic journey through the Underworld taken by the hero twins, the Sun and the Moon, with underlying meanings about the conflict between good and evil and the cycles of heavenly bodies. The game ended when the ball passed through the stone ring, and then one player (or perhaps one team) became a human sacrifice to the gods.

The dramatic ball court is a fitting setting for the ritualistic game. It features the Temple of the Jaguar on the long east wall and another temple at the far north end. Phenomenal decorative reliefs cover the walls. The acoustics of the court are also amazing. A person standing in one temple can hear a conversation taking place in the temple at the other end. Similar ball courts existed at most major urban centers of the Maya and other Mesoamerican peoples, with some variations in the designs. Many still stand.

CONNECTION The same qualities of grandeur and spectacle seen in the *Colosseum* and *The Great Ball Court* are present in many sports arenas today, including the *Olympic Stadium at Munich* (Fig. 2.44, page 54).

ART THAT ILLUSTRATES LEISURE ACTIVITIES

Throughout history and across cultures, artists have recorded the spectacles, leisure activities, and forms of entertainment in their cultures.

Images of Athletes

The focus figure for this section comes from the Minoan culture on the island of Crete. The fresco wall painting *Bull Jumping* or *Toreador Fresco* (Fig. 15.13), dating from c. 1550–1450 BCE, is part of a group of murals with bulls as subject matter, located in the ruins of the palace at Knossos. It may refer to the mythical Minotaur, half-man and half-bull beast, to whom young men and women were sacrificed. The bull also symbolizes fertility and strength.

The contestants are trim, youthful, and idealized. They demonstrate their courage with every leap and tumble, as they face the fury of the bull and all he stands for. The overall forms are flowing, undulating, and floating, as if referring to the ocean that surrounds the islands. The massive bull seems graceful and the figures seem weightless, as if suspended in water. In ancient Mediterranean civilizations, gender was often indicated by dark (male) and light (female) skin tones.

Athletes are often depicted in an ideal manner, as in the *Bull Jumping* fresco and again in the vase painting of *Ball Players* (Fig. 15.14), which shows some of the very ballplayers who would have competed on the Maya ball court in Figure 15.12. Team members are covered with elaborate dress and heavy padding, especially on the chest and knees. This was eye-catching attire that also provided necessary protection from the hard ball. Patterns and insignia cover the players' clothing, and they are adorned with earrings and a large animal headdress, showing that ballplayers enjoyed considerable status in Mayan society. In usual Mayan fashion, the painting combines outlined, dark

15.13 *Bull Jumping,* Crete, c. 1550–1450 BCE. Wall painting, 24 1/2″ high. Palace complex at Knossos.

Youthful acrobats leap over the back and the horns of a bull.

15.14 *Ball Players,* Mexico, 11th–13th centuries. Vase painting. Maya.

Elaborate padding and costumes were worn by Mayan ball players.

15.15 *Acrobat*, Mexico, Early Pre-Classical, 1200–600 BCE. Light clay, 10″ × 6 1/2″. National Museum of Anthropology, Mexico City.

The ancient contortionist is the inspiration for the clever composition of this small sculpture.

silhouette forms and patterned areas. The figures, though stylized, seem powerful and lithe.

Also from Mexico comes the *Acrobat* (Fig. 15.15), from the ancient village of Tlatilco located outside Mexico City, discovered in 1940. Like the *Bull Jumping* figures, this *Acrobat* from 1220–600 BCE is rendered in a simplified way, with smooth outer lines and relatively few anatomical details. He has a relatively naturalistic face framed with a stylized, incised hair treatment and articulated toes. The head is disproportionately large, with a concentrating, straining expression. Compositionally, the bent arms and legs create diagonals that frame the face. Graves contained burial offerings that included figurines of females, ball-players, musicians, dancers, and acrobats. Clearly these artifacts indicate that these ancient peoples prepared for an afterlife full of entertainment.

Music and Dance Imagery

Artworks that depict music and dance can tell us about the musical forms of cultures now long lost, and about the social, political, and religious framework into which

music fits. The sculpture and two paintings in this section give visual form to performing events.

The focus figure is from seventeenth-century Holland, a painting of a young boy engrossed in playing his flute by Judith Leyster, a prolific artist whose work was well known at the time, a rare accomplishment for a woman in a predominantly male art world. *Boy Playing a Flute* (Fig. 15.16), from 1630–1635, is considered her masterpiece. Leyster captures the pride and the enthusiasm of the young musician as he glances at his audience, likely looking for their approval. The mellow tones of the painting suggest the soft tones of the flute. In the shallow space, the boy is balanced compositionally with the instruments hanging on the wall.

Holland at the time was predominantly middle class and Protestant, so music was not written for grand productions for the nobility or for elaborate rituals for the Catholic Church, but was often performed in the middle-class home. Leyster painted the boy as an ordinary child, playing for his own pleasure and that of his family, in a home graced with several musical instruments.

In contrast to the detail and individuality shown in *Boy Playing a Flute*, our next sculpture is a more abstracted work, where the smooth curves of the musician and instrument almost become as one. In the Cycladic Islands off

15.16 JUDITH LEYSTER. *Boy Playing a Flute*, Netherlands, 1630–1635. Oil, 28 1/2″ × 24 1/4″. National Museum, Stockholm, Sweden.

This painting documents the presence of music in ordinary middle-class homes in the Netherlands in the 17th century.

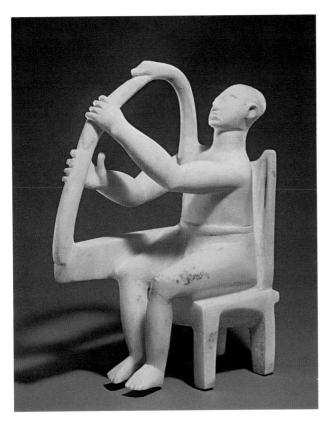

Greece, sculptures of male musicians were found buried in graves along with plank marble goddess figures like that in Figure 7.4. The *Harp Player*, from c. 2500–1100 BCE (Fig. 15.17), is smoothly carved with clear, simplified forms. Precise attention was given to the hands and fingers, as in his thumb that plucks invisible strings. The upper torso, arms, and head are exaggerated or stylized. The proportions of the musician figures appear standardized, with a fixed ratio of height to width, perhaps reflecting the mathematical relationship of musical intervals. The *Harp Player* is better viewed in profile, rather than from the front.

Just as the *Boy Playing a Flute* reflects the Northern European Protestant middle class from which it came, the Egyptian wall painting of *Musicians and Dancers* (Fig. 15.18) reflects its culture's style of entertainment and its fixation with funerary rituals and the afterlife. Traditionally, living relatives celebrated the anniversaries of the dead

15.17 *Harp Player*, Cycladic culture, c. 2500–1100 BCE. Marble, approx. 14″ × 3″. Metropolitan Museum of Art, New York, Rogers Fund, 1947 (47.100.1).

Musician and instrument seem almost combined in the simplified, smooth forms.

15.18 *Musicians and Dancers*, Egypt, c. 1400 BCE. Fresco, 12″ × 27″. From the tomb of Nebamun, Thebes. The British Museum, London.

In the bottom area of this painting, the style of depicting the human form is unusually free, relaxed, and unstructured when compared to the more typical, formal style, seen at the top of this painting.

in their tombs, some of which were quite large and elaborate and featured fresco wall paintings. In *Musicians and Dancers*, from the tomb of Nebamun, dated c. 1400 BCE, four finely dressed women sit casually at the bottom right, with one playing an oboe-like instrument while others clap in rhythm. The cone on top of each woman's head was made of perfumed animal tallow, which would melt and run down their bodies, covering them with fragrant oil. To the right are barely clad dancers and stacked wine jars.

The painting style at the bottom of this fresco is relaxed as well, which contrasts with the formal depictions of higher-ranking Egyptians, at top. The ladies' hair is loose, the soles of their feet are shown, and two face the viewer head-on rather than in the typical Egyptian profile. The lively dancers are smaller, indicating their lesser rank. The whole scene gives the feeling of levity and pleasure meant both for the spirit of the deceased and for the living.

ART IN ENTERTAINMENT

This section contains works that straddle the borders dividing art, popular culture, and entertainment. In addition to their striking visual elements, most of these artworks also have components of sound, music, movement, or dance.

Art and Dramatic Productions

The visual arts have long been part of dramatic productions, especially in masks, puppetry, set design, costumes, and graphics. Theater has in turn influenced the visual arts, particularly **Performance Art**.

Our focus figure is by Henri-Marie-Raymond de Toulouse-Lautrec, who lived in the cabaret and theater district of Montmartre, Paris, in the 1880s. There he became friends with artists, entertainers, street people, and prostitutes, many of whom became the focus of his work. Other visual artists have produced graphics for the performing arts, but Lautrec is well known for his street posters of Paris nightlife, which reached a wide audience consisting of people who probably did not attend art galleries and salons. A favorite subject was *Jane Avril* (Fig. 15.19), a singer and dancer at the famous cabaret Moulin Rouge. This 1899 poster captures the provocative essence of the cabaret. Avril's sensuous silhouette is composed of simple, fluid shapes filled with bright, flat colors. The

coiling snake emphasizes her curves and suggests that she is a temptress, like Eve to Adam. Her written name balances the negative space and at the same time visually supports her exaggerated back bend. Toulouse-Lautrec was influenced by shallow space, decorative color, and the fluid contour line of Japanese prints. His work strongly influenced later graphic designers.

In addition to producing posters, artists have created objects used in live performances, including props, backdrops, and puppets. In many cases, like Lautrec's posters, these visual elements are essential for conveying the theme and mood of the performance.

Puppetry is an art form at least four thousand years old. Japan has a traditional form of "doll drama" called *Bunraku* (Fig. 15.20), which was originally performed by traveling troupes. Doll dramas continue today. The naturalistic puppets are one-half life-size with articulated hands, heads, eyes, brows, and mouths. Only male characters have articulated legs, because female puppets wear long robes. Wearing elevated sandals, the master puppeteer, whose face we see, holds the puppet up and works the head and facial features with one hand and the doll's right hand with the other. Assistants covered in black control

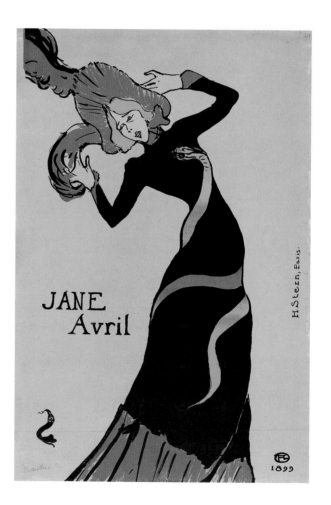

15.19 HENRI DE TOULOUSE-LAUTREC. *Jane Avril*, Paris, France, 1899. Lithographic poster, 22″ × 14″.

Artists have often provided imagery for theater or dance that captures the essence of the performance.

15.20 *Bunraku* performance on stage, Japan, c. 20th century.

Ancient doll dramas are preserved in Japan as national treasures.

the left hand and the feet. Lengthy practice and discipline are required to get all actions precisely synchronized, as they work in full view of the audience. The puppeteers are accompanied by a singer-narrator and a musician playing a three-stringed instrument called a samisen. The singer describes the scenes, voices all the roles, and makes comments to enhance the drama. All the elements, including the voices, the puppets, the movements, and the music, combine to create an art form that Japan recognizes as a national treasure.

Puppetry took a new form in the mid-1990s on the Broadway stage with Disney's *The Lion King* (Fig. 15.21), which featured a unique combination of human-puppet characters, created and directed by Julie Taymor. Her background includes Indonesian masked dance, Bunraku puppetry, and Western opera. Because the puppeteer-actors

15.21 JULIE TAYMOR (designer and director). Scene from *The Lion King*, New York City, USA, opened mid-1990s.

Elements of art, theater, and popular culture mix in the design and performance of this Broadway play.

are visible, both the story and the process of telling the story unfold simultaneously. This is especially appropriate because the animal-characters endure humanlike rites of passage and a search for identity. In our example, the dancers perform high, graceful leaps, mimicking antelopes' movements, and their costumes are coordinated with those of the puppets. Again, the visuals capture the essence of the dramatic performance.

Set design is another area of significant overlap between the visual arts and performing arts, but of course in a different way than the Lautrec poster of *Jane Avril*. In 1958, U.S. artist Robert Rauschenberg, choreographer Merce Cunningham, and composer Morton Feldman created an innovative and provocative work entitled *Summerspace* (Fig. 15.22), with John Cage as musical director, first performed at the American Dance Festival. All components were performed together but were also independent of one another, with aspects of improvisation and chance. Cunningham conceived of space as a continuum, without a focal point for the dancers. Conceptually, this was like some abstract painting in which there is no figure that is more important than the background. Cunningham was also influenced by Albert Einstein's theory of relativity, which posited that there are no fixed points in space. Rauschenberg designed the sets and costumes to echo the dance that had no center point but moved from all points

on the stage. The dancer's costumes were covered with dots (or points) like the set, giving each element equal visual importance.

In recent years, the performing arts have had a great influence on the visual arts, especially in **performance art**, a visual art form that incorporates live action and mixed media and is presented before an audience. The first performances were 1960s "Happenings" organized by Allan Kaprow, who believed that art, like life, should be unstable, transitory, and ambiguous. What *happened* was what was important. This opposes much previous Western thought, which regarded artworks as pure, transcendent, universal objects meant to endure. Kaprow felt that art should mesh with life, rather than interpret life experience. During happenings, participants and audience were often one and the same.

For *Household*, Kaprow set the happening to begin at a specific time in a dump area in Ithaca, New York, close to Cornell University. It began as male participants built a tower of garbage, while women built a nest of twigs and string, suggesting the traditional domain of each gender. From inside the nest, the women began screeching at the men, who brought a wrecked car and smeared it with strawberry jam. The women left their nest and began licking the jam off the car (Fig. 15.23) while the men destroyed the nest. Afterward, the men wiped the jam off the car

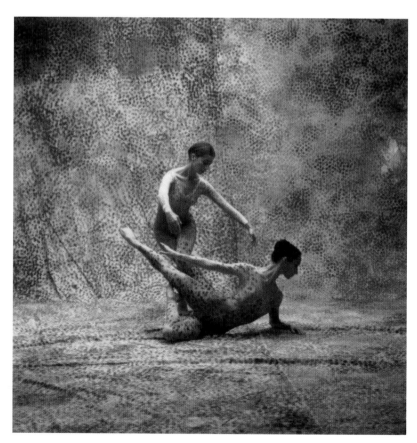

15.22 *Summerspace.* Music by Morton Feldman, choreography by Merce Cunningham, set and costumes by Robert Rauschenberg; John Cage, Musical Director of the Cunningham Dance Company. Premiered at the American Dance Festival at Connecticut College, New London, Connecticut. Dancers: Viola Farber (standing) and Carolyn Brown.

A visual artist provided the design of the costumes and backdrops in this experimental dance production.

15.23 ALLAN KAPROW. *Household*, May 1964. Performance "Happening." Commissioned by Cornell University, New York.

Happenings were events that began with a simple premise but progressed in unexpected ways through spontaneity and improvisation.

with white bread and ate it, while the women retaliated by decimating the men's tower. The event continued with violence until the men demolished the car and set it on fire. In silence, all participants watched the car burn, and then departed without words. *Household* was bizarre, surreal, and ambiguous like a dream, and Kaprow welcomed individual interpretations.

Musical Instruments and Dance

The visual arts and music also overlap, but in ways different from visual art and theater. Historically, artists have made musical instruments and continue to do so today. Aspects of dance recall the visual arts, and artists have provided props for dancers.

The focus figure is an artwork that is also a musical instrument. The beautifully crafted *Lyre* (Fig. 15.24) of wood, lapis lazuli, and gold and shell inlay was found in the royal Mesopotamian tomb of Queen Puabi, dated c. 2685 BCE. Similar to a harp, the instrument's wooden sound box and body are composed of clean rectangles and subtle curves, with decorative sculpture and scenes as accents. The stunning blue-bearded bull is made of gold and lapis lazuli, an imported semiprecious stone. It is naturalistic with highly stylized details, such as the outlined eyes and patterned beard. Bearded bulls were symbols of royalty.

15.24 *Lyre*, Ur (Iraq), c. 2685 BCE. Wood, gold and shell inlay, lapis lazuli, 5′ 5″ high. Sound box from tomb of Queen Puabi. University of Pennsylvania Museum.

Beautiful design and expert craftsmanship distinguish this lyre, which was part of an ancient royal burial.

15.25 *Asmat Hand Drum*, Indonesia, c. 1950. Painted wood, lizard skin, rattan, 45″ high. Southwest Asmat coast. From the collection of Tobias Schneebaum, New York.

To make this drum, the center of a log was hollowed out. The exterior, along with the handle, was then shaped and carved from that same piece of log.

Beneath the bull's head are four scenes made of shell inlaid in bitumen. They may depict a fantastic banquet, fables, or the myth of Gilgamesh. Characters include a young man flanked by two human-headed bulls, and four-legged creatures acting as servants: a lively dog with a dagger carries a table, followed by a lion with a platter and a large jar. Below them, a donkey musician plays a lyre like the one it adorns. Such a grandly made lyre is both a visual and musical work of art.

Just as fables or myths are important components of the *Lyre*, ritual is an important dimension for the *Asmat Hand Drum* (Fig. 15.25). In both cases, it is not enough that

the drum or lyre function musically, but also that they are beautifully crafted works of art. In Melanesia, men make and use very large as well as small drums that are used in ceremonies for a boy's initiation, to placate ancestor spirits who died because of an enemy raid, and for magical rites. This mid-sized drum is carried in one hand, while the lizard skin head is struck with the other. The slender, hourglass-shaped drums were usually decorated with ancestral and head-hunting symbolism, represented in the figures on the handles.

Turning to dance, the North American Sioux *Open Circle Dance* (Fig. 15.26) was part of the annual celebration of the springtime rebirth of nature. The dancer performs to a rapid rhythm, using twenty-eight hoops made of wood or reeds. All movements have spiritual significance and together are visualizations suggesting the unity of all things in the universe, as well as individual growth, change, and metamorphosis. Some parts of the dance re-create the image of an eagle soaring in flight, suggesting that parts of nature (including human beings) belong to the spiritual world in the heavens. Another configuration represents the caterpillar, which, during the dance, will become a graceful butterfly. The rigorous performance climaxes with the "Hoops of Many Hoops," when all things of the universe come together as part of a hopeful Sioux prophecy for peace among all people. This dance is an elaborate variation of older forms that has been developed because of the interest of tourists. Once again, entertainment, art, and ritual mix.

The Dogon people in Mali connect the dance, costume, and the *Kanaga* mask (Fig. 15.27). The performers are members of a male masked society called the *awa*, who, in their dance, tell their culture's story about how death entered the world. The masking and the red color of the costume are believed to catch, manipulate, and rechannel vital forces that could pose potential danger to the community if unleashed. Kanaga masks are worn three days after a death in the community, when the spirit of the deceased is believed to leave the body. The masks, carved by the performers, have several interpretations, such as a bird in flight, a mythological crocodile, or a god in the act of creation.

ART AND VISUAL CULTURE

The last several decades have been unique in human history, because of the impact of mass media. **Visual Culture** is an area of academic study that deals with the totality of images and visual objects produced in industrial and postindustrial nations, and the ways that those images are disseminated, received, and used.

15.26 KEVIN LOCKE. Performing the *Open Circle Dance*, USA, 20th century. Sioux.

Hoop dances are performed by one dancer with many hoops, who spins them to create shapes that are symbolically important for the story being told through the dance.

Today, an almost constant barrage of images comes to us from art, advertising, information design, gaming, news organizations, science, and education. Researchers in biology, medicine, and astronomy are making visualizations of things that are not visible. Surveillance is part of the public space. Ordinary people are constantly making and circulating images with cell phones and camcorders. Visual culture scholars study visual media of all sorts, as well as the "centrality of vision and the visual world in producing meanings, establishing and maintaining aesthetic values, gender stereotypes and power relations within cultures" (Rogoff 1998:14). Image competes with word as our main mode of communication and of understanding the global culture. Scholars also maintain that our eager consumption of images fills our lives with virtual experiences that replace real life. These images generate emotions related to pleasure, anxiety, power, and fantasy. Vision is associated with the **gaze** (discussed on page 177 in relation to sexuality and on page 372 in relation to race), because power relationships are embedded in "who is looking at whom."

Visual culture is also concerned with **spectacle**, or any kind of public show on a grand scale. This event could be the opening ceremonies for the Olympic Games, the miles of neon lights on the Las Vegas strip, a celebrity making an entrance, a grand immersive video installation like Pipilotti Rist's *Pour Your Body Out* (Fig. 15.1), or a Hollywood blockbuster movie with special effects and enhanced sound. The value of these objects or events lies in their images.

Visual culture is transnational. In some cases, it may not make sense to identify the source of some art

15.27 *Kanaga Masked Dancers*, Mali, 20th century. Dogon.

In Africa, the masquerade is the art form that combines dance, music, and carving (masks).

by geography. If an artist grew up in Tokyo, now lives in Paris, and makes art installations in Rio de Janeiro, is that art Japanese, French, or Brazilian? Pictures reflect the complexity, ambiguities, and contradictions of the world today. No one "world picture" comes through the study of visual culture; rather, we experience multiple viewpoints and meanings may shift from person to person, and from country to country. Things are becoming more complex rather than simple.

> **CONNECTION** Chapter 4 provided more in-depth discussion for deriving meaning, or multiple meanings, from artworks.

Visual culture studies more than just art and entertainment, which are the subjects of this chapter. Yet contemporary art, popular culture, and entertainment provide a good introduction to visual culture studies, and that is the focus of the rest of this chapter.

Film, Television, and Cartoons

Art and entertainment heavily overlap in film, television, and cartoons, where at times the same work easily can be classified in any or all of these media. Film, television, and cartoons are all based on sequential images. Narrative is a key element in most. All are dependent upon technology, specifically commercial printing, photography, sound recording, and digital imaging. Film and television are fertile areas of investigation for visual culture scholars, because of the embedded social messages and, in the case of Hollywood films, the quality of spectacle. Many films and television programs have influenced fine artists.

> **CONNECTION** Nam June Paik's multi-imaged *Electronic Superhighway* (Fig. 3.1, page 55) is a good example of art that refers to entertainment technologies.

Cartoons have a long history in drawing, printmaking, and newspapers, where they entertain or promote political causes (like Honoré Daumier's political cartoon in Fig. 11.29). In comics, the sequential images tell a story. First introduced in Sunday supplements in newspapers more than a century ago, early comics were marked by great experimentation. *Gasoline Alley* (Fig. 15.28) is part of a later development in comics, with more elaborate storytelling and memorable characters. Although *Gasoline Alley* was usually concerned with humble yet humorous domestic issues, occasionally the writer/artist Frank King

lavished beautiful graphic arabesques and visual fantasies over the comic space. Our example, with a boy and his Uncle Walt doodling designs with a compass, echoes concurrent developments in abstraction in art. Once considered solely popular culture, comics have recently been featured in major exhibitions at top art museums, and some artists work in the comic-strip format. Comics continue today, and many future classics may be wrapped up with the news in your daily paper.

The motion picture was born of the marriage of photography and electricity. Early experiments in film soon led to elaborate productions with experienced actors. Film quickly became distinct from theater. The movable camera removed all boundaries from the staged space, and sequences could be shot on soundstages or anywhere in the world. Sound was added to the action in 1927, which made or broke many actors' careers.

> **CONNECTION** An example of Eadweard Muybridge's sequential images, which are early experiments to capture motion with photography, is *Handspring, a flying pigeon interfering, June 26, 1885* (Fig. 12.23, page 351).

Many films are considered classics, almost works of art, in addition to their entertainment value. The 1930s and 1940s were considered the Golden Age of Hollywood, with large studios producing romances, comedies, thrillers, and musicals, as well as grandiose and expensive productions like *Gone with the Wind*. Ambitious filmmaking was not limited to the United States, as classics came from many countries. The 1940s was also the Golden Age of Mexican cinema, and the 1944 film *Maria Candelaria (Xochimilco)* (Fig. 15.29), directed by Emilio Fernández, shared the prize for best film at the Cannes Film Festival. While the story has its weaknesses, the cinematography by Gabriel Figueroa is breathtaking. The film also documents the now-lost culture that flourished in the floating gardens of Xochimilco, which once produced most of the food and flowers for Mexico City.

> **CONNECTION** Like *Maria Candelaria*, *Gone with the Wind* is an epic, dramatic film that deals with a lost way of life. In Chapter 5, page 120, read about its recent restoration and the controversy it sparked.

During this era, television came into its own as an important and almost omnipresent media, adding more

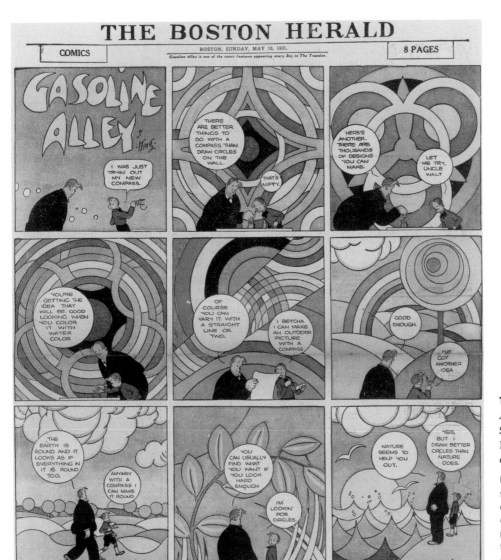

15.28 FRANK KING. *Gasoline Alley*, USA, 1931. Newspaper Sunday page, detail, published May 10, 1931; 23″ × 17″. Private collection.

Rather than advancing the story lines in the weekday editions, the Sunday editions of this comic strip were often philosophical observations on the nature of life or explorations of the world.

15.29 *Maria Candelaria*, Mexico, 1943. Directed by Emilio Fernández, starring Dolores del Río and Pedro Armendáriz. Cinematography by Gabriel Figueroa.

This film is from the golden age of Mexican cinema.

Art and Visual Culture **453**

15.30 *I Love Lucy*, USA, 1951–1957. Television video, situation comedy (sitcom). CBS Entertainment, A Division of CBS, Inc. Images of Lucille & Desi Arnaz are licensed by Desilu, Too, LLC.

This series is considered one of the all-time classics of American television.

layers to our complex visual culture. Television in essence shrank the world as people could witness events from far-off places right in their living rooms on the small screen. Television became broadly popular in the 1950s. Most of the early television shows evolved from radio programs, such as the quiz show, talk show, travelogue, and sitcom (situation comedy). Later programming expanded to investigative reporting, political coverage, educational programs, music videos, reality TV, and makeover series.

One icon of American family humor is *I Love Lucy* (Fig. 15.30). Performed and filmed before a live audience, this sitcom was rated number one in its time. Even the 1953 inauguration of President Dwight D. Eisenhower drew fewer viewers than the episode showing the birth of little Ricky. Although the scripts were undoubtedly effective, much of the humor was communicated visually, through facial expression, gesture, and body language. Notice how clearly the idea of conflict and outraged surprise is communicated in Figure 15.30. Still in syndication, *I Love Lucy* remains a popular favorite.

Television and movies have borrowed from art and vice versa. From 1995 through 2003, U.S. artist Matthew Barney created the *Cremaster* cycle of films, juxtaposing historical and autobiographical imagery with bizarre creatures, bodily orifices, and so on. Rather than presenting a narrative, the ravishing imagery promotes personal, free-associative meanings. Much of the films' content deals with gender identity, and many characters have mutant, ambiguous, or partially formed genitalia. Audiences are either repulsed or fascinated. All *Cremaster* films borrow from Hollywood types; for example, *Cremaster 1* references the Busby Berkeley musical extravaganza. Barney also creates individual artworks related to his films, such as *Cremaster 1: The Goodyear Chorus* (Fig. 15.31), a color print, based on a film still.

Animation grew out of flip books, in which a series of drawn images seem to move as book pages are flipped rapidly. Early animation features gained a wide following beginning in the 1930s. Animation is labor-intensive if completely hand-drawn; for example, an average of 14,000 drawings are required for a ten-minute animation sequence. **Traditional animation** is drawn on transparent sheets, so that foreground action figures can be separated and moved across an unchanging background. **Claymation**, a relatively early form of animation, uses clay sculptures that are photographed while being moved in tiny increments. **Computer animation** is a new form that allows characters to be plotted as a series of points and vectors and made to move with mathematical computation. Disney and Warner Brothers were two pioneers in the animation industry, but other studios and independent producers now exist.

Hayao Miyazaki's *Spirited Away* (Fig. 15.32), 2002, is considered to be an animation movie masterpiece. The story concerns Chihiro, a ten-year-old girl separated from her parents in a fantastic and sometimes frightening land. In the process of reuniting with them, she grows up. Miyazaki created scenes with fantastic structures and broad vistas that are amazingly beautiful, are often vast and ornate, and draw from a variety of historical and global sources. Likewise, lush landscapes abound. Miyazaki is known for his elaborate hand-drawn architectural interiors and diverse characters.

Video Games and Electronic Toys

Currently in the field of entertainment, video games and electronic toys are a major new component in contemporary visual culture. Some artists are experimenting with the medium to see if it can be used to deliver an artistic experience. For example, the video and installation artist Bill Viola (see Figure 12.9 on page 340), with the

15.32 HAYAO MIYAZAKI. Still from *Spirited Away*, Japan, 2002. Feature-length animated movie.

Making drawings move is the great appeal of animation.

15.33 *Boy Controlling a Robot.* 2010.

Art, design, technology, and entertainment are integrated in new ways in the 21st century.

of Southern California Game Innovation Lab, is working on a video game entitled *The Night Journey.* Unlike many action-packed video games, the plan for The Night Journey is to slow the viewers down so that they travel mindfully through a mysterious landscape.

Other electronic toys and games expand our experiences and populate our living spaces with innovations that have only been imagined in the past. Just one example of present developments is the robotic toy seen in Figure 15.33, *Boy Controlling a Robot.* This instance of interactive play shows a boy steering and manipulating a looming, almost frightening, robot twice his size. Robotic toys

are increasingly popular in the toy market, including new robotic versions of the old, such as stuffed pets, model cars, dolls and warriors, plus a huge assortment of character-like robots that come in all sizes and shapes.

Undoubtedly in the years to come, the evolution of technology and media based art will bring more complex and exotic forms of entertainment, coexisting side-by-side with previous traditional forms that continue to be enjoyed. Art, design, technology, and entertainment will be integrated in new ways, and will include functionality and educational purposes as well. The future is almost here.

POSTSCRIPT

FINDING ART AND USING IT IN YOUR LIFE

The overall purpose of this book has been to inquire into human creativity, and therefore our own creativity. We have seen that art is something that human beings have to do, through the ages, throughout the world. And what about you? Art is already part of your life. With a little effort, you can make it even more enriching for you. Here are some suggestions on how you may do that.

Seeing Original Artwork. One of the most thrilling ways to enjoy art is to see it in person! Nothing can describe the awesome feeling of standing in front of the *Great Pyramids* at Gizeh, or walking through the Mayan ruins at *Chichén Itzá*, or experiencing the space in the church of *St. Peter's* in Rome. If distant travel is not possible, you probably have many opportunities to see original artwork within a reasonable drive from your home. Here are some places to seek out art.

- **Museums and Galleries:** Almost all communities of any size support museums and galleries, ranging from modest to grand. Although local museums may not display the most famous "masterpieces," they contain works of real value that are rewarding to study and may surprise the first-time visitor. When you are in a city in the United States or abroad where a major museum or an archeological site is located, such as the Metropolitan in New York City or the tomb of Shi Huangdi in Shaanxi, China (Fig. 5.24), make it a point to spend some time there.
- **Schools:** Student art is extraordinarily inventive, spontaneous, and expressive. Art exhibits can be found in the hallways and libraries of elementary and secondary schools. On a professional or near-professional level, you can find art at most colleges and universities. Undergraduate and graduate student art is often high-quality, exciting work. Art department galleries show the work of faculty and professional artists both to enrich the art program and to expose the academic community to this art. These exhibits are often free and open to the public. Large universities sponsor major exhibitions, like the art of the Peruvian Moche at a University of California at Los Angeles gallery (Fig. 9.12). A phone call to the school is all it takes to find out about the schedules of the exhibits.
- **Civic Buildings, Private Institutions, and Corporations:** Often, government buildings have been designed by accomplished architects, and the buildings are examples of fine works of architecture. In your area, post offices, courthouses, and the like may have distinctive designs as well as display paintings, sculptures, and art treasures. Other places to look

for art in your community are banks, libraries, and hospitals. Many of these institutions have their own collections to enhance their interiors. Often, libraries will have exhibition space available and will host artworks by local artists. Some hospitals collect art. For example, an impressive collection of contemporary artwork can be found in the University Hospitals of the University of Iowa in Iowa City. Many corporations have large art collections displayed in their corporate offices.

- **Public Art:** Since the 1930s, the United States has had a great tradition of art in public places. More recently, the Percent for the Arts Programs have incorporated art into all new government-funded buildings and in redevelopment areas where private investors are receiving tax abatements. You may be able to find excellent art in transportation centers, at bus stops, and along jogging paths, river walks, and historic trails.
- **Historic Homes, Mansions, and Palaces:** The homes of historic or celebrated people sometimes become museums for public viewing, such as *Monticello*, which was built by Thomas Jefferson. This house is full of art treasures and Jefferson's own amazing inventions. Also, the Palace of *Versailles* and the *Forbidden City* are now open to everyone, examples of magnificent opulence originally known to only a few. In the United States are several mansions formerly belonging to wealthy entrepreneurs who bequeathed their estates as museums. Every city and town has a chamber of commerce that can aid the visitor in finding these interesting sites.
- **Places of Worship:** Churches, temples, synagogues, and mosques are rich places to look for art. Besides their architectural designs, they likely are decorated with both old and contemporary artworks. A place of worship may have exquisite stained-glass windows, as seen in the twelfth-century *Chartres Cathedral* (Fig. 8.39 and 8.40), fine paintings, sculptures, or elaborate tile work.
- **Parks:** Many parks are designed by landscape architects, so the gardens, walks, lakes, and so on are carefully planned. The *Boboli Gardens* in Florence, Italy, boast two museums. The well-known *Central Park* in New York City (Fig. 15.8), planned in the nineteenth century, has an art museum, several theaters, a zoo, and many more features. It is also the home of several commemorative sculptures. The open-air park brings art and nature into one enjoyable and relaxing environment. Most community parks are free to the public or charge a small parking fee to help with maintenance.
- **Art Online:** Art is available in many forms on the Internet. Most museums and many galleries have Web sites where you can find information about current exhibitions and permanent collections. Commercial galleries also have Web sites focused on the sale of artwork. Artists have their own Web sites that feature their work. To find artists' Web sites, inquire at arts organizations or do a Web search on art resources or media art centers. They will likely have links to artists' pages or feature recent artists' projects.

Art in Everyday Life. The art in our everyday lives is art in the broadest sense of the word, consisting of aesthetic objects that surround us. You may be aware of some of this, but much is taken for granted. Your home is both aesthetic and functional and is on a continuum with the nineteenth-century Sioux *Tipis* (Fig. 6.33) and Frank Lloyd Wright's *Fallingwater* (Fig. 6.34). Your utensils, dishes, and furniture have aesthetic and design qualities, whether they were mass produced or made by an artist/craftsperson. Notice the quality of light in your room, or the ceramic bowl that holds your serving of soup. Make choices about the space you live in, and the shapes and colors with which you surround yourself. To enjoy art more, make a conscious effort to see it and observe it in both your life and your environment. You might be surprised at how often art is right in front of you!

Develop your own artistic expression. All human beings have the potential to be creative. One of the best ways to enjoy art is to make art, even if you are not an art student or if you question your skills. Studio classes are available for the taking and can be found at local art museums, schools, and community centers. If you would rather study art than make it, look for art history courses available at colleges and museums. If you would rather not take a formal course in studio work or art history, then try it on your own. Many fine artists and learned persons in the world are self-trained. Whatever you choose, have a great time!

Living with Art in Your Home. Start or continue your own collection of work you enjoy and like to look at. There are several resources from which to draw your collection, and the first is right in your home. Frame some work of your own or that of a family member. Children are prolific artists and will have several selections from which to choose. You can purchase art at a reasonable price from student exhibitions and art sales at art schools and departments. Students are both encouraged and gratified when their work is purchased.

Seek out artists in your area and make an appointment to see their work in their studios. Some artists are open to barter or to swapping services in place of a cash transaction.

Many museums have museum stores where reproductions of major works are sold at affordable prices. Sculpture replicas are also available. If you prefer original art, some museums have sales and rental galleries. Of course, galleries are another outlet where you can purchase original art.

Arts and Crafts Fairs are fun and great for purchasing artwork directly from the artists. The artists set up displays of their work and sell it directly to the public. They are usually happy to talk about their work. Many of the artists are working on the site, which makes these fairs all the more interesting and enjoyable.

Congratulations! You have finished this book. The authors wish you well as you personally continue your exploration into the art world, which is inherently *your* world.

Students installing an art exhibition.

Support artists in your community. Check out exhibitions at your local university or community college. Many excellent works are on display in these galleries.

GLOSSARY

A

Abstract Expressionism An art movement that emerged after World War II that emphasized spontaneous artistic self-expression, non-representational imagery, and distinct paint application; most abstract expressionist works were paintings.

abstracted texture A distortion, a simplification, or an exaggeration of an actual texture.

Abstraction Visual imagery in art that does not copy reality. This might be achieved by simplifying, distorting, or exaggerating objects from nature.

academy An institution developed in various cultures to educate artists and to set strict standards and guidelines for art works.

accent Special attention given to any element of a composition in order to attract the viewer's eye to it. This may be done by giving an element a brighter color, isolating it, or enlarging it in order to accent it. Any visual device may be used in an accent.

achromatic value scale (ak-ruh-MAT-ik) A chart indicating tonal variations, without color, consisting only of grays.

acropolis (ah-KRAH-pul-us) The highest ground in an ancient Greek city; originally fortified and, later, the site of temples.

acrylic A water-soluble, permanent synthetic paint that was developed in the 1960s.

action painting A process used in creating a non-objective painting whereby the artist makes gestural movements to produce expressive brush strokes, drips, and splashes.

actual line Physical lines made with material that have more length than depth.

additive color system Color that is created by mixing light rays. When the three primary colors (red, blue, and green) are mixed, a white light is produced. Cyan, yellow, and magenta are the secondary colors in this system.

additive process Any art-making process in which materials are built up to create the final product.

adobe (ah-DOH-bee) Sun-dried brick made of straw and clay.

aerial perspective The blurring of forms, colors, and values as they recede into the background. This is sometimes referred to as *atmospheric perspective*, as receding forms in space take on the colors and tones of the natural atmosphere.

Aesthetics (es-THET-iks) A branch of Western philosophies that is concerned with the critical reflections on art, on beauty, and on taste.

afterimage A phenomenon that occurs after staring at an area of color for a while, then glancing at a white ground. The eye will see the complementary color.

airbrush A small spray gun attached to a compressed air source that atomizes liquid paint, allowing it to be sprayed onto a surface.

akua'ba A female doll used as a fertility aid by young Asanti women in Ghana

alla prima (ah-la PREE-mah) A technique in painting in which pigment is laid directly on the surface without any underpainting.

alternating rhythm Two or more different visual elements are repeatedly placed side by side or in a grid, which produces a regular and anticipated sequence.

altar A specifically prepared area or platform designed for a worship place.

ambient light The light all around us in the world.

amphitheater (am[p]-feh-THEE-et-er) An oval, semi-circular, or circular arena surrounded by tiers of seats.

amulet (AM-yoo-let) A charm worn to protect one from evil.

analogous colors Colors (**hues**) that are placed next to one another on the **color wheel**.

Ancestor Dreaming A system of spiritual beliefs for the Aboriginal people in Australia that accounts for creation and the cosmos.

animation A series of drawings that vary slightly from one to the next, so that the figures within the drawings appear to move.

animé A contemporary style of animation that originates in Japan.

animism The belief that all things in nature contain a spiritual force or soul.

anthropomorphic Giving human characteristics and attributes to a nonhuman being.

apotheosis (ah-poth-ee-OH-sus) The raising of human beings to a divine level, or to be deified.

aquatint A printmaking process related to etching in which the metal plate is covered with a powder of acid-resistant resin to create a tonal area.

arabesque (ar-ah-BESK) Intricate interlocking surface decorations usually of spiral forms, knots, and flora. There is no suggestion of human forms in the designs.

arcade A line of arches placed side by side on piers or columns that may be freestanding or attached to a wall.

arch A curved structure made of stone or brick that supports weight over an opening.

Archaic A period in Ancient Greece when artwork shifted from featuring primarily abstract decoration to emphasizing more nature-based or figurative work; roughly 700-500 BCE.

architecture The science and art of designing buildings and other structures that are both aesthetic and functional.

armature The underlying framework on which clay, wax, or plaster is placed; used in making sculpture.

artifact An object made by one or more human beings and usually categorized by time and culture.

assemblage (ah-sem-BLAHZH) Sculptures made from various found objects or prefabricated parts that are put together.

asymmetrical balance Balance that is achieved in a composition by arranging dissimilar elements so that they exist in groupings of equal visual weight and attention.

Athena Greek goddess of war, wisdom, and crafts.

atlatl (AHT-[uh]-lat-[uh]l) A stick thrower, or a device that aids the throwing of a stick or spear.

atmospheric perspective *See* **aerial perspective**.

atrium (AY-tree-um) The entrance room with an open skylight in a Roman house. Also, the attached, open-colonnaded court at the entrance of a Christian basilica.

attic The uppermost story in a structure.

Automatism A process for artmaking that incorporates intuition, spontaneity, unconscious behavior, and the accidental.

avant-garde (av-an[t]-GAR) Late-nineteenth- and twentieth-century artists who develop new concepts in their work.

avatar (av-uh-TAR) In Hinduism, the manifestation of a deity, or an aspect of a deity.

B

ba Part of the human soul, in ancient Egyptian beliefs. *See also* **ka**.

balance Visual equilibrium in a composition; achieved by organizing the weight and attention of all elements in an artwork. Types of balance are **symmetrical**, **asymmetrical**, and **radial**.

baldacchino (bal-dah-KEE-no) A canopy placed over a throne or an altar, sometimes resting on columns.

balustrade (BAL-us-trade) A railing supported by short pillars.

bargeboards Boards that conceal roof timbers projecting over gables; often decorated.

Baroque (bah-ROHK) A style of architecture and art in seventeenth- and eighteenth-century Western cultures (specifically in Europe) characterized by exaggeration, overstatement, and a flare for artifice and the theatrical.

barrel vault *See* **vaulting**.

bas relief (bah reh-LEEF) *See* **relief**.

base The lowest part of an Ionic or a Doric column.

binder A liquid, gel, or wax that holds pigment particles together and dries to create a paint layer.

biomorphic shape An irregular shape that resembles living forms.

bitumen A natural, tar-like substance.

black figure A style of Greek pottery that has been decorated with dark figures placed on a lighter background of red clay.

bodhisattva (boh-dih-SAHT-vah) In Buddhist beliefs, those humans who have attained the level of Buddhahood but choose to postpone their achieving Nirvana to remain on Earth to help others.

brackets In traditional Chinese architecture, clusters of interlocking pieces of wood shaped like inverted pyramids at the tops of upright posts, directly beneath the roof.

Buddha A person who has achieved a state of complete spiritual enlightenment; one who has attained Nirvana; the Buddha is Siddhartha Gautama, the spiritual leader from India who founded Buddhism.

Buddhism An Asian religion with the belief that the rejection of personal desires will lead to complete spiritual enlightenment.

buon fresco (true fresco) A form of fresco painting in which wet pigment is applied to a wet plaster wall, with very durable results.

burin A sharp pointed tool used to incise or engrave a plate or block in the printmaking process.

bust A sculpture of a human being that includes only the head and shoulders.

buttressing A mass of brick or stone that supports a wall or an arch; a *flying buttress* is a buttress placed some distance from the structure it is supporting, and it is connected to the main structure with an arch.

Byzantine A cultural style dating from 527 to 1453 CE and associated with Byzantium (especially Constantinople, now Istanbul, Turkey).

C

caliph A successor of Mohammed in the Islamic faith and recognized as their religious leader.

calligraphy (keh-LIG-reh-fee) Handwriting that is considered exceptionally beautiful.

canon (KAN-on) A rule of proportion that meets the requirements of a specific cultural aesthetic.

cantilever (kant-el-EE-ver) A structure in architecture that extends or protrudes horizontally beyond its support.

capital Uppermost element on a column, serving as a transition from the shaft to the lintel.

caricature The exaggeration of natural features usually seen for comic or satirical effect.

carving A type of sculpture in which unwanted materials are removed from a large block of material like stone, wood, or Styrofoam.

caryatid (kar-ee-AYT-id) A supporting element, like a column, that is carved to represent a female figure. A male supporting figure is called an *atlantid*.

cast, casting A process in which a mold of a form is made, then a liquid material is poured in and allowed to harden. The mold is then removed, leaving a sculptural replica of the original form.

catacombs (KAT-eh-kohmz) Subterranean chambers used for the burial of the dead.

cathedral (keh-THEE-drel) A church that is the official seat of a bishop.

centaur (SEN-tar) A half-man, half-horse creature, from fables.

ceramic Pottery and objects made of clay.

chalk A soft, white form of limestone, shaped into sticks and used for drawing; colored pigments can be added for colored chalk.

charcoal A carbon stick created from burnt wood, used for drawing.

chatras Stacked stone disks on a pole, seen on the top of Hindu temples.

Chi-Rho (ki roh) The initials of Christ's name in Greek.

chiaroscuro (kee-ar-eh-SK[Y]OOR-oh) In a drawing, the use of various tones (black, white, and grays) to create the illusion of volume.

chroma (KRO-ma) Brightness or dullness of a hue, or intensity.

chromatic Of or relating to color

Christianity Religions founded on the life and teachings of Jesus

cili An ancient symbol of wealth, fertility, and luck. It appears in the shape of a woman's head with a large, fanlike headdress radiating from it.

cire perdue (seer per-DOO) *See* **lost wax**.

city-state An autonomous political entity, consisting of a city and its surrounding territory.

civilization A highly structured society, with a written language or a very developed system of communication, organized government, and advances in the arts and sciences.

Classical The art of ancient Greece during the fifth century BCE, based on ideal proportion grounded in the human figure. The term also refers to a style that is clear and rational. Western art aesthetics are heavily influenced by Classical Greek art, seen in Roman, Romanesque, Renaissance, and Neoclassical styles.

Classical Baroque The Baroque style that also contains classical characteristics, especially in architecture. *See* **Baroque style**.

claymation A method of animation using clay figures moving in small increments in place of drawings.

clerestory (KLEER-stor-ee) An area of wall that contains windows and that rises above roof areas that surround it.

codex (codices) Early books made of parchment, vellum, deerskin, or bark paper, which were bounded on one side, or folded into fan-like pleats.

collaboration Arrangement in which two or more artists work together on one artwork.

collage (kuh-LAZH) A two-dimensional composition in which paper, cloth, or other materials are glued to a surface.

colonnade (kol-uh-NADE) A row of columns that supports an entablature or lintel.

color wheel A circular arrangement of the hues of the spectrum.

column A cylinder consisting of a base, shaft, and capital (top element) that usually supports a roof. However, freestanding columns sometimes function as monuments. *See* **Orders**.

combine Works that are both painting and sculpture.

complementary colors Hues that are located directly opposite each other on the color wheel.

complete frame system A structural system originated in China, with brackets, cantilevers, and totally non-load-bearing walls.

composition The organization of the elements of an artwork in such a way that harmony, balance, unity, and variety are achieved.

computer animation Totally digital animation; in some forms, characters can be plotted as a series of points and vectors and made to move with mathematical computation.

conceptual Artwork whose primary purpose is to convey an idea or a concept in any medium. Printed text is often included.

condottiere Mercenary soldiers who fought for various city-states during the European Renaissance.

contained style In a sculpture, all the forms are kept within the overall outer shape.

content An artwork's themes or messages, conveyed through subject matter, symbols, or iconography.

context Consists of the external conditions that surround a work of art, such as historical events, religious attitudes, social norms, and so on.

contour line The outline of a shape.

contrapposto (kon-trah-POS-toh) A standing position in which the body weight rests on one straight leg, with the other leg relaxed and bent, giving the torso an s-shaped curve.

cool [colors] Generally, blues, greens, and purples.

corbel (KOR-bul) Stones or bricks stacked so that each new layer projects beyond the layer below it; corbels can be arranged to create a corbeled arch or corbeled vault.

Corinthian Order (kuh-RIN-thee-en) *See* **Orders**.

cornice (KOR-niss) A projecting horizontal element that crowns a structure.

cosmos A systematic, orderly, harmonious universe.

craft A category of art that requires special manual skills and is often functional in origin.

crayon A small stick used as drawing material, with pigment held together by a wax binder.

cross-contours Repeated lines that go around an object or a form to express its three-dimensionality.

cross-hatching *See* **hatching**.

cross vault *See* **vaulting**.

crypt An underground chamber usually located in a church below the altar, sometimes used for burials.

Cubism An art style in which multiple viewpoints or facets are represented within one point of view. Analytical Cubism broke down forms, while Synthetic Cubism used collage and assemblage to represent parts of objects in order to visually play with illusions and reality.

culture The totality of ideas, customs, skills, and arts that belong to a people or group; or a particular people or group, with their own ideas, customs, and arts.

cultural style The recurring and distinctive features in many works of art emanating from a particular place and era, which allow them to be seen as a distinct and coherent group

cuneiform (kyoo-NAY-uh-form) A system of writing with wedge-shaped characters, used in the ancient Near East.

curvilinear Consisting of visual elements that are made up of or allude to curved lines.

D

Dada, Dadaist Of or relating to an art movement characterized by works with fantastic or incongruous imagery.

daguerreotype (deh-GARE-[e]-o-type) A photographic process invented in the nineteenth century for fixing an image on a silver-coated metal plate.

deconstruction A method for analyzing works of art developed in the late twentieth century, in which artworks are treated as texts that can have a variety of meanings, based on the person who perceives them, emphasizing subjectivity.

Deconstructivist A contemporary architectural style in which building parts are disassembled and reassembled in an almost sculptural fashion, without regard to the function of the building.

decoration An adornment or an embellishment on an object or structure intended to give visual pleasure.

direction The course of movement, as in horizontal, vertical, diagonal, or meandering.

digital art Art that is made with the assistance of electronic devices, or intended to be displayed on a computer.

diptych (DIP-tik) A two-paneled painting, often hinged.

disciplines Branches of art-making activity, such as painting or sculpture.

distemper A painting process using pigments mixed with egg yoke, egg white, glue, or size.

distortion The changing of an accepted perception of a form or object so that it may be barely or not at all recognizable.

dome A hemisphere used to cover an open interior space, made of an arch rotated 360 degrees on a vertical axis.

Doric Order *See* **Orders**.

drum A solid cylindrical stone that is stacked with others to create the shaft of a column, or a hollow cylinder base that supports a dome.

drypoint An etching, which is a kind of printmaking, in which the design is scratched into the surface of a metal plate.

dynasty A powerful group or family that rules a territory or nation for an extended period.

E

earthenware Ceramic ware made of slightly porous clay fired at a low temperature.

earthworks In art, the earth itself as sculptural material.

eccentric rhythm A perceived pattern that has irregular repetition of elements or irregular spacing between elements.

eave, eaves The edge of the roof that overhangs the wall.

edition A number of **prints** made from a specific printing process in one single batch. Each batch is then numbered, i.e., first edition, second edition, etc.

egg tempera Paint created by grinding dry pigment into egg yolk, which is the binder.

embroidery Sewing a design or image with colored threads into a fabric.

emphasis A device in art that draws the attention of the viewer to one or more focal points in an artwork.

encaustic (en-KAH-stik) A paint medium in which pigments are mixed into heated beeswax.

engaged column A column partly embedded in a wall.

English Perpendicular *See* **Gothic**.

engraving The process of incising or scratching lines on a hard material, such as wood or a metal plate.

entablature (in-TAB-leh-chur) In classical Greek architecture, the part of the building that is above the capital of the supporting columns. It consists of three parts: the architrave, the frieze, and the pediment.

entasis (EN-teh-sis) An apparent swelling or bulging in the shaft of a Doric column.

Epicureanism (ep-i-kyoo-REE-en-izm) An ancient Greek philosophy that advocated intelligent pleasure-seeking in life, because death was the end to existence.

equestrian An artwork that depicts a figure mounted on a horse.

etching The creation of lines or areas on glass or a metal plate, using acid that eats into the exposed surface but leaves coated, protected areas unchanged. When etched plates are inked, they can be used in printmaking.

Eucharist (YOO-keh-rist) The Sacrament of Holy Communion in the Christian faith. The ritual involves the symbolic transformation of bread and wine into the sacrificial body and blood of Jesus Christ.

Expressionism (Expressionist) An art movement in early-twentieth-century Europe that focused on capturing the subjective feeling toward objective reality. The movement developed a bold, colorful, and vigorous style, especially in painting.

F

fabricated, fabrication Artworks created with industrial and commercial processes or materials, such as welding or neon lighting; often fabricated works are designed by the artist but made by a professional in the fabrication process.

façade (feh-SAHD) The front facing of a building.

Fauvism (FOH-vizm) An early-twentieth-century art movement in Europe led by Henri Matisse that focused on bright colors and patterns. The term comes from the French word *fauve*, meaning "wild beast."

Feminism, Feminist Criticism Artwork or art criticism based on the idea that women should have political, economic, and social rights that are equal to those of men.

fengshui (FUNG-shway) The science and art of arranging architecture and furnishings to allow for a good flow of energy. The term comes from the Chinese words for *wind* and *water*.

fetish An object that is empowered with supernatural powers.

feudalism (FYOOD-el-izm) An economic and political system in rural societies in which the land is owned and controlled by a few warrior-rulers, and the rest of the people work the land as peasants.

finial (FIN-ee-el) A crowning ornament or knob.

flute, fluting Narrow vertical channels carved from top to bottom into the shafts of columns.

Fluxus A late-twentieth-century art movement that sought to create a kind of anti-art or non-art; art was conceived as an artist-initiated experience rather than an object.

flying buttress *See* **buttressing**.

focal point Main area of visual concentration in an artwork.

Foreshortening In a two dimensional artwork, creating a sense of space by enlarging areas of an object that are close to the viewer, and shrinking the parts that are farther away.

form The total appearance and organization of an artwork; also, a shape or structure in an artwork.

formal analysis The study of artwork that focuses on the elements of the language of art and the principles of composition.

formal qualities All that makes up an artwork, such as the formal elements (line, value and light, color, shape, space, texture, volume and mass, time, and motion), the medium, proportion, size, and subject matter.

formalism Artworks based solely on formal qualities.

formalist criticism The analysis and critique of an artwork based on its composition and the arrangement of its elements and principles.

found objects Already existing objects incorporated into a sculpture or assemblage. Ready-mades refer to found objects that are presented almost in their original form as finished sculptures.

freestanding Sculpture in the round, intended to be seen from many viewpoints.

French Gothic *See* **Gothic**.

fresco A painting made on plaster; in *true fresco*, water-based pigments are painted directly on a wet lime plaster ground and bind with the plaster when dry; in *dry fresco*, the paint is applied to dry plaster.

fresco secco (dry fresco) A form of fresco painting in which paint is applied to a dry plaster wall.

frieze (freez) A decorative band in the central section of the entablature in classical Greek architecture, or a decorative band on a building.

frontal A quality of sculpture in the round when it is meant to be viewed from one side only.

Futurism An art movment in Italy around 1910 that celebrated the speed, energy, change, and upheaval of the machine age.

G

gaze An analysis in artwork of who is looking at whom, and the often-implied power relationship of autonomous subject (who gazes) and subservient object (the object of the gaze)

genre painting (ZHAH[n]-reh) Paintings that contain subject matter of everyday life.

geodesic dome (jee-oh-DEES-ik) A dome shape made of framework consisting of interlocking polygonal units, developed by R. Buckminster Fuller.

geometric pattern Repeated objects, lines, or shapes based on mathematical concepts, such as the circle, square, or rectangle, and regular intervals.

gesso A common ground made of very fine powdered white chalk suspended in glue (the traditional method) or acrylic medium (modern gesso).

gesture A quickly sketched image that captures the essence of the form of the subject.

gild, gilding Coating or layering a surface with gold, gold leaf (a very thin layer of gold), or a gold color.

glaze In painting, a thin layer of glossy, transparent color applied on top of previously painted, dry areas of the painting; in ceramics, a hard, waterproof, often glossy coating fired onto the clay surface of pottery or sculpture.

glyph (glif) A figure or character that has symbolic meaning and is most often carved in relief.

Gothic The history, culture, and art of western Europe from the twelfth through the fourteenth centuries. Local variations include French Gothic and the English Perpendicular Style.

Gothic Revival A 19th century style of art that evoked Medieval Gothic architecture, craft, and painting.

gothic vault A type of vaulting featuring pointed arches

gouache (gwash) Painting with opaque watercolors.

graffiti Writing or drawing written or painted on public walls.

graver An incising tool used by printmakers and sculptors.

groin vault *See* **vaulting**.

ground A coating on a support that affects its surface quality, for example, making it rough or non-absorbent or smooth, and so on.

guilds (gilds) Organizations of merchants, artisans, and craftsmen that developed in medieval Europe.

H

handscroll A long piece of paper or cloth that is unrolled in one hand and re-rolled in the other to view individual scenes and read text.

Happening An art event that is planned by the artist and that may be performed spontaneously and solicit participation of its audience. This art form was invented by Allan Kaprow.

Harlem Renaissance A revival and celebration of African American culture, values, and aesthetics, which were expressed through all the arts in the 1920s and 1930s in the United States.

harmony The quality of relating the visual elements of a composition through the repetition of similar characteristics. A pleasing visual interaction occurs through harmony.

hatching The placing of lines side by side in parallel groups to create values and tones. Layers of such line groups create crosshatching.

Hellenistic The culture that flourished around Greece, Macedonia, and some areas bordering the Mediterranean Sea from around 323 to 31 BCE.

hieratic scaling (hi-uh-RAT-ik) A system of proportion of figures or subject matter in a work of art that gives emphasis to what or who is considered to be the most important; for example, the largest figure would be the most important or highest in rank.

hieroglyphic (hi-ro-GLIF-ik) Ancient picture writing, especially that used by the Egyptian culture.

Hinduism The dominant religion of India whose basic beliefs encompass the cycle of reincarnation and a supreme being in many forms.

horizon line In linear perspective, a horizontal line that represents eye level.

hue The pure state of color that the eye sees in the spectrum.

Humanism A system of thought that emphasizes human reason, justice, and ethics above supernaturalism and superstition.

hydria (HI-dree-ah) A Greek ceramic water jar, usually with two handles.

hypostyle (HI-puh-style) A large hall in which a grid of columns support the roof.

I

icon A visual image, pictorial representation, or symbol that may have religious or political connotations.

iconoclasm (eye-KON-uh-klazm) The act of destroying religious images or opposing their veneration.

iconography (eye-keh-NOG-reh-fee) The study of visual images and symbols within their cultural and historical contexts.

idealism An artistic interpretation of the world as it should be according to respective cultural aesthetics. Generally, all flaws and imperfections found in nature are removed.

idealized A style of art in which natural imagery is modified in a way that strives for perfection according to the values and aesthetics of a particular culture.

ideological criticism Art criticism that is rooted in the writings of Karl Marx and deals with the political underpinnings of art.

illumination A drawing or painting that decorates a hand-copied book or text.

imago mundi (im-AG-o MUN-dee) Image of the world.

impasto (im-PAHS-toe) Paint that has been thickly applied to the ground.

implied line A drawn line having missing areas that are visually completed by the viewer.

Impressionism A late-nineteenth-century painting style, originating in Western Europe, that attempts to capture subtle light qualities or fleeting moments with small strokes of strong color.

incised A kind of mark that is made by carving or gouging into a surface with a sharp instrument.

inlay To piece together or insert materials, such as ivory or colored wood, into a surface.

installation An art piece usually of mixed media that is organized for and placed in a specific space.

intaglio (in-TAH-lee-oh) A printmaking process in which lines are incised or etched into a metal plate, which is then inked and wiped so that the ink remains only in the incised lines and then transferred to paper.

intensity Brightness or dullness of a hue, or chroma.

International style A style developed in the thirteenth and fourteenth centuries in Europe with characteristics of French Gothic and Sienese art. Later, in the twentieth century, a style of architecture based on simple geometric forms without adornment.

invented [texture] An imaginary surface quality created by the artist.

Ionic Order (EYE-on-ik) *See* **Orders**.

irregular shape A shape that is complex, often organic or biomorphic, that has no simple name.

Islam The religion of Muslims as revealed to the prophet Mohammed and recorded in the Holy Koran, or Quran.

isometric perspective A perspective system for rendering a three-dimensional object on a two-dimensional surface by drawing all horizontal edges at a 30-degree angle from a horizontal base. All the verticals are drawn perpendicularly from the horizontal base.

J

Judaism Religion and way of life of the Jewish people, based on Mosaic law.

juxtapose To place contrasting elements, images, or ideas side by side.

K

ka Part of the spirit or soul of a human being in ancient Egyptian culture. *See also* **ba**.

kachina (kuh-CHEE-nuh) A spirit doll of the Pueblo culture in North America.

Kami (kah-mee) Spirits or deities in the Shinto religion, believed to dwell in nature and in charismatic people.

karma (KAR-muh) The consequences of the actions of this life, which influence the next reincarnation.

keystone The center wedge-shaped stone in an arch that fixed in place the other stones of the arch.

Kitab Khana In the Ottoman Empire, a royal atelier of artists and craftspersons who copied and illuminated books; also a library for storing books.

kinetic Sculpture that moves.

kitsch (kich) Works that are done in what is considered to be poor taste.

kiva (KEE-vuh) An underground, circular ceremonial structure of the Pueblo culture in North America.

Koran (koo-RAN) The sacred book of the Islamic religion; also *Quran*.

L

labret (LA-bret) A mouth ornament.

lacquer A resinous varnish that adds a rich sheen to a surface.

lamassu (lah-MAH-soo) A winged, human-headed bull, from Assyria.

laminated Composed of layers of glued or fused material.

lapis lazuli (LAP-is LAHZ-eh-lee) A semiprecious stone with a deep blue color.

line An element in art with length but negligible width.

line quality Attributes of a line, such as jagged, flowing, rough, angular, and so on.

linear perspective *See* **perspective**.

lintel (LINT-el) In architecture, a horizontal member spanning an opening, and usually carrying a weight from above.

lithography (lith-OG-reh-fee) A form of printmaking, invented in the nineteenth century, based on the principle that water and oil do not mix.

living rock Natural rock formation that may become incorporated in a sculpture or a building.

load bearing structure A kind of building in which all areas of the walls support the structure above them, and the walls have few openings.

local colors The natural color of an object

lost wax [*cire perdue*] A sculptural method in which a cast is made from a wax model by coating the model with an investment material that can be heated to high temperatures. The wax melts away, leaving a negative mold of the model, into which molten metal is poured or clay is pressed, creating a hollow duplicate of the original wax work.

M

malagan or **malanggan** (mah-lah-gan *or* mah-lang-gan) The carvings and ritual pieces created to honor the dead in Papua New Guinea; also, the festivals for which the carvings are made.

mana (MAH-na) Supernatural power or influence that flows through some individuals or resides in some objects.

mandala (MUN-duh-luh) A design with geometric elements that delineates deities, the universe, and wholeness in Hinduism or Buddhism.

masjid (MUS-jid) Mosque.

masquerade (mas-ker-ADE) A ceremony or a festive gathering in which masks and costumes are worn.

mass (volume) An area of occupied space. *Mass* usually refers to a solid occupying a space, while *volume* may refer to either a solid mass or an open framework occupying a space.

mausoleum (maw-seh-LEE-um) A stately tomb usually built above the ground.

medieval (meh-DEE-vel) Of or like the period between ancient and modern times.

medium, media Traditional and nontraditional materials used to make art, such as charcoal, paint, clay, bronze, video, or computers.

megalithic (meg-ah-LITH-ik) A structure built with huge stones, especially ancient or Neolithic monuments or tombs.

Mesoamerica (mes-oh-eh-MER-i-kah) The Central American regions of Mexico, Guatemala, El Salvador, and Belize.

Mesolithic (mes-oh-LITH-ik) The middle Stone Age, between the Paleolithic and Neolithic eras, marked by the earliest use of local and permanent food sources.

metaphor An image or visual element that is primarily descriptive of one thing, but is used to describe something else.

Middle Ages A period between ancient and modern times, often used in reference to Europe from the fifth through the fourteenth centuries.

mihrab (MEE-rahb) In a mosque, a niche in the wall that faces Mecca.

minaret A prayer tower that is part of an Islamic mosque.

minbar (MIN-bar) In an Islamic mosque, the pulpit for the imam, a Muslim spiritual and political leader.

Minimalism, Minimalist A nonobjective art movement in the twentieth century in the United States in which artists reduced their images and objects to pure form. These images and forms were called *primary structures*.

mixed media The mixing of art materials and forms in creating an artwork.

moai (moh-eye) A large, stone figure from the Easter Islands (Rapa Nui).

mobile A hanging kenetic sculpture whose movement is determined by air currents.

modeling The process of making a sculpture in which malleable substances such as clay or wax are pushed or pulled into a shape.

Modernism A period of Western art, primarily in the twentieth century, during which innovation and self-critical practice were emphasized.

module, modular Distinct units or sections; a composition that incorporates modules.

monochromatic An artwork that contains the hue, tints, and shades of only one color.

monolithic A large, single block or column.

Monotheism A religion distinguished by the belief in only one god.

monotype A printmaking process involving drawing or painting directly on a plate, resulting in only one impression of an image.

montage (mahn-TAHZH) A composite created by combining several separate pictures or separate clips from movies or videos.

mosaic (mo-ZAY-ik) An image or decoration created by covering a surface with small pieces of variously colored material, such as metal, glass, or stone.

mosque (mosk) An Islamic place of worship.

motif (mo-TEEF) A design or image in a composition that takes on visual significance.

mudra (MOO-druh) A hand gesture with symbolic meaning in Hindu and Buddhist art.

multipoint perspective A kind of drawing that depicts forms in space as receding to two or more vanishing points not on the same horizon line.

muqarna or **mukarna** (moo-KAR-na) Numerous niches and niche fragments, or hanging vaults, clustered in a honeycomb-like pattern, that appear in Islamic domes, arches, portals, and window openings.

mural Images painted directly on a wall, or covering a wall.

N

natural pattern Repeated elements that resemble each other, but are not exactly alike; the interval between elements may be irregular.

natron A naturally occurring soda ash used in the mummification process.

Naturalism, Naturalistic A style of art with imagery that resembles what we see in the world around us.

necropolis (neh-KROP-eh-lis) The city of the dead.

negative space Voids within an artwork.

Neoclassic, Neoclassical, Neoclassicism An 18th century revival of the Classical Greek and Roman styles in art and architecture, as well as styles from the European Renaissance.

Neolithic (nee-oh-LITH-ik) A period of the Stone Age in which humans used polished stone tools and developed agriculture; the New Stone Age.

niche (nich) A recess in a wall, usually designed to hold a decorative or votive object.

neutral Low-intensity colors.

neo-modernist Contemporary art movements and art criticism that responds to and critiques modernism.

nirvana (nir-VAH-nah) The ultimate release from the cycle of reincarnation in the Buddhist and Hindu faiths, achieved by the expulsion of individual passion, hatred, and delusion. The attainment of total peace.

nonobjective Artwork that has no imagery that resembles the natural world.

O

obelisk (OB-eh-lisk) A tall, four-sided monolith that is tapered at its apex into a pyramid form.

oblique perspective A method of showing three-dimensional objects in a drawing by rendering all receding planes at thirty degrees from the ground line.

obsidian (ob-SID-ee-en) A dark, volcanic glass.

oculus (AH-kyoo-lus) The round opening in the center of a dome.

odalisque (OH-deh-lisk) A Turkish harem girl.

oil paint A painting medium in which powdered pigments are ground into a slow-drying oil (usually linseed).

one-point perspective A drawing in which all front-facing planes are shown as parallel to the picture plane, and all other planes recede to a single point.

Op Art A 1960s style of art that created unusual visual vibrations with contrasting colors or closely placed lines.

Orders In Classical Greek architecture, an Order consists of a column with a specific style of base, shaft, capital, and entablature that is decorated and proportioned to the Classical Greek canon. The types of Orders are: Doric, Ionic, Corinthian, Tuscan, Roman Doric, and Composite.

organic architecture A style of American architecture developed by Louis Sullivan and Frank Lloyd Wright that incorporated flowing natural forms in its design.

organic A shape that seems to be drawn from nature or that is like nature; not geometric.

oriki A Yoruba praise poem

outline A line that strictly adheres to the perimeter of a shape, without variations in line thickness.

P

pagan A follower of a polytheistic religion, or an irreligious or a hedonistic person.

pagoda (peh-GO-deh) A multistoried, Asian, towerlike temple with upward sweeping roofs over each story.

paint, painting media Colored pigment ground with a binder, having a semiliquid or paste consistency.

Paleolithic (pay-lee-oh-LITH-ik) Old Stone Age, dating from 25,000 to 8000 BCE; the era of hunters and gatherers.

pantheism A belief that a divine spirit permeates everything in the universe.

papyrus (peh-PI-rus) A tall water plant, abundant around the Nile River, used for making an early form of paper.

pastels Sticks of colored pigments held together by wax or glue, used for drawing.

pathos The power to provoke compassion.

patriarch The male head of a family or family line.

patron A person who supports the artist and the arts.

pattern In art, a repetition of any element in the composition.

pedestal (PED-es-tel) The base of a column or colonnade in Classical architecture, or a base on which a sculpture or a vase may be placed.

pediment (PED-eh-ment) A low, pitched gable resting on columns, a portico, a door, or a window.

pencil A graphite rod in a wood or metal holder, used for drawing.

pendentive (pen-DENT-iv) The triangular concave sections that are created when a dome is supported by a base of arches.

Performance, Performance Art Influenced by the "Happening," performance art consists of live-action events staged as artworks.

personification May be an idea, a virtue/vice, a philosophy, or a force, represented in human form.

perspective A system of rendering the illusion of three-dimensional depth on a flat, two-dimensional surface.

pharaoh (FA-ro) Title of kings in ancient Egypt.

phenomenology The study of phenomena, such as art, from the point of view of a conscious and perceiving subject.

photography Traditionally, a light-sensitive surface such as film is exposed to light through a lens, which creates a negative image on the film; in digital photography, light-sensors in the camera record a light array, creating an image that is displayed on a screen.

photomontage A composition of many photographs, or of one using many prints to create a new image.

photo silk screen A variation on regular screen printing, in which photographs are used with special chemicals to block areas of ink, resulting in an image.

piazza (pee-AT-za) An open court or plaza.

pictograph (PIK-to-graf) A picture or picture-like symbol used in early writing to convey an idea or information.

picture plane The flat, two-dimensional surface of a drawing, a print, or a painting.

pier A solid stone or masonry support, usually rectangular.

pigments Colors in powder form, mixed with binders to create paint.

pillar Any freestanding, column-like structure that does not conform to the Classical Orders. A pillar may or may not be cylindrical.

pinnacle Usually a pointed or conical ornamentation that is placed on a spire or a buttress.

planar space The vertical and horizontal space of a surface for a drawing or painting.

pointed arch As opposed to the rounded arch, this structure narrows upward to a point.

Pointillism An art movement in Europe in the late nineteenth century in which artists applied daubs of pure pigment to a ground to create an image. The paint daubs appear to blend when viewed from a distance.

polytheism The belief in many gods with distinct functions.

Pop Art An art movement in the mid-twentieth century that used common commercial items as subject matter, including newspapers, comic strips, celebrities, political personalities, Campbell's soup cans, and Coca-Cola bottles. Usually created as satire, these artworks glorified the products of mass popular culture and elevated them to twentieth-century icons.

portal An opening, a door, an entrance, or a gate.

portico (POR-ti-ko) A porch or covered walkway, with columns on one side supporting the roof.

post and lintel system A method of construction that uses posts to support a crossbeam that can bear the weight of the roof.

Postimpressionism The late-nineteenth-century movement in European painting that followed Impressionism, in which artists emphasized their subjective viewpoint or the formal qualities of the painting.

Postmodernism The late-twentieth-century movement in art, based to some extent on deconstructivism and accommodating a wide range of styles.

Post-structuralism Various branches of art criticism that are a reaction against Structuralism and hold that there is not one single meaning in an artwork, but rather multiple meanings.

power figure A carved figure that is empowered with magic, which can heal and protect. *See* **fetish**.

Pre-Columbian Refers to civilizations that thrived in the Western Hemisphere before the arrival and impact of Christopher Columbus and the conquests that followed.

primary colors In any medium, those colors that, when mixed, produce the largest range of new colors.

print In printmaking, an image created by pressing an inked plate onto a surface; in photography, a photograph usually made from a negative.

printmaking The process of making multiple artworks or impressions, usually on paper, using a printing plate, woodblock, stone, or stencil.

proportion The size relationship, or relative size, of parts of objects or imagery to a whole or to each other.

Psychoanalytic Criticism Art criticism that holds that art should be studied as the product of individuals who are shaped by their pasts, their unconscious urges, and their social histories.

pueblo (PWEB-lo) A type of communal housing built by Native Americans, primarily in the Southwest.

pylon (PIE-lan) A truncated pyramid form usually seen in Egyptian monumental gates.

Q

quatrefoil The shape of a four-leafed clover that is found in architectural plans or a **niche** containing **relief** sculpture.

Quran (koo RAN) Variation of *Koran*.

R

radial balance Visual equilibrium achieved when all the elements in a composition radiate outward from a central point.

ready-mades *See* **found objects**.

Realism A nineteenth-century style of art that depicts everyday life without idealism, nostalgia, or flattery.

rectilinear (rek-teh-LIN-ee-er) Consisting of straight lines set at 90-degree angles in a composition.

reflected [light] The brightness and color of light that is bounced off of objects in the environment.

Reformation (ref-or-MAY-shun) A sixteenth-century European movement aimed at reforming the Catholic Church, but resulting in the establishment of the Protestant churches.

refracted light The range of colors visible when a prism breaks a light beam into a spectrum of color, or in a rainbow after a storm.

register A band that contains imagery or visual motifs; often, several registers are stacked one above the other to convey a narrative sequence.

regular rhythm Standardized visual elements repeated systematically with consistent intervals.

regular shape Geometric shapes with names like circle, square, triangle, etc.

reinforced concrete Also known as ferroconcrete, features steel reinforcing bars embedded in concrete, which makes the concrete much stronger and less brittle.

relational aesthetics Art criticism that focuses on human relationships and social spaces, rather than emphasizing art objects in private galleries, homes, or museums.

relative [color] *See* **relativity of color perception.**

relativity of color perception To the human eye, colors appear different depending upon their surroundings; for example, a tan color might appear greenish when surrounded by strong red, and conversely appear reddish when surrounded by a strong green.

relic A sacred fragment of an object, a deceased saint, or an ancestor.

relief Sculpture that projects from or is carved into a flat surface. When the sculptural form is at least half round or more, it is called a *high relief*; when it is less, it is called a *low* or *bas relief*.

relief printing A group of printmaking techniques in which areas not to be printed are cut away from the printing surface, so that the areas to be printed are left higher.

reliquary (REL-i-kwer-ee) A vessel or receptacle designed to house a holy relic.

Renaissance (ren-eh-SAHNZ) A rebirth of learning and the arts in the fourteenth through the seventeenth centuries in Europe, along with the revival and study of ancient Greek and Roman cultures.

render, rendered To depict or execute in an art form.

representational art Art that presents nature, people, and objects from the world in a recognizable form.

retablo (reh-TAH-blo) A small votive painting.

rhythm A form of repetitive beats that are usually seen in a composition as a pattern. This is accomplished by repeating one or more of the formal elements in the organization of a work.

ribbed vault *See* **vaulting**.

ridgepole The beam running the length of the building, located under the highest point of a gabled roof.

Rococo (ro-ko-KO) The style of art, architecture, music, and decorative arts from early-eighteenth-century Europe, made primarily for the upper class.

Romanesque (Roman-like) An architectural style in Medieval Europe that contained massive walls, barrel vaults, and rounded arches. Romanesque churches had cross-shaped plans.

Romanticism An art movement in nineteenth-century Europe that focused on the intuitive, emotional, and picturesque. It rejected the carefully planned and rationalized compositions of the Renaissance and added a sense of mysticism to art.

rose window A large, circular, stained-glass window in a Gothic church, composed of many parts.

rotunda (ro-TUN-dah) A round building, hall, or room, usually roofed with a dome.

S

saltcellar A dish or a container designed to hold salt.

samurai (SAM-uh-rye) In feudal Japan, a member of the warrior class.

sanctuary A sacred or holy place in a church or temple.

sanskrit (SAN-skrit) The classic Indo-Aryan language from the fourth century BCE, still used in some Buddhist rituals.

sarcophagus (sar-KOF-eh-gus) A coffin.

sarsen A type of sandstone monolith found in ancient ruins, such as Stonehenge in England.

saturation The intensity or brightness of a color.

satyr A part-human part-goat creature who is associated with the beliefs of the ancient Greek god Dionysos.

scale The apparent size of an object or image that is measured by comparing it to other objects and images that are recognized as being normal sized.

scarification (skar-i-fi-KAY-shun) The cutting or scratching of the skin in various designs that will heal as permanent body decoration.

secondary colors Colors that result when any two primary colors are mixed in a particular medium.

semiotics The study of signs and symbols in written and verbal communication.

seppuku (seh-POO-koo) A Japanese ceremony of taking one's life.

serigraphy (seh-RIG-reh-fee) A printmaking technique in which ink is applied through a stencil that has been adhered to a stretched cloth.

shade The addition of black to a hue.

shading In drawing, carefully manipulating gradations in values to create the appearance of natural light on objects.

shah (shah) A title of the former rulers of Iran.

shaman (SHAH-men) A person, priest, or priestess who is empowered to use magic to cure and heal, imbue an object with magic, control spirits and commune with ancestors, and foretell the future.

shape A flat, two-dimensional element with a defined outline and usually without interior detail.

Shinto (SHIN-to) A major Japanese religion, with emphasis on ancestor and nature worship.

Shiva (SHEE-veh) Hindu god of destruction and reproduction.

shogun (SHO-gun) Any of the various hereditary leaders of Japan until 1867, who were the real rulers instead of the emperors.

silk screen *See* **serigraphy**.

silverpoint A thin rod of silver that leaves marks on paper or wood coated with layers of gesso as a ground.

simulated [texture] Painting or drawing a texture so that it seems like it could be felt.

site-specific sculpture A sculpture designed to fit into and interact with the elements in one specific location.

skeletal In architecture, relating to a framework of steel that is covered with a "skin" of glass or other light materials.

skene The background building to a performance stage in Greek theater.

slip A liquid clay, often applied to the clay vessel before firing to create surface designs.

spandrel (SPAN-drel) The area between two arches or alongside one arch, or the space between the ribs of a vault.

spectacle Public show on a grand scale.

spectrum The breakdown of white light into its components of red, orange, yellow, green, blue, indigo, and violet.

sphinx (sfinks) A figure made up of a human head and a lion's body, likely of Egyptian origin.

spire A pointed roof of a tower or steeple.

squinches The spatial areas created when a dome is placed on a square or a polygonal base.

stained glass Pieces of colored glass arranged to create an abstract composition or representational image.

stainless steel Steel alloyed with chromium, which is virtually rust-free and corrosion-free.

steel frame construction A kind of structure in which a steel framework serves as a skeleton to support multistoried buildings.

stele (STEE-leh); *pl.* **stelae** (STEE-lee) A stone slab or tablet that is carved with images and/or inscriptions usually in commemoration of a person or an event.

still life An assembled composition of objects set up by the artist to use as subject matter for an artwork.

Stoicism (STO-i-siz-em) Indifference to pleasure or pain.

structural systems Organized methods of construction that result in functional and durable buildings. These systems must endure the forces of gravity and weather as well as forces within the building itself.

Structuralism Art criticism that holds that the understanding a single work of art is based on the overall structure of art and the complex interrelationship of all its parts, because structure gives the meaning to an artwork like a sentence determines the meaning of individual words within it.

stucco (STUK-oh) A plaster material that may be used for reliefs and architectural ornamentation, such as moldings and cornices. It is also a wall covering made of a thin layer of cement.

stupa (STOO-pah) A dome-shaped Buddhist shrine.

style Specific recognizable attributes and characteristics that are consistent and coherent in the artwork within a historical period, within a cultural tradition, or of an individual artist.

subject matter The specific idea of an artwork.

subtext The underlying ideas or messages in an artwork.

subtractive color system Any system of color mixing in which the addition of more colors gives a duller result.

Subtractive process or method (sculpture) A technique in which a sculptural material, such as stone or wood, is carved away to produce a form.

sultan (SULT-n) A former ruler of Turkey, or a Muslim ruler.

support A surface upon which a two-dimensional artwork, such as a painting, is made.

Suprematism A twentieth-century art style in which artists express their true reality through totally non-objective compositions in painting.

Surreal, Surrealism (ser-REE-el-izm) An art movement in early-twentieth-century Europe influenced by the work of Sigmund Freud. Fantastic and dreamlike imagery drawn from the subconscious; or automatic drawing similar to doodling.

suspension and tensile construction A kind of construction in which steel cables are attached to vertical pylons or masts that can support structures like bridges, exhibition tents, or sports arenas.

symbol A visual element that represents something else, often an abstract concept like peace.

symbolic geometry The use of geometry to demarcate sacred alignments in nature; the use of geometric shapes in art and architecture to symbolize divine attributes.

symmetrical balance Balance achieved by distributing equal weight evenly throughout a composition. If an imaginary line could be drawn vertically down an artwork that has symmetrical balance, one side would mirror the other.

sympathetic magic A form of ritual or prayer that is directed to an image or an object in order to bring about a desired result, such as a successful hunt.

T

tabernacle A sacred place that holds the Holy Eucharist in the Christian religion.

taboo Forbidden for general use; usually applied to sacred rituals, places, or objects.

tactile texture A physical surface variation that can be perceived by the sense of touch.

Tapestry, tapestries A heavy fabric woven with designs or images, intended as a wall hanging or furniture covering.

tempera (TEM-per-ah) Painting with pigments mixed with size, casein, or egg yolk.

tensile strength (TEN-sil) The degree to which a material can withstand stretching, stress, or tension.

terra-cotta (TER-eh KOT-ah) A low-fired ceramic clay, such as that found in red-earth flowerpots.

tertiary colors (TUR-shee-er-ee) Colors that result from the mixing of one primary color and a neighboring secondary color.

tetrahedron (teh-trah-HEE-dren) A solid contained by four triangular planar faces.

texture A surface characteristic that is or appears to be tactile.

thatch A roof covering made of straw or reeds.

three-point perspective A drawing in which only one point of each volume is closest to the viewer, and all planes recede to one of three points.

time The art element that is involved in performances or video work, or is required in the viewing of static artwork.

tint The result when white is mixed with a color.

tone *See* **value**.

Torah The holy scroll of the Hebrews containing the Pentateuch, their first five books of scriptures.

torana (TO-rah-nah) Gateway in the stone fence surrounding a stupa, located at the cardinal points.

totem The emblem or symbol of a family clan.

Tourist Art Art that is based on a particular ethnic tradition, but is specifically created to sell to tourists.

tracery The ornamentation of the upper part of a Gothic window. *Plate tracery* was carved through solid stone, while *bar tracery* was incorporated in the mullions of a window.

traditional animation A style of animation that is completely hand-drawn and painted.

transept (TRAN-sept) In cross-shaped buildings, the lesser space that intersects the main space at a ninety degree angle.

triumphal arch A freestanding Roman arch commemorating an important event.

trompe l'oeil (tromp-LOY) Illusionistic painting that fools viewers into believing that they are seeing actual three-dimensional objects instead of their representation.

truss Wooden or metal beams arranged in connected triangles to make a framework.

tufa (TOO-feh) A porous rock formed from deposits of springs. The material can be easily carved when first exposed to air, then hardens with age.

two-point perspective A drawing in which no planes are parallel to the picture plane, but all recede to one of two points on the horizon.

tympanum (TIM-peh-num) In architecture, a half-circular space below an arch, and above a doorway or window.

U

ukiyo-e (oo-kee-yo-ay) A kind of Japanese print or painting; literally, "pictures from the floating world."

unity A quality achieved in an artwork when the artist organizes all the compositional elements so that they visually work together as a whole.

V

value The lights and darks in a composition; sometimes referred to as *tone*.

vanishing point In linear perspective, a point on the horizon line where parallel lines converge.

Vanitas (VAH-nee-tas) A style of Dutch painting in which the theme is the transitory nature of earthly things along with the inevitability of death.

variety Opposing or contrasting visual elements in a composition that add interest without disturbing its unity.

Vaulting, vaults A system of masonry roofing or ceiling construction based on the principle of the arch. There are several types of vaults: The *barrel* vault is a single arch extended in depth from front to back, forming a tunnel-like structure; a *groin* or a *cross* vault is formed with two barrel vaults positioned at 90-degree angles so as to cross or intersect one another; a *ribbed* vault is a variation of the groin vaulting system in which arches diagonally cross over the groin vault forming skeletal ribs; a *dome* is formed by rotating arches on their vertical axis to form a hemispheric vault.

vellum (VEL-um) A fine kind of parchment.

video; video art Art made with recording cameras and displayed on monitors, and having moving imagery.

vignette (vin-YET) A decorative design that might be used on a page of a book or in a drawing, print, or painting; the outer edges of the composition are softened or blurred.

visual culture Art criticism that integrates and studies all of the visual components of contemporary culture, including fine art, television, advertising, and so on.

visual texture The rendering of illusionary texture on a surface or a ground. This texture may be simulated, abstracted, or invented.

volume *See* **mass**.

votive painting A gift given to a deity in the form of a painting.

voussoir (voo-SWAR) Wedge-shaped stone used to build an arch or a vault.

W

warm colors Generally, reds, oranges, and yellows.

wash A thin layer of watery paint.

watercolors Pigments suspended in a water-soluble glue and applied to paper in transparent layers.

woodcut A kind of printmaking done by cutting away nonprinting areas from the surface of a block of wood.

Y

Yakshi (yah-shee) A lesser Hindu and Buddhist female divinity, associated with fertility and vegetation; the male counterpart is the Yaksha.

Z

Zen A variation of Buddhism, practiced mostly in Japan, Vietnam, and Korea, that seeks intuitive illumination of the mind and spirit, primarily through meditation.

ziggurat (ZIG-oo-rat) A terraced, flat-topped pyramid surmounted by a temple, from the ancient Near East.

BIBLIOGRAPHY

Abbate, Francesco, ed. *Precolumbian Art of North America and Mexico.* Translated by Elizabeth Evans. London: Octopus Books, 1972.

Abbott, Helen, et al., eds. *The Spirit Within: Northwest Coast Native Art from the John H. Hauberg Collection.* New York: Rizzoli, 1995.

Abiodun, Rowland, Henry J. Drewal, and John Pemberton III, eds. *The Yoruba Artist: New Theoretical Perspectives on African Arts.* Washington, DC: Smithsonian Institution Press, 1994.

Adachi, Barbara. "Living National Treasures." *Japanese Encyclopedia.* Tokyo: Kodansha, 1983, pp. 60–61.

Adams, Laurie Schneider. *A History of Western Art.* New York: McGraw-Hill, 1997.

Albarn, Keith, Jenny Miall Smith, Stanford Steele, and Dinah Walker. *The Language of Pattern: An Inquiry Inspired by Islamic Decorations.* New York: Harper and Row, 1974.

Alva, Walter, and Christopher B. Donnan. *Royal Tombs of Sipan.* Los Angeles: The Fowler Museum of Cultural Heritage, University of California, Los Angeles, 1993.

American Film Institute. "Preservation." *American Film Institute.* http://afionline.org (accessed July 16, 1998).

Andah, Bassey W. "The Ibadan Experience to Date." In *Museums and Archeology in West Africa,* edited by Claude Daniel Ardouin. Washington, DC: Smithsonian Institution Press, 1997.

Anderson, Richard L. *Calliope's Sisters: A Comparative Study of Philosophies of Art.* Englewood Cliffs, NJ: Prentice Hall, 1990.

Ardouin, Claude Daniel, ed. *Museums and Archeology in West Africa.* Washington, DC: Smithsonian Institution Press, 1997.

Arnason, H. H. *History of Modern Art.* Englewood Cliffs, NJ: Prentice Hall, 1986.

Atkins, Robert. *Art Speak: A Guide to Contemporary Ideas, Movements, and Buzzwords, 1945 to the present.* New York: Abbeville Press, 1997.

Auping, Michael. *Jenny Holzer.* New York: Universe Publishing, 1992.

Baines, John, and Jaromir Malak. *Cultural Atlas of the World: Ancient Egypt.* New York: Facts on File, 1994.

Barrie, Dennis. "The Scene of the Crime." *Art Journal* 50, no. 3 (Fall 1991): 29–32.

Barrow, Terrence. *An Illustrated Guide to Maori Art.* Honolulu: University of Hawaii Press, 1984.

Barrow, Tui Terrence. *Maori Wood Sculpture of New Zealand.* Rutland, VT: Charles E. Tuttle, 1969.

Baumann, Felix, and Marianne Karabelnik, eds. *Degas Portraits.* London: Merrell Holberton, 1994.

Beaver, R. Pierce, et al., eds. *Eerdmans' Handbook to the World's Religions.* Grand Rapids, MI: William B. Eerdmans, 1982.

Beck, James, and Michael Daley. *Art Restoration: The Culture, the Business and the Scandal.* New York: W. W. Norton, 1993.

Becker, Carol. "Art Thrust into the Public Sphere." *Art Journal* 50, no. 3 (Fall 1991): 65–68.

Beckwith, John. *Early Medieval Art.* New York: Praeger, 1973.

Benton, Janetta Rebold. *The Medieval Menagerie: Animals in the Art of the Middle Ages.* New York: Abbeville Press, 1992.

Benton, Janetta Rebold, and DiYanni, Robert. *Arts and Culture: Volume II.* Upper Saddle River, NJ: Prentice Hall, 1998.

Bernadac, Marie-Laure. *Louise Bourgeois.* Paris: Flammarion, 1996.

Berrin, Kathleen, ed. *The Spirit of Ancient Peru: Treasures from the Museo Arqueológico Rafael Larco Herrera.* London: Thames and Hudson, 1997.

Bersson, Robert. *Worlds of Art.* Mountain View, CA: Mayfield, 1991.

Bertelli, Carlo. *Mosaics.* New York: W. H. Smith, 1989.

Bianchi, Emanuela. *Ara Pacis Augustae.* Rome, Italy: Fratelli Palombi Editori, 1994.

Blair, Sheila S., and Bloom, Jonathon M. *Art and Architecture of Islam 1250–800.* Yale University Press, New Haven, c 1994.

Blake, Nayland, Lawrence Rinder, and Amy Scholder, eds. *In a Different Light: Visual Culture, Sexual Identity, Queer Practice.* San Francisco: City Light Books, 1995.

Blier, Suzanne Preston. *The Royal Arts of Africa.* New York: Harry N. Abrams, 1998.

Bluemel, Carl. *Greek Sculptors at Work.* New York: Phaidon, 1969.

Blunden, Caroline, and Mark Elvin. *The Cultural Atlas of the World: China.* Alexandria, VA: Stonehenge Press, 1991.

Blunt, Wilfrid. *Isfahan, Pearl of Persia.* London: Elek Books, 1966.

Boardman, John. *Greek Art.* London: Thames and Hudson, 1996.

Bond, Anthony, and Joanna Woodall. *Self Portrait: Renaissance to Contemporary.* London: National Portrait Gallery, 2005.

Boyd, Andrew. *Chinese Architecture and Town Planning 1500 B.C.–A.D. 1911.* London: Alec Tiranti, 1962.

Brainard, Shirl. *A Design Manual.* Upper Saddle River, NJ: Prentice Hall, 1998.

Brotherston, Gordon. *Painted Books from Mexico: Codices in UK Collections and the World They Represent.* London: The British Museum Press, 1995.

Brown, Kendall H., et al. *Light in Darkness: Women in Japanese Prints of the Early Shwa (1926–1945).* Los Angeles: Fisher Gallery, University of Southern California, 1996.

Buehler, Alfred, Terry Barrow, and Charles P. Mountford. *The Art of the South Sea Islands.* New York: Crown, 1962.

Burson, Nancy. *Faces.* Santa Fe, NM: Twin Palms, 1993.

Burton, Rosemary, and Richard Cavendish. *Wonders of the World.* Chicago: Rand McNally, 1991.

Bushnell, G. H. S. *Ancient Arts of the Americas.* New York: Praeger, 1965.

Cahill, James. *The Lyric Journey: Poetic Painting in China and Japan.* Cambridge, MA: Harvard University Press, 1966.

Cameron, Elisabeth L., with Doran H. Ross. *Isn't S/he a Doll? Play and Ritual in African Sculpture.* Los Angeles: UCLA Fowler Museum of Cultural History, 1996.

Canaday, John. *Mainstreams of Modern Art.* New York: Holt, Rinehart and Winston, 1959.

Cantrell, Jacqueline Phillips. *Ancient Mexico: Cultural Traditions in the Land of the Feathered Serpent.* Dubuque, IA: Kendall/Hunt, 1984.

Carpenter, T. H. *Art and Myth in Ancient Greece.* London: Thames and Hudson, 1991.

Caruana, Wally. *Aboriginal Art.* London: Thames and Hudson, 1993.

Casson, Lionel. *Ancient Egypt.* New York: Time-Life Books, 1971.

Caygill, Marjorie, and John Cherry. *A. W. Franks: Nineteenth Century Collecting and the British Museum.* London: The British Museum Press, 1997.

Center for African Art. *ART/artifact: African Art in Anthropology Collections.* New York: Prestel Verlag, 1989.

Chandra, Pramod. *The Sculpture of India 3000 BC–AD 1300.* Washington, DC: The National Gallery of Art, 1985.

Chicago, Judy. *Through the Flower: My Struggles as a Woman Artist.* Garden City, NY: Doubleday, 1975.

Chui, Hu. *The Forbidden City, Collection of Photographs.* Beijing: China Photographic Publishing House, 1995.

Clark, Kenneth. *Animals and Men: Their Relationship as Reflected in Western Art from Prehistory to the Present Day.* New York: William Morrow, 1977.

Clark, Kenneth. *The Nude: A Study in Ideal Form.* Princeton, NJ: Princeton University Press, 1956.

Clearwater, Bonnie. *Mark Rothko: Works on Paper.* New York: Hudson Hills Press, 1984. Distributed by Viking Penguin.

Cocke, Thomas. *900 Years: The Restorations of Westminster Abbey.* London: Harvey Miller, 1995.

Coe, Michael, Dean Snow, and Elizabeth Bensen. *The Cultural Atlas of the World: Ancient America.* Richmond, VA: Stonehenge Press, 1990.

Coe, Michael D. *The Maya.* New York: Thames and Hudson, 1982.

Collcutt, Martin, Marius Jansen, and Isao Kumakuro. *Cultural Atlas of the World: Japan.* Alexandria, VA: Stonehenge Press, 1991.

Collier's. *Photographic History of World War II.* New York: P. F. Collier and Son, 1946.

Collignon, Maxime. *Manual of Mythology in Relation to Greek Art.* New Rochelle, NY: Caratzas Brothers, 1982.

Colton, Joel. *Great Ages of Man: Twentieth Century.* New York: Time-Life Books, 1968.

Colvin, Howard. *Architecture and the After-life.* New Haven and London: Yale University Press, 1991.

Compassion and Protest: Recent Social and Political Art from the Eli Broad Family Foundation Collection. New York: Cross River Press, a Division of Abbeville Press, 1991.

Corbin, George A. *Native Arts of North America, Africa, and the South Pacific.* New York: Harper and Row, 1988.

Cotterell, Arthur. *The First Emperor of China.* New York: Holt, Rinehart and Winston, 1981.

Cowart, Jack, et al. *Georgia O'Keeffe: Art and Letters.* Washington, DC: The National Gallery of Art, 1987.

Craven, Roy C. *Indian Art: A Concise History.* London: Thames and Hudson, 1997.

Crimp, Douglas. "The Photographic Activity of Postmodernism." In *Postmodern Perspectives: Issues in Contemporary Art,* edited by Howard Risatti, 131–139. Englewood Cliffs, NJ: Prentice Hall, 1990.

Culbertson, Judi, and Tom Randall. *Permanent Parisians: An Illustrated Guide to the Cemeteries of Paris.* Chelsea, VT: Chelsea Green, 1986.

Cunningham, Lawrence S., and John J. Reich. *Culture and Values: A Survey of the Western Humanities, Volume II.* Fort Worth, TX: Harcourt Brace College Publishers, 1998.

Cuttler, Charles D. *Northern Painting from Pucelle to Bruegel: Fourteenth, Fifteenth and Sixteenth Centuries.* New York: Holt, Rinehart and Winston. 1968.

Davies, J. G. *Temples, Churches and Mosques: A Guide to the Appreciation of Religious Architecture.* New York: The Pilgrim Press, 1982.

Dawson, Barry, and John Gillow. *The Traditional Art of Indonesia.* London: Thames and Hudson, 1994.

de Franciscis, Alfonso. *Pompeii: Civilization and Art.* Naples, Italy: Edizioni Interdipress, 1997.

De la Mora, Sergio. *Forging a National and Popular Art Cinema in Mexico: "María Candelaria."* Accessed online in June 2010 at http://www.sdlatinofilm.com/trends5.html.

DeMott, Barbara. *Dogon Masks: A Structural Study in Form and Meaning.* Ann Arbor, MI: UMI Research Press, 1982.

Denyer, Susan. *African Traditional Architecture.* New York: Africana Publishing, 1978.

Derson, Denise. *What Life Was Like on the Banks of the Nile, Egypt 3050–30 BC.* Alexandria, VA: Time-Life Books, 1996.

Desai, Vishakha N., and Darielle Mason. *Gods, Guardians and Lovers: Temple Sculptures from North India A.D. 700–1200.* New York: The Asia Society Galleries; Ahmedabad: Mapin Publishing, 1993.

Dewald, Ernest T. *Italian Painting.* New York: Holt, Rinehart and Winston, 1965.

de Zegher, M. Catherine. *Inside the Visible: An Elliptical Traverse of 20th Century Art.* Cambridge: MIT Press, 1996.

Dickerson, Albert I., ed. *The Orozco Frescoes at Dartmouth.* Hanover, NH: The Trustees of Dartmouth College, 1962.

Drewal, Henry John, and John Pemberton III, with Rowland Abiodun. *Yoruba, Nine Centuries of African Art and Thought.* New York: Center for African Art, 1989.

Duiker, William J., and Jackson J. Spielvogel. *World History.* 4th ed. Belmont, CA: Thomson/Wadsworth, 2004.

Durand, Jorge, and Douglas S. Massey. *Miracles on the Border: Retablos of Mexican Migrants to the United States.* Tucson and London: University of Arizona Press, 1995.

Ebrey, Patricia Buckley. *Cambridge Illustrated History of China.* London: Cambridge University Press, 1996.

Edwards, Jim. *Precarious Links: Emily Jennings, Hung Liu, Celia Munoz.* San Antonio, TX: San Antonio Museum of Art, 1990.

Edwards, I. E. S. *The Treasures of Tutankhamun.* New York: Penguin Books, 1977.

Elkins, James. *Visual Studies: A Skeptical Introduction.* New York: Routledge, 2003.

Encyclopedia Americana. S.v. "Central Park," by Harry L. Coles; "China: Theater," by Chia-pao Wan; "Globe Theater," by Bernard Beckermen; "Japan: Doll Drama," by Donald Richie; "Disneyland and Disney World," "Epcot," "Palenque," by Pedro Armillas; "Zoological Gardens," by William Bridges. Danbury, CT: Grolier, 1986.

Encyclopedia Britannica Online. S.v. "Animal Behaviour: Behaviour of Animals in Groups." *http://www.eb.com:180/cgi-bin/g?DocF=macro/5000/62/94.html* (accessed May 19, 1998).

Etienne, Robert. *Pompeii: The Day a City Died.* New York: Harry N. Abrams, 1992.

Ezra, Kate. *Art of the Dogon.* New York: The Metropolitan Museum of Art, 1988.

Fagan, Brian M. *Rape of the Nile.* Kingston, RI: Moyer Bell, 1992.

Fagg, William. *Yoruba: Sculpture of West Africa.* New York: Alfred A. Knopf, 1982.

Feder, Norman. *American Indian Art.* New York: Harry N. Abrams, 1995.

Feest, Christian F. *Native Arts of North America.* New York: Oxford University Press, 1980.

Fichner-Rathus, Lois. *Understanding Art.* Boston, MA: Wadsworth/Cengage, 2010.

Fiero, Gloria. *The Humanistic Tradition.* Madison, WI: WCB Brown and Benchmark, 1995.

Fiodorov, B., ed. *Architecture of the Russian North, 12th through 19th Centuries.* Leningrad: Aurora Art Publishers, 1976.

Fisher, Robert E. *Mystics and Mandalas: Bronzes and Paintings of Tibet and Nepal.* Redlands, CA: The University of Redlands, 1974.

Flaherty, Thomas H. *Incas: Lords of Gold and Glory.* Alexandria, VA: Time-Life Books, 1992.

–––. *The American Indians: The Spirit World.* Alexandria, VA: Time-Life Books, 1992.

–––. *The Mighty Chieftains.* Alexandria, VA: Time-Life Books, 1993.

Flaherty, Thomas H., ed. *Aztecs: Reign of Blood and Splendor.* Alexandria, VA: Time-Life Books, 1992.

Fleming, William. *Arts and Ideas.* 3rd ed. New York: Holt, Rinehart and Winston, 1970..*Frank Gehry: Pritzker Architect Prize Laureate 1989.* http://www.pritzkerprize.com/gehry.htm (accessed April 13, 2004).

Frankfort, Henri. *The Art and Architecture of the Orient.* New Haven, CT: Yale University Press, 1970.

Furst, Peter T., and Jill L. Furst. *North American Indian Art.* New York: Rizzoli, 1982.

Gardner, Joseph L. *Mysteries of the Ancient Americas.* Pleasantville, NY: Reader's Digest, 1986.

Gardner, Paul. *Louise Bourgeois.* New York: Universe Publishing, 1994.

Getty, Adele. *Goddess, Mother of Living Nature.* London: Thames and Hudson, 1990.

Getz-Preziosi, Pat. *Early Cycladic Sculpture: An Introduction.* Malibu, CA: J. Paul Getty Museum, 1994.

Gilbert, Creighton. *History of Renaissance Art Throughout Europe.* New York: Harry N. Abrams, 1973.

Gillon, Werner. *A Short History of African Art.* New York: Penguin Books, 1991.

Godfrey, Tony. *Painting Today.* Phaidon, 2005.

Goggin, Mary-Margaret. "'Decent' vs. 'Degenerate' Art: The National Socialist Case." *Art Journal* 50, no. 4 (Winter 1991): 84–93.

Goodman, Susan Tumarkin, ed. *Russian Jewish Artists in a Century of Change 1890–1990.* Munich: Prestel-Verlag, 1995.

Gowing, Lawrence. *Lucien Freud.* London: Thames and Hudson, 1982.

Graves, Eleanor. *Life Goes to War: A Picture History of World War II.* Boston, MA: Little, Brown, 1977.

Graze, Sue, Kathy Halbreich, and Roberta Smith. *Elizabeth Murray: Paintings and Drawings.* New York: Harry N. Abrams, in association with the Dallas Museum of Art and the MIT Committee on the Visual Arts, 1987.

Greenberg, Clement. "Avant-Garde and Kitsch." *Partisan Review* 6 (Fall 1939). Reprinted in Greenberg, *Art and Culture: Critical Essays.* Boston: Beacon Press, 1961.

Gregory, Richard L. *Eye and Brain: The Psychology of Seeing.* 5th ed. Princeton, NJ: Princeton University Press, 1997. *Grolier Encyclopedia.* S.v. "Pacifism and Non-violent Movements," "Gandhi's Campaigns." 1996.

Grube, Ernst J. *The World of Islam.* New York: McGraw-Hill, 1977.

Gruzinski, Serge. *The Aztecs: Rise and Fall of an Empire.* New York: Harry N. Abrams, 1992.

"Guernica." www.web.org.uk/picasso/guernica.html (accessed March 15, 2004).

Guiart, Jean. *The Arts of the South Pacific.* New York: Golden Press, 1963.

Guilbaut, Serge. *How New York Stole the Idea of Modern Art: Abstract Expressionism, Freedom, and the Cold War.* Translated by Arthur Goldhammer. Chicago and London: University of Chicago Press, 1983.

Hadington, Evan. *Lines to the Mountain Gods.* New York: Random House, 1987.

Hanson, Allan, and Louise Hanson, eds. *Art and Identity in Oceania.* Honolulu, HI: University of Hawaii Press, 1990.

Harle, J. C. *The Art and Architecture of the Indian Subcontinent.* London: Penguin Books, 1986.

Harris, Ann Sutherland, and Linda Nochlin. *Women Artists 1550–1950.* New York: Alfred A. Knopf, 1984.

Hartt, Frederick. *History of Italian Renaissance Art: Painting, Sculpture, Architecture.* Englewood Cliffs, NJ: Prentice Hall, 1969.

Hawthorn, Audrey. *Kwakiutl Art.* Seattle and London: University of Washington Press, 1979.

Hay, John. *Masterpieces of Chinese Art.* Greenwich, CT: New York Graphic Society, 1974.

Heartney, Eleanor. "Pornography." *Art Journal* 50, no. 4 (Winter 1991): 16–19.

Hedgecoe, John. *Henry Moore,* Nelson, London: Simon and Schuster, New York, 1968.

Helm, Mackinley. *Mexican Painters: Rivera, Orozco, Siqueiros, and Other Artists of the Social Realist School.* New York: Dover, 1941.

Hershey, Irwin. *Indonesian Primitive Art.* New York: Oxford Press, 1991.

Heusinger, Lutz. *Michelangelo.* Florence, Italy: Scala; New York: Riverside, 1989.

Hillier, J. *Japanese Colour Prints.* London: Phaidon, 1991.

Historical Anatomies on the Web, http://www.nlm.nih.gov/exhibition/historicalanatomies/home.html. Accessed March 2010

Hoffman, Katherine. *Concepts of Identity: Historical and Contemporary Images and Portraits of Self and Family.* New York: HarperCollins, 1996.

Holm, Bill. *Northwest Coast Indian Art: An Analysis of Form.* Seattle: University of Washington Press, 1995.

Holt, Elizabeth Gilmore, ed. *Literary Sources of Art History: An Anthology of Texts from Theophilus to Goethe.* Princeton, NJ: Princeton University Press, 1947.

Holt, John Dominis. *The Art of Featherwork in Old Hawaii.* Honolulu: Topgallant, 1985.

Honour, Hugh, and John Fleming. *The Visual Arts: A History.* Englewood Cliffs, NJ: Prentice Hall, 1995.

Hooks, Bell. *Art on My Mind: Visual Politics.* New York: New Press, 1995.

Hopkins, Jerry. *Yoko Ono.* New York: Macmillan, 1986.

Howard, Jeremy. *Art Nouveau: International and National Styles in Europe.* Manchester, UK: Manchester University Press, 1996.

Hughes, Robert. *American Visions.* New York: Alfred A. Knopf, 1997.

Hulton, Paul, and Lawrence Smith. *Flowers in Art from East and West.* London: British Museum Publications, 1979.

Huntington, Susan L., and John C. Huntington. *Leaves from the Bodhi Tree.* Seattle: University of Washington Press, 1990.

Identity and Alterity: Figures of the Body 1895–1995. Edited by Manlio Brusatin and Jean Clair. Venice, Italy: Marsilio, 1995. Exhibition catalog of La Biennale di Venezia 46, esposizione internazionale d'arte.

Indych, Anna. "Nuyorican Baroque: Pepón Osorio's *Chucherías.*" *Art Journal* 60, no. 1 (Spring 2001): 72–83.

Internet Medieval Sourcebook. www.fordham.edu/halsall/sbook.html (accessed March 30, 2004).

Ivory: An International History and Illustrated Survey. New York: Harry N. Abrams, 1987.

J. Paul Getty Museum Handbook of the Collections. Malibu, CA: J. Paul Getty Museum, 1991.

Janson, H. W. *History of Art.* New York: Harry N. Abrams, 1995.

Jellicoe, Geoffrey, and Susan Jellicoe. *The Landscape of Man.* London: Thames and Hudson, 1987.

Jonaitis, Aldona. *From the Land of the Totem Poles.* New York: American Museum of Natural History, 1988.

Jones, Alexander. *The Jerusalem Bible.* Garden City, NY: Doubleday, 1966.

Jones, Amelia, ed. *Sexual Politics: Judy Chicago's Dinner Party in Feminist Art History.* Berkeley: University of California Press, 1996.

Kaplan, Janet A. "*Give and Take* Conversations." *Art Journal* 61, no. 2 (Summer 2002): 68–97.

Kaprow, Allen. *Assemblage, Environments and Happenings.* New York: Harry N. Abrams, 1961.

Kearney, Richard, and David Rasmussen, eds. *Continental Aesthetics: Romanticism to Postmodernism, An Anthology.* Malden, MA: Blackwell Publishers LTD, 2001.

Kessler, Adam T. *Empires Beyond the Great Wall: The Heritage of Genghis Khan.* Los Angeles: Natural History Museum of Los Angeles County, 1994.

Kettering, Alice McNeil. "Gentlemen in Satin: Masculine Ideals in Later Seventeenth-Century Dutch Portraiture." *Art Journal* 56, no. 2 (Summer 1997): 41–47.

Kienholz, Edward, and Nancy Reddin Kienholz. *Kienholz: A Retrospective.* New York: Whitney Museum of American Art, 1996.

Kirsh, Andrea. *Carrie Mae Weems.* Washington, DC: The National Museum of Women in the Arts, 1993.

Kitchen, K. A. *Pharaoh Triumphant: The Life and Times of Ramesses II.* Cairo, Egypt: American University in Cairo Press, 1982.

Koons, Jeff. *The Jeff Koons Handbook.* New York: Rizzoli, 1992.

Kopper, Phillip. *The Smithsonian Book of North American Indians before the Coming of the Europeans.* Washington, DC: Smithsonian Books, 1986.

Kulka, Tomas. *Kitsch and Art.* University Park: Pennsylvania State University Press, 1996.

Kundera, Milan. *The Unbearable Lightness of Being.* Translated by Michael Henry Heim. New York: Harper and Row, 1984.

Kuroda, Taizo, Melinda Takeuchi, and Yuzo Yamane. *Worlds Seen and Imagined: Japanese Screens from the Idemitsu Museum of Art.* New York: The Asia Society Galleries; Abbeville Press, 1995.

Laude, Jean. *African Art of the Dogon.* New York: Viking Press, 1973.

Lauer, David A., and Stephen Pentak. *Design Basics.* Boston, MA: Thomson/Wadsworth, 2008.

Lazzari, Margaret, and Clayton Lee. *Art and Design Fundamentals.* New York: Van Nostrand Reinhold, 1990.

Lee, Sherman E. *A History of Far Eastern Art.* New York: Harry N. Abrams, 1973.

Levenson, Jay A. *Circa 1492.* New Haven, CT: Yale University Press, 1991.

Levi, Peter. *The Cultural Atlas of the World: The Greek World.* Alexandria, VA: Stonehenge Press, 1992.

Lewis, Bernard. *Islam and the Arab World.* New York: Alfred A. Knopf, 1976.

Lewis, Phillip. "Tourist Art, Traditional Art and the Museum in Papua New Guinea." In *Art and Identity in Oceania,* edited by Allan Hanson and Louise Hanson. Honolulu: University of Hawaii Press, 1990.

Lincoln, Louise. *Assemblage of Spirits: Idea and Image in New Ireland.* New York: George Braziller, 1987.Linker, Kate. *Love for Sale: The Words and Pictures of Barbara Kruger.* New York: Harry N. Abrams, 1990.

Lion King: The Broadway Musical ("Circles of Sound," by Lebe M, "New Visions for Pride Rock," by Eileen Blumenthal and Julie Taymor). *Stagebill,* 1998.

Lippard, Lucy R. *Mixed Blessings: New Art in a Multicultural America.* New York: Pantheon Books, 1990.

Lippard, Lucy. *The Pink Glass Swan: Selected Feminist Essays on Art.* New York: New Press, 1995.

Lossing, Benson J. *Mathew Brady's Illustrated History of the Civil War.* Washington, DC: Fair Fax Press; Barre Publishing, 1912.

Lowe, Sarah M. *Frida Kahlo.* New York: Universe Publishing, 1991.

Lundquist, John M. *The Temple: Meeting Place of Heaven and Earth.* London: Thames and Hudson, 1993.

Lyle, Emily, ed. *Sacred Architecture in the Traditions of India, China, Judaism and Islam.* Edinburgh: Edinburgh University Press, 1992.

Machida, Margo. "Out of Asia: Negotiating Asian Identities in America." In *Asia America: Identities in Contemporary Asian American Art.* New York: The Asia Society Galleries; New Press, 1994.

Mackenzie, Lynne. *Non-Western Art: A Brief Guide.* Upper Saddle River, NJ: Prentice Hall, 2001.

Malone, Maggie, and Hideko Takayama. "A Japanese Buying Spree: The Tycoon Who Spent $160 Million at Auctions." *Newsweek,* May 28, 1990, p. 75.

Mann, A. T. *Sacred Architecture.* Rockport, MA: Element, 1993.

Marcus, George E. "Middlebrow into Highbrow at the J. Paul Getty Trust." In *Looking High and Low,* edited by Brenda Jo Bright and Liza Bakewell. Tuscon: University of Arizona Press, 1995.

Mariani, Valerio. *Michelangelo the Painter.* New York: Harry N. Abrams, 1964.

Mathieu, Paul. *Sex Pots, Eroticism in Ceramics:* Rutgers University Press, New Brunswick, New Jersey. c 2003.

Matilsky, Barbara C. *Fragile Ecologies: Contemporary Artists' Interpretations and Solutions.* New York: Rizzoli, 1992.

Matt, Leonard von, Mario Moretti, and Guglielmo Maetzke. *The Art of the Etruscans.* New York: Harry N. Abrams, 1970.

McLanathan, Richard. *The American Tradition in the Arts.* New York: Harcourt Brace and World, 1968.

Mead, Sidney Moko. *Te Maori: Maori Art from New Zealand Collections.* New York: Harry N. Abrams, 1984.

Media Scape. New York: Solomon R. Guggenheim Museum, 1996.

Miller, Kimberly J. "Battle for Iwo Jima." http://www.usmc.mil (accessed 1997).

Miller, Arthur G. *The Painted Tombs of Oaxaca, Mexico: Living with the Dead.* Cambridge: Cambridge University Press, 1995.

Miller, Mary Ellen. *The Art of Mesoamerica from Olmec to Aztec.* New York: Thames and Hudson, 1986.

Mirzoeff, Nicholas, ed. *The Visual Culture Reader.* London and New York: Routledge, 1998.

———. *An Introduction to Visual Culture.* London; New York: Routledge, 1999.

Mitchell, W. J. T., ed. *Art and the Public Sphere.* Chicago and London: University of Chicago Press, 1992.

Mitchell, W. J. T., and Margaret Dikovitskaya. *An Interview with W. J. T. Mitchell, Gaylord Donnelley Distinguished Service Professor of English and Art History, University of Chicago, 11 January 2001.* http://humanities.uchicago.edu/faculty/Mitchell/Dikovitskaya_interviews_Mitchell.pdf.

Monod-Bruhl, Odette. *Indian Temples.* London: Oxford University Press, 1951.

Morgan, William N. *Prehistoric Architecture in the Eastern United States.* Cambridge, MA: MIT Press, 1980.

Moynihan, Elizabeth B. *Paradise as a Garden in Persia and Mughal India.* London: Scolar Press, 1979.

Munroe, Alexandra. *Japanese Art After 1945: Scream Against the Sky.* New York: Harry N. Abrams, 1994.

Murray, Jocelyn. *The Cultural Atlas of the World: Africa.* Alexandria, VA: Stonehenge Press, 1992.

Murray, Peter, and Linda Murray. *The Art of the Renaissance.* New York: Praeger, 1963.

Nagle, Geraldine. *The Arts-World Themes.* Madison, WI: Brown and Benchmark, 1993.

Nemser, Cindy. *Art Talk: Conversations with 15 Women Artists.* New York: HarperCollins, 1995.

Newhall, Beaumont. *History of Photography from 1839 to the Present Day.* New York: Museum of Modern Art, 1964.

Newland, Amy and Chris Uhlenbeck, eds. *Ukiyo-e to Shin Hanga: The Art of Japanese Woodblock Prints.* New York: Mallard Press, 1990.

Newton, Douglas. *New Guinea Art in the Collection of the Museum of Primitive Art.* New York: Publishers Printing–Admiral Press, 1967.

Nochlin, Linda. *Women, Art, and Power and Other Essays.* New York: Harper and Row, 1988.

Northern, Tamara. *The Art of Cameroon.* Washington D.C.: The Smithsonian Institute, 1984.

Norwich, John Julius, ed. *Great Architecture of the World.* New York: Bonanza Books, 1979.

Nou, Jean-Louis, Amina Okada, and M. C. Joshi. *Taj Mahal.* New York: Abbeville Press, 1993.

Ocvirk, Otto G., Robert E. Stinson, Philip R. Wigg, Robert O. Bone, and David L. Clayton. *Art Fundamentals: Theory and Practice.* Madison, WI: Brown and Benchmark, 1998.

Of Sky and Earth: Art of the Early Southeastern Indians. Edited by Roy S. Dickens. Dalton, GA: Lee Printing Company, 1982. Published in conjunction with the exhibition shown at the High Museum of Art, Atlanta, GA.

O'Hara, Frank. *Robert Motherwell.* New York: Museum of Modern Art, 1965.

Ohashi, Haruzo. *The Japanese Garden: Islands of Serenity.* Tokyo: Graphic-sha, 1997.

Oliver, Douglas L. *The Pacific Islands.* Honolulu: University of Hawaii Press, 1989.

O'Neill, John P., ed. *Mexico: Thirty Centuries of Splendor.* New York: Metropolitan Museum of Art, 1990.

Pacific: A Companion to the Regenstein Halls of the Pacific. Edited by Ron Dorfman. Chicago: Field Museum of Natural History, 1991. Field Museum Centennial Collection.

Papanek, John L. *Mesopotamia: The Mighty Kings.* Alexandria, VA: Time-Life Books, 1995.

Papanek, John L., ed. *Africa's Glorious Legacy, Lost Civilizations.* Alexandria, VA: Time-Life Books, 1994.

———. *Ancient India, Land of Mystery.* Alexandria, VA: Time-Life Books, 1994.

Pasztory, Esther. *Aztec Art.* New York: Harry N. Abrams, 1983.

Pelrine, Diane M. *Affinities of Form: Arts of Africa, Oceania and the Americas from the Raymond and Laura Wielgus Collection.* Munich: Prestel-Verlag, 1996.

Pendlebury, J. D. S. *A Handbook to the Palace of Minos at Knossos.* London: Macmillan, 1935.

Penny, David W. *Art of the American Indian Frontier: The Chandler-Pohrt Collection.* The Detroit Institute of Art. Seattle: University of Washington Press, 1992.

Perani, Judith, and Fred T. Davidson. *The Visual Arts of Africa: Gender, Power and Life Cycle Rituals.* Upper Saddle River, NJ: Prentice Hall, 1998.

Perchuk, Andrew. "Hannah Wilke [exhibition at] Ronald Feldman Fine Arts." *Artforum* (April 1994): 93–94.

Phipps, Richard, and Richard Wink. *Invitation to the Gallery.* Dubuque, IA: Wm. C. Brown, 1987.

Pierson, William H., and Martha Davidson. *Arts of the United States: A Pictorial History.* New York: McGraw-Hill, 1960.

Preble, Duane, Sarah Preble, and Patrick L. Frank. *ArtForms.* Upper Saddle River, NJ: Prentice Hall, 1999.

Ragghianti, Carlo Ludovico, and Licia Ragghianti Collobi. *National Museum of Anthropology, Mexico City.* New York: Newsweek (Simon and Schuster), 1970.

Ramseyer, Urs. *The Art and Culture of Bali.* Singapore and Oxford: Oxford University Press, 1986.

Rawson, Jessica, ed. *The British Museum Book of Chinese Art.* London: Thames and Hudson, 1992.

Reilly, Maura. "The Drive to Describe: An Interview with Catherine Opie." *Art Journal* 60, no. 2 (Summer 2001) 83–95.

Rhodes, Colin. *Outsider Art, Spontaneous Alternatives.* World of Art. New York: Thames and Hudson, 2000.

Richter, Anne. *Arts and Crafts of Indonesia.* San Francisco: Chronicle Books, 1994.

Risatti, Howard, ed. *Postmodern Perspectives: Issues in Contemporary Art.* Englewood Cliffs, NJ: Prentice Hall, 1990.

Rochfort, Dennis. *Mexican Muralists.* New York: Universe Publishing, 1993.

Ross, Doran H. "Akua's Child and Other Relatives: New Mythologies for Old Dolls." In *Isn't S/he a Doll? Play and Ritual in African Sculpture,* by Elisabeth L. Cameron, 43–57. Los Angeles: UCLA Fowler Museum of Cultural History, 1996.

Rowland, Anna. *Bauhaus Source Book.* New York: Van Nostrand Reinhold, 1990.

Roy, Christopher. *Art and Life in Africa: Selections from the Stanley Collection, Exhibitions of 1985 and 1992.* Iowa City: University of Iowa Museum of Art, 1992.

Rubin, Barbara, Robert Carlton, and Arnold Rubin. *Forest Lawn: L.A. in Installments.* Santa Monica, CA: Westside Publications, 1979.

Santini, Loretta. *Pompeii and the Villa of the Mysteries.* Narni-Terni, Italy: Editrice Plurigraf, 1997.

Sasser, Elizabeth Skidmore. *The World of Spirits and Ancestors in the Art of Western Sub-Saharan Africa.* Lubbock: Texas Tech University Press, 1995.

Saunders, J. B. de C. M., and Charles O'Malley. *The Illustrations from the Works of Andreas Vesalius of Brussels.* New York: Dover, 1950.

Sayre, Henry M. *The Object of Performance: The American Avant-Garde since 1970.* Chicago: University of Chicago Press, 1989.

Schmitz, Carl A. *Oceanic Art: Myth, Man and Image in the South Seas.* New York: Harry N. Abrams, 1971.

Schwarz, Hans-Peter. *Media-Art-History.* Munich: Prestel-Verlag, 1997.

Seaford, Richard. *Pompeii.* New York: Summerfield Press, 1978.

Setton, Kenneth M., et al. *The Renaissance, Maker of Modern Man.* Washington, DC: National Geographic Society, 1970.

Sharer, Robert, and Sylvanus Morley. *The Ancient Maya.* Stanford, CA: Stanford University Press, 1994.

Sharp, Dennis. *A Visual History of Twentieth Century Architecture.* Greenwich, CT: New York Graphic Society, 1972.

Shearer, Alistair. *The Hindu Vision: Forms of the Formless.* London: Thames and Hudson, 1993.

Sheets, Hilary. "Click Here for Enlightenmnet." *ARTnews,* April 2010. Accessed online in June 2010 at http://www.artnews.com/issues/article.asp?art_id=2910.

Shohat, Ella, and Robert Stam. "Narrativizing Visual Culture," in *The Visual Culture Reader,* ed. by Nicholas Mirzoeff. London and New York: Routledge, 1998.

Sickman, Lawrence, and Alexander Soper. *The Art and Architecture of China.* New Haven, CT: Yale University Press, 1971.

Silva, Anil de, Otto von Simons, and Roger Hinks. *Man Through Art, War and Peace.* Greenwich, CT: New York Graphic Society, 1964.

Simmons, David. *Whakairo Maori Tribal Art.* New York: Oxford University Press, 1985.

Simon, Joan, ed. *Bruce Nauman.* Minneapolis: Walker Art Center, 1994.

Sitwell, Sacheverell. *Great Palaces.* New York: Hamlyn, 1969.

Skinner, Charles Montgomery. *Myths and Legends of Our Own Land.* Philadelphia and London: J. B. Lippincott, 1924.

Skira, Albert. *Treasures of Asia: Chinese Painting.* Cleveland, OH: World, 1960.

Slatkin, Wendy. *Women Artists in History: From Antiquity to the Present.* Upper Saddle River, NJ: Prentice Hall, 1997.

Smith, Bradley, and Wan-go Wen. *China: A History in Art.* New York: Doubleday, 1979.

Snellgrove, David L., ed. *The Image of the Buddha.* Paris: UNESCO (United Nations Educational, Scientific and Cultural Organization); Tokyo: Kodansha, 1978.

Solomon-Godeau, Abigail. "The Other Side of Vertu: Alternative Masculinities in the Crucible of Revolution." *Art Journal* 56, no. 2 (Summer 1997): 55–61.

Sontag, Susan. *Against Interpretation and Other Essays.* New York: Farrar, Straus and Giroux, 1966.

Spayde, Jon. "Cultural Revolution." *Departures* (September/October 1995): 115–123, 154–157.

Sporre, Dennis J. *The Creative Impulse: An Introduction to the Arts.* Upper Saddle River, NJ: Prentice Hall, 1996.

Staccioli, R. A. *Ancient Rome: Monuments Past and Present.* Rome: Vision, 1989.

Staniszewski, Mary Anne. *Believing Is Seeing: Creating a Culture of Art.* New York: Penguin Books, 1995.

Stanley-Baker, Joan. *Japanese Art.* London: Thames and Hudson, 1984.

Sterling, Charles. *Still Life Painting: From Antiquity to the Twentieth Century.* 2nd ed. rev. New York: Harper and Row, 1980.

Stewart, Gloria. *Introduction to Sepik Art of Papua New Guinea.* Sydney, Australia: Garrick Press, 1972.

Stewart, Hilary. *Looking at Indian Art of the Northwest Coast.* Seattle: University of Washington Press, 1979.

Stierlin, Henri. *Art of the Aztecs and Its Origins.* Translated by Betty and Peter Ross. New York: Rizzoli, 1982.

Stierlin, Henri. *The Pharaohs, Master-Builders.* Paris: Terrail, 1992.

Stokstad, Marilyn. *Art History.* Upper Saddle River, NJ: Prentice Hall, 1995.

Stooss, Toni, and Thomas Kellein, eds. *Nam June Paik: Video Time–Video Space.* New York: Harry N. Abrams, 1993.

Stuart, Gene S., and George E. Stuart. *Lost Kingdoms of the Maya.* Washington, DC: National Geographic Society, 1993.

Sullivan, Michael. *Art and Artists of Twentieth-Century China.* Berkeley: University of California Press, 1996.

Sutton, Peter C. *The Age of Rubens.* Boston: Museum of Fine Arts, Boston: 1993.

Swann, Peter C. *Chinese Monumental Art.* New York: Viking, 1963.

Tadashi Kobayashi. *Ukiyo-e: An Introduction to Japanese Woodblock Prints.* Tokyo: Kodansha, 1992.

Tallman, Susan. "General Idea." *Arts Magazine* (May 1990): 21–22.

Tannahill, Reay. *Food in History.* New York: Stein and Day, 1973.

Tansey, Richard G., and Fred S. Kleiner. *Gardner's Art Through the Ages.* Fort Worth, TX: Harcourt Brace College Publishers, 1996.

Taylor, Pamela York. *Beasts, Birds and Blossoms in Thai Art.* Kuala Lumpur, Malaysia: Oxford University Press, 1994.

Taylor, Simon. "Janine Antoni at Sandra Gering." *Art in America* 80 (October 1992).

Tello, J. C. "Arte Antiguo Peruano." *Inca: Revista de Estudios Antropolico.* Vol. 2. Lima, Peru: Universidad de San Marcos de Lima, 1924.

Terrace, Edward L. B., and Henry G. Fisher. *Treasures of Egyptian Art from the Cairo Museum.* London: Thames and Hudson, 1970.

Thomas, Nicholas. *Oceanic Art.* London: Thames and Hudson, 1995.

Thucydides. *The Peloponnesian War.* Translated by Rex Warner. Baltimore: Penguin Books, 1954.

Time-Life Books. *Lost Civilizations: Anatolia—Cauldron of Cultures.* Richmond, VA: Time-Life Books, 1995.

Tom, Patricia Vettel. "Bad Boys: Bruce Davidson's Gang Photographs and Outlaw Masculinity." *Art Journal* 56, no. 2 (Summer 1997): 69–74.

Townsend, Richard F., ed. *The Ancient Americas: Art from Sacred Landscapes.* Chicago: Art Institute of Chicago, 1992.

Tregear, Mary. *Chinese Art.* London: Thames and Hudson, 1991.

Truettner, William H. *The Natural Man Observed: A Study of Catlin's Indian Gallery.* Washington, DC: Smithsonian Institution Press, 1979.

Turner, Jane, ed. *The Dictionary of Art.* New York: Grove, 1996.

Vercoutter, Jean. *The Search for Ancient Egypt.* New York: Harry N. Abrams, 1992.

Vickers, Michael, ed. *Pots and Pans.* Oxford: Oxford University Press, 1986.

Vogel, Susan. *Africa Explores: 20th Century African Art.* New York: Center for African Art, 1991.

Vogel, Susan Mullin. *African Art, Western Eyes.* New Haven and London: Yale University Press, 1997.

Von Blum, Paul. *The Art of Social Conscience.* New York: Universe Books, 1976.

von Hagen, Victor W. *The Desert Kingdoms of Peru.* London: Weidenfeld and Nicolson, 1965.

Vroege, Bas, and Hripsim Visser, eds. *Oppositions: Commitment and Cultural Identity in Contemporary Photography from Japan, Canada, Brazil, the Soviet Union and the Netherlands.* Rotterdam: Uitgeverij, 1990.

Wallach, Alan. *Exhibiting Contradiction: Essays on the Art Museum in the United States.* Amherst: University of Massachusetts Press, 1998.

Wallis, Brian, ed. *Hans Haacke: Unfinished Business.* New York: The New Museum of Contemporary Art; Cambridge: MIT Press, 1986.

Washburn, Dorothy, ed. *Hopi Kachina: Spirit of Life.* San Francisco: California Academy of Sciences, 1980. Distributed by the University of Washington Press. Weibiao, Hu. *Scenes of the Great Wall.* Beijing: Wenjin Publishing House, 1994.

Weintraub, Linda, ed. *Art What Thou Eat: Images of Food in American Art.* Mount Kisco, NY: Moyer Bell, 1991.

Wescoat, James L., Jr., and Joachim Wolschke-Bulmahn. *Mughal Gardens: Sources, Places, Representations and Prospects.* Washington, DC: Dumbarton Oaks Research Library and Collection, 1996.

Wheat, Ellen Harkins. *Jacob Lawrence: American Painter.* Seattle: University of Washington Press, 1986.

Willett, Frank. *African Art.* New York: Thames and Hudson, 1993.

———. *Ife in the History of West African Sculpture.* New York: McGraw-Hill, 1967.

Willis, Deborah, ed. *Picturing Us: African American Identity in Photography.* New York: New Press, 1994.

Willis-Braithwaite, Deborah. *VanDerZee Photographer 1886–1983.* New York: Harry N. Abrams, 1993.

Wilson, David M., and Ole Klindt-Jensen. *Viking Art.* Minneapolis: University of Minnesota Press, 1980.

Wilson, Sir David M., ed. *The Collections of the British Museum.* Cambridge: Cambridge University Press, 1989.

Wingert, Paul S. *An Outline of Oceanic Art.* Cambridge, MA: University Prints, 1970.

———. *Art of the South Pacific.* New York: Columbia University Press, 1946.

Winkelmann-Rhein, Gertraude. *The Paintings and Drawings of Jan "Flower" Bruegel.* New York: Harry N. Abrams, 1968.

Witherspoon, Gary. *Language and Art of the Navajo Universe.* Ann Arbor: University of Michigan Press, 1977.

Wolff, Janet. *The Social Production of Art.* New York: New York University Press, 1984.

Yau, John. "Hung Liu [exhibition at] Nahan Contemporary." *Artforum* (March 1990):162.

Yenne, Bill, and Susan Garratt. *North American Indians.* China: Ottenheimer, 1994.

Yood, James. *Feasting: A Celebration of Food in Art.* New York: Universe Publishing, 1992.

Zarnecki, George. *Art of the Medieval World.* New York: Harry N. Abrams, 1975.

Zelanski, Paul, and Mary Pat Fisher. *Design Principles and Problems.* Fort Worth, TX: Harcourt Brace College Publishers, 1996.

Zelevansky, Lynn, et al. *Love Forever: Yayoi Kusama 1958–1968.* Los Angeles: Los Angeles County Museum of Art, 1998.

Zigrosser, Carl. *Prints and Drawings of Käthe Kollwitz.* New York: Dover, 1969.

CREDITS

American Art Museum Washington DC/Art Resource NY; **bottom** Erich Lessing/Art Resource NY; **Page 107 top left** Reuters/CORBIS; **top right** Ando or Utagawa (1797–1858)/Leeds Museums and Galleries (City Art Gallery) U.K./The Bridgeman Art Library; **bottom** John James Audubon The Birds of America Plate #26: Carolina Parrot 1827–38 Hand-colored engraving and aquatint on paper North Carolina Museum of Art Transfer from the North Carolina State Library G.74.27.1/26; **Page 108** Lindsay Hebberd/CORBIS; **Page 109 top left** New Guinean (20th century)/Museum of Fine Arts Houston Texas USA/Funded by Lester Smith in honour of Harry H. Cullen/The Bridgeman Art Library; **top right** Heini Schneebeli/The Bridgeman Art Library; **bottom right** The Proportions of the human figure (after Vitruvius) c.1492 (pen & ink on paper) Vinci Leonardo da (1452–1519)/Galleria dell' Accademia Venice Italy/The Bridgeman Art Library; **Page 110 top right** Bildarchiv Preussischer Kulturbesitz/Art Resource NY; **left** Museum of Northern Arizona; **Page 111** Michael S. Yamashita/CORBIS; **Page 112** Mark Karrass/Corbis; **Page 113 top** Carnegie Museum of Art; **bottom left** Andrea Jemolo/CORBIS; **Page 114** Kunsthistorisches Museum; **Page 115 top** Art Resource Inc.; **bottom right** Scala/Art Resource NY; **Page 116** Adam Woolfitt/Encyclopedia/CORBIS; **Page 117 top left** Tibor Bognár/Terra/CORBIS; **center left** Robert Holmes/Terra/CORBIS; **Page 118** Giraudon/Art Resource NY; **Page 119** Photononstop/SuperStock; **Page 120** Sunset Boulevard/Corbis; **Page 121 top** age fotostock/SuperStock; **bottom left** Vatican Museums and Galleries Vatican City Italy/The Bridgeman Art Library; **bottom right** Vatican Museums and Galleries Vatican City Italy/Alinari/The Bridgeman Art Library; **Page 122 bottom left** mediacolor's/Alamy; **bottom right** CNN/Getty Images; **Page 123** SEF/Art Resource NY; **Page 124 top left** The Metropolitan Museum of Art; **top right** GALERIE LELONG; **bottom** San Diego Museum of Man

Page 127 Images & Stories/Alamy; **Page 129 top** Bison carving c.12000 BC (ivory) Paleolithic/Private Collection/Ancient Art and Architecture Collection Ltd./The Bridgeman Art Library; **bottom left** Erich Lessing/Art Resource NY; **Page 130 center right** © Wolfgang Kaehler/CORBIS; **center left** The Newark Museum/Art Resource NY; **bottom left** Werner Forman/Topham/The Image Works; **top right** Réunion des Musées Nationaux/Art Resource NY; **Page 131 top left** Catalhoyuk Research Project; **top right** Shimizu Kohgeisha Co. Ltd. Permission Ryoko-in Management; **center right** Pei Cobb Freed & Partners; **bottom center** Jennifer Steele/Art Resource NY/© Aboriginal Artists Agency Limited; **Page 132 top left** Ali Meyer/Corbis; **center right** Digital Image © The Museum of Modern Art/Licensed by Scala/Art Resource NY 130.1946a–c © 2008 Artists Rights Society (ARS) NY/ProLitteris Zürich; **Page 133 center left** Smithsonian American Art Museum Washington DC/Art Resource NY; **bottom left** Werner Forman/Art Resource; **center right** The Art Gallery Collection/Alamy; **Page 134** Colorphoto Hans Hinz; **Page 135 top left** Jennifer Steele/Art Resource NY/© Aboriginal Artists Agency Limited; **top right** © Charles & Josette Lenars/CORBIS; **bottom** Gianni Dagli Orti The Picture Desk Limited/CORBIS; **Page 136** 1988 Sue Coe/Courtesy Galerie St. Etienne New York; **Page 137 top left** Photograph © Museum of Fine Arts Boston; **bottom left** Ashmolean Museum Oxford UK; **Page 138 top** The Newark Museum/Art Resource NY; **bottom right** The Newark Museum/Art Resource NY; **Page 139 top left** Museo Nazionale Preistorico Etnografico; **bottom** Edith C. Blum Collection Art Institute Bard College. © 2004 Andy Warhol Foundation for the Visual Arts/Artists Rights Society (ARS) New York; **Page 140** Réunion des Musées Nationaux/Art Resource NY; **Page 141 top left** © 2004 The Whitney Museum of American Art. © Wayne Thiebaud/Licensed by VAGA New York NY; **bottom right** Shimizu Kohgeisha Co. Ltd. Permission Ryoko-in Management; **Page 142 bottom left** Werner Forman/Topham/The Image Works; **center right** The Metropolitan Museum of Art Rogers Fund 1919. (19.164) Photograph © 1998 The Metropolitan Museum of Art; **Page 143 top** Artichoke halved 1930 (gelatin silver print) Weston Edward Henry (1886–1958)/Fred Jones Jr. Museum of Art University of Oklahoma USA/Museum Purchase 1937/The Bridgeman Art Library; **bottom** © Edimédia/CORBIS; **Page 144** Just Art Gallery; **Page 145 top left** Freer Gallery of Art; **bottom** Copyright 2006 Judy Chicago/Artists Rights Society (ARS) New York; **Page 146 top right** © Estate of Duane Hanson/Licensed by VAGA New York NY; **center right** Janine Antoni. Gnaw 1992. Courtesy of the artist and Luhring Augustine New York; **Page 147** Russell Thompson/Arkansas Office Inc.; **Page 148 top right** Catalhoyuk Research Project; **center right** © Dewitt Jones/CORBIS; **Page 149 top left** © Wolfgang Kaehler/CORBIS; **bottom right** Scala/Art Resource NY; **Page 150 bottom left** Scala/Art Resource NY; **center left** Erich Lessing/Art Resource NY; **Page 151 top left** Robert Newcombe/Nelson-Atkins Museum of Art; **top right** Royal Tropical Institute Amsterdam; **Page 152 bottom left** Werner Forman/Art Resource NY; **center right** Alan Schein Photography/Corbis; **Page 153 top left** H. Mark Weidman Photography/Alamy; **bottom left** Scala/Art Resource NY; **Page 154 top right**

Stephen A. Edwards; **top left** Richard Glover/Terra/Corbis; **Page 155 top left** Tibor Bognar/Alamy; **bottom right** Pei Cobb Freed & Partners; **Page 156 bottom** Robert Holmes/Corbis; **center right** Tibor Bognár/Terra/CORBIS

Page 157 Ellen McKnight/Alamy; **Page 159 top right** The Art Archive/Museum of Anatolian Civilisations Ankara/Gianni Dagli Ort/Picture Desk; **Page 160 bottom right** North Carolina Museum of Art/Fine Art/CORBIS; **bottom center** Museo Larco Lima – Perú; **top right** Erich Lessing/Art Resource NY; **center left** © The Trustees of the British Museum; **center** The Detroit Institute of Arts; **Page 160 center right** Standing Female Figure Bamana Mali 19th–20th century (wood copper beads and metal)/Detroit Institute of Arts USA/Bequest of Robert H. Tannahill/The Bridgeman Art Library; **Page 161 top left** Scala/Art Resource NY; **top right** The Trustees of The British Museum/Art Resource NY; **top center** Victoria & Albert Museum London/Art Resource NY; **Page 162 center left** Erich Lessing/Art Resource NY; **bottom left** Araldo de Luca/Corbis Art/Corbis; **top right** Araldo de Luca/Corbis Museum/Corbis; **Page 163 bottom left** Library of Congress; **top right** The Museum of Modern Art New York. The Museum of Modern Art New York/Art Resource NY. Art/Marisol Escobar/Licensed by VAGA New York NY; **center right** The Museum of Modern Art/Licensed by SCALA/Art Resource NY; **Page 164** Ali Meyer/Corbis; **Page 165 left** Ashmolean Museum; **bottom right** © The Trustees of the British Museum; **Page 166** © The Trustees of the British Museum; **Page 167** Scala/Art Resource NY; **Page 168** The Detroit Institute of Arts; **Page 169 top left** Standing Female Figure Bamana Mali 19th–20th century (wood copper beads and metal)/Detroit Institute of Arts USA/Bequest of Robert H. Tannahill/The Bridgeman Art Library; **top right** North Carolina Museum of Art/Fine Art/CORBIS; **Page 170** Scala/Art Resource NY; **Page 171** Photograph © 1993 The Metropolitan Museum of Art; **Page 172** National Gallery London/Art Resource NY; **Page 173 top** The Art Archive/Bodleian Library Oxford/The Picture Desk; **bottom right** Museum of Fine Arts Boston; **Page 174 bottom left** Scala/Art Resource NY; **bottom right** Museo Larco Lima – Perú; **Page 175 top** The Trustees of The British Museum/Art Resource NY; **bottom right** Tokyo National Museum c/o DNP Archives.com Co. Ltd; **Page 176** Victoria & Albert Museum London/Art Resource NY; **Page 177** Charles Walker/Topfoto/The Image Works; **Page 178** Réunion des Musées Nationaux/Art Resource NY; **Page 179 top** Réunion des Musées Nationaux/Art Resource NY; **bottom right** LYNN HERSHMAN; **Page 180** Zindman/Fremont/Mary Boone Gallery; **Page 181 top left** courtesy Regen Projects Los Angeles © Catherine Opie; **top right** Metropolitan Museum Of Art New York/© 2004 The Georgia O Keeffe Foundation/Artists Rights Society (ARS) New York; **Page 182** Hirshhorn Museum and Sculpture Garden; **Page 183 top left** Photo: Allan Finkelman Art © Louise Bourgeois Trust/Licensed by VAGA New York NY; **bottom left** Robert Miller Gallery; **Page 184** Photograph © Justin Kerr; **Page 185 top left** Museo Larco Lima – Perú; **top right** Erich Lessing/Art Resource NY; **bottom left** Photo © 1985 Dirk Bakker Detroit Institute of Arts

Page 187 American Museum of Natural History; **Page 189** Réunion des Musées Nationaux/Art Resource NY; **Page 190 center left** Gianni Dagli OrtiThe Picture Desk Limited/CORBIS; **center right** Francis G. Mayer/Fine Art/CORBIS; **top left** American Museum of Natural History; **bottom right** The Detroit Institute of Arts; **center** Kennet Havgaard/Aurora/Getty Images; **top right** Skyscan/Terra/Corbis; **top center** © Sylvain Sonnet/Corbis; **Page 191 top left** Nimatallah/Art Resource NY; **center** Andy Clarke 2010/Used under license from Shutterstock.com; **center left** © Kelly-Mooney Photography/Corbis; **top right** Liu Liqun/Corbis; **Page 191 top center** J. Paul/Getty Museum; **center right** Robert Harding Picture Library; **Page 192 top right** © Roger Wood/CORBIS; **br** mediacolor's/Alamy; **top left** Richard A Cooke III/Stone/Getty Images; **Page 193 bottom left** Scala/Art Resource NY; **top right** Erich Lessing/Art Resource NY; **center right** Giraudon/Art Resource NY; **Page 194** Nimatallah/Art Resource NY; **Page 195** Nimatallah/Art Resource NY; **Page 196 top left** Sandro Vannini; **bottom right** Gianni Dagli OrtiThe Picture Desk Limited/CORBIS; **Page 197** Angelo Hornak/Corbis Art/CORBIS; **Page 198** Robert Harding Picture Library; **Page 199** Borromeo/Art Resource NY; **top left** Robert Harding Picture Library; **Page 200** Nelson-Atkins Museum of Art Kansas; **Page 201** Princeton University Press/Art Resource NY; **Page 202** Francis G. Mayer/Fine Art/CORBIS; **Page 203** The Art Archive/Unterlinden Museum Colmar/Picture Desk; **Page 204 top left** Art Resource NY; **center right** Just Art Gallery; **Page 205 top left** Jorge Durand; **bottom right** Colorphoto Hans Hinz; **Page 206** Erich Lessing/Art Resource NY; **Page 207 top left** Photograph © Justin Kerr; **bottom right** Photograph © 1990 The Metropolitan Museum of Art NY; **Page 208 bottom left** Museum of Northern Arizona; **bottom right** The Detroit Institute of Arts; **Page 209** Kennet Havgaard/Aurora/Getty Images; **Page**

INDEX

Page numbers in *italics* refer to
pages that contain illustrations